Frommer's®

Montana & Wyoming
6th Edition

by Eric Peterson

Here's what the critics say about Fro.

"Amazingly easy to use. Very portable, very complete."
—*Booklist*

"Detailed, accurate, and easy-to-read information for all price ranges."
—*Glamour Magazine*

"Hotel information is close to encyclopedic."
—*Des Moines Sunday Register*

"Frommer's Guides have a way of giving you a real feel for a place."
—*Knight Ridder Newspapers*

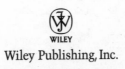

WILEY

Wiley Publishing, Inc.

About the Author

A Denver-based freelance writer, **Eric Peterson** has written and contributed to numerous Frommer's guides covering the American West, from Montana to Texas. He has also recently written several coffee table books and *Ramble: A Field Guide to the USA* (www.speckpress.com). He worked in the Yellowstone laundry plant in Gardiner, Montana, in 1992 and can't keep himself away for very long.

Published by:

Wiley Publishing, Inc.

111 River St.
Hoboken, NJ 07030-5774

ISBN-13: 978-0-471-77818-9
ISBN-10: 0-471-77818-4

Editor: Cate Latting
Production Editor: Jana M. Stefanciosa
Cartographer: Roberta Stockwell
Photo Editor: Richard Fox
Production by Wiley Indianapolis Composition Services

Front cover photo: Glacier National Park: alpine flowers and trees
Back cover photo: Madison River: man fly-fishing

For information on our other products and services or to obtain technical support, please contact our Customer Care Department within the U.S. at 800/762-2974, outside the U.S. at 317/572-3993 or fax 317/572-4002.

Wiley also publishes its books in a variety of electronic formats. Some content that appears in print may not be available in electronic formats.

Manufactured in the United States of America

5 4 3 2 1

Contents

List of Maps

To my parents, Pete and Vicki

Acknowledgments

The author wishes to thank for their help Tom and Mona Mesereau of Mesereau Public Relations, Jeff Brown and Julianne Baker of the Yellowstone Association Institute, Jackie Skaggs of Grand Teton National Park, Cheryl Matthews and Lee Whittlesey of Yellowstone National Park, Melissa Wilson of Glacier National Park, Carol Beck-Edgar of the Flathead CVB, Claudia Wade of the Park County Travel Council, Susan Doherty, Cyndy Andrus of the Bozeman CVB, Darren Rudloff of the Cheyenne Area CVB, Rick Hoeninghausen of Xanterra Parks & Resorts, and Cinda Culton of the Grand Teton Lodge Company.

—Eric Peterson

An Invitation to the Reader

In researching this book, we discovered many wonderful places—hotels, restaurants, shops, and more. We're sure you'll find others. Please tell us about them, so we can share the information with your fellow travelers in upcoming editions. If you were disappointed with a recommendation, we'd love to know that, too. Please write to:

Frommer's Montana & Wyoming, 6th Edition
Wiley Publishing, Inc. • 111 River St. • Hoboken, NJ 07030-5774

An Additional Note

Please be advised that travel information is subject to change at any time—and this is especially true of prices. We therefore suggest that you write or call ahead for confirmation when making your travel plans. The authors, editors, and publisher cannot be held responsible for the experiences of readers while traveling. Your safety is important to us, however, so we encourage you to stay alert and be aware of your surroundings. Keep a close eye on cameras, purses, and wallets, all favorite targets of thieves and pickpockets.

Other Great Guides for Your Trip:

Frommer's Yellowstone & Grand Teton National Parks

Frommer's Rocky Mountain National Park

Frommer's National Parks of the American West

RV Vacations For Dummies

Frommer's USA

Frommer's Utah

Frommer's Colorado

Frommer's Star Ratings, Icons & Abbreviations

Every hotel, restaurant, and attraction listing in this guide has been ranked for quality, value, service, amenities, and special features using a **star-rating system.** In country, state, and regional guides, we also rate towns and regions to help you narrow down your choices and budget your time accordingly. Hotels and restaurants are rated on a scale of zero (recommended) to three stars (exceptional). Attractions, shopping, nightlife, towns, and regions are rated according to the following scale: zero stars (recommended), one star (highly recommended), two stars (very highly recommended), and three stars (must-see).

In addition to the star-rating system, we also use **seven feature icons** that point you to the great deals, in-the-know advice, and unique experiences that separate travelers from tourists. Throughout the book, look for:

Finds	Special finds—those places only insiders know about
Fun Fact	Fun facts—details that make travelers more informed and their trips more fun
Kids	Best bets for kids and advice for the whole family
Moments	Special moments—those experiences that memories are made of
Overrated	Places or experiences not worth your time or money
Tips	Insider tips—great ways to save time and money
Value	Great values—where to get the best deals

The following **abbreviations** are used for credit cards:

AE	American Express	DISC	Discover	V	Visa
DC	Diners Club	MC	MasterCard		

Frommers.com

Now that you have the guidebook to a great trip, visit our website at **www.frommers.com** for travel information on more than 3,000 destinations. With features updated regularly, we give you instant access to the most current trip-planning information available. At Frommers.com, you'll also find the best prices on airfares, accommodations, and car rentals—and you can even book travel online through our travel booking partners. At Frommers.com, you'll also find the following:

- Online updates to our most popular guidebooks
- Vacation sweepstakes and contest giveaways
- Newsletter highlighting the hottest travel trends
- Online travel message boards with featured travel discussions

What's New in Montana & Wyoming

Montana and Wyoming are known for their rugged beauty, outdoor recreational opportunities, Wild West history, and wide-open spaces. These are sparsely populated areas, where getting around means long hours in a car and where visitors get to see a section of America that is little changed from the way it was when pioneers moved through in covered wagons. Change comes slowly here—that's one of the things we like so much about these states—but gradually we are seeing more paved roads, more chain motels and restaurants, and at least a few of the more upscale facilities we expect to find in America's more modern cities.

Following are some of the recent changes in Montana and Wyoming, and we'll be watching with anticipation, and just a bit of trepidation, as these states move toward joining the modern world.

GLACIER NATIONAL PARK Admission fees to the park went up in 2005. The new fee is $25 per vehicle for up to 7 days ($15 in winter) or $12 per person for those on foot, bicycles, and motorcycles ($10 in winter). In 2006, construction on Going-to-the-Sun Road will intensify, meaning regular 30-minute to 2-hour delays for several years. For more information, see chapter 5.

MISSOULA, THE FLATHEAD & THE NORTHWEST CORNER **Missoula** The **Rocky Mountain Elk Foundation** cut the ribbon on a terrific new **visitor center** (5705 Grant Creek Rd.; ✆ 406/523-4545) in November 2004

that puts the old facility to shame. **Pearl Café and Bakery** (231 E. Front St.; ✆ 406/541-0231) opened in summer 2004 and quickly won a local following.

The Swan Valley The luxurious **Resort at Paws Up** (40060 Paws Up Rd.; ✆ 800/473-0601), opened in 2005, 199 years after Meriwether Lewis paid a visit to the property. See p. 124.

Whitefish The Big Mountain Resort saw **Morning Eagle Lodge** (Big Mountain Village; ✆ 800/858-4157), welcome its first guests to the most posh lodging on the slopes during the 2004–05 ski season. Below, **Averill's Lodge at Whitefish Lake** (1399 Wisconsin Ave.; ✆ 800/735-8869) was hammering away at press time to open the town's first four-season luxury resort by wintertime 2006. Downtown, the **Corner House Grille** (147 Central Ave.; ✆ 406/863-2323) opened in 2003 and quickly emerged as a dining standout.

See chapter 6 for more information.

HELENA & SOUTHWESTERN MONTANA **Butte** As the mining gash known as the **Berkeley Pit** is Butte's most-visited attraction, plans called for a $185,000 face-lift of the area for fall 2006, including a playground, restrooms, expanded interpretive displays, and a bronze statue of "The Auditor," the mysterious dreadlocked dog that wandered this desolate moonscape for 17 years. In 2005, **The Mai Wah** (17 W. Mercury St.; ✆ 406/723-3231) unveiled its long-awaited permanent exhibit, "The Butte

Chinese Experience," telling this fascinating story with artifacts, images, and interpretive displays. The landmark saloon known as the **M&M Cigar Store** (9 N. Main St.; ℂ **406/723-7612**) never closed between 1890 and 2003 but shut down for 2 years until reopening in time for St. Patrick's Day 2005.

See chapter 7 for more information.

THE HI-LINE & NORTH-CENTRAL MISSOURI RIVER COUNTRY Great Falls Two new standout eateries—the **Beargrass Grille** (518 Central Ave.; ℂ **406/453-1277**) and **The Breaks** (202 2nd Ave. S.; ℂ **406/453-5980**)—opened in 2005 and 2004, respectively, and emerged as the city's leading culinary lights.

The Rocky Mountain Eastern Front The Nature Conservancy sold paleontological hot spot **Egg Mountain** to Montana State University; public tours are no longer available.

The Hi-Line: U.S. 2 The **H. Earl Clack Museum** (ℂ **406/265-4000**) relocated to Havre's Holiday Village Mall, 1753 W. U.S. 2. In Fort Peck, the **Fort Peck Interpretive Center and Museum** (Yellowstone Rd.; ℂ **406/526-3493**) opened in 2005. The big attraction is a terrifying, fleshed-out replica of the most complete Tyrannosaurus rex skeleton ever found, unearthed nearby in 1997.

See chapter 8 for more information.

BOZEMAN, SOUTH-CENTRAL MONTANA & THE MISSOURI HEADWATERS Bozeman Unspooling in early October, **Hatch** (ℂ **406/586-2635**) is an audiovisual arts festival that began in 2004. The dinosaur exhibits at the **Museum of the Rockies** (600 W. Kagy Blvd.; **406/994-2251**) are in the midst of a makeover. The first two phases—the **Hall of Horns and Teeth** and the **Mesozoic Media Center**—opened in 2005 and 2006, respectively. Phase three, the **Hall of Giants,** populated with animatronic

dinosaurs, is slated for ribbon-cutting in 2007.

The Gallatin Valley Moonlight Basin (ℂ **877/822-0430**) opened in 2003, making it the country's first new destination ski resort in 20 years. In 2005, **Big Sky Resort** (ℂ **800/548-4486**) and Moonlight Basin connected their trail systems, making for a combined 5,300 acres of terrain—making for the largest ski area in the United States.

See chapter 9 for more information.

BILLINGS & EASTERN MONTANA Longtime Billings dining stalwart **Walkers Grill** (2700 1st Ave. N.; ℂ **406/245-9291**) moved into posh new digs in 2004, taking over the first floor of a new brick loft building in the heart of downtown. See chapter 10 for more information.

YELLOWSTONE NATIONAL PARK The **Bar N Ranch** (890 Buttermilk Creek Rd., West Yellowstone; ℂ **406/646-0300**) opened as a swank but rustic guest lodge and cabin complex in 2004. Park **admission fees** went up in 2005: Entrance for up to 7 days costs $25 per vehicle and covers both Yellowstone and Grand Teton national parks. A snowmobile or motorcycle pays $20 for 7 days, and someone who comes in on bicycle, skis, or foot pays $12. In mid-2004, a judge overturned a previous ruling enforcing a **snowmobiling ban;** snowmobiling will be allowed through 2007, but a long-term policy has yet to be settled upon. Due to an ongoing renovation, the **Old Faithful Inn** (ℂ **307/344-7311**) had a short season in 2005, and plans called for it to be closed for part of the 2006 summer as well. See chapter 11 for more information.

JACKSON HOLE & GRAND TETON NATIONAL PARK Jackson Hole Mountain Resort (ℂ **307/733-2292**) announced it would close the resort's famed tram after summer 2006. At press time, JHMR was still discussing replacement solutions for the tram. The ultraposh **Four Seasons Resort Jackson Hole** (7680 Granite Loop, Teton Village; © **307/ 732-5000**) opened in December 2004. The former chef of the Million Dollar Cowboy Bar steakhouse opened **Burke's Chop House** (72 S. Glenwood St.; © **307/733-8575**) in 2004. See chapter 12 for more information.

CODY & NORTH-CENTRAL WYOMING   Sadly, our favorite restaurant in Cody—Stefan's—closed in 2004. **Bison Willy's Base Camp,** 1625 Alger St., Cody; © **877/587-0629**), a home converted into a hostel of sorts, opened in 2005 near downtown. See chapter 13.

SHERIDAN & EASTERN WYOMING The proprietors of **The Occidental Hotel** (10 N. Main St., Buffalo; © **307/684-0451** have done a wonderful job of restoring the historic structure, opening a number of rooms in 2005 and 2006. See chapter 14.

SOUTHERN WYOMING   Cheyenne After a long period of decline, the historic **Plains Hotel** (1600 Central Ave.; © **866/ 275-2467**) enjoyed a much-needed restoration in 2003. Across the street, the newly restored **Cheyenne Depot** (121 W. 15th St.) has emerged as a social and cultural hot spot, its plaza hosting the annual pancake breakfast during **Cheyenne Frontier Days** and Friday evening concerts in the summertime.

Laramie   The Brick Bed & Breakfast (105 S. 5th St.; © **800/788-4626**) opened in 2004 and immediately set the standard for Laramie's small population of B&Bs.

See chapter 15 for more information.

1

The Best of Montana & Wyoming

A mix of the rugged Wild West, the even more rugged Rocky Mountains, and a few almost-modern cities—or what we might call overgrown cow towns—make the states of Montana and Wyoming a delightful vacation spot. This is especially true for people who savor outdoor adventures, but it's also the case for those looking to discover a part of the United States that many of us have seen only in the movies and on television (and that's a rather distorted view). Here you'll find some of the most breathtaking scenery in America; a vast array of wildlife that not only thinks it owns the place, but actually does; and even some first-class Western-style lodges, restaurants, and museums.

Following are what we consider some of the best experiences in Montana and Wyoming, highlights to help you begin planning your trip.

1 The Best Vacation Experiences

- **Glacier National Park** (MT): The best vacation spot in Montana is also the most obvious one. By the standard of other crowded national parks, this spectacular country is virtually undiscovered. See chapter 5.
- **Yellowstone National Park** (WY): It's the crown jewel of American parks, and it remains the prime attraction in the Rocky Mountains. This unique park offers visitors an extraordinary combination of wilderness, wildlife, and geothermal wonders. See chapter 11.
- **Grand Teton National Park** (WY): The Grand Tetons are an excellent short course in Rocky Mountain parks for travelers with less time: magnificent peaks rising from the Snake River plain, alpine lakes, wildflowers, and wildlife, in a relatively small park that can be seen in a few days. See "Grand Teton National Park" in chapter 12.

2 The Best Outdoor Adventures

- **Exploring the Bob Marshall Wilderness** (MT): The 1.5-million-acre Bob Marshall Wilderness Complex in northwest Montana is one of America's most spectacular wild places. Lace up your hiking boots, tie on your bandanna, and take to the high country in Montana's northwest corner. See section 7, "The Bob Marshall Wilderness Complex," in chapter 6.
- **Enjoying the Yellowstone Backcountry** (WY): Outfitters from ranches around Yellowstone National Park will take you into the deep wilderness that surrounds the busy attractions at the

park's center, and there you'll get a flavor of the wild as rich as the Rockies can offer. If you have experience, you can go on your own—paddling Yellowstone Lake, backpacking along Slough Creek, or telemark skiing the powder around Shoshone Lake. See chapter 11 for details.

3 The Best Wildlife Viewing

- **Glacier National Park** (MT): The experience of watching wildlife amid the imposing terrain of Glacier National Park is tough to beat. With a little energy, you can see mountain goats, moose, elk, and other native animals in their natural habitat. Keep a good distance, and be aware of any and all bear restrictions and regulations—the grizzly is the park's unofficial mascot. See chapter 5.
- **The Bob Marshall Wilderness Complex** (MT): Just south of Glacier, in the Bob Marshall Wilderness Complex, roam a full complement of Rocky Mountain wildlife—although you have to wander into the backcountry to find it. See section 7, "The Bob Marshall Wilderness Complex," in chapter 6.
- **The Lamar Valley** (WY): You can see wildlife in many parts of Yellowstone, including the meadows across from the Old Faithful complex. But the richest trove of wildlife is in the park's northeast corner, in the valley nicknamed "The Serengeti of North America." See chapter 11.

4 The Best Winter Vacations

- **Skiing at Big Sky and Moonlight Basin** (MT; ℂ **800/548-4486** or 877/822-0430): In 2005, Big Sky and Moonlight Basin connected their trail systems, making for a combined 5,300 acres of terrain—the largest ski area in the country. See p. 227.
- **Wintering at Old Faithful** (WY): The chilly season in Yellowstone is increasingly popular, and it's bound to be even more so now that the Old Faithful Snow Lodge has been transformed into a handsome, comfortable facility. You can take a Snowcoach into the park, or cross-country ski or snowshoe to the Lonestar Geyser and other attractions. See p. 303.
- **Skiing at Jackson Hole Mountain Resort** (WY; ℂ 307/733-2292): Jackson Hole offers a vertical drop that will take your breath away. There are a variety of ways to get to the bottom, from double black diamonds to intermediate slopes. Skiers who like a challenge should come here and mix the visit with some ballooning, tours of the elk refuge, and other adventures. See p. 311.

5 The Best Hotels & Resorts

- **Many Glacier Hotel** (Glacier National Park, MT; ℂ **406/892-2525**): The best thing about Many Glacier, apart from its elegant mien, its friendly service, and its cozy rooms, is the setting, along Swiftcurrent Lake and in the shadows of Mount Grinnell and Mount Wilbur. See p. 82.
- **The Pollard** (Red Lodge, MT; ℂ **800/765-5273**): You can join Buffalo Bill on the guest register at The Pollard, a historic spot that proves that a hotel doesn't need to sprawl all over the place to set the highest standard of comfort and elegance. See p. 238.
- **Old Faithful Inn** (Yellowstone National Park, WY; ℂ **307/344-7311**): If you

Montana

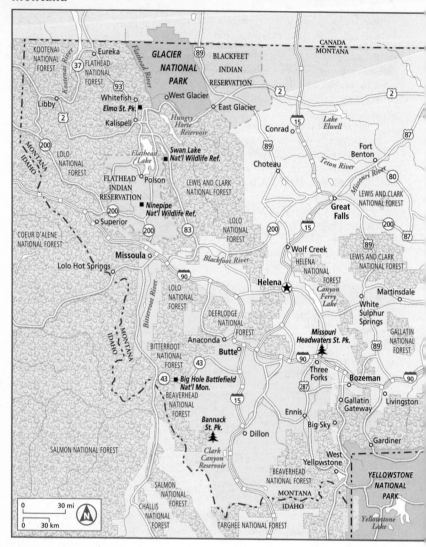

ever wonder whether there is really art in architecture, look at the way the rustic simplicity and monumental structure of this inn make a perfect fit just across the way from one of nature's most astonishing creations. A lattice of logs climbs to an 85-foot ceiling. You can find peace in the upper balconies, or join the convivial crowds around the big stone fireplace below. See p. 305.

• **Four Seasons Resort Jackson Hole** (Jackson, WY; ℡ **307/732-5000**): The newest—and most deluxe—

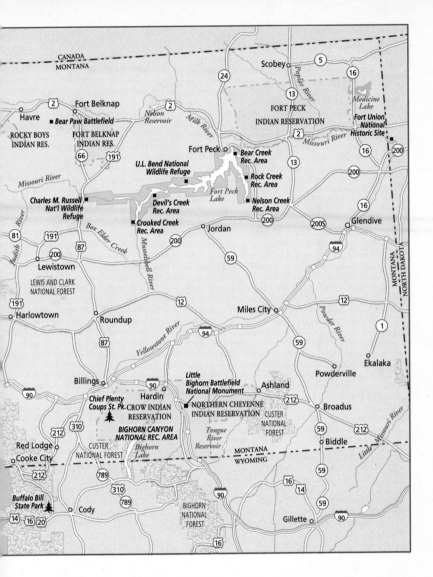

lodging option in Teton Village, the ultrastylish Four Seasons opened in December 2004 and immediately set a new standard for ski-in, ski-out luxury. See p. 320.

- **The Occidental Hotel** (Buffalo, WY; © 307/684-0451): Born as a tent in 1878, The Occidental has burned to the ground and been lost in a poker game in its storied history. After 8 years and $1.2 million of restoration, the grand hotel reopened in 2002. See p. 380.

Wyoming

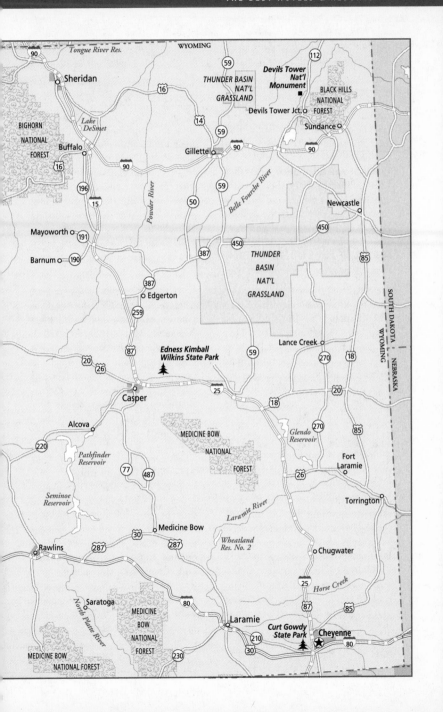

6 The Best Guest Ranches

- **Triple Creek Ranch** (Darby, MT; ✆ **406/821-4600**): This place is wonderful. It's pretty much the perfect guest ranch, where guests are pampered like European royalty, and the prices reflect it. It has all the traditional dude ranch activities, as well as a pool and a fitness room. See p. 110.

- **Lone Mountain Ranch** (Big Sky, MT; ✆ **800/514-4644**): Lone Mountain Ranch is a winter and summer resort that has views into the Spanish Peaks Wilderness Area. In winter there are 45 miles of cross-country trails over terrain that will challenge every level of skier. In summer, you can ride, hike, fish, or simply relax and eat in the popular restaurant. There are bird walks with naturalists and forays into Yellowstone. See p. 230.

- **Lost Creek Ranch** (Moose, WY; ✆ 307/733-3435): Positioned next door to a national park and possessing a beautiful view of the Tetons on one side and the Gros Ventres on the other, Lost Creek layers on the comforts and activities. You can ride, hike, swim, fish, float, play tennis, shoot skeet, play billiards, and eat gourmet food. Regulars return every year. There are only 10 cabins, but if you can get a reservation, it's worth it. See p. 322.

7 The Best Bed & Breakfasts

- **The Garden Wall Inn** (Whitefish, MT; ✆ **888/530-1700**): This delightful B&B, built in the 1920s, is full of charm—all of the furnishings are period antiques, including clawfoot tubs and Art Deco dressers. Gourmet breakfasts include specialties like wild huckleberry crepes. See p. 137.

- **The Sanders B&B** (Helena, MT; ✆ **406/442-3309**): Built in 1875, this historically important B&B has been beautifully restored. You'll relax on original furniture under the eyes of portraits hung by the original owner, U.S. Sen. Wilbur Fiske Sanders. See p. 156.

- **Lehrkind Mansion** (Bozeman, MT; ✆ **800/992-6932**): Located in the Historic Brewery District, the Lehrkind Mansion looks like something out of a fairy tale. Everything, from the rare 1897 Regina music box in the parlor to the many original fixtures in the bathrooms, is period—with the exception of the hot tub. See p. 219.

- **Charley Montana Bed & Breakfast** (Glendive, MT; ✆ **888/395-3207**): This majestic neoclassical mansion houses a top-flight B&B in what was once the palatial, 26-room abode of rancher Charles Krug. See p. 258.

- **Bentwood Inn** (Jackson, WY; ✆ **307/739-1411**): This B&B is an architectural marvel: a 6,000-square-foot log mansion with 43 corners. See p. 319.

- **The Mayor's Inn** (Cody, WY; ✆ **888/217-3001**): This two-story A-frame, built in 1905 for Mayor Frank Houx, is now one of Cody's best B&Bs. The fully licensed bar on the enclosed back porch is the perfect spot to unwind. See p. 359.

- **Spahn's Big Horn Mountain Bed and Breakfast** (Big Horn, WY; ✆ 307/674-8150): With a 100-mile view from a secluded peak tucked amid the Bighorn Mountains, this rustic hideaway features a massive three-story living area and rooms decorated with country quilts and lodgepole furniture. See p. 377.

8 The Best Restaurants

- **The Tupelo Grille** (Whitefish, MT; ✆ **406/862-6136**): Whitefish's best restaurant specializes (surprisingly) in spicy New Orleans–style food: the Cajun Creole combo (a platter of shrimp Creole, crawfish étouffée, and chicken and sausage jambalaya) is a specialty. See p. 142.
- **The Dining Room at Chico Hot Springs** (Pray, MT; ✆ **800/468-9232**): The vegetables served here are grown at the resort's own greenhouse. The game is raised here, and it's served expertly, along with beef, lamb, and other Rocky Mountain staples. Portions are generous and beautifully presented. See p. 235.
- **Park Street Grill and Cafe** (Gardiner, MT; ✆ **406/848-7989**): Adding a dash of zest to the staid meat-and-potatoes dining scene, the menu here is a refreshing mix of Italian entrees, fresh seafood, and chicken, pork, and beef dishes. For dessert, the huckleberry crème brûlée is out of this world. See p. 270.
- **The Blue Lion** (Jackson, WY; ✆ **307/733-3912**): This is an old stalwart, still serving some of the best food in the region, with delicious game dishes like grilled elk loin in peppercorn sauce, and fresh seafood flown in daily. See p. 323.
- **Jenny Lake Lodge Dining Room** (Grand Teton National Park; ✆ **307/733-4647**): The five-course dinners here (from prime rib of buffalo to smoked sturgeon ravioli) are so good you might be distracted from the spectacular scenery just outside the window. You may be roughing it in the park, but you'll need to dress properly at this establishment. See p. 344.

9 The Best Fly-Fishing

- **The Madison** (MT): Brown trout aren't native to this area, but no one's asking them to leave—on this popular river running from Yellowstone National Park into Montana, they're the big attraction. The Madison converges with its "holy trinity" counterparts, the Jefferson and Gallatin, near Three Forks, but lots of anglers fish it around Yellowstone. See chapters 9 and 11.
- **The Snake** (WY): It seems somehow fitting that the menacing-sounding Snake River is home to a feisty strain of cutthroat trout, making it one of the most satisfying Western rivers to fish. See chapter 12.

10 The Best Golf Courses

- **Old Works** (Anaconda, MT): Jack Nicklaus has created a course that is as much fun to play as it is beautiful to look at. The course wonderfully integrates the rocky bluffs, the historic nature of the old copper-processing sites, and prairie grasses and sage. See p. 162.
- **Teton Pines** (Jackson, WY): You won't find a more beautiful view from any golf course in the country—except maybe the neighboring Jackson Hole club—with the granite Grand Teton looming over every shot. See p. 313.
- **The Powder Horn** (Sheridan, WY): Under the majestic Bighorn Mountains, this gorgeous 27-hole course mixes Scottish-style golf, wide-open fairways, and some serious target practice. See p. 375.

11 The Best Museums

- **Lewis and Clark National Historic Trail Interpretive Center** (Great Falls, MT; ☏ **406/727-8733**): This offers a great perspective on the "Corps of Discovery," from its conception back East to its endpoint at the mouth of the Columbia River at the Pacific Ocean. Films, lectures, and demonstrations are among the offerings. See p. 192.
- **Museum of the Rockies** (Bozeman, MT; ☏ **406/994-2251**): The centerpiece of this first-rate museum is the fabulous dinosaur exhibit. The exhibit, which is in the midst of a makeover, is shaping up to be one of the premiere paleontology attractions in the world. See p. 217.

- **Buffalo Bill Historical Center** (Cody, WY; ☏ **307/587-4771**): An art museum, a firearm gallery, the memorabilia of the West's great showman, and exhibits about the Plains Indians comprise the finest museum in the Rocky Mountains. See p. 356.
- **National Historic Trails Interpretive Center** (Casper, WY; ☏ 307/261-7700): This excellent facility uses state-of-the-art exhibits to give us modern travelers an idea of what life on the "road" was like to the emigrants who passed through here in the mid-1800s on the Oregon, Mormon, California, and Pony Express trails. See p. 387.

12 The Best Performing Arts & Cultural Festivals

- **International Wildlife Film Festival** (Missoula, MT; ☏ **406/728-9380**): This film festival has become a required festival for international filmmakers who specialize in wildlife. It goes for a week in early to mid-May, and includes panel discussions and workshops, as well as screenings of the world's best wildlife films. See p. 97.
- **Montana Cowboy Poetry Gathering** (Lewistown, MT; ☏ **406/538-5436**): Held each year in mid-August, this is a rhyming good time

for the bowlegged and horse-drawn set. In addition to a healthy dose of range rhyme, there are arts-and-crafts shows, and booths full of leather. See p. 200.
- **Cheyenne Frontier Days** (Cheyenne, WY; ☏ **800/227-6336**): The "Daddy of 'em All," Cheyenne Frontier Days is a 10-day Western spectacle of parades, rodeo, dances, and concerts. It's safe to say that this is the most vivid demonstration of Western hospitality you'll encounter in the modern world. See p. 396.

2

Planning Your Trip to Montana & Wyoming

Few things can ruin a much-anticipated vacation more than poor planning: for instance, arriving at a national park in mid-January, only to discover that it's almost totally closed by snow until early May, or discovering that you missed by 2 days that dog-sled race you would have loved to see. This chapter is designed to assist you in sorting out the details that could make the difference between a trip you'll never forget and one you'd rather not remember.

1 The Regions in Brief

Planning a trip to Montana and Wyoming can be done in several ways. Those interested in a particular activity, such as hiking, might choose two or three locations and divide their time among them. Conversely, one could first select a destination, such as one of the national parks or an Old West town, and then determine the activities to be pursued there.

This book is organized geographically. Because these states are so large, many visitors will limit their vacations to one or two regions.

MONTANA

GLACIER COUNTRY & THE NORTH-WEST CORNER This includes Glacier National Park, the Flathead Valley and northwest corner of the state, and Missoula, one of Montana's three largest cities. The national park draws millions of visitors annually who come to see its soaring peaks, varied wildlife, and innumerable lakes and streams. The **Going-to-the-Sun Road,** a 50-mile scenic highway that cuts through the heart of the park from southwest to northeast, makes Glacier surprisingly accessible.

Elsewhere in the region, the increasingly popular Big Mountain draws downhill skiers, and Flathead Lake is a magnet because of its excellent watersports and quality golf courses. One of the fastest-growing areas in the state, the **Flathead Valley** shelters an interesting mix of residents: Farmers and loggers share ski lifts and trout streams with transplanted urbanites and big-bucks entrepreneurs, all looking for their slice of paradise. On the southern edge of the region is **Missoula,** a vigorous college town with good restaurants, interesting shops, and bits of Montana history.

SOUTHWESTERN MONTANA This area in the central part of the state is extremely diversified. **Helena,** a town centered on arts and politics (though not necessarily in that order), has a beautiful historic district filled with classic architecture, and access to tremendous fishing on the Missouri River. **Butte,** on the other hand, is working hard to overcome the decay caused by the exploitation, then abandonment, of its mines. Other areas in this part of the state are full of lore. Vigilantes and corrupt sheriffs dominate the stories of the "ghost towns" of Virginia City and Nevada City, both of which are kept alive today by tourists seeking a realistic glimpse into America's past, and Bannack, an abandoned ghost town that's now a state park.

MISSOURI RIVER COUNTRY One of the least populated areas in the state, this region stretches from the mountains to the eastern border and is distinguished by prairies that roll along for hundreds of miles. **Great Falls,** the region's largest city, is a mecca for those interested in the story of famed explorers Lewis and Clark. U.S. 2, or the **Hi-Line**—that long stretch of pavement that runs across the northern part of the state—cuts by a series of farms and ranches that perpetuate the homesteader life. New farming equipment and satellite dishes are just modern polish on an old tune.

SOUTH-CENTRAL MONTANA (YELLOWSTONE COUNTRY) Though this region is almost a twin of the northwest part of the state in many ways—a nearby national park, renowned ski resorts, a university, lots of tourists—it has a unique personality. The city of **Bozeman** is home to Montana State University and a vibrant downtown. Anglers come from all over the world to fish these blue-ribbon trout streams, but the main attraction in this part of the state is **Yellowstone National Park.** Still, even the valleys that lead to it—the Madison, Gallatin, and Paradise—are spectacular destinations themselves.

EASTERN MONTANA The geography in this part of Montana is similar to its neighboring region to the north, but there are more people and more things to do here. **Billings** is the supply center for eastern Montana and northern Wyoming. It's easily the largest city in Montana and has prospered without the helpful hand of tourism that the western side of the state has seen. The Bighorn Canyon and

the Yellowtail Dam draw their share of visitors, especially hunters and anglers, but this region's main attraction is **Little Bighorn Battlefield,** where Gen. George Armstrong Custer led the Seventh Cavalry to defeat at the hands of the Sioux and the Northern Cheyenne.

WYOMING

YELLOWSTONE PLATEAU Yellowstone sits atop a volcanic caldera that periodically blows its top—once every 600,000 years, give or take—but in the interim provides a largely intact ecosystem in this park of 2.2 million acres. Protected from major development by the National Park Service, Yellowstone provides habitat no longer found elsewhere in the Lower 48, and is home to herds of bison, elk, grizzly bears, trumpeter swans, Yellowstone cutthroat trout, and more subtle beauties such as wildflowers and hummingbirds. The geothermal area is greater than any other in the world, with mud pots, geysers, and hot springs of all colors, size, and performance, indicative of a complex natural plumbing system that pulls water down into the earth's crust and regurgitates it at high temperatures. More than three million visitors come here annually, not just to pay homage to Old Faithful, but also to fish, hike, camp, and boat.

THE TETONS & JACKSON HOLE The Tetons are a young range, abrupt and sharp-edged as they knife up from the plain below. And while the photogenic peaks get top billing, it's the valley of Jackson Hole that provides the more varied environments and experiences. **Grand Teton National Park** offers some of the most stunning scenery most of us will ever see—shimmering lakes, thickly carpeted forests, and towering peaks that are blanketed with snow throughout most of the year. It's an easy-to-see park—you can catch its breathtaking beauty on a quick drive—but you'll find lakes and waterfalls

The Regions of Montana & Wyoming

Eastern Montana **6**

Eastern Wyoming **10**

Flathead & Northwest Corner **2**

Glacier National Park **1**

Jackson Hole &
    Grand Teton National Park **8**

North Central Montana **4**

North Central Wyoming **9**

South Central Montana **5**

Southern Wyoming **11**

Southwestern Montana **3**

Yellowstone National Park **7**

and even better views and adventures if you leave your car and take to the trails and waterways. The Tetons are especially popular with mountain climbers, who scale its peaks year-round. Elsewhere in the valley you can float the lively Snake River, visit the National Elk Refuge in the winter, or play cowboy at one of the dude and guest ranches that dot the valley. Skiers and snowboarders have a blast at the resorts here, as well as Grand Targhee on the other side of Teton Pass. And the snug town of **Jackson,** with its antler-arched town square and its busy shops, offers everything from classy art galleries to noisy two-steppin' cowboy bars.

NORTH-CENTRAL WYOMING This is the sort of basin settlers were looking for when they came this way in the 19th century—mountain ranges on all sides cradling wide, ranchable bottomlands, and some mineral wealth to pay for ranch kids' college educations. More and more, though, the oil and gas development, sheep herding and cattle driving, and beet- and wheat-growing are giving way to recreation and tourism. The beautiful mountains here—the Wind Rivers, the Owl Creeks, the Absarokas, the east side of the Bighorns—get less attention than the Tetons, but that only makes them more attractive. Historically, the area learned its lessons in tourism from the West's greatest showman, Buffalo Bill Cody, who helped build the fun-loving town that still bears his name. The rodeo and great museum of **Cody** are joined by other attractions, including the **Bighorn**

Canyon National Recreation Area, the hot springs of **Thermopolis,** and the **Wind River Indian Reservation,** home to the Shoshone and Arapaho peoples.

EASTERN WYOMING The plains don't begin when you pass east over the Continental Divide; there's another mountain range to cross, and then another—first the Bighorns, then the Black Hills—before you're really out there on the howling flats. The **Bighorns** are a treasure of steep canyons, snow-crowned peaks, good fishing, and good hiking, and at their feet sit two of Wyoming's nicest communities, **Sheridan** and **Buffalo.** Some of the prize ranches in this valley have become some of the best dude ranches in the country. Farther east, across the plains beyond the energy boomtown of Gillette, stands the unmistakable geological landmark that is **Devils Tower,** and along Wyoming's eastern border rise the Black Hills. The region's other claim to fame lies in its history. This is the land of Butch Cassidy and his Hole-in-the-Wall Gang (also known as the Wild Bunch), of cattle rustlers, cowboys, and outlaws.

SOUTHERN WYOMING To the millions of drivers who cross Wyoming on I-80, this is the empty quarter, consisting of mostly barren, windswept plains. But it also has its own mountainous corner—the craggy Medicine Bow—a lot of history, and mineral wealth of many varieties, from natural gas to trona. More discerning travelers will not see a wasteland: They'll follow the routes of

---

Tips **Weather & Road Conditions**

For up-to-date information on current weather, contact the **National Weather Service** at ☏ **406/449-5204** in Montana, or 307/772-2468 in Wyoming, or online at **www.wrh.noaa.gov.** For statewide **road conditions,** contact the **Montana Department of Transportation** (☏ **800/226-7623,** or 511 in Montana; www.mdt.mt.gov) or the **Wyoming Department of Transportation** (☏ **888/996-7623** in Wyoming, or 307/772-0824; www.wyoroad.info).

Oregon Trail pioneers (you can still find the wagon-wheel ruts and graves), get off the freeway to visit historic sites like Fort Laramie, and throw out a fishing line on the North Platte near Saratoga or in Flaming Gorge Reservoir south of Green River. In this country you'll find both old and new—from the historic getaway of Saratoga to the capital city of Cheyenne, where the city throws the biggest rodeo party in the West during July's Cheyenne Frontier Days.

2 Visitor Information

MONTANA

Travel Montana, P.O. Box 200533, 301 S. Park St., Helena, MT 59620-0133 (© **800/VISIT-MT** [800/847-4868] or 406/841-2870; TDD 406/841-2702; www.visitmt.com), provides information about Big Sky country and specific locales in Montana.

It puts out two well-designed editions of the *Montana Vacation Guides*—one for summer, one for winter—plus the *Montana Travel Planner,* which provides more detailed information, including contacts with agencies that can provide information, travel services such as airlines and rental-car agencies, and listings by town of places to stay and eat, with charts specifying price ranges and such amenities as hot tubs and access for travelers with disabilities. Travel Montana will also send you separate guides to some of Montana's more popular sports: snowmobiling, fishing, and skiing; as well as site-specific guides for each of six travel regions: Glacier Country in the northwest, Gold West Country in the southwest, Russell Country in north-central Montana, Yellowstone Country in south-central Montana, Missouri River Country in the northeast, and Custer Country in the southeast.

For additional information about attractions, facilities, and services at specific Montana destinations—national parks, cities, or towns—contact the **Montana Chamber of Commerce,** Box 1730, Helena, MT 59624 (© **406/463-2370;** www.montanachamber.com), for the address and phone number of the nearest chamber office.

WYOMING

The **Wyoming Business Council Travel & Tourism Division,** I-25 at College Drive, Cheyenne, WY 82002 (© **800/225-5996** or 307/777-7777; www.wyomingtourism.org), distributes summer and winter editions of the *Travelers Journal,* an informative guide with information about sights and towns in the state's five travel areas—Devils Tower/Buffalo Bill Country in the north and east, Oregon Trail/Rendezvous Country in central Wyoming, Medicine Bow/Flaming Gorge along the southern border, Jackson Hole/Jim Bridger Country in the west, and Grand Teton and Yellowstone—as well as special features on everything from geology to adventure travel. They also furnish maps, cultural and park guides, and other information.

3 Money

Compared with much of America, Montana and Wyoming are a bargain. Especially when you get away from the national parks and major resorts, you'll find that lodging and dining is relatively inexpensive. However, you might need to budget a bit more for transportation here, mainly because distances between destinations are so great. In Montana, Canadian currency is usually accepted at the current conversion rate, especially near the border.

ATMs

The easiest and best way to get cash away from home is from an ATM (automated teller machine). The **Cirrus** (© **800/424-7787;** www.mastercard.com) and **PLUS** (© **800/843-7587;** www.visa.com) networks span the globe; look at the back of your bank card to see which network you're on, then call or check online for ATM locations at your destination. Be sure you know your personal identification number (PIN) before you leave home and be sure to find out your daily withdrawal limit before you depart. Remember that many banks impose a fee every time a card is used at a different bank's ATM, and that fee can be higher for international transactions (up to $5 or more) than for domestic ones (where they're rarely more than $1.50). On top of this, the bank from which you withdraw cash may charge its own fee. To compare banks' ATM fees within the U.S., use www.bankrate.com. For international withdrawal fees, ask your bank.

CREDIT CARDS

Credit cards are a safe way to carry money: They also provide a convenient record of all your expenses, and they generally offer relatively good exchange rates. You can also withdraw cash advances from your credit cards at banks or ATMs, provided you know your PIN. Keep in mind that you'll pay interest from the moment of your withdrawal, even if you pay your monthly bills on time.

TRAVELER'S CHECKS

You can buy traveler's checks at most banks. They are offered in denominations of $20, $50, $100, $500, and sometimes $1,000. Generally, you'll pay a service charge ranging from 1% to 4%.

The most popular traveler's checks are offered by **American Express** (© **800/807-6233** or 800/221-7282 for card holders—this number accepts collect calls, offers service in several foreign languages, and exempts Amex gold and platinum cardholders from the 1% fee.); **Visa** (© **800/732-1322**)—AAA members can obtain Visa checks for a $9.95 fee (for checks up to $1,500) at most AAA offices or by calling © **866/339-3378;** and **MasterCard** (© **800/223-9920**).

American Express, Thomas Cook, Visa, and **MasterCard** offer **foreign currency traveler's checks,** which are useful if you're traveling to one country, or to the euro zone; they're accepted at locations where dollar checks may not be.

If you carry traveler's checks, keep a record of their serial numbers separate from your checks in the event that they are stolen or lost. You'll get a refund faster if you know the numbers.

4 When to Go

Summer, autumn, and winter are the best times to visit the Northern Rockies. The days are sunny, the nights are clear, and humidity is low. A popular song once romanticized "Springtime in the Rockies," but that season—or what most people think of as springtime—lasts about 2 days in early June. The rest of the spring season is likely to be chilly with snow or rain; most of the annual moisture in these states falls during March and April.

Summer is the best season to visit for hiking, fishing, camping, and wildlife watching. It will be warm during the day and cool at night. In **Montana,** average highs in July run from 69°F (21°C) in **West Yellowstone** to 89°F (32°C) in **Miles City,** and lows at night from 40°F (4°C) to 60°F (16°C). In **Wyoming,** the average high temperatures in July range from 80°F (27°C) to 90°F (32°C)—at high elevations, it almost never gets above 100°F (38°C), and it's dry. The plains tend to get hotter than the mountains.

Montana's Average Monthly Temperatures (High/Low)

		Jan	Feb	Mar	Apr	May	June	July	Aug	Sept	Oct	Nov	Dec
Billings	°F	32/14	38/19	45/25	57/34	67/44	77/52	86/58	85/57	72/47	61/37	45/26	36/18
	°C	0/–10	4/–7	7/–4	14/1	19/6	25/11	30/14	29/14	23/8	16/3	7/–3	2/–8
Bozeman	°F	33/12	38/16	46/22	55/30	65/38	73/44	82/49	81/48	71/40	58/31	42/21	34/13
	°C	1/–11	3/–9	8/–6	13/–1	18/3	23/7	28/9	27/9	22/4	14/–1	6/–6	1/–11
Missoula	°F	30/15	37/20	46/25	57/32	66/39	74/46	84/50	83/49	72/41	57/31	41/24	31/17
	°C	–1/–9	3/–7	8/–4	14/0	19/4	23/8	29/10	28/9	22/5	14/–1	5/–4	–1/–8
W. Yellow-stone	°F	24/0	31/3	38/9	48/20	59/29	69/35	79/40	77/37	66/29	53/22	35/10	25/2
	°C	–4/–18	–1/–16	3/–13	9/–7	15/–2	21/2	26/4	25/3	19/–2	12/–6	2/–12	–4/–17

Wyoming's Average Monthly Temperatures (High/Low)

		Jan	Feb	Mar	Apr	May	June	July	Aug	Sept	Oct	Nov	Dec
Casper	°F	34/13	38/16	45/22	56/29	67/39	79/47	87/54	86/53	74/43	61/33	44/22	35/15
	°C	1/–11	3/–9	7/–6	13/–2	19/4	26/8	31/12	30/12	23/6	16/1	7/–6	2/–9
Cheyenne	°F	38/16	40/18	44/22	54/30	64/39	75/48	83/55	80/53	72/44	60/34	46/24	40/18
	°C	3/–9	4/–8	7/–6	12/–1	18/4	24/9	28/13	27/12	22/7	16/1	8/–4	4/–8
Cody	°F	36/13	40/16	47/22	57/31	66/40	76/48	85/54	83/54	72/43	61/34	46/23	38/16
	°C	2/–11	4/–9	8/–6	14/–1	19/4	24/9	29/12	28/12	22/6	16/1	8/–5	3/–9
Devils Tower	°F	34/5	39/10	48/19	59/28	69/38	79/47	87/53	87/50	76/40	63/28	45/17	36/7
	°C	1/–15	4/–12	9/–7	15/–2	21/3	26/8	31/12	31/10	24/4	17/–2	7/–8	2/–14
Jackson	°F	27/5	33/8	41/16	52/25	63/31	72/37	82/41	80/39	71/31	59/23	40/16	28/6
	°C	–3/–15	1/–13	5/–9	11/–4	17/–1	22/3	28/5	27/4	22/–1	15/–5	4/–9	–2/–14
Sheridan	°F	33/9	38/14	46/21	57/30	67/40	76/48	86/54	86/52	74/42	61/32	46/20	36/12
	°C	1/–13	3/–10	8/–6	14/–1	19/4	24/9	30/12	30/11	23/6	16/0	8/–7	2/–11
Yellowstone	°F	29/10	34/13	40/18	50/26	61/34	70/41	80/47	79/45	68/38	55/29	39/19	31/12
	°C	–2/–12	1/–11	4/–8	10/–3	16/1	21/5	27/8	26/7	20/3	13/–2	4/–7	–1/–11

Fall brings spectacularly clear days, cool clear nights, and calm winds up until late October, when things get iffy again. Weather is changeable, however, and snow is possible—likely, even—in the high country, so don't try an extended backpacking trip unless you are experienced and well prepared. Actually, this is a requirement year-round; you can get caught in mountain snowstorms in July and August.

Winter is a glorious season here, though it can be very cold. Lows in Havre, Butte, West Yellowstone, and Jackson average single digits in January. And it can be very windy in some parts of these states, especially on the plains. But the air is crystalline, the snow is powdery, and the skiing is fantastic. If you drive around Montana and Wyoming in the winter *always* carry sleeping bags, extra food, flashlights, and other safety gear. You need to be prepared to survive if your car breaks down or you get stuck in a blizzard or snow squall. Every resident has a horror story about being caught outside unprepared. Only the north entrance at Yellowstone National Park is open to automobiles in the winter. Lodging is available in the park only at Mammoth and Old Faithful. Ski resort towns like Jackson and Kalispell stay lively all winter, but summer tourist towns like Cody are quiet.

MONTANA & WYOMING CALENDAR OF EVENTS

January

Montana Pro Rodeo Circuit Finals. Montana's best cowboys compete in the final round of this regional competition in Great Falls. Call © **406/727-8900** for information. Second or third weekend in January.

International Pedigree Stage Stop Sled Dog Race. Some of the top mushers in the world compete in this race around the Wind River Mountains. It's run in stages, with festive overnight stops in towns along the way. Call © **307/ 734-1163** (www.wyomingstagestop. org). Late January to early February.

February

Race to the Sky. This weeklong event is the longest continuous dog-sled race in the Lower 48. It starts in Helena and ends in Missoula. Call © **406/881- 3647** (www.racetothesky.org) for information. Mid-February.

Winter Carnival. Novelty ski races and rodeo events take center stage during this Jackson, Wyoming, event that includes cowboy poetry readings, Dutch-oven cook-offs, and a barn dance. Call © **307/733-3316** (www. jacksonholechamber.com) for information. Mid-February.

Wyoming Snow Sculpting Competition. When Laramie's weather is at its frostiest, teams come from all over to make snow into art. Call © **307/ 745-7339** for information. Late February.

Wyoming State Winter Fair. They hold this one indoors in Lander, except for the chariot races. There are booths galore, music, entertainment, a livestock competition, and a big dance. Call © **307/332-3892** for information. Late February or early March.

March

C. M. Russell Auction of Original Art. The finest Western art auction in the country, with exhibitors and attendees from around the world. Great Falls, Montana. Call © **406/761- 6453** for information. Mid-March.

St. Patrick's Day in Butte. This wild and woolly (and often booze-soaked) outdoor party pays homage to Butte's Irish heritage. Call © **406/723-3177** for more information. March 17.

April

Cowboy Songs and Range Ballads. With scholarly underpinning, the Buffalo Bill Historical Center in Cody, Wyoming, stages a gathering of real cowboy song and storytelling. Call © **307/587-4771** (www.bbhc.org) for the schedule. Early April.

May

International Wildlife Film Festival. A unique, juried film competition in Missoula, Montana, with more than 100 entries from leading wildlife filmmakers. Call © **406/728-9380** (www. wildlifefilms.org). Early to mid-May.

Miles City Bucking Horse Sale. A "3-day cowboy Mardi Gras," this stock sale in Miles City, Montana, features street dances, parades, barbecues, and, of course, lots of bucking broncos. Call © **406/234-2890** (www.buckinghorse sale.com) for information. Third weekend in May.

Elk Antler Auction. Nearly 10,000 pounds of bull-elk antlers are auctioned off in Jackson's town square. Call © **307/733-3316** (www.jackson holechamber.com) for information. Third Saturday in May.

June

Plains Indian Powwow. Indian dancers from around the region compete in various dance categories, accompanied by traditional drum groups, on the Robbie Powwow Garden next to the Buffalo Bill Historical Center in Cody, Wyoming. Call © **307/587-4771** (www.bbhc.org) for information. Mid-June.

Chugwater Chili Cook-Off. Thousands of hot-food pilgrims come to Chugwater, Wyoming, to taste the spicy contenders in this contest. Call ✆ 307/422-3345 (www.chugwater chilicookoff.com) for information. Mid-June.

Lewis & Clark Festival. Commemoration of Lewis and Clark's journey in and around Great Falls, Montana, with historic reenactments, buffalo roasts, and float trips. Call ✆ 406/452-5661 for information. Late June.

Eastern Shoshone Indian Days Powwow. A celebration of American Indian tradition and culture that's followed by one of Wyoming's largest powwows and all-Indian rodeos, in Fort Washakie, Wyoming. Call ✆ 307/332-9106 for information. Late June.

July

Cody Stampede. There are rodeo nights all summer in Cody, but this long weekend is the big one, and the rodeo ring excitement carries over to street dances, fireworks, and food. Call ✆ 800/207-0744 (www.codystampede rodeo.org) for details. July 1 to July 4.

Legend of Rawhide Reenactment. An overeager gold miner comes to an untimely end in this production of the popular Western legend in Lusk, Wyoming. Call ✆ 800/445-8838 (www.legendofrawhide.com) for information. Second weekend in July.

International Climbers Festival. Speakers, music, demonstrations, and climbing at the famed Wild Iris and other rock faces in Fremont County attract rock climbers from around the world to this gathering in Lander, Wyoming. Call ✆ 307/349-1561 (www.climbersfestival.org). Second weekend in July.

North American Indian Days. The Blackfeet Reservation hosts a weekend of native dancing, singing, and drumming, with crafts booths and games, in Browning, Montana. Call ✆ 406/338-7276 for information. Mid-July.

Yellowstone Jazz Festival. This music camp gathers young musicians for tutelage by some big names from the jazz world, followed by a series of performances in Powell and Cody, Wyoming. Call ✆ 307/587-3898 for information. Mid-July.

Grand Teton Music Festival. Fine musicians from around the world join this orchestra every summer. A varied classical repertoire includes numerous chamber concerts and some premieres in Teton Village, Wyoming. Call ✆ 307/733-3050 (www.gtmf.org) for information. Mid-July to the end of August.

Cheyenne Frontier Days. One of the country's most popular rodeos, the "daddy of 'em all" entertains huge crowds for a full week in Cheyenne, Wyoming. Call ✆ 800/227-6336 (www.cfdrodeo.com) for information. Last week in July.

Evel Knievel Days. Butte honors its favorite son and one-time problem child, daredevil Evel Knievel, with parades, stunt shows, and children's events. Call ✆ 406/494-2825 (www.knievelweek.com) for more information. Last week in July.

August

Happy Jack Music Festival. Bluegrass and fiddles prevail over this festival of mountain music in Curt Gowdy State Park near Cheyenne, Wyoming. Call ✆ 307/777-7519 (www.happyjack festival.com) for information. Mid-August.

Sweet Pea Festival. A full-fledged arts festival in Bozeman, Montana, with fine art, musicians, and various entertainment for all ages. Call ✆ 406/586-4003 for information. First full weekend in August.

Grand Targhee Bluegrass Festival. A 3-day celebration of music, arts, food, and entertainment in Jackson, Wyoming. Call ✆ 800/827-4433 (www.jacksonholechamber.com) for information. Mid-August.

Crow Fair. By far one of the biggest and best American Indian gatherings in the Northwest, with dancing, food, and crafts in Crow Agency, Montana. Call ✆ **406/638-3700** for information. Mid-August.

Montana Cowboy Poetry Gathering. A 3-day event featuring readings and entertainment from the real McCoys in Lewistown, Montana. Call ✆ **406/538-8278** for information. Mid-August.

September

Nordicfest. A Scandinavian celebration in Libby, Montana, featuring a parade, a juried craft show, headliner entertainment, and an international Fjord horse show. Call ✆ **800/785-6541** (www.libbynordicfest.com) for information. First weekend following Labor Day.

Western Design Conference. Western-style furniture and clothing fashions on the runway, in Cody, Wyoming. Call ✆ **888/685-0574** (www.westerndesign conference.com) for more information. Third week in September.

Buffalo Bill Historical Center Art Show and Patrons Ball. With a big art sale to support the museum, and a black-tie dinner and ball, this is one of the Rockies' premier (and only) formal social events. Cody, Wyoming. For information call ✆ **307/578-5002** (www.bbhc.org). Late September.

October

Hatch Fest. Unspooling over 6 days, this audiovisual arts festival in Bozeman includes film screenings, workshops, filmmaker Q&As, and live music after dark. For information, call ✆ **406/586-2635** (www.hatchfest. com). Early October.

Glacier Jazz Stampede. This 3-day event brings ragtime, swing, and blues musicians to multiple venues in Kalispell. Call ✆ **406/755-6088** (www.glacierjazz.com) for more information. Early October.

December

Christmas Strolls and Parades. Statewide, Montana and Wyoming. Check with local chambers of commerce for specific dates and locations.

5 Travel Insurance

The cost of travel insurance varies widely, depending on the cost and length of your trip, your age and health, and the type of trip you're taking, but expect to pay between 5% and 8% of the vacation itself.

TRIP-CANCELLATION INSURANCE Trip-cancellation insurance will help retrieve your money if you have to back out of a trip or depart early, or if your travel supplier goes bankrupt. Permissible reasons for trip cancellation can range from sickness to natural disasters to the State Department declaring a destination unsafe for travel.

For more information, contact one of the following recommended insurers:

Access America (✆ 866/807-3982; www.accessamerica.com); **Travel Guard International** (✆ 800/826-4919; www.travel guard.com); **Travel Insured International** (✆ 800/243-3174; www.travel insured.com); and **Travelex Insurance Services** (✆ 888/457-4602; www.travelex-insurance.com).

MEDICAL INSURANCE Most health insurance policies cover you if you get sick away from home—but check, particularly if you're insured by an HMO.

LOST-LUGGAGE INSURANCE On flights within the U.S., checked baggage is covered up to $2,500 per ticketed passenger. On international flights (including

U.S. portions of international trips), baggage coverage is limited to approximately $9.07 per pound, up to approximately $635 per checked bag. If you plan to check items more valuable than what's covered by the standard liability, see if your homeowner's policy covers your valuables, get baggage insurance as part of your comprehensive travel-insurance package, or buy Travel Guard's "BagTrak" product.

If your luggage is lost, immediately file a lost-luggage claim at the airport, detailing the luggage contents. Most airlines require that you report delayed, damaged, or lost baggage within 4 hours of arrival. The airlines are required to deliver luggage, once found, directly to your house or destination free of charge.

6 Health & Safety

GENERAL AVAILABILITY OF HEALTHCARE

Hospitals with 24-hour emergency rooms can be found in most cities and large towns in Montana and Wyoming, as well as Yellowstone National Park, which has three clinics within its borders.

COMMON AILMENTS

GIARDIA   Lakes and streams in Montana and Wyoming are often host to giardia and other intestinal parasites. When hiking or backpacking, bring plenty of water. Drink from a lake or stream only if you treat the water first by filtering it, boiling it, or adding iodine pills.

HYPOTHERMIA   Hypothermia occurs when your body gets so cold that it can no longer warm itself. It's aggravated by exhaustion, wetness, and wind, and is a leading cause of death among outdoor recreationists. It is not limited to cold weather; you can get hypothermia on a summer day that suddenly turns stormy. Always dress in layers and be prepared for bad weather, especially if you will be away from your car or lodging for an extended amount of time. When a partner gets hypothermia, you should join him or her in a sleeping bag and use your body warmth to assist.

WILDLIFE CONCERNS   Be especially cautious around wildlife, particularly with children. Bison are not big sheepdogs, and bears are not stuffed animals; they are wild animals that can turn on you suddenly if you get too close. Never—I repeat, never—get between a mother bear and her cub. If you're exploring during the summer, carry a can of pepper spray (bear mace), an effective deterrent to bears, available at local sporting goods stores.

HIGH-ALTITUDE HAZARDS   Peaks in Wyoming and Montana top out over 10,000 feet, and much of both states' terrain is over a mile high. For many visitors, this is a big jump in altitude—give yourself a few days to acclimate before you embark on strenuous exercise.

EXTREME WEATHER EXPOSURE   The weather in the Northern Rockies is capricious—it can snow in July, or give you serious sunburn in February. If your wilderness activity takes you to a body of water, have extra clothes available in case you get wet, preferably wool and fleece fabrics, which wick away moisture. Many Western streams, rivers, and lakes are glacier-fed and run high during spring; they can be difficult to negotiate and are extremely cold. Winter backcountry explorers should always be equipped with a shovel, a sectional probe, and an avalanche transceiver, since avalanches are common.

WHAT TO DO IF YOU GET SICK AWAY FROM HOME

In most cases, your existing health plan will provide the coverage you need. But double-check; you may want to buy **travel medical insurance** instead. (See the section on insurance, above.) Bring your insurance ID card with you when you travel.

If you suffer from a chronic illness, consult your doctor before your departure. For conditions like epilepsy, diabetes, or heart problems, wear a **MedicAlert Identification Tag** (© **800/825-3785;** www.medic alert.org), which will immediately alert doctors to your condition and give them access to your records through MedicAlert's 24-hour hot line.

Pack **prescription medications** in your carry-on luggage, and carry prescription medications in their original containers, with pharmacy labels—otherwise they won't make it through airport security. Also bring along copies of your prescriptions in case you lose your pills or run out. Don't forget an extra pair of contact lenses or prescription glasses.

7 Specialized Travel Resources

TRAVELERS WITH DISABILITIES

Most disabilities shouldn't stop anyone from traveling. There are more options and resources out there than ever before. Wyoming and Montana are not necessarily ahead of the curve when it comes to accessible facilities: There are only a handful of accessible trails in the main attraction—the national parks.

The U.S. National Park Service offers a **Golden Access Passport** that gives free lifetime entrance to all properties administered by the National Park Service—national parks, monuments, historic sites, recreation areas, and national wildlife refuges—for persons who are visually impaired or permanently disabled, regardless of age. You may pick up a Golden Access Passport at any NPS entrance fee area by showing proof of medically determined disability and eligibility for receiving benefits under federal law. Besides free entry, the Golden Access Passport also offers a 50% discount on federal-use fees charged for such facilities as camping, swimming, parking, boat launching, and tours. For more information, go to www.nps.gov/fees_passes.htm or call © **888/467-2757.**

The **Montana Independent Living Project,** 1820 11th Ave., Helena, MT 59601 (© **800/735-6457** or 406/442-5755), operates an information and referral service for travelers with disabilities, providing information relating to such topics as accessibility, recreation, and transportation.

Many travel agencies offer customized tours and itineraries for travelers with disabilities. Among them are **Flying Wheels Travel** (© **507/451-5005;** www.flying wheelstravel.com); **Access-Able Travel Source** (© **303/232-2979;** www.accessable.com); and **Accessible Journeys** (© **800/846-4537** or 610/521-0339; www.disabilitytravel.com). **Avis Rent a Car** has an "Avis Access" program that offers such services as a dedicated 24-hour toll-free number (© **888/879-4273**) for customers with special travel needs; special car features such as swivel seats, spinner knobs, and hand controls; and accessible bus service.

Organizations that offer assistance to disabled travelers include **MossRehab** (www.mossresourcenet.org), the **American Foundation for the Blind (AFB)** (© **800/232-5463;** www.afb.org), and **SATH** (Society for Accessible Travel & Hospitality) (© **212/447-7284;** www. sath.org)

The community website **iCan** (www. icanonline.net/channels/travel/index.cfm) has destination guides and several regular columns on accessible travel. Also check out the quarterly magazine **Emerging Horizons** www.emerginghorizons.com); and *Open World* magazine, published by SATH (see above).

GAY & LESBIAN TRAVELERS

Wyoming and Montana do not have the reputation of being the gay-friendliest states in the Union, especially in the wake of the Matthew Shepherd murder in Laramie in 1998. But larger cities tend to have a gay scene of some kind, especially Missoula and Bozeman in Montana, and there is little for gay travelers to worry about. However, some of the more rural destinations are still rife with homophobia.

The **International Gay & Lesbian Travel Association (IGLTA)** (✆ **800/ 448-8550** or 954/776-2626; www.iglta. org) is the trade association for the gay and lesbian travel industry, and offers an online directory of gay- and lesbian-friendly travel businesses; go to their website and click on "Members."

Based in Red Lodge, Montana, **Out-West Global Adventures** (✆ **800/743-0458** or 406/446-1533; www.outwest adventures.com) offers gay and lesbian adventure travel packages, including ranching vacations in Montana and back-packing trips in Yellowstone. **Now, Voyager** (✆ **800/255-6951;** www.now voyager.com) is a well-known San Francisco–based gay-owned and -operated travel service.

SENIOR TRAVEL

Most lodging establishments and museums in Montana and Wyoming offer discounts to seniors. Mention the fact that you're a senior citizen when you make your travel reservations. Although all of the major U.S. airlines except America West have canceled their senior discount and coupon book programs, many hotels still offer discounts for seniors. In most cities, people over the age of 60 qualify for reduced admission to theaters, museums, and other attractions, as well as discounted fares on public transportation.

Members of **AARP** (formerly known as the American Association of Retired Persons), 601 E St. NW, Washington, DC 20049 (✆ **888/687-2277;** www. aarp.org), get discounts on hotels, airfares, and car rentals. AARP offers members a wide range of benefits, including *AARP: The Magazine* and a monthly newsletter. Anyone over 50 can join.

The **U.S. National Park Service** offers a **Golden Age Passport** that gives seniors 62 years or older lifetime entrance to all properties administered by the National Park Service—national parks, monuments, historic sites, recreation areas, and national wildlife refuges—for a one-time processing fee of $10, which must be purchased in person at any NPS facility that charges an entrance fee. Besides free entry, a Golden Age Passport also offers a 50% discount on federal-use fees charged for such facilities as camping, swimming, parking, boat launching, and tours. For more information, go to www.nps.gov/ fees_passes.htm or call ✆ **888/467-2757.**

Many reliable agencies and organizations target the 50-plus market. **Elderhostel** (✆ **877/426-8056;** www.elder hostel.org) arranges study programs for those aged 55 and over (and a spouse or companion of any age) in the U.S. and in more than 80 countries around the world. Most courses last 5 to 7 days in the U.S. (2–4 weeks abroad), and many include airfare, accommodations in university dormitories or modest inns, meals, and tuition. **ElderTreks** (✆ **800/741-7956;** www.eldertreks.com) offers small-group tours to off-the-beaten-path or adventure-travel locations, restricted to travelers 50 and older. **INTRAV** (✆ **800/ 456-8100;** www.intrav.com) is a high-end tour operator that caters to the mature, discerning traveler, not specifically seniors, with trips around the world that include guided safaris, polar expeditions, private-jet adventures, and small-boat cruises down jungle rivers.

Recommended publications offering travel resources and discounts for seniors include: the quarterly magazine *Travel 50 & Beyond* (www.travel50andbeyond. com); *Travel Unlimited: Uncommon Adventures for the Mature Traveler* (Avalon); *101 Tips for Mature Travelers,* available from Grand Circle Travel (© **800/221-2610** or 617/350-7500; www.gct.com); and *Unbelievably Good Deals and Great Adventures That You Absolutely Can't Get Unless You're Over 50* (McGraw-Hill), by Joann Rattner Heilman.

FAMILY TRAVEL

Montana and Wyoming are full of great family destinations, especially Yellowstone, Grand Teton, and Glacier national parks. Many properties in these areas have family cabins that include kitchens, and most motels have family rooms or suites tailored to the needs of parents with their kids. To locate those accommodations, restaurants, and attractions that are particularly kid-friendly, refer to the "Kids" icon throughout this guide.

Familyhostel (© **800/733-9753;** www. learn.unh.edu/familyhostel) takes the whole family, including kids ages 8 to 15, on moderately priced domestic and international learning vacations. Lectures, field trips, and sightseeing are guided by a team of academics.

Recommended family travel Internet sites include **Family Travel Forum** (www. familytravelforum.com), a comprehensive site that offers customized trip planning; **Family Travel Network** (www.familytravel network.com), an award-winning site that offers travel features, deals, and tips; **Traveling Internationally with Your Kids** (www.travelwithyourkids.com), a comprehensive site offering sound advice for long-distance and international travel with children; and **Family Travel Files** (www. thefamilytravelfiles.com), which offers an online magazine and a directory of off-the-beaten-path tours and tour operators for families.

Family groups should always ask about discounts for attractions and accommodations. If you plan to stay a week at a ski resort or dude ranch, you may find a better value by renting a condominium or lodge than multiple rooms. Ski areas often offer packages that include accommodations and lift tickets; check with a ski resort's reservation service for current prices. Before booking any type of room, event, or activity, be sure to inquire whether there are discounts for children or age restrictions.

A National Parks Pass costs $50 and provides free admission into any national park requiring an entry fee. Not only will the pass admit you and any passengers in your vehicle at all parks where a per-vehicle fee is charged, but it also will admit you and your spouse, parents, and children at parks where a per-visitor fee is charged. Valid for 1 full year from first use in a national park, the pass can be purchased at park entrance stations and visitor centers, or by phone (© **888/GO-PARKS**) or online (www.nationalparks.org).

Montana Kids (www.montanakids. com) is a website from Travel Montana that's both for kids, with games and such, and their parents, with information about places to go and things to do with families. As for books, *Frommer's Family Vacations in the National Parks* (Wiley Publishing, Inc.) is an excellent resource; and *How to Take Great Trips with Your Kids* (The Harvard Common Press) is full of good general advice that can apply to travel anywhere.

WOMEN TRAVELERS

Founded in 1982 and the first of its kind, **AdventureWomen** in Bozeman (© **800/ 804-8686,** or 406/587-3883 outside the U.S.; www.adventurewomen.com) offers customized trips to just about anywhere in the world for active and adventurous women, age 30 and older. In Montana, the company guides hiking trips as well as skiing and guest-ranch trips.

Check out the award-winning website **Journeywoman** (www.journeywoman. com), a "real life" women's travel information network where you can sign up for a free e-mail newsletter and get advice on everything from etiquette and dress to safety; or the travel guide *Safety and Security for Women Who Travel* by Sheila Swan and Peter Laufer (Travelers' Tales, Inc.), offering common-sense tips on safe travel.

TRAVELING WITH PETS

While Montana and Wyoming seem like natural destinations for bringing Fido along, the national parks are absolutely awful destinations for pets—they aren't allowed on the trails or many in-park hotels. If your itinerary is focused on national forests and dog-friendly cabin resorts, however, it can be workable to bring a dog on the trip.

Keep in mind that dogs must be leashed at all times on all federal and state lands. However, because many of the public lands in these states have bears and other wildlife, there are sometimes site-specific regulations regarding pets. Aside from regulations, be attentive to your pet's well-being. Just as people need extra water in this dry climate, so do pets. And keep in mind that trails are often rough, and jagged rocks can cut the pads on your dog's feet. Remember, too, that dogs that usually spend most of their time sleeping aren't used to 10-hour hikes up mountainsides.

8 Planning Your Trip Online

SURFING FOR AIRFARES

The "big three" online travel agencies— **Expedia.com, Travelocity.com,** and **Orbitz.com**—sell most of the air tickets bought on the Internet. (Canadian travelers should try expedia.ca and Travelocity. ca; U.K. residents can go for expedia. co.uk and opodo.co.uk.) Each has different business deals with the airlines and may offer different fares on the same flights, so it's wise to shop around. Expedia and Travelocity will also send you **e-mail notification** when a cheap fare becomes available to your favorite destination. Of the smaller travel agency websites, **SideStep** (www.sidestep.com) has gotten the best reviews from Frommer's authors. It's a browser add-on that purports to "search 140 sites at once," but in reality only beats competitors' fares as often as other sites do.

Also remember to check **airline websites,** especially those for low-fare carriers such as Southwest, JetBlue, AirTran, WestJet, or Ryanair, whose fares are often misreported or simply missing from travel agency websites. Even with major airlines, you can often shave a few bucks from a fare by booking directly through the airline and avoiding a travel agency's transaction fee. But you'll get these discounts only by **booking online:** Most airlines now offer online-only fares that even their phone agents know nothing about. For the websites of airlines that fly to and from your destination, go to "Getting There," p. 31.

Great **last-minute deals** are available through free weekly e-mail services provided directly by the airlines. Most of these are announced on Tuesday or Wednesday and must be purchased online. Most are only valid for travel that weekend, but some (such as Southwest's) can be booked weeks or months in advance. Sign up for weekly e-mail alerts at airline websites or check mega-sites that compile comprehensive lists of last-minute specials, such as **Smarter Travel** (smartertravel.com). For last-minute trips, **site59.com** and **lastminutetravel. com** in the U.S. and **lastminute.com** in Europe often have better air-and-hotel package deals than the major-label sites. A website listing numerous bargain sites and airlines around the world is **www.itravelnet.com**.

If you're willing to give up some control over your flight details, use what is called an **"opaque" fare service** like **Priceline** (www.priceline.com; www.priceline.co.uk for Europeans) or its smaller competitor **Hotwire** (www.hotwire.com). Both offer rock-bottom prices in exchange for travel on a "mystery airline" at a mysterious time of day, often with a mysterious change of planes en route. The mystery airlines are all major, well-known carriers—and the possibility of being sent from Philadelphia to Chicago via Tampa is remote; the airlines' routing computers have gotten a lot better than they used to be. But your chances of getting a 6am or 11pm flight are pretty high. Hotwire tells you flight prices before you buy; Priceline usually has better deals than Hotwire, but you have to play their "name our price" game. If you're new at this, the helpful folks at **BiddingForTravel** (www.biddingfortravel.com) do a good job of demystifying Priceline's prices and strategies. Priceline and Hotwire are great for flights within North America and between the U.S. and Europe. But for flights to other parts of the world, consolidators will almost always beat their fares. **Note:** In 2004 Priceline added nonopaque service to its roster. You now have the option to pick exact flights, times, and airlines from a list of offers—or opt to bid on opaque fares as before.

SURFING FOR HOTELS

Shopping online for hotels is generally done one of two ways: by booking through the hotel's own website or through an independent booking agency (or a fare-service agency like Priceline; see below). These Internet hotel agencies have multiplied in mind-boggling numbers of late, competing for the business of millions of consumers surfing for accommodations around the world. This competitiveness can be a boon to consumers who have the patience and time to shop and compare the online sites for good deals—but shop they must, for prices can vary considerably from site to site. And keep in mind that hotels at the top of a site's listing may be there for no other reason than that they paid money to get the placement.

Of the "big three" sites, **Expedia** offers a long list of special deals and "virtual tours" or photos of available rooms so you can see what you're paying for (a feature that helps counter the claims that the best rooms are often held back from bargain-booking websites). **Travelocity** posts unvarnished customer reviews and ranks its properties according to the AAA rating system. Also reliable are **Hotels.com** and **Quikbook.com.** An excellent free program, **TravelAxe** (www.travelaxe.net), can help you search multiple hotel sites at once, even ones you may never have heard of—and conveniently lists the total price of the room, including the taxes and service charges. Another booking site, **Travelweb** (www.travelweb.com), is partly owned by the hotels it represents (including the Hilton, Hyatt, and Starwood chains) and is therefore plugged directly into the hotels' reservations systems—unlike independent online agencies, which have to fax or e-mail reservation requests to the hotel, a good portion of which get misplaced in the shuffle. More than once, travelers have arrived at the hotel, only to be told that they have no reservation. To be fair, many of the major sites are undergoing improvements in service and ease of use, and Expedia will soon be able to plug directly into the reservations systems of many hotel chains—none of which can be bad news for consumers. In the meantime, it's a good idea to **get a confirmation number** and **make a printout** of any online booking transaction.

In the opaque website category, **Priceline** and **Hotwire** are even better for

Frommers.com: The Complete Travel Resource

For an excellent travel-planning resource, we highly recommend **Frommers. com** (www.frommers.com), voted Best Travel Site by *PC Magazine*. We're a little biased, of course, but we guarantee that you'll find the travel tips, reviews, monthly vacation giveaways, bookstore, and online-booking capabilities thoroughly indispensable. Among the special features are our popular **Destinations** section, where you'll get expert travel tips, hotel and dining recommendations, and advice on the sights to see for more than 3,500 destinations around the globe; the **Frommers.com Newsletter,** with the latest deals, travel trends, and money-saving secrets; our **Community** area featuring **Message Boards,** where Frommer's readers post queries and share advice (sometimes even our authors show up to answer questions); and our **Photo Center,** where you can post and share vacation tips. When your research is done, the **Online Reservations System** (www.frommers. com/book_a_trip) takes you to Frommer's preferred online partners for booking your vacation at affordable prices.

hotels than for airfares; with both, you're allowed to pick the neighborhood and quality level of your hotel before offering up your money. Priceline's hotel product even covers Europe and Asia, though it's much better at getting five-star lodging for three-star prices than at finding anything at the bottom of the scale. On the downside, many hotels stick Priceline guests in their least desirable rooms. Be sure to go to the BiddingForTravel website (see above) before bidding on a hotel room on Priceline; it features a fairly up-to-date list of hotels that Priceline uses in major cities. For both Priceline and Hotwire, you pay upfront, and the fee is nonrefundable.

Note: Some hotels do not provide loyalty program credits or points or other frequent-stay amenities when you book a room through opaque online services.

SURFING FOR RENTAL CARS

For booking rental cars online, the best deals are usually found at rental-car company websites, although all the major online travel agencies also offer rental-car reservations services. Priceline and Hotwire work well for rental cars, too; the only "mystery" is which major rental company you get, and for most travelers the difference between Hertz, Avis, and Budget is negligible.

9 The 21st-Century Traveler

INTERNET ACCESS AWAY FROM HOME
WITHOUT YOUR OWN COMPUTER

To find cybercafes in Montana and Wyoming, check **www.cybercaptive.com** and **www.cybercafe.com**. In many areas in Wyoming and Montana, however,

Internet access can be hard to come by, and finding a public library that offers free access can be a better bet.

Aside from libraries and cybercafes, most **youth hostels** nowadays have at least one computer you can get to the Internet on. Avoid **hotel business centers,** which often charge exorbitant rates.

Most major airports now have **Internet kiosks** scattered throughout their gates. These give you basic Web access for a per-minute fee that's usually higher than cybercafe prices.

WITH YOUR OWN COMPUTER

More and more hotels, cafes, and retailers are signing on as Wi-Fi (wireless fidelity) "hotspots." Mac owners have their own networking technology: Apple AirPort. **T-Mobile Hotspot** (www.t-mobile.com/hotspot) serves up wireless connections at more than 1,000 Starbucks coffee shops nationwide. **Boingo** (www.boingo.com) and **Wayport** (www.wayport.com) have set up networks in airports and high-class hotel lobbies. iPass providers (see below) also give you access to a few hundred wireless hotel lobby setups. To locate other hotspots that provide **free wireless networks** in cities around the world, go to **www.personaltelco.net/index.cgi/WirelessCommunities**.

For dial-up access, most business-class hotels throughout the world offer dataports for laptop modems, and a few thousand hotels in the U.S. and Europe now offer free high-speed Internet access. In addition, major Internet Service Providers (ISPs) have **local access numbers** around the world, allowing you to go online by placing a local call. The **iPass** network also has dial-up numbers around the world. You'll have to sign up with an iPass provider, who will then tell you how to set up your computer for your destination(s). For a list of iPass providers, go to www.ipass.com and click on "Individuals Buy Now." One solid provider is **i2roam** (© **866/811-6209** or 920/235-0475; www.i2roam.com).

Wherever you go, bring a **connection kit** of the right power and phone adapters, a spare phone cord, and a spare Ethernet network cable—or find out whether your hotel supplies them to guests.

USING A CELLPHONE ACROSS THE U.S.

Just because your cellphone works at home doesn't mean it'll work elsewhere in the country (thanks to our nation's fragmented cellphone system). It's a good bet that your phone will work in major cities. But take a look at your wireless company's coverage map on its website before heading out—T-Mobile, Sprint, and Nextel are particularly weak in rural areas. If you need to stay in touch at a destination where you know your phone won't work, **rent** a phone that does from **InTouch USA** (© **800/872-7626;** www.intouchglobal.com) or a rental-car location, but beware that you'll pay $1 a minute or more for airtime.

If you're venturing deep into national parks, you may want to consider renting a **satellite phone ("satphones"),** which are different from cellphones in that they connect to satellites rather than ground-based towers. A satphone is more costly than a cellphone but works where there's no cellular signal and no towers. Unfortunately, you'll pay at least $2 per minute to use the phone, and it only works where you can see the horizon (usually not indoors). In North America, you can rent Iridium satellite phones from **RoadPost** (© **888/290-1606** or 905/272-5665; www.roadpost.com). InTouch USA (see above) offers a wider range of satphones but at higher rates.

If you're not from the U.S., you'll be appalled at the poor reach of our GSM (Global System for Mobiles) wireless network, which is used by much of the rest of the world (see below). Your phone will probably work in most major U.S. cities; it definitely won't work in many rural areas. (To see where GSM phones work in the U.S., check out www.t-mobile.com/coverage/national_popup.asp.) And you may or may not be able to send SMS (text messaging) home—something Americans tend not to do anyway, for various cultural and technological reasons. (International budget travelers like to send text messages home because it's much cheaper than making international calls.) Assume nothing—call your wireless provider and get the full scoop. In a worst-case scenario, you can always rent a phone; InTouch USA delivers to hotels.

10 Getting There

BY PLANE

Travelers flying into Montana can choose to land in one of the state's six major airports: Billings, Bozeman, Great Falls, Helena, Kalispell, or Missoula. Air service to these airports is provided by the following airlines: **Delta** (© 800/221-1212; www.delta.com), **Frontier** (© 800/432-1359; www.flyfrontier.com), **Northwest** (© 800/225-2525; www.nwa.com), and **United** (© 800/241-6522; www.ual.com). Delta and United's commuter affiliate is **SkyWest** (© 800/453-9417; www.skywest.com), and Northwest's is **Horizon** (© 800/547-9308; www.horizonair.com). The busiest of the smaller connection airlines is **Big Sky** (© 800/237-7788; www.bigskyair.com).

In Wyoming, Jackson, Casper, Cheyenne, Cody, Gillette, Laramie, Riverton, Rock Springs, and Sheridan have airports with commercial intrastate airline service. Presently, the airlines serving the state are **Delta** (© 800/221-1212; www.delta.com) and **United** (© 800/241-6522; www.ual.com), with service to Jackson by **American Airlines** (© 800/433-7300; www.aa.com), **Northwest** (© 800/225-2525; www.nwa.com), and **Big Sky Airlines** (© 800/237-7788; www.bigskyair.com). Commuter carriers in Wyoming include **SkyWest** (© 800/453-9417; www.skywest.com) and **Great Lakes Aviation** (© 800/554-5111; www.greatlakesav.com).

Montana and Wyoming's airports are dwarfed by **Denver International Airport** in Colorado and **Salt Lake City International Airport** in Utah. However, connecting flights are available from Denver and Salt Lake to almost all of the regional airports in Montana and Wyoming, and—if you have time—renting a car in one of these larger cities can make for a nice scenic drive to your final destination.

FLYING FOR LESS: TIPS FOR GETTING THE BEST AIRFARE

Passengers sharing the same airplane cabin rarely pay the same fare. Travelers who need to purchase tickets at the last minute, change their itinerary at a moment's notice, or fly one-way often get stuck paying the premium rate. Here are some ways to keep your airfare costs down.

- Passengers who can book their ticket **long in advance,** who can **stay over Saturday night,** or who **fly midweek** or **at less-trafficked hours** may pay a fraction of the full fare. If your schedule is flexible, say so, and ask if you can secure a cheaper fare by changing your flight plans.
- You can also save on airfares by keeping an eye out in local newspapers for **promotional specials** or **fare wars,** when airlines lower prices on their most popular routes. You rarely see fare wars offered for peak travel times, but if you can travel in the off-months, you may snag a bargain.
- Search **the Internet** for cheap fares (see "Planning Your Trip Online," earlier in this chapter).
- **Consolidators,** also known as bucket shops, are great sources for international tickets, although they usually can't beat the Internet on fares within North America. Start by looking in Sunday newspaper travel sections; U.S. travelers should focus on the *New York Times, Los Angeles Times,* and *Miami Herald.* For less-developed destinations, small travel agents who cater to immigrant communities

in large cities often have the best deals. *Beware:* Bucket shop tickets are usually nonrefundable or rigged with stiff cancellation penalties, often as high as 50% to 75% of the ticket price, and some put you on charter airlines, which may leave at inconvenient times and experience delays. Several reliable consolidators are worldwide and available on the Net. **STA Travel** is now the world's leader in student travel, thanks to its purchase of Council Travel. It also offers good fares for travelers of all ages. **ELTExpress (Flights.com)** (© **800/ TRAV-800;** www.eltexpress.com) started in Europe and has excellent fares worldwide, but particularly to that continent. It also has "local" websites in 12 countries. **FlyCheap** (© **800/FLY-CHEAP;** www.1800fly

cheap.com) is owned by package-holiday megalith MyTravel and so has especially good access to fares for sunny destinations. **Air Tickets Direct** (© **800/778-3447;** www.air ticketsdirect.com) is based in Montreal and leverages the currently weak Canadian dollar for low fares; it'll also book trips to places that U.S. travel agents won't touch, such as Cuba.

• Join **frequent-flier clubs.** Accrue enough miles, and you'll be rewarded with free flights and elite status. It's free, and you'll get the best choice of seats, faster response to phone inquiries, and prompter service if your luggage is stolen, your flight is canceled or delayed, or if you want to change your seat. You don't need to fly to build frequent-flier miles—**frequent-flier credit cards** can provide

---

⌢Tips Getting Through the Airport

• Arrive at the airport 1 hour before a domestic flight and 2 hours before an international flight; if you show up late, tell an airline employee and she'll probably whisk you to the front of the line.

• Beat the ticket-counter lines by using airport electronic kiosks or even online check-in from your home computer, from where you can print out boarding passes in advance. Curbside check-in is also a good way to avoid lines.

• Bring a current, government-issued photo ID such as a driver's license or passport. Children under 18 do not need government-issued photo IDs for domestic flights, but they do for international flights to most countries.

• Ship it—don't stow it: Though pricey, it's sometimes worth it to travel luggage-free. Specialists in door-to-door luggage delivery include **Virtual Bellhop** (www.virtualbellhop.com), **SkyCap International** (wwww.skycap international.com), **Luggage Express** (www.usxpluggageexpress.com), and **Sports Express** (www.sportsexpress.com).

• Use a TSA-approved lock for your checked luggage. Look for Travel Sentry certified locks at luggage or travel shops and Brookstone stores (or online at www.brookstone.com).

• Speed up security by removing your jacket and shoes before you're screened. In addition, remove metal objects such as big belt buckles. If you've got metallic body parts, a note from your doctor can prevent a long chat with the security screeners.

thousands of miles for doing your everyday shopping.

LONG-HAUL FLIGHTS: HOW TO STAY COMFORTABLE

Long flights can be trying; stuffy air and cramped seats can make you feel as if you're being sent parcel post in a small box. But with a little advance planning, you can make an otherwise unpleasant experience almost bearable.

- Your choice of airline and airplane will definitely affect your leg room. Find more details at www.seatguru.com, which has extensive details about almost every seat on six major U.S. airlines. For international airlines, research firm Skytrax has posted a list of average seat pitches at www.airlinequality.com.
- Emergency exit seats and bulkhead seats typically have the most legroom. Emergency exit seats are usually held back to be assigned the day of a flight (to ensure that the seat is filled by someone able-bodied); it's worth getting to the ticket counter early to snag one of these spots for a long flight. Many passengers find that bulkhead seating (the row facing the wall at the front of the cabin) offers more legroom, but keep in mind that bulkheads are where airlines often put baby bassinets, so you may be sitting next to an infant.
- To have two seats for yourself in a three-seat row, try for an aisle seat in a center section toward the back of coach. If you're traveling with a companion, book an aisle and a window seat. Middle seats are usually booked last, so chances are good you'll end up with three seats to yourselves. And in the event that a third passenger is assigned the middle seat, he or she will probably be more than happy to trade for a window or an aisle.
- Ask about entertainment options. Many airlines offer seatback video systems where you get to choose your movies or play video games—but only on some of their planes. (Boeing 777s are your best bet.)
- To sleep, avoid the last row of any section or a row in front of an emergency exit, as these seats are the least likely to recline. Avoid seats near highly trafficked toilet areas. Avoid seats in the back of many jets—these can be narrower than those in the rest of coach class. You also may want to reserve a window seat so that you can rest your head and avoid being bumped in the aisle.
- Get up, walk around, and stretch every 60 to 90 minutes to keep your blood flowing. This helps avoid **deep vein thrombosis**, or "economy-class syndrome," a potentially deadly condition that can be caused by sitting in cramped conditions for too long. Other preventative measures include drinking lots of water and avoiding alcohol (see next bullet).
- Drink water before, during, and after your flight to combat the lack of humidity in airplane cabins—which can be drier than the Sahara. Bring a bottle of water on board. Avoid alcohol, which will dehydrate you.
- If you're flying with kids, don't forget to carry on toys, books, pacifiers, and chewing gum to help them relieve ear pressure buildup during ascent and descent. Let each child pack his or her own backpack with favorite toys.

BY CAR

In Montana, **I-90** runs west to east from St. Regis to Wyola, near the Wyoming border southeast of Billings. **I-94** goes east from Billings to Glendive and the North Dakota border. **U.S. Highway 2,** called the "Hi-Line," is another east-west alternative, stretching across the northern reaches of Montana from Bainville to Troy. The major interstate traversing the state from north to south is **I-15,** from Sweetgrass to Monida.

Wyoming is crossed through the southern part of the state by **I-80,** a huge trucker route from Pine Bluffs in the east to Evanston in the west. **I-90** begins in the north-central part of the state near Ranchester and comes out in the northeast near Beulah. Just outside Buffalo is I-90's junction with **I-25,** a north-south route that runs through Cheyenne. The western part of the state north of Rock Springs is dominated by U.S. highways and secondary state-maintained roads.

BY TRAIN

Amtrak's *Empire Builder* (© **800/872-7245;** www.amtrak.com) provides daily rail service along the northern tier of Montana, traveling west from Chicago and east from Seattle. The train stops at Wolf Point, Glasgow, Malta, Havre, Shelby, Cut Bank, Browning, East Glacier, Essex, West Glacier, Whitefish, and Libby.

11 Packages for the Independent Traveler

Package tours are simply a way to buy the airfare, accommodations, and other elements of your trip (such as car rentals, airport transfers, and sometimes even activities) at the same time and often at discounted prices.

One good source of package deals is the airlines themselves. Most major airlines offer air/land packages, including **American Airlines Vacations** (© 800/321-2121; www.aavacations.com), **Delta Vacations** (© 800/221-6666; www.deltavacations.com), **Continental Airlines Vacations** (© 800/301-3800; www.co

vacations.com), and **United Vacations** (© 888/854-3899; www.unitedvacations.com). Several big **online travel agencies**—Expedia, Travelocity, Orbitz, Site59, and Lastminute.com—also do a brisk business in packages.

Travel packages are also listed in the travel section of your local Sunday newspaper. Or check ads in the national travel magazines such as *Arthur Frommer's Budget Travel Magazine, Travel & Leisure, National Geographic Traveler,* and *Condé Nast Traveler.*

12 Escorted General-Interest Tours

Escorted tours are structured group tours, with a group leader. The price usually includes everything from airfare to hotels, meals, tours, admission costs, and local transportation.

Several regional companies provide small, personalized escorted tours of specific areas in Montana and Wyoming. These include **Great Divide Wildlands Institute** (© 406/683-4669; www.greatdividetours.com), **Montana High Country Tours** (© 406/834-3469; www.mhct.com), **Yellowstone Safari** (© 866/586-1155; www.yellowstonesafari.com), **AdventureBus** (© 888/737-5263; www.adventurebus.com), and **Off the Beaten**

Path (© 800/445-2995; www.offthebeatenpath.com). National companies that provide tours in Montana and Wyoming, often including Glacier, Yellowstone, and Grand Teton national parks, include **Maupintour** (© 800/255-4266; www.maupintour.com) and **Tauck Tours** (© 800/788-7885; www.tauck.com). National bus-tour company **Gray Line** (© 800/443-6133 or 307/733-4325; www.graylinejh.com) offers tours originating in the Jackson Hole area. **Amtrak** (© 800/872-7245; www.amtrak.com) also offers tour packages in Montana.

Tips **Ask Before You Go**

Before you invest in a package deal or an escorted tour:

- Always ask about the **cancellation policy.** Can you get your money back? Is there a deposit required?
- Ask about the **accommodations choices and prices** for each. Then look up the hotels' reviews in a Frommer's guide and check their rates online for your specific dates of travel. Also find out what types of rooms are offered.
- Request a complete **schedule** (escorted tours only).
- Ask about the **size** and demographics of the group (escorted tours only).
- Discuss what is included in the **price** (transportation, meals, tips, airport transfers, and so forth). (escorted tours only)
- Finally, look for **hidden expenses.** Ask whether airport departure fees and taxes, for example, are included in the total cost—they rarely are.

---

13 The Active Traveler

INFORMATION ON PUBLIC LANDS

Much of the fun to be had in the Northern Rockies takes place out of doors. Throughout this book, you'll find contact information for national and state parks, national forests, and the like. Here are some key statewide and regional resources. The **U.S. Forest Service** has information about national forests and wilderness areas in Montana, as well as **Bridger-Teton National Forest** in Wyoming, at the Northern Region Office, Federal Building, 200 E. Broadway, Box 7669, Missoula, MT 59807 (© **406/329-3511;** www.fs.fed.us/r1). The rest of Wyoming's forests, as well as **Thunder Basin National Grassland,** are covered by the Rocky Mountain Region Office, P.O. Box 25127, Lakewood, CO 80225 (© **303/275-5350;** www.fs.fed.us/r2).

The federal **Bureau of Land Management** also manages millions of acres of recreational lands and can be reached at its Wyoming state office, 5353 Yellowstone Rd., Cheyenne, WY 82009 (© **307/**775-6256), or its Montana state office, 5001 Southgate Dr., Billings, MT 59101 (© **406/896-5000**).

For information on Montana state parks, fishing, and hunting, get in touch with **Montana Fish, Wildlife, and Parks,** 1420 E. 6th Ave., P.O. Box 200701, Helena, MT 59620 (© **406/444-2535;** http://fwp.state.mt.us). This organization also offers a 900-number information line (© **900/225-5397**) on a wide variety of recreational topics for $1.50 per minute. In Wyoming, contact **Wyoming State Parks and Historic Sites,** 2301 Central Ave., Cheyenne, WY 82001 (© **307/777-6303;** http://wyoparks.state.wy.us). For hunting and fishing, contact **Wyoming Game and Fish,** 5400 Bishop, Cheyenne, WY 82003 (© **307/777-4600;** http://gf.state.wy.us).

ACTIVITIES A TO Z

BACKCOUNTRY SKIING There is nothing as thrilling as skiing deep, untracked powder in completely wild terrain. To enjoy this sport you need a good set of telemark skis, good information about where to go, and expert knowledge of snow conditions and avalanche risks. Among the best places to pursue this sport is **Togwotee Pass** in Bridger-Teton National Forest in Wyoming. Otherwise, check at local ski shops and ask at the headquarters of national forests and state parks. The **Jackson Hole Mountain Resort** decided in 1999 to allow skiers to ski beyond the boundaries of areas it grooms and patrols—as long as they sign waivers. Check with other ski resorts about out-of-bounds forest areas that might be accessible for backcountry adventures.

BIKING   Mountain biking is a fast-growing sport. Some folks take it easy, pedaling their way to wild country on smooth, easy-grade paths; others are looking for a fast ride down on bumpy, steep trails. Bring your own bike or rent from a local bike shop that will likely assist you in finding the best spots to ride. Bicycling on roads is also popular, but there are limitations: While automobile traffic on many roads is light, there isn't much room, because most of the roads have skimpy shoulders—Yellowstone roads are among the worst. Nor are drivers in this region terribly respectful of bicyclists. So be watchful, research your routes so you can keep to the wider roads, and always wear that helmet.

BOATING & SAILING   Serious sailors are not likely to put down roots at this altitude; even weekend sailors would be wise to look elsewhere for their kind of fun. But if you insist on trying, you'll find a few sails spread on the bigger lakes of these mountains. You can take a pretty big boat on pretty big **Flathead Lake, Jackson Lake,** or even **Yellowstone Lake,** if you're careful about the weather. Smaller boats like Hobie Cats, in some ways, better suit the sudden, swirling winds typical of these mountains.

Powerboating is another matter; if you've got a motor, pack a lunch and head for any of the many lakes that dot Montana and Wyoming's landscape. **Canyon Ferry** is a popular Montana water-skiing spot, and you'll see Wyoming powerboats cruising **Boysen Reservoir** or the many impoundments on the **North Platte.** Just make sure to check around locally regarding access if you're uncertain about it. All types of boats are available locally for rent.

CROSS-COUNTRY SKIING   If you don't plan to pound down the backcountry powder on telemark skis, but you want to get out in the snow, cross-country skiing can be practiced on any relatively flat, open meadow or plain where there's snow on the ground, or along old roads in the region's forests. Scores of guest ranches now groom trails for both track and skate skiing, and almost every ski resort in the region has a trail. If you

---

Fun Fact **Are You a Dude or a Guest?**

A century ago, it was common courtesy in the West for ranches to feed and lodge travelers who stopped by on their treks across the great empty spaces. Gradually it became acceptable to accept a few dollars from guests, and by the 1920s a ranch visit was a full-fledged vacation.

When you make your ranch reservations, it's wise to know the difference between a "dude ranch" and a "guest ranch." A dude ranch typically requires a 1-week minimum stay, and they give you the whole package: riding, fishing, trips to the rodeo, and family-style meals. Dude ranchers look down their noses at "guest" ranches, which will take guests staying just 1 night and charge extra for activities such as riding.

don't want to pay to ski, **Forest Service logging roads** are typically used for cross-country trails. Many golf courses are also regularly groomed for track skiing; some are even lighted for night skiing. The best place to cross-country ski in Montana is **West Yellowstone,** training ground of U.S. Nordic and Biathlon ski teams; in Wyoming, the **Jackson Hole** area and **Grand Teton National Park.**

DOWNHILL SKIING   There are 13 downhill ski areas in Montana and 11 in Wyoming, scattered amid the towering mountain ranges found predominantly in the western parts of both states. Breathtaking summit vistas are standard fare. Usually operating from late November to mid-April, and with comparatively shorter lift lines and less expensive lift tickets than most other ski areas in the country, Montana and Wyoming ski resorts are great values for the ski enthusiast. Don't fret if you're not skiing black-diamond runs; all ski resorts have acres of beginner and intermediate trails, and seasoned instructors provide lessons at extremely affordable prices. More and more often, you'll find telemark skiers honing their skills on packed resort slopes. The best skiing in Montana can be found at **Big Sky Resort,** near Bozeman, which is the biggest ski area in Montana, with runs for all abilities. West of Glacier National Park, Whitefish's Big Mountain prides itself on a family atmosphere. In Wyoming, the Jackson Hole area wins hands down, with the **Jackson Hole Ski Resort, Snow King,** and **Grand Targhee** ski hills just a short drive apart.

DUDE RANCHES   The dude ranch is the fabled Western experience come to life: daily rides by horseback, cowboy coffee beneath an expansive blue sky, campfire singalongs, and homemade food served in rustic lodges. Accommodations are usually in a comfortable cabin or lodge. You need not have any riding experience before your visit; ranch hands are trained to assist even the greenest of greenhorns. For additional information on dude ranches in both Montana and Wyoming, as well as other Western states, contact **Dude Ranchers' Association,** P.O. Box 2307, Cody, WY 82414 (℃ **307/587-2339;** www.dude ranch.org). The best dude ranches can be found in the **Paradise and Gallatin valleys** in southwest Montana, and in the **Sheridan** area and the **Wapiti Valley** west of Cody in Wyoming.

FISHING   Montana and Wyoming have long been known for world-class fly-fishing, their streams and creeks teeming with native trout—rainbow, brook, brown, mackinaw, golden, and cutthroat—as well as kokanee salmon, yellow perch, largemouth bass, and northern pike. Warm-water species include sauger, channel catfish, and smallmouth bass. Best places to fish in Montana: on any one of the world-class, blue-ribbon streams in the southwest part of the state. In Wyoming, head for the waters of the **North Platte River** near Saratoga and the Miracle Mile, or the high lakes of **the Wind River Indian Reservation.**

GOLF   Golfers may be pleasantly surprised at the number of exceptional courses found in both states, particularly in Bigfork and Anaconda, Montana. Summer's long days make this a perfect place to play a round, especially when you take into consideration that average daily temperatures and humidity are much lower here than at destinations in Florida. Reserve tee times well in advance. Best Montana courses: the **Old Works, Anaconda; Eagle Bend, Whitefish.** In Wyoming: the **Jackson Hole Golf and Tennis Club; Teton Pines, Jackson.**

HIKING   Hiking gives you the added bonus of moderate to strenuous cardiovascular exercise while you're seeing the sights. Remember, though, that these are the mountains, and the elevation you gain over the course of the hike is a much

Fishing Licenses

Both Montana and Wyoming require fishing licenses, which are available from most sporting goods stores, outfitters, or tackle shops. Yellowstone National Park requires an additional fishing permit (see chapter 11), and American Indian tribes located in the two states have special regulations and may require permits for fishing in their waters.

In Montana, all nonresident anglers 15 and older are required to buy fishing licenses. Those under 15 do not need a fishing license as long as they are with an adult who has a valid fishing license. A license for the period of March 1 through the following February is $60. A consecutive 2-day license is $15. In addition to fishing licenses, however, nonresident anglers of all ages must also possess conservation licenses, which cost $9.25 each. For information, contact the Montana Department of Fish, Wildlife, and Parks, 1420 E. 6th Ave., Helena, MT 59620 (© **406/444-2535;** http://fwp.state.mt.us).

You'll also need a Wyoming state fishing license if you plan to fish that state's waters. An adult nonresident license costs $10 per day and $75 for the season. Youth fees (ages 14–18) are $3 per day and $15 for the season. A $10 Conservation Stamp is also required for all licenses except the 1-day variety. No license is required for kids under 14, as long as they are accompanied by an adult who has a valid fishing license. You'll also have to check creel limits, which vary from year to year and place to place. Information is available from the Wyoming Game and Fish Department (© **307/777-4600;** http://gf.state.wy.us).

better indication of how difficult the hike will be than the actual distance traveled. Be sure to wear comfortable hiking shoes that have been broken in, and if you plan on hiking in prime grizzly country, be sure to carry bear mace and check with rangers for what to do in case you actually see a bear. Best place to take a hike in Montana: Glacier National Park. In Wyoming: the Wind River Mountains or Bighorn Mountains.

MOUNTAINEERING: ROCK & ICE CLIMBING The Northern Rockies provide superb opportunities for climbers to experience the year-round beauty of Montana and Wyoming's mountains, whether you seek a daylong rock climb during the height of summer in Montana's Beartooths or a technical climb up one of the faces of the Tetons. Ice climbing is becoming a hot ticket in the dead of winter, when many of the world's finest climbers congregate in Cody, Wyoming, for unforgettable winter mountaineering. Not for the faint of heart, the sport is highly technical and requires extreme fitness and stamina. Best place to climb in Montana: **Granite Peak,** the state's highest. In Wyoming: **Grand Teton National Park** or **Wild Iris** south of Lander.

SNOWBOARDING Forget all those stereotypes you've heard about snowboarders: This sport is a simple combination of speed, air, and style. If you've never done it, realize that you may have a very sore butt during your first few days, although seasoned shredders swear that the learning curve is much shorter than that for skiing. Experienced snowboarders will find Montana and Wyoming ski areas to be snowboard-friendly. If you're really into riding, ask around at local ski shops for winter backcountry options or summer snowboarding—**Glacier Park's Logan Pass** is a popular Fourth of July hike-'n'-ride destination. Best place in Montana and Wyoming: **The Big Mountain.**

SNOWMOBILING   With more than 3,000 miles of trails in Montana and 1,300 in Wyoming, snowmobilers have a vast winter playground to explore. Though rental shops are plentiful, machines are in high demand, so you're wise to make a reservation well in advance. Though snowmobiling doesn't require an extreme level of physical fitness, you have to be able to adequately handle the snowmobile and be well versed in safety measures since avalanches are common in the areas some of these trails traverse. Best bets for snowmobiling in Montana: **West Yellowstone** and the **Seeley Lake Valley.** In Wyoming: **Yellowstone National Park** and the surrounding national forest lands.

WATERSPORTS: CANOEING, KAYAKING & RAFTING   Paddlers have a wealth of choices here. Montana is particularly rich in rivers worth floating: the Flathead, the Blackfoot, the Madison, the Clarks Fork near Missoula, the Dearborn, the Yellowstone, and even the big old Missouri. In Wyoming there is less variety, but you'll find some fine stretches of river on the Snake, the Platte, the Hoback, and Clarks Fork through Sunlight Basin. If you choose white-water rafting, leave the driving to someone else (that is, sign up with an outfitter that will provide an experienced person to pilot your craft), though you may be asked to paddle. The smaller rivers have no dams to regulate flows, which means kayakers seeking fast, scary runs should come during runoff in June,

while canoeists wanting to relax and bird-watch can easily handle the upper Snake or Flathead late in the summer. For thrills, try the **Yellowstone River** at Gardiner, Montana, and the **Snake River** in Wyoming.

CHOOSING AN OUTFITTER

If you're just getting started as an outdoor adventurer, it might be wise to hire an outfitter to train and guide you in the ways of the wild. Even if you're experienced, you might prefer to pay someone else to handle the logistics of food, shelter, and planning, so you can just enjoy yourself.

When considering an outfitter, think about things like group size, activity level, and guide expertise. Do you mind sleeping in a tent every night? Do you want to travel with a small group or be part of a larger one? With strangers, or friends? Is your fitness level appropriate to the type of trip you want to take? Honestly evaluate your own limitations, your health, your outdoor experience, and your travel comfort zone.

Make sure that the company is up-to-date with government permits and insurance. Find out how well the company knows the area where you're going, and ask for references from people they've taken on similar trips. Inquire about your guide's background and experience. Get a firm price, including extras like airport transfers, meals, or equipment rentals.

Though this book discusses regional outfitters, you can also find an outfitter through **The Montana Outfitters and Guides Association,** 2033 11th Ave., #8, Helena, MT 59601 (© **406/449-3578;** www.moga-montana.org), and the **Wyoming Outfitters and Guide Association,** P.O. Box 2650, Casper, WY 82602 (© **307/265-2376;** www.wyoga.org).

Among reputable national and international companies that offer outdoor adventure trips in this region, including multi-activity excursions: Austin-Lehman Adventures (© 800/575-1540; www.austinlehman.com); Backroads (© 800/462-2848; www.backroads.com); GORP-travel (© 877/440-4677; www.gorptravel.com); Moguls Mountain Travel (© 888/604-5848; www.moguls.com); and The World Outdoors (© 800/488-8483; www.theworldoutdoors.org).

14 Getting Around

BY CAR

With a weak public transportation infrastructure and long distances between towns, an automobile is essential in these parts, particularly if you plan to get off the beaten path (the exception would be a ski vacation where you stay at the resort). Most paved roads are well maintained—in fact, road-repair crews are a much bigger hazard than potholes. Be forewarned that many of the less-accessible places require driving down dirt or gravel roads, far from the nearest tow truck.

If you plan to get off the highway, rent accordingly: You'll need front-wheel drive at least, and if you're going onto the bentonite roads of the desert or foothills, you'd better get four-wheel-drive. In the winter, even the interstates can turn glassy and treacherous.

Car rentals are available in every sizable city in the state and at airports. Widely represented agencies include **Alamo** (© 800/462-5266; www.alamo.com), **Avis** (© 800/331-1212; www.avis.com), **Budget** (© 800/527-0700; www.budget.com), **Enterprise** (© 800/261-7331; www.enterprise.com), **Hertz** (© 800/654-3131; www.hertz.com), **National** (© 800/227-7368; www.nationalcar.com), and **Thrifty** (© 800/847-4389; www.thrifty.com). Detailed lists of car-rental agencies in particular areas are included throughout the book.

Speed limits in Montana are 75 mph on interstates and 70 mph or slower on secondary roads, depending on the road condition and contour. The interstate speed limit in Wyoming is 75 mph, while the speed limits for two-lane roads throughout the state are as posted (usually 55 or 65 mph). The limits are enforced fairly strictly, particularly in construction areas, where fines are doubled.

Take extra precautions when driving in winter, since some highways may be restricted to four-wheel-drive vehicles or those equipped with tire chains or snow tires (these highways will be clearly marked), or may be closed for hours and even—in cases of severe mudslides—months. Also, some roads (including several in Yellowstone and Glacier national parks) are always closed in winter. Make sure you have the following safety items: a shovel and a small bag of sand or cat litter in case you get stuck in snow or ice; a first-aid kit; jumper cables; wool blankets or sleeping bag; and an ice scraper/snow brush. Always carry drinking water, summer or winter.

Above all, winter motorists need to drive slower, not make any sudden turns or stops, and watch for wildlife: Some animals gravitate to the warmth of asphalt during cold weather.

15 Tips on Accommodations

You won't find many high-priced multi-story luxury hotels here, such as those in major cities on the East and West coasts. Montana and Wyoming are mostly rural areas—some would argue that even the cities here are just overgrown cow towns—and the preponderance of accommodations choices will fall into one of four categories: major chains such as Best Western, Comfort Inn, and Super 8; small independent motels or clusters of cabins; historic hotels and bed-and-breakfast inns; and ranch resorts, where lodging is secondary to the myriad activities offered.

You usually won't have too much trouble finding a bed for the night, even without reservations, except in and near the national parks during summer, and during major events such as Cheyenne's Frontier Days. Winter can also be a problem for those looking for a room; not because they're all booked but because a lot of lodgings (and restaurants as well) simply shut down after the summer crowds have left.

SAVING ON YOUR HOTEL ROOM

The **rack rate** is the maximum rate that a hotel charges for a room. Hardly anybody pays this price, however. To lower the cost of your room:

- **Ask about special rates or other discounts.** Always ask whether a room less expensive than the first one quoted is available, or whether any special rates apply to you. You may qualify for corporate, student, military, senior, or other discounts. Mention membership in AAA, AARP, frequent-flier programs, or trade unions, which may entitle you to special deals as well. Find out the hotel policy on children—do kids stay free in the room or is there a special rate?
- **Dial direct.** When booking a room in a chain hotel, you'll often get a better deal by calling the individual hotel's reservation desk than at the chain's main number.
- **Book online.** Many hotels offer Internet-only discounts, or supply rooms to Priceline, Hotwire, or Expedia at rates much lower than the ones you can get through the hotel itself.

Shop around. And if you have special needs—a quiet room, a room with a view—call the hotel directly and make your needs known after you've booked online.

- **Remember the law of supply and demand.** Resort hotels are most crowded and therefore most expensive on weekends, so discounts are usually available for midweek stays. Business hotels in downtown locations are busiest during the week, so you can expect big discounts over the weekend. Many hotels have high-season and low-season prices, and booking the day after high season ends can mean big discounts.
- **Look into group or long-stay discounts.** If you come as part of a large group, you should be able to negotiate a bargain rate, since the hotel can then guarantee occupancy in a number of rooms. Likewise, if you're planning a long stay (at least 5 days), you might qualify for a discount. As a general rule, expect 1 night free after a 7-night stay.
- **Avoid excess charges and hidden costs.** When you book a room, ask whether the hotel charges for parking. Use your own cellphone, pay phones, or prepaid phone cards instead of dialing direct from hotel phones, which usually have exorbitant rates. And don't be tempted by the room's minibar offerings: Most hotels charge through the nose for water, soda, and snacks. Finally, ask about local taxes and service charges, which can increase the cost of a room by 15% or more. If a hotel insists upon tacking on a surprise "energy surcharge" that wasn't mentioned at check-in or a "resort fee" for amenities you didn't use, you can often make a case for getting it removed.
- Consider the pros and cons of **all-inclusive** resorts and ranches. The

term "all-inclusive" means different things at different hotels. Many all-inclusive properties will include three meals daily, horseback riding, children's programs, spa entry, and other amenities. In general, you'll save money going the all-inclusive way—as long as you use the facilities provided. The downside is that your choices are limited and you're stuck eating and playing in one place for the duration of your vacation.

- **Book an efficiency.** A room with a kitchenette allows you to shop for groceries and cook your own meals. This is a big money saver, especially for families on long stays.
- **Consider enrolling in hotel "frequent-stay" programs,** which reward repeat customers who accumulate enough points or credits to earn free hotel nights, airline miles, complimentary in-room amenities, or even merchandise. These are offered not only by many chain hotels and motels (Hilton HHonors, Marriott Rewards, Wyndham ByRequest, to name a few), but individual inns and B&Bs. Many chain hotels partner with other hotel chains, car-rental firms, airlines, and credit card companies to give consumers additional ways to accumulate points in the program.

LANDING THE BEST ROOM

Somebody has to get the best room in the house. It might as well be you. You can start by joining the hotel's frequent-guest program, which may make you eligible for upgrades. A hotel-branded credit card usually gives it owner "silver" or "gold" status in frequent-guest programs for free. Always ask about a corner room. They're often larger and quieter, with more windows and light, and they often cost the same as standard rooms. When you make your reservation, ask if the hotel is renovating; if it is, request a room away from the construction. Ask about nonsmoking rooms, rooms with views, rooms with twin, queen-, or king-size beds. If you're a light sleeper, request a quiet room away from vending machines, elevators, restaurants, bars, and discos. Ask for one of the rooms that have been most recently renovated or redecorated.

If you aren't happy with your room when you arrive, say so. If another room is available, most lodgings will be willing to accommodate you.

16 Recommended Books & Films

In addition to the books discussed below, those planning an extended trip to Yellowstone and/or Grand Teton national parks will find an abundance of information in *Frommer's Yellowstone & Grand Teton National Parks* (Wiley Publishing, Inc.).

FICTION   Start with some classics: A. B. Guthrie's *The Big Sky* (Houghton Mifflin, 1947) is now a Montana classic, as is Owen Wister's *The Virginian* (Macmillan, 1929), set in frontier Wyoming. Then move on to contemporary fiction, like the classic fly-fishing novella *A River Runs Through It* (University of Chicago Press, 1976) by Norman Maclean. *Fool's*

Crow (Viking Penguin, 1986) by James Welch (a native Montanan) and *Heart Mountain* (Viking Penguin, 1989) by Gretel Ehrlich are fictional stories that revolve around American Indian and Asian characters. Annie Proulx's *Close Range Wyoming Stories* (Scribner, 1999) and *Bad Dirt: Wyoming Stories 2* (Scribner, 2004) are recent additions by a fine writer who's spent considerable time around Sheridan. Poet James Glavin's beautifully written *The Meadow* (Henry Holt, 1992) is set in the Tie Siding area of southeast Wyoming.

Montana is fortunate to have the best of its literature compiled in one volume, *The*

Last Best Place (University of Montana Press, 1988), the definitive anthology of Montana writings, from American Indian myths to contemporary short stories.

NONFICTION   Novelist Ivan Doig wrote a beautiful memoir about his youth in Montana, *This House of Sky* (Harcourt Brace Jovanovich, 1978). Gretel Ehrlich's *The Solace of Open Spaces* (Viking Penguin, 1986) is a beautifully written, evocative account of Wyoming ranch life. Paul Schullery's *Searching for Yellowstone* (Mariner Books, 1997) is a great look at the ecology of the world's first national park and mankind's impact on it. Eric Sorg's *Buffalo Bill: Myth and Reality* is an informative read about the man who truly defined the mythos of the West.

If your interests lean more toward geography, check out the *Roadside Geology of Montana* (Mountain Press, 1986) by David Alt and Donald W. Hyndman, and the similar *Roadside Geology of Wyoming* (Mountain Press, 1988) by David R. Largeson and Darwin R. Spearing.

HISTORY   Perhaps the best, and easiest, read about the history and culture of Montana is found between the covers of *Montana, High, Wide and Handsome* (University of Nebraska Press, 1983), written by Joseph Howard and first published in 1944. Another interesting historical tome is Aubrey Haines' two-volume *The Yellowstone Story* (University Press of Colorado, 1977).

FILMS   Hollywood adapted Norman Maclean's *A River Runs Through It* in 1992 with Brad Pitt; *Rancho Deluxe* (1975) is set in Livingston, Montana, and depicts a rapidly changing place though cattle rustlers played by Jeff Bridges and Sam Waterston; *Little Big Man* (1970) is a revisionist Western that covers Custer's Last Stand and much more. Wyoming films of note include the made-for-HBO *The Laramie Project* (2001), an adaptation of a stage play about the murder of gay college student Matthew Shepard, and *Close Encounters of the Third Kind* (1977), Steven Spielberg's UFO epic that climaxes at Devils Tower National Monument.

FAST FACTS: **Montana & Wyoming**

American Express American Express travel-service representatives are located across the state. To automatically connect with the nearest agent, call 🛈 **800/221-7282**.

Area Codes The statewide area code for Montana is **406**. Wyoming's area code is **307**. Intrastate long-distance calls also require these prefixes.

ATM Networks Automated teller machines are generally available for cash transactions at any time of the day; most are compatible with the Cirrus, Cash Card, and PLUS system networks.

Business Hours Most businesses in these states operate at least 5 days each week and many are also open on weekends. Generally speaking, retail shops open around 10am and close at 6pm. During the two peak tourist seasons in summer and winter, many businesses extend their hours. In smaller towns, don't be surprised to find a hastily penned note on the door if the snow or sunshine conditions are perfect: Many business owners have been known to take their share of "powder days" with no advance notice.

Car Rentals See "Getting Around," p. 40.

Driving Rules See "Getting Around," p. 40.

Embassies & Consulates See chapter 3, "For International Visitors."

Emergencies Throughout most of Montana and Wyoming, call ℂ **911** for any emergency requiring the police, firefighters, or emergency medical technicians. Where 911 is not available, dial **0** and the operator will connect you to the appropriate emergency service provider.

Gambling The legal gambling age in Montana is 18, and it's a habit that's easily indulged—you'll find video gambling machines in restaurants, taverns, and filling stations. The two most popular are poker and keno (a game of chance similar to bingo). In Wyoming, gambling is illegal.

Information See section 2, "Visitor Information," earlier in this chapter.

Internet Access The Internet has come to Montana and Wyoming, with a number of lodgings and campgrounds providing easy hookups or Wi-Fi access. There are also several cybercafes in these states, and Internet access is often available at public libraries.

Liquor Laws The legal age for the purchase or consumption of alcohol is 21 in both states. All liquor stores in Montana are state-controlled with minimum hours of 10am to 6pm, although individual stores may be open longer. Most are closed on Sunday. Liquor may also be bought at bars with package licenses during their operating hours. Beer and wine are available at convenience stores and supermarkets from 8:30am to 2am.

Lost & Found Be sure to tell all of your credit card companies the minute you discover your wallet has been lost or stolen and file a report at the nearest police precinct. Your credit card company or insurer may require a police report number or record of the loss. Most credit card companies have an emergency toll-free number to call if your card is lost or stolen; they may be able to wire you a cash advance immediately or deliver an emergency credit card in a day or two. Visa's U.S. emergency number is ℂ **800/847-2911** or 410/581-9994. American Express cardholders and traveler's check holders should call ℂ **800/ 221-7282**. MasterCard holders should call ℂ **800/307-7309** or 636/722-7111. For other credit cards, call the toll-free number directory at ℂ **800/555-1212**.

If you need emergency cash over the weekend when all banks and American Express offices are closed, you can have money wired to you via **Western Union** (ℂ **800/325-6000**; www.westernunion.com).

Identity theft or fraud are potential complications of losing your wallet, especially if you've lost your driver's license along with your cash and credit cards. Notify the major credit-reporting bureaus immediately; placing a fraud alert on your records may protect you against liability for criminal activity. The three major U.S. credit-reporting agencies are **Equifax** (ℂ **800/766-0008**; www.equifax.com), **Experian** (ℂ **888/397-3742**; www.experian.com), and **TransUnion** (ℂ **800/680-7289**; www.transunion.com). Finally, if you've lost all forms of photo ID call your airline and explain the situation; they might allow you to board the plane if you have a copy of your passport or birth certificate and a copy of the police report you've filed.

Newspapers & Magazines Checking out a community's local newspaper can provide a fascinating look into the personality of the area. Montana's major daily newspapers are *The Missoulian* (www.missoulian.com), the *Great Falls Tribune* (www.greatfallstribune.com), and the *Billings Gazette* (www.billings gazette.com). In Wyoming, the *Casper Star-Tribune* (www.trib.com) is the only statewide paper, while the *Wyoming Tribune-Eagle* (www.wyomingnews.com) is Cheyenne's daily. Magazines of note include *Big Sky Journal* (www. bigskyjournal.com) and *Montana Magazine* (www.montanamagazine.com).

Passports **For residents of the United States:** Whether you're applying in person or by mail, you can download passport applications from the U.S. State Department website at **http://travel.state.gov**. To find your regional passport office, either check the U.S. State Department website or call the **National Passport Information Center** toll-free number (© **877/487-2778**) for automated information.

For residents of Canada: Passport applications are available at travel agencies throughout Canada or from the central **Passport Office**, Department of Foreign Affairs and International Trade, Ottawa, ON K1A 0G3 (© **800/567-6868**; www.ppt.gc.ca).

For residents of the United Kingdom: To pick up an application for a standard 10-year passport (5-year passport for children under 16), visit your nearest passport office, major post office, or travel agency or contact the **United Kingdom Passport Service** at © **0870/521-0410** or search its website at www. ukpa.gov.uk.

For residents of Ireland: You can apply for a 10-year passport at the **Passport Office**, Setanta Centre, Molesworth Street, Dublin 2 (© **01/671-1633**; www.irl gov.ie/iveagh). Those under age 18 and over 65 must apply for a €12 3-year passport. You can also apply at 1A South Mall, Cork (© **021/272-525**), or at most main post offices.

For residents of Australia: You can pick up an application from your local post office or any branch of Passports Australia, but you must schedule an interview at the passport office to present your application materials. Call the **Australian Passport Information Service** at © **131-232**, or visit the government website at www.passports.gov.au.

For residents of New Zealand: You can pick up a passport application at any New Zealand Passports Office or download it from their website. Contact the **Passports Office** at © **0800/225-050** in New Zealand or 04/474-8100, or log on to www.passports.govt.nz.

Police Dial © **911**, or **0** (for the operator).

Safety See section 6, "Health & Safety," earlier in this chapter.

Smoking In 2005, Montana enacted a law banning smoking in public buildings and restaurants; bars have until 2009 to comply. In Wyoming, most restaurants have separate smoking and nonsmoking areas, and most hotels in both states have nonsmoking rooms.

Taxes Montana has no state sales tax, but there is a lodging tax of 7%, and certain resort communities can also charge a tax of up to 3% for goods and services.

Wyoming's state sales tax is 4%, and local communities can add up to 1% more. Communities can impose a lodging tax of up to 4%.

Time Zone Montana and Wyoming are located in the Mountain Time zone and both states observe daylight saving time from spring to fall.

Useful Phone Numbers **U.S. Dept. of State Travel Advisory** (© 202/647-5225; staffed 24 hr.); **U.S. Passport Agency** (© 202/647-0518); U.S. **Centers for Disease Control International Traveler's Hotline** (© 404/332-4559).

3

For International Visitors

The pervasiveness of American culture around the world may make you feel that you know the USA pretty well, but leaving your own country still requires an additional degree of planning. This chapter will help prepare you for the more common problems that visitors may encounter.

1 Preparing for Your Trip

ENTRY REQUIREMENTS

Immigration laws are a hot political issue in the United States these days, and the following requirements may have changed somewhat by the time you plan your trip. Check at any U.S. embassy or consulate for current information and requirements. You can also plug into the **U.S. State Department**'s Internet site at **www.travel.state.gov**.

VISAS The U.S. State Department has a **Visa Waiver Program** allowing citizens of certain countries to enter the United States without a visa for stays of up to 90 days. At press time these included Andorra, Argentina, Australia, Austria, Belgium, Brunei, Denmark, Finland, France, Germany, Iceland, Ireland, Italy, Japan, Liechtenstein, Luxembourg, Monaco, the Netherlands, New Zealand, Norway, San Marino, Slovenia, Spain, Sweden, Switzerland, and the United Kingdom. Citizens of these countries need only a valid passport and a round-trip air or cruise ticket in their possession upon arrival. If they first enter the United States, they may also visit Mexico, Canada, Bermuda, and/or the Caribbean islands and return to the United States without a visa. Further information is available from any U.S. embassy or consulate. Canadian citizens may enter the

United States without visas; they need only proof of residence.

Citizens of all other countries must have (1) a valid passport that expires at least 6 months later than the scheduled end of their visit to the United States, and (2) a tourist visa, which may be obtained without charge from any U.S. consulate.

OBTAINING A VISA To obtain a visa, the traveler must submit a completed application form (either in person or by mail) with a 1½-inch-square photo, and must demonstrate binding ties to a residence abroad. Usually you can obtain a visa at once or within 24 hours, but it may take longer during the summer rush from June through August. If you cannot go in person, contact the nearest U.S. embassy or consulate for directions on applying by mail. Your travel agent or airline office may also be able to provide you with visa applications and instructions. The U.S. consulate or embassy that issues your visa will determine whether you will be issued a multiple- or single-entry visa and any restrictions regarding the length of your stay.

British subjects can obtain up-to-date passport and visa information by calling the **U.S. Embassy Visa Information Line** (© **0891/200-290**) or by visiting the "Visas to the U.S." section of the

American Embassy London's website at www.usembassy.org.uk.

MEDICAL REQUIREMENTS Unless you're arriving from an area known to be suffering from an epidemic (particularly cholera or yellow fever), inoculations or vaccinations are not required for entry into the United States. If you have a medical condition that requires syringe-administered medications, carry a valid signed prescription from your physician. The Federal Aviation Administration (FAA) no longer allows airline passengers to pack syringes in their carry-on baggage without documented proof of medical need. If you have a disease that requires treatment with narcotics, you should also carry documented proof with you—smuggling narcotics aboard a plane is a serious offense that carries severe penalties in the U.S.

For HIV-positive visitors, requirements for entering the United States are somewhat vague and change frequently. For up-to-the-minute information contact **AIDSinfo** (© **800/448-0440,** or 301/519-6616 outside the U.S.; www.aidsinfo.nih.gov) or the **Gay Men's Health Crisis** (© **212/367-1000;** www.gmhc.org).

DRIVER'S LICENSES Foreign driver's licenses are usually recognized in the U.S., but you may want to get an international driver's license if your home license is not in English.

PASSPORT INFORMATION

For information on how to get a passport, go to "**Passports**" in the "**Fast Facts:** Montana & Wyoming" section of chapter 2—the websites listed provide downloadable passport applications as well as the current fees for processing passport applications. For an up-to-date, country-by-country listing of passport requirements around the world, go to the "Foreign Entry Requirement" Web page of the U.S. State Department at **http://travel.state.gov**.

Note: The International Civil Aviation Organization has recommended a policy requiring that *every* individual who travels by air have a passport. Many countries are now requiring that even children have their own passports to travel internationally.

FOR RESIDENTS OF CANADA

There are three ports of entry into Montana from Canada (and vice versa) that are open 24 hours a day: **Roosville,** the farthest west, en route from Cranbrook, B.C. (© **406/889-3865**); **Sweetgrass,** in the center near Glacier National Park, en route from Calgary (© **406/335-2434**); and **Raymond,** the farthest east en route from Regina (© **406/895-2664**). There are also 12 seasonal ports, which vary their hours and seasons of operation. For information on whether or not a specific seasonal port is open, contact one of the 24-hour ports.

CUSTOMS
WHAT YOU CAN BRING IN

For details regarding U.S. Customs and Border Protection, consult your nearest U.S. embassy or consulate, or **U.S. Customs** (© **202/927-1770;** www.customs.ustreas.gov).

WHAT YOU CAN BRING HOME
Canadian Citizens

For a clear summary of Canadian rules, write for the booklet *I Declare,* issued by the **Canada Border Services Agency** (© **800/461-9999** in Canada, or 204/983-3500; **www.cbsa-asfc.gc.ca**).

U.K. Citizens

For information, contact **HM Customs & Excise** at © **0845/010-9000** (from outside the U.K., 020/8929-0152), or consult their website at **www.hmce.gov.uk**.

Australian Citizens

A helpful brochure available from Australian consulates or Customs offices is *Know Before You Go.* For more information, call the **Australian Customs Service** at ℂ **1300/363-263,** or log on to **www. customs.gov.au**.

New Zealand Citizens

Most questions are answered in a free pamphlet available at New Zealand consulates and Customs offices: *New Zealand Customs Guide for Travellers, Notice no. 4.* For more information, contact **New Zealand Customs,** The Customhouse, 17–21 Whitmore St., Box 2218, Wellington (ℂ **04/473-6099** or 0800/428-786; **www.customs.govt.nz**).

HEALTH INSURANCE

Although it's not required of travelers, health insurance is highly recommended. Unlike many European countries, the United States does not usually offer free or low-cost medical care to its citizens or visitors. Doctors and hospitals are expensive, and in most cases will require advance payment or proof of coverage before they render their services. Policies can cover everything from the loss or theft of your baggage and trip cancellation to the guarantee of bail in case you're arrested. Good policies will also cover the costs of an accident, repatriation, or death. Packages such as **Europ Assistance's "Worldwide Healthcare Plan"** are sold by European automobile clubs and travel agencies at attractive rates. **Worldwide Assistance Services, Inc.** (ℂ **800/777-8710;** www. worldwideassistance.com) is the agent for Europ Assistance in the United States.

Though lack of health insurance may prevent you from being admitted to a hospital in nonemergencies, don't worry about being left on a street corner to die: The American way is to fix you now and bill the living daylights out of you later.

INSURANCE FOR BRITISH TRAVELERS Most big travel agents offer their own insurance, and will probably try to sell you their package when you book a holiday. Think before you sign. **Britain's Consumers' Association** recommends that you insist on seeing the policy and reading the fine print before buying travel insurance. **The Association of British Insurers** (ℂ **0171/600-3333;** abi.org.uk) gives advice by phone and publishes the free *Holiday Insurance,* a guide to policy provisions and prices. You might also shop around for better deals: Try **Columbus Travel Insurance Ltd.** (ℂ **0870/033-9988;** www.columbus direct.net).

INSURANCE FOR CANADIAN TRAVELERS Canadians should check with their provincial health plan offices or call **HealthCanada** (ℂ **866/225-0709;** www.hc-sc.gc.ca) to find out the extent of their coverage and what documentation and receipts they must take home in case they are treated in the United States.

MONEY

CURRENCY The U.S. monetary system is very simple: The most common **bills** are the $1 (a "buck"), $5, $10, and $20 denominations. There are also $2 bills (seldom encountered), $50 bills, and $100 bills (the last two are usually not welcome as payment for small purchases). All the paper money was recently redesigned, making the faces on them disproportionately large, but the old-style bills are still legal tender.

Coins come in seven denominations: 1¢ (1 cent, or a penny); 5¢ (5 cents, or a nickel); 10¢ (10 cents, or a dime); 25¢ (25 cents, or a quarter); 50¢ (50 cents, or a half dollar); the gold-colored Sacagawea coin, worth $1; and the rare silver dollar.

Note: The "foreign-exchange bureaus" so common in Europe are rare even at airports in the U.S., and nonexistent outside major cities. It's best not to change foreign money (or traveler's checks denominated in a currency other than U.S. dollars) at a small-town bank, or even a branch in a big city; in fact, leave any currency other than U.S. dollars at home— it may prove a greater nuisance to you than it's worth.

TRAVELER'S CHECKS Traveler's checks are widely accepted, but make sure that they're denominated in U.S. dollars; foreign-currency checks are often difficult to exchange. The three traveler's checks that are most widely recognized—and least likely to be denied—are **Visa, American Express,** and **Thomas Cook.** Be sure to record the numbers of the checks, and keep that information in a separate place in case they get lost or stolen.

CREDIT CARDS & ATMs Credit cards are the most widely used form of payment in the United States: **Visa** (Barclaycard in Britain), **MasterCard** (Euro-Card in Europe, Access in Britain, Chargex in Canada), **American Express, Diners Club,** and **Discover.** There are, however, a handful of stores and restaurants in Montana and Wyoming that do not take credit cards, so be sure to ask in advance.

The easiest and best way to get cash away from home is from an ATM (automated teller machine). The **Cirrus** (© **800/424-7787;** www.mastercard.com) and **PLUS** (© **800/843-7587;** www.visa.com) networks span the globe; look at the back of your bank card to see which network you're on, then call or check online for ATM locations at your destination. Be sure you know your personal identification number (PIN) and daily withdrawal limit before you depart. *Note:* Remember that many banks impose a fee every time you use a card at another bank's ATM, and that fee can be higher for international transactions (up to $5 or more) than for domestic ones (where they're rarely more than $2). In addition, the bank from which you withdraw cash may charge its own fee. To compare banks' ATM fees within the U.S., use **www.bankrate.com**. For international withdrawal fees, ask your bank.

SAFETY
GENERAL SAFETY SUGGESTIONS
While tourist areas are generally safe, crime is on the increase everywhere, and U.S. urban areas tend to be less safe than those in Europe or Japan. You should always stay alert. This is particularly true of large U.S. cities. It is wise to ask your hotel front desk staff or the city's or area's tourist office if you're in doubt about which neighborhoods are safe.

Avoid deserted areas, especially at night, and don't go into public parks at night unless there's a concert or similar occasion that will attract a crowd.

Avoid carrying valuables with you on the street, and don't display expensive cameras or electronic equipment. If you are using a map, consult it inconspicuously—or better yet, try to study it before you leave your room. Hold onto your pocketbook, and place your billfold in an inside pocket. In theaters, restaurants, and other public places, keep your possessions in your sight.

Always lock your room door—don't assume that once inside your hotel you are automatically safe and no longer need to be aware of your surroundings.

DRIVING SAFETY Driving safety is important, too. Although carjackings are practically unheard of in Montana and Wyoming, keep your vehicle's door locked at all times, just to be on the safe side. If you have an accident, even on the highway, stay in your car with the doors locked until you assess the situation or until the police arrive. Always try to park in well-lit and well-traveled areas if possible. If you leave your rental car unlocked and empty of your valuables, you're probably safer than locking your car with valuables in plain view. If someone attempts to rob you or steal your car, don't try to resist the thief/carjacker—report the incident to the police department immediately by calling © 911.

2 Getting to the U.S.

There are no direct flights from any foreign countries to either Montana or Wyoming. Travelers have to go through one of the hub cities. However, several major U.S. airlines with international connections serve the states.

International travelers heading for Montana and Wyoming will likely be flying through Seattle, Denver, or Salt Lake City. One of the charms of Montana and Wyoming is that they are remote, but this remoteness means that it takes longer to reach them.

The major airports in Montana are Billings, Bozeman, Great Falls, Helena, Kalispell, and Missoula; and in Wyoming the major airports are in Casper and Jackson. **Delta** and **Northwest** serve most of these cities, and **United** and **United Express** also provide some service.

AIRLINE DISCOUNTS   Smart travelers can reduce the price of a plane ticket by shopping around. Overseas visitors, for example, can take advantage of the APEX (Advance Purchase Excursion) reductions offered by all major U.S. and European carriers. For more money-saving airline advice, see "Getting There," in chapter 2. For the best rates, compare fares and be flexible with the dates and times of travel.

IMMIGRATION & CUSTOMS CLEARANCE   Visitors arriving by air, no matter what the port of entry, should cultivate patience and resignation before setting foot on U.S. soil. Getting through immigration control may take as long as 2 hours on some days, so be sure to have this guidebook or something else to read. This is especially true in the aftermath of the September 11, 2001, terrorist attacks, when U.S. airports have considerably beefed up security clearances. People traveling by air from Canada, Bermuda, and certain Caribbean countries can sometimes clear Customs and Immigration at the point of departure, which is much faster.

In contrast, for the traveler arriving by car or rail from Canada, the border-crossing formalities have been streamlined to the vanishing point. People traveling by air from Canada, Bermuda, and some places in the Caribbean can sometimes clear Customs and Immigration at the point of departure, which is much quicker.

3 Getting Around the U.S.

BY PLANE   Some large airlines offer travelers on their transatlantic or transpacific flights special discount tickets under the name **Visit USA,** allowing mostly one-way travel from one U.S. destination to another at very low prices. These discount tickets must be purchased abroad in conjunction with your international fare. This system is the easiest, fastest, cheapest way to see the country. Obtain information well in advance from your travel agent or the airline, since the conditions attached to these discount tickets can be changed without advance notice.

BY TRAIN   International visitors (excluding Canadians) can also buy a USA Rail Pass, good for 15 or 30 days of unlimited travel on **Amtrak** (© **800/USA-RAIL;** www.amtrak.com). The pass is available through many overseas travel agents. Prices valid for travel across the United States in 2005 for a 15-day pass were $295 off-peak, $440 peak; a 30-day pass costs $385 off-peak, $550 peak. Fares are significantly cheaper, however, within particular regions. See Amtrak's website for the cost of travel within the western, eastern, or northwestern United States. With a foreign passport, you can also buy passes direct from some Amtrak locations, including San Francisco, Los Angeles, Chicago, New York, Miami,

Boston, and Washington, D.C. Reservations are generally required and should be made as early as possible. Regional rail passes are also available.

Amtrak (© **800/872-7245**) stops along Montana's northern tier at Browning, Cut Bank, Essex, Glacier National Park, Glasgow, Havre, Libby, Malta, Shelby, West Glacier, Whitefish, and Wolf Point. Amtrak doesn't run through Wyoming.

BY BUS Bus travel is often the most economical form of public transit for short hops between U.S. cities, but it can also be slow and uncomfortable—certainly not an option for everyone (particularly when Amtrak, which is far more luxurious, offers similar rates). **Greyhound/Trailways** (© **800/231-2222;** www.greyhound.com), the sole nationwide bus line, offers an **International Ameripass** that must be purchased before coming to the United States, or by phone through the Greyhound International Office at the Port Authority Bus Terminal in New York City (© **212/971-0492**). The pass can be obtained from foreign travel agents or through Greyhound's website (order at least 21 days before your departure to the U.S.) and costs less than the domestic version. The 2005 passes cost as follows: 4 days ($179), 7 days ($239), 10 days ($289), 15 days ($349), 21 days ($419), 30 days ($479), 45 days ($529), or 60 days ($639). You can get more info on the pass at the website, or by calling © **402/330-8552.** In addition, special rates are available for seniors, students, and children.

BY CAR The most cost-effective, convenient, and comfortable way to travel around the United States is by car. The interstate highway system connects cities and towns all over the country; in addition to these high-speed, limited-access roadways, there's an extensive network of federal, state, and local highways and roads. Some of the national car-rental companies include **Alamo** (© 800/462-5266; www.alamo.com), **Avis** (© 800/331-1212; www.avis.com), **Budget** (© 800/527-0700; www.budget.com), **Enterprise** (© 800/261-7331; www.enterprise.com), **Hertz** (© 800/654-3131; www.hertz.com), **National** (© 800/227-7368; www.nationalcar.com), and **Thrifty** (© 800/847-4389; www.thrifty.com).

If you plan on renting a car in the United States, you probably won't need the services of an additional automobile organization. If you're planning to buy or borrow a car, automobile-association membership is recommended. See "Automobile Organizations" under "Fast Facts: For the International Traveler," below, for more information.

FAST FACTS: For the International Traveler

Automobile Organizations Auto clubs will supply maps, suggested routes, guidebooks, accident and bail-bond insurance, and emergency road service. The **American Automobile Association (AAA)** is the major auto club in the United States. If you belong to an auto club in your home country, inquire about AAA reciprocity before you leave. You may be able to join AAA even if you're not a member of a reciprocal club; to inquire, call AAA (© **800/222-4357**; http://travel.aaa.com). AAA has a nationwide emergency road service telephone number (© **800/AAA-HELP**).

Business Hours See "Fast Facts: Montana & Wyoming" in chapter 2.

Currency & Currency Exchange   See "Money" in section 1, "Preparing for Your Trip," earlier in this chapter.

Electricity   Like Canada, the United States uses 110–120 volts AC (60 cycles), compared with 220–240 volts AC (50 cycles) in most of Europe, Australia, and New Zealand. If your small appliances use 220–240 volts, you'll need a 110-volt transformer (bring one with you—they're hard to find in the U.S.) and a plug adapter with two flat, parallel pins.

Embassies & Consulates   All embassies are located in the nation's capital, Washington, D.C. Some consulates are located in major U.S. cities, and most nations have a mission to the United Nations in New York City. If your country isn't listed below, call for directory information in Washington, D.C. (© 202/555-1212) for the number of your national embassy.

The embassy of **Australia** is at 1601 Massachusetts Ave. NW, Washington, DC 20036 (© 202/797-3000; www.austemb.org). There are consulates in New York, Honolulu, Houston, Los Angeles, and San Francisco.

The embassy of **Canada** is at 501 Pennsylvania Ave. NW, Washington, DC 20001 (© 202/682-1740; www.canadianembassy.org). Canadian consulates are in Buffalo (N.Y.), Detroit, Los Angeles, New York, and Seattle.

The embassy of **Ireland** is at 2234 Massachusetts Ave. NW, Washington, DC 20008 (© 202/462-3939). Irish consulates are in Boston, Chicago, New York, and San Francisco.

The embassy of **Japan** is at 2520 Massachusetts Ave. NW, Washington, DC 20008 (© 202/238-6700; www.embjapan.org). Japanese consulates are located in Atlanta, Kansas City, San Francisco, and Washington, D.C.

The embassy of **New Zealand** is at 37 Observatory Circle NW, Washington, DC 20008 (© 202/328-4800; www.emb.com/nzemb). New Zealand consulates are in Los Angeles, Salt Lake City, San Francisco, and Seattle.

The embassy of the **United Kingdom** is at 3100 Massachusetts Ave. NW, Washington, DC 20008 (© 202/462-1340). Other British consulates are in Atlanta, Boston, Chicago, Cleveland, Houston, Los Angeles, New York, San Francisco, and Seattle.

The only foreign consulate in Wyoming or Montana is the **Norwegian Consulate**, P.O. Box 2529, Billings, MT 59103 (© 406/252-3441). A number of countries have consulates in Denver, and some also are represented in Salt Lake City.

Emergencies   Call © **911** to report a fire, call the police, or get an ambulance. This is a toll-free call (no coins are required at public telephones). In a very few rural areas, it may be necessary to dial "0" for the operator, who can then connect you to the proper emergency service.

Gasoline (Petrol)   Petrol is known as gasoline (or simply "gas") in the United States, and petrol stations are known as both gas stations and service stations. Gasoline costs less than half as much here as it does in Europe (about $2.25 per gallon at press time), and taxes are already included in the printed price. One U.S. gallon equals 3.8 liters or .85 imperial gallons.

Holidays   Banks, government offices, post offices, and many stores, restaurants, and museums are closed on the following legal national holidays: January 1 (New Year's Day), the third Monday in January (Martin Luther King, Jr.,

Day), the third Monday in February (Presidents' Day, Washington's Birthday), the last Monday in May (Memorial Day), July 4 (Independence Day), the first Monday in September (Labor Day), the second Monday in October (Columbus Day), November 11 (Veterans Day/Armistice Day), the fourth Thursday in November (Thanksgiving Day), and December 25 (Christmas). Also, the Tuesday following the first Monday in November is Election Day and is a federal government holiday in presidential-election years (held every 4 years, and next in 2008).

Legal Aid   The foreign tourist will probably never become involved with the American legal system. If you are "pulled over" for a minor infraction (speeding, for example), never attempt to pay the fine directly to a police officer; this could be construed as attempted bribery, a much more serious crime. Pay fines by mail, or directly into the hands of the clerk of the court. If accused of a more serious offense, say and do nothing before consulting a lawyer. Once arrested, a person can make one telephone call to a party of his or her choice. Call your embassy or consulate.

Liquor Laws   See "Fast Facts: Montana & Wyoming" in chapter 2.

Mail   Mail can be sent to you, in your name, c/o General Delivery at the main post office of the city or region where you expect to be (call Ⓒ **800/275-8777** or see www.usps.gov for information on the nearest post office). The addressee must pick up mail in person and must produce proof of identity. Most post offices will hold your mail for up to 1 month. Post office hours vary greatly, but most are open at least Monday through Friday from 8am to 5pm.

Generally found at intersections, mailboxes are blue with a red-and-white stripe and carry the inscription U.S. MAIL. If your mail is addressed to a U.S. destination, don't forget to add the five-digit postal code (or zip code) after the two-letter abbreviation of the state to which the mail is addressed.

At press time, domestic postage rates were 24¢ for a postcard and 39¢ for a letter. For international mail, a first-class letter of up to 1 ounce costs 84¢ (63¢ to Canada and Mexico); a first-class postcard costs 75¢ (55¢ to Canada and Mexico); and a preprinted postal aerogramme costs 75¢.

Taxes   In the United States there is no value-added tax (VAT) or other indirect tax at the national level. Every state, county, and city has the right to levy its own local tax on all purchases. Montana has no state sales tax, but there is a lodging tax of 7%, and certain resort communities can also charge a tax of up to 3% for goods and services. Wyoming's sales tax is 4% statewide, and local communities can add up to 2% more. Wyoming also allows communities to impose a lodging tax of up to 4%.

Telephone, Telegraph, Telex & Fax   The telephone system in the United States is run by private corporations, so rates, especially for long-distance service and operator-assisted calls, can vary widely. Generally, hotel surcharges on long-distance and local calls are astronomical, so you're usually better off using a **public pay telephone,** which you'll find clearly marked in most public buildings and private establishments as well as on the street. Convenience grocery stores and gas stations always have them. Many convenience groceries and packaging services sell **prepaid calling cards** in denominations up to $50; these can be the least expensive way to call home. Many public phones at airports now accept

American Express, MasterCard, and Visa credit cards. **Local calls** made from public pay phones in most locales cost either 25¢ or 35¢. Pay phones do not accept pennies, and few will take anything larger than a quarter.

Most long-distance and international calls can be dialed directly from any phone. **For calls within the United States and to Canada,** dial 1 followed by the area code and the seven-digit number. **For other international calls,** dial 011 followed by the country code, city code, and the telephone number of the person you are calling.

Calls to area codes **800, 888, 877,** and **866** are toll-free. However, calls to numbers in area codes **700** and **900** (chat lines, bulletin boards, "dating" services, and so on) can be very expensive—usually a charge of 95¢ to $3 or more per minute, and they sometimes have minimum charges that can run as high as $15 or more.

For **reversed-charge or collect calls,** and for person-to-person calls, dial 0 (zero, not the letter O) followed by the area code and number you want; an operator will then come on the line, and you should specify that you are calling collect, or person-to-person, or both. If your operator-assisted call is international, ask for the overseas operator.

For **local directory assistance** ("information"), dial 411; for long-distance information, dial 1, then the appropriate area code and 555-1212.

Telegraph and telex services are provided primarily by Western Union. You can bring your telegram into the nearest Western Union office or dictate it over the phone (© **800/325-6000**). You can also telegraph money, or have it telegraphed to you, very quickly over the Western Union system, but this service can cost as much as 20% of the amount sent.

Most hotels have **fax machines** available for guest use (be sure to ask about the charge to use it), and many hotel rooms are even wired for guests' fax machines. A less expensive way to send and receive faxes may be at stores such as **The UPS Store** (formerly Mail Boxes Etc.), a national chain of packing service shops (look in the Yellow Pages directory under "Packing Services").

There are two kinds of telephone directories in the United States. The **White Pages** list private households and business subscribers in alphabetical order. The inside front cover lists emergency numbers for police, fire, ambulance, poison-control center, and so on. The first few pages will tell you how to make long-distance and international calls. Government numbers are usually printed on blue paper within the White Pages. The **Yellow Pages** list all local services, businesses, industries, and houses of worship according to activity with an index at the front or back. The Yellow Pages also include city plans or detailed area maps, postal zip codes, and public-transportation routes.

Time The continental United States is divided into **four time zones:** Eastern Standard Time (EST), Central Standard Time (CST), Mountain Standard Time (MST), and Pacific Standard Time (PST). Alaska and Hawaii have their own zones. For example, noon in New York City (EST) is 11am in Chicago (CST), 10am in Denver (MST), 9am in Los Angeles (PST), 8am in Anchorage (AST), and 7am in Honolulu (HST).

Daylight saving time takes effect at 2am the first Sunday in April until 2am the last Sunday in October except in Arizona, Hawaii, the U.S. Virgin Islands, and Puerto Rico. (Indiana began observing daylight saving time in Apr 2006.) Daylight saving moves the clock 1 hour ahead of standard time. (A new law will extend daylight saving in 2007; clocks will change the 2nd Sun in Mar and the 1st Sun in Nov.)

Montana and Wyoming are located in the Mountain Time zone and both states observe daylight saving time.

Tipping   Tipping is so ingrained in the American way of life that the annual income tax of tip-earning service personnel is based on how much they should have received in light of their employers' gross revenues. Accordingly, they may have to pay tax on a tip you didn't actually give them.

Here are some rules of thumb:

In hotels, tip **bellhops** at least $1 per bag ($2–$3 if you have a lot of luggage) and tip the **chamber staff** $1 to $2 per day (more if you've left a disaster area for him or her to clean up, or if you're traveling with kids and/or pets). Tip the **doorman** or **concierge** only if he or she has provided you with some specific service (for example, calling a cab for you or obtaining difficult-to-get theater tickets). Tip the **valet-parking attendant** $1 every time you get your car.

In restaurants, bars, and nightclubs, tip **service staff** 15% to 20% of the check, tip **bartenders** 10% to 15%, tip **checkroom attendants** $1 per garment, and tip **valet-parking attendants** $1 per vehicle. Tip the **doorman** only if he has provided you with some specific service (such as calling a cab for you). Tipping is not expected in cafeterias and fast-food restaurants.

Tip **cabdrivers** 15% of the fare.

As for other service personnel, tip **skycaps** at airports at least $1 per bag ($2–$3 if you have a lot of luggage) and tip **hairdressers** and **barbers** 15% to 20%.

Tipping ushers at movies and theaters, and gas-station attendants, is not expected.

Toilets   You won't find public toilets or restrooms on the streets in most U.S. cities, but they can be found in hotel lobbies, bars, restaurants, museums, department and discount stores, railway and bus stations, or service stations. Note, however, that some establishments display a notice that toilets are for the use of patrons only. Paying for a cup of coffee or a soft drink will qualify you as a patron. If possible, avoid the toilets at parks and beaches, which tend to be dirty.

4

Suggested Montana & Wyoming Itineraries

Montana and Wyoming are two of the bigger states in the country, and all of that land and sky makes for something of a blank canvas when it comes to planning a trip to theses parts. Most visitors come here to see their natural wonders in general and Yellowstone, Grand Teton, and Glacier national parks in particular, but there is plenty to see beyond their boundaries: top-notch museums; fun college, resort, and authentic Western towns; crystal-clear lakes and rivers for paddling and fishing; and vast tracts of open space.

As far as a time commitment goes, 1 week is a bit short for a trip to Montana and Wyoming, but you can scratch the surface of one region in that time—say, Yellowstone or the Flathead Valley in Montana. Two weeks is much better, giving the opportunity to delve deeper into one region or travel between the Greater Yellowstone Ecosystem and Glacier National Park.

But with all of that real estate, it's important to not stretch yourself too thin: It's better to be out on the trails in the Rockies than behind the wheel of a car. Take time to explore places well off the beaten tourist track and breathe the fresh air, take in the views, and really, truly get away from it all.

1 Montana & Wyoming in 1 Week

This route brings you to the northwest corner of Wyoming and south-central Montana: the 18-million-acre parcel known as the Greater Yellowstone Ecosystem.

Day ❶: Arrive in Jackson, Wyoming 🌣🌣

Start your Rocky Mountain getaway in the world-class resort town of Jackson. Serviced by more airlines than any other town in the state, Jackson is relatively easy to get to and a comfortable launching pad for a Montana/Wyoming vacation. Check out **Town Square,** with its famed antler arches, and the downtown area for window-shopping and lunch, before heading up to the **National Museum of Wildlife Art** (p. 315) for the afternoon. In the evening, drive to **Teton Village** or nearby **Wilson** for dinner, perhaps with a stop to

fish on the **Snake River** en route, or if time permits, a ride up the tram at the **Jackson Hole Mountain Resort.** Take your pick of lodgings in and around Jackson. See p. 306.

Day ❷: Grand Teton National Park 🌣🌣🌣

But of course you didn't come to Wyoming for the civilization. Get up early and head immediately for **Grand Teton National Park.** Stop at the visitor center in **Moose** before catching a boat across **Jenny Lake** to the trail leading up **Cascade Canyon;** take it at least to **Hidden Falls** and **Inspiration Point,** but

Montana & Wyoming in 1 & 2 Weeks

FLATHEAD VALLEY **9-11** Glacier NP

CANADA
USA

Historic Mining Town

Milk River

12-13
Flathead Lake
Big Fork

15

Missouri River

Missoula
Great Falls

14

90

Helena

M O N T A N A

Butte

8

Bozeman

Nevada City

7

Livingston

Yellowstone River

94

IDAHO

Bannack

Virginia City

6

PARADISE VALLEY

90

3-5

Yellowstone NP

15

John D. Rockefeller, Jr.
Memorial PKWY

90

2

Snake R.

25

1

Jackson

W Y O M I N G

Green R.

Sweetwater R.

North Platte R.

80

0   100 mi
0   100 km

WEEK 1
❶ Jackson, WY
❷ Grand Teton National Park
3-5 Yellowstone National Park
❻ The Paradise Valley and Bozeman, MT
❼ Bozeman, MT

WEEK 2
❽ Butte, Helena, and Great Falls, MT
9-11 Glacier National Park
12-13 The Flathead Valley
⓮ Montana's Gold West Country

you'll get away from most of the crowds if you continue up the canyon for another mile or two. Either bring lunch with you or come down to one of the numerous eateries in the park. Spend the afternoon ogling the majestic mountains from the numerous overlooks, and take a stroll around **Willow Flats** looking for moose or up **Signal Mountain** (you can drive to the summit as well) for a magnificent perspective. For hungry, budget-minded types, we love the nachos at **Deadman's Bar** in Signal Mountain Lodge (p. 347). Spend the night in one of the park's lodgings or campgrounds. See p. 343.

Day ❸: Arrive in Yellowstone National Park ✸✸✸

You got a taste of the in-your-face grandeur of the Tetons, now it's time for the subtler, wilder confines of **Yellowstone National Park,** and its amazing amalgam of wildlife, geysers, and hiking trails. You'll drive out of **Grand Teton National Park** through the **John D. Rockefeller Jr. Memorial Parkway** before entering Yellowstone, and will soon arrive at the trail head to **Lewis River Channel** to Shoshone Lake, the largest backcountry lake in the lower 48. Pack a lunch or plan for a late lunch at **Old Faithful,** where you'll spend the night after a stop at **West Thumb** en route. In the evening, watch the famed geyser erupt then stroll the boardwalks for a glimpse at some of the lesser-known thermal features here: Castle, Grand, and Riverside geysers are all awe-inspiring sights to behold. Stay at one of the myriad lodging options at Old Faithful; eat here as well. See p. 300.

Days ❹ & ❺: Yellowstone National Park ✶✶✶

You've whet your Yellowstone appetite. Now you've got 2 full days to get your fill of hiking, wildlife-watching, sightseeing, or whatever else might tickle your fancy. We recommend visitors spend the first half of Day 4 exploring the **Grand Canyon of the Yellowstone** area, gawking from the overlooks but also hiking one of the **rim trails**, or to **Clear Lake** and **Lily Lake**, or down the metal staircase known as **Uncle Tom's Trail** for an unbeatable perspective of the base of **Lower Falls**. Drive up to Tower-Roosevelt in the afternoon to unwind on the porch at **Roosevelt Lodge** (p. 303), where you'll sleep in a dinky cabin after enjoying a cookout on the trail. The next day, you're in prime position for an early start of wildlife-watching in the **Lamar Valley**— "the Serengeti of North America." Have lunch in Cooke City and perhaps do a little fishing in Trout Lake or Soda Butte Creek, before reversing course for **Mammoth Hot Springs.** After walking the boardwalk here, have dinner at the **Park Street Grill** (p. 270) in Gardiner, Montana, or have a quick bite at Mammoth

before heading to **Boiling River** for a soak before the sun sets. Stay in either Mammoth or Gardiner. See p. 285.

Day ❻: The Paradise Valley ✶✶ & Bozeman, Montana ✶✶

From Mammoth or Gardiner, drive north on U.S. 89 up the idyllic **Paradise Valley** to **Livingston, Montana.** Wander downtown Livingston, visiting one of the town's three museums, check out a gallery or two, and have a bite to eat. Next, drive west on I-90 to downtown **Bozeman, Montana,** for the evening. Spend the afternoon strolling **Main Street** and settle on a restaurant downtown—there are plenty to choose from—and perhaps a watering hole for an after-dinner drink. As for accommodations close to downtown, we can't recommend the **Lehrkind Mansion** enough (p. 219).

Day ❼: Bozeman, Montana ✶✶

After breakfast at the Lehrkind or at one of the noshing spots on Main, head south to the **Museum of the Rockies** (p. 217), on the campus of Montana State University. This top-flight museum offers a lens into one of the best and brightest paleontology programs in the country and a look at the largest collection of American dinosaurs in the world. Either have lunch at the museum cafe or head back downtown, before venturing south into the **Gallatin National Forest** for an afternoon hike or fishing expedition. For dinner, try **The Mint** (p. 220) in nearby Belgrade, a very Montana kind of place.

2 Montana & Wyoming in 2 Weeks

Start with the preceding 1-week itinerary, then from Bozeman, Montana, make your way northwest to Glacier Country and the Flathead Valley and many more of the natural wonders that give the Treasure State its nickname.

Days ❶ to ❼: Montana & Wyoming in 1 Week

Follow the itineraries outlined above.

Day ❽: Butte, Helena ✶ & Great Falls, Montana

This is a big driving day, covering about 80 miles on I-90 west and another 150 miles on I-15 north. But it also puts you within a relatively short drive of **Glacier National Park** and gives you an opportunity to visit one or both of Great Falls' terrific museums: the **Lewis and Clark National Historic Trail Interpretive Center** (p. 192) and the **C.M. Russell Museum Complex** (p. 191). We're also suckers for the **Sip 'n Dip Lounge** (p. 194), the kitschiest watering hole in the West. En route from Bozeman, stop for a peek at the **Berkeley Pit** in Butte and lunch on **Last Chance Gulch** in Helena.

Days ➒, ➓ & ⓫: Glacier National Park ⟡⟡⟡

Visit another museum in Great Falls or head directly to **Glacier National Park.** Before ascending **Logan Pass** on Going-to-the-Sun Road, stop at Sunrift Gorge for a hike up toward Siyeh Pass, where there's a nice view of a hanging glacier. Camp or stay at one of the many nice hostelries in the park; eat in the park as well. The next day take your pick of activities: **rafting** out of West Glacier; **hiking** to Avalanche Lake or another trail; or **sightseeing** in Glacier's many nooks and crannies. Stay in the park again on night 10, or take your choice of one of the hostelries in the gateways of East Glacier, West Glacier, St. Mary, Essex, or Polebridge. Explore more of Glacier by car or foot on day 11 before leaving the park for Whitefish. In Whitefish, stay at **The Garden Wall Inn** (p. 137) and walk downtown for dinner.

Days ⓬ & ⓭: The Flathead Valley ⟡⟡

Use Whitefish as a base for exploring the Flathead Valley. After breakfast, take a scenic cruise or fishing charter on **Flathead Lake,** then spend the remainder of the day in **Bigfork,** shopping, strolling, and having dinner at one of the terrific eateries. Perhaps take in a play at the **Bigfork Summer Playhouse** (p. 116). Stay at one of the many lodgings in or around Bigfork for the evening. On the next day, drive south to **Missoula** for a peek at the **Rocky Mountain Elk Foundation Visitor Center** (p. 101) and the University of Montana campus, before getting in one last hike in the **Rattlesnake Wilderness Area** just outside of town. In the evening, venture into downtown Missoula for dinner and drinks. See p. 104.

Day ⓮: Explore Montana's Gold West Country

You might end your trip in Missoula and spend the final day enjoying a slow start and a good breakfast. But if your schedule allows, take the day for a scenic drive through the Bitterroot Valley, south of town via U.S. 93, and over Lost Trail Pass. From there, you'll have an opportunity to visit one of Montana's historic mining towns: Virginia City, Nevada City, or Bannack. (The latter is a ghost town that's now a state park.) From any of these, you're in good position to get to Salt Lake City, if you arrived by air, and I-15, if you're driving home. See p. 107.

3 Yellowstone & Grand Teton National Parks for Families

Yellowstone and Grand Teton national parks can be challenging destinations for families. Many of the recreational activities (particularly hiking) can be taxing for little ones, who might also find too much time in the car a bit of a bore. The following itinerary offers a few tips to get the most out of a week in the parks for everybody.

Day ➊: Arrive in Cody, Wyoming ⟡

Cody is the ideal gateway for a family vacation in Yellowstone: Kids will surely enjoy the shootouts in front of the **Irma**

Hotel (p. 359) downtown, and the nightly **Cody Nite Rodeo** (p. 357) has kiddie rides beforehand and a participatory "calf scramble" that allows youngsters

Yellowstone & Grand Teton National Parks for Families

1 Cody, WY
2 Arrive in Yellowstone National Park
3-4 Explore Yellowstone National Park
5-6 Grand Teton National Park
7 Jackson, WY

to get in on the action and chase a bewildered calf around the arena in between the events. (The kids are trying to grab the coveted ribbon tied to the animal.) Older kids might even like the **Buffalo Bill Historical Center** (p. 356). As for food and lodging, try **Maxwell's** (p. 361) and the **Buffalo Bill Village Resort** (p. 358).

Day **2**: Arrive in Yellowstone National Park ✸✸✸

Head straight into **Yellowstone** on Day 2, stopping for a picnic along the shore of **Yellowstone Lake** once you've entered. **West Thumb** is an excellent primer for introducing tykes to the park's geothermal underpinnings. Spend the night at **Old Faithful,** where you can see more incredible displays produced by the heat, water, and geology below. See p. 271.

Days **3** & **4**: Explore Yellowstone ✸✸✸

While many hikes in the first itinerary in this chapter may not be suitable for all children, we like two in particular for people of all ages: **Artist Paint Pot Trail** south of Norris, and the **Forces of the Northern Range Self-Guiding Trail** near Mammoth. Both are short, level, and give a good glimpse at different phenomena that have shaped Yellowstone's ecosystem over the eons. On Day 3, tackle Artist Paint Pot Trail, then wander Norris' boardwalks before making your way to Mammoth for the evening. Get a room, cabin, or campsite here and hit **Boiling River** (p. 285) for a soak before exploring more thermal features at Mammoth via boardwalk. The next morning, you're in prime position for the Forces of Nature Self-Guiding Trail, which gives a look at the effects of a forest fire, before driving west for an afternoon exploring the Lamar Valley in search of wildlife— the **Yellowstone Association Institute** offers customizable expeditions that will allow mom and dad a break from the wheel. Spend the night at **Roosevelt Lodge** (p. 303)—a family favorite—after enjoying a signature chuck-wagon cook-out on the trail.

Days ❺ & ❻: Grand Teton National Park ⓡ⭐⭐

It's a pretty good drive from Roosevelt to Grand Teton, so plan a stop at the **Grand Canyon of the Yellowstone** and picnic in the southern reaches of the park en route. You'll probably get your first peek at the Tetons in the early afternoon. Pick a base in the park—your choices range from campgrounds to luxury cabins—and stick with it. **Colter Bay Village** (p. 345)

is a particularly family-friendly spot, and gives you the opportunity to set out to moose-watch in Willow Flats or around Jackson Lake Lodge. The next day, take the boat across **Jenny Lake** and hike as far up Cascade Canyon as you see fit. In the afternoon, take a **scenic cruise** on Jackson Lake. See p. 327.

Day ❼: Jackson, Wyoming ⓡ⭐

Your last day will be well spent in Jackson. At Town Square, there are nightly shootouts and stagecoach rides. You might check out the alpine slide or miniature golf at Snow King Resort (p. 312), or the excellent National Museum of Wildlife Art, which has kid-oriented interpretation and activities. Grab dinner at Billy's Giant Hamburgers at the Cadillac Grille (p. 324) and stay at the Virginian Lodge (p. 318); it has a big grassy courtyard centered on a pool. Jackson has an airport and is an easy drive from I-15 at Idaho Falls.

4 Exploring the Wild West Past of Montana & Wyoming

Many visitors come to the region for the sublime views and superb recreation, but many others come in search of the real West that's slowly but surely fading into the history books. There are pockets of fascinating history that shaped the nation's culture and textbooks, vestiges of the Old West amid the developments of the new in Wyoming to Montana.

Day ❶: Arrive in Cheyenne, Wyoming

Begin your day downtown at the beautifully restored Union Pacific Depot and the **Cheyenne Depot Museum** (p. 398) for a look at how the railroad shaped the history of this part of the West. Pick up their brochure *Tracking Trains in Cheyenne* and dig a little deeper into this fascinating chapter. Another interesting (and intertwined) tale is told at the **Cheyenne Frontier Days Old West Museum** (p. 398). Stay at the historic **Plains Hotel** (p. 400) downtown after a dinner at the **Little Bear Inn** (p. 401).

Day ❷: Laramie & Saratoga

On your second day, head west into Laramie for a visit to the **Wyoming Territorial Prison State Historic Site** (p. 405) and then continue into the Snowy Range Mountains to visit **Saratoga, Centennial,** and/or **Woods Landing** and stay for the night. Saratoga's historic Hotel Wolf and Woods Landing are particularly interesting. See p. 407.

Day ❸: Casper & Buffalo ⓡ

Return to Laramie and drive north through the Shirley Basin on U.S. 287 and Wyo. 487 to Casper and the excellent **National Historic Trails Interpretive**

Exploring the Wild West Past of Montana & Wyoming

Historic Mining Town

CANADA
USA

Havre
Chinook
Bear Paw Battlefield

Great Falls

Missouri River

MONTANA

Butte

Yellowstone River

MONTANA'S GOLD WEST COUNTRY

IDAHO

Little Bighorn Battlefield NM

Yellowstone NP

Sheridan
Cody

Snake R.

Buffalo

WYOMING

Hole-in-the-Wall

Casper

Green R.
Sweetwater R.
North Platte R.

Laramie
Saratoga
Cheyenne

0   100 mi
0   100 km
N

❶ Cheyenne, WY
❷ Laramie and Saratoga, WY
❸ Casper and Buffalo
❹-❺ Sheridan & vicinity
❻ Cody, WY
❼ Chief Joseph Scenic Highway

Center (p. 387). Perhaps lunch at the **Wonder Bar** (p. 390) before continuing north to **Hole-in-the-Wall** (p. 380), a hide-out favored by Butch Cassidy and the Sundance Kid. Stay in Buffalo at **The Occidental Hotel** (p. 380). Explore Buffalo's other historic attractions, Fort Phil Kearny and the Jim Gatchell Memorial Museum, while in town.

Days ❹ & ❺: Sheridan & Vicinity

From Buffalo, continue north on I-25 to Sheridan, for a look at its numerous **historic attractions** (p. 375). Use Sheridan as a base for exploring the rest of the area, especially **Little Bighorn Battlefield National Monument** (p. 253), the site of Custer's infamous Last Stand. If you're looking for a knowledgeable guide, Ron Spahn of Spahn's Big Horn Mountain Bed and Breakfast offers daylong **historic and cultural tours** (p. 374) of the area, including spots well off the beaten track.

Day ❻: Cody

No Old West trip would be complete without a visit to the town founded by and bearing the name of William "Buffalo Bill" Cody. The **Buffalo Bill Historical Center** (p. 356) is a must-visit, with a great look into the life of Cody himself as well as many other aspects of the area's history. Stay at **Pahaska Tepee Resort** (p. 359), Buffalo Bill's old hunting lodge, or in town at the Mayor's Inn.

Day ❼: Chief Joseph Scenic Highway

From Cody, drive north out of town and get on the **Chief Joseph Scenic Highway** (p. 352), which connects to the Beartooth Scenic Byway, an awe-inspiring route into **Yellowstone National Park.** The road follows the route taken by the Nez Perce tribe, which fled the U.S. Army and its attempt to force relocation to Oklahoma. The flight of the Nez Perce in summer 1877 snaked through Yellowstone but ended in Hi-Line country at **Bear Paw Battlefield** (p. 204). From here, you could head in that direction and later hit Butte and Montana's Gold West Country for a look at the region's mining history, or into Yellowstone for an adapted version of the first itinerary in this chapter. The **Yellowstone Association Institute** (p. 277) also offers a number of history-oriented classes and expeditions.

5

Glacier National Park

Majestic and wild, this vast preserve overwhelms visitors, beckoning with stunning mountain peaks (many covered year-round with glaciers), verdant mountain trails that cry out for hikers, and the sheer diversity of its plant and animal life. The unofficial mascot in these parts is the grizzly, a refugee from the high plains.

Named to describe the slow-moving glaciers that carved awe-inspiring valleys throughout this expanse of over 1 million acres, Glacier National Park exists because of the efforts of George Bird Grinnell, a 19th-century magazine publisher and cofounder of the Audubon Society. Following a pattern established with Yellowstone and Grand Teton, Grinnell lobbied for a national park to be set aside in the St. Mary region of Montana, and in May 1910 his efforts were rewarded. Just over 20 years later, it became, with its northern neighbor Waterton Lakes National Park in Canada, Glacier-Waterton International Peace Park—a gesture of goodwill and friendship between the governments of two countries.

Today you'll see nature at work here: The glaciers are receding (the result of global warming, some say) and avalanches have periodically ravaged Going-to-the-Sun Road, the curving, scenic 50-mile road that bisects the park. Fires in 2003 charred more than 100,000 acres of forest, about 10% of the park's total acreage.

If your time is limited, simply motor across Going-to-the-Sun Road, viewing the dramatic mountain scenery. Visitors with more time will find diversions for both families and hard-core adventurers; while some hiking trails are suitable for tykes, many more will challenge those determined to conquer and scale the park's tallest peaks. Glacier's lakes, streams, ponds, and waterfalls are equally engaging. Travelers board cruise boats to explore the history of the area; recreational types can fish, row, and kayak.

However, to truly experience Glacier requires slightly more effort, interest, and spunk than a drive through. Abandon the pavement for even the shortest and easiest hiking trail and you'll discover a window into Glacier's soul.

1 Just the Facts

GETTING THERE

The closest cities to the park with airline service are **Kalispell,** 29 miles southwest of the park, **Missoula,** 150 miles south, and **Great Falls,** 150 miles southeast.

Glacier Park International Airport, north of Kalispell at 4170 U.S. 2 (© **406/257-5994;** www.glacierairport.com), is serviced by SkyWest, Horizon, Big Sky, and Northwest. **Great Falls International Airport** (© **406/727-3404;** www.gfairport.com) is served by these same airlines, as is **Missoula International Airport** (© **406/728-4381;** www.msoairport.com), which has flights from Allegiant and United as well.

If you're driving, you can reach the park from U.S. highways 2 and 89. Rental cars are available in Kalispell, Great Falls, Missoula, Whitefish, East Glacier, and West Glacier. **Avis, Budget, Hertz,** and **National** all have counters at the above airports.

Amtrak's Empire Builder (© **800/872-7245;** www.amtrak.com), a Chicago-Seattle round-trip route, makes daily stops at West Glacier and Essex year-round and East Glacier from May 1 to October 1.

ACCESS/ENTRY POINTS

There are six paved entrances that provide vehicular access to Glacier National Park, but if you are traveling by car, you will most likely use **West Glacier** and **St. Mary.** These entrances are located at either end of Going-to-the-Sun Road, with West Glacier on the southwest side and St. Mary on the east. From the park's western boundary, you can enter at **Polebridge** to access Bowman and Kintla lakes or enter at the **Camas Creek** entrance and take the Camas Road to Going-to-the-Sun. The **Many Glacier** entrance provides access to the Many Glacier Hotel, Swiftcurrent Lake, and many backcountry trails. The **Two Medicine** entrance is only about 4 miles north of East Glacier Park on Mont. 49, with auto access to Lower Two Medicine Lake and Two Medicine Lake, as well as hiking trails to Pumpelly Pillar and over Pitamakan Pass. Four miles south of the Two Medicine entrance, the **East Glacier** entrance is for hikers only—it is not a paved entry point for cars—for access to trails at the southeastern corner of the park. **Essex** is strictly a backcountry access point to Scalplock Mountain and backcountry campgrounds along Ole Creek and Park Creek. **Cut Bank** is a dirt road, closed in winter, with backcountry access only to Triple Divide Pass and the northern route to Pitamakan Pass.

Caution: Entrance to the park is severely restricted during winter months when the alpine section of Going-to-the-Sun Road is closed. See section 2, "Driving in the Park," below, for more information.

VISITOR CENTERS

To receive information about the park before your trip, contact the superintendent, **Glacier National Park,** West Glacier, MT 59936 (© **406/888-7800;** www.nps.gov/ glac). The **Glacier Natural History Association** offers numerous publications; for a catalog, contact the association at P.O. Box 310, West Glacier, MT 59936 (© **406/ 888-5756;** fax 406/888-5271; www.glacierassociation.org).

For up-to-date information on park activities once you arrive, check in at visitor centers located at **Apgar, Logan Pass,** and **St. Mary.** Apgar is open from May through October (and weekends during the winter), Logan Pass from mid-June to late September; and St. Mary from mid-May to mid-October. Park information may also be obtained from the **Many Glacier Ranger Station** or park headquarters in **West Glacier.** General park information about Glacier is available at © **406/888-7800** and www.nps.gov/glac, and about Waterton at © **403/859-5133,** or on the Web at **http:// parkscanada.pch.gc.ca/waterton**. The **Alberta Information Center** is located in a conspicuously modern building in West Glacier, providing information about Waterton-Glacier and other attractions in Alberta. There are also numerous exhibits about Canadian life and culture.

FEES & BACKCOUNTRY PERMITS

Rangers are on duty at most entry points to collect fees, issue backcountry permits, and answer questions.

Glacier National Park

Apgar Visitor Center **2**
Cut Bank Ranger Station **11**
Granite Park Chalet **5**
Lake McDonald Lodge **3**

Logan Pass Visitor Center **7**
Many Glacier Lodge **9**
Polebridge Entrance **1**
St. Mary Visitor Center **10**

Sperry Chalet **8**
Waterton Lakes National
Park Entrance **4**
Weeping Wall **6**

FEES Admission to the park for up to 7 days costs $25 per vehicle ($15 in winter) or $12 per person for those on foot, bicycles, and motorcycles ($10 in winter). A season pass costs $30 and allows unlimited entry to Glacier National Park for 1 year. The National Park, Golden Age, and Golden Access passes are also honored (see section 7, "Specialized Travel Resources," in chapter 2). Camping fees are $12 to $17 per night at the park's drive-in campgrounds. A separate entrance fee is charged for visitors to Waterton Lakes National Park (see "A Side Trip to Waterton Lakes National Park," later in this chapter).

Tips **Traveling through the Park without a Car**

Glacier's signature red **Jammer** buses are now in service after a restoration project that began in 1999. For schedules, contact **Glacier Park, Inc.** (*©* **406/892-2525**). GPI also operates a **hiker's shuttle** that makes regular stops at popular trail heads. **Suntours** (*©* **800/786-9220**) originate from East Glacier, Browning, and St. Mary. The reasonable rates start at $65 for a 6-hour tour led by a knowledgeable guide from the Blackfeet Nation.

BACKCOUNTRY PERMITS   You must obtain backcountry permits in person from the Apgar Backcountry Office, St. Mary Visitor Center, or the ranger stations at Many Glacier, Polebridge, or Two Medicine. Visitors who enter Glacier's backcountry from the Canadian side (at Goat Haunt or Belly River in Waterton) can get a permit at the Waterton Visitor Reception Centre, but only with a credit card. **During summer months,** permits may be obtained no earlier than 24 hours before your visit. There is a $4 per-person per-night charge for backcountry camping. Permits are good only for the prearranged dates and locations, with no more than 3 nights allowed at a single campground. Campsites are limited. A single site has a maximum occupancy of four persons. Stoves are required in most areas (no open fires), and pets are not permitted on the trails.

To ensure a spot and avoid the hassle, order an Advance Reservation Backcountry Trip planner from **Backcountry Reservations** (*©* **406/888-7800**), GNP, West Glacier, MT 59936; sending them your dates with a check for $20 between June 15 and October 31 will reserve your spot in the wilderness.

Due to lower demand in winter, camping permits are available up to 7 days in advance. A few rules do take effect beginning each November 20, so double-check at visitor centers for details.

SPECIAL REGULATIONS & WARNINGS

Park regulations here are similar to those in other lands administered by the National Park Service, and generally prohibit damaging the natural resources. Pets must be leashed and are not allowed on trails. In addition, RVs and other vehicles longer than 21 feet or wider than 8 feet are prohibited on the 24-mile stretch of Going-to-the-Sun Road between Avalanche Campground and Sun Point on St. Mary Lake. Snowmobiling is prohibited in the park.

WHEN TO GO

Glacier is magnificent at any time of the year, but it's not always easily accessible. Most visitors come in **summer,** and it seems as if they all drive along Going-to-the-Sun Road. The 52-mile two-lane road is generally open from early June to mid-October, depending upon the weather. During summer months, sunrise is around 5am, and sunset at nearly 10pm, so there's plenty of time for exploring. The shoulder seasons of **spring and fall** see budding wildflowers and seasonal colors, but these sights can be viewed only from the park's outer boundaries and a limited stretch of the scenic highway.

In **winter,** road access is limited. Going-to-the-Sun Road is plowed to Lake McDonald Lodge on the west side of the park, 12 miles from West Glacier, but the remainder of the road is closed. Snowmobiles are prohibited. All unplowed roads become trails for snowshoers and cross-country skiers, who rave about the vast wonderland. Guided trips are a great way to experience the park in winter, or you can strap on a pair of snow-shoes and explore it on your own. A popular skiing expedition is to go as far up Going-to-the-Sun Road as your energy permits. Wintertime temperatures average between 15°F (–9°C) and 30°F (–1°C), but extreme lows can reach 30°F below (–34°C). Average winter snowfall is almost 12 feet, and it snows about half of the days from November through February.

AVOIDING THE CROWDS

If you want to avoid the crowds, travel in the off season before mid-June, when the park begins to fill, and after Labor Day, when families traveling with youngsters have returned home (Aug is the busiest month). If that's not possible, consider the following: Since most people congregate close to the major hotels, find a trail head that is equidistant from two major points and head for the woods.

Going-to-the-Sun Road is nearly always jammed in the summer daylight hours. If you can, make the trip before 8:30am. In July and August, the parking lot at Logan Pass Visitor Center fills to capacity. Try to visit early in the day or late in the afternoon.

RANGER PROGRAMS

When you enter the park, you'll be given the park's publication, *The Glacier Explorer*, which lists the naturalist-led programs offered at Glacier and Waterton. There are a wide variety of hikes, boat trips, campfire programs, family programs, and other activities. Many are accessible for those in wheelchairs. There are also campfire presentations given by members of local tribes. Most programs are free, although those including boat trips may have a small fee associated. For schedules, check the park newspapers or call ✆ **406/888-7800.**

TIPS FOR TRAVELERS WITH PHYSICAL DISABILITIES

Information on facilities and services for those with disabilities is available at any of the visitor centers in the park, although most of the park's developed areas are fully accessible by wheelchair. The park's *Accessibility in Glacier National Park* publication describes current programs and services for visitors with disabilities.

FOR THE VISUALLY IMPAIRED Audiotapes, park brochure recordings, and tactile nature items are available at the Apgar, Logan Pass, and St. Mary visitor centers. All other park facilities—restrooms, restaurants, campgrounds, gift shops—are accessible with some assistance.

FOR THE MOBILITY IMPAIRED The Trail of the Cedars, Oberlin Bend Trail, Goat Lick Overlook Trail, and Running Eagle Falls Nature Trail are wheelchair accessible. A bike path at Apgar also provides magnificent views of the park's scenery. Wheelchairs are available for loan at the Apgar, Logan Pass, and St. Mary visitor centers and almost all of the park's facilities are fully accessible.

⟨Kids⟩ Especially for Kids

The park has a *Junior Ranger Newspaper* available at the visitor centers that lists seven activities to introduce youngsters between 6 and 12 years of age to the habitats in Glacier. Kids must complete five activities to receive a badge. Children are also welcome on most interpretive activities, but should be accompanied by an adult.

Vehicle Regulations

Park regulations prohibit vehicles more than 21 feet long or 8 feet wide on the 24-mile stretch of Going-to-the-Sun Road between Avalanche Campground and Sun Point on St. Mary Lake. If you are traveling in a vehicle exceeding the 21-foot limit, park it at one of the parking areas located at Avalanche Campground and Sun Point and let someone else do the driving (see "Traveling through the Park without a Car," above).

FOR THE HEARING IMPAIRED   Interpreters provide written synopses of most slide and campfire programs. If you plan on hiking, note that five of the park's self-guided nature trails have printed brochures available at the trail head. General park information is available by TDD at ℭ **406/888-7806.** An interpreter may be available to sign at ranger programs. Call ℭ **406/888-7930** 2 weeks in advance to make arrangements.

ORGANIZED TOURS & ACTIVITIES

Narrated boat tours 𝕒𝕒 from Lake McDonald, St. Mary, Two Medicine, and Many Glacier are offered daily from mid-June to mid-September by Glacier Park Boat Company. These excursions combine an hour-long lake cruise with a short hike or picnic. Spectacular views of Lake McDonald, the Grinnell Glacier, and the panoramic rugged cliffs ringing St. Mary Lake are just a few of the photo opportunities you may have. The boats typically depart every hour, at least five times each day, although schedules are subject to change in late season or if the weather is inclement. Fees run no more than $15, and kids 4 to 12 are half-price. For more information, contact **Glacier Park Boat Co.** at P.O. Box 5262, Kalispell, MT 59903 (ℭ **406/257-2426;** www.glacier parkboats.com). Listed below are seasonal phone numbers for cruises at the following locations: **Lake McDonald** (ℭ **406/888-5727**), **Many Glacier** (ℭ **406/732-4480**), **Two Medicine** (ℭ **406/226-4467**), and **St. Mary** (ℭ **406/732-4430**).

Unique **Jammer tours** are given along Going-to-the-Sun Road and north to Waterton, in 33 restored classic bright red coaches from the 1930s, long identified with Glacier. Their drivers provide insightful commentary about the park and its history, and you don't have to worry about how close you may be to the edge of the often-precipitous road! For schedules contact **Glacier Park, Inc.** (ℭ **406/892-2525**). Historical-cultural **25-passenger motorcoach tours** of the Going-to-the-Sun Road conducted by knowledgeable guides from the Blackfeet Nation originate from East Glacier, Browning, and St. Mary. The reasonable rates start at $65 for a 6-hour trip. Contact **Suntours** (ℭ **800/786-9220**).

SPECIAL ACTIVITIES

Scenic helicopter tours of Glacier are offered by **Glacier Heli Tours** (ℭ **800/879-9310**) and **Kruger Helicopters** (ℭ **406/387-4565**). Prices start at about $100 per person for four people for a half-hour trip.

The **Glacier Institute** conducts field classes in the summer that examine Glacier's cultural and natural resources. These 1- to 5-day courses include instruction, transportation, park fees, and college credit. Instructors are highly skilled in their area of expertise, bringing to each course an intimate knowledge of the region and subject matter. The classroom is Glacier National Park and, during the park's off season, other areas in northwest Montana. Courses cover such topics as alpine wildflowers, Glacier's grizzlies, weather systems, and nature photography. Contact the institute for a copy of its current catalog at 137 Main St., P.O. Box 1887, Kalispell, MT 59903 (**☎ 406/ 755-1211;** www.glacierinstitute.org). Prices typically range from $50 to $350 per course.

2 Driving in the Park

Because of the massive piles of rock that surround a visitor, it is impossible to drive through Glacier without drawing comparisons to Grand Teton. At Teton, unless you hit the hiking trails, the mountains keep their distance. But, in Glacier, as you drive, the mountain peaks envelop you.

GOING-TO-THE-SUN ROAD

If you plan only a day or two in Glacier, the most important thing to do is to drive **Going-to-the-Sun Road,** the 50-mile road that bisects the park between West Glacier and St. Mary. Points of interest are clearly marked along this road, and correspond to the park brochure *Points of Interest Along the Going-to-the-Sun Road,* which is available at visitor centers. Bring plenty of film.

The road gains more than 3,400 feet in 32 miles, and is very narrow in places. Visitors with a fear of heights should take a van tour or shuttle. Because of the road's narrowness, oversize vehicles and trailers must use U.S. 2.

As you begin the drive from the West Glacier entrance, you'll pass the largest of the 653 lakes in Glacier—**Lake McDonald.** Numerous turnouts along the way present opportunities to photograph the panoramic views of the lake with its mountainous backdrop. You can see **Sacred Dancing Cascade** and **Johns Lake** after an easy, half-mile hike from the roadside through a hemlock and red cedar forest. The trail head for this hike is 2 miles north of the Lake McDonald Lodge along Going-to-the-Sun Road.

The **Trail of the Cedars** is a short, handicapped-accessible boardwalk trail through terrain thickly carpeted in vibrant, verdant hues. This is also the beginning of the Avalanche Lake Trail, a 2.1-mile hike (one-way) to the foot of Avalanche Lake, one of the most popular day hikes in the park. The trail head is about 5½ miles north of Lake McDonald Lodge, just past the Avalanche Creek Campground.

Almost exactly halfway along Going-to-the-Sun is the overlook for Heaven's Peak, the massive snow-covered mountain to the south that you've just driven around. This is also the jumping-off point for **The Loop Trail,** which can take you to the Granite Park Chalet. Just 2 miles farther is the **Bird Woman Falls Overlook.** Bird Woman Falls drops in a wondrous bounty of water from a hanging valley above the road. Next along the road is the oft-photographed **Weeping Wall,** which is a wall of rock with water pouring forth.

At the 32-mile mark from West Glacier is **Logan Pass,** one of the park's busiest areas and the starting point for the hike to **Hidden Lake,** likely the park's most popular trail. There's a visitor center here atop the Continental Divide, with a bookstore and a small display about the wildlife, flora, and geology of the area.

As you continue the drive downhill, you'll reach the turnout for **Jackson Glacier,** the most easily recognizable glacier in the entire park; followed by **Sunrift Gorge** and **Sun Point,** which are accessible via two short trails rife with wildlife.

Note: Beginning in 2006, construction on Going-to-the-Sun Road will cause 30-minute delays from June 15 to September 15, and up to 2-hour delays before and after that period. The project is slated to last several years.

WINTER ROAD CONDITIONS   Going-to-the-Sun Road is open seasonally, usually from early June to mid-October, depending on weather conditions. Call the park at ✆ **406/888-7800** to find out when tentative openings and closings are scheduled. During the winter, you may drive Going-to-the-Sun Road for 10 miles from West Glacier along Lake McDonald to the road closure; this is a popular destination for cross-country skiers.

OTHER DRIVES

ALONG THE LOWER EDGE OF THE PARK   Circumnavigating the lower half of the park is easily accomplished in 1 long day. After a leisurely breakfast in West Glacier, you'll be in East Glacier in plenty of time for lunch at the Glacier Park Lodge (see section 6, "Where to Stay," in this chapter) and at St. Mary or Many Glacier for dinner.

The road between West Glacier and East Glacier—it's approximately 57 miles—is a well-paved, two-lane affair that winds circuitously around the western and southern borders of the park and follows the Middle Fork of the Flathead River. As you descend to the valley floor, you'll travel through beautiful, privately owned Montana ranch and farm land. Shortly after entering the valley, look to the north and admire the park's massive peaks. The **Goat Lick** parking lot, on U.S. 2 just east of Essex, gets you off the beaten path and provides a view down into a canyon carved by the Flathead River. If you have time, take the short hike down to the stream.

Beyond East Glacier, as you head east on Mont. 49 and north toward Two Medicine, you'll notice that the earth appears to fall off. The contrast is inescapable—mountains tower in the west, but to the east the Hi-Line begins, sporting a horizon that extends so far and so flat as to seemingly lend credence and legitimacy to the Flat Earth Society. But round a bend on Two Medicine Road and suddenly you'll find yourself faced with three mountains (Appistocki Peak, Mount Henry, and Bison Mountain) bare of vegetation but as red as their Southwestern counterparts. Ten miles later, continuing the route northward on U.S. 89, you'll come across a wide panorama of mountain peaks, valleys, ridges, and forested mountains that truly characterizes Glacier's personality. Conclude the bottom half of your long loop by wending downward from these high elevations to the village of St. Mary.

TO POLEBRIDGE   There are two ways to see the park's western boundary and to access the Polebridge area in the north: One is slow and uncomfortable, the other slightly faster and more comfortable. The **North Fork Road** from Columbia Falls takes about an hour to negotiate. It's a sometimes-paved, mostly gravel and pothole

---

Tips Picnic Paradise

The best picnicking spot on the Going-to-the-Sun Road is at the **Sun Point Lake** parking area, which is also the trail head for the .7-mile-round-trip path that follows the shoreline of the lake and leads to Baring Falls. It's located about 9 miles east of the Logan Pass Visitor Center, or 9 miles west of the St. Mary Visitor Center. From the picnic area, the views across the lake to the mountains are unrivaled in the park. For a truly spectacular experience, get there at sunrise.

Tips Glacier's Best Photo Ops

Get up early to catch Glacier's best photo ops. Near bodies of water, the sunrise provides an unrivaled multitude of oranges, blues, and yellows. Then, as the earth warms, lakes are transformed to fog-covered valleys, creating a mystical photographic opportunity.

One of the most picturesque spots is the west end of St. Mary Lake; not only does it paint the lake orange and yellow, it paints the mountains red and orange. A close runner-up is the view west from an overlook across St. Mary Lake to Wild Goose Island in the foreground and the peaks and glaciers at the west end of the lake. Logan Pass, when it's carpeted with wildflowers (late June to early Aug), is not to be missed.

Late-day photos of the Garden Wall from west of Logan Pass are also very dramatic.

stretch that follows the North Fork of the Flathead River. Not much is there besides water and scenery, but the area around Polebridge is a popular place to take in Montana's natural beauty without modern-day distractions like telephones and TVs.

The **Inside North Fork Road,** just north of Apgar, also runs to Polebridge. However, it's totally unpaved, takes an hour longer, and is much harder on driver, passenger, and equipment. Take the faster route instead and spend that extra hour relaxing on a riverbank.

3 Outdoor Pursuits

BIKING   Opportunities for biking in the park are limited, since bikes may be ridden only on established roads, bike routes, or in parking areas, and are not allowed on trails. Restrictions apply to the most hazardous portions of Going-to-the-Sun Road during peak travel times from around mid-June to Labor Day; call ahead to find out when the road will be closed to bikers. During low-visibility periods caused by fog or darkness, a white front light and a back red reflector are required. A few shared campsites for bicyclists are held until 9pm at Apgar, Sprague Creek, Fish Creek, Many Glacier, Two Medicine, Avalanche, Rising Sun, and St. Mary campgrounds, for $3 per person. Before Logan Pass opens and after it closes, Going-to-the-Sun Road is also popular with bikers, provided it is not knee-deep with snow.

From June 15 to Labor Day, bikes are prohibited between Apgar and Sprague Creek campgrounds between 11am and 4pm in both directions, and from Logan Creek to Logan Pass (eastbound) between 11am and 4pm. It takes about 3 hours and 45 minutes to ride from Sprague Creek to Logan Pass.

BOATING   You can take advantage of some of those 653 lakes with a boat rental at various spots. Motor size is restricted to 10 horsepower on most lakes, and a detailed list of other regulations is available at park headquarters and staffed ranger stations. Park rangers may inspect or board any boat to determine regulation compliance. At Apgar and Lake McDonald, you will find kayaks, canoes, rowboats, and motorboats. Only human-powered or electric motorboats are available at Two Medicine. At Many

Glacier you can rent kayaks, canoes, and rowboats. For details, call **Glacier Park Boat Co.** at (© **406/257-2426** or browse **www.glacierparkboats.com**.

FISHING   Glacier's streams and lakes are habitat for whitefish, kokanee salmon, arctic grayling, and five kinds of trout. Try the North Fork of the Flathead to fish for cutthroat and bull trout and any of the park's three larger lakes (Bowman, St. Mary, and McDonald) for rainbow, brook trout, and whitefish. State of Montana fishing licenses are generally not required within the park's boundaries, although you will need one on the North Fork and Middle Fork of the Flathead River. Also, keep in mind that since the eastern boundary of the park abuts the Blackfeet Indian Reservation, you may find yourself fishing in their territorial waters. To avoid a problem, purchase a $10 use permit from businesses in the gateway towns; the permit covers fishing, hiking, and biking in the reservation. Fishing outside the park in Montana waters requires a state license; check in at a local fishing shop to make certain you're within the law. For equipment or sage advice, or to schedule a guided foray ($275 for two people for a half-day), contact **Glacier Anglers** (© **800/235-6781**) at the Glacier Outdoor Center in West Glacier.

HIKING   Glacier is a park that is best seen on foot. Its 1,600 square miles have over 150 trails, totaling more than 750 miles. You can hike over 100 miles along the Continental Divide alone.

Trail maps are available at outdoor stores in Whitefish and Kalispell, as well as at the major visitor centers and ranger stations in the park. Before striking off into the wilderness, however, check with the nearest ranger station to determine the accessibility of your destination, trail conditions, and recent bear sightings. Also note that the trail maps don't show elevation changes or many terrain features beyond lakes and the tallest peaks. If you plan to do any extensive hiking, it is best to purchase a U.S. Geological Survey (USGS) topographic map, available at outdoor sporting goods stores and the USGS website (www.usgs.gov).

The Park Service asks you to stay on trails to keep from eroding the fragile components of the park. Also, don't traverse snowbanks, especially the steeper ones. You should have proper footwear and rain gear, enough food, and, most important, enough water, before approaching any trail head. A can of pepper spray can also come in handy when you're in grizzly habitat. If you're planning to hike in Canada, be sure the bear spray is USEPA approved.

See section 4, "Exploring the Backcountry," below, for information on some of the longer hiking trails and further information on backpacking.

If you plan an extended hike, let someone know your route and your expected time of return. Take a flashlight, in case you take longer than you think. Carry a map, rain gear, and extra clothing. Drink lots of water.

Among the park's shorter and easier trails is the **Trail of the Cedars Nature Trail** (.25 miles round-trip; access is across from the Avalanche Campground Ranger Station), an easy, level trail that's wheelchair accessible. It has interpretive signs along the way. The **Hidden Lake Overlook Nature Trail** ⊕ (3 miles round-trip; accessed from the Logan Pass Visitor Center) is an easy-to-moderate interpretative trail that climbs 460 feet to an overlook of scenic Hidden Lake. It's a popular trail, but by hiking past the overlook to the lake, you'll avoid some of the crowds, and you might even see a mountain goat.

The Loop (8 miles round-trip; access is on Going-to-the-Sun Rd., about halfway between Avalanche Campground and Logan Pass Visitor Center) offers a moderate hike that climbs to Granite Park Chalet and back. Many people use it as a continuation of the Highline Trail, but this is the section to do if you're not quite so adventurous (the Highline Trail is almost 8 miles long; see "Exploring the Backcountry," below). If you want to spend the night in the chalet, contact **Glacier Wilderness Guides** for reservations (📞 **800/521-7238**). (See the descriptions of the chalets in section 5, "Camping," below.)

The **Sun Point Nature Trail** (1.4 miles round-trip; access is 9 miles west of St. Mary at the Sun Point parking area) is an easy walk on gentle slopes that presents commanding views of Baring Falls. Among the favorite hikes (because of its beautiful scenery) is the **Iceberg Lake Trail** 🔎🔎 (9.5 miles round-trip; access at a trail head in a cabin area east of the Swiftcurrent Coffee Shop and Campstore). This is a moderate hike that traverses flower-filled meadows to a jewel of a high lake backed against a mountain wall. Even in summer, there may be snow on the ground and ice floating in the lake. Look for mountain goats or bighorn sheep on the cliffs above. And, as in many of the park's backcountry areas, keep an eye out for the grizzlies.

Swiftcurrent Nature Trail 🔎 (2.4 miles round-trip; access is at a picnic area ½ mile west of the hotel turnoff) is a fun and easy hike along the lake shore, through the woods, and near a marsh, so you may see deer and birds—keep an eye out for blue grouse. If you have time, continue on the trail as it circles Lake Josephine, another easy hike, adding 2.8 miles to the trip. Dramatic Mount Gould towers above the far end of Lake Josephine, and midsummer wildflowers can be spectacular. A longer, 10-mile round-trip trail to Grinnell Glacier, the park's largest, is also accessed from this area.

The very easy **Running Eagle Falls Trail** (.6 mile round-trip; access is 1 mile west of the Two Medicine entrance) winds through a heavily forested area to a large, noisy waterfall. The popular **Twin Falls Trail** (7.6 miles round-trip; accessed from Two Medicine Campground) is an easy hike to scenic Twin Falls. Hikers can walk the entire distance to Twin Falls on a clearly identified trail, or boat across Two Medicine Lake to the foot of the trail head, and hike the last mile. The **St. Mary Falls Trail** 🔎🔎 (1.6 miles round-trip; accessed from Jackson Glacier Overlook) is a fairly easy walk that takes you to rushing falls of the St. Mary River. The roar of the cascade is prodigious and satisfying.

HORSEBACK RIDING   You can bring your own horses and pack animals into the park, but restrictions apply to private stock. A free brochure detailing regulations regarding horseback riding is available from the National Park Service.

Guided horseback riding at Lake McDonald and Many Glacier is provided by Mule Shoe Outfitters (📞 **406/888-5121** or 406/732-4203; www.mule-shoe.com). They offer hourly ($28) and full-day rides ($120) into the nearby wilderness. Glacier Gateway Trailrides (📞 **406/226-4408**) offers similar rides from corrals at East Glacier.

MOUNTAIN CLIMBING   The peaks of Glacier Park rarely exceed 10,000 feet in elevation, but don't let the surveyors' measurements fool you. Glacier has some incredibly difficult climbs, and you must inquire at the ranger station regarding climbing

---

⟨Tips⟩ Bear Warning!

To remind you yet again: Glacier is grizzly country. Make noise when you hike, don't cook near where you sleep, and don't sleep in the same clothes you cooked in.

conditions and closures. In general, the peaks are unsuitable, except for experienced climbers or those traveling with experienced guides; park administration does not recommend climbing because of the unstable nature of the rock.

RAFTING & FLOAT TRIPS   Though the waters that are actually in the park don't lend themselves to white-water rafting, the forks of the Flathead River are some of the best in the northwest corner of the state. For just taking it easy and floating on your back in the summer sun, the North Fork of the Flathead River stretching from Polebridge to Columbia Falls and into Flathead Lake is ideal. Portaging in Polebridge can be difficult, however. The same may be said for the Middle Fork of the Flathead, at the southern border of the park.

For white-water voyagers, the North Fork of the Flathead River (Class II, III) and the Middle Fork (Class III) are the best bets. Inquire at any ranger station for details and conditions, since flow rates change dramatically as snow melts or storms move through the area.

The Middle Fork is a little more severe; the names of certain stretches (such as the Narrows, Jaws, and Bonecrusher) are terror-inspiring in themselves. To assuage that terror, several outfitters offer expert and sanctioned guided trips.

Established in 1975, **Glacier Raft Company,** P.O. Box 210, West Glacier, MT 59936 (© **800/235-6781** or 406/888-5454; www.glacierraftco.com), is Montana's oldest raft company. Their trips range from half-day trips for $43 to $56 per person, full-day excursions for $74 per person, 2-day trips for $299 per person, to 3-day outings for $420 per person. Their prices include all necessary equipment and food. They also offer scenic trips and inflatable kayak rentals among other services. Other local raft guides include **Great Northern Whitewater,** P.O. Box 270, West Glacier, MT 59936 (© **800/735-7897** or 406/387-5340; www.gnwhitewater.com); Montana Raft Company, P.O. Box 330, West Glacier, MT 59936 (© **800/521-7238** or 406/387-5555); and **Wild River Adventures,** P.O. Box 272, West Glacier, MT 59936 (© **800/700-7056** or 406/387-9453; www.riverwild.com).

SNOWSHOEING & CROSS-COUNTRY SKIING   Glacier has numerous cross-country trails, the most popular of which is the **Upper Lake McDonald Trail** to the Avalanche picnic area. This 8-mile trail offers a relatively flat route up Going-to-the-Sun Road with views of McDonald Creek and the mountains looming above the McDonald Valley. For the advanced skier, the same area presents a more intense 11-mile trip that heads northwest in a roundabout fashion to the Apgar Lookout. The most popular trail on the east side is the **Autumn Creek Trail** near Marias Pass. However, avalanche paths cross this area, so inquire about current weather conditions. Yet another popular spot is in Essex along the southern boundary of the park at the Izaak Walton Inn (p. 84). In West Glacier, **Glacier Outdoor Center** (© **800/235-6781**) rents snowshoes and cross-country ski packages for $10 and $15 per day, respectively.

4 Exploring the Backcountry

Glacier offers every kind of backcountry experience, from short day hikes to 2-week treks. Consider your fitness level, backcountry experience, and interests, and then get some advice from one of Glacier's rangers. They can provide you with area maps, but a topographical map is highly recommended if you're going for more than a short walk.

Backcountry campgrounds have maps at the entrance to show you the location of each campsite, the pit toilet, food-preparation areas, and, perhaps most important, food-storage areas. If you fish while camping, it's recommended you exercise catch-and-release so as to avoid attracting wildlife in search of food. If you eat the catch, be certain to puncture the air bladder and throw the entrails into deep water at least 200 feet from the nearest campsite or trail. You will need a permit to camp; see "Backcountry Permits," in section 1 of this chapter.

GUIDED BACKCOUNTRY TRIPS   Glacier Wilderness Guides (© 800/521-7238 or 406/387-5555; www.glacierguides.com) is the exclusive hiking guide service in the park. From May through September, it organizes custom trips and offers weekly departures for 3- and 6-day trips. Prices vary, but you can figure on spending $100 to $140 per person per day. It also rents equipment and can arrange trips where you stay indoors at night.

NOTABLE BACKCOUNTRY HIKING TRAILS

DAWSON-PITAMAKAN LOOP ☀ This difficult, 19-mile loop traverses Rising Wolf Mountain, at 9,513 feet the area's most prominent feature. There are backcountry campsites at Old Man Lake and at No Name Lake. The trail offers splendid panoramas of the park's interior and of many alpine lakes. You'll encounter lots of steep ups and downs: The elevation change is 2,400 feet. The trail head is at Two Medicine Campground.

KINTLA LAKE TO UPPER KINTLA LAKE TRAIL   This 24-mile round-trip hike skirts the north shore of Kintla Lake above Polebridge for about 7 miles before climbing a couple of hundred feet. This stretch of the hike is a breeze. However, once you hit Kintla Creek you may want to reconsider going any farther. With 12 miles under your belt at this point, climbing 3,000 feet may not seem like a great idea. The trail, once it breaks into the clear, offers views of several peaks, including Kinnerly Peak to the south of Upper Kintla Lake. The trail head is located 14 miles north of Polebridge after a drive along a gravel road, at the western tip of Kintla Lake.

BOWMAN LAKE TRAIL ☀☀ This especially scenic trail (14 miles to Brown Pass) is similar to the Kintla Lake hike in difficulty, and, like the Kintla Trail, passes a lake on the north. After a hike through the foliage, the trail climbs out of reach of anyone in bad shape, then ascends 2,000 feet in less than 3 miles to join the Kintla Trail at Brown Pass. A left turn takes you to Kintla Lake (23 miles to the Kintla Lake trail head), a right takes you to Goat Haunt at the foot of Waterton Lake (9 miles). To reach the Bowman Lake trail head, go ⅓ mile north of Polebridge, then turn east (right) up the Bowman Creek road. The road ends after 6 miles at the southeast end of Bowman Lake, from which the trails radiate.

QUARTZ LAKE TRAIL   Accessed from the Bowman Creek trail head, the entire loop is 12 miles, running up and over an 1,800-foot ridge and then dropping down to the south end of Lower Quartz Lake. From there it's a level 3-mile hike to the west end of Quartz Lake, then it's 6 miles back over the ridge farther north (and higher up) before dropping back to Bowman Creek. An interesting aspect of this trail is evidence of the Red Bench Fire of 1988, which took a chunk out of the North Fork area.

THE HIGHLINE TRAIL   This easy-to-moderate 12-mile round-trip hike, which gains only 200 feet in elevation, begins at the Logan Pass Visitor Center and skirts the Garden Wall at elevations of more than 6,000 feet to Granite Park Chalet. Keep an eye on your watch to be certain you'll have enough time for the return hike to Logan Pass. You can continue on from the chalet to "the Loop," the aptly named section of

Going-to-the-Sun Road where the trail actually terminates (an additional 3.2 miles), although to make sure you can get back to your car by nightfall, you'll need to plan for a shuttle.

PIEGAN PASS TO MANY GLACIER If you're looking for a longer, tougher hike from Logan Pass, try this one. You pick up the trail at Siyeh Bend, about 3 miles on the east side of Logan Pass Visitor Center. It's a 13-mile walk up over Piegan Pass, past Grinnell Glacier and Grinnell Lake to Josephine and Swiftcurrent lakes before reaching Many Glacier Lodge. There are many long, steep stretches, going both up and down.

5 Camping

INSIDE THE PARK

Stop at any ranger station for information on closures and availability, and consult the chart below for information on amenities and fees.

There are a variety of camping opportunities here. Campgrounds accessible by paved roads include **Apgar,** near the West Glacier entrance; **Avalanche Creek,** just up from the head of Lake McDonald; **Fish Creek,** on the west side of Lake McDonald; **Many Glacier,** in the northeast part of the park; **Rising Sun,** on the north side of St. Mary Lake; **St. Mary,** on the east side of the park; and **Two Medicine,** in the southeast part of the park near East Glacier. **Sprague Creek,** near the West Glacier entrance, offers a paved road but does not allow towed vehicles. There are also five campgrounds accessed by narrow dirt roads. Though utility connections are not provided at these sites, fireplaces, picnic tables, washrooms (with sinks and flush toilets), and cold running water are located at each campground. Campsites are available on a first-come, first-served basis, payable by cash or check, except for Fish Creek and St. Mary campgrounds, where sites can be reserved by Discover, Masterccard, and Visa through the **National Park Service Reservation System** (© **800/365-2267;** http://reservations.nps.gov).

A few shared sites for bicyclists are held until 9pm at Apgar, Sprague Creek, Avalanche, Fish Creek, Many Glacier, Two Medicine, Rising Sun, and St. Mary campgrounds, for $3 per person.

THE CAMPGROUNDS

Despite its proximity to the center of the hotel and motel activity, the **Many Glacier Campground** ⁂ is a well-treed campground with more privacy than you'd expect. The campground has adequate space for small motor homes and pickup truck/camper combinations, but space for vehicles pulling trailers is limited. It is a veritable mecca for tent campers. The **Avalanche Campground** is situated in the bottom of the valley near Lake McDonald in a heavily treed area immediately adjacent to the river. The **Two Medicine Campground** ⁂ lies in the shadow of the mountains near three lakes and a stream. It is a well-treed area that has beautiful sites, plenty of shade, and opportunities to wet a fishing line. Two Medicine is a little out of the way of the typical Glacier traveler, and may offer a little more solitude. The **Cut Bank Campground** road is not paved, but it's only 5 miles from the pavement to the ranger station and campground. The road and campground are best suited to recreational vehicles 21 feet or shorter.

CHALETS

Two of the park's most popular destinations, Granite Park and Sperry Chalets—National Historic Landmarks built by the Great Northern Railway between 1912 and

Amenities for Each Campground in Glacier National Park

Campground	# of Sites	Fee	Max RV Length	Flush Toilets	Disposal Stations	Boat Access
Apgar	4	$15	25 sites; up to 40'	Yes	Yes	Yes
Avalanche	87	$15	50 sites; up to 26'	Yes	Yes	No
Bowman Lake*	48	$12	RVs not recommended	No	No	Yes
Cut Bank*	19	$12	RVs not recommended	No	No	No
Fish Creek	178	$17	3 sites; up to 35'	Yes	Yes	No
Kintla Lake*	13	$12	RVs not recommended	No	No	Yes
Logging Creek*	8	$12	RVs not recommended	No	No	No
Many Glacier	110	$15	13 sites; up to 35'	Yes	Yes	Yes
Quartz Creek*	7	$12	RVs not recommended	No	No	No
Rising Sun	83	$15	3 sites; up to 30'	Yes	Yes	Yes
St. Mary	148	$17	25 sites; up to 35'	Yes	Yes	No
Two Medicine	99	$15	13 sites; up to 32'	Yes	Yes	Yes

Campgrounds are accessible only by narrow dirt roads. RVs are not recommended.

1914—are subjects of an extensive restoration project. The **Granite Park Chalet** is a hiker's shelter only. Guests must bring their own food, water, cooking and eating utensils, flashlights, and sleeping bags. Rooms and beds are provided, as are a kitchen with a cooking stove and dining room. No public water is available, so bring your own. The chalet has 12 rooms (all single bunk beds), and sleeps two to six per room. Cost is about $70 per night per person, plus a one-time $10 per-person fee if you want bed linens. To get there, you'll have to walk about 3 miles from The Loop trail head off Going-to-the-Sun Road, or about 6 miles on the trail to Swiftcurrent Pass at the end of Many Glacier Road from the east side.

The **Sperry Chalet** is an impressive stone structure in the center of the wilderness. Here you'll get a room (with linens) plus three meals daily, but no bathing facilities except cold water, and the modern composting toilets are outside. Rates are $155 for the first person in a room plus $100 for each additional person, and include all meals. To get there, walk about 4 miles from the road, up Snyder Creek, then toward Gunsight Mountain. The trail head is opposite the entrance to Lake McDonald Lodge on the lower portion of Going-to-the-Sun Road.

For reservations at either chalet, contact **Belton Chalets** at (© **888/345-2649** or 406/387-5654; www.graniteparkchalet.com or www.sperrychalet.com).

CAMPGROUNDS IN GATEWAY COMMUNITIES

During the busy season, it's recommended that you reserve a spot at these campsites at least 1 month in advance.

IN EAST GLACIER

Y Lazy R Situated just off U.S. 2, this campground is conveniently located within walking distance of East Glacier and is the closest to town and its laundry facilities. Plan to arrive early if you want to snag one of the few sites with trees. The Y Lazy R is a great value and an ideal place to plant the RV before heading off to explore the region.
P.O. Box 146, East Glacier, MT 59434. © **406/226-5505**. 10 tent sites, 30 RV sites. $15 tent; $18 full hookup. No credit cards.

IN ST. MARY

Johnson's of St. Mary   April through September (depending on the weather), this is where you want to camp if you can get a spot. The campground is located near the southern end of Lower St. Mary Lake and provides an inexpensive overnight stop with access to the east side of the park and the tourist facilities at the St. Mary Lodge. There are also showers ($3), a laundromat, and an 18-hole miniature golf course.

St. Mary, MT 59417. ℂ 406/732-4207. www.johnsonsofstmary.com. 40 tent sites, 82 RV sites. $18 tent; $25 RV with electricity and water only; $28–$30 full hookup; $20 motor home, no hookup. MC, V.

IN WEST GLACIER

Glacier Campground   This campground—1 mile west of West Glacier on U.S. 2—is the closest campground outside the park. Set amid a forested area overgrown with evergreens, it's a quiet, comfortable, shady place to retreat. Most sites have water and electric hookups; the balance is perfect for tent camping. Five rather primitive cabins are also available, but furnishings are modest: sleeping beds with mattresses and electricity, but no plumbing or kitchen facilities. Recreational facilities include volleyball, horseshoes, and a basketball court; also on the premises are an excellent Cajun restaurant, a laundromat, and a small general store.

P.O. Box 447, 12070 U.S. 2, West Glacier, MT 59936. ℂ 888/387-5689 or 406/387-5689. www.glaciercampground. com. 80 tent sites, 80 RV sites, 5 cabins. $19 tent; $20–$26 RV; $35–$45 cabin. MC, V.

Lake Five Resort   Located 3 miles west of West Glacier and approximately 1 mile from U.S. 2 is this cabin and campground arrangement, an alternative to potentially crowded park campgrounds. Situated on a 235-acre lake surrounded by private homes and summer cottages, the resort is far from the madding crowd (though still close to the park itself). Seven of the nine cabins are on the lakefront, all of them equipped with bathrooms and showers. The only distraction may be the sound of powerboats.

540 Belton Stage Rd., West Glacier, MT 59936. ℂ 406/387-5601. www.lakefiveresort.com. 9 cabins, 6 tepee lodges, 45 sites with electricity and water (14 of which have sewer hookups). $30–$35 site; $100–$145 cabin; $50–$60 tepee. No credit cards.

BACKCOUNTRY CAMPING

If it's the backcountry you're bent on seeing, Glacier has 63 backcountry campgrounds. Fortunately, many are at lower elevation, so inexperienced backpackers have an opportunity to take advantage of them. For an accurate depiction of your itinerary's difficulty, and advice on what may be needed, check with rangers in the area you contemplate visiting. The primary source of danger is bears. Backcountry permits are available at ranger stations, and can be made in person up to 24 hours in advance. There are separate fees for advance reservations ($20) and backcountry camping ($4 per person per night). See "Backcountry Permits," in section 1 of this chapter.

6 Where to Stay

Television reception is limited in the Glacier National Park area, so if TV is important to you, check not only that the lodging facility has in-room TVs, but also call and ask just what channels they get.

INSIDE THE PARK

With only one exception, Glacier Park, Inc. (GPI), operates the hostelries in Glacier National Park. Lake McDonald Lodge, Glacier Park Lodge, and Many Glacier Hotel are first-tier properties that have been popular destinations since early in the 20th century.

Swiftcurrent Motor Inn is typical of the casual motel-style properties at the other end of the spectrum, providing decent but undistinguished accommodations for less money. Although the lodges have a considerable charm, they don't have spas, air-conditioning, or in-room televisions.

Reserve well in advance. August dates may fill before the spring thaw. For more information on the following properties or to make a reservation, contact **Glacier Park, Inc.,** P.O. Box 2025, Columbia Falls, MT 59912 (© **406/892-2525;** fax 406/892-1375; www.glacierparkinc.com). GPI does not accept pets at any of its facilities.

Apgar Village Lodge   The Apgar Village Lodge is located on the south end of Lake McDonald and is one of two lodgings in Apgar Village. There's a wide variety of lodging available here, but the best places—reserve early—are along Lake McDonald Creek and on the banks of the lake. There are nine river cabins, and several motel rooms overlooking the creek. The cabins are much nicer than they look on the outside. Five large cabins have been completely remodeled, with two bedrooms; most of them have kitchens with stoves and refrigerators. Some of the small ones tend to be a little dark.

Apgar Village, Box 410, West Glacier, MT 59936. © 406/888-5484. Fax 406/888-5273. www.westglacier.com. 28 cabins, 20 motel rooms. $90–$227 cabin; $72–$95 double motel room. AE, DISC, MC, V. Closed early Oct to Apr. *In room:* TV, no phone.

Glacier Park Lodge ✶✶   Actually just outside the southeast entrance at East Glacier Park, this is the flagship inn of the park, an imposing timbered lodge that stands as a stately tribute to the Great Northern Railroad and its early attempts to lure tourists to Glacier. The carefully manicured lawn and ever-blooming wildflowers frame the grounds in colors spectacular enough to rival the mountain backdrop. The interior features massive Douglas fir pillars, some 40 inches in diameter and 40 feet tall. In fact, stand in the middle of the lobby and look up—you'll discover beams, carved from massive trees, that are the structural supports for the entire building. Skylights, wrought-iron chandeliers, and a desk hewn from a 36-inch-diameter log add to the Old West flavor.

Rooms are well furnished, but showers are elbow-banging small, and sinks are significantly smaller than those found in today's modern hotels and motels. A wooden deck outside the lounge provides an excellent spot for cocktails, reading, or a late-afternoon snooze. A glass-enclosed breezeway connects the main building to the west wing; the oak chaise longues found there are an ideal spot from which to watch a sunrise. There's even an immaculately groomed executive-style golf course. The Trading Post offers traditional souvenirs, as well as nicely crafted American Indian artwork and clothing. Some evenings, members of the Blackfeet tribe recount their history around the fireplace.

East Glacier, MT 59434. © 406/892-2525. Fax 406/892-1375. www.glacierparkinc.com. 154 units. $149–$199 double; $399 suite. AE, DISC, MC, V. Closed early Oct to late May. **Amenities:** Restaurant; lounge; outdoor pool; 9-hole golf course; activities desk. *In room:* No phone.

Lake McDonald Lodge ✶✶   The Lake McDonald Lodge feels like a genuine mountain lodge. Although this two-story building doesn't have the same towering ceilings and open spaces as other park hotels, it has a warm, cozy feel inspired by its wood construction. Lodge rooms, located on the second and third floor of the lodge (no elevator), are pleasantly decorated and have a historic feel, while the motel units are simple but well maintained. The well-preserved cottages are located in multi-unit

The Other Gateway Communities

If the convenience of staying on Glacier's back porch is important to you, the places listed on the following pages are your best bets. See "Where to Stay" in the Whitefish, Kalispell, and Columbia Falls sections of chapter 6 for listings of places that might be more in line with your needs if the park is merely a 1- or 2-day part of your vacation.

cottage buildings in a wooded area. Situated on the shore of the park's largest lake, the lodge provides a marvelous central base for exploring the western part of the park. The lodge is a center for boating activity; scenic cruises depart daily and canoe rentals are popular. Common lounging areas are furnished with heavy couches, sofas, and chairs that surround a stone fireplace. A post office and sundries store are also on the grounds. The entire lodge is nonsmoking.

Glacier National Park, MT 59936. © 406/892-2525. Fax 406/892-1375. www.glacierparkinc.com. 62 units in lodge and motel, 38 cottage units. $154 lodge room; $115 motel unit; $101–$154 cottage. AE, DISC, MC, V. Closed late Sept to late May. **Amenities:** 2 restaurants; lounge; post office. *In room:* No phone.

Many Glacier Hotel ★★★   Many Glacier is a vast, sprawling four-story structure on Swiftcurrent Lake. It's the most popular lodging in the park, and with good reason. The setting is beautiful, and there are a wide variety of activities to embark on from here—boating, hiking, and bird-watching, to name but a few. Most of the rooms are a little larger than the ones usually associated with a Northern Pacific hotel. But this was never a "railroad hotel." Completed in 1915, it was one of a network of chalets—others were Sperry and Granite—that visitors rode to on horseback. The chalets were set a day's ride apart.

Rooms, decorated in keeping with the hotel's historic roots, are located in the main lodge around the balconies overlooking the lobby or in the adjoining annex. The lakeside rooms offer great views of Swiftcurrent Lake. If you plan to use your room only as a place to crash at the end of the day, save money by booking one of the smaller units. You'll almost certainly see bears wandering around Many Glacier in August when the huckleberries ripen. All units are nonsmoking.

Glacier National Park, MT 59936. © 406/892-2525. Fax 406/892-1375. www.glacierparkinc.com. 216 units. $120–$199 double; $236 suite. AE, DISC, MC, V. Closed mid-Sept to mid-June. **Amenities:** Dining room; coffee shop; lounge; nightly cabaret performances begin midsummer. *In room:* No phone.

Rising Sun Motor Inn   Located 6½ miles from St. Mary, just off Going-to-the-Sun Road, the Rising Sun consists of a complex made up of a restaurant, a motor inn, cottages, a camp store, a gift shop, and a service station. The basic motel rooms are just that—basic but uninspiring motel rooms—but are completely adequate for a good night's rest and in an excellent location for those who want to explore the eastern side of the park from Going-to-the-Sun Road. The cottages (you rent half of a duplex) are more interesting but a bit on the rustic side. All units here are nonsmoking.

Glacier National Park, MT 59936. © 406/892-2525. Fax 406/892-1375. www.glacierparkinc.com. 63 units. $99–$115 double; $101 cottage. AE, DISC, MC, V. Closed mid-Sept to mid-June. **Amenities:** Dining room. *In room:* No phone.

Swiftcurrent Motor Inn ★ *Value*   The Swiftcurrent Motor Inn is located about a mile upstream from Many Glacier Hotel, but it attracts an entirely different crowd.

The people who stay here are younger, less well-to-do, and primarily active types interested in spending lots of time exploring the backcountry trails. Like Many Glacier, the inn is set against a mountain backdrop in what is considered a hiker's paradise. Motel rooms here have standard motel decor—functional but nothing special; cabins are a bit more interesting, with one or two bedrooms, and perhaps a bathroom (communal facilities are nearby). All units are nonsmoking. The Swiftcurrent was built in 1936 as a motor hotel, the first in the park specifically directed at tourists arriving by car rather than by train. There are three circles of cabins and two motel-style units, all set back in the trees. The inn sits in a wildlife migratory path, so you likely will see bear, elk, and moose in the parking lot. The Italian Garden Ristorante serves a mean garlic and artichoke-heart pizza. There's also a camping supplies store on the property.

Glacier National Park, MT 59936. ✆ 406/892-2525. Fax 406/892-1375. www.glacierparkinc.com. 88 units and cabins, most cabins without private bathroom. $99–$115 double in motor inn; $45–$77 double in cabin. AE, DISC, MC, V. Closed mid-Sept to mid-June. **Amenities:** Restaurant; coin-operated laundry. *In room:* No phone.

Village Inn at Apgar   Not to be confused with Apgar Village Lodge (see above), the Village Inn at Apgar is the smallest of the properties operated by GPI in Glacier. Located in Apgar Village, the inn is convenient to the general store, cafes, and boat docks. Like its counterparts throughout the park, the Village Inn is comfortably outfitted with modest furnishings, making it a cozy and convenient place to set up camp. All 36 rooms are located on two floors of the inn and 12 of them have kitchenettes. Apgar Village bustles with activity during the summer and is a great choice for families.

Glacier National Park, MT 59936. ✆ 406/892-2525. Fax 406/892-1375. www.glacierparkinc.com. 36 units. $113–$179 double. AE, DISC, MC, V. Closed early Oct to late May. *In room:* Kitchenette, no phone.

IN GATEWAY COMMUNITIES
IN EAST GLACIER

Backpacker's Inn   This dorm-style hostel consists of a private cabin and a shared coed cabin that sleeps eight. At $12 per person, the price is right, but don't expect much more than a bed. The rooms are booked out of Serrano's restaurant (see "Where to Dine," below).

P.O. Box 94, East Glacier, MT 59434. ✆ 406/226-9392. 16 beds in 3 cabins. $12 per person in coed dorm; $25 for 1 person and $35 for 2 in private cabin. DISC, MC, V. Closed mid-Oct to Apr. *In room:* No phone.

Brownies Grocery and AYH Hostel *(Value*   Reservations are recommended at this popular combination grocery store/hostel, which offers comfortable rooms at extremely affordable prices. Dorm and family rooms are located on the second floor of a rustic, older log building with several common rooms for guests to share, including a porch, kitchen, bathrooms, and laundry.

P.O. Box 229, East Glacier, MT 59434. ✆ 406/226-4426 or 406/226-4456. 10 units, all with shared bathroom. AYH members $13–$26 or $38 family room; nonmembers $16–$29 or $38 family room. Family rooms sleep 2–6. MC, V. Closed Oct to early May, depending on the weather. *In room:* No phone.

Jacobson's Cottages   Located in a nicely wooded area, these quaint cottages are small but comfortable. All have cable TV and one has a kitchen. Entertainment and good food are short walks away with Restaurant Thimbleberry a half-block down the street, and Two Medicine an 11-mile drive. The cottages are available seasonally, and reservations are recommended.

120 Mont. 49 (P.O. Box 454), East Glacier, MT 59434. ✆ 888/226-4422 or 406/226-4422. Fax 406/226-4425. 12 cottages. $55–$80 double. AE, DISC, MC, V. Closed Nov–Apr. *In room:* Cable TV, no phone.

Mountain Pine Motel   This property is a one-story, 1950s-style motel that provides clean, well-furnished rooms equipped with cable TV. It is in a shaded, timbered area along Mont. 49. Most standard rooms have two queen-size beds, reading chairs and table, chest, and bathrooms with tub/shower combinations. There is also a large three-bedroom log house available with a view of the mountains. All units are nonsmoking.

Mont. 49, East Glacier, MT 59434. ✆ **406/226-4403**. 25 units. $58–$64 double. AE, DC, DISC, MC, V. Closed Oct–Apr. *In room:* TV.

IN ESSEX

Izaak Walton Inn 🟊🟊 *(Finds)*   Built in 1939, this inn originally housed railway workers. It now has three floors of rooms, a restaurant, and a tavern. The rooms are not large, but they are beautifully kept, with wood-paneled walls and various Western touches and a private bathroom. Some have, in addition to the double beds, futon couches that can be folded out for another bed. The halls are decorated in railroad memorabilia. The converted cabooses are similarly decorated (with kitchenettes to boot), and what train buff can resist the temptation of spending the night in a genuine caboose? Unlike a lot of Glacier lodging establishments, the inn is booming in winter. Skiers are attracted to its 30 miles of groomed trails, and it offers a number of skiing packages.

290 Izaak Walton Inn Rd., Essex, MT 59916. ✆ **406/888-5700**. Fax 406/888-5200. www.izaakwaltoninn.com. 33 units plus 4 caboose cottages. $107–$148 double; $222–$242 suite; $675 caboose for a 3-night minimum stay. MC, V. **Amenities:** Restaurant (Continental); lounge; sauna. *In room:* Kitchenette, no phone.

IN POLEBRIDGE

North Fork Hostel and Square Peg Ranch   Formerly called the Quarter Circle MC Ranch and located inside the park, this lodge was moved to its present location near Polebridge in the late 1960s, and is ideal for the back-to-nature traveler. It now sits within a stone's throw of the North Fork of the Flathead River and right across the river from Glacier National Park. Accommodations are rustic, with a mountain-cabin feel—there's no electricity in Polebridge, so lighting is powered by kerosene and propane, and heat is from an old-fashioned woodstove. There are separate facilities for men and women, as well as couples' accommodations, washrooms with hot showers, and clean outhouses. There are also several small cabins suitable for families. Hostel guests should bring linens or sleeping bags (sheets are available for rent) and flashlights. The Square Peg Ranch offers two rustic log homes, with similar decor to the hostel, and a few bare-bones tepees and campsites for $10 a night. The log homes have solar-heated showers, or guests can use the hostel showers, and there are outhouses. The hostel and cabins have complete kitchen facilities, and there's a relaxing wood-fired hot tub outside for everyone. Equipment rentals and Internet access are also available here.

80 Beaver Dr., Polebridge, MT 59928. ✆ **406/888-5241** or 406/253-4321. www.nfhostel.com. 12 bunks, 2 cabins, 2 log homes. $15 bunk; $35 cabin; $70 log home. AE. Closed mid-Oct to Apr. **Amenities:** Communal kitchen; Jacuzzi. *In room:* No phone.

Polebridge Mercantile and Cabins *(Value)*   There is no electricity and no running water in the cabins here, let alone bedding—it's bring-your-own sleeping bag or linens at the Merc. The most expensive "luxury" cabin has a bathroom and running water in the kitchenette. Each cabin has a propane cooking stove and lights, and the views out over the west side of Glacier National Park make the price tag a steal, especially if you brought the kids. This may sound a tad too rough and primitive, but Polebridge is actually a happening spot in the summer when all the river rats and seasonal residents converge for good times and tall tales about the rapids they've run and their mountaineering adventures. There is a great bakery here, too.

P.O. Box 280042, Polebridge, MT 59928. ℂ **406/888-5105**. www.members.tripod.com/polebridge. 4 cabins. $35–$45 cabin. MC, V. *In room:* Kitchenette, no phone.

IN ST. MARY

The Resort at Glacier 🐾   Situated at the St. Mary end of Going-to-the-Sun Road, this lodge is another member of the minority of park properties that aren't managed by GPI. The main lodge and attendant rooms are standard Montana fare, with tasteful ironwood furnishings. Lodging is in three different areas in close proximity to the center of the complex; lodge and motel rooms are nicely done motel-style units that may have two single beds or a queen-size. The nicest units are the cabins, which boast living areas with dining tables, kitchenettes with microwaves and minifridges, and queen-size beds in a separate sleeping area. All rooms have phones; most have TVs and air-conditioning. The surrounding complex includes a market, several restaurants, and a lounge.

U.S. 89 and Going-to-the-Sun Rd., St. Mary, MT 59417. ℂ **800/368-3689** or 406/732-4431. Fax 406/732-9265. www.glcpark.com. 124 units, including 57 hotel rooms, 48 lodge rooms and suites, and 19 cabins and cottages. $85–$140 double hotel rooms; $145–$350 cabin or cottage; and $160–$250 lodge room or suite. AE, DISC, MC, V. **Amenities:** 3 restaurants (fine dining/cafe/pizza); 2 lounges; activities desk; coin-operated washers and dryers. *In room:* A/C, TV, fridge, kitchenettes, coffeemaker, hair dryer, iron.

IN WEST GLACIER

Belton Chalets and Lodge   A National Historic Landmark, this facility across from the railroad station has been completely restored to the elegance of an early-20th-century hotel. The rooms are small, simple, and old-fashioned; the cottages have a few modernities (fridges, microwaves, coffeemakers). But the feel of the place is comfortable and the staff is very friendly. Many of the rooms have their own balcony looking out over the rounded timber hills in the near distance, the foothills to Glacier National Park.

12575 U.S. 2, West Glacier, MT 59936. ℂ **888/235-8665** or 406/888-5000. Fax 406/888-5005. www.beltonchalet. com. 25 units, 2 cottages. $130–$270 early June to early Sept; $95–$200 early Sept to early June. Rates include complimentary continental breakfast. AE, MC, V. **Amenities:** Restaurant (see "Where to Dine," below); lounge; spa; game room. *In room:* No phone.

Glacier Outdoor Center 🐾   Built in three stages since 1996, the cabins at the Glacier Raft Company's headquarters are delightful, functional, and tasteful. They sport trout, moose, and bears on everything from dishes to lampshades. Backing up to the Flathead National Forest just west of the park entrance on U.S. 2, the cabins are nestled well off the road around a grassy glen with a picnic area, volleyball court, and a trout pond where casting clinics are held in the summer. Each cabin has a fully equipped kitchen, one or two bedrooms, and a private deck with a barbecue; the two-bedroom units can sleep up to 14 people.

U.S. 2, P.O. Box 210D, West Glacier, MT 59936. ℂ **800/235-6781** or 406/888-5454. www.glacierraftco.com. 9 cabins. $230–$345 per cabin per night; lower rates in winter. AE, DISC, MC, V. **Amenities:** Activities desk. *In room:* Kitchens.

Great Northern Chalets 🐾   This small, family-oriented resort located near West Glacier offers log chalets that have balconies facing landscaped flower gardens and a pond, with mountain views in the distance. Two types of chalets are offered, the largest being a beautifully furnished two-story, two-bedroom unit with three queen-size beds, a full bathroom upstairs, and half bathroom downstairs. Smaller chalets have one large upstairs bedroom with two queen-size beds, and a downstairs level with a full-size sleeper sofa and a kitchen with service for six.

12127 U.S. 2, West Glacier, MT 59936. ✆ 800/735-7897 or 406/387-5340. Fax 406/387-9007. www.gnwhitewater. com. 5 units. $200–$300 double. AE, DISC, MC, V. Closed late Oct to Mar. **Amenities:** 16-ft. indoor Jacuzzi; volleyball court; fly-fishing instruction. *In room:* No phone.

Vista Motel *(Value* Perched atop a hill at the west entrance to Glacier National Park, the Vista boasts tremendous views of the mountains. It's strictly a strip motel, old but pretty well preserved. The owner is a serious Denver Broncos fan, if that influences your choice one way or the other. Accommodations are not luxurious, but rooms are clean and comfortable, the cabins can easily house a family, and it's cheaper than the competition.

11955 U.S. 2 East (P.O. Box 90), West Glacier, MT 59936. ✆ 406/888-5311. Fax 406/888-9027. 25 units, including 5 cabins. $65–$120 double. AE, DISC, MC, V. Closed late Sept to Apr. **Amenities:** Outdoor heated pool. *In room:* No phone.

West Glacier Motel *(Value* Formerly the River Bend Motel, this property has two locations. Half of the units are in West Glacier on Going-to-the-Sun Road, about a mile from the park entrance, and a second set of units is another mile away on a forested piece of ground that presents panoramic views of the park. This 1950s-style motel has a great location, the prices can't be beat during peak season, and rates drop dramatically the week before Labor Day. The Western-style cabins are better suited to family use, since they come with two or three queen-size beds.

200 Going-to-the-Sun Rd., West Glacier, MT 59936. ✆ 406/888-5662. www.westglacier.com. 32 units. $88 motel room double; $125–$156 cabin. AE, DISC, MC, V. Closed early Oct to Apr. *In room:* TV, kitchens in cabins, no phone.

7 Where to Dine

INSIDE THE PARK

Food options inside the park are primarily limited to dining rooms operated by GPI. Breakfasts range from $4.50 to $9, lunch entrees are $6 to $12, and most dinner entrees $10 to $25.

You'll find above-average food served at above-average prices in the dining rooms at the major properties. Glacier Park Lodge has the **Great Northern Steak & Rib House,** which has Western decor and a menu of beef, barbecued ribs, fish, and chicken, plus a full breakfast buffet; and **The Sunset Lounge,** which offers a bar menu of sandwiches and appetizers. At Lake McDonald Lodge you'll find **Russell's Fireside Dining Room** ⚡, which has a hunting lodge atmosphere with rough-hewn beams and hunting trophies, and specializes in American standards, including beef tenderloin, roast duckling, seared mountain trout, roast turkey, Alaskan salmon, and steaks; there's also a full breakfast buffet. Also at Lake McDonald Lodge is the **Stockade Lounge,** which serves a bar menu of sandwiches and appetizers, and **Jammer Joe's,** a pizzeria/family restaurant. Many Glacier Hotel has the **Ptarmigan Dining Room,** which has Swiss decor in keeping with the lodge, emphasizing spectacular mountain views, and serves continental and Swiss cuisine plus a breakfast buffet. Many Glacier also has the **Swiss Room and Interlaken Lounge,** with a bar menu of sandwiches and appetizers, and **Heidi's,** a fast-food counter known for its huckleberry frozen yogurt. The dining rooms open with the park and close sometime in September, depending on the facility. At each dining room, breakfast is served from 6:30 to 9:30am; lunch from 11:30am to 1:30pm; and dinner from 5:30 to 9:30pm. Coffee and snack shops open either at 7 or 8am and close at 9pm. All of the above restaurants are nonsmoking.

The alternatives include second-tier restaurants close to the hotels, most of which are comparable to chain restaurants in both quality and price. The **Two Dog Flats Grill** at the Rising Sun Motor Inn serves "hearty American fare"; the Swiftcurrent Motor Inn restaurant is the **Italian Gardens Ristorante.** Lunch and dinner feature combinations of salads, sandwiches, pasta dishes, and "create your own" pizzas. At Apgar you'll find a deli and a family dining arrangement.

IN GATEWAY COMMUNITIES
IN EAST GLACIER
Two Sisters Cafe, north of St. Mary on U.S. 89 in Babb (© **406/732-5535**), may serve up the very best pie in the area, with a fun atmosphere and a huge license plate collection. Susan and Beth Higgins, the eponymous sisters that run the place, specialize in creative "New American" fare, with a menu that often changes but typically includes dishes like cioppino, herb risotto, and chipotle barbecued chicken. The restaurant is open daily from late May to mid-September from 8am to 10pm and accepts MasterCard and Visa.

Restaurant Thimbleberry ✿✿ AMERICAN   Locally famous for its incredible pies, the Thimbleberry also serves great omelets for breakfast, sandwiches and salads for lunch, and an excellent cornmeal-dusted St. Mary Lake whitefish for dinner. Serving self-described "slow food," this is a good choice for vegetarians or people looking for something other than a Montana steak or hamburger. And if you've never had fry bread, then the Thimbleberry is the place to try it.

1112 Mont. 49, East Glacier. © 406/226-5523. Breakfast items $3–$7; main courses $4.50–$8 lunch, $12–$18 dinner. No credit cards. Daily 6:30am–10pm. Closed Oct to mid-May.

Serrano's ✿ MEXICAN   In East Glacier, if you're going to eat only one dinner, eat it at Serrano's. The farther north you go, the warier you should be of Mexican restaurants. But Serrano's only claims a kind of Mexican-California-Southwest influence, and the food succeeds very well. The seafood enchilada, with shrimp and scallops, is excellent, especially when accompanied by one of the restaurant's fabulous margaritas. Or, if you prefer, have a beer from the large selection of microbrews. Serrano's has an outstanding local reputation, so don't be surprised if you encounter masses of people during the height of summer.

29 Dawson Ave., East Glacier. © 406/226-9392. Reservations recommended. Main courses $9–$15. AE, DISC, MC, V. Daily 5–10pm. Closed Oct–Apr.

IN POLEBRIDGE
Northern Lights Saloon (Finds) AMERICAN/ECLECTIC   When people don't mind traveling over 30 miles of bumpy gravel road, when they don't blink an eye as they hit yet another gaping pothole and lose a hubcap or bend a rim, they must know something you don't about wherever it is they're going—in this case, the Northern Lights Saloon. This small restaurant, located squarely in the middle of nowhere, attracts summer crowds that often have to wait patiently outside for a table to clear, in anticipation of the well-prepared and reasonable gourmet specials and fresh strawberry-rhubarb pie. Picnic tables, a volleyball net, and the peaks of Glacier Park are there to make the wait as painless as possible. You won't find a place with more character or a friendlier staff.

Polebridge. ⓒ **406/888-5669.** Reservations not accepted. Main courses $9–$17. MC, V. Late May to mid-Sept daily 4–10pm; mid-Sept to late May Fri–Sat 4–9pm, Sun 9am–3pm. Bar open later.

IN WEST GLACIER

The Belton Tap Room and Grille AMERICAN   This restaurant, located in restored buildings that were once the Great Northern Railroad Chalet, serves up respectable food geared toward American tastes—steaks, buffalo, chicken, ribs, trout, and salmon. And although this place is deep within the heart of the meat-and-pota-toes Rockies, there are a number of vegetarian selections. A large stone fireplace domi-nates the taproom, which serves several kinds of brewed-in-Montana beers.

12575 U.S. 2, West Glacier (across from the west entrance to the park and from the Glacier Amtrak Station). ⓒ **406/888-5000.** Dinner $9–$25. AE, MC, V. Daily 5–10pm. Bar open later.

Glacier Highland Restaurant ⚘ *Value* AMERICAN   This is the spot to satisfy the sweet tooth; a baker is on hand, so the pies are well worth the stop, and the cinnamon rolls are breakfast giants. The Highland Burger is, by any standard, a great hunk of beef, and the fresh trout is a dinner specialty.

U.S. 2, West Glacier. ⓒ **406/888-5427.** Breakfast items $4–$8.50; main courses $5–$8.50 lunch, $10–$18 dinner. AE, DISC, MC, V. Daily 7am–10pm. Closed mid-Nov to Mar.

ESSENTIAL SERVICES

EAST GLACIER   East Glacier has a gas station, post office, several gift shops, a small market with a limited supply of fresh meats and produce as well as beer and wine, and a modest supply of fishing and camping accessories.

WEST GLACIER   A gas station, general store, laundromat, photo shop, rafting companies, post office, gift shop, bar, and restaurant are located just outside the West Glacier entrance to the park.

ST. MARY   The **St. Mary Supermart** (ⓒ **406/732-4431**) will never be confused with a metropolitan-area supermarket, but it's the closest thing you will find in any of the park gateway cities except Kalispell, which is 80 miles due west. Fresh produce, canned goods, and beverages, including beer and wine, will be found here, but you can expect to pay tourist-town prices. There's also a post office.

8 A Side Trip to Browning & the Blackfeet Indian Reservation

127 miles NW of Great Falls; 69 miles E of West Glacier; 160 miles W of Havre

According to American Indian legend, the Blackfeet were named because their moc-casins were blackened with soot from fires or paint. Siksika, the "Blackfooted People," became their tribal name, and they eventually grew into four bands: the Blackfeet in Montana and the Kaina, Pikani, and Siksika of Alberta, Canada. Today the Blackfeet maintain a humble existence near the beautiful lands that were once their own, with about half of the tribal enrollment of 14,000 living on the reservation near the east side of Glacier National Park. **Browning,** the tribal headquarters, is a gateway town to Glacier, but many visitors pass through quickly in anticipation of the end of the prairies and the beginning of the mountains.

ESSENTIALS

GETTING THERE   To reach Browning, follow U.S. 89 south from St. Mary for 32 miles, or take U.S. 2 east from East Glacier for 12 miles. Browning is about 69 miles east of West Glacier on U.S. 2.

SPECIAL EVENTS Browning holds **North American Indian Days** in mid-July. This 4-day celebration draws visitors from across the region to view American Indian dance competitions, games, and sporting events at the Blackfeet Tribal Campgrounds, which are adjacent to the **Museum of the Plains Indian.**

WHAT TO SEE & DO

The **Museum of the Plains Indian,** U.S. 2 and 89 (© **406/338-2230**), is a fairly modest effort, but it has one of the best collections of Indian garb in the West. It also features some very good art by local Blackfeet artists. Admission is free.

A large and eclectic art collection is on display in the **Blackfeet Heritage Center and Art Gallery** (© **406/338-5661**), at the intersection of U.S. highways 2 and 89. There are historic artifacts alongside contemporary works, as well as a nicely stocked gift shop. The place is open daily May through September and weekdays year-round.

9 A Side Trip to Waterton Lakes National Park

190 miles NW of Great Falls; 342 miles S of Edmonton, Alberta

Waterton Lakes National Park and Glacier are in many ways one park separated by an international boundary. The terrain is much the same. But Canada is a foreign country, and you'll be pleasantly reminded of that in a visit to Waterton, where you can still get British high tea and a biscuit, if you're so inclined.

Waterton is where the Canadian mountains meet the vast rolling prairies, so there's an incredible variety of flowers and animals here. As you travel along the high ridge you'll see meadows and boggy areas that are ideal habitat for moose; later, you'll find yourself surrounded by lakes, as the Canadian Rockies fill the horizon. The area is also a haven for elk, mule deer, and bighorn sheep, and both grizzly and black bears are found in the park.

Compared with its counterparts in the Lower 48, Waterton is a tiny park; the total size is only 203 square miles. However, the park has great historical significance: Based on more than 200 identified archaeological sites, historians think that aborigines first populated the area 11,000 years ago.

The parks have been designated the Waterton/Glacier International Peace Parks to commemorate the "long history of peace and friendship" between the United States and Canada. Waterton Lakes was made a national park in 1895, with Glacier being designated 15 years later. The joint international designation came in 1932, and in 1995, the peace park became a World Heritage Site.

ESSENTIALS

American and Canadian money is freely accepted in both Glacier and Waterton. Stores provide change in the local currency after adjusting for the current exchange-rate differential.

GETTING THERE From the eastern entrance of Glacier National Park at St. Mary, drive north through Babb, until you reach the intersection of Mont. 17—it's very well marked. Head northwest to the Canadian border, where Mont. 17 becomes Alberta 6 (remember, you need proof of citizenship—and a driver's license doesn't always work). Head down into the valley until you reach the park entrance on your left.

FEES & BACKCOUNTRY PERMITS Park entrance costs C$6 (about US$5) per person, at a maximum of C$15 (US$12) per vehicle. Day hiking does not require a permit, but backcountry overnight trips do, at a cost of C$9 (US$7) per person per day. Permits may be obtained at the visitor center up to 24 hours in advance of your trip, or they may be reserved by calling ☎ **403/859-5133**.

VISITOR INFORMATION   The Visitor Reception Centre is just inside the park, on the same road you used coming in (☎ **403/859-5133**). Online, visit **www.parkscanada. gc.ca/waterton**.

EXPLORING THE PARK

Unlike most "park villages," Waterton village actually is a village. It looks like it would be a nice place to live. As you drive along the perimeter of the lake headed for Waterton Village, you'll pass three large lakes, the habitat of bald eagles that often perch atop the snags of dead trees. The park bears a striking resemblance to Grand Teton National Park in Wyoming in that its attractions spread across a narrow valley floor. But the valley is narrower and three-fourths of it is surrounded by peaks, so the overall effect is cozier, but equally dramatic.

By most standards, it's also windier here—though locals say that they don't acknowledge the wind unless there are whitecaps in the restroom toilets at The Prince of Wales Hotel (see "Where to Stay," below). The Prince of Wales actually does sway noticeably in a high wind, although signs assure you that it is not a concern.

Hiking, biking, and boating on the lake are the most popular pastimes. Most of the 120 miles of trails are easily accessible from town. They range in difficulty from short strolls to steep treks for overnight backcountry enthusiasts.

BIKING   All of Waterton's roads are open for bicycling, but because they are shared with automobiles, they are narrow and potentially hazardous. Waterton allows biking on some trails. Check at the visitor center to find out which ones.

HIKING   The first thing a lot of people do at Waterton Park is hike the **Bear's Hump Trail** ⚑⚑. It is the park's most popular path—but not necessarily the easiest. The trail starts at the visitor center. Only about .75 mile long, it gains 700 feet in elevation from bottom to top. That is steep, squared. You'll be rewarded with a panoramic view of the park. The hike is called Bear's Hump because of the shape of the mountain, not because you're likely to run into bears—though, of course, you never know.

Right at the edge of Waterton Park, at **Cameron Falls,** Cambrian rocks are exposed from the period 600 million years ago when life exploded on earth. This is the oldest exposed formation in the Rocky Mountains. The falls are spectacular, too.

For nearly 20 years, the 11-mile **Crypt Lake Trail** ⚑⚑⚑ has been rated as one of Canada's best hikes—except for those prone to seasickness, since the trail head is reached by taking a 2-mile boat ride across Upper Waterton Lake. Contact **Waterton Shoreline Cruise Company** (☎ **403/859-2362**) for details regarding the boat shuttle. After that, the trail leads past Hellroaring Falls, Twin Falls, and Burnt Rock Falls before reaching Crypt Falls and a passage through a 60-foot rock tunnel. The elevation gain is 2,300 feet, but veterans say the hike is doable in 3 hours, one-way.

A second extended tour starts at the marina and heads south across the international boundary to **Goat Haunt,** Montana, an especially popular trip because of the sightings of bald eagles, bears, bighorn sheep, deer, and moose, as well as numerous unusual geologic formations.

The **International Peace Park Hike** is a free guided trip held on Saturdays from the end of June to the end of August. Participants meet at the Bertha trail head at

10am and spend the day on an 8.5-mile trail that follows Upper Waterton Lake. At the end of the trail, hikers return via boat to the main dock. Adult fare is C$15 (US$12); children's fare is C$7 (US$6).

There is a wonderful nature trail in **Red Rock Canyon,** a short, easy trek through time—.7 mile, 65 million years—to when the shallow sea that once lay here exposed and then oxidized mudstone rock to the color of a merlot. The rocks are banded with white slashes—portions that didn't oxidize because they were not exposed to the air from the receding and returning sea. The Red Rock Canyon Road is also an area of fairly frequent bear sightings.

WHERE TO STAY

For complete lodging information, contact **central reservations** for the Waterton area (© **800/215-2395;** www.trailofthegreatbear.com).

While **The Prince of Wales Hotel** (see below) is clearly the flagship on this lake, alternative arrangements can be made at **Kilmorey Lodge** (© **403/859-2334;** www.kilmoreylodge.com). This cozy country inn on Emerald Bay, at the north end of the lake, has an antique decor. Bedrooms have down comforters and a dining room and lounge are on the premises. Standard doubles are C$123 (US$98), and credit cards are accepted. The **Waterton Lakes Lodge** (© **888/985-6343** or 403/859-2150; www.watertonlakeslodge.com) opened in July 1997. Located in the heart of Waterton Village, the lodge offers lake and mountain views, and some rooms have fireplaces, whirlpool tubs, and kitchenettes. Other facilities include a health center, spa, and indoor pool. Rates start at C$175 (US$140); credit cards are accepted. The facility closes from October through April.

The Prince of Wales Hotel 🏛🏛🏛   The stunning Prince of Wales compares with the finest park hostelries in Montana and Wyoming. Built in 1927 by the Great Northern Railway, the hotel boasts soaring roofs, gables, and balconies that convey the appearance of a giant alpine chalet. Rooms, though small, have aged well, with dark-stained, high-paneled wainscoting and heavily upholstered chairs. Standard rooms have double beds and/or twins; suites have king-size beds. Bathrooms have European-style tubs with wraparound curtains and tiny washbasins. The choice accommodations here would be one of the pricey lakeside rooms, but if you're on a budget, ask about the rooms facing the mountains. Rates from opening through mid-June are lower than rates the rest of the season.

The lobby, like many of the old railroad hotels, is wood, wood, and more wood—in this case accented by tufted furniture and carpeting. Two-story-tall windows overlook the lake and village, only minutes away by footpath. If you don't spend the night at the Prince of Wales, at least stop in for a traditional British afternoon tea, served daily from 2 to 5pm in the hotel lobby. All in all, the experience is very European—the gift shop even sells English bone china and Waterford crystal. The entire facility is nonsmoking.

Waterton Lakes National Park, AB T0K 2M0. © **403/859-2231,** or 406/892-2525 in winter. Fax 403/859-2630. www.glacierparkinc.com. 87 units. C$199–C$399 (US$159–US$319) double; C$599–C$799 (US$479–US$639) suite. AE, DISC, MC, V. Closed late Sept to early June. **Amenities:** Restaurant; lounge; gift shop.

CAMPING

At the west end of the village is **Townsite Campground** 🏕, a Parks Canada–operated facility with 235 sites that's an especially popular jumping-off spot for campers headed into the park's backcountry. Prices range from C$21 (US$17) to C$33 (US$26); half of the sites have electricity and sewage disposal. Also available on the premises are kitchen shelters, washrooms, and shower facilities. The site is perched right on the lake, so views are excellent and trails await evening strollers. The campground is open from late April to early October.

There are also more than 10 designated **wilderness campgrounds** with dry toilets and surface water, some of which have shelters. Every person that stays overnight here must obtain a permit from the park at a price of C$7 (US$6) per day.

WHERE TO DINE

All of the village's restaurants and retail outlets are within a 4-block area around Waterton Avenue (which the locals call Main St.). So despite the fact that many buildings aren't numbered, you'll have no problem finding places to eat or shop.

The **Bighorn Grill** (© 403/859-2150) at the Waterton Lakes Lodge offers casual dining (mostly beef and seafood) and spectacular views. The **Royal Stewart Dining Room** (© 403/859-2231) serves breakfast, lunch, dinner, mostly continental and English fare, and high tea in the lobby of The Prince of Wales Hotel.

You'll find luxurious surroundings, and slightly higher prices, at **Kootenai Brown Dining Room** (© 403/859-2211) at the Bayshore Inn, considered the luxury spot on the lake. The order of the day is steaks, chicken, rack of lamb, and the occasional seafood entree; the dining room is also open for breakfast and lunch.

New Frank's Restaurant (© 403/859-2240), located on Waterton's main street, serves both conventional Western fare that includes beef, chicken, and spaghetti, and a Chinese menu that includes an all-you-can-eat evening buffet, as well as breakfast and lunch.

6

Missoula, the Flathead & the Northwest Corner

The northwest corner of Montana is the mythological Montana, the one you probably envisioned when you set out for the Big Sky. This is the country of snow-capped mountains and crystal lakes. It's a land of barely explored wilderness and steel-toed lumberjacks, a land peopled with the ghosts of trappers, mountain men, and Blackfeet Indians.

It's also a booming recreational area. The geographic center of the region is Flathead Lake, which boasts the somewhat cumbersome distinction of being the "largest natural freshwater lake west of the Mississippi." The lake was gouged during the last glaciation about 12,000 years ago. It is very deep in places—386 feet out toward the middle—with 128 miles of shoreline, much of it taken up by vacation homes. Anglers will appreciate the fact that trophy trout, salmon, perch, and whitefish all take up residence here. And vacationers seeking a quiet getaway will be pleased by the fact that despite the busy summer season on the lake, it doesn't feel crowded, and there are plenty of places to get out of earshot of everyone.

Besides Flathead Lake, the area from Whitefish to Missoula offers plenty of opportunities for hiking, biking, fishing, boating, golf, parasailing, and nearly every other outdoor activity known to man. In winter, you'll find fine alpine ski areas, excellent cross-country skiing, snowshoeing, snowboarding, and inner-tubing.

Also here is the nation's largest wilderness complex, the **Bob Marshall–Great Bear–Scapegoat Wilderness,** which includes some of the most rugged, beautiful, untrammeled country in the Lower 48 states. The magnificent Chinese Wall, a vast monolith on the spine of the Continental Divide, is a symbol of wilderness in Montana, as is the grizzly bear, the king of the wild even when humans venture in for a visit.

1 Scenic Drives

Two major roads run through the northwest corner: U.S. 93, which runs north to south, and U.S. 2, which runs east to west. Mont. 200, one of the state's most scenic drives, bisects the lower section of the region.

U.S. 93 heads north from the Bitterroot Valley south of Missoula to the Canadian border. Much of the road slices beneath jagged peaks poking at the skyline. It's especially pretty early in the morning or early evening, when the light softens the rugged landscape. North of Missoula in the Flathead Valley near St. Ignatius and the spectacular Mission Mountains, the valley opens. At **Polson,** you've reached the southern portion of Flathead Lake, which stretches 28 miles to the north. In some places it is 8 miles wide. North of the lake are Kalispell, Whitefish, and Columbia Falls, gateway

Northwestern Montana

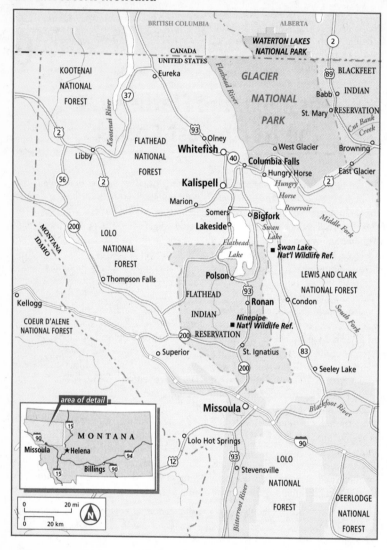

towns to nearby Glacier National Park. The last oasis in Montana is the border village of Eureka, just minutes south of the Canadian border.

Plan on spending an afternoon making your way around Flathead Lake, which is ringed by snowcapped mountains and bright blue skies. On the east side, you can pick ripe cherries and explore the art galleries and Western boutiques of Bigfork. On the west side, you might sample a creamy huckleberry shake, poke through the antiques stores, and visit an award-winning winery.

2 Missoula ⭐

200 miles E of Spokane, Washington; 213 miles NE of Lewiston, Idaho; 339 miles W of Billings; 115 miles NW of Helena; 115 miles S of Kalispell

Missoula has been growing by leaps and bounds for a decade, and the reason is clear: The city is in a beautiful valley along the Clark Fork River, with a relatively mild climate more influenced by the Pacific Northwest than by the high Rockies. One could say the same about the local culture.

Since this is the home of the University of Montana, the crowds in Missoula's vibrant downtown are more often young and Birkenstocked than grizzled and cowboy-booted. Also in the mix are many prominent Western writers who live in or near the city; the result is an intellectual and cultural outpost.

Activity in the great outdoors—be it fly-fishing on Rock Creek, skiing at Snowbowl, hiking in the Selway-Bitterroot, or cross-country skiing on Lolo Pass—is probably what most attracts these types to the area. The outdoors figures heavily in Missoula-area politics as well. There is a strong proenvironment sentiment among the populace.

ESSENTIALS

GETTING THERE   **Allegiant** (✆ 800/432-3810), **Horizon** (✆ 800/547-9308), **SkyWest** (✆ 800/327-2850), **Big Sky** (✆ 800/237-7788), **United** (✆ 800/241-6522), and **Northwest** (✆ 800/225-2525) all have flights into the **Missoula International Airport** (✆ 406/728-4381), northwest of downtown on U.S. 93.

I-90 leads into Missoula from the west (Washington State and Idaho) and the east (Billings and Bozeman). From Salt Lake City, I-15 leads up through Idaho and intersects with I-90 at Butte. For information on **road conditions** in Missoula, call ✆ **406/728-8553** or **511** for road conditions statewide. Avalanche information can be obtained by calling the **West Central Montana Avalanche Center** (✆ 800/281-1030 or 406/549-4488).

The **bus terminal**, 1600 W. Broadway (✆ **406/549-2339**), is served by **Greyhound** (✆ **800/231-2222**; www.greyhound.com) for national travel and **Rimrock Stages** (✆ **800/255-7655**; www.rimrocktrailways.com), which serves intrastate Montana travelers from Missoula to Whitefish.

VISITOR INFORMATION   The **Missoula Convention and Visitors Bureau,** 1121 E. Broadway, Suite 103, Missoula, MT 59802 (✆ **800/526-3465** or 406/532-3250; www.missoulacvb.org), has brochures, city maps, and area maps for outdoor activities, shopping, dining, and tours for most of northwestern Montana.

GETTING AROUND   Several rental-car agencies, including **Avis** (✆ 800/831-2847 or 406/549-4711), **Budget** (✆ 800/527-0700 or 406/543-7001), **Hertz** (✆ 800/654-3131 or 406/549-9511), and **National** (✆ 800/227-7368 or 406/543-3131), maintain counters at the airport; or try **Rent-a-Wreck,** 1905 W. Broadway (✆ 406/721-3838). **Airport Shuttle** (✆ 406/543-9416) operates a transit service to and from the airport.

Missoula's city bus line is **Mountain Line Transit** (✆ **406/721-3333**; www.mountainline.com). It doesn't run late at night or on Sundays.

Taxi service is available 24 hours a day through **Yellow Cab** (✆ **406/543-6644**).

ORIENTATION   Missoula's layout is a tad confusing, so make sure you have a good city map. Remember that downtown is bisected by the Clark Fork River, and become

---

Baseball under the Stars

Missoula is home to minor league baseball's **Missoula Osprey,** an affiliate of the Arizona Diamondbacks in the Pioneer League. For ticket information, call ⓒ **406/543-3300** or visit www.missoulaosprey.com.

---

acquainted with the locations of the three bridges, which provide access to the university and points south. Trails alongside the river are suitable for strolling, though you'll share them with runners and bikers.

SPECIAL EVENTS   The International Wildlife Film Festival ✪, founded by internationally known bear biologist Dr. Charles Jonkel in 1977, recognizes scientific accuracy, artistic appeal, and technical excellence through a juried competition. Highlights of the 1-week festival, held annually in early to mid-May, include four daily screenings, workshops and panel discussions, a wildlife photo contest, and various wildlife art displays. Contact the festival (ⓒ **406/728-9380;** www.wildlifefilms.org) for details. **Out to Lunch at Caras Park** (ⓒ **406/543-4238**) is a popular summer series featuring live entertainment and numerous food vendors from 11am to 1:30pm every Wednesday June through August.

GETTING OUTSIDE

One of the first things you notice if you look up in Missoula is a giant "M" on Mount Sentinel. The trail to the M is a popular hike, a steep zigzag that rewards the determined hiker with panoramic views of the valley. Mount Sentinel is also a favorite spot for hang gliding. You can obtain information and maps of recreation areas before leaving town at the **Bureau of Land Management,** 3255 Fort Missoula Rd. (ⓒ **406/329-3914**).

ORGANIZED ADVENTURES   Adventure Connections (ⓒ **800/441-2286** or 406/549-5034; www.montanatravel.com) is a recommended four-season outfitter, specializing in fly-fishing and snowmobiling trips. The outfitter **10,000 Waves** (ⓒ **800/ 537-8315** or 406/549-6670; www.10000-waves.com) presents an opportunity to go hiking or rafting and absorb some Montana history in the process. The company offers two tours that focus on **Garnet Ghost Town,** one of the best-preserved old mining camps in the West.

BIKING

The best place to cycle is at the **Rattlesnake National Recreation Area.** To get there, drive northeast on Van Buren to Rattlesnake Drive. Be sure to consult one of the free trail maps available at bike shops before setting out. Bikes are prohibited in the wilderness portion of the recreation area. **Montana Snowbowl** ski area also has trails for the serious mountain biker. For information, contact ⓒ **406/549-9777.** To rent bikes, contact **Open Road Bicycles and Nordic Equipment,** 517 S. Orange St. (ⓒ **406/ 549-2453**), or **Missoula Bicycle Works,** 708 S. Higgins Ave. (ⓒ **406/721-6525**).

CROSS-COUNTRY SKIING

There are hundreds of square miles of cross-country ski terrain within 30 miles of Missoula. In nearby Garnet, the absence of gold turned a once-prosperous mining town into a ghost town that's now become a magnet for cross-country skiers at the **Garnet Resource Area.** With more than 50 miles of trails and a remote location, this area offers a delightful backcountry experience. And while out there, many like to stay

Missoula

ACCOMMODATIONS ■
Best Western Grant Creek Inn **24**
Doubletree Hotel Missoula-
    Edgewater **18**
Goldsmith's Inn **19**
Mountain Valley Inn **1**
Ruby's Inn **22**

ATTRACTIONS ●
Aerial Fire Depot & Smokejumper
    Center Art Museum **25**
Art Museum of Missoula **8**
Historic Ninemile Remount
    Depot Visitor Center **21**
Historical Museum
    at Fort Missoula **4**
Missoula Carousel **13**
Rocky Mountain Elk
    Foundation **23**

DINING/NIGHTLIFE ◆
Bernice's Bakery **26**
The Bridge **15**
Butterfly Herbs **12**
Charlie B's **7**
The Depot **5**
The Fire Place **2**
The Hob Nob **16**
The Kettlehouse Brewing Co. **14**
Nap's **3**
Oxford Cafe **9**
Pearl Café and Bakery **17**
Red Bird **11**
Sean Kelly's **10**
Shadows Keep **27**
Two Sisters **6**

SERVICES ●
Missoula Convention
    & Visitors Bureau **20**

MONTANA
Missoula
Helena

See Inset Below

DOWNTOWN

Railroad
Broadway
Reserve St.
Rodgers
Russell
Clark Fork River
Wyoming
S. 3rd
U.S. Highway 93
S. 4th
S. 5th
S. 6th
Orange
Higgins
Burlington
Stephens
Brooks
Arthur
South
South
S. Higgins
Reserve St.
SW Higgins
Hamilton
39th St.

0   1 mi
0   1 km

Downtown Missoula

Clark Fork River
Broadway
Nora
McCormick
Owen
Alder
Spruce
Railroad
Orange
Rose
Ryman
Pine
Wood
Orange
Main
Higgins
Pattee
Washington
Adams
Jefferson
Madison
Monroe
Jackson
Van Buren
Bank
Kiwanis
Levasseur
Clay
Front
Chestnut
S. 4th

0   1/2 mi
0   0.5 km

in Garnet's **old-fashioned miner's cabins** (see "Where to Stay," later in this chapter). Getting there can be an arduous task in winter. Take I-90 east to Mont. 200, turn east for 5 miles to Garnet Range Road, and then go south along the Forest Service Road.

There are 150 miles of marked cross-country ski trails scattered through the **Lolo National Forest** (© 406/329-3750). Popular areas include **Pattee Canyon, Seeley Lake,** and **Lolo Pass.** The Pattee Canyon Complex, 5½ miles south of town, offers several groomed trails that range in difficulty from a short 1.6km trail to a longer 5.4km trail, but the snow level varies from year to year. At Lolo Pass, there's a National Forest information center at the top of the pass with maps and permit sales. To get there, take U.S. 12 west from Lolo for about 30 miles.

Twenty miles from Missoula, the **Lubrecht Experimental Forest** (© 406/243-7463), operated by the University of Montana's forestry department, has six ski trails and numerous logging roads. To reach Lubrecht from Missoula, take I-90 east to exit 109 and follow Mont. 200 northeast to Greenough. Turn right just past the post office, and less than a half-mile down that road is the Lubrecht camp.

DOWNHILL SKIING

Montana Snowbowl   Snowbowl has a vertical drop of 2,600 feet, much of it in the form of steep runs suitable only for experts. There's not a lot of terrain for beginners here, but the hard-core skier will have a ball. Eighty percent of the runs are for intermediate, expert, and advanced skiers, with another 500 acres for the extreme skier. Snowbowl has reasonably priced rooms for rent during the winter, with and without private bathrooms. Rentals and instruction are also available.

Snowbowl Rd., P.O. Box 8107, Missoula, MT 59807. © 800/728-2695 or 406/549-9777. www.montanasnowbowl. com. Lift tickets $34 adults, $14 children 6–12; senior, student, night, and half-day rates available. Late Nov to early Apr Fri–Sun. From I-90, exit at Reserve St.; head north on Grant Creek Rd., and turn left on Snowbowl Rd.

FISHING

The **Clark Fork River,** which runs through town, has had its share of environmental problems and concerns over the years. A cleanup effort that began in the 1970s has helped, but it's never going to be an angler's first choice. The **Bitterroot River** and **Rock Creek** are better bets. Though Rock Creek has been known as a blue-ribbon trout stream, the Bitterroot is also a good spot for those who want to pull in a trout or two, and it has multiple public-access areas near the highway. The Missoula office for the **Montana Department of Fish, Wildlife, and Parks** (© 406/542-5500) will direct you to some fine fishing spots, including Siria, a more remote site 30 miles up Rock Creek Road.

Whether guiding you along Missoula's Clark Fork River or helping you pick out the perfect fly, **Grizzly Hackle,** 215 W. Front St. (© 800/297-8996 or 406/721-8996; www.grizzlyhackle.com), can help you with your fly-fishing vacation. Seasoned guides lead you to fishing holes along the Lower Clark Fork, the Bitterroot, the Missouri, and the Blackfoot rivers, as well as Rock Creek, in search of native rainbow, Westslope cutthroat, and brown trout. The company also runs the **Lodge on Butler Creek,** not far from Missoula, where rooms rent for $165 per night for two, and other overnight accommodations. Grizzly Hackle advocates barbless hooks and catch-and-release fishing, donating heavily to river restoration projects and angling-oriented charities.

GOLF

Farther north, there are a number of great golf courses, but in Missoula the golf is only average. The 9-hole **Highlands Golf Club,** located at 102 Ben Hogan Dr. (© 406/728-7360), is a short, hilly, public course with wickedly gyrating greens. A round runs

$12 to $15. There's also the par-29 executive **Linda Vista,** 4195 Miller Creek Rd. (© **406/251-3655**), with greens fees of $12 to $14, and another 9-hole course on the **University of Montana** campus (© **406/728-8629**), with greens fees of $11 to $13. The **Larchmont Golf Course,** 3200 Old Fort Rd. (© **406/721-4416**), the only 18-hole public course within city limits, is a long, fairly tough track that the big hitters will like. Greens fees are $24 to $26.

HIKING

An easy hike follows the **Kim Williams Trail,** along either side of the Clark Fork River through downtown. The trail is named for a deceased, much-beloved newspaper columnist. Just outside of town is the **Rattlesnake National Recreational Area and Wilderness.** To get there, drive northeast on Van Buren to Rattlesnake Drive. The Rattlesnake covers 59,000 acres, 33,000 of which are congressionally designated wilderness. Camping is prohibited within 3 miles of the road because of the heavy use the area receives. Drive northeast on Van Buren to Rattlesnake Drive.

There are two state parks in the Missoula area: **Beavertail Hill** (© **406/542-5500**) is located on the Clark Fork and is open May through September, with excellent river access and shady cottonwood trees lining the riverbanks. There is a day-use charge of $5; campers pay $15 per night. **Council Grove State Park** (© **406/542-5200**) is where the Hellgate Treaty establishing the Flathead Indian Reservation was signed. Open for day use only (free), the park has interpretive displays and picnic facilities. Take the Reserve Street exit from I-90 and drive 2 miles south, then 10 miles west on Mullan Road.

The **Lolo Trail** is an interesting hike. This trail was created by the constant use of the Nez Perce, Salish, and other tribes who lived in the area and moved back and forth across Lolo Pass.

You can explore a half-mile section of the original trail at Howard Creek, 18 miles west of the intersection of U.S. 93 and U.S. 12 in Lolo. Or hike a 5-mile section of the trail from Lee Creek Campground to the Idaho border. The campground is about 26 miles west of the highway intersection in Lolo.

SNOWMOBILING

The areas around Missoula have more than 500 miles of groomed snowmobile trails in a number of popular areas. In Lolo Pass, for instance, there are 150 miles of groomed trails connecting the Lolo and Clearwater national forests. There are four other nearby designated areas—Superior, Skalkaho Pass, Seeley Lake, and Lincoln—each with approximately as many miles of groomed trails. For a guide to area snowmobiling, contact the Missoula Convention and Visitors Bureau (© **800/526-3465**).

WHITE-WATER RAFTING & KAYAKING

Lewis & Clark Trail Adventures, 912 E. Broadway (© **800/366-6246** or 406/728-7609; www.trailadventures.com), offers no-nonsense white-water rafting on the Salmon River during excursions through the heart of the Frank Church No Return Wilderness. The main trip is on a 120-mile stretch of Idaho white water, where you can expect to see mountain goats, bighorn sheep, elk, deer, eagles, and otters. Other excursions take in the Lochsa River, the Alberton Gorge of the Clark Fork River, and the Missouri River (through areas in which Lewis and Clark made their famous trek). Trips run May through September. Hiking, biking, and historic tours on the Lolo Trail are also available. Five-day trips on the Salmon River run from $895 per adult.

One-day trips on the Lochsa or through Alberton Gorge range from $70 to $115 per adult. Guided hikes on the Lolo Trail are between $139 (1 day) and $655 (3 days) per adult. Children's rates are about 30% lower.

The Clark Fork and the Blackfoot rivers are the settings for white-water adventure with **10,000 Waves** ⋆ (𝒞 **800/537-8315** or 406/549-6670; www.10000-waves. com). Half-day and full-day floats feature thrilling white-water rapids along high mountain rivers and through steep, narrow canyons. Half-day trips are $50 per person; full-day floats cost $78 (includes a great lunch). The company uses self-bailing rafts, which enable the paddler to focus on the sport, not survival. If you want an even bigger thrill, consider a guided kayak trip. Rates are $38 for 2 hours, $65 for a half-day, and $85 for a full day. 10,000 Waves also offers a rafting and kayaking trip and guided tour of Garnet Ghost town for $90.

Montana River Guides (𝒞 **800/381-7238** or 406/273-4718; www.montanariver guides.com) is another good option, offering paddling instruction as well as rafting expeditions. Half-day trips run $45; full-day and dinner trips are $69. The most gonzo approach is a guided "river-boarding" trip—akin to sledding on the river on a board designed for the purpose—for $85 to $105.

SEEING THE SIGHTS

You can organize your own tour and check out the architectural highlights of the "Garden City" by picking up a copy of the *Historical Walking/Driving Tour* brochure. For further information, contact the **Missoula Historic Preservation Office** (𝒞 **406/ 523-4706**).

The **Farmers Market** ⋆ (𝒞 **406/777-2636**) at Market Plaza (located at the north end of Higgins Ave., where it meets with Railroad and Alder sts.) is the place to be during summer for organic vegetables, fresh flowers, and assorted culinary pleasures. It's open Saturday from 9am to noon May through late October, as well as Tuesday from 5:45 to 7:15pm in July and August.

Aerial Fire Depot and Smokejumper Center   This is the nation's largest training base for smokejumpers—firefighters who parachute into remote areas of national forests to combat wildfires. This facility offers a fascinating look at the life of a Western firefighter, beginning with the days when pack animals were an important part of backcountry fire fighting, through the 1939 advent of the smokejumper, up to today's heroes. The Aerial Fire Depot Visitor Center features murals, educational videos, a reconstructed lookout tower, and exhibits of firefighters that illustrate the lives and history of these rescue workers. The center also talks about the important role of fire in forest ecology.

Adjacent to Missoula International Airport, U.S. 10 W. 𝒞 406/329-4934. Free admission. Daily 8:30am–5pm. Tours available on the hour beginning at 10am; no tours noon–2pm; last tour begins 4pm. Closed between Labor Day and Memorial Day weekend.

Art Museum of Missoula ⋆   Located downtown in the historic Carnegie Library (1903), this museum's permanent collection includes about 600 works by about 200 artists, with a special emphasis on contemporary works by Montana and Native American artists. Changing exhibits feature regional, national, and international art; recent displays showcased works by Bozeman's Keith Goodheart and Livingston's Russell Chatham. Associated programs include films, concerts, lectures, tours, and children's events. A renovation and expansion were underway at press time, with the grand opening of the museum's new contemporary wing slated for fall 2006. Until that time,

the contemporary collection was being housed in the lobby of the Florence Building, 111 N. Higgins Ave.

335 N. Pattee St. (C) **406/728-0447.** www.artmissoula.org. Free admission; suggested donation $2. Tues–Fri 10am–5pm (until 7pm Thurs); Sat 10am–3pm. Closed Sun–Mon.

Historical Museum at Fort Missoula Fort Missoula, one of Montana's first military posts, was established in 1877, the year Chief Joseph of the Nez Perce led his tribe toward Canada. Now the home of the National Guard and Reserve units, Fort Missoula has as its main attraction this museum, which houses displays that detail the fort's history and rotating exhibits in its indoor galleries. Outside, the campus is also home to several historic buildings moved to the site, including a one-room schoolhouse, a homestead cabin, an 1863 church, and other buildings.

Building 322, Fort Missoula Rd. (C) **406/728-3476.** www.fortmissoulamuseum.org. $3 adults, $2 seniors, $1 students, free for children under 6; $10 maximum per family. Memorial Day to Labor Day Mon–Sat 10am–5pm, Sun noon–5pm; Rest of year Tues–Sun noon–5pm.

Historic Ninemile Remount Depot Visitor Center This visitor center, along with the Smokejumper Center, will educate you in the early methods of rugged firefighting in the northern Rockies, when pack animals were a vital part of a firefighter's "equipment." Listed on the National Register of Historic Places, the depot appears today much as it did when the Civilian Conservation Corps constructed it in the 1930s, complete with live pack mules. All tours are self-guided.

20325 Remount Rd., Huson, MT 59846. (C) **406/626-5201.** Free admission. Daily 9am–5pm. Closed between Labor Day and Memorial Day weekend. Drive 22 miles west of Missoula on I-90, then 4 miles north of exit 82.

Rocky Mountain Elk Foundation ✯ *Kids* Though a relatively young conservation organization, the Rocky Mountain Elk Foundation has made a large contribution to conserving elk and elk habitat. Now it has a visitor center that does that contribution proud: a dazzling new facility that opened in November 2005. Encompassing ecology, biology, game management, and hunting, the center does a nice job telling the story of elk in North America, from their peak population of 10 million to their overhunted low point of just 90,000 (c. 1900), to their rebound to a million head today. The exhibits are interactive, covering everything from the unusual elk bugle to conservation legends, and many of them are geared toward children. Many visitors come simply to

---

Kids **Especially for Kids**

A remarkable community effort, the **Missoula Carousel** ((C) **406/549-8382;** www.carrousel.com) was a project begun with nothing more than unrealistic optimism. During planning, funding, and assembly stages of the project, Missoula relied on the kindness of others to make it happen. The hand-carved and -painted horses are the result of thousands of hours of labor from volunteer workers, most of whom were novices trained in the art of carving and painting. A treat for kids, adults will also marvel at this merry-go-round by the river at downtown's **Caras Park,** which is located at the spot where Higgins Avenue crosses the Clark Fork River. The carousel is open daily year-round, with 50¢ rides for children under 18 and seniors and $1.50 rides for adults. Immediately west of the carousel building is another fun community project: a fantasy-themed playground dubbed Dragon Hollow.

see the world record antler racks on display here—one of them measures 448 inches in all, adding up every last fork and tine. Allow 1 hour.

5705 Grant Creek Rd. (just north of I-90, exit 101). © 406/523-4545. www.rmef.org. Free admission. Mon–Fri 8am–6pm; Sat–Sun 9am–6pm.

SHOPPING

Global Village World Crafts, 519 S. Higgins Ave. (© **406/543-3955**), is a project of the Jeannette Rankin Peace Resource Center, selling jewelry, clothing, and musical items from communities around the world. **Butterfly Herbs,** 232 N. Higgins Ave. (© **406/728-8780**), features an eclectic collection of items, including fresh herbs, jewelry, coffee mugs, teapots, and handmade paper and candles. If you begin to feel the bohemian spirit and suddenly want your own pair of Birkenstocks, just go next door to **Hide & Sole,** 236 N. Higgins Ave. (© **406/549-0666**), for reshodding.

Pipestone Mountaineering, 129 W. Front St. (© **406/721-1670**), has an excellent range of outdoor gear for serious climbers, river runners, and campers. **The Trail Head,** 221 E. Front St. (© **406/543-6966;** www.trailheadmontana.net), is another good outdoors store, with gear for snowshoers, kayakers, and just about everybody in between.

Missoula is home to an impressive literary community, and the city's bookstores are among the state's best, including **Fact and Fiction,** 220 N. Higgins Ave. (© **406/ 721-2881**). The largest newsstand in Missoula is the **Garden City News,** 329 N. Higgins Ave. (© **406/543-3470**), which specializes in daily newspapers from both coasts, as well as from the Rocky Mountain area. Vintage, rare, and first-edition books are available from **Bird's Nest Books** (© **406/721-1125**) at 219 N. Higgins Ave.

If you're looking for clothes, the **Macy's,** 110 N. Higgins Ave. (© **406/542-6000**), is an old standard and Missoula's only downtown department store. **Rainbow's End,** at 113 W. Main St. (© **406/829-1800**), is the last refuge of hippie clothing for women.

If you haven't found that perfect Montana gift yet, try the **Moose Creek Mercantile,** 314 N. Higgins Ave. (© **406/543-6503**), which offers a vast selection, much of it in wildlife themes.

Monte Dolack is one of the best-known artists in Montana. His often-humorous posters and prints are available at 139 W. Front St. in the **Monte Dolack Gallery** (© **406/549-3248**). The gallery also features works of other prominent Montana artists, including Mary Beth Percival. Other worthwhile galleries include **Art Attic,** 123 South Ave. W. (© **406/728-5500**), and the **Montana Museum of Art and Culture** in the PAR/TV Building on the campus of the University of Montana (© **406/ 243-2019**).

WHERE TO STAY

You won't find a whole lot of lodging variety within Missoula's city limits: It's dominated by chains, with a smattering of independents and Victorian-era B&Bs. For a distinctive night's sleep, try roughing it in a historic cabin. Information on rental of **old-fashioned miner's cabins** at the ghost town of Garnet is available by contacting the **Garnet Preservation Association,** 3255 Fort Missoula Rd., Missoula, MT 59804 (© **406/329-1031;** www.garnetghosttown.org). The cabins are available for $30 to $40 a night from December through April, when they are typically accessible only on skis, snowshoes, or snowmobiles. Rustic cabins and lookouts are also available for rent through the **National Forest Service,** 200 E. Broadway (P.O. Box 779), Missoula, MT 59807

(© **406/329-3511**). Get information on camping at Missoula's **Bureau of Land Management,** 3255 Fort Missoula Rd., Missoula, MT 59804 (© **406/329-3914**).

HOTELS & MOTELS

Best Western Grant Creek Inn   Situated close to a freeway off-ramp (I-90, exit 101), this Best Western is a good chain property in Missoula. The quality of the rooms and services is what you'd normally associate with a higher-priced chain, including complimentary wireless high-speed Web access. There are a good variety of options here. Deluxe suites have a fireplace, two big television sets, a dining area, a desk, a closet, and a view. Conventional rooms have two queen-size beds or one king-size. There are several restaurants and bars nearby.

5280 Grant Creek Rd., Missoula, MT 59808. © **888/543-0700** or 406/543-0700. Fax 406/543-0777. www.bestwestern. com/grantcreekinn. 126 units. $85–$125 double; $139–$169 suite. Rates include hot breakfast buffet. AE, DC, DISC, MC, V. **Amenities:** Indoor pool; exercise room; Jacuzzi; sauna. *In room:* A/C, TV w/pay movies, dataport, coffeemaker, hair dryer, iron.

Doubletree Hotel Missoula-Edgewater ⭐   This is the premier hotel facility in Missoula, and a 2002 renovation further cemented its superiority. Located on the north bank of the Clark Fork, the upper-end rooms offer a good deal of space with a beautiful view of the river and the University of Montana. Rooms on the second level have balconies, some overlooking the swimming pool. The property is geared toward business travelers, with meeting rooms and business services (such as wireless Internet access) available. The lobby area is nicely finished, with a gift shop that sells Western American souvenirs, clothing, and trinkets. The Finn and Porter restaurant, specializing in steaks, seafood, and chops, is just off the lobby. The wooden deck outside the lounge is a fine spot for a cocktail over the Clark Fork River.

100 Madison St., Missoula, MT 59802. © **800/222-8733** or 406/728-3100. 171 units. $79–$225 double; $185–$275 suite. AE, DISC, MC, V. **Amenities:** Restaurant (steaks/seafood); lounge; outdoor heated pool; exercise room; outdoor Jacuzzi; airport shuttle; business center; laundry service. *In room:* A/C, cable TV w/pay movies, dataport, coffeemaker, hair dryer, iron.

The Fort at Lolo Trail Center *(Finds)*   This hot-springs resort, 25 miles west of Lolo and only 7 miles from the Montana-Idaho border, is an especially popular winter destination—the cross-country skiing on Lolo Pass is excellent, as is the snowmobiling. The Fort has recently upgraded its facilities, adding a large new building that houses the educational Lewis & Clark Exhibition Center, two hot tubs utilizing natural spring water, a dinner theater, and a convention center. There are 18 rooms in the lodge and 12 in a motel-style unit. It's called the Fort because the design is reminiscent of television's old Fort Apache. The motel rooms are large and less expensive than those in the lodge, but they are spare in the decor department. Since the fabled **Lolo Hot Springs,** 38500 W. U.S. 12 (© **406/273-2290;** www.lolohotsprings.com), are a separate operation, there's a fee to soak in them. They also have four new rental cabins on the property, under different ownership than the Fort, for $75 double.

38600 W. U.S. 12, Lolo, MT 59847. © **406/273-2201.** www.lolotrailcenter.com. 30 units, 18 tepees. $79–$139 double. DISC, MC, V. **Amenities:** Restaurant; lounge; 2 indoor Jacuzzis. *In room:* No phone.

Goldsmith's Inn ⭐   This beautiful 1911 brick home is Missoula's only riverside B&B, right on the Clark Fork River just across from the University of Montana. (The home is the former residence of Clyde Duniway, the second president of the University of Montana.) Four of the seven rooms are suites with private sitting rooms, and all rooms have private bathrooms and attractive Victorian furnishings. Some also have fireplaces or reading nooks. Request the Clarkfork Suite to get a Japanese bath to soak in while looking out at the river. The Goldsmith's fabulous ice cream is a Missoula favorite, and you can get some right next door at Goldsmith's Waterfront Pasta House.

809 E. Front St., Missoula, MT 59802. (C) **866/666-9945** or 406/728-1585. www.goldsmithsinn.com. 7 units. $69–$134 double. Rates include full breakfast. DISC, MC, V. *In room:* A/C, cable TV, fridge, hair dryer, iron.

Mountain Valley Inn (★ (*Value*) This one-time chain property has evolved into a first-rate independent, as new ownership has poured money back into the place. Rooms are fresh and clean, with small bathrooms with tub/shower combos; two nicely renovated family suites are available. There's also a small library/guest lounge and a barbecue restaurant on the property.

420 W. Broadway, Missoula, MT 59802. (C) **800/249-9174** or 406/728-4500. www.mountainvalleyinnmissoula.com. 60 units. $55–$69 double; $129 suite. Rates include complimentary cookies and full breakfast. AE, DISC, MC, V. **Amenities:** Restaurant (barbecue); exercise room; coin-op washers and dryers; dry cleaning; Wi-Fi network. *In room:* A/C, cable TV, coffeemaker, hair dryer, iron.

Ruby's Inn (★ (*Kids*) Just south of I-90 at the west end of town, Ruby's can't be missed—just look for the big neon lips. The somewhat garish sign belies a top-notch independent motel run by Ruby Erck for over 30 years, with fresh, clean rooms. Executive rooms are twice as big, and the honeymoon suite has a four-poster king-size bed and a two-person hot tub. The best feature might be the "backyard," along Grant Creek with fishing access (and grills to cook your catch) and a creek-side Jacuzzi.

4825 N. Reserve St., Missoula, MT 59808. (C) **800/221-2057** or 406/541-7829. Fax 406/541-7829. 126 units. $95–$100 double; $125–$149 suite. Complimentary afternoon refreshments and hot breakfast buffet. AE, DC, DISC, MC, V. Pets accepted, $10 fee. **Amenities:** Seasonal outdoor pool; health club access to Gold's Gym; outdoor Jacuzzi; courtesy car; coin-op washers and dryers; dry cleaning. *In room:* A/C, cable TV, dataport, kitchenette, coffeemaker, hair dryer, iron.

WHERE TO DINE

Thanks to the university and a relatively cultured populace, Missoula is blessed with an excellent variety of restaurants, ranging from organic vegetarian to full-blown carnivorous. In addition to the options discussed below, we suggest **The Hob Nob,** 531 S. Higgins Ave. ((C) **406/541-4622**), for great breakfasts like homemade corned beef hash, sourdough flapjacks, and migas. A stone's throw from the carousel, **Nap's,** 231 W. Front St. ((C) **406/829-1207**), is a burger fanatic's dream, frying up enormous 12-ouncers, as well as steaks, salads, and sandwiches. Good for kids and pizza lovers, **The Fire Place,** 241 W. Main St. ((C) **406/728-2579**), cooks up gourmet pizza in a central open kitchen.

EXPENSIVE

The Depot (★ STEAKS/SEAFOOD A Missoula institution, The Depot is known for its upscale atmosphere and good food. The decor is along the contemporary cowboy and Western theme, with an inviting brick bar that looks out onto an active rail yard and more than 20 colorful paintings by Larry Pirnie. You might try the scallop casserole: scallops and mushrooms in white wine, Swiss cheese, and cream sauce. The beef menu features prime rib, New York strip, and filets; specialties include the garlic-roasted filet and a fresh range veal chop served with fresh mushrooms and heavy cream. There is a huge wine list. Among the finest recent vintages are some hard-to-find 1989 bordeaux (at $98–$145 a bottle). There's also a more casual pub area called **The Deck,** serving a less expensive array of burgers and sandwiches.

201 W. Railroad Ave. (C) **406/728-7007**. Reservations recommended. Main courses $13–$33. AE, DC, DISC, MC, V. Sun–Thurs 5:30–10:30pm; Fri–Sat 5:30–11pm. Bar open later.

Pearl Café and Bakery ♨ STEAKS/SEAFOOD/ECLECTIC   Named for chef/owner Pearl Cash, this swank new eatery opened in summer 2004 and immediately rose into the upper echelon of Missoula's culinary landscape. Cash, who has operated several acclaimed restaurants in the area since the 1970s, delivers a sumptuous menu of creative regional standards, such as braised bison short ribs with huckleberry sauce, served with roasted butternut squash, and duckling with pomegranate-cherry sauce and wild rice risotto. Located in half of the historic former Missoula Mercantile Warehouse, Pearl has three distinct dining areas: a sleek but casual bar area out front that takes only walk-ins; a first-floor dining room with warm peach and brick walls; and an upstairs mezzanine with wrought-iron railings and an air of elegance. The wine list is excellent.

231 E. Front St. ℂ **406/541-0231.** www.pearlcafeandbakery.com. Reservations recommended. Main courses $17–$29. AE, MC, V. Mon–Sat 5–10pm.

Red Bird ♨ ECLECTIC   The small, intimate Red Bird is tucked in the alley on the ground floor of the Art Deco Florence Building. Chef Jim Tracey changes the menu seasonally, but the entrees are fresh and superbly prepared year-round. One of Tracey's personal favorites is a grilled escolar. It's served in a pool of vanilla bean–infused coconut milk, alongside fried green tomatoes and a green onion and corn-rice cake, for a remarkable presentation. Other dishes include hand-cut beef, bison, and lamb plates, as well killer homemade desserts.

120 W. Front St. ℂ **406/549-2906.** www.redbirdrestaurant.com. Reservations recommended. Main courses $15–$24. AE, DISC, MC, V. Tues–Sat 5–9:30pm.

Shadows Keep ♨ STEAKS/SEAFOOD   After the landmark Greenough Mansion at the Highlands Golf Club burned to the ground in 1992, this castlelike restaurant, serving some of the area's best food, took its place on the very same foundation. Positioned on the bluffs of southeast Missoula, Shadows Keep oozes class, from the 30-foot ceiling in the bar to the panoramic views of the city and surrounding mountains. Shadows Keep is known for its rack of lamb and salmon entrees, as well as its rich and decadent desserts. The lounge and terrace offer a more casual setting and a menu of appetizers, salads, and small plates.

102 Ben Hogan Dr. ℂ **406/728-5132.** www.shadowskeep.com. Main courses $15–$25. AE, DISC, MC, V. Daily 5–10pm.

MODERATE

The Bridge ♨ ITALIAN/ECLECTIC   Established in 1971, The Bridge is one of the granddaddies of Missoula's dining scene, and it's easy to see (and taste) why it's still going strong. It's a bustling restaurant that shares space with the Crystal Theater, Missoula's artiest movie house. Order several appetizers rather than a dinner—they'll all be delicious and it's the best way to sample the restaurant's variety. Stalwart entrees are the flat iron steak, Thai seafood stew, and *linguica paella,* with sausage, clams, mussels, prawns, salmon, and sole. There are also a number of thin-crusted pizzas and hints of Asian and African cuisine on the menu. The Bridge is within walking distance of the major hotels, so you can take a nice stroll across the river to get there. Alternatively, you can dine in your room: The delivery number is ℂ **406/542-0002.**

515 S. Higgins Ave. ℂ **406/542-0638.** www.bridgebistro.com. Main courses $13–$19. AE, DISC, MC, V. Sun–Thurs 5–10pm; Fri–Sat 5–11pm.

Two Sisters ♨♨ NEW AMERICAN/ECLECTIC   Two Sisters is the sister restaurant of an eatery near Glacier National Park in Babb. Looking for a four-season town, older sister Beth Higgins relocated to Missoula—and younger sister Susan comes down from Babb in the winter. The pair won over locals with creative cuisine and a colorful, whimsical downtown space. The dinner menu is a standout, including fresh and simple dishes like chicken satay, linguine with clams, and a chèvre-stuffed tenderloin. Barbecue fans will like the chipotle barbecue chicken, while herbivores tend to gush over the terrine, layered in polenta and served on a sweet red-pepper coulis. There are also dishes with influences from down south, such as fried catfish and New Orleans–style cioppino. Breakfasts include eggs Benedict, oatmeal, and quiche; lunches are soups, salads, and sandwiches.

127 W. Alder. (② 406/327-8438. Reservations accepted. Breakfast $3.50–$8; lunch $4–$9; dinner $8–$25. MC, V. Sun–Tues 8am–3pm; Wed–Sat 8am–10pm.

INEXPENSIVE

Bernice's Bakery ⊛ BAKED GOODS   Bernice's has been one of Missoula's most beloved culinary spots since the late 1970s. This small, out-of-the-way place, known for its delicious baked goods, is a great place for breakfast. In addition to an outstanding soft homemade granola, Bernice's sells buttery croissants filled with flavored cream cheeses, an excellent complement to the freshly brewed organic coffee that's also a staple. Organic juices and teas are available, too. This is also a great dessert spot—the cream puffs are out of this world—and a good choice for lunch as well.

190 S. 3rd St. W. (② 406/728-1358. Most items $2–$5. DISC, MC, V. Daily 6am–8pm.

The Oxford Cafe AMERICAN   Even if you don't eat at the Ox, as it's known, you really should go in and look around. Established in 1883, this distinctly Montanan cafe is a Missoula institution, adorned with beer signs, a long bar, a breakfast counter, a bison head, and an endless stream of eccentrics, cowboys, and bikers. Chicken-fried steaks are the specialty of the house; the Ox had sold more than 150,000 at last count. When a customer orders the brains and eggs—admittedly not very often—the waitress shouts to the cook, "He needs 'em!" The Oxford card room is the gathering place for the toughest, tightest poker players in western Montana. Other restaurants come and go, but the Ox endures, a testament to overflowing breakfast plates, live keno calling, and bottled American beer. As proprietor Ralph Baker put it, "The place hasn't closed in so long, we don't even know where the keys are."

337 N. Higgins Ave. (② 406/549-0117. Breakfast $3–$11; lunch $3–$7; dinner $6–$11. AE, DISC, MC, V. Daily 24 hr.

MISSOULA AFTER DARK
WATERING HOLES FOR ANY TASTE

There are plenty of watering holes in Missoula, whether your buzz of choice is alcohol or caffeine induced. **Sean Kelly's,** 130 W. Pine (② **406/542-1471**), serves Irish pub–style food—bangers and mash, pot roast, Irish stew—in addition to your alcoholic beverage of choice. The weekend jazz is wonderful, and there are also pool tables in the back. **Butterfly Herbs** at 232 N. Higgins Ave. (② **406/728-8780**) has a distinct 1960s feel. It's the perfect place to order up an ordinary cup of java, or an exotic beverage from an extensive specialty espresso menu. Bold, bawdy, and bedecked with black-and-white photos of regulars, **Charlie B's,** 428 N. Higgins Ave. (no phone), is one of the best dives in the northwest, serving a cross section of Missoula: blue-collar types, professionals, and college kids. The exterior doesn't have a sign; just follow the laughter and chatter. The **Kettlehouse Brewing Co.** at 602 Myrtle St. (② **406/728-1660**) is a great neighborhood brewery that supplies many local restaurants. Its taproom—which is open Monday through Saturday from noon to 9pm—is a funky hangout with old couches and a jovial atmosphere.

THE PERFORMING ARTS

The **Montana Repertory Theater,** located at the University of Montana campus (© **406/243-6809;** www.montanarep.org), is the state's only Equity company, performing new and classical works. The **Missoula Children's Theater** is the largest touring children's theater in the United States, performing original musical productions and featuring hundreds of talented children from communities across the States, Canada, and the Pacific Rim. The theater season starts early in June and continues through the end of March. The **Missoula Community Theater** provides a year-round calendar of family entertainment. Both the Children's Theater and the Community Theater are located at 200 N. Adams St. (© **406/728-1911;** www.mctinc.org).

The **Missoula Symphony Orchestra and Chorale,** 320 E. Main St. (© **406/721-3194;** www.missoulasymphony.org), is composed of university students, Missoula residents, and other regional musicians, often performing with featured guests in the University Theater on campus. The **String Orchestra of the Rockies,** P.O. Box 8265, Missoula, MT 59807 (© **406/728-8203;** www.sor-montana.org), a statewide professional string ensemble, is based in Missoula and performs almost exclusively there. At the University of Montana's **Music Recital Hall** (© **406/243-6880**), the school's music department often brings in outstanding musicians to perform. Regularly scheduled recitals include solo and ensemble performances by faculty and students.

3 A Detour into the Bitterroot Valley ⓧ

Extends 89 miles S of Missoula to the Idaho border

Although in part a bedroom community for Missoula, the Bitterroot Valley has become a second home and retirement paradise for folks who have fallen in love with the Missoula-area mountains, but not with the Missoula-area traffic. Though not as well-known as other areas of the state, the fly-fishing in the Bitterroot River is excellent, making it a preferred destination for anglers in the know.

The Bitterroot has the reputation as Montana's banana belt because the microclimate in the valley offers a long growing season. A lot of Missoula-area golf fanatics head to Hamilton in February because the golf course there greens up for play much earlier than the ones even a few miles farther north.

GETTING AROUND & VISITOR INFORMATION   For maps, brochures, and sage advice about the area and its happenings, consult the **Bitterroot Valley Chamber of Commerce,** which has offices at 105 E. Main St., Hamilton, MT 59840 (© **406/363-2400;** www.bvchamber.com).

DRIVING TOURS

If you'd like to take a driving tour through the area (see the "Southwestern Montana" map, in chapter 7), travel south on U.S. 93 to Florence, then cross the Bitterroot River and travel south on Mont. 203/263 through a 32-mile area filled with interesting landmarks, reconnecting with U.S. 93 at Hamilton. On your trip back, take U.S. 93 south through Hamilton and Victor, Darby, and Sula. As an alternative, continue south beyond Sula to Mont. 43, the road that leads to Wisdom. Doing so will take you winding through the valley and canyons of the Bitterroot Mountains, and you'll finally emerge at the Big Hole Battlefield.

If you are feeling very brave, and you don't mind getting your car beaten up on a rough dirt road, take the Skalkaho Pass Road to the east of Hamilton. Pick up Mont. 38 just south of Hamilton—up Skalkaho Creek. The pavement runs out after a few miles, and you'll drive over a rocky, pitted, narrow road up through the Sapphire Mountains. Go slowly; the drop-offs here are as extreme as those along Going-to-the-Sun Road in Glacier National Park, but without the guardrails. The views of forested hills are unsurpassed. It takes about 2 hours to cover the 54 miles to the **Anaconda Pintler Scenic Route,** Mont. 1, which you pick up around Georgetown Lake.

GETTING OUTSIDE

The Bitterroot Valley runs south along the Bitterroot River between the Bitterroot Range to the west and the Sapphire Mountains to the east. The Bitterroot Range is the site of the Selway-Bitterroot Wilderness, which at 1.3 million acres is one of the nation's largest wilderness areas. Numerous trail heads are located off major highways between Lolo and Darby. You can get information about hiking in the wilderness from the Bitterroot National Forest's **Darby Ranger District office,** 712 N. Main, Darby, MT 59829 (© **406/821-3913**), open Monday through Friday from 8am to 4:30pm.

The Lake Como Recreation Area is a popular day-use and camping area with swimming, hiking, and boating. To get there, go 4 miles north from Darby on U.S. 93. Turn west on Lake Como Road and go about 2½ miles to the area. There are 22 camping units in two different campgrounds for $8 to $14 a night and a "rustic" cabin on the lake for $60 per night. Reservations for the cabin are available through the Darby Ranger District office (see above); a lottery is held in March.

If it's fly-fishing you're seeking, check out **Chuck Stranahan's Flies and Guides,** P.O. Box 594, Hamilton, MT 59840 (© **406/363-4197**; www.riverbendfly.com), one of the longest-running acts in the Montana guiding business. Owner Chuck Stranahan is a nationally known fly-tier, with a number of his patterns chosen for the Jack Dennis fly-tying book, the bible of the business. He excels in instruction. His company customizes trips for its customers, with an emphasis on the Bitterroot River, though trips also go to other rivers in western Montana. Guided trips or personal instruction cost $345 to $450 per day for one or two people.

SEEING THE SIGHTS

The west side of the valley has fishing access as well as places to shop, eat, and stay. The historic section of the valley is on the east side of the river, and is accessible at Florence, Stevensville, Victor, Pinesdale, and Hamilton.

Following are a lot of the attractions you'll come across if you start driving at the north end of Mont. 203/269 and head south.

Eight miles south of Florence on Mont. 203, you'll hit the **Lee Metcalf National Wildlife Refuge** (© **406/777-5552**; http://leemetcalf.fws.gov), which is free and is open daily from dawn to dusk. This wetland habitat is the result of dikes and dams that impound the water of several streams. It has helped to improve migratory waterfowl habitats and has created a nesting success, but a number of other species benefit as well, including osprey and deer. A short loop trail, open from mid-July to mid-September, leads around several ponds and blinds in the refuge's southwest corner. The picnic area is open year-round and has 2 miles of walking trails. Hunting for waterfowl is permitted on designated ponds during the fall duck-hunting season. Bow hunting for deer is permitted in season as well. Near the entrance is the well-preserved exterior of the 1885 **Whaley Homestead,** an excellent example of vernacular frontier architecture. You can drive around the refuge on the dirt road and come out in Stevensville, the next stop on the tour.

Stevensville is the oldest town in Montana, the result of the early missionary work of the indefatigable Jesuit Fr. Pierre DeSmet, who founded **St. Mary's Mission** in 1841. Capped with a bell tower, the mission is a small structure paneled with logs and white boards and an important place in the development of Montana—it was the first permanent structure in the state to be built by European Americans. John Owen bought the mission from the Jesuits in 1850 and established a trading post, Fort Owen. Though the issue of who first found gold in Montana will doubtless never be established, in Owen's diary in 1852 he wrote: "Hunting gold. Found some."

From here, continue south on Mont. 203 to Hamilton and the Marcus Daly Mansion. Montana copper king Marcus Daly never did anything on a small scale, and his house is no exception. The **Marcus Daly Mansion** (© 406/363-6004; www.daly mansion.org) is a spectacular Georgian Revival mansion with classical porticoes. It occupies 24,000 square feet on three floors, with 25 bedrooms, 15 bathrooms, and 7 fireplaces. The mansion was finished in 1910, after Daly's death, and his widow, Margaret, lived there in the summers until her own death in 1941. It's open 10am to 4pm daily from Memorial Day weekend to Labor Day weekend, as well as on weekends and December. Admission costs $7 for adults, $6 for seniors, $4 for students 12 to 18, and $3 for kids 6 to 11 (free for under 6).

On the opposite side of the river, the village of Hamilton, several blocks long and 4 blocks wide, is worth a leisurely stroll since most of the businesses here are small, locally owned, and often interesting. For outdoor gear, head to **Bob Ward & Sons,** 1120 N. 1st St. (© **406/363-6204**), for a good selection of fishing, skiing, camping, and hunting equipment. Nearby is **Robbins,** 209 W. Main St. (© **406/363-1733**), a nice shop that sells home furnishings, crystal, china, and gourmet kitchen accessories. The **BiblioJoe,** 252 W. Main St. (© **406/363-5220**), sells all manner of espresso drinks and adjoins the **Chapter One** bookstore, featuring new and used books and periodicals. Perhaps the most remarkable store in Hamilton is the **Main Street Rug Co.** (© **406/363-0338**), 126 W. Main St., which has a vast collection of Oriental rugs for sale.

WHERE TO STAY

Hamilton Super 8, 1325 N. 1st St., Hamilton, MT 59840 (© **800/800-8000** or 406/363-2940), is a clean, typically budget-minded motel with a location central to the Bitterroot Valley. The same holds true for the **Best Western Hamilton Inn,** 409 S. 1st St., Hamilton, MT 59840 (© **800/426-4586** or 406/363-2142), though the advantage here is the presentation of an excellent breakfast buffet, and the fact that some rooms are equipped with microwaves and refrigerators. Double rooms at both properties run around $60 to $80 per night.

Deer Crossing Bed & Breakfast ℜ   The 25 acres of land surrounding this pleasant, modern inn served as an apple orchard in the 1920s, and innkeepers Stu and Linda Dobbins still utilize the remaining trees to present lucky fall guests with delicious pies. The main house features three rooms and a pair of suites, ranging from the thoroughly Western Charlie Russell Suite (with a minibar, fridge, and Jacuzzi) to the small, understated Moose Meadows Room, with a plush quilt and a private entry. The property's original homesteader's cabin is still standing, renovated to serve as a rustic rental cabin. There's another cabin, the Montanan, that's a bit more modern, with a television and a small kitchenette. Given a choice between a room and a cabin, go with the cabin.

396 Hayes Creek Rd., Hamilton, MT 59840. © 800/763-2232 or 406/363-2232. Fax 406/375-0771. www.deercrossing montana.com. 7 units, including 2 suites and 2 cabins. $99 double; $139 suite; $149 cabin. Lower rates mid-Oct to mid-Apr. AE, DISC, MC, V. Pets accepted in cabins. *In room:* Cable TV, kitchenette, no phone.

Triple Creek Ranch 🐾🐾🐾   This is one of the most elegant, and expensive, guest ranches in the West, with just about every imaginable amenity and activity. The ranch is an adults-only resort that encourages guests to relax and do things according to their own schedules. The luxury cabins have a sitting area, king-size bed, wet bar, fireplace, and double steam shower. Tennis rackets, fly-fishing gear, and horses are available to guests. The ranch is the only Montana property to meet the Relais & Châteaux standards. The *Wall Street Journal* called a stay here "roughing it Robin Leach style."

The on-site **Triple Creek Dining Room** serves gourmet cuisine for breakfast, lunch, and dinner. It's open to the public in the evenings, but during the summer season—June, July, and August—it's filled with resort guests, and it's very difficult to get a reservation.

5551 W. Fork Rd., Darby, MT 59829. © 406/821-4600. Fax 406/821-4666. www.triplecreekranch.com. 19 cabins. $510–$995 per couple per night. Rates include meals, drinks, and activities. AE, DISC, MC, V. **Amenities:** Restaurant; outdoor heated pool; putting green; tennis court; exercise room; outdoor Jacuzzi; concierge; bike rental; activities desk; business center; limited room service; massage. *In room:* A/C, cable TV, dataport, kitchenettes, minibar, fridge, coffeemaker, hair dryer, iron, safe.

WHERE TO DINE

Don't expect a whole lot in the way of fine dining in the Bitterroot Valley. If all your outdoor activities have you craving a juicy steak, try **Victor Steakhouse,** 2426 Meridian Rd., Victor (© **406/642-3300**). Dinner entrees are $10 to $25. The **Spice of Life Cafe,** 163 S. 2nd St. in Hamilton (© **406/363-4433**), has offerings ranging from a Bitterroot strip steak to Thai curry noodles. **Maggie's** at 217 W. Main St. in Hamilton (© **406/363-4567**) is a good breakfast and lunch place in a spare cafe-style setting.

A SIDE TRIP: SKIING & HOT SPRINGS AT LOST TRAIL PASS

Lost Trail Pass is a remote and undiscovered corner of Montana about 80 miles south of Missoula on the Idaho border. This area is heavily timbered but not heavily populated. It's also off the beaten path because most travelers use I-15. This corner of the state is very pretty—with pine-covered peaks replacing the forbidding rock crags that dominate the skyline farther north.

With Lost Trail Powder Mountain, Lost Trail Hot Springs, and Camp Creek Inn, this pass area is an unforgettable winter vacation destination for those who loathe big crowds and the attendant ski scene.

Lost Trail Powder Mountain ski area recently expanded into a long, steeper area adjacent to the original hill, with five lifts in all. Overall, the runs are mostly intermediate, with lots of light powder. If you like to ski the bumps but aren't a fanatic about it, the moguls develop on the intermediate runs in the afternoon, just in time to wear you out completely. The lift ticket prices are an excellent value at $28 for adults and $18 for children 6 to 12; kids under 6 ski free. For more information, contact Lost Trail Powder Mountain, P.O. Box 311, Conner, MT 59827. Ski reports are available during the season at © **406/821-3211** or online at **www.losttrail.com**. The ski area is 90 miles south of Missoula at the Montana-Idaho border, ¼ mile from U.S. Highway 93.

Just down the hill to the north from the ski area is the unpretentious lodge and hot springs, **Lost Trail Hot Springs Resort,** 8221 U.S. 93 S., Sula, MT 59871 (© **800/825-3574** or 406/821-3574; www.losttrailhotsprings.com). The lodge arranges summer raft trips, horseback riding, and fishing. It isn't fancy by urban standards, but the food in the restaurant, which overlooks the hot-springs pool, is good, especially if you enjoy basic American grub—burgers and pizzas. Nightly rates are $55 to $120 for lodge rooms, and $95 to $175 for cabins. If you come just to soak, it's $6 for adults, less for seniors and children.

4 The Flathead Indian Reservation & the Mission Valley

42 miles N of Missoula; 75 miles S of Kalispell

The Confederated Salish and Kootenai tribes make their home on the Flathead Indian Reservation, with tribal headquarters for the 1.3-million-acre reservation in Pablo. The tribes, however, own only slightly more than 50% of the land within reservation boundaries.

The change in culture for the tribes came quickly when fur traders, homesteaders, and the missionaries of the Catholic Church headed west. Founded in the early 1850s by Jesuit priests, the town of **St. Ignatius** (located 32 miles north of Missoula on U.S. 93) is nestled in the heart of the Mission Valley. One of the valley's larger small towns, St. Ignatius has a modest Flathead Indian Museum and trading post on the highway.

Wildlife conservation and land management have played big parts in the lives of the tribal members. The **Mission Mountain Wilderness** was the first wilderness area officially designated as such by a tribe in the United States. Hiking in the wilderness area requires the purchase of a tribal permit ($8 for 3 days or $14 for a year) from the **Flathead Reservation Confederated Salish-Kootenai Tribes,** Box 278, Pablo, MT 59855 (© **406/675-2700;** www.cskt.org). The Mission Mountain Wilderness is located in the Mission Mountain Range, east of U.S. 93. Numerous gravel roads lead up to the trail heads.

The St. Ignatius Mission, P.O. Box 667, St. Ignatius, MT 59865 (© **406/745-2768**), was established in 1854 as an offshoot of the missionary work of the famous Jesuit Fr. Pierre DeSmet. A Fr. Hoecken began the mission in a small log cabin, which is still on the premises and serves as the visitor center. In 1891, the mission added this magnificent brick church in its ministry to the Indians. The ceiling is decorated with 58 murals, depicting scenes from the Old and New Testaments, by Brother Joseph Carignano, an Italian Jesuit without formal art training. The mission is 2 blocks off U.S. 93.

The National Bison Range ⊛ (© **406/644-2211;** www.fws.gov/bisonrange/nbr), just west of St. Ignatius on reservation land, is just 7 miles southwest of Charlo on County Road 212. The 18,500 acres here contain between 350 and 500 bison, the remnants of a national bison herd that once totaled 60 million. The visitor center has a small display about the history and ecology of bison in America. The 19-mile Red Sleep Road goes through four different habitat types—grasslands, riparian, montane forest, and wetlands. In addition to the bison, you'll see deer, bighorn sheep, antelope, and maybe an occasional coyote or black bear. There's a trail here for people with physical disabilities. Gates are open from 7am to dusk daily year-round; the visitor center is open from 8am to 6pm weekdays, 9am to 6pm weekends in summer, and 8am to 4:30pm weekdays in winter. Cost is $4 per car (free in winter).

If you're more interested in feathers than in fur, check out the **Ninepipe National Wildlife Refuge** (© **406/644-2211;** www.fws.gov/bisonrange/ninepipe), which is next to U.S. 93, 5 miles south of Ronan. Established in 1921, the refuge has 2,000 acres of water, marsh, and grassland for the double-crested cormorant and the great blue heron, among other migrating birds. The refuge is open daily from dawn to dusk, although portions are closed during the fall and early winter hunting season and the bird-nesting season in spring and early summer. Admission is free. Fishing is permitted in some areas of the adjacent Pablo Reservoir, but a tribal permit is required ($17 for 1 day, $43 for 3 days). For information on tribal fishing regulations, call © **406/675-2700.**

WHERE TO STAY & DINE   The **Ninepipes Lodge,** 41000 U.S. 93, Charlo, MT 59824 (© **406/644-2588;** www.ninepipes.com), across from the Ninepipe National Wildlife Refuge, is a pleasant motel, with 25 rooms decorated with lodgepole furniture and a wildlife/nature theme. Your choice of king-size, queen-size, double, or twin beds is offered, and all units have TVs and telephones. Double rates are $63 to $73. There is also a restaurant on the premises, offering American selections for all three meals. Also adjacent and under the same management is the **Ninepipes Museum of Early Montana** (© **406/644-3435**), which contains early Western art, American Indian beadwork, wildlife displays, a life-size diorama of an Indian camp scene, and other displays on the area's history. Admission costs $4 for adults, $3 for students, and $2 for children 6 to 12, and is free for children under 6 who are accompanied by an adult. Call for current hours.

A SIDE TRIP TO HOT SPRINGS

Hot Springs is a funky little town of hand-painted signs and potholed streets, tucked into a cul-de-sac of low Montana mountains. Lots of visitors swear by the local waters' therapeutic qualities, especially as a palliative for arthritis. Situated southwest of Polson, just off Mont. 28, the tiny community is about 1½ hours from Flathead Lake.

The 1928 **Symes Hotel** ⚘, 209 Wall St. (© **888/305-3106** or 406/741-2361; www.symeshotsprings.com), is a vaguely pink, Alamo-like structure that aspires to be Art Deco. You can rent rooms or just tubs in stalls that can be filled with the famous waters. Some rooms have their own tubs, and there are two small pools and a large soaking tub outside. Rooms run from $37 to $117 a night, in a bewildering combination of options (you get claw-foot tubs and the occasional TV, but no phones). There's also a day spa, a yoga studio, and a restaurant on the property. A motel with housekeeping apartments, the **Hot Springs Spa,** 308 N. Spring St. (© **406/741-2283**), is less distinguished option. Many of its rooms have soaking tubs; rates range from $35 to $60.

Wild Horse Hot Springs (© **406/741-3777**), 5 miles northeast of town, offers a rather primitive soak in blue concrete tubs. This place is located several miles down a dirt road. The private rooms are each outfitted with a "plunge" (private pool), toilet, shower, steam room, and furniture that your grandmother would have found old-fashioned. But some people swear by the place and come back every single year. There are only two rooms to sleep in here, priced at $55 to $65 a night. A soak costs $5 an hour per person.

The free **Camas Bath** is located at the end of Spring Street, a small concrete pool with the same valuable waters. For more information, contact the **Hot Springs Chamber of Commerce,** P.O. Box 580, Hot Springs, MT 59845 (© **406/741-2662;** www.hotsprgs.net/hscofc).

5 The Flathead Lake Area: Somers, Polson & Bigfork ⭐⭐

Bigfork: 92 miles N of Missoula; 15 miles SE of Kalispell

This is one of the most beautiful areas in Montana. Glacier National Park's towering peaks rise from the valley floor on the east and the mountains of the Flathead National Forest define the edge of the valley to the west. This is a land of forests, cattle, and alfalfa—with a velvet-green valley floor, green and granite mountains, and, on a sunny day, a dramatic deep-blue ceiling.

This part of Montana seems to offer something for everyone, whether your interests lie indoors or out. There are watersports on the lake and hikes that lead to sparkling mountain streams with views. But if you want to shop or see a play, you can easily spend your day inside the boutiques, galleries, and theater of Bigfork.

With much of this area lying within the tribal lands of the Salish-Kootenai, there is also a long-standing American Indian heritage.

ESSENTIALS

GETTING THERE   Bigfork is located near the northeastern shores of Flathead Lake, 15 miles southeast of Kalispell by car, at the intersection of Mont. 35 and Mont. 83. Polson is at the southern tip of the lake, 33 miles southwest of Bigfork via Mont. 35 and 60 miles north of Missoula via U.S. 93. The nearest airports are **Glacier Park International** (✆ 406/257-5994), north of the lake between Kalispell and Columbia Falls, and the **Missoula International Airport** (✆ 406/728-4381) in Missoula. Bigfork is just over a 30-minute drive from Glacier Park International; Polson is roughly midway between the two airports. For rental cars, **Avis** (✆ 800/331-1212), **Budget** (✆ 800/527-0700), **Hertz** (✆ 800/654-3131), and **National** (✆ 800/227-7368) maintain counters at each airport.

VISITOR INFORMATION   Your best bet for information on the south end of the lake is the **Port Polson Chamber of Commerce,** P.O. Box 667, Polson, MT 59860 (✆ 406/883-5969; www.polsonchamber.com). For goings-on north, contact the **Bigfork Chamber of Commerce,** P.O. Box 237, Bigfork, MT 59911 (✆ 406/837-5888; www.bigfork.org). The **Flathead Convention and Visitor Bureau** (✆ 406/756-9091; www.fcvb.org), **Travel Montana** (✆ 800/847-4868), and **Glacier Country** (✆ 800/338-5072) can supplement this information.

GETTING OUTSIDE

The Flathead is one of those rare places where you see the serious golfer and the serious backpacker in the same spot, sometimes in the same body. The golfing is excellent on several courses, and the backpacking, hiking, and fishing are even better. Fishing, boating, and "yachting" are popular sports for those who can afford to practice them. If your plans take you to one of the lakes or trails on the Salish-Kootenai Reservation, don't forget to buy a tribal permit.

BOATING

With Flathead Lake being the largest natural freshwater lake west of the Mississippi River, you can bet that this is a big boating destination. Boat rentals are available at the **Bigfork Marina and Boat Center** (✆ 406/837-5556), **Kwa Taq Nuk Resort** (✆ 800/882-6363), **Bayview Resort and Marina** (✆ 406/837-4843), and **Marina Cay Resort** (✆ 406/837-5861).

A sailboat excursion is available from **Averill's Flathead Lake Lodge** (© **406/837-5569**) on two classic racing sloops designed by L. Francis Herreshoff. Fewer than a dozen of these 50-foot "Q-Boats" remain in the world. There are a couple of 2-hour cruises daily from late May to mid-October. Fixed-keel sailboats can be launched at the state parks around Flathead Lake. Big Arm, Yellow Bay, and Somers have fishing accesses. Because winds may blow hard during the afternoon, only ballasted boats are recommended on the main portion of the lake.

The Montana Department of Fish, Wildlife, and Parks has designated a **Flathead Lake Marine Trail,** showing point-to-point campsites and landing points that a human-powered craft like a canoe or kayak can reach in 1 day. You can obtain a brochure on the trail from the **MFW&P** (© **406/752-5501;** www.fwp.state.mt.us) or from the **Flathead Convention and Visitor Bureau** in Kalispell (© **406/756-9091**).

CRUISES

Excursion cruises are a good way for visitors to check out Flathead Lake. The 65-foot *Far West* (© **406/857-3203**) is one of the area's oldest, with daily scenic cruises and occasional Sunday brunch cruises. **Pointer Scenic Cruises** (© **406/837-5617**) offers charter rides on high-speed powerboats that cruise to ancient pictographs viewable only by boat; this company also offers explorations of Wild Horse Island, dinner cruises, and custom tours. The *Princess* cruise boat (© **406/883-2448**) takes a 1½-hour tour, leaving the Kwa Taq Nuk resort marina in the early afternoon and making a loop around Wild Horse Island (no stops) before heading back. If it's a Montana sunset you're after, take the 2-hour sunset cruise, departing in the late afternoon, and look west.

FISHING

Fishing the southern half of Flathead Lake requires a Salish-Kootenai tribal permit, which you can purchase at stores in Polson or at the tribal headquarters in Pablo. The brochure *Fishing the Flathead* is available from the **Flathead Convention and Visitor Bureau** (© **406/756-9091**). It provides information on 14 different fishing opportunities, as well as an outline of the licensing and catch-and-release regulations. This brochure includes information on Whitefish, Flathead, and Swan lakes, and several lesser-known lakes where you can catch fish but avoid crowds. To increase your odds of snagging something besides a log, contact **Glacier Fishing Charters** (© **406/892-2377**). Also, "Shorty" George's **A-Able Fishing** (© **800/231-5214** or 406/257-5214; www.aablefishing.com) will outfit a fishing trip with guides who know the area.

GOLF

There are two golf courses—one terrific, the other just pretty good—overlooking the shores of Flathead Lake. In Polson, the 18-hole **Polson Country Club** public course is the pretty good one, situated just off the lake on U.S. 93 (© **406/883-8230;** www.polsoncountryclub.com). A round of 18 holes is $28 to $35. The course is fairly short—under 6,800 yards from the tips and only 6,079 from the white tees—but it's very pretty and beautifully maintained.

The terrific course is **Eagle Bend Golf Club** (© **406/837-7300;** www.golfmt.com), a challenging Jack Nicklaus–designed track with views of Flathead Lake and the surrounding mountains, located in Bigfork just off the highway on Holt Drive. The 18-hole course is only 6,200 yards from the white tees, but it's harder than Chinese arithmetic. There are 27 excellent holes of golf here. Greens fees range from $30 to

The Flathead Valley

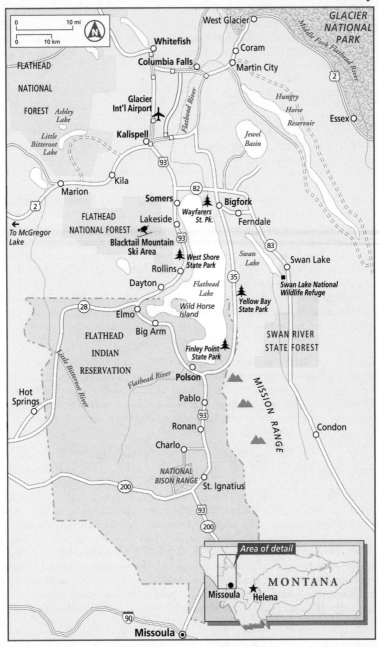

$71 for 18 holes, depending on what time of year and what time of day. *Golf Digest* has called this one of the country's top 50 courses. Be sure to call ahead for a tee time.

There are seven more courses in the area. Contact the **Flathead Valley Golf Association** (© **800/392-9795;** www.golfmontana.com) for a free visitor's guide and information regarding all of the courses.

HIKING

This is bear country, and hikers should work to avoid confrontations by making noise and being watchful. Don't surprise them and they won't surprise you.

Besides strolling by the lake at one of the marinas or state parks, the best bet for trekking is in the **Jewel Basin,** a designated hiking area north of Bigfork. More than 30 miles of trails make it a great place for day hiking as well as overnights. Before dropping into the actual basin, you'll get a great look at the Flathead Valley and Flathead Lake. For free maps of some of the more popular trails, inquire locally at one of the **Forest Service** offices in Kalispell (© **406/755-5401**) or Bigfork (© **406/837-5081**). To reach the head of the hiking area, take Mont. 83 from either Bigfork or Somers, turn north onto Echo Lake Road, and follow the signs.

A short hike, not far from Bigfork and about 45 minutes from the trail head, will take you to **Estes Lake.** Take County Road 209 out of Bigfork. Turn south at the Ferndale fire station. When the road forks, take the right fork, County Road 498. It's about a 7-mile drive from there to the parking area.

A slightly more ambitious, but still short, hike goes up to **Cold Lakes** in the **Mission Mountain Wilderness.** Take Mont. 83 south to County Road 903. Turn right (west), then follow the road to the trail head. The hike is about an hour one-way.

RAFTING

The **Flathead Raft Company** (© **800/654-4359** or 406/883-5838; www.flathead raftco.com) runs half of its outfit from Polson at Riverside Park on U.S. 93, and half from Bigfork. Tours go down the South Fork of the Flathead River and include a swing through the Buffalo Rapids and Kerr Dam. Half-day trips are $32 to $40, and full-day scenic trips range from $65 to $80. Meals and overnight trips are also available.

SKIING

The relatively new **Blacktail Mountain Ski Area** (© **406/844-0999;** www.blacktail mountain.com) is a big step toward making the Flathead Lake region a full-blown year-round resort area. There's an average annual snowfall of 250 inches, which ought to be enough. The area is on over 1,000 acres of national forest, served by two double chairs, a triple lift, and a handle tow. The hill is excellent for beginner and intermediate skiers, with 1,440 vertical feet of drop. Seventy percent of the runs are rated intermediate and only 15% are black diamonds. There are two restaurants, a lounge, ski rental, and a ski school. Lift tickets cost adults, $30 full day, $22 half-day; 13 to 18 years old, $20 full, $16 half; 8 to 12 years old, $13 full, $10 half; ages 70 and older and 7 and younger, free. Lifts open at 9:30am and close at 4:30pm, Wednesday through Sunday and holidays. The area is located 14 miles west of Lakeside on Blacktail Mountain Road.

EXPLORING THE AREA

Bigfork Summer Playhouse   Bigfork has earned a fine regional reputation for its summer stock theatrical productions, performed by rising college-age stars. Performances of Broadway shows are scheduled from the end of May until early September. Recent productions include *Grease, Chicago,* and *Anything Goes.*

526 Electric Ave., Bigfork. © 406/837-4886 for showtimes and reservations. www.bigforksummerplayhouse.com. Ticket prices vary.

Miracle of America Museum   This eccentric but interesting museum contains an extensive collection of odds and ends dedicated to explaining the development of America, with specific attention to the Constitution and the Bill of Rights. Like most of these efforts, the place is heavily weighted toward the military side of the story, with plenty of guns, uniforms, and battle memorabilia. But unlike a lot of the roadside museums, there is at least some effort to explain what you're looking at. There's also a collection of antique Harley-Davidsons, some dating back to 1912, and odds and ends ranging from comic books and Bibles to a two-headed calf trophy and a statue of a winged monkey.

58176 U.S. 93, Polson, MT 59860. © 406/883-6804. www.cyberport.net/museum. $4 adults, $1 for children 3–12 (free for under 3). Summer daily 8am–8pm; rest of year Mon–Sat 8am–5pm, Sun 1:30–5pm.

The Mission Mountain Winery   Montana's only winery is located here on Flathead Lake, producing award-winning merlot along with chardonnay and pale ruby champagne. Tours of the small facility are free and take about 15 minutes. The winery produces 6,500 cases of wine a year. Although most of the wines produced here are white, the winery considers the reds to be the finer vintages. The pinot noir grapes are grown in vineyards around Flathead Lake.

82420 U.S. 93, Dayton. © 406/849-5524. www.missionmountainwinery.com. May–Oct tastings daily 10am–5pm.

SHOPPING

Bigfork's main street, Electric Avenue, is littered with a variety of galleries, gift shops, boutiques, and bookstores. And it's only 4 blocks long. **Twin Birch Square,** at 459 Electric Ave., is a two-level, pine-log shopping mall where you'll find **Artisans** (© 406/837-2789), featuring functional art from all over the country; and **Rock 'n' River** (© 406/837-7275), a nice shop with Montana monogrammed shirts, blankets, and a variety of gifts. At **Electric Avenue Books,** 524 Electric Ave. (© 406/837-6072), browsers are invited to peruse a book or a field journal, or even tickle the ivories on the resident piano. The **Eric Thorsen Fine Art Gallery,** 547 Electric Ave. (© 406/837-4366), handles artwork from the well-known sculptor. He is best known for the sculptures he has created for Trout Unlimited, the Wild Turkey Federation, and Ducks Unlimited (at last count more than 12,000 fund-raising pieces in total). His two-level gallery is a display case for bronze and wood creations; on the second level is the artist's studio, where visitors are encouraged to observe the artist at work.

Doors away is the gallery of **Ken Bjorge** (© 406/837-3839), 570 Electric Ave., who also creates life-size studies of wildlife in bronze. Don't be surprised to find yourself standing next to a 6-foot-tall crane or eagle while he works his craft in your presence. Across the street from Bjorge's studio is **Two River Gear** (© 406/837-3474), which deals in fly-fishing equipment and info, and Patagonia wear. **Artfusion,** 471 Electric Ave. (© 406/837-3526), is an eclectic gallery that represents more than 60 contemporary Montana artists and craftspeople. Around the corner at **Bay Books & Prints,** 350 Grand Ave. (© 406/837-4646), there are rare books and first editions. The owners carry an extensive collection of books about the explorers Lewis and Clark, some very rare and in good condition.

If you're looking for an authentic yet unusual gift item with a Western theme, visit **Electric Avenue Gifts** (© 406/837-4994), 459 Electric Ave. At **Brookies Cookies,** 191 Mill St. (© 406/837-2447; www.brookiescookies.com), you'll find blue-ribbon

---

Moments **A Visit to Wild Horse Island**

Wild Horse Island, one of the largest islands in the inland United States, is run as a wildlife preserve by the Montana Department of Fish, Wildlife, and Parks (© **406/752-5501**). It contains one of the last remnants of Montana's endangered Palouse prairie plant and provides a habitat for bighorn sheep, mule deer, coyotes, and a few wild horses. The island was originally created more than 17,000 years ago as a result of heavy glacial activity that formed the entire area. Sensitivity by the human visitors who visit this unusual environmental preserve is essential—please leave no traces of your visit. The park is open for day use only, and can be reached only by boat. Take your own or rent one from the **Sunny Shores Resort** (© **406/849-5622**). Several boat tours go to Wild Horse Island as well. You can take one from Bigfork with **Pointer Scenic Cruises** (© **406/837-5617**). *Note:* There are no visitor services on the island.

---

cookies and other baked goods, baked fresh daily. And for delectable jams and syrups, try **Eva Gates Homemade Preserves,** 456 Electric Ave. (© **406/837-4356**), which has been in the business since 1949.

Shopping in **Polson** at the other end of Flathead Lake is less of an upscale experience. There is a good antiques store, though, the **Antique Emporium,** actually two shops at 323–325 Main St. (© **406/883-3045**). Out on U.S. 93, there is a three-store strip mall, the anchor store for which is **Three Dog Down,** 61547 U.S. 93 (© **800/ DOG-DOWN**). This funky down outlet sells comforters, coats, pillows, duvets, and other cold-weather gear. Owner Robert A. Ricketts is a former opera singer who moved from Cincinnati to Polson to start a low-key dream business. Prices for high-quality down goods are lower here than in more fashionable metropolitan stores.

WHERE TO STAY

There are five campgrounds in Flathead Lake state parks, each located at a different point around the lake: Big Arm (© **406/849-5255**) and West Shore (© **406/844-3066**) on the west side of the lake; and Finley Point (© **406/887-2715**), Yellow Bay (© **406/752-5501**), and Wayfarers (© **406/837-4196**) on the east shore. The phone numbers are operational only in summer. You can also call © **406/752-5501** for information on any of these state park campgrounds, which are open May through September and charge $15 per night.

Accommodations on and near the lake include guest ranches, water-oriented resorts with the gamut of recreational opportunities, and basic motels that offer clean but modest rooms.

Averill's Flathead Lake Lodge ★★★ *Kids*   For an all-around vacation experience, this is the best on the lake. A beautiful log lodge surrounded by thousands of acres of forest serves as your home base for all activities, which include horseback riding, boating, and fishing. The Western experience is done up right at this place, complete with singalongs, campfires, and barn dances. The location and the atmosphere of this place (the Averills perfectly combine a ranching lifestyle with the summer vacation experience) make this one of the top picks in the state. Scattered around the property are 20 two- and three-bedroom cabins, featuring simple Western-style furnishings. Inside the lodge are 19 guest rooms, just as woodsy but smaller, that sleep up to four and have

My, what an inefficient way to fish.

Ring toss, good. Horseshoes, bad.

Faster! Faster! Faster!

We take care of the fiddly bits, from providing over 43,000 customer reviews of hotels, to helping you find our best fares, to giving you 24/7 customer service. So you can focus on the only thing that matters. Goofing off.

travelocity

You'll never roam alone.™

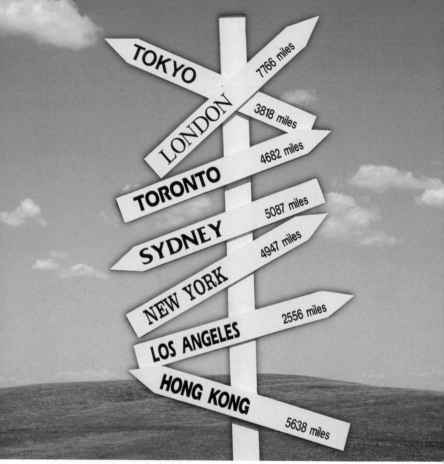

queen-size beds and a pair of twin beds in a loft. Meals are served family-style in the main lodge—the food is top-notch.

P.O. Box 248, Bigfork, MT 59911. © 406/837-4391. Fax 406/837-6977. www.averills.com. 19 lodge rooms, 20 cabins. $2,793 per adult per week (based on 1-week minimum stay); $1,152–$2,086 children 3–18; $147 children under 3. Rates include all meals and ranch activities. AE, MC, V. **Amenities:** 4 tennis courts; extensive watersports equipment; children's program; activities desk; babysitting. *In room:* No phone.

Best Value Port Polson Inn   Although it's right on the highway, this is a very nice motel with an excellent view of the lake. The rooms are large and very clean, and there are two apartments and three suites that are especially good for families. The outdoor hot tub has a view of the lake, a perfect setting for unwinding after a day of fishing or hiking. Some rooms have kitchens and/or views overlooking the lake and the Mission Mountains. The rates are considerably lower in winter.

502 U.S. 93 E., Polson, MT 59860. © 888/315-2378 or 406/883-5385. Fax 406/883-3998. www.bestvalueinn.com. 43 units. $89–$125 double; $225 apt. Rates include continental breakfast. AE, DISC, MC, V. **Amenities:** Exercise room; indoor and outdoor Jacuzzis; sauna. *In room:* A/C, cable TV, kitchen, hair dryer, iron.

The Candlewycke Inn ★★ *Finds*   Tucked away on 10 acres of pine forest at the foot of the Swan Mountains, this luxurious and large B&B is a modern home that innkeepers Megan and Steve Ward converted into a first-rate inn. The parlor, with 30-foot ceilings and an exposed pine staircase, draws you into a comfortable living space bedecked with an attractive selection of folk art. The large rooms have private bathrooms, and range from the somewhat frilly Botanical (with a canopied king-size bed, large bathroom, and private entry) to the rugged Wilderness (adorned with animal hides and a king-size bed with a log frame). There's a trail system on the property, an immaculate lawn, and all sorts of little touches (such as antlers converted to back scratchers). The breakfasts, anything from salmon quiche to wild rice and mushroom soufflés, are tailored to the tastes of guests.

311 Aero Lane, Bigfork, MT 59911. © 888/617-8805 or 406/837-6406. www.candlewyckeinn.com. 5 units. $130–$145 double; $195 suite. Rates include full breakfast. AE, MC, V. **Amenities:** Outdoor Jacuzzi; game room; lawn games; washers and dryers. *In room:* Cable TV, dataport, fridge, hair dryer, iron.

Kwa Taq Nuk Resort at Flathead Bay ★   This Best Western affiliate is a top-draw resort managed and owned by the Salish and Kootenai Indian tribes. It's the nicest property on the Polson end of the lake and offers a restaurant, marina, and art gallery. It's also the best decorated, with interesting and artful American Indian works on the walls. Lakeside rooms have commanding views, enhanced by decks furnished with chairs and cocktail tables. All the rooms are large and amply furnished.

The main lobby level is home to both a lounge and a restaurant, which provide stunning lakeside views. You can also eat or drink in the sunshine out on the deck. The retail operation is a combination gift shop/art gallery, so you'll find typical tourist souvenirs as well as authentic Western art produced by regional artists. The lower level has a large, comfortable sitting area with a large-screen cable television, swimming pool, and casino. This is the most expensive property on this end of the lake, but the amenities make it worth the extra money.

303 U.S. 93, Polson, MT 59860. © 800/882-6363 or 406/883-3636. Fax 406/883-5392. www.kwataqnuk.com. 112 units. $95–$135 double. AE, DC, DISC, MC, V. **Amenities:** Restaurant (steakhouse); lounge; indoor and outdoor pools; Jacuzzi; watersports rentals; concierge; activities desk; business center; dry cleaning. *In room:* A/C, cable TV, dataport, coffeemaker, hair dryer, iron.

Marina Cay Resort and Conference Center ✸ Boasting the most protected harbor on the lake, Marina Cay is a nice resort right on the water on the outskirts of Bigfork. The rooms are very large, and most open to a view on the water. The place attracts a few celebrities, including actress Jodie Foster, the Miami Heat's Shaquille O'Neal, and writer Stephen King. Rooms here are sizable, and there is a wide variety to choose from, but the walls in the older buildings are thin and noise carries easily from room to room.

Two restaurants serves food year-round: the **Bay Club,** a solid fine-dining option, and **Champs,** with a sports-bar, casino-style atmosphere; both will cook fish you catch from the lake or nearby rivers. The summer-only **Tiki** lounge serves drinks by the pool under flaming gas lamps.

180 Vista Lane, Bigfork, MT 59911. ℂ 800/433-6516 or 406/837-5861. Fax 406/837-1118. www.marinacay.com. 125 units. $89–$159 room; $199–$359 condo; $229–$429 suite. AE, DC, DISC, MC, V. **Amenities:** Restaurant; lounge; outdoor pool; 2 Jacuzzis; extensive watersports rentals; concierge. *In room:* A/C, cable TV, kitchenettes, coffeemaker, hair dryer, iron.

Mountain Lake Lodge Unlike many of its peers, Mountain Lake Lodge focuses on accommodations, not recreation, and its single-mindedness shows. The highlights of the hotel, located 5 miles south of Bigfork, are the idyllic courtyard—with a pool, waterfall, and the best view on the lake—and the rooms, each with a sitting area, fireplace, lake view, and deck or patio. Located in one of five buildings, all have a king-size bed in an imposing log frame and a queen-size sofa sleeper; many have Jacuzzis. The restaurant, **Louis',** serves steak and seafood, or you can grab a cherry-smoked pizza in the pub. The entire property is nonsmoking.

1950 Sylvan Dr., Bigfork, MT 59911. ℂ 877/823-4923 or 406/837-3800. Fax 406/837-3861. www.mountainlake lodge.com. 30 units. $99–$225 double; $125–$275 suite. AE, DISC, MC, V. **Amenities:** Restaurant; lounge; seasonal outdoor pool; exercise room; Jacuzzi. *In room:* A/C, cable TV, kitchen, fridge, coffeemaker, hair dryer, iron.

Swan River Inn ✸ Located in the heart of Bigfork, the Swan River Inn has a decidedly European feel, injected with a fair amount of whimsy to boot. Each of the six rooms is quite distinctive. The large log-cabin suite is decorated to resemble, well, a log cabin. The Arabian suite is an Aladdin-style fantasy come to life. The Art Deco suite hearkens back to the 1920s. All have beautifully restored bathrooms.

Upstairs, the **Swan River Cafe and Dinner House** serves steak, pork loin, rack of lamb, and a number of chicken and pasta dishes. In contrast to the Swiss architecture of the building's exterior, the **Grotto** is a second restaurant that converted an average lounge into a beautiful French-inspired facility complete with heavy wood furniture, stucco walls, and wrought-iron fixtures.

360 Grand Ave., Bigfork, MT 59911. ℂ 406/837-2220. Fax 406/837-2327. www.swanriverinn.com. 6 units. $140–$195 summer; $90–$135 winter. AE, DISC, MC, V. **Amenities:** 2 restaurants.

WHERE TO DINE

Bigfork has cornered the market on fine dining on the lake. Flathead residents from Whitefish and Kalispell routinely make their way to Bigfork to eat and take in a play at the Bigfork Summer Playhouse. For a burger, a beer, or a game of pool, head over to the smoky, kitschy **Village Well** (℡ **406/837-5251**), which makes a pretty good pizza to boot.

Coyote Roadhouse Grill ✸✸ ECLECTIC Master chef and spice fanatic Gary Hastings labels the Coyote's cuisine "Southwestern/Tuscan/Mayan/Cajun," so it's a little hard to know what to expect. It's no big deal, because the food is uniformly superb—some locals swear the Cajun food here is better than what you get in New Orleans, where Hastings used to work. Located in the Coyote Roadhouse bed-and-breakfast in Ferndale, about 10 miles southeast of Bigfork, the restaurant always has a gumbo and jambalaya plate on the menu, but Hastings is forever experimenting and tinkering in the kitchen. On a given night, you might get veal saltimbocca or any number of fiery Mayan or Southwestern dishes. The seafood is flown in fresh twice weekly, and the chile peppers for the Mayan red chile sauce (usually served on a char-broiled pork tenderloin or crab cakes) are imported from Mexico. The atmosphere is rustic yet refined, and the dining room has a nice mountain view.

600 Three Eagle Lane, Ferndale. ⓒ **406/837-4250**. www.coyoteroadhouse.com. Reservations required. Main courses $22–$33. No credit cards. Wed–Sun 5:30–8:30pm. Closed Oct to mid-May.

La Provence 🟥🟥 FRENCH/MEDITERRANEAN   Marc Guizol, the affable chef/owner of La Provence, made his way to Bigfork after his culinary career took him to the Ritz-Carlton in Naples and Caesar's Palace in Las Vegas. In his own eatery (occupying the space formerly filled by the Bridge Street Gallery Restaurant), Guizol's experience shines. The dinner menu is filled with lovingly prepared French standards, from escargot on a potato cake to roasted duck and grilled filet mignon. He also seasonally mixes in a few game dishes and classic European desserts. The room itself is an airy, pleasant space with a simple country French flair. For lunch, the restaurant serves light fare: quiche, pastries, and sandwiches.

408 Bridge St., Bigfork. ⓒ **406/837-2923**. www.bigforklaprovence.com. Reservations recommended. Lunch $5.50–$7.50; dinner $15–$30. AE, MC, V. Mon–Sat 11am–2pm and 5–9pm. Closed Mon in winter.

Showthyme 🟥🟥 ECLECTIC   When you ask locals what the best restaurant in town is, they'll more often than not tell you Showthyme—the restaurant that's located next to the summer playhouse. The atmosphere is a little bit New York, a little bit Montana. With a chef named Blu Funk and a manager named Rose Funk, you know the food has to be colorful. And it is: The Funks serve up everything from rack of lamb to sirloin steaks to chiles rellenos, all with a touch of creative flair. The king salmon is excellent, as is the seared yellowfin topped with wasabi aioli.

548 Electric Ave., Bigfork. ⓒ **406/837-0707**. Reservations recommended. Main courses $12–$25. AE, DISC, MC, V. Sun–Thurs 5–9pm; Fri–Sat 5–9:30pm. Closed Jan.

Tiebuckers Pub and Eatery AMERICAN   Located in the old railroad depot in the sleepy town of Somers, Tiebuckers is a good restaurant that is prized by the locals. The fresh fish and steamed clams keep the crowds coming, but the menu also offers a good variety of beef and pasta. The ribs in Grandpa's Sauce (a family secret) are also excellent. If your tastes skew toward the exotic, the restaurant also occasionally serves game: Buffalo, ostrich, or alligator might be available on a given night. There's also a pub menu with sandwiches and other inexpensive dishes.

75 Somers Rd., Somers. ⓒ **406/857-3335**. Reservations required for parties of 8 or more. Main courses $9–$23. AE, DISC, MC, V. Summer Tues–Sat 5–10pm; winter Tues–Sat 5–9pm. Closed Nov.

THE PERFORMING ARTS

In addition to the troupe of the Bigfork Summer Playhouse (see "Exploring the Area," earlier in this chapter), Flathead Lake visitors can take in a play by the **Port Polson Players** (ⓒ **406/883-9212**), a talented group of thespians who take to the stage at various area venues. Call for current information on plays, ticket prices, event dates, and times.

6 The Swan Valley

Extends 91 miles S of Bigfork; Southern End: 33 miles E of Missoula; 90 miles W of Helena

The 50-mile stretch of Mont. 83 from Columbia Falls to Swan, Condon, and Seeley lakes is isolated from Flathead Lake's tourist attractions. Though less traveled, the road boasts vistas even more lovely than those seen from U.S. 93, its cousin to the west. Opportunities for watching wildlife are quite good, and Seeley, Summit, and Alva lakes—all excellent recreational areas—lie close to the highway.

Swan Valley seems more authentically "Montana" than other, busier areas, perhaps because the area isn't developed for tourists. Though some think the timber industry clear-cuts are an eyesore, the remainder of this thinly populated area is crowned with snowcapped mountains and accessible lakes. Swan Valley seems remote compared to the nearby larger towns—an hour from Missoula, 2 hours from Helena—and it looks like it will remain relatively undiscovered for some time. In winter, snowmobiling, cross-country skiing, and even sled-dog mushing are the sports of choice in this out-of-the-way wonderland. Be sure to watch out for deer year-round along Mont. 83, especially at dawn and dusk—and remember, they usually travel in small groups.

Seeley Lake is one of the places where you can see the loon. Henry David Thoreau described the bird's call as a "long-drawn, unearthly howl, probably more like that of a wolf than any other bird." The loon is a symbol of north-country wilderness, and an appropriate one for this quiet and beautiful area.

ESSENTIALS

GETTING THERE   Other than being air-dropped, the only way to get into the Swan Valley is motor vehicle via Mont. 83. Airports in **Kalispell** (© **406/257-5994**) and **Missoula** (© **406/728-4381**) are almost equidistant from the Swan. The town of Seeley Lake is 48 miles from Missoula. Take Mont. 200 east from Missoula 33 miles to Mont. 83 north. It's 42 miles from Kalispell to Swan Lake in the northern portion of the valley. Take U.S. 93 south to Mont. 82 east, then Mont. 83 south. For weather reports, call © **406/449-5204** or 511 for road conditions statewide.

VISITOR INFORMATION   The Swan Valley isn't exactly a self-promoter. Though several businesses rely on tourists, the valley-wide tendency is to remain small. The **Seeley Lake Chamber of Commerce,** P.O. Box 516, Seeley Lake, MT 59868 (© **406/677-2880;** www.seeleylakechamber.com), can send you information on local happenings. For general information about Glacier Country, which includes the Swan Valley, call © **800/338-5072** or check out www.glacier.visitmt.com.

GETTING OUTSIDE

Densely forested and marked by a sparkling chain of lakes, the Seeley–Swan Valley offers a variety of activities for the outdoor enthusiast, with a vast network of Forest Service trails making year-round recreational opportunities for hiking, mountain biking, fishing, cross-country skiing, and snowmobiling. The **Seeley Lake Ranger District,** Seeley Lake (© **406/677-2233;** www.fs.fed.us/r1/lolo), will provide you with a detailed map of these trails upon request. The district office is 3 miles north of Seeley Lake near mile marker 18 of Mont. 83. One of the most popular summer activities is the **Clearwater River Canoe Trail,** a 3½-mile leisurely run down the river to the north end of Seeley Lake. The put-in is at the end of Forest Service Road 17597 and ends at the canoe landing at the ranger station.

The Forest Service publishes *Seeley Lake Area Recreation Opportunities*, which outlines a number of hikes in the national forest and wilderness areas. You can pick up a copy at the Lolo National Forest ranger district office, located at 3583 Mont. 83 just north of the town of Seeley Lake, or request one by phone (© **406/677-2233**). For a fairly short and interesting family hike, try the **Morrell Falls Trail**, a 2.5-mile hike from the trail head to a series of cascades, the largest of which drops 90 feet. From Clearwater Junction, travel north on Mont. 83 for 15 miles. Turn east on Cottonwood Lakes Road 477 and go 1¼ miles. Turn north on West Morrell Road 4353, then go 6 miles. Turn east on Pyramid Pass Road 4364 and go a quarter-mile. Turn north on Morrell Falls Road 4364 and go a mile to the trail head.

OUTFITTERS & GUIDES   Swan Valley is home to several experienced guides who know parts of this vast territory like the toughened backs of their leathery hands. Guided pack trips on horseback usually run from $175 to $250 per person per day, with a normal trip into the Bob Marshall Wilderness usually lasting a week. **Buck Creek Guide Service** (© **406/754-2471**) offers trips that focus on natural history and local culture, as well as big-game-hunting expeditions. **JM Bar Outfitters** (© **406/825-3230;** www.jmbaroutfitters.com) offers trail rides and fishing trips in the summer and hunting trips in the fall and winter. Call for prices. In Clearwater, **Monture Crick Outfitters** (© **888/420-5768** or 406/244-5763; www.montana outfitter.com) offers summer backpacking trips, hunting, and fishing in the Bob Marshall Wilderness.

WHERE TO STAY

The Lodges on Seeley Lake *(finds*   One of only two lodges right on Seeley Lake, this 1920 lodge and cabins operation is secluded and offers plenty of space to stretch out. The cabins are spacious and beautifully decorated, complete with upholstered chairs and queen-size beds. All the rooms have televisions and private bathrooms. There's also a summer-only bunkhouse that sleeps eight for $275 a night. Fortunately, the modern conveniences have been added without sacrificing the rustic feeling of the lodge. The best thing here though, remains the peaceful views of the lake from the beachfront, and of the wilderness beyond. The lodges have complimentary boats for guests to take out for fishing or recreation.

2156 Boy Scout Rd. (P.O. Box 568), Seeley Lake, MT 59868. © **800/900-9016.** Fax 406/677-3806. www.lodgeson seeleylake.com. 11 units. $121–$185 double. MC, V. **Amenities:** Watersports equipment. *In room:* TV, kitchen, no phone.

Swan River Lodge *(Value*   This is a good budget option in the Swan Valley. The rooms are fairly ordinary, though the setting is spectacular. And the building is pretty, a two-level log structure that doesn't look like your typical roadside motel. Several restaurants are nearby, and you can also arrange accommodations for your horse.

Between mile markers 46 and 47 on Mont. 83 (P.O. Box 1278), Condon, MT 59826. © **877/588-7926** or 406/754-2688. 22 units. $56–$65 double. Rates include continental breakfast. AE, DC, DISC, MC, V. Pets accepted. *In room:* Cable TV.

GUEST RANCHES & RESORTS

Double Arrow Resort *★*   Double Arrow is 2 miles south of Seeley Lake on Mont. 83, near the Bob Marshall Wilderness Area. The resort has just about any activity that a Montana-bound vacationer could want—golf, tennis, fishing, riding, hiking, and mountain biking. There are also guided fly-fishing and float trips available on the Blackfoot River. In the winter, there's cross-country skiing, snowmobiling, and sleigh

riding. You can get accommodations suited to nearly any taste, from relatively inexpensive rooms in the main lodge, to cabins, to a full-size, four-bedroom lodge all to yourself. The cabins are large and comfortably furnished, with sitting areas featuring upholstered chairs and sofas.

Rides to trail heads in the wilderness area offer opportunities for guests to explore Clearwater Valley, Horseshoe Hills, and the Morrell Falls National Recreation Trail. Two all-weather tennis courts and an enclosed pool with a hot tub keep guests busy afterward. There's also an 18-hole golf course. The public is welcome at **The Seasons Restaurant,** which offers fine dining—mostly well-prepared beef and seafood, but there are vegetarian selections as well—and a Sunday brunch on special occasions.

P.O. Box 747, Seeley Lake, MT 59868. ⓒ **800/468-0777** or 406/677-2777. Fax 406/677-2922. www.doublearrow resort.com. 26 units. $90–$175 double; $175–$725 2- to 4-bedroom lodges. Call for off-season rates. AE, DISC, MC, V. **Amenities:** Restaurant; lounge; indoor pool; golf course; outdoor tennis courts; indoor Jacuzzi; watersports equipment; activities desk; massage. *In room:* Kitchen, no phone.

Lake Upsata Guest Ranch ✿✿

This family-oriented guest ranch is located along the southern border of the Bob Marshall Wilderness Area within shouting distance of Missoula and Seeley Lake. You stay in delightful but rustic cabins that have shower-only bathrooms (no tubs). Horseback riding is the number-one activity at the ranch, although fly-fishing instruction (on the nearby Blackfoot River) is also arranged for guests. Hiking is another key experience, and the managers have organized several hikes that allow visitors to see wildlife and learn about the area's flora. Other activities here include tours to the nearby ghost town of Garnet, and tube riding and kayaking on the lake. Meals are served family-style in the main lodge. The food is excellent; daily menus change and include baked ham, Yankee pot roast, salmon, and roast turkey.

135 Lake Upsata Rd., P.O. Box 6, Ovando, MT 59854. ⓒ **800/594-7687.** www.upsata.com. 8 cabins. $220 per adult per night; $190 per child (ages 6–11) per night. 4-day minimum stay. Rates include all meals and activities. MC, V. Pets accepted. **Amenities:** Dining room; hot tub; watersports equipment; activities desk; washer and dryer. *In room:* Fridge, coffeemaker.

The Resort at Paws Up ✿✿✿

Opened in 2005—199 years after Meriwether Lewis climbed Sentinel Rock on the property—this cattle ranch-turned-ultraposh-resort is situated along 7 miles of the Blackfoot River on 37,000 pristinely rugged acres. Lavish Western accommodations come in several varieties, ranging from timber duplexes to 2,400-square-foot guest homes to the historic 1908 Morris House next to Elk Creek, which sleeps eight. With 300-thread-count linens, bath salts, outdoor hot tubs, and DVD libraries among the standard amenities, the common thread is luxury, which even extends into Paws Up's ecoresort "Tent City," where roughing it includes feather beds, electricity, and running water. It's certainly not cheap, but Paws Up's rate includes just about every imaginable recreational activity, and then some: hiking on the resort's 25 miles of trails; horseback riding; sport shooting; ATV rides; swimming in the river and other natural holes; boating and watersports; and snowmobiling, cross-country skiing, and sleigh rides in winter. There are all sorts of custom packages geared toward anglers, couples, and equestrians. Some include dinner and breakfast; three-meal-a-day packages are available to other guests for about $110 a day.

40060 Paws Up Rd., Greenough, MT 59823. ⓒ **800/473-0601.** Fax 406/244-5201. www.pawsup.com. 9 cabins. $248–$1,295 per person per night. Some packages include all meals and activities. AE, DC, DISC, MC, V. About 30 miles east of Missoula via Mont. 200. **Amenities:** 2 restaurants; outdoor heated pool; spa; exercise room; extensive watersports equipment; concierge; activities desk; room service; massage; courtesy car; dry cleaning; Wi-Fi network. *In room:* A/C, cable TV w/DVD player, dataport, kitchenette, coffeemaker, hair dryer, iron.

Tamaracks Resort 🎣   Tamaracks started out as a homestead in 1916 and became a resort in 1930. It is right on Seeley Lake with 1,700 feet of lakefront. The resort has a 1940s feel to it, with lots of room between the cabins, screened-in porches, and an attached campground (sites run $25 a night). The cabins are clean and comfortable, and there is also a trio of full-fledged log homes for those in need of more space (the largest is 2,500 sq. ft.). Every cabin and home has a full kitchen. The resort offers boat and canoe rental, a basketball court, horseshoe pits, and volleyball in the summer, and cross-country ski, skate, and snowmobile rentals in winter.

Mont. 83, Mile 17, P.O. Box 812, Seeley Lake, MT 59868. © **800/477-7216** or 406/677-2433. Fax 406/677-3503. www.tamaracksresort.com. 15 cabins, including 3 log homes. $75–$205 cabin; $150–$420 log home. MC, V. **Amenities:** Watersports and winter sports equipment; lawn games; activities desk. *In room:* TV, kitchen, no phone.

WHERE TO DINE

In Seeley Lake, the local's choice for breakfast or lunch is the **Filling Station Restaurant and Bar** (© **406/677-2080**), and the best fried takeout option is undoubtedly **Double Front Chicken** (© **406/677-2980**). Both restaurants are in the heart of town. In Swan Lake, try the **Laughing Horse Lodge** on Mont. 83 (© **406/886-2080**), which serves hearty meals and uses fresh, locally grown ingredients.

Lindey's Prime Steak House STEAKS   Apart from the dining room at the Double Arrow Resort (see "Where to Stay," above), this is easily the best restaurant in the area. A carbon copy of a sister restaurant in Minnesota that has achieved national acclaim, Lindey's makes ordering easy: There are only three dinner choices—chopped sirloin, prime sirloin, and special sirloin—all of which are accompanied by the restaurant's excellent greaseless hash browns plus a tossed green salad. For smaller appetites, there's a special "dinner-sharing" arrangement that allows two people to order one steak and two plates for an additional $6.25. Seating is in a comfortable glass-enclosed space with views overlooking the lake and the seaplane landing area. Bay Burgers is the lunch outlet, serving juicy burgers and little else.

Mont. 83, Seeley Lake. © **406/677-9229.** Lunch $5–$6.50; dinner $11–$24. MC, V. May–Sept daily 11am–10pm; Oct–Apr 15 Thurs–Mon 11am–3pm and 5–9pm. Closed Apr 16–30.

7 The Bob Marshall Wilderness Complex ★★

45 miles S of Big Fork; 78 miles NE of Missoula; 80 miles W of Great Falls

The Bob Marshall Wilderness Complex is the largest wilderness area in the Lower 48 states, covering 1.5 million acres, or about 2,400 square miles. We hate to keep picking on Rhode Island for these comparisons, but the Bob, as it is usually called, is more than twice the size of that state.

The complex includes the Bob Marshall Wilderness proper, and the Great Bear and Scapegoat wilderness areas. It abuts Glacier National Park, creating a huge area of relatively untouched country extending nearly half the width of Montana from the Canadian border. Marshall himself was one of the earliest advocates of wilderness for its own sake in the U.S., and the wild lands that bear his name were among the areas designated by the federal Wilderness Act of 1964. The Great Bear and Scapegoat were set aside in the 1970s.

Just south of Glacier National Park, the complex occupies nearly the entire territory that lies between the boundaries of U.S. 2 to the north, Mont. 83 to the west, Mont. 200 to the south, and U.S. highways 287 and 89 to the east. Access points along these roads occur infrequently and are poorly marked, so keep your eyes peeled.

The wilderness area has become very popular with hikers and horse-packers over the years, leading to a curious pattern of trail deterioration. Federal budget austerity allows the U.S. Forest Service little funding for trail maintenance, and while heavy traffic on the most popular trails has led to their erosion, many of the secondary trails have virtually disappeared. Quite a few trails that are marked on topographical maps of the area are faint or nonexistent on the ground. You should know fundamental trail-finding and direction skills—how to read a topo map—in case a trail dies out or is covered by snow banks.

EXPLORING THE AREA

For information, maps, and advice about traveling in the Bob Marshall Wilderness complex, contact one of the six ranger stations monitoring the wilderness. In the **Lewis and Clark National Forest:** Rocky Mountain Ranger District, 1102 Main Ave. NW, Box 340, Choteau, MT 59242 (℃ **406/466-5341**). In the **Flathead National Forest:** the Glacier View and Hungry Horse Ranger Districts, 8975 U.S. 2 E., Hungry Horse, MT 59919 (℃ **406/387-3800**), or the Swan Lake Ranger District, 200 Ranger Station Rd., Bigfork, MT 59911 (℃ **406/837-7500**). In the **Lolo National Forest:** Seeley Lake Ranger District, HC 31 Box 3200, Seeley Lake, MT 59868 (℃ **406/677-2233**). In the **Helena National Forest:** Lincoln Ranger District, Box 219, Lincoln, MT 59639 (℃ **406/362-4265**). An excellent guidebook to the area is *Hiking Montana's Bob Marshall Wilderness,* by Erik Molvar (Falcon Press). The **Bob Marshall Foundation,** P.O. Box 903, Whitefish, MT (℃ **406/863-5411;** www.bob marshallfoundation.com), is a good resource as well.

The most popular destination in the Bob is the **Chinese Wall,** a striking rock formation that stands more than 1,000 feet tall and stretches for 22 miles through the wilderness on the western boundary of the **Sun River Game Preserve.** One of the more well-traveled trails and easy accesses to the Chinese Wall is along the South Fork of the Sun River on the Holland Lake–Benchmark Trail (see below). From the east, reach the Chinese Wall by taking Trail 202 at Benchmark for 5 miles to Trail 203, then continue on this trail for roughly 11 miles before taking the Indian Creek Trail, Trail 211, to the south end of the Chinese Wall at White River Pass, elevation 7,590 feet. The Chinese Wall is unmistakable and is one of the most recognizable geologic formations in Montana. The USGS topographical maps for the trip are Slategoat Mountain, Prairie Reef, and Amphitheatre Mountain.

Advice for Day-Trippers

Day hiking is best done near **Holland Lake.** Take Mont. 83 south 61 miles from Bigfork, or north 20 miles from Seeley Lake, to reach the **Holland Lake Lodge** (℃ **877/925-6343** or 406/754-2282; www.hollandlakelodge.com) and the trails. Trail 42 from the north side of Holland Lake connects with Trail 110 to reach the Necklace Lakes just inside the Wilderness boundaries. To reach the Holland Lake Falls and Upper Holland Lake before crossing the Wilderness boundary at Gordon Pass, take Trail 415 a short way until it joins Trail 35. This trail, taken to its end, stretches from the western boundary into the center of the park near the South Fork of the Flathead River (not a day hike). Rooms at the lodge run $95 to $115 per person, double occupancy, all meals included.

The high meadows at the base of the wall are very fragile, and overnight camping is prohibited along the base between Cliff and Salt mountains. So plan your trip to allow time to reach a camping area away from this section of the wall.

Towering peaks run great lengths through the Bob and stand as some of the tallest, and certainly the most dramatic, sites in the northwest part of the state outside Glacier National Park. **Holland Peak,** just north of Holland Lake on the wilderness area's western boundary, is a spectacular 9,356-foot giant that can be seen from afar but cannot be accessed directly. A short day hike is available from the Holland Lake Lodge (see "Advice for Day-Trippers," above, for directions to the lodge) into the wilderness to **Holland Falls.** The distance from the trail head to the falls is only about 1.5 miles, an easy hike with only 240 feet of elevation gain. This trail is designated for hikers only; bikes, horses, and other pack animals are prohibited.

Once inside the wilderness area, **Big Salmon Lake** is a wonderful destination for the photographer, capturing the length and the beauty of Holland Peak's east face. To reach Big Salmon Lake, take Trail 42 from the Holland Lake Lodge on the west side of the Bob to Trail 110. It's a very long day hike, and a reasonable 2-day hike through the Swan Range to Big Salmon Lake.

Located one-third of the way in on the **Holland Lake–Benchmark Trail** (a 60-mile trail across the midsection of the Bob that, following a series of shorter trails, takes roughly a week to traverse), Salmon Lake is simple purity without sight or sound of civilization. This trail also runs just south of the Chinese Wall.

North, in the Great Bear, is the impressive **Great Northern Mountain.** This 8,705-foot peak towers over the northeast part of the Great Bear Wilderness and can be viewed from many different points along the roadsides near the wilderness areas. You'll need a couple of vehicles if you don't have someone who can pick you up where you exit the Bob at the end of your journey. Park at Holland Lake if you plan on making it your terminus, or at Benchmark, west of Augusta, if you plan on ending there.

If you begin on the east side, the Holland Lake–Benchmark Trail follows the South Fork of the Sun River on trails 202 and 203 before moving west along Indian Creek on Trail 211. This takes you, as mentioned above, to the south end of the Chinese Wall at White River Pass. From there, you'll take Trail 138 along the South Fork of the White River until you reach the White River and Trail 112. This trail takes you to the South Fork of the Flathead River at White River Park. Across the river, you'll find Murphy Flats and Trail 263 along the river to Trail 110. This long trail takes you along Big Salmon Lake and the Swan Range, and then to Holland Lake outside the Bob's western boundary.

To reach the summit of Great Northern, you'll have to do some off-trail hiking— 8 miles, if you make a round-trip. From Martin City, just northeast of Columbia Falls on U.S. 2, take the East Side Reservoir Road (38) for just over 15 miles to Highline Loop Road (1048). Take this road for just more than a half-mile across the bridge to the "trail head." Start along the left side of the creek until the landscape opens up. Trudge up to the ridge, then along it, to Great Northern's summit.

The majestic **Scapegoat Mountain** is the dominating jewel of the Scapegoat Wilderness Area. Surrounded by cliffs, this 9,204-foot summit is easily the most prominent feature in the southern part of the wilderness complex.

Wildlife abounds in the Bob, with grizzly bears being the most feared and the most difficult to spot. Moose and deer are common. Elk gather each fall for mating at the base of the Chinese Wall in the Sun River Game Preserve on the wilderness's east side.

There are lots of birds, including the ptarmigan, a brown quail-like bird that changes the color of its plumage each winter to snow white.

HELPFUL TIPS Some things to remember when camping: Before you set out, contact and consult a ranger at one of the district ranger stations mentioned above about distances, the wisdom of your itinerary, and restrictions. You can also pick up a topographical map. Carry plenty of water and water containers. Remember when loading up your pack that this is the weight you'll likely endure for a week or so. Restrictions are few. No vehicles are allowed in the area, including bicycles. To get around in the Bob you either walk or ride on an animal's back. It might also help to remember, too, that hunting is allowed in many areas, making backpacking in the Bob a little less inviting in the fall. Wear bright colors and make lots of noise.

8 Kalispell ⟨⋆

115 miles N of Missoula; 249 miles E of Spokane, Washington

Located smack-dab in the center of Montana's primary vacation and tourism region, Kalispell isn't as much a destination for recreational visitors as are Whitefish and Big-fork, but it is a good base for exploring the area and has a number of attractions in its own right. The city, which is also a business and industrial center, is in a beautiful setting and conveniently located for visits to Flathead Lake, skiing in Whitefish, or hiking and touring in Glacier National Park. If you come to Kalispell after visiting Glacier or the Bob Marshall Wilderness, it will seem positively urban. It has all the modern inconveniences, including a large mall and long waits at traffic lights. But it has managed to preserve a good deal of its historical character, and has a colorful arts and dining scene.

ESSENTIALS

GETTING THERE **Glacier Park International Airport** (✆ 406/257-5994) is located north of town at 4170 U.S. 2. **America West** (✆ 800/235-9292), **Delta** (✆ 800/221-1212), **Horizon** (✆ 800/547-9308), **Northwest** (✆ 800/225-2525), and **Big Sky** (✆ 800/237-7788) have daily flights.

U.S. 2 will get you here from the east or west. From Missoula, U.S. 93 leads north into town on a scenic 120-mile route that takes you past Flathead Lake. The drive usually takes a solid 2½ hours, no matter what the season. RVs amble along the gradually curving road during summer (to the frustration of most other drivers!), and icy conditions warrant added caution and reduced speeds during the winter.

Amtrak stops at the Whitefish depot, just 15 miles north of Kalispell. The bus terminal is located at 1301 S. Main St. (✆ 406/755-4011).

VISITOR INFORMATION The **Flathead Convention and Visitor Bureau** is located at 15 Depot Park, Kalispell, MT 59901 (✆ 406/756-9091; www.fcvb.org), and not only offers practical information concerning Kalispell, but provides information on year-round lodging, activities, and attractions, including Glacier National Park, Big Mountain Ski Resort, and Flathead Lake.

GETTING AROUND Rental-car companies **Avis** (✆ 800/831-2847), **Budget** (✆ 800/527-0700), **Hertz** (✆ 800/654-3131), and **National** (✆ 800/227-7368) maintain counters at the airport.

For 24-hour taxi service, call **Kalispell Taxi and Airport Shuttle** (✆ 406/752-4022) or **Flathead-Glacier Transportation** (✆ 406/892-3390).

GETTING OUTSIDE

Kalispell itself isn't exactly a destination for the person looking for outdoor recreation, but its location between Glacier National Park and Flathead Lake makes it a good home base for those exploring this region, during both the summer and ski seasons.

BIKING   Since motor vehicle traffic on U.S. 2 or U.S. 93 make them less than ideal for bike riding, cyclists usually head to the back roads. **Whitefish Stage Road** runs parallel to U.S. 93 (from U.S. 93, go east on Reserve St. to reach it) and offers some great views of the mountains in a bucolic environment. For area information, as well as all kinds of bicycle accessories, try **Bike Rite** at 110 E. Idaho St. (© **406/756-0053**).

FISHING   There is good fishing on the main Flathead River between Columbia Falls and Kalispell for trout and whitefish. There is good shore access at Pressentine, which is 5 miles north of Kalispell on U.S. 2 (follow the fishing access signs). Or you can float from Pressentine down river to Old Steel Bridge.

GOLF   **Buffalo Hill** (© **888/342-6319** or 406/756-4530; www.golfbuffalohill.com), just off U.S. 2 north of town at 1176 N. Main St., is an older course that's very hilly, with lots of trees and lots of memorable holes that can have serious golfers brushing up on their cursing. Cost is $30 to $51 for 18 holes, depending on the month and time of day. Carts are $12 to $14.

HIKING   **Lone Pine State Park** (© **406/755-2706**) is an attractive state park with a few hiking trails. Go west on U.S. 2. At the intersection with Meridian, you'll see signs for the park sending you left (south). Take this road for about 5 miles (in the curve to your right, the road becomes Foys Lake Rd.) to the park. Once you're there, take in the views of the valley below or hike on the trails. The day-use fee is $5.

SEEING THE SIGHTS

Woodland Park, on the east edge of town at Woodland Park Drive, is a little spot that offers visitors a place to sit down in the sun and relax if they want to kill a few hours outside without killing themselves. There's a lagoon with ducks and a swimming pool. Walking tracks skirt the park. Another worthwhile attraction is the **Museum at Central School,** 124 2nd Ave. E. (© **406/756-8381**), dedicated to preserving Kalispell's history.

Conrad Mansion   ⋪   This 26-room Victorian mansion takes up most of a city block. Built in 1895 by Missouri River freighter Charles E. Conrad, the mansion has been beautifully restored and outfitted with the original furnishings. All tours of the mansion are guided and last about an hour; tour guides are dressed in Victorian costume and explain the history of Conrad and his palatial home. Some highlights: an amazing collection of dolls and toys from three generations of the Conrad family, meticulously kept clothing from the 19th century, and the annual Christmas bazaar in late October. The beautifully kept grounds also make for a peaceful locale for a short walk or a picnic.

330 Woodland Ave. © 406/755-2166. www.conradmansion.com. $8 adults, $7 seniors, $3 children under 12. Mid-May to mid-Oct daily 10am–5pm; Christmas tours offered in Dec Wed–Sun. Located 6 blocks east of Main St.

Hockaday Museum of Art   ⋪   The charming Hockaday contains art formerly located in the Carnegie Library. The museum focuses on the works of Montana artists, both contemporary and historic, including Russell Chatham, Ace Powell, and Robert Scriver. There are tours, a gift shop, and an "Arts in the Park" program each July. The Hockaday has a very fine regional reputation for the quality of its programs.

302 2nd Ave. E. $©$ **406/755-5268.** www.hockadayartmuseum.org. $5 adults, $4 seniors, $2 students, and free for children under 12. Summer Tues–Fri 10am–6pm, Sat 10am–5pm, Sun noon–4pm; winter Tues–Sat 10am–5pm.

SHOPPING

Although not a major shopping destination, Kalispell has enough to offer if your money is burning a hole in your pocket. The **Kalispell Center Mall** at 20 N. Main St. ($©$ **406/751-5051**) has more than 40 stores and restaurants. Just up the street, downtown Kalispell has a few stores of its own. **Norm's News,** 34 Main St. ($©$ **406/ 755-5466**), has the latest newspapers from around the globe as well as a comprehensive magazine rack and espresso bar. **Books West** ($©$ **406/752-6900**) is the downtown bookshop on 101 Main St. The **Western Outdoor Store** ($©$ **406/756-5818**), 48 Main St., has a vast collection of Western gear for sale—4,000 pairs of cowboy boots, sterling silver Western belt buckles, and, for the wannabe dude, cowboy hats in all sizes and shapes. There's also an antiques store in the basement. The **Rocky Mountain Outfitter** ($©$ **406/752-2446**), 135 Main St., has all the gear you'll need for hiking nearby trails and scaling the peaks. You can also rent kayaks and canoes if you want to head out on the water on your own.

Mark Ogle Gallery, 101 E. Center St. ($©$ **406/752-4217**), features a selection of wildlife paintings and prints by its eponymous owner. **Columbine Glassworks** ($©$ **406/752-7174**) at 140 Main St. has stained glass and artworks in many other media.

WHERE TO STAY

Double J Econo Lodge *Value* Formerly the Diamond Lil, this boisterous hotel is on the nondescript south side of town and offers lodging for considerably less. The rooms are fairly large; unfortunately, they all face the parking lot or the swimming pool and hot tubs. There is a casino associated with the hotel that doubles as a watering hole.

1680 U.S. 93 S., Kalispell, MT 59901. $©$ **800/843-7301** or 406/752-3467. Fax 406/752-3489. www.diamondlil.com. $83–$99 double. AE, DC, DISC, MC, V. **Amenities:** Lounge/casino; outdoor heated pool; Jacuzzi; coin-op washers and dryers. *In room:* Cable TV, coffeemaker, hair dryer.

Four Seasons Motor Inn *Value* This is a very nicely kept older, independent motel. The rooms are in three different buildings that flank the parking area. They're bright, clean, and large, with full tub/shower combos. They are pleasantly decorated with nice artwork of Flathead Lake and Glacier National Park scenes. Some have fridges and/or modem-ready phones. None of them has a view to speak of, but this motel offers a nice, inexpensive alternative to the chains. Rates are about 30% lower in the off season.

350 N. Main, Kalispell, MT 59901. $©$ **800/545-6399** or 406/755-6123. Fax 406/755-1604. www.fourseasonsmotor inn.com. 97 units. $76–$110 double. AE, DISC, MC, V. Pets accepted. **Amenities:** Restaurant; indoor Jacuzzi; Wi-Fi network. *In room:* A/C, TV, coffeemaker, hair dryer.

Hampton Inn *&* Kalispell's Hampton Inn is an attractive three-story brick structure surrounded by lovely landscaping. The fairly large rooms have one king-size bed or two queen-size. The lobby has a comfortable sitting area in front of a large dome fireplace, enhanced by colorful log furniture with leather cushions. A business center provides a personal computer, fax-modem lines, calculators, copy machines, and a printer for guests; there is also free wireless Internet access.

1140 U.S. 2 W., Kalispell, MT 59901. $©$ **800/HAMPTON** or 406/755-7900. Fax 406/755-5056. www.northwest inns.com. 120 units. $108–$168 double; $200–$250 suite. Rates include continental breakfast. AE, DISC, MC, V. **Amenities:** Indoor pool; exercise room; indoor Jacuzzi; courtesy car; coin-op washers and dryers; Wi-Fi network. *In room:* A/C, TV/VCR, dataport, fridge, coffeemaker, hair dryer, iron.

The Kalispell Grand Hotel ⟨⟩   The Kalispell Grand is a historic hotel (1912) done in the Old West tradition. Located downtown, the hotel has been beautifully refurbished, right down to the pressed-tin ceiling and elegant oak staircase. By today's standards the rooms are small, as are the bathrooms, but the historic ambience and fresh feel make the lack of space worthwhile. The lobby is the hotel's centerpiece, with cherrywood walls, a small art gallery, and an air of Victorian elegance.

100 Main St., Kalispell, MT 59901-4452. ⟨⟩ 800/858-7422 or 406/755-8100. Fax 406/752-8012. www.kalispell grand.com. 40 units. $91–$135 double. Rates include continental breakfast. AE, DC, DISC, MC, V. Pets accepted. **Amenities:** Restaurant; spa. *In room:* A/C, TV, dataport (w/free high-speed Internet access), hair dryer.

WHERE TO DINE
MODERATE
Alley Connection CHINESE   The best place in the valley for Chinese cuisine, the Alley Connection took several years to reach its current state of grace. What started out as a small, one-room operation has become two tastefully but simply decorated dining rooms that serve up excellent fare. Meals of chow mein, sweet-and-sour pork, and Szechuan chicken may be ordered separately or in the more popular family-style. Lunch is a great deal for less than $6, and service is always quick and dependable.

22 1st St. ⟨⟩ 406/752-7077. Reservations recommended. Lunch $3.75–$6; dinner $6–$13. AE, DISC, MC, V. Mon–Thurs 11am–2:30pm and 5–9pm; Fri–Sat 11am–2:30pm and 5–9:30pm. Closed Sun.

Cafe Max ⟨⟩⟨⟩ CONTINENTAL   Cafe Max brings a dash of New York–style culinary glitz to the Flathead Valley. Owned by chef Doug Day, the place is small, elegant, busy, and always booked. The food is excellent, elegantly prepared and presented. While the menu changes often, two standbys are the wild Alaskan salmon with a champagne-shallot sauce and the grilled filet mignon. (The rack of lamb also gets high marks.) There are also some soup entrees, such as Montana buffalo with barley and shrimp and roasted red-pepper bisque. In the end, the layout is one of intimacy and class, and this is the town's romantic hot spot. The restaurant serves beer and wine only, but its eclectic wine list is one of Kalispell's best.

121 Main St. ⟨⟩ 406/755-7687. Reservations strongly recommended. Main courses $12–$28. AE, MC, V. Tues–Sun 5–9pm. Closed Sun in winter.

Painted Horse Grille ⟨⟩ ECLECTIC AMERICAN   A relatively new entry in the Kalispell dining landscape, this restaurant is located in a space that was a bar until it was gutted in 1999. Now a sleek, long room decorated in mellow earth tones, the Grille has quickly become a local favorite in the winter and starts drawing in tourists when the snow melts. The approach is to bring in the best of various culinary traditions (namely French, American, Asian, and Italian) to its varied menu. For lunch, we recommend the delectable paella or shellfish linguine. The dinner specialties are the roasted rack of lamb and the roast curried duck. You might even find a Cajun dish or a buffalo steak among the daily specials.

110 Main St. ⟨⟩ 406/257-7035. Reservations recommended. Lunch $6–$7; dinner $14–$24. AE, MC, V. Mon–Fri 11:30am–2:30pm; Mon–Sat 5:30–9pm.

INEXPENSIVE
The Bulldog Pub and Steakhouse STEAKS/SEAFOOD   Decorated in the style of an English pub, the Bulldog is a steak joint with a sense of humor. The menu is fairly varied, if conventional, but the prime rib and barbecue chicken breasts in huckleberry barbecue sauce stand out. If you're feeling adventurous, try the full elephant

roasted on a spit for $29,000 (it's on the menu, really!). The waitress assured us that it could be ready in 15 minutes because the elephants are parboiled ahead of time.

1711 U.S. 93 S. ℂ 406/752-7522. Lunch $5–$7; dinner $8–$16. AE, DISC, MC, V. Mon–Wed 11am–10pm; Thurs 11am–11pm; Fri 11am–midnight; Sat 4pm–midnight. Bar open later.

The Knead Café ⊀ STEAK/SEAFOOD/ECLECTIC   A funky, bohemian bakery, The Knead Café is a great lunch spot and a good destination for a more upscale dinner. The brightly decorated walls are covered with the work of local artists, and the whole place has an arty, breezy atmosphere. The food is tasty and designed to please meat-eaters and vegetarians alike. Lunch runs the gamut from falafel to Thai chicken curry burritos and buffalo burgers. At dinner, try the Salmon Wellington or a hanger steak. The Knead also has a stellar weekend brunch.

25 2nd Ave. W. ℂ 406/755-7510. Reservations accepted for large parties only. Breakfast $4–$7; lunch $6–$8; dinner $7–$12. MC, V. Mon–Fri 10:30am–3:30pm and 5–10pm; Sat 8am–3:30pm and 5–10pm; Sun 9am–3pm.

Norm's News 𝒦𝒾𝒹𝓈 BURGERS   Established in 1938, Norm's is a classic old-fashioned soda fountain, with racks of magazines and newspapers and an assortment of 300 kinds of candy, which should perk the kids up after a long day. It's quite a sight, from the Rock-ola jukebox to the ornate back bar carved from Mediterranean cypress. The menu is as basic as it gets: burgers, hot dogs, and fries, plus a wide variety of sundaes, ice-cream sodas, and hard-packed ice cream. Try a Glacier Supreme, a concoction of 7-Up, syrup, and whipped cream, after exploring the real thing.

34 Main St. ℂ 406/755-5466. Reservations not accepted. Most items $3–$6. No credit cards. Mon–Sat 9am–6pm; Sun 11am–4pm.

9 Whitefish ⊀⊀

12 miles N of Kalispell

Whitefish has boomed as a resort community, attracting people from all over the country and making it Montana's fastest-growing area. Longtime residents have feared it will become another Aspen or Jackson Hole, but that hasn't quite happened yet. In fact, Whitefish is still relatively sedate.

Whitefish is almost two different towns—the town itself and the Big Mountain ski area. The busy season in town is the summer, and room rates are correspondingly higher there during warm weather. This may seem odd for a ski town, but Glacier National Park attracts about two million visitors a year, while the ski area brings in only about 300,000.

Up on the mountain, however, the peak season is winter, especially during Christmas vacation time. So if you don't mind the winding 5-mile drive up (or down) the Big Mountain road, you can find slightly less expensive accommodations in the appropriate season.

ESSENTIALS

GETTING THERE   Whitefish is easier to get to than virtually any other Montana vacation town. It's a quick drive up U.S. 93 from Kalispell. For the local weather forecast, call ℂ 406/755-4829.

Glacier Park International Airport (ℂ 406/257-5994) is 10 minutes away between Columbia Falls and Kalispell. **America West** (ℂ 800/235-9292), **Delta** (ℂ 800/221-1212), **Horizon** (ℂ 800/547-9308), **Northwest** (ℂ 800/225-2525), and **Big Sky** (ℂ 800/237-7788) have daily flights.

The **Amtrak** (© **800/USA-RAIL;** www.amtrak.com) station on N. Central Avenue, with two trains daily—one eastbound and one westbound—is shared with **Burlington Northern** at the edge of downtown in a renovated and charmingly attractive depot. The bus terminal is also located at the train depot, with daily service to and from Missoula from **Rimrock Stages** (© **406/755-4011**).

VISITOR INFORMATION   The **Whitefish Chamber of Commerce** (© **877/ 862-3548** or 406/862-3501; www.whitefishchamber.com) is located downtown at 520 E. 2nd St. Here you'll find just about everything you need in the way of brochures, area maps, and travel information.

GETTING AROUND   **Budget** (© **800/248-7604**) and **National** (© **800/227- 7368**) maintain counters at Glacier Park International Airport. Other companies renting cars in Whitefish include **Avis** (© **800/331-1212**) and **Hertz** (© **800/654-3131** or 406/862-1210). **Whitefish Taxi** can be reached at © **406/862-0587.**

SPECIAL EVENTS   Whitefish is home to the **Winter Carnival** ☆ (© **406/862- 3501**), a wild and woolly event held annually in mid-January since 1960. It includes a parade, children's events, a disco party, a snow-sculpting competition, and a battle of the bands at local bars. Of special note is the Penguin Plunge, where a group of brave locals take a dip in frigid Whitefish Lake in the name of charity.

GETTING OUTSIDE

Whitefish is truly a paradise for outdoors enthusiasts, with ski slopes, hiking trails, watersports opportunities, and Glacier National Park just down the road. For all kinds of outdoor equipment or apparel, check out **Sportsman & Ski Haus** at the Mountain Mall (© **406/862-3111**) or **Ski Mountain Sports,** 238 Central Ave. (© **406/ 862-7541**). **The Wave,** 1250 Baker Ave. (© **406/862-2444**), is a first-rate new aquatic and fitness facility, with several pools, weight machines and free weights, massage therapists, and much more.

BIKING

Although there are some road-biking opportunities here, biking in Whitefish really means mountain biking. The same old logging roads that make the hiking only average (see below) make the mountain biking excellent. Big Mountain has added 20 miles of single-track bike trails. The trails are free, but the area offers a ride to the top on the chairlift for you and your bike for $15. **The Big Mountain Resort** (© **406/862-2900;** see "Downhill Skiing," below), offers five graded mountain-biking trails, the longest of which, graded as intermediate, is 8 miles. There's also a short half-mile trail for beginners and two expert trails of about a mile each. The resort offers guided mountain tours ($35–$56) and private mountain-biking lessons. Trails lead across the mountain to entrances at Glacier National Park, Whitefish Lake, and Hell-roaring Basin. Bicycle rentals are available as well. Another Whitefish operation shares the expertise for mountain bikers seeking adventure on seemingly undiscovered paths. **Glacier Cyclery and Fitness,** 326 E. 2nd (© **406/862-6446**), provides excellent service and maintenance as well as rentals, area maps, and up-to-date information for the serious mountain biker. This outfit has been ranked among the 100 best cycle shops in a pool of 6,800 independent dealers. For a less challenging ride, you can make the 20-mile round-trip on paved roads from downtown Whitefish to the head of Whitefish Lake. Most of the route follows East Lakeshore Drive and offers views of the lake.

BOATING & SWIMMING

The boating is excellent on Whitefish Lake, and the lifeguard-staffed City Beach abuts the west side of town. You can rent water-skiing boats, fishing boats, paddle boats, and personal watercraft from the **Whitefish Lake Lodge Marina** (© **406/862-9283**), which is operated by Whitefish Lake Lodge (see "Where to Stay," later in this section) between mid-May and mid-September. Fees vary from $15 for a canoe or kayak (1-hr. minimum) to $80 per hour for a water-ski boat (2-hr. minimum). There are twilight boat cruises on Sunday and Thursday evenings that leave at 5:30pm ($20 adults).

CROSS-COUNTRY SKIING

The Big Mountain Resort (see "Downhill Skiing," below) offers 12km of very challenging cross-country trails. The **Glacier Nordic Club** maintains 15km of trails on the Whitefish Lake Golf Course (see "Golf" below) and another 1.6km across the street near the Grouse Mountain Lodge.

These provide an excellent outing on the hilly golf course. A small donation allows skiers to enjoy both sides of the street, and yearly passes are available. For information, contact the **Grouse Mountain Lodge** (© **406/862-3000**). The **Flathead Convention and Visitor Bureau** (© **406/756-9091**) provides a free outline of trails in or near Whitefish, as well as a list of equipment sales and rental operations.

DOG-SLEDDING

Dog-Sled Adventures (© **406/881-2275;** www.dogsledadventuresmontana.com) lets you explore the mountains around Whitefish "at the speed of dog." The guided 12-mile rides in two-person or family-size sleds run through Stillwater State Forest, 2 miles north of Olney. Each trip takes about 1½ hours and the sleds are equipped with blankets to keep you warm. Many of the dogs pulling the sleds were rescued by the owners from unwanted homes or animal shelters and trained as sled dogs. A sled ride costs about $75 per adult, with steep discounts for kids, and includes a cup of hot chocolate and homemade cookies at the end of your ride.

DOWNHILL SKIING

The Big Mountain Resort 🌟🌟 *(Finds)*   This resort offers lots of powder, lots of skiing in the trees, and plenty of runs for every level of skier. With an annual snowfall of 300 inches, a vertical drop of 2,500 feet, a brand-new superpipe for the snowboarding crowd, and virtually no lines, the Big Mountain is one of the best ski areas in the northwestern United States. More than half the mountain is geared to the intermediate skier, but there is plenty of terrain for experts and beginners. The expert runs are pretty steep—not as steep as those at Wyoming's Jackson Hole Ski Area, but steep enough. There are never any crowds at Big Mountain, even in the holiday seasons, so although the prices have gone up a bit over the years, you can still spend your time skiing rather than waiting in lift lines.

Ski school options include half-day group lessons for kids ($70) and half-day private sessions for adults ($160). There's also a full-service ski-rental shop.

For après-ski food and entertainment, the Big Mountain holds its own, with 10 restaurants in the village or on the hill. Our choice for food and beverage at the mountain is **Moguls Village Pub,** a casual, full-service restaurant and bar with a menu chock-full of Italian and American food. **Summit House** is a cafeteria that dishes up burgers and the like during the daytime; Mexican buffet dinners are served on some evenings. The **Hellroaring Saloon and Eatery** serves both lunch

A Brewery in Whitefish

The glass-enclosed brewing "tower" at the **Great Northern Brewing Company,** on Central and Railway (© **406/863-1000**), gave birth to the original Black Star beer; the company has since split from Black Star with six other products. The tasting room is open daily from noon until 8pm (until 6pm Mon–Thurs in the winter); guests are limited to one freebie before they have to pony up for their beers. There's also a coffeehouse open from 8am to 7pm.

and dinners in a typical après-ski atmosphere. **The 'Stube** is the mountain's rowdiest watering hole, with a mechanical bull and a chuck wagon–style dinner.

In summer, you can take gondola rides to the top of the mountain ($10 adults, $8 children 7–18 and seniors 70 and over), go horseback riding with **Big Sky Rides** (© **406/755-7433**), or mountain bike on the trails (bike rentals are available). A new warm-weather diversion is **Walk-in-the-Treetops** ($48 for 3 hr.), a harnessed adventure that goes 70 feet aboveground into the forest's canopy.

P.O. Box 1400 (12 miles north of Whitefish on Big Mountain Rd.), Whitefish, MT 59937. © 800/858-5439 or 406/862-2900. Fax 406/862-2955. www.big-mountain.com. Lift tickets $49 adults, $41 seniors 62 and over, $36 children 7–18; half-day and night rates available. AE, DISC, MC, V. Late Nov to Apr daily. From Whitefish, head north on Baker Ave. over the viaduct to Wisconsin Ave. for 3 miles until you see the flashing yellow light. Turn right on Big Mountain Rd. and proceed 8 miles to the Big Mountain Village.

FISHING

It's not the Madison Valley, but Whitefish does have some hot spots for anglers wanting to try their hand. **Tally Lake** is a deep hole located north of Whitefish off U.S. 93. Five miles north of town, turn left onto the Tally Lake Road (signs will direct you). You can expect cutthroat, rainbow, kokanee, brook trout, and whitefish.

In town, across the viaduct toward the Big Mountain, lies **Whitefish Lake.** If you can handle the summer bustle, the lake offers some pretty good lake trout. Northern pike can be found here, and rainbow and cutthroat can be nabbed on dry flies in the evening. The **Lakestream Flyshop,** 334 Central Ave. (© **406/862-1298;** www.lakestream.com), is the best resource in town for information about fly-fishing the Flathead River and local streams. It's also a great spot for a fly-fisherman to construct a wish list, since the store sells all types of fly-fishing equipment, clothing, books, flies, dust catchers, and memorabilia. The staff here provides full-service fly-fishing, tying, and rod-building services, in addition to good advice. Guided trips are $375 a day, $275 for a half-day.

GOLF

The **Whitefish Lake Golf Club** ⚐, U.S. 93 N. (© **406/862-4000;** www.golfwhitefish.com), is the only 36-hole golf course in the state. Built in the 1930s, the golf club's trees have grown up considerably in the time since.

While not especially long, the course offers a wide variety of shots that will require you to use all the clubs in your bag (and maybe some you forgot). Almost all the fairways are lined with trees. There are few fairway bunkers, but they have strategic placement around the greens. Both 18-hole setups measure a little more than 6,500 yards from the tips. There is also a driving range and putting green. This course may not be as good as Meadow Lake (see the "Golf" section in "Columbia Falls," later in this chapter), but it is a very fun track. Greens fees are $34 to $41 for 18 holes, $19 to $22 for 9 holes. Carts rent for $26.

HIKING

The hiking in the immediate Whitefish area is not great. For the most part, trails either stay in the woods so that you don't see anything except trees, or they go along old logging roads—which make for good mountain biking, but less interesting hiking. The most popular trail in town is the **Danny On Trail** to the summit of the Big Mountain. Named for a Forest Service ecologist who was killed in a ski accident on the Big Mountain in 1979, it begins in the Big Mountain Village and ascends the south face of the mountain on four different paths. There's about a 4-mile trek from the top of the lift along the ridge to Flower Point and back. It takes about 2 hours. The most demanding walk is 5.75 miles from the base of the ski area to the top of the hill and then along the ridge. You can ride the lift back down. Snow can be a problem in late spring and even the early months of summer.

SNOWBOARDING

Snowboarders will find kindred spirits—as well as an extensive line of boards and apparel—at **Stumptown Snowboards** (© **406/862-0955**) at 128 Central Ave. The staff here will fill you in on the local snowboarding scene on the Big Mountain (where the shop has a smaller annex) and other spots in the Flathead Valley.

SNOWMOBILING

Contact the **Flathead Snowmobile Association** (© **406/752-1580**) for current conditions and advice. The **Flathead Convention & Visitors Bureau** (© **406/756-9091**) prints a brochure, *Snowmobiling Montana's Flathead Valley,* with information on guides, trails, and snowmobile-friendly accommodations. For rentals contact **J&L RV Rentals** in Columbia Falls (© **406/892-7666;** www.jandlrvrentals.com).

SHOPPING

The main shopping area of Whitefish is on Central Avenue and stretches for 3 blocks. For a ski town, the shopping frenzy is fairly subdued. The largest bookshop in town is **Bookworks,** 244 Spokane Ave. (© **406/862-4980**), which stocks the best in nature books, regional writing, and children's literature; it's also the source of current hardcover and paperback bestsellers. The **Artistic Touch,** 209 Central Ave. (© **406/862-4813**), sells self-described "Montana crafts of merit." The gallery is operated by a jeweler who exhibits an eclectic, diverse group of sculptures in all types of media—expect glazed wall sculptures, pottery mobiles suspended from the ceiling, wood and wire combinations, and even a full-size, handmade marimba. **The Tomahawk Trading Company,** 131 Central Ave. (© **406/862-9199**), has a large selection of Indian-made jewelry. The **Bear Mountain Mercantile,** 237 Central Ave. (© **406/862-8382**), is chock-full of gimcracks, knickknacks, and souvenirs, many with a bear theme. **Two Medicine Gallery,** 123 Central Ave. (© **406/862-0744**), is one of our favorites, stocking a mix of antique books, interesting decor, and eclectic art. There are 12 art galleries in Whitefish that participate in a "First Thursdays" program on Thursday nights from July to October.

For a behind-the-scenes look at some of the local farms and their offerings, contact **FarmHands** (© **406/862-5356**) for a free map of Flathead Valley farms that produce everything from goats to garlic and also welcome visitors.

WHERE TO STAY
IN & AROUND TOWN

Whitefish might just have the best range of accommodations in all of Montana, with everything from mom-and-pop motels to graceful inns to slope-side condos. There's a **Super 8,** 800 Spokane Ave. (*℃* **800/800-8000** or 406/862-8255), with doubles for $65 to $100 nightly. **The Pine Lodge,** 920 Spokane Ave. (*℃* **800/305-7463** or 406/862-7600; www.thepinelodge.com), is a good independent option, with doubles for $75 to $125.

Best Western Rocky Mountain Lodge *₢*

Located on the U.S. 93 commercial strip just south of downtown, this is a very fine Best Western. The larger rooms have their own wet bars and fireplaces. There are king- and queen-size beds, and balconies and Jacuzzis in the higher-priced rooms. This is an especially good option for those passing through on their way to or from Glacier, and aren't concerned with proximity to downtown Whitefish or Big Mountain. The outdoor year-round pool is a nice perk, as is the Wi-Fi network, which covers the lobby and select rooms.

6510 U.S. 93 S., Whitefish, MT 59937. *℃* **800/862-2569** or 406/862-2569. Fax 406/862-1154. www.rockymtnlodge. com. 79 units. $69–$119 double; $99–$169 suite. Rates include continental breakfast. AE, DC, DISC, MC, V. **Amenities:** Outdoor heated pool; exercise room; outdoor Jacuzzi; courtesy car; business center; dry cleaning. *In room:* A/C, cable TV, dataport, fridge, coffeemaker, hair dryer, iron.

Duck Inn *Value*

This is the best value in the Whitefish area. The building is right off the U.S. 93 strip, overlooking the Whitefish River. The rooms are very large, every one with a fireplace and a private bathroom with a deep soak tub. There is a lovely lobby area, a broad-windowed room overlooking the river. Even though it's right in town, the location gives the illusion of the serene, quiet countryside. The owners also own a car-rental agency, and guests at the inn get unlimited mileage with their rentals.

1305 Columbia Ave., Whitefish, MT 59937. *℃* **800/344-2377** or 406/862-3825. www.duckinn.com. 10 units. $69–$109 double. Rates include continental breakfast. AE, DISC, MC, V. **Amenities:** Car-rental desk. *In room:* A/C, cable TV, hair dryer.

The Garden Wall Inn *₢₢* *Finds*

While it's right on the main Whitefish drag, The Garden Wall Inn is a world of its own. Owners Rhonda Fitzgerald and Chris Schustrom clearly take pride in providing all of the little luxurious extras. The inn is full of country charm—it was built in 1923, and all of the furnishings are period antiques, including claw-foot tubs and Art Deco dressers, depending on your room. Every detail is just about perfect, right down to the towels, which are large and fluffy enough to dry two adults. Since Rhonda and Chris are both trained chefs, breakfast is a gourmet event (wild huckleberry crepes are just the tip of the iceberg) with an emphasis on locally produced ingredients, and afternoons end with hors d'oeuvres and beverages. They're also avid outdoors buffs: Ask them for tips before you head out on that excursion to Glacier or Big Mountain.

504 Spokane Ave., Whitefish, MT 59937. *℃* **888/530-1700** or 406/862-3440. www.gardenwallinn.com. 4 units. $125–$145 double; $215 suite. Rates include full breakfast and afternoon refreshments. AE, MC, V. *In room:* No phone.

Good Medicine Lodge *₢*

The Good Medicine Lodge is an already excellent place that is continually improving itself. Two of the best rooms have gas-log stoves and new furnishings. Several second-floor rooms have beautiful views of the Big Mountain, and ground-floor rooms have porches with garden access. Rooms are large, modern, and clean, and decorated with various themes, like golf, Western, and Native American.

The clientele tends to be the active type, but there are also older folks from warmer climes who come to Whitefish for a white Christmas—or other special occasions.

537 Wisconsin Ave., Whitefish, MT 59937. © **800/860-5488** or 406/862-5488. Fax 406/862-5489. www.goodmedicine lodge.com. 9 units. $95–$220 double. Rates include full breakfast. AE, DISC, MC, V. **Amenities:** Jacuzzi; coin-op washer and dryer; Wi-Fi network. *In room:* A/C, hair dryer.

Grouse Mountain Lodge 🖈🖈

Immediately adjacent to the 18th hole of one of Whitefish Lake's two golf courses, Grouse Mountain Lodge is one of Montana's premier vacation lodge properties, and it was nicely spiffed up for its 20th anniversary in 2004. The lodge combines luxury accommodations, fine service, and good food to provide a memorable experience. Standard hotel-like rooms are called the executive rooms, overlooking the golf course from the third floor, with vaulted ceilings and large living areas. The loft rooms have a sleeper sofa, fridge and microwave downstairs, and a staircase leading to an upper bedroom, where there is a king-size bed and a curtained-off area with two twins. The lodge has three places to eat: a casual grill, an outdoor patio, and the fine-dining **Wine Room.**

2 Fairway Dr., Whitefish, MT 59937. © **800/321-8822** or 406/862-3000. Fax 406/862-0326. www.grousemountain lodge.com. 145 units. $129–$229 double; $185–$259 loft. AE, DISC, MC, V. **Amenities:** 3 restaurants; indoor pool; golf course; 2 outdoor Jacuzzis; sauna; game room; concierge; activities desk; car-rental desk; courtesy car; business center; dry cleaning; Wi-Fi network. *In room:* A/C, cable TV, dataport, coffeemaker, hair dryer.

Hidden Moose Lodge 🖈 *(Finds)*

The centerpiece of this small independent property is the vaulted, high-ceilinged great room with the vast river-rock chimney fireplace. But the large, comfortable rooms are nicely done as well. Guests can savor their gourmet breakfast on their own decks if they wish. Even the bathroom mirrors are appointed with handmade ironwork. Their sign on the road is almost invisible, so it's important to know that the lodge is located about 1½ miles from town on the road to Big Mountain.

1735 E. Lakeshore Dr. (on the road to Big Mountain), Whitefish, MT 59937. © **888/733-6667** or 406/862-6516. Fax 406/862-6514. www.hiddenmooselodge.com. 12 units. $99–$199 depending on season. Rates include full breakfast. AE, DISC, MC, V. **Amenities:** Outdoor Jacuzzi. *In room:* Cable TV/DVD player, fridge.

North Forty Resort

Nestled in the pines along Mont. 40 between Whitefish and Columbia Falls, the North Forty is a great place to stay if you don't like being in town but still want to be close. Even the smaller duplex cabins all have large living areas, fireplaces, kitchens, front porches, and barbecue grills. North Forty is located in a serene and quiet area off the main highway, and there is a cross-country ski/hiking trail located at the north end of the property.

3765 Mont. 40 W. (P.O. Box 4250), Whitefish, MT 59937. © **800/775-1740** or 406/862-7740. Fax 406/862-7741. www.northfortyresort.com. 30 units. Summer $169 double; winter $109 double. AE, DISC, MC, V. Pets accepted. **Amenities:** Outdoor Jacuzzi; Wi-Fi network. *In room:* Cable TV, dataport, kitchen, coffeemaker.

Whitefish Lake Lodge Resort 🖈

The two-story condos available here are very nice, but may be soon overshadowed by those in Averill's Lodge at Whitefish Lake, the long-in-progress four-season luxury resort at the same address. The bold new building opened for New Year's 2006 after several years of delays. The existing resort condos include a very large tiled kitchen, a dining area, a deck overlooking Whitefish Lake and the marina, and a large loft bedroom, as well as a downstairs bedroom. The living rooms are tastefully appointed and mirrors on the far wall make the large rooms look even larger. In summer, there is a full-service marina with boat rentals; in winter, there are also hotel-style rooms normally in a rental pool for $120 double, when available, which is fairly rare.

1399 Wisconsin Ave., Whitefish, MT 59937. ℂ 800/735-8869 or 406/862-2929. Fax 406/862-3550. www.wfll.com. 28 units. Condos $345–$385. AE, MC, V. **Amenities:** Outdoor pool; indoor and outdoor Jacuzzi; watersports rentals; coin-op washers and dryers. *In room:* TV, kitchen.

ON THE BIG MOUNTAIN

The Big Mountain is a full-service ski area, working to attract local skiers, Canadian and American vacationers, and families. It provides a wide variety of accommodations to fit almost every pocketbook. You can reach central reservations at ℂ 800/858-5439. Be sure to ask about discounted lift and lodging packages. If you're looking for a house or condo instead of a hotel, inquire at **Big Mountain Lodging** (ℂ 800/243-7547; www.stayatbigmountain.com) and **Big Mountain Alpine Homes** (ℂ 800/858-5439; www.stayatbigmountain.com). Most are available for rent on a nightly basis, although some require longer stays. You can get a low-end condo or house for as little as $280 a night, or a glorious ski home for as much as $1,250. A video-rental library is available, as is a heated indoor pool.

Alpinglow   The closest lodging to the lifts, Alpinglow is located virtually at the base of the gondola in the Big Mountain Village. The rooms are standard fare, clean and done in pastels, but those on the valley side offer spectacular views of Flathead Lake. On a clear day, you can see almost to Polson. The restaurant has broad picture windows, a deck looking out over the lift base, and a beautiful bar serving wine and microbrews. The Alpinglow was the first recreational condo built in Montana, and it's showing its age a bit, but renovations have kept it quite livable.

Big Mountain Village, Whitefish, MT 59937. ℂ 800/754-6760 or 406/862-6966. Fax 406/862-0076. www.alpinglow. com. 54 units. $125–$140 double. AE, DISC, MC, V. **Amenities:** Restaurant; 2 outdoor Jacuzzis; sauna; coin-op washers and dryers. *In room:* A/C, cable TV.

Edelweiss *Kids*   The Edelweiss has some very nice large rooms, all with kitchens, full bathrooms, and fireplaces, and configurations ranging from basic studios to condo units with lofts and two bathrooms. Many of the rooms have panoramic views of the valley below, and all of them have a small balcony or patio. Convenient to the lifts, the Edelweiss has a large hot tub and a Finnish dry-heat sauna. Residents also have access to an indoor swimming pool.

3840 Big Mountain Rd., Whitefish, MT 59937. ℂ 800/858-5439 or 406/862-5252. Fax 406/862-0586. www.stayat edelweiss.com. 50 units. $130–$170 double. AE, MC, V. **Amenities:** Indoor Jacuzzi; sauna; coin-op washers and dryers. *In room:* Cable TV/VCR, kitchen.

Hibernation House *Value*   This is the least expensive place on the hill, popular with high school and college groups, ski teams, and families on budgets. And if you'll be on the slopes all day and just want a clean bed, this will do just fine. All of the rooms are exactly alike: pretty small with a double bed and a set of bunk beds. Each room has its own television—a relatively recent development—but people still like to congregate in the lobby, where there is a large-screen TV. You can ski right to the back door on a groomed trail, and it is only a short walk to a lift in the morning. Another perk: The buffet breakfast is quite good.

3812 Big Mountain Rd., Whitefish, MT 59937. ℂ 800/858-5439 or 406/862-1982. Fax 406/862-1956. www.stayat bigmountain.com. 42 units. $70–$95 double. Rates include full breakfast. AE, DISC, MC, V. **Amenities:** Outdoor Jacuzzi; coin-op washers and dryers. *In room:* Cable TV.

Kandahar Lodge ⊛   Kandahar combines the genteel ambience of a European inn with the requirements of an upscale modern ski hotel. The rooms are large and elegantly appointed, featuring pine walls, leather furnishings, and down comforters. About a third of the units are outfitted with kitchenettes, and the large loft bedrooms have vaulted ceilings. Overall, the lodge is one of the best (and priciest) lodging options on Big Mountain. Likewise, the Cafe Kandahar is the best restaurant on the mountain, serving seafood and other Continental standards.

3824 Big Mountain Rd., Whitefish, MT 59937. ℂ **800/862-6094** or 406/862-6098. Fax 406/862-6095. www.kandahar lodge.com. 48 units. $119–$259 double; $219–$699 suite. AE, DISC, MC, V. **Amenities:** Restaurant; lounge; exercise room; spa; indoor and outdoor Jacuzzis; sauna; business center; massage; coin-op washers and dryers. *In room:* Cable TV, kitchenettes, fridge, coffeemaker, microwave.

Kintla Lodge ⊛   A grand native log-and-stone lodge that echoes the architecture in Glacier National Park, Kintla is one of the newest accommodations on the mountain, opening in 1998. It is very upscale, and has an elevator serving its four floors. (That's something people appreciate more than you might think after a day of skiing.) But it's not cheap: A three-bedroom, three-bathroom unit goes for $600 a night in peak holiday season (mid-Dec through New Year's). All units have wood-clad French doors opening onto a patio, stone flooring in the entry and kitchens, individual ski storage, and tastefully simple pine furnishings. Best of all, Kintla is only 20 feet from Big Mountain's Tenderfoot lift. There is no restaurant on the premises, but the village's tonier shops are located on the ground level outside.

Big Mountain Village, Whitefish, MT 59937. ℂ **800/858-4157** or 406/862-1960. Fax 406/862-2955. www.stayatbig mountain.com. 14 units. $150–$450 1- to 3-bedroom unit. AE, DISC, MC, V. **Amenities:** Outdoor Jacuzzi; sauna; shopping arcade. *In room:* Cable TV/VCR.

Morning Eagle Lodge ⊛⊛   The newest lodging option on Big Mountain, Morning Eagle welcomed its first guests during the 2003–04 ski season and immediately entrenched itself as the most posh address on these slopes. The units range from studios to lavish three-bedroom affairs, all with similar contemporary, mildly Western decor: granite countertops, checkered Berber carpet and slate flooring, large tiled bathrooms, and fully equipped kitchens. The studios here are about 500 square feet, whereas the largest three-bedroom, three-bathroom units are about three times that size. The rooms have great views, pull-out sleeper sofas, washer/dryer units, and private balconies. There is a ski room downstairs, and a rooftop deck—a great perk, featuring outdoor heaters, a barbecue, and a 10-person hot tub.

Big Mountain Village, Whitefish, MT 59937. ℂ **800/858-4157** or 406/862-1960. Fax 406/862-2955. www.stayatbig mountain.com. 49 units. $175–$475 1- to 3-bedroom unit. AE, DISC, MC, V. **Amenities:** Outdoor Jacuzzi; sauna; shopping arcade. *In room:* Cable TV/DVD player, kitchen, hair dryer, iron.

Ptarmigan Village ⊛   This is an extensive condo setup that is spread over a lower portion of the Big Mountain. The units are pretty snazzy, featuring vaulted ceilings, fireplaces, fully equipped kitchens, and some unexpected touches: wood stoves, grills, CD players, and spiral staircases. The decks overlook a woody area where signs warn about increased black bear activity in the summer—there's a hiking trail here, too, if the bears don't scare you off. There's also a nice fishing pond where kids can spy on the turtles hiding in the reeds in summer.

3000 Big Mountain Rd. (P.O. Box 458), Whitefish, MT 59937. ℂ **800/552-3952** or 406/862-3594. Fax 406/862-6664. www.ptarmiganvillage.com. 50 units. $90–$205 condo. AE, DISC, MC, V. **Amenities:** Indoor and outdoor pools; tennis courts; indoor Jacuzzi; sauna; coin-op washers and dryers. *In room:* Cable TV/VCR, kitchen.

CAMPING

Whitefish Lake State Park is tucked on the outskirts of town in a nicely wooded area on Whitefish Lake. Call the **Department of Fish, Wildlife, and Parks (℃ 406/752-5501)** for additional information. The **Whitefish KOA Kampground (℃ 800/562-8734** or 406/862-4242) is about 2 miles south of town on U.S. 93 and has RV and tent sites ($20–$60 each) and 10 small cabins ($30–$65).

WHERE TO DINE

A good cup of organic coffee and a selection of baked goods are available at the **Montana Coffee Traders,** located at 110 Central Ave. (℃ **406/862-7667**), which also houses a nifty used bookstore and a nice place to sprawl out on a couch and read a book. **Loula's Café,** located downstairs at 300 E. 2nd St. (℃ **406/862-5614**), serves traditional American breakfasts and salads and sandwiches for lunch in an attractive setting. **The Buffalo Cafe,** 514 3rd St. (℃ **406/862-2833**), is Whitefish's best breakfast spot—try their legendary bacon-and-egg-filled pies. And for plump subs for lunch and Mexican fare for dinner, try **Quickee,** 28 Lupfer Ave. (℃ **406/862-9866**)—just look for the house with the gas pump above the door.

Corner House Grille ⋪⋪ STEAKS/SEAFOOD   Owned by William Foley, the CEO of one of the country's largest insurance companies, the Corner House Grille opened in late 2003 and immediately vaulted into the upper echelon of Whitefish's bustling culinary strata. The masculine dining room is one of the state's most elegant, with white tablecloths and a rich, romantic atmosphere. The food blends French and Continental influences, Asian sauces and other far-flung preparations, and regional ingredients, with terrific results. Representative dishes from the continually evolving menu include sesame mooshu duck and goat cheese tempura for starters, fennel-dusted Florida grouper with white corn sauce, and grilled buffalo hanger steak with truffle herb fries. The wine list and the desserts—including a heavenly crème brûlée—are excellent.

147 Central Ave. ℃ **406/863-2323.** Main courses $22–$35. Reservations accepted. AE, DISC, MC, V. Wed–Mon 5–10pm (closed Mon in winter).

Mambo Italiano ITALIAN   A swank, dimly lit *ristorante*, Mambo Italiano has the locals raving and the tourists lined up around the block. The color scheme and the music are both loud—the bright walls are multicolored and the stereo blasts Sinatra, Louis Prima, and Dean Martin—but it complements the rich Italian fare quite nicely. For an appetizer, you can't miss with the Italian Tootsie Rolls: egg wrappers stuffed with ricotta, mozzarella, and pesto. Cooked in an open central kitchen, main courses range from crackly crust pizza to *Pappa Biagio Bolognese* (ribbon noodles baked with meat sauce and mozzarella) and *Pollo Con Formaggio* (a breaded chicken cutlet dripping with four cheeses).

234 E. 2nd St. ℃ **406/863-9600.** Main courses $7–$15. Reservations accepted weekdays only. AE, DISC, MC, V. Mon–Sat 5–10pm (until 9pm Labor Day to Memorial Day).

Pollo Grill AMERICAN   This farmhouse-themed restaurant, located between Whitefish and the Big Mountain, has an unofficial motto: "People don't go away hungry." You can get a spit-roasted chicken or duck if you're after the house specialties, but the eatery also serves up a good steak and fresh salmon if your tastes tend toward the bovine or the aquatic. Most dishes come with a choice of two sides from a long list that includes garlic mashed potatoes, English cucumber salad, and braised red cabbage. The wine list is excellent.

1705 Wisconsin Ave. ℂ **406/863-9400.** Reservations recommended. Main courses $12–$24. AE, DISC, MC, V. Summer daily 5–10pm; winter daily 5–9pm.

Truby's ⚓ PIZZA/STEAKS   Even if you're not crazy about pizza, you'll likely appreciate Truby's eclectic approach to the popular dish. Here you can get wood-fired, Thai-style, Athenian, veggie, or design-your-own pizza. The crusts are thin and hand-tossed, and toppings range from Cajun andouille sausage and Jamaican jerked chicken to feta cheese and mandarin oranges. Pastas, steaks, seafood specials, baby back ribs, and burgers made of a mix of beef and buffalo on focaccia bread round out the menu. Truby's has a happening atmosphere with a comfortable bar, lots of customers, and a cheerful staff. The wine list features 150 different bottles.

115 Central Ave. ℂ **406/862-4979.** Reservations not accepted. Main courses $8–$21. AE, DISC, MC, V. Daily 5–10pm. Limited menu (pizza and salads) until midnight Fri–Sat.

The Tupelo Grille ⚓⚓ CONTINENTAL/CAJUN   The Tupelo is Whitefish's best restaurant, especially for those with a taste for spicy New Orleans–style food. Creole chicken and dumplings in a rosemary-tomato cream sauce and a Cajun Creole combo (a platter of shrimp Creole, crawfish étouffée, and chicken and sausage jambalaya) are specialties. The menu is full of creative variations on staples from both North and South (for instance, buffalo stroganoff, low-country shrimp and grits, and sesame and black-pepper seared ahi), and the atmosphere is pleasant, mildly contemporary, with big, comfortable booths and tables.

17 Central Ave. ℂ **406/862-6136.** Reservations recommended for large parties. Main courses $14–$24. AE, MC, V. Daily 5:30–9:30pm.

Wasabi ⚓ SUSHI   Few locals thought that a sushi joint in Whitefish would fly, but it turned out to be a fortuitous decision by proprietor/chef Scott Nagel. The contemporary space is a real eye-catcher, with wasabi-green walls, an orange ceiling, and a large mirror displaying the chefs hard at work above checkerboard floors. The menu runs the whole gamut of sushi, from California rolls to six-fish rainbow rolls, and also includes a nice selection of Asian-influenced grilled poultry and seafood. There's beer, wine, and six varieties of sake, but no liquor. The establishment also encompasses the adjacent **Ginger Grill,** a casual East-meets-West eatery, and the snazzy **419 Wine and Oyster Bar** upstairs.

419 E. 2nd St. ℂ **406/863-9283.** Reservations recommended. Sushi $4–$15 per order; main courses $8–$28. MC, V. Tues–Sun 5–10pm.

Whitefish Lake Restaurant ⚓ CONTINENTAL   There are Montanans who will enter the Whitefish Lake Restaurant as their horse in the "best restaurant in the state" sweepstakes. Located at the public golf course, it is generally conceded to be the best restaurant in the Whitefish area. It's housed in a building that was constructed in 1936 as a WPA project. The dining room has an almost churchlike atmosphere: dark and quiet, with large log beams and a large stone fireplace providing warmth on chilly evenings. The menu for the evening meal covers the culinary landscape, from vegetable strudel to 12-ounce prime rib, rack of lamb, and roast duckling; fresh seafood may include lobster, king crab, halibut, or Pacific salmon. The wine list is impressive, as is the bar's martini menu. As formal as a golf club ever gets, it's the only place in Whitefish that approaches dressy.

U.S. 93 N. (at the Whitefish Lake Golf Course). ℂ **406/862-5285.** Reservations recommended. Lunch $6–$10; dinner $16–$24. AE, DISC, MC, V. Summer daily 11am–3pm and 5:30–10pm; winter Sun–Thurs 5:30–9pm, Fri–Sat 5:30–9:30pm.

WHITEFISH AFTER DARK

The summer-only **Alpine Theatre Project** (© 406/862-7469; www.alpinetheatre project.org) and the year-round **Whitefish Theatre Company** (© 406/8625371; www.whitefishtheatreco.org) stage musicals and dramas at the O'Shaughnessy Center in downtown Whitefish. There's also a pretty good bar scene: Start your crawl at **Flanagan's Central Station,** 125 Central Ave. (© 406/862-8888), a high-ceilinged joint with live rock, jazz, bluegrass, and funk and a good bar menu. Follow that with a time-out at **Casey's,** 101 Central Ave. (© 406/862-8150), which is seedier but has more character; its clientele tends to be older and more local, and the walls are covered with wildlife pictures and patriotic slogans. A third stop could be at the **Great Northern Bar and Grill,** 27 Central Ave. (© 406/862-2816), which is pretty upscale. This place is jumping on weekend nights. Your final stop: the **Bulldog Saloon,** 144 Central Ave. (© 406/862-5636). Not just a bar, the Bulldog turns out a pretty mean burger, too.

10 Columbia Falls

11 miles N of Kalispell; 9 miles E of Whitefish

Columbia Falls gets a bad rep not only for being the home of Plum Creek, a smoke-billowing institution seen for miles even at night, but also for its not-so-subtle image as a tourist trap. And unlike Great Falls, where the falls are out of town and (gasp!) dammed, Columbia Falls goes you one better by not having any falls at all. The redeeming features and equalizers are the town's proximity to Glacier National Park, and lodging rates that are somewhat less expensive—it's a good fallback location if you have trouble finding a room in Whitefish. Residents here are real Montanans, something of a rarity in an area being inundated with out-of-staters setting up house.

ESSENTIALS

GETTING THERE   Glacier International Airport (© 406/257-5994) is 10 minutes away on U.S. 2 between Columbia Falls and Kalispell. **America West** (© 800/235-9292), **Delta** (© 800/221-1212), **Horizon** (© 800/547-9308), **Northwest** (© 800/225-2525), and **Big Sky** (© 800/237-7788) have daily flights. The closest **Amtrak** station is in Whitefish, 10 miles to the northwest.

VISITOR INFORMATION   The **Columbia Falls Area Chamber of Commerce,** P.O. Box 312, Columbia Falls, MT 59912 (© 406/892-2072; www.columbiafalls chamber.com), can provide you with pertinent area information. The chamber and the **U.S. Forest Service** jointly operate an information cabin in Maranette Park on U.S. 2 near the center of town. You can also get Columbia Falls information from the **Glacier Country Regional Tourism Commission** (© 800/338-5072; www.glacier. visitmt.com).

GETTING AROUND   The only car-rental agency actually located in Columbia Falls city limits is **Dollar,** 5506 U.S. 2 W. (© 406/892-0009).

GETTING OUTSIDE

Two of the best-kept secrets in this part of the state are the **North** and **South Lion lakes.** To find them, follow the signs to the west side of the Hungry Horse Reservoir. Less than 5 miles after turning off of Mont. 40, you will come to a cutoff to the North Lion Lake and, within a hundred yards, arrive at South Lion Lake.

Both are well protected, quiet, and for the most part undiscovered by tourists—excellent for picnicking, fishing, or swimming.

There is a road around **Hungry Horse Reservoir,** a 110-mile round-trip that you can start from the town of Hungry Horse. Hungry Horse is 9 miles south of West Glacier or 6 miles east of Columbia Falls on U.S. 2. This is an excellent drive for seeing wildlife. You're almost certain to see at least an elk, and maybe a moose or bear. It's also a great place for fishing.

GOLF

Columbia Falls is home to one of Montana's best golf courses, **Meadow Lake** (© **406/892-2111;** www.meadowlakegolf.com) at the Meadow Lake Resort, see "Where to Stay," below. About 6,700 yards from the back tees, the course is very challenging, especially the greens, which are "speed sensitive" and have lots of nearly invisible breaks in them. The fairways are fairly wide but lined with intimidating large trees. Greens fees are $24 to $52 for 18 holes, depending on the time of year and day. Carts rent for $12 to $14 per seat.

HIKING

Columbia Mountain, Glacier National Park, and the Jewel Basin are nearby, but the **Great Northern** is the grandpappy of 'em all in these parts. If you want a leisurely stroll with moderate difficulty, stick to the Danny On Trail on the Big Mountain in Whitefish. If you want 8 hours of hardship, then the Great Northern is for you. To get there, take U.S. 2 to Martin City, then turn onto the East Side Reservoir Road for 15 miles. At that point, turn east to Highline Loop Road, and from here you should be able to see the approach route. The hike goes up the 8,705-foot-high Great Northern Mountain in the Great Bear Wilderness. While there's not an official trail, enough people have beaten a path to the summit that one is clear enough to make out. This isn't a leisurely walk, nor is it the most publicized hike in the area, but it is the most rewarding for those willing to make the effort. The views of Glacier and the Hungry Horse Reservoir are remarkable.

EXPLORING THE TOWN: KITSCH & CAMP

Remember when your dad used to drive the family to the ocean or the mountains for the annual family vacation? Whenever you passed the "Tent of Miracles" or the "Cave of 10,000 Rattlesnakes" or the "Fabulous Mystery House," you'd beg Dad to stop. He always ignored you and drove on as if you hadn't spoken. Columbia Falls offers you the chance to find out what attractions like these are all about.

Big Sky Waterslide & Miniature Greens, at the junction of U.S. highways 2 and 206 (© **406/892-5025**), is the main attraction and a good place to cool off. It is the largest such park in the state of Montana. If you've always wanted to reenact the snow scenes from *The Shining* without the snow (and who hasn't?), then the **Amazing Fun Center,** at U.S. 2 E., Coram (© **406/387-5902**), is your place. Like rats hunting for an odorless cheese, tourists often enter the Fun Center's maze and emerge hours later. If mazes aren't your bag, the place also has go-karts and other games. The **House of Mystery,** 7800 U.S. 2 E., Columbia Falls (© **406/892-1210**), offers a vortex (you'll just have to go in to find out) and other bewilderments.

WHERE TO STAY

Bad Rock Country Bed and Breakfast ✸ Ⓕⁱⁿᵈˢ   This is a great choice for those who want to use Columbia Falls as a base for visiting both Glacier and Whitefish but want to avoid the hustle and bustle of being right on the highway. Nestled in a green meadow at the base of the Swan Mountains, this is a very good B&B with three rooms in the main house and two duplex cabins on the grounds. The cabins are newer, built with square-cut pine logs and furnished with custom lodgepole pine trappings and fridges, microwaves, and coffeemakers. In the main house, the best room is no. 2, with a four-poster queen-size bed, Asian art on its red walls, and a private balcony perfect for watching the sunset. The Bad Rock is known for its lavish breakfasts, which begin with fresh fruit, end with a sweet dessert, and might have biscuits and gravy or French toast stuffed with green apples.

480 Bad Rock Dr., Columbia Falls, MT 59912. (℃) **888/892-2829** or 406/892-2829. Fax 406/892-2930. www.badrock. com. 3 main house units, 4 cabin units. $159–$179 double. Rates include full breakfast. AE, DC, MC, V. **Amenities:** Outdoor Jacuzzi; game room. *In room:* A/C, hair dryer.

Meadow Lake Resort 🎿 Meadow Lake offers a wide variety of excellent accommodations in a modern-resort style. Development focuses on the golf course, which is one of the best in the state. Rooms are stylish in the modern sense, and many of the condo units have Jacuzzis. The resort has a recreation center with Nautilus weight machines and aerobic equipment. There is a large pool and hot tub. The inn features standard-size hotel rooms with a king-size bed, double sleeper sofa, a large bathroom with double vanity sinks, and a veranda or patio. The condos come in suites (a single room with kitchen, bathroom, and, usually, a Jacuzzi), or one- and two-bedroom versions. They all have fireplaces, full kitchens, convenient washer and dryer access, private deck with barbecue, VCR, and stereo. Even if you haven't come for golf, this is still the best place to spend the night.

100 St. Andrews Dr., Columbia Falls, MT 59912. (℃) **800/321-4653** or 406/892-8700. Fax 406/892-8731. www.meadow lake.com. 24 units in inn plus a wide variety of condos and rental homes. $95–$165 at inn; $130–$445 condo or home. AE, DC, MC, V. **Amenities:** Restaurant; lounge; indoor and outdoor heated pools; 18-hole golf course; exercise room; spa; Jacuzzi; sauna; children's program; game room; activities desk; courtesy car; massage; dry cleaning and laundry service. *In room:* A/C, TV/VCR, kitchen, coffeemaker.

Western Inn/Glacier Mountain Shadow Resort *(Value)* This recently renovated, low-cost hostelry offers clean, comfortable accommodations with prices to match their modesty. Single rooms come with one queen-size bed, and double rooms have two queen-size beds. The accommodations are no better or worse than those found in a typical low-cost national chain. Also available for rent are 13 RV campsites (about $25 each).

At the intersection of U.S. 2 and U.S. 206, Columbia Falls, MT 59912. (℃) **406/892-7686.** Fax 406/892-4575. 22 units. $75–$115 double; $175 suite. Rates include continental breakfast. AE, DISC, MC, V. **Amenities:** Outdoor heated pool; 2 indoor Jacuzzis; coin-op washers and dryers. *In room:* TV.

WHERE TO DINE

The Back Room of the Nite Owl *(Value)* AMERICAN This old-fashioned roadside diner is just off the main drag in Columbia Falls. You'll be pleasantly surprised by what the joint has to offer—the roasted chicken, spareribs, and country ribs (small chunks cooked in barbecue sauce) are all delicious and reasonably priced. Fry bread is the house specialty and comes with meals instead of standard bread items. The Sunday pizza, fried chicken, and salad buffet is a bargain for $8.

U.S. 2 E. (near the intersection with 4th Ave.). (℃) **406/892-3131.** Most items $6–$13. AE, DISC, MC, V. Mon–Sat 4–10pm; Sun 2–10pm.

7

Helena & Southwestern Montana

This is where Montana came of age, changing in a few short years from an isolated outback of fur traders and rugged explorers to a series of bustling, boisterous mining camps, where fortunes were made and lost overnight. Butte was once the "Richest Hill on Earth," and gold strikes were also made at Helena's Last Chance Gulch and Virginia City's Alder Gulch. Bannack, another gold-mining boomtown, was the first territorial capital.

The area has calmed down somewhat since then. Butte's Berkeley Pit, full of toxic water, is a Superfund site. The Anaconda copper smelter is shut down, and the Old Works is now a golf course.

Helena is the businesslike state capital, the seat of Montana's politics.

But in the Big Hole Valley, you can still see some ranching and farming done the old-fashioned way. There are plenty of fishing and outdoor opportunities all over the mountains that cloak southwestern Montana.

While signs of modern American life are now rampant, many cross sections of this region's storied past have been meticulously preserved. The old prison at Deer Lodge can give you an eye-opening perspective on frontier justice, and the preserved mining towns of Nevada City and Virginia City provide a taste of the boomtown, mining-camp life.

1 Scenic Drives

Two high-speed highways—interstates 90 and 15—intersect in the region, but the best roads to take are the well-maintained back roads: state and county highways that follow unlikely and out-of-the-way paths. Traveling from Anaconda to Dillon could be done via the interstate in good time, just over an hour. But a better, less-frequented route through the Big Hole Valley runs east of the Continental Divide and the Anaconda-Pintler Wilderness Area. A good stopping point is Wisdom, which has the dubious distinction of being one of the coldest places in the Lower 48, and the turnoff for the Big Hole National Battlefield. Driving farther south on Mont. 278 takes you to Jackson, then Bannack State Park, before ending at I-15 south of Dillon. From Dillon, drive north on Mont. 41 to Twin Bridges and the junction with Mont. 287. This road runs south through the Old West towns of Sheridan, Laurin, Alder, Nevada City, and Virginia City, before ending in Ennis at the junction with U.S. 287.

DRIVING TOUR 1: THE BIG HOLE VALLEY

This short loop tour takes you through the Big Hole Valley, nicknamed "Land of 10,000 Haystacks." Begin in Dillon, the largest of the towns in this area, and keep your eye out for white-tailed and mule deer in the morning and early evening. Travel

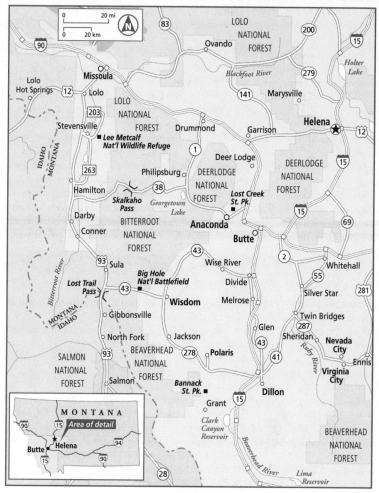

north on I-15 to Divide, then take Mont. 43 southwest to Wisdom. This is a tiny town with little other than its residents and the scenery to recommend it, but the Big Hole National Battlefield (described in detail later in this chapter) is a short drive west on Mont. 43 and is well worth the trip.

Then head back to Wisdom and take Mont. 278 south toward Dillon. Along the way, stop in Jackson for a soak in the hot springs, or tour Montana's territorial capital city, Bannack, in Bannack State Park (see section 6, later in this chapter) just 28 miles farther, off Mont. 278. As you stroll the boardwalks you'll discover the ease with which you can lose yourself in the state's early history—a microcosm that reflects the entire Old West. This drive is great during the summer, when haystacks fill the fields and the Bannack Days celebration re-creates early events in Montana's history. It's not so tame during winter months, though, when roads are icy and caution is required.

DRIVING TOUR 2: THE PINTLER SCENIC ROUTE

This tour is best enjoyed during summer, when area attractions open their doors to visitors and long summer days extend daylight hours.

This scenic route takes you from the mining city of Anaconda on a loop tour with ghost towns, historic buildings, and wildlife. Starting in Anaconda—where you can visit the copper-smelting display at the Copper Village Museum or admire an old Art Deco theater, **The Washoe,** which was ranked fifth in the nation by David Naylor *(American Picture Palaces)* for its architectural value—you'll head on little-traveled roads into a mountainous area that rivals any in the state.

Northwest of Anaconda on Mont. 1 lies **Georgetown Lake,** a popular tourist destination in both summer and winter, when anglers and skiers flock to the lake and nearby ski area, **Discovery.** There are dog-sled races here on winter Sundays. Continue on Mont. 1 to Drummond, known as the "Bull Shipper's Capital of the World."

Heading southeast on I-90 will take you to **Deer Lodge,** home to the state prison, historic **Grant-Kohrs Ranch,** and the **Montana Auto Museum,** which features a slightly depleted collection of 120 antique automobiles—restored, original models from the early 1900s to the 1960s. County Road 273 takes you back to Anaconda.

2 Helena ⓒ★

64 miles N of Butte; 115 miles SE of Missoula; 89 miles S of Great Falls

Cradled in the foothills of the Montana Rockies, Helena is the focal point of the state's politics and culture. During the week, it's a bustling community of politicians, lobbyists, and bureaucrats. On the weekends, however, it seems they all turn into outdoors fanatics, heading to the lakes and mountains. Helena is also a haven for artists and other creative types, evidenced by the galleries that dot the streets once dominated by mining-era saloons and houses of ill repute.

In its early days, Helena was a wild-and-woolly boomtown, built on gold mining. Last Chance Gulch was named when four miners said they had one last chance to hit it big in the West—and they did. The town boomed in the gold rush of 1865. During the height of this prosperity, only Manhattan could boast more millionaires than the small Montana city. And along the way, the town recorded an alarming number of murders and robberies. Then, in 1935, earthquakes devastated the town. Beginning October 3, more than 2,000 tremors rocked the city, causing millions of dollars in damage.

After Helena took state capital rights from Virginia City in 1875, Marcus Daly, the Butte copper king with more than just a bystander's interest in the capital's location, decided to steal it away from Helena and move it to Anaconda, 25 miles from Butte. As we all now know, Daly's efforts proved unsuccessful, but he started a political war that echoes throughout the state even today.

GETTING THERE   SkyWest/Delta (ⓒ 800/453-9417), **Horizon** (ⓒ 800/547-9308 or 406/442-0930), **Northwest** (ⓒ 800/225-2525), and **Big Sky** (ⓒ 800/237-7788) provide commuter links to larger airports in Montana and other Western states from **Helena Regional Airport** (ⓒ 406/442-2821), northeast of the city on Skyway Drive off U.S. 15.

The **bus depot** is located at 3100 U.S. 12 E. (ⓒ **406/442-5860**), with service on **Rimrock Stages,** a Trailways affiliate (ⓒ **800/255-7655;** www.rimrocktrailways.com) that links with Greyhound.

Helena

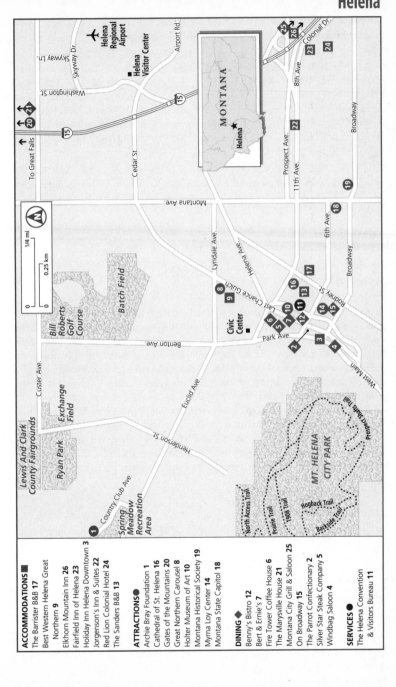

ACCOMMODATIONS ■
The Barrister B&B **17**
Best Western Helena Great
  Northern **9**
Elkhorn Mountain Inn **26**
Fairfield Inn of Helena **23**
Holiday Inn Helena Downtown **3**
Jorgenson's Inn & Suites **22**
Red Lion Colonial Hotel **24**
The Sanders B&B **13**

ATTRACTIONS ●
Archie Bray Foundation **1**
Cathedral of St. Helena **16**
Gates of the Mountains **20**
Great Northern Carousel **8**
Holter Museum of Art **10**
Montana Historical Society **19**
Myrna Loy Center **14**
Montana State Capitol **18**

DINING ◆
Benny's Bistro **12**
Bert & Ernie's **7**
Fire Tower Coffee House **6**
The Marysville House **21**
Montana City Grill & Saloon **25**
On Broadway **15**
The Parrot Confectionary **2**
Silver Star Steak Company **5**
Windbag Saloon **4**

SERVICES ●
The Helena Convention
  & Visitors Bureau **11**

Driving from the east or west, take I-90; turn north on I-15 and head toward Helena. From the north or south, I-15 leads right into town.

VISITOR INFORMATION A good starting point for local activities and area maps is the **Helena Convention and Visitor's Bureau** at 225 Cruse Ave., Suite A, Helena, MT 59601 (*©* **800/743-5352** or 406/447-1530; fax 406/447-1532; www. helenacvb.visitmt.com). There is an information office run by the chamber out near the airport at Cedar Street off I-15. Another source is **Gold West Country** (a branch of Travel Montana, the mother lode for brochures and information about the region and the state) 1155 Main St., Deer Lodge, MT 59722 (*©* **800/VISIT-MT** or 406/ 846-1943; http://goldwest.visitmt.com).

GETTING AROUND Car-rental agencies at the airport include **Avis** (*©* 800/ 831-2847 or 406/442-4440), **Hertz** (*©* 800/654-3131 or 406/449-4167), and **National** (*©* 800/227-7368 or 406/442-8620). **Enterprise** (*©* 800/736-8222 or 406/449-3400) is in town at 1521 N. Montana Ave.

GETTING OUTSIDE

Just beyond the city limits, the area is chock-full of recreational opportunities, with blue-ribbon trout streams, downhill ski areas, and millions of acres of public land.

FISHING

There are several stretches of prime fishing along the upper stretch of the Missouri River. The section from **Toston Dam** downstream to **Canyon Ferry Lake** offers brown and rainbow trout in the 2- to 10-pound class. Floating with large streamers, wet flies, and lures is the most popular and productive way to catch these fish as they make their way upriver to spawn. The fishing gets progressively better from late spring to fall. The section below **Hauser Dam** to **Beaver Creek** offers a chance for really big trout. Other popular fishing areas include **Park Lake** 15 miles southwest of Helena, **Lake Helena,** and the **Smith River** to the east of the Big Belt Mountains.

Paul Roos Outfitters, 418 N. Last Chance Gulch (*©* **800/858-3497** or 406/442-5489; www.paulroosoutfitters.com), offers customized fly-fishing trips on the Smith River, considered in fishing circles one of the best in the state, and in the world. The company offers all-inclusive 3-day trips ($1,525) and 5-day trips ($3,250) from mid-May to mid-July, as well as day trips on the Missouri River.

HIKING

Mount Helena City Park covers 628 acres on Mount Helena, a 5,468-foot peak that looks out over the city. Nine trails cover the park, the easiest of which, the **1906 Trail,** follows the base of the limestone cliffs past Devil's Kitchen to the 5,468-foot summit. To reach the 1906 Trail, take W. Main south of downtown and turn right on Reeder's Village Drive. Drive up the hill to the dead end and you're at the trail head. **Hogback Trail** is a rough and rocky hike that leads from the peak to the exposed Hogback Ridge. Contact the Helena Convention and Visitor's Bureau (*©* **406/447-1530**) for information.

There are more than 700 miles of trails in the Helena National Forest. The **Trout Creek Canyon Trail** offers a spectacular view of Hanging Valley. Helena is also the gateway to the **Gates of the Mountains Wilderness.** For a serious hike in the wilderness area, you can go to **Mann Gulch,** the site of a forest fire in August 1949. Sixteen firefighters parachuted into Mann Gulch at about 6pm on August 5. Within 2 hours, all but three had perished. The incident is the subject of Norman Maclean's book,

Young Men and Fire. You can get more information about hiking into Mann Gulch from the Helena Ranger district ((C) **406/449-5490**).

ROCKHOUNDING

Helena was founded on gold mining, and the area is still rightly famous for its gemstones, particularly Montana sapphires. Sapphires, a variety of the mineral corundum, are harder than any natural stone except a diamond. The Helena area has several commercial areas that allow visitors to dig for sapphires. Diligent treasure seekers can also uncover garnets, moss agates, fossils, and hematite. The **Spokane Bar Sapphire Mine & Gold Fever Rock Shop,** 5360 Castles Rd. ((C) **406/227-8989;** www.sapphire mine.com), south of Hauser Lake lets groups dig buckets for about $60. The record sapphire taken from here was 155 carats.

SKIING

Great Divide Ski Area   Great Divide is primarily a local ski hill, not a destination resort, but the resort has added a half-pipe and night lights while expanding to 1,600 acres. Belying a 1,500-foot vertical drop, it is also pretty tough (15% beginner, 40% intermediate, and 45% advanced), although the Lower Mountain offers wide-open runs that cater to novice and intermediate skiers. There are a total of 139 trails on a trio of mountains served by five double chairs and a surface tow.

There is also the Beginner's Backyard with a free lift and free ski-instruction sessions for entry-level skiers every day and a terrain park for snowboarders. Private lessons are also available through the ski school.

P.O. Box SKI, Marysville, MT 59640. (C) 406/449-3746. Snow reports 406/447-1310. www.greatdividemontana.com. Lift tickets $29 adults, $14–$24 students and seniors, free for children 5 and under with adult; rate reductions at noon and 4pm and Wed–Thurs Jan–Apr. Mid-Nov to early Apr Wed–Sun 9am–4pm with some night skiing. Take exit 200 off I-15, then go west on Mont. 279 to Marysville Rd.

SNOWMOBILING

Three major trail systems are within a 30-minute drive of Helena. The Minnehaha-Rimini area grooms 120 miles of trails, and the Marysville and Magpie-Sunshine areas, with views into the Gates of the Mountains Wilderness, each groom 45 miles of trails. For details on these trails, as well as special event information, contact the **Helena Snowdrifters Snowmobile Club** at P.O. Box 5505, Helena, MT 59604 ((C) **406/443-0108** or 406/458-5423).

WATERSPORTS

Canyon Ferry Lake Recreation Area, managed by the Bureau of Reclamation ((C) **406/475-3310** or 406/475-3921), is a 25-mile-long lake within 20 minutes of Helena. In the spring, summer, and fall, the lake is primarily a rainbow trout fishery, but it does have numerous campgrounds, picnic areas, and boat ramps. The lake is especially popular with water-skiers, jet-skiers, and water-tubers, though you'll see sailboats racing as well. This is also a prime bird-watching area—hundreds of eagles migrate through Canyon Ferry each year from mid-October to mid-December, but the numbers are declining in tandem with those of spawning kokanee salmon below the dam.

Watersports fans also head to two Helena-area state parks that are centered on manmade lakes: **Spring Meadow Lake** (day use only) and **Black Sandy** at Hauser Reservoir (campsites: $15). Spring Meadow is a 30-acre, spring-fed lake on Helena's western edge, noted for its clarity and depth. Open to nonmotorized boats only, the lake is popular for swimming and fishing. To reach Spring Meadow Lake, take U.S. 12 west, then head north on Joslyn to Country Club. One of the only public parks on the shores of Hauser Reservoir, Black Sandy is an extremely popular weekend boating, fishing, and water-skiing takeoff point. To get to Hauser Reservoir, drive 7 miles north of Helena on I-15, then 4 miles east on Route 453, then follow signs 3 miles north on a county road. Information on both is available by calling © **406/495-3270** and each sports a $5 per vehicle day-use fee.

SEEING THE SIGHTS

A walking tour of the city will give you a capsule of the history of the Old West. For pointers on where to explore, contact the **Helena Convention and Visitor's Bureau** (© **800/743-5352** or 406/442-1530) and request one of the excellent walking tour brochures by the Montana Historical Society.

Last Chance Gulch was so named because a quartet of gold-seeking prospectors declared the spot to be their "last chance" to strike it rich. It came to be one of the richest gold-producing areas in the world and remains one of Helena's main streets. Located downtown, this historic area combines Helena's colorful past with a contemporary freshness. Architecturally significant buildings, many of which are listed on the National Register of Historic Places, house espresso shops and boutiques, while ultramodern sculptures depict historical events. Interpretive markers are scattered along the pedestrian mall, with historical information relating to period construction. **Kumamoto Prefecture** in Japan is Montana's "sister state," and the prefecture maintains a cultural center at 34 N. Last Chance Gulch (© **406/449-7904**). Visitors are welcome, and it's free. For a great place to play chess or checkers, head to the south end of Last Chance Gulch, where you'll find concrete tables with checkerboard tile inlays.

In Jefferson City, 15 miles south of Helena via I-15, the **Tizer Botanic Gardens & Arboretum,** 38 Tizer Lake Rd. (© **406/933-8789;** www.tizergardens.org), is the only botanic garden in the vicinity, a peaceful display of bulbs, perennials, roses, and other plants crisscrossed by paths. It's open May through September; admission is $4 (free for kids under 6).

Archie Bray Foundation   Archie Bray, a Helena resident and enthusiastic supporter of the arts, established this artistic colony for potters in 1951 at the brickyard and kilns of the Western Clay Manufacturing Company. Over the years it has become a premier testing ground for ceramic artists, working together to share ideas and techniques. Various playful sculptures dot the lawns. Of special note are several larger, freestanding monuments by Robert Harrison, including *A Potter's Shrine,* dedicated to Bray and incorporating some materials up to 100 years old; *Tile-X,* stacked drain tiles in the shape of a pyramid; and *Aruina,* a monument of brick and tile whose four arches frame the surrounding Helena landscape. Because of the intimate nature of each individual resident's art-making process, visitors are asked to respect their privacy. Allow 1 to 2 hours.

2915 Country Club Ave. © **406/443-3502.** www.archiebray.org. Free admission. Gallery Mon–Sat 10am–5pm, Sun 1–5pm, with ceramic art for sale. Visitors may take a self-guided walking tour of the grounds during daylight hours.

Cathedral of St. Helena   Completed in 1924, the Cathedral of St. Helena was modeled on a church in Vienna, Austria. Its beautiful twin 230-foot spires seem ready to soar heavenward on their own, filigreed and light. The cathedral is decorated with magnificent Bavarian stained-glass windows, hand-carved oak pews, hand-forged bronze light fixtures, and Carrara marble statues. At one time it was open to all who wandered by, but there are now times when the cathedral is left unattended and the doors are locked. So if you want to see the inside, it is best to call ahead. Masses are held here daily.

530 N. Ewing. ℂ **406/442-5825.** Open to public; hours vary. Call to arrange a free group tour.

Gates of the Mountains Boat Tours
Meriwether Lewis coined the name "Gates of the Mountains" while plying this portion of the Missouri with his party. At almost every bend in the waterway, the towering rock formations seemed to block their passage, only to magically open up as they drew closer. Visitors can have an experience similar to Lewis's through a boat tour of this scenic riverway on the *Pirogue*, the *Sacajawea II*, or the *Hilger Rose*. The 105-minute excursions take you through the mountain "gates," past prehistoric pictographs on the limestone rocks, to a picnic area where wildlife-viewing opportunities abound. You can choose to return on a later boat and take a hike into the nearby Gates of the Mountains Wilderness Area.

P.O. Box 478, Helena, MT 59624. ℂ **406/458-5241.** www.gatesofthemountains.com. $10 adults, $9 seniors, $6 children 4–17, free for children under 4. Memorial Day to late Sept; call for cruise schedule departures and returns. From Helena, drive 18 miles north on I-15 to exit 209 (Gates of the Mountains).

Holter Museum of Art ☆
Considered one of the premier galleries in the state, the Holter displays artwork in 7,200 square feet and features 10 to 14 different shows each year, all of which include an intriguing diversity of media and styles. Specializing in contemporary art of the Northwest region, the museum provides exhibition space for local as well as nationally prominent artists, and is definitely worth an hour of time. The museum also runs a summer arts-education program for youngsters and adults and is home to a slick gift shop. Allow 1 or 2 hours.

12 E. Lawrence St. ℂ **406/442-6400.** www.holtermuseum.org. Free admission. Mid-June to early Sept Mon–Fri 10am–6pm, Sat 10am–5pm, Sun noon–5pm; early Sept to mid-June Tues–Sat 10am–5pm, Sun noon–5pm.

Last Chance Tour Train
A train engine on wheels pulls you around Helena on a tour of its historic sites, including the Atlas Block, the Montana Club, and the old governor's mansion. This is an excellent way to get oriented in Helena and learn a few things about the city at the same time. The tours last 1 hour.

Tours leave from the Montana Historical Society Building, 225 N. Roberts. ℂ **888/423-1023** or 406/442-1023. www.lctours.com. $6.50 adults, $6 seniors, $5.50 children 4–12, free for children under 4. Mid-May to mid-Sept; tour times vary seasonally.

The Montana Historical Society Museum ☆
The Montana Historical Society maintains a library and archives, as well as a museum. The **Montana Homeland Gallery** displays the history of Montana going back over 11,000 years. On display are petroglyphs, dinosaur bones, and implements of the earliest American Indians and first European settlers. Walls are adorned with calendars dating from 1906, some of which have profit-and-loss calculations scribbled on them by their rancher-owners. The **Mackay Gallery** has a permanent display of original Charlie Russell masterpieces—more than 60 artworks, including oils, watercolors, sculptures, and Russell's famous illustrated letters—that showcase one of the West's most remarkable artists. The **Northeast and Haynes galleries** house seasonal exhibits. The mounted hide of Big Medicine, a sacred, rare white bison that lived on Montana's National Bison Range from 1933 to 1959, is on display on the second-floor mezzanine.

Guided tours of the original **governor's mansion** ($4 adults, $1 children 5–18, $10 maximum per family), located at 304 N. Ewing, are also available through the society.

This Queen Anne–style mansion with a distinctive checkerboard background was constructed in 1888 for entrepreneur William A. Chessman and his family. The state acquired the mansion in 1913 and governors resided here for half a century, during which time the mansion lost much of its original historical flavor. However, a major restoration of the building was undertaken beginning in 1969, and much of its allure has been recovered. From May to September, tours operate on the hour from noon to 4pm Tuesday through Sunday, and Saturdays from noon to 4pm the rest of the year. Allow about 2 hours.

225 N. Roberts St. ℂ 406/444-2694. www.montanahistoricalsociety.org. $5 adults, $1 children 5–18, free for children under 5, with a $12 maximum per family. Mon–Sat 9am–5pm (Thurs until 8pm). Library and archives: Tues–Fri 9am–5pm; Sat 9am–1pm.

Montana State Capitol   Several years ago Montana's beautiful state capitol building underwent extensive renovations, revitalizing the historic grandeur that was lost during construction in the 1960s. Situated on 14 acres, the building was designed by architects Charles Bell and John Kent in the late 1800s. It's decorated in the French Renaissance style with frescoes, a grand stained-glass dome, and murals. The dome, faced with copper, rises 165 feet. Inside are murals by noted Montana artists Charlie Russell, Edgar Paxson, and Ralph DeCamp, including Russell's famed *Lewis and Clark Meeting Indians at Ross' Hole.* The grounds and flower gardens of the state capitol building in Helena are a designated state park, visited by thousands of people each year.

Montana Ave. and 6th St. ℂ 406/444-4789. www.montanacapitol.com. Free admission; no charge for tours. Building Mon–Fri 8am–5pm. May–Sept Montana Historical Society gives daily tours on the hour Mon–Sat 9am–3pm, Sun 11am–4pm; rest of year (even-numbered years only) tours on the hour Sat 10am–2pm.

SHOPPING

Last Chance Gulch is a 4-block-long pedestrian mall. Though it is not exclusively a shopping area, the office buildings are liberally interspersed with boutiques, restaurants, pubs, and places for the kids to play. Informational kiosks are located in the center of this walking mall and at its north end. **Main News,** 9 N. Last Chance Gulch (ℂ **406/442-6424**), is a tobacco shop with various statewide, regional, and city newspapers. It's located in the **Atlas Block,** one of a group of historically significant architectural structures in Last Chance Gulch. Helena's main areas were leveled several times in the last 125 years or so, once by earthquakes (in 1935) and several times by fire in the 19th century and again in 1928. In response to the fires, builders in the Atlas Block carved images of salamanders, which in mythology are impervious to fire. **Lasso the Moon,** 25 S. Last Chance Gulch (ℂ **406/442-1594**), is a classic toyshop, featuring rack after rack of unique toys that aren't stocked by the mass-market retailers. Next door at 21 S. Last Chance Gulch, is the **Ghost Art Gallery** (ℂ **406/443-4536**), which features art on Western and nature themes. Another good gallery is **Upper Missouri Artists,** 7 N. Last Chance Gulch (ℂ **406/457-8240**).

   The attractive **Great Northern Town Center** is an emerging retail area just west of the intersection of Lyndale Avenue and Last Chance Gulch. Here, **Cobblestone Clothing,** 828 Great Northern Blvd., Suite 103 (ℂ **406/449-8684**), sells upscale women's apparel with a hint of the New West; **Grand Junction Mercantile,** 825 Great Northern Blvd. (ℂ **406/442-6210**), is the place for gifts. There is also a new eight-screen movie theater here.

ESPECIALLY FOR KIDS

Great Northern Carousel *Kids* Privately built by the developer of the Great Northern Town Center, this new carousel is an enchanting work of art, with a definitive Montana spin—there are hand-carved bison, grizzly bears, dinosaurs, otters, and bighorn sheep alongside the horses, frogs, and pigs. There is also the Painted Pony Ice Cream Parlor and a gift shop on-site.

924 Bicentennial Plaza (at the Great Northern Town Center). ☎ 406/457-5353. $1 per ride. Memorial Day to Labor Day Sun–Thurs 10am–9pm, Fri–Sat 10am–10pm; rest of year Sun–Thurs 11:30am–8pm, Fri 11:30am–9pm, Sat 10am–8pm.

The Parrot Confectionery *Kids* Kids and adults alike will love this colorful candy store, established in 1922. The Parrot serves up its original cherry phosphates and caramel-cashew sundaes from the soda fountain, beneath its charming collection of ceramic elephants. Family-owned, The Parrot has provided gourmet chocolate and candy to Helena for more than 80 years, and loyal customers attest that the place and its products haven't changed a bit over time. In addition to its Helena clientele, The Parrot supplies candy to chocoholics from nearly every state in the union. It's known for its signature parrot confection, chocolate-covered caramels, and many other candies. They also have a "secret recipe" chili for lunch.

42 N. Last Chance Gulch. ☎ 406/442-1470. Mon–Sat 9am–6pm (soda fountain open until 5:30pm).

WHERE TO STAY

There's no shortage of good accommodations in Helena, with a bevy of historic inns and a number of business-oriented hotels and motels that cater to traveling politicos of all stripes. Aside from the options discussed below, you might try the **Holiday Inn Helena Downtown,** 22 N. Last Chance Gulch (☎ 406/443-2200), a seven-story brick edifice with double rates of $85 to $105. The **Fairfield Inn of Helena,** 2150 11th Ave. (☎ 800/228-2800 or 406/449-9944), is another good option, with doubles for $75 to $85 and an indoor pool, as is the independent **Elkhorn Mountain Inn,** 1 Jackson Creek Rd. at I-15, exit 187 (☎ 406/442-6625; www.elkhorninn. com), a top-drawer mom-and-pop just south of Helena with a double rate of $71.

The Barrister Bed-and-Breakfast ✦ Located directly across the street from the Cathedral of St. Helena, The Barrister is one of many elegant homes near the original governor's mansion. Built in 1874 and listed on the National Register of Historic Places, this Queen Anne–style gem was renovated in 1992 and opened as a B&B in 1993. The rooms are large and elegantly furnished with antiques. Each has a private bathroom—though some are across the hall. A nice touch is that each room has a black-and-white photo of what it looked like in the 19th century, courtesy of the Montana Historical Society. Most of the rooms are somewhat frilly, aside from the manly Captain's Suite, with a rich red carpet and a nautical theme. The third floor is a two-bedroom apartment that rents for $150 per night but is usually leased on longer term, by the week or month. The common areas include a parlor, sun porch, den, TV room/library, laundry room, and office with high-speed DSL Internet connection.

416 N. Ewing St., Helena, MT 59601. ☎ 800/823-1148 or 406/443-7330. Fax 406/442-7964. http://thebarrister mt.tripod.com. 5 units. $95–$150 double. Rates include full breakfast. AE, DC, DISC, MC, V. Pets accepted. **Amenities:** TV room/library; office w/high-speed Internet connection. *In room:* A/C, cable TV w/VCR, dataport, hair dryer, no phone.

Best Western Helena Great Northern ✦ Helena's newest hotel has rich, somewhat masculine rooms with two queen-size beds or a king-size, high ceilings, railroad-themed art, and a striking red contrast wall. Some of the rooms have fridges, and six of them open up to both the hall and the indoor pool. The hotel is the anchor of the new Great Northern Town Center development, and is adjacent to a steakhouse on one side and a health club on the other. It's a bit outside of walking distance to downtown Helena, but worth the short drive because of the rooms' freshness and comfort, which overshadow the downtown Holiday Inn. There's a restaurant attached, the **Silver Star Steak Company** (see "Where to Dine," below), that is under different ownership but will deliver to your room. The entire property is nonsmoking.

835 Great Northern Blvd., Helena, MT 59601. ℭ **800/829-4047** or 406/457-5500. www.gnhotelhelena.com. 101 units. $95–$135 double; $135–$145 suite. AE, DC, DISC, MC, V. **Amenities:** Indoor pool; exercise room; indoor Jacuzzi; courtesy car; business center; Wi-Fi network; limited room service; coin-op washers and dryers; dry cleaning. *In room:* A/C, cable TV w/pay movies, dataport (w/complimentary high-speed Internet), coffeemaker, hair dryer, iron.

Jorgenson's Inn & Suites *Value*

Jorgenson's has been a Helena institution since the 1950s, and offers a relative bargain. As you might expect in an older place, the rooms are a little smaller than those in most newer motels, but they have been religiously renovated, modernized, and refurbished throughout the years; some have microwaves and fridges. Guests also have access to the fully equipped fitness center across the street.

1714 11th Ave., Helena, MT 59601. ℭ **800/272-1770** or 406/442-1770. Fax 406/449-0155. 116 units. www.jorgensons inn.com. $59–$109 double. AE, DC, DISC, MC, V. **Amenities:** Restaurant; lounge/casino; small indoor pool; access to nearby fitness center; courtesy car. *In room:* A/C, cable TV, dataport, coffeemaker.

Red Lion Colonial Hotel

This is a fairly upscale property, with a spiral stairway inside that you might expect Scarlett O'Hara to come sweeping down at any moment. The rooms are huge by any standard, and the location right by the interstate is convenient for travelers. Some rooms also offer panoramic views of the valley and mountains beyond. The suites include king-size beds, refrigerators, and microwaves; some have private Jacuzzis.

2301 Colonial Dr. (just off I-15 at U.S. 12), Helena, MT 59601. ℭ **800/733-5466** or 406/443-2100. Fax 406/449-8815. www.redlion.com. 149 units. $79–$129 double. AE, DC, DISC, MC, V. **Amenities:** Restaurant; lounge; indoor and outdoor heated pools; room service; Jacuzzi; dry cleaning. *In room:* A/C, cable TV w/pay movies, dataport, coffeemaker, hair dryer, iron.

The Sanders B&B *ƐƐ*

The Sanders is a lesson in Montana history all on its own. Built and owned by Wilbur Fisk Sanders in 1875, the B&B has been beautifully restored by Bobbi Uecker (no relation to former ballplayer Bob) and Rock Ringling (a fourth-generation descendant of the famous circus family). Sanders was Montana's first U.S. senator and made his reputation by vigorously prosecuting the infamous Plummer gang in Virginia City. The Uecker-Ringlings are only the third owners of the property, and they purchased it with nearly all of its furnishings, most once owned by Sanders himself. As a result, guests sleep on beds from 1875 and look at the same pictures that Sanders did. (One was painted by his wife, an important Western suffragette in her day.) Bobbi's enthusiasm shows in every detail, from the savory breakfasts, where she's willing to accommodate every kind of dietary restriction, to the advice she can offer on Helena's restaurants and attractions. Our favorite accouterment is the elephant "bridle" in the Sanders Suite, marked with a big round disc reading "The Greatest Show on Earth." Wonder where they got that?

328 N. Ewing, Helena, MT 59601. ℭ **406/442-3309.** Fax 406/443-2361. www.sandersbb.com. 7 units. $110–$125 double. Rates include full breakfast and afternoon refreshments. AE, DC, DISC, MC, V. **Amenities:** Wireless DSL. *In room:* A/C, TV/VCR, dataport, hair dryer.

CAMPING

Kim's Marina and RV Resort, 8015 Canyon Ferry Rd. (20 miles west of town), Helena, MT 59601 (℗ **406/475-3723;** www.kimsmarina.com), has a complete resort facility that includes comfortable cabins situated on the lakefront. Canoes, deck boats, and paddle boats are for rent on a daily basis. You'll find 50 tent and 60 RV sites as well as tennis, volleyball, horseshoes, and boat rentals. **The Lakeside Resort,** 11 miles east of Helena on York Road near Hauser Lake (℗ **406/227-6413**), is an RV park that is open year-round with 70 full hookups and an on-site bar, restaurant, beach, and picnic area. North of town 3 miles on Montana Avenue is the **Helena Campground and RV Park,** with green grass and shade, an all-you-can-eat breakfast, and an ice-cream social in the summer. It's located at 5820 N. Montana Ave. (℗ **406/458-4714;** www.helenacampgroundrvpark.com). At all three, the going rate for a site with hookups is $25 to $32.

For more primitive sites, the Bureau of Reclamation and Bureau of Land Management jointly run several campgrounds between Townsend in the south and Helena along U.S. 287 at Canyon Ferry Lake. From south to north, they are: **Indian Road Recreation Area** (1 mile north of Townsend on U.S. 287, mile marker 75), Silos (7 miles north of Townsend on U.S. 287, mile marker 70), and **White Earth Campground** (13 miles north of Townsend on U.S. 287 to Winston). The Indian Road Recreation Area offers a fishing pond for children and visitors with disabilities.

WHERE TO DINE

Fire Tower Coffee House, 422 N. Last Chance Gulch (℗ **406/495-8840**), is a nice place to sit in an overstuffed chair and have a cup of coffee, muffin, or sandwich. Wagon ride dinners are available for $59 per person through **Last Chance Ranch,** 2884 Grizzly Gulch (℗ **406/442-2884**).

Benny's Bistro ✦ CREPES/ECLECTIC   This breezy cafe has a jazz theme, with horns and woodwinds on the brick walls and a piano—manned during dinner on Fridays—and big windows that face the street. The open kitchen in the back specializes in crepes for dinner, stuffing them with everything from curried shrimp to smoked salmon to veggies and brie. Beyond the delectable crepes, the dinner menu includes a killer (and meatless) Mediterranean polenta, pesto-stuffed scallops, and a tenderloin steak (this is Montana, after all). Lunches consist of gourmet sandwiches of focaccia-style bread; breakfasts are scones, frittatas, and fruit crisps. This is the spot to eat downtown if you're looking for casually upscale, but not stuffy.

108 E. 6th Ave. ℗ **406/443-0105.** Breakfast $1.50–$4.50; lunch $5.50–$7; dinner $12–$21. MC, V. Mon–Fri 8:30am–3pm; Thurs–Sat 5:30–9pm. Closed Sun.

Bert & Ernie's AMERICAN   A stalwart bar and grill in downtown Helena since 1974, Bert & Ernie's has occupied its present Last Chance Gulch location (a former clothing store) since 1990 and remains a good, reliable pick for a casual lunch or dinner. The fun atmosphere with the requisite clutter hanging from the walls (stuffed animals, neon signs, stained glass, and such) is a good match for the menu, a mix of sandwiches, burgers, Mexican fare, and dinner entrees like Atlantic mussels, jambalaya, and steaks. Attached and under the same ownership is the intimate **Sommeliers,** an upscale wine bar that serves appetizers and desserts.

361 N. Last Chance Gulch. ℗ **406/443-5680.** Reservations accepted. Main courses $7–$25. AE, DISC, MC, V. Sun–Thurs 10am–9pm; Fri–Sat 10am–10pm.

The Marysville House ✦ STEAKS/SEAFOOD   Every Rocky Mountain state has a barely surviving ghost town with a still-great steakhouse. Marysville, an 1870 gold-mining town, once boasted a population of 4,000—now it's 70. And The Marysville House is the steakhouse that's still going strong, selling the most lobster of any eatery in the state. Located in what was once a train depot, The Marysville House serves steaks, crab legs, and cold, smooth beer in a rustic setting. The no-nonsense meals come with corn on the cob and beans. Guests have their choice of dining inside or out. And how's this for low-key Americana: Meals are served on paper plates, horse-shoes and a marshmallow-roasting fire pit can be found outside, and you can eat at a picnic table on the deck.

153 N. Main St., Marysville, MT (a 45-min. drive from Helena). © **406/443-6677**. www.marysvillemontana.com. Reservations for groups of 10 or more only. Dinner $13–$37. MC, V. Year-round Wed–Sun; hours vary with the seasons; opens about 5pm. From Helena, take U.S. 15 North to exit 200, Mont. 279. Go north on Mont. 279 for 23 miles; turn left at the sign for Marysville for 6 miles to find this living ghost town.

Montana City Grill and Saloon STEAKS   This is a nice, sunny bar and grill that specializes in beef, fish, chicken, pasta, seafood, and ribs. The house specialty is the huckleberry barbecue sauce, which the cook liberally slathers on pork ribs, chicken, and pork chops. The pastel-and-wood dining room is adjoined by the bar, which has a pool table and one of the clearest big-screen televisions in the state. On weekends, the restaurant often features dinner themes, such as Cajun, Italian, or seafood.

Montana City, 5 miles south of Helena on I-15. © **406/449-8890**. Reservations accepted for large parties only. www.montanacitygrill.com. Main courses $13–$30; sandwiches and burgers $6–$8. AE, DC, DISC, MC, V. Mon–Thurs 5am–9pm; Fri–Sat 5–10pm; Sun 8am–9pm. Closed Mon and Tues in winter.

On Broadway ✦✦ ITALIAN   Located in a historic brick building near Last Chance Gulch, On Broadway is the place to go in Helena for good Italian food. It's got a warm atmosphere, brick walls contrasting with ferns and two levels of dining, and exceptional food, with artful combinations of meats and vegetables, fresh herbs, and pasta highlighting the menu. A local favorite is the Chicken alla Broadway, a chicken breast topped with fresh mushrooms and cheese, then baked in a Mornay sauce with mozzarella. The fish menu is the most imaginative, headed up by blackened tuna and oven-roasted salmon.

106 Broadway. © **406/443-1929**. Reservations not accepted. Main courses $11–$25. AE, DISC, MC, V. Mon–Thurs 5:30–9:30pm; Fri–Sat 5:30–10pm.

Silver Star Steak Company ✦ STEAKS/SEAFOOD   The culinary anchor of the new Great Northern Town Center development, the Silver Star is an intimate, contemporary space with hints of the new West and a traditional menu. If a tad unadventurous, the food is quite good, with a nice selection of steaks—recommended are the Tucson Sirloin with spicy lime sauce and the Silver Star Signature Steak, an eight-ounce sirloin served Oscar-style—and seafood. The latter includes halibut stuffed with brie and crab and roasted salmon. There is a less expensive menu served in the bar, with burgers and other dishes running $8 to $16. Lunch includes salads, sandwiches, and pasta dishes.

833 Great Northern Blvd. © **406/495-0677**. Reservations recommended. Lunch $7–$15; dinner $17–$28. AE, DISC, MC, V. Mon–Sat 11:30am–2:30pm; daily 5–10pm. Bar open later.

Windbag Saloon ✦ AMERICAN   Helena residents love this restaurant like you'd love an eccentric aunt: She's the most interesting relative you have and you always have a great time at her place. Who cares if she has a checkered past? So what if one of the cleanest and most respected bordellos in all of Montana once operated in the location where the restaurant now enjoys its own flourishing business? At least it's respectable now, continuing the location's tradition as a focal part of Helena's nightlife. Try one of a long list of microbrews, or order something from the extensive collection of appetizers, before moving on to the Little Ida sandwich, 10 ounces of ground sirloin with peppers and onions, and fries so thick you'll barely be able to finish a serving. Seafood is flown in twice weekly, steaks are hand-cut on the premises, and the daily quiches are top of the line.

19 S. Last Chance Gulch. (© 406/443-9669. Lunch $6–$11; dinner $8–$23. AE, DISC, MC, V. Mon–Fri 11am–2pm; Sat 11:30am–2:30pm; Mon–Sat 5:30–9:30pm.

NIGHTLIFE & THE PERFORMING ARTS

Make it a point to visit the state-of-the-art **Myrna Loy Center for the Performing and Media Arts** ✯, 15 N. Ewing St. (© **406/443-0287;** www.myrnaloycenter.com). Formerly the county jail, the Myrna Loy (named after the silver-screen legend who was one of Helena's most famous residents) is today a multidisciplinary cultural center. Within its castlelike facade are a 55-seat cinema and a 250-seat performance hall, along with a gallery that focuses on regional art. Other playgoing opportunities include productions by **Grandstreet Theatre,** 325 N. Park Ave. (© **406/447-1574;** www.grandstreet.net), and the **Montana Shakespeare Company** (© **406/449-4466;** www.montanashakespeare.org), who take to the stage June through August at Performance Square in downtown Helena.

Of the Queen City's watering holes, we like **Miller's Crossing,** 52 S. Park Ave. (© **406/442-3290**), for the live music, neighborhood atmosphere, and Blackfoot River Brewing suds on tap, and the popular **Brewhouse Pub & Grille,** 939½ Getchell St. (© **406/457-9390**), atop the Lewis & Clark Brewing Company in the Great Northern Town Center area.

3 Butte & Anaconda

Butte: 64 miles S of Helena; 120 miles SE of Missoula; 82 miles W of Bozeman; 150 miles NW of West Yellowstone

Butte may not be most people's idea of a vacation destination, but in many ways the city is the hidden soul of Montana. Butte's emergence in the 19th century as a hellraising, wide-open mining town drew a lot of people to the state, including a variety of racial and ethnic groups. Butte has always been a strong union town in a state and region that disdain union activity. This union and socialist tradition from the rip-roaring days has made a lasting contribution to a strong progressive political tradition.

Butte used to be called "the richest hill on earth," for its production of copper, silver, and other precious metals, and during the 1880s, Butte was the world's largest copper producer. In 1955, the world's richest hill became the beginning of one of the world's largest holes, the Berkeley Pit, which provided more cost-efficient open-pit mining of copper. The pit grew and grew and almost swallowed the town. But after the mine closed in the 1980s, groundwater seeped up through the maze of tunnels below, creating a gigantic pollution problem. The town's drinking water—and very survival—was threatened by this toxic sea, but the problem is now being addressed by a brand-new, $20-million water treatment plant that opened in 2003.

If you can look past the signs of decline that remain from the end of the mining era, Butte is full of rich history, colorful citizens, and a sort of blue-collar San Francisco–style

---

(Tips) **Travel Tip**

When traveling to this part of the state, many folks decide to fly into Salt Lake City, Utah. It's a 5½-hour drive north through some spectacular country to get to this neck of the woods.

---

charm. Physically, Butte is built along the sides of steep hills, which provides a great vantage point on the valley below. It also boasts Montana Tech, an arm of the University of Montana system and one of the top-rated engineering schools in the country.

Anaconda was the "company town" formed when copper king Marcus Daly extended his copper empire 24 miles west. The community was spared the name "Copperopolis."

ESSENTIALS

GETTING THERE The **Bert Mooney Airport** (© **406/494-3771**), is served by **Horizon** (© **800/547-9308**) and **SkyWest** (© **800/453-9417**). The **Greyhound** station in Butte is located at 101 E. Front St. (© **406/723-3287**). For current **weather information,** call © **406/329-4840** or 511.

VISITOR INFORMATION The **Butte Convention and Visitors Bureau Information Center,** 1000 George St., Butte, MT 59701-7901 (© **800/735-6814** or 406/723-3177; www.buttecvb.com), is located just off exit 126 near the intersections of I-15 and I-90. The center is a user-friendly facility just off the freeway, close to a wetlands area where you can take a breather from driving while watching wild ducks, geese, and muskrats go about their business.

The **Anaconda Chamber of Commerce,** 306 E. Park, Anaconda, MT 59711 (© **406/563-2400;** www.anacondamt.org), can give you information on Butte's sister city. For brochures devoted to area attractions and driving tours, contact **Travel Montana's Gold West Country** (© **406/846-1943**).

GETTING AROUND Car-rental agents in Butte include **Avis** (© 406/494-3131), **Budget** (© 406/494-7573), **Enterprise** (© 406/494-1900), **Hertz** (© 406/782-1054), and **Statewide Rent-a-Car** (© 406/723-4366).

The **Butte–Silver Bow Transit System** city buses run from 6:45am to 6:15pm Monday through Friday and 8:45am to 4:45pm on Saturday; for information on fares and stops, call © **406/497-6515. Mining City Taxi** (© **406/723-6511**) provides local transportation 24 hours a day.

SPECIAL EVENTS Butte has a heavy Irish heritage from its days as a mining boomtown. This legacy shines brightly (almost too brightly) on **St. Patrick's Day** 𝄞, when this mining museum of a town throws a shamrock-tinted bash that is the big event of the year—even the banks shut down. The March 17 celebration is one of the biggest St. Patrick's Day parties outside of New York City, but be forewarned: It tends to be very rowdy and very drunk.

If you want a more family-friendly Irish festival, try **An Ri Ra,** an annual 3-day tradition in mid-August. Another fun annual event—which began in 2002—is **Evel Knievel Days,** held in late July and featuring motorcycle stunt shows, a parade, and an appearance by the legendary daredevil himself. Contact the **Butte CVB** (© **800/735-6814**) for the dates and times of these activities.

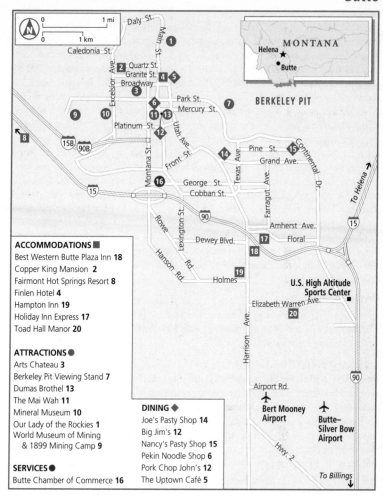

ACCOMMODATIONS ■
Best Western Butte Plaza Inn **18**
Copper King Mansion **2**
Fairmont Hot Springs Resort **8**
Finlen Hotel **4**
Hampton Inn **19**
Holiday Inn Express **17**
Toad Hall Manor **20**

ATTRACTIONS ●
Arts Chateau **3**
Berkeley Pit Viewing Stand **7**
Dumas Brothel **13**
The Mai Wah **11**
Mineral Museum **10**
Our Lady of the Rockies **1**
World Museum of Mining
   & 1899 Mining Camp **9**

SERVICES ●
Butte Chamber of Commerce **16**

DINING ◆
Joe's Pasty Shop **14**
Big Jim's **12**
Nancy's Pasty Shop **15**
Pekin Noodle Shop **6**
Pork Chop John's **12**
The Uptown Café **5**

GETTING OUTSIDE

Lost Creek State Park (© **406/542-5500**), a few miles outside of Anaconda, is a great place to camp or hike, or simply sit and admire the scenery. At the end of the road into the park, a short path will take you to pretty Lost Creek Falls, which tumble over a 50-foot drop. There are also mountain goats and bighorn sheep in residence. Several hiking trails lead off from the road. Among the most interesting things here are the rocks. Exposed on the tops of some cliffs is the 1.3-billion-year-old Newman Formation, a Precambrian rock that's among the oldest exposed rocks in the Lower 48 states. This is a primitive park, without services (and without charge). There are 25 campsites, suitable mostly for tents and car campers. To get to the park, drive 1½ miles east of Anaconda on Mont. 1, then 2 miles north on County Road 273, then 6 miles west on Lost Creek Rd.

GOLF

The **Old Works** ★★, 1205 Pizzini Way, Anaconda (© **406/563-5989;** www.old works.org), is a golf course and a work of art. This is your tax dollars at work, and you should feel good about it. The course is built on a Superfund site that had been a blight on the landscape since 1884, when the upper works began to process 500 tons of copper ore daily under Marcus Daly's voracious eye. By 1887 the lower works were necessary because of the demand. The Old Works closed in 1902, when the new Washoe Smelter—the big tower you can see from anywhere in the valley—took over all the processing. Jack Nicklaus designed the golf course, a tough but fair layout that even eight-handicappers are willing to play from the white tees. The black sand traps, the old processing works, and the vast, forbidding black tailings piles are all worked beautifully into the layout of the course. This is one of the finest courses not just in Montana, but in America. To reach the course, which is open from mid-May to the end of October, take Commercial Street to North Cedar Street, turn north, then east (right) on Pizzini Way. Peak season greens fees are $38 to $41 for 18 holes per person; cart rentals are $13 per person.

There's also an 18-hole course ($29–$39) at nearby **Fairmont Hot Springs Resort** (see "Where to Stay," later in this chapter). **Highland View Golf Course** (© **406/ 494-7900**), at Stodden Park in Butte, has two separate 9-hole courses: a par 3 ($10) and a regulation ($12).

ROCK CLIMBING

Spire Rock and the Humbug Spires are the two most popular routes for rock climbers. The **Bureau of Land Management** (© **406/533-7600**) can refer guides and provide other climbing information.

ROCKHOUNDING

From the Continental Divide east of Butte through the mountains to the south, diligent rockhounders can find smoky quartz, amethyst, epidote, and tourmaline. Ask the curator at the **Mineral Museum** (see "Seeing the Sights," below) on the Montana Tech campus for leads on local hot spots. The **Butte Mineral and Gem Club,** P. O. Box 4492, Butte, MT 59702, has mining claims on **Crystal Park** about 70 miles southwest of Butte that are free and open to the public. From Butte go south on I-15 and west on Mont.43; just past Wise River, turn south on the Pioneer Mountains Scenic Byway and drive about 20 miles to Crystal Park.

SKIING

In addition to **Discovery Ski Area,** Butte visitors are within range of **Maverick Mountain** (see section 4, "Dillon & the Big Hole," later in this chapter).

Tips Butte Touring Tips

From June through September, the **Butte Trolley** tour leaves from the Butte Visitor Center for a 1½-hour tour of the city's key attractions. Driver/tour guides are chosen for their knowledge of the town's history. Call © **406/723-3177** for schedules and other information. Year-round **Old Butte Historical Tours** (© **406/ 498-3424;** www.buttetours.info) offers historic walking tours covering old speakeasies, brothels, hotels, and more.

Discovery Ski Area   This is another Montana ski resort that falls somewhere in the middle of the pack if you make a list ranking them for nearly any category. The 614 skiable acres here are nicely spread among beginner, intermediate, and expert runs. Five kilometers (3 miles) of groomed trails will satisfy the Nordic skier, or you can blaze your own trail through untracked snow.

While the scenery equals or exceeds that of other areas in the state, the real plus here is the resort's proximity to **Fairmont Hot Springs Resort** (see "Where to Stay," below), a four-season facility where soaking and swimming are year-round favorites. Ski rentals and instruction are available (private lessons are $35 per hour) as well as cafeteria-style food. There are no hotels at the ski area; the nearest accommodations are at Fairmont Hot Springs or in Butte and Anaconda.

P.O. Box 221, Anaconda, MT 59711. ℭ 406/563-2184. www.skidiscovery.com. Full-day lift tickets $30 adults, $15 children 12 and younger and seniors; half-day $22 beginning at 12:30pm. From Anaconda, drive west on Mont. 1 for 20 miles to Georgetown Lake. Turn right (north) at the DISCOVERY SKI AREA sign. Continue north for 4½ miles to the ski area.

SNOWMOBILING

Call the Butte office of the **Beaverhead-Deerlodge National Forest** (ℭ 406/494-2147) for information on nearby trails, most of which explore the Georgetown Lake area. The four major trail systems include Carp Ridge, which terminates at the Anaconda-Pintler Wilderness boundary; Echo Lake, at the midpoint of Georgetown Lake and Discovery Ski Area; Peterson Meadows, a popular spot for cookouts and picnics; and Red Lion Racetrack Lake, with ridge-top views of surrounding peaks.

SEEING THE SIGHTS

For information on the **Pintler Scenic Route,** a driving tour that begins in Butte, see section 1 of this chapter.

The Berkeley Pit is rumored to be visible from the moon. It is located just off the Continental Drive in Butte. Starting in 1955, nearly 1.5 billion tons of material were removed from the pit—including more than 290 million tons of copper ore—before mining ceased in 1982. A short walk through a dimly lit tunnel (fully accessible for those with disabilities) takes you to an observation deck where you can view the pit, which is doggedly filling with groundwater. Unfortunately, the water flows through several thousand miles of underground pit tunnels through the mineralized zones and becomes heavily acidic en route to the surface. In 2003, a newly built water treatment plant began processing the polluted water, sidestepping the possibility that the toxic water would seep into the city's drinking water and render the town pretty much uninhabitable. The viewing stand is at the east end of Mercury Street on the fringes of the downtown area, and is open to the public ($1 admission) during daylight hours May through September. A good online resource is **www.pitwatch.org**. As the Pit is Butte's most-visited attraction, plans called for a $185,000 face-lift of the area for fall 2006, including a playground, restrooms, expanded interpretive displays, and a bronze statue of "The Auditor," the mysterious dreadlocked dog who wandered this desolate moonscape for 17 years until his passing in 2003.

The 585-foot **Anaconda Smelter Stack,** just off Mont. 1 on the outskirts of Anaconda, is one of the tallest standing brick structures in the world and is designated a Montana State Park, though there is no public access to the structure. Once considered the largest copper-smelting stack in the entire world, all 58 stories of the desolate shaft rise starkly to meet the Montana sky. A few interpretive displays detail the smelter stack's history and construction.

Fun Fact **Butte's "Favorite" Son**

Daredevil extraordinaire Evel Knievel was born and raised in Butte before he went on to jump (or attempt to jump) his motorcycle over every imaginable obstacle. It seems that Knievel was something of a juvenile delinquent during adolescence, picking just about every available lock in town. But the city buried the hatchet in 2002 by establishing the **Evel Knievel Loop,** a drive around town marked by plaques, in conjunction with the first annual **Evel Knievel Days,** an annual festival held in late July or early August that commemorates Knievel's life with stunt shows, parades, and kids' events. Call © **406/494-2825** or visit **www.knievelweek.com** for more information.

Arts Chateau ⊛ Built in 1898 for Charles Clark, son of copper king William A. Clark, the Butte–Silver Bow Arts Chateau is an impressively restored mansion and art gallery. Stained-glass windows, beveled glass, ornate wrought iron, and intricately detailed woodwork contribute to the mansion's early-20th-century elegance. The home's magnificent staircase leads to a second-story museum, filled with period furniture, and the gallery, which houses traveling displays by Montana artists in a much more modern setting. The two galleries have exhibits that change every 6 weeks. Other highlights include the fourth-floor ballroom, which replicates a grand hunting lodge, and the first-floor gift shop, with hundreds of made-in-Montana items for sale. Under the same umbrella, the year-round **Butte-Silver Bow Arts Center,** 124 S. Main St., has a coffee shop (the Venus Rising Espresso House), and arts store, and regular films and musical entertainment.

321 W. Broadway, Butte. © **406/723-7600.** www.bsbarts.org. $4 adults, $3 seniors, $2 children, free for children, or $10 family of 4. Summer Mon–Sat 10:30am–5:30pm; winter Sat 11am–5pm or by appointment. Tours available.

Dumas Brothel Opened in 1890 as a "parlor house," the Dumas was once at the heart of Butte's red-light district. It was the city's longest-running house of prostitution, closing in 1982. Under the guidance of Rudy Giecek, the Dumas Brothel has been turned into a museum of prostitution. When the long-closed rooms in the basement were opened, they revealed "intact time capsules"—cigarette packs, liquor bottles, playing cards, and a rare White Cross model no. 26 metal vibrator, made in the pre–World War I era. *Note:* The museum has had funding problems in recent years; it's probably best to call in advance.

45 E. Mercury St., Butte. © **406/494-6908.** www.thedumasbrothel.com. Tours $6 per person. May–Aug daily 10am–5pm. Closed Sept–Apr.

The Mai Wah ⊛ Adjacent to China Alley, the Mai Wah and Wah Chong Tai buildings stand as tributes to Butte's early Chinese population, which numbered 400 in 1890. With a first-floor mercantile and second-floor noodle parlor, The Mai Wah provided a segment of the city's ethnic community with jobs after the mines were exhausted. Today the buildings house exhibits and memorabilia honoring the rich Asian history of the area. In 2005, The Mai Wah's long-awaited permanent exhibit, "The Butte Chinese Experience," opened to the public, telling this fascinating story with artifacts, images, and interpretive displays.

17 W. Mercury St., Butte. © **406/723-3231.** www.maiwah.org. $3 adults, free for children. Memorial Day to Labor Day Tues–Sun 11am–5pm.

Mineral Museum   This museum displays only a percentage of the mineral specimens that belong to Montana Tech's geology department, though that still makes for a pretty impressive mineral display. The explanation of the minerals consists of their identification and place of origin. One display features a comprehensive display of fluorescent minerals, starkly illuminated by ultraviolet lights. One of the area's most exciting discoveries, a 28-ounce gold nugget found in the Highland Mountains south of Butte, is also on display.

Montana Tech Campus. ℂ **406/496-4414**. www.mbmg.mtech.edu/museum.htm. Free admission. Memorial Day to Labor Day daily 9am–6pm; Rest of year Mon–Fri 9am–4pm; In May and Sept–Oct Sat–Sun 1–5pm. From the center of Butte, take Park St. west to the Montana Tech Campus and follow the signs to the museum.

Our Lady of the Rockies   When you look up to the eastern heights above Butte, you'll see the large white statue of Our Lady of the Rockies in a notch at the top of a hill. The 90-foot statue was built "in the likeness of Mary, Mother of Jesus," and is dedicated to all women, and especially mothers. Private cars are not allowed up to the site, but you can get a close-up view of the statue on 2½-hour bus tours. If you don't have time for a tour, but are interested in learning more about Our Lady of the Rockies, visit the information center and gift shop for a look at a panoramic mural of the statue. There is also a 30-minute video detailing the construction: 400 tons of concrete were used just for the statue's base.

Butte Plaza Mall, 3100 Harrison Ave. ℂ **800/800-LADY** or 406/782-1221. www.ourladyoftherockies.org. Free admission to information center and gift shop. Summer Mon–Sat 9am–5pm, Sun 10am–5pm; winter limited hours. Tours depart daily during summer. $12 for adults, $10 seniors 55 and over, $9 children 13–17, $5 children 5–12, and free for children under 5.

Washoe Theater ⚑   The Washoe shares the distinction with New York City's Radio City Music Hall of being the last two theaters done in the Art Deco style, and the Washoe is actually the more impressive. The brick exterior is unremarkable, and when you see it you'll wonder what all the fuss is about. But inside, this is a true movie palace. Considered one of the most architecturally significant theaters in the country, it's a work of art in cerulean, salmon, beige, and yellow, with a fabulous curtain. If you arrive at midday, the theater is usually closed—it's still a working first-run movie theater and doesn't open until evening. But if someone is there, they'll turn on the lights and let you look around. Or you can take a trolley tour through the Anaconda Chamber to get a guaranteed peek.

305 Main St., Anaconda. ℂ **406/563-6161**. Movie tickets $4 adults, $3 children 11 and under. Fri–Tues open 8pm; Wed–Thurs, 7pm.

⌐Tips   **Anaconda Touring Tips**

You can take the **Vintage Bus Tour of Historic Anaconda** from the Anaconda Chamber of Commerce, 306 E. Park St. (ℂ **406/563-2400**), Monday through Saturday at 10am and 2pm, from mid-May to mid-September. The cost is $6 adults, $2 children 6 and under. The tour includes a stop and inside tour of the fabulous Washoe Theater, which usually is open only at 8pm. The chamber also has a historical walking tour brochure for $2, but you won't see the inside of the Washoe unless you get lucky.

World Museum of Mining & 1899 Mining Camp ☆ This popular museum is a re-creation of the 1899 Hellroarin' Gulch mining town. It's on the site of the Orphan Girl mine, which, though not a blockbuster by Butte standards, managed to produce 7.6 million ounces of silver, along with lead and zinc. The mining town is set up with typical businesses and buildings of the mining era here, with explanations of each of their functions in the community. There's also a hard-rock mining hall with tools of the trade and examples of types of framing timbers used underground. In summer 2005, the museum started an evening dinner theater with melodramas based on Butte's colorful history ($10 per person, or $15 for the dinner theater plus admission to the museum). Call for the current schedule.

155 Museum Way, P.O. Box 33. ✆ **406/723-7211.** www.miningmuseum.org. $7 adults, $5 children 13–18, $2 children 5–12, free for children 5 and under. Apr–Oct daily 9am–5:30pm, last ticket sold at 4:30pm. From the center of Butte, take Park St. west to the Montana Tech Campus. Continue on Park through the campus and make a left at Museum Way.

WHERE TO STAY

Beyond the options listed below, we recommend the new **Holiday Inn Express,** 1 Holiday Park Dr. (✆ **800/465-4329** or 406/494-6999), with rates of $83 to $103 double and suites for $109 to $119, and the newer **Hampton Inn,** 3499 Harrison Ave. S. (✆ **800/426-7866** or 406/494-2250), with double rates of $95 to $115.

Best Western Butte Plaza Inn ☆ This property is the best motel in the area because of its facilities, services, and location next to the freeway. Rooms, with modern decor, are small but quiet and clean, all with either king- or queen-size beds, with complimentary broadband access through the TV. The European breakfast buffet, included in the room price, includes thinly sliced meats and cheeses, fruits, muffins, hot or cold cereals, and juices and coffee. Next door, **Perkins Family Restaurant** is open 24 hours a day and serves traditional family fare. On-site, **Hops** is a pub and casino decorated in the style of an English pub.

2900 Harrison Ave., Butte, MT 59701. ✆ **800/543-5814** or 406/494-3500. Fax 406/494-7611. www.bestwestern.com/butteplazainn. 134 units. $85–$93 double. Rates include breakfast buffet. AE, DISC, MC, V. Pets accepted, $50 deposit. **Amenities:** Restaurant; lounge; indoor pool; exercise room; indoor Jacuzzi; sauna; courtesy car; business center; Wi-Fi network; room service; massage; coin-op washers and dryers; dry cleaning. In room: A/C, cable TV w/pay movies, dataport, coffeemaker, hair dryer, iron.

Copper King Mansion ☆ This combination museum and bed-and-breakfast inn is an ideal choice for those who want to savor the historic ambience of one of the most lavish homes of the late 19th century. The huge home was built for mining magnate William A. Clark in 1888 for $260,000. There are 30 rooms on three floors, decorated in a lush "modern Elizabethan" style. While the inn's exterior has seen better days, the interior features remarkably intricate woodwork and a large number of opulent pieces of period furniture collected by the inn's owners. There are even a few original items from the period of Clark's ownership. In the third-floor ballroom, there's an 814-pipe Estey organ as well as a private collection of clothing and memorabilia dating back to the late 1800s; a small chapel is discreetly located to the side.

All of the guest rooms but one are very large and beautifully furnished. There are parquet floors downstairs, and the octagon-shaped reception room, the billiard room, and the library all reflect Clark's love of luxury. Antique lamps and chandeliers, ornate frescoed ceilings, and etched amber transoms complement the rooms' original furniture, including two matching African mahogany sleigh beds. If you stay at the B&B,

you can sleep in the copper king's room, but you have to get up early. April through September, public tours ($7 per person) start at 9am and run until 5pm, when the mansion is closed to the public so that the night's guests can be admitted.

219 W. Granite St., Butte, MT 59701. © 406/782-7580. www.thecopperkingmansion.com. 5 units, 2 with shared bathrooms. $65–$95 double. Rates include full breakfast and a complimentary tour. AE, DISC, MC, V. In room: No phone.

Fairmont Hot Springs Resort 🐾 *(Kids)*   This oasis between Butte and Missoula is a great place for families, with a 350-foot water slide and a pair of Olympic-size pools, a small wildlife zoo, and a playground. Parents will enjoy the wide range of activities as well, from golf and tennis to cross-country skiing in the winter. Plus, of course, the hot springs. Discovery Ski Area is only 30 minutes away. The standard rooms are fairly typical, hotel-style accommodations, but they all have balconies, and the suites are as large and snazzy as one could want, sleeping as many as eight guests each. Many of the suites also have fully equipped kitchens, and, by resort standards, the cost is modest.

1500 Fairmont Rd., Fairmont, MT 59711. © 800/332-3272 or 406/797-3241. www.fairmontmontana.com. 152 units. $114–$375 double; $159–$435 suites. AE, DC, DISC, MC, V. **Amenities:** 2 restaurants; lounge (w/casino); 2 indoor and 2 outdoor hot-springs pools; 18-hole golf course; tennis courts; 2 steam rooms; courtesy car; room service; massage; Wi-Fi network; coin-op washers and dryers. In room: A/C, cable TV w/pay movies and video games, dataport, kitchen (in the suites), coffeemaker, hair dryer, iron.

Finlen Hotel   Butte's most historic hotel, the 1924 Finlen was modeled after New York's Astor Hotel after its mining-era predecessor was razed. The lobby is elegant, with soaring copper-accented columns, crystal chandeliers, and marble walls, inside an attractive nine-story, brick facade. Some rooms are nicer than others, but they are clean and well maintained, with small bathrooms and a typical motel feel (lacking historic ambience). There is also a motel-style annex with slightly lower rates that represents more than half of the rooms.

100 E. Broadway, Butte, MT 59701. © 800/729-5461 or 406/723-5461. www.finlen.com. 53 units. $44–$58 double; $65 suite. AE, DC, DISC, MC, V. **Amenities:** Lounge. In room: A/C, TV, dataport.

Toad Hall Manor 🐾   In 2003, Glen Johnson converted his palatial, 11,000-square-foot home on the 16th hole of the Butte Country Club into a splendid B&B. The early 1990s home has a more historic feel than you'd think, and a quartet of whimsical guest rooms named for characters in the children's classic *The Wind in the Willows*. We like Mr. Mole's Hide-away, with its great mountain views and stately walnut furnishings, but for a splurge, Sir Badger's Suite might be the best room in the city, with two bedrooms, a walk-in closet, and a two-person Jacuzzi, occupying the entire fifth floor. The breakfasts are unique, with such dishes as Swedish wheat and eggs and Polynesian French toast. The entire place has high-speed wireless Internet access.

1 Green Lane, Butte, MT 59701. © 866/443-8623 or 406/494-2625. Fax 406/494-8025. www.toadhallmanor.com. 4 units. $99–$165 double. Rates include full breakfast. AE, DC, DISC, MC, V. **Amenities:** Massage; Wi-Fi network. In room: Cable TV, dataport, hair dryer, iron.

WHERE TO DINE

Butte's ethnic tradition is most evident in its food, with pasties (pronounced *pass*-tees, or *pah*-stees if you're British) ranking high on the list. If you've never tried one of these Cornish meat-filled pastries, you're in for a treat. Try **Joe's Pasty Shop**, 1641 Grand Ave. (© **406/723-9071**) or **Nancy's Pasty Shop**, 2810 Pine St. (© **406/782-7410**). Another local delicacy that should not be missed is a $3 breaded pork chop sandwich from **Pork Chop John's**, 8 W. Mercury St. (© **406/782-0812**). This bare-bones, blue-collar diner is a Butte landmark, and the sandwiches, wrapped in wax paper and topped with pickles, mustard, and onions, are the best deal in town.

Big Jim's STEAKS/SEAFOOD   This is a classic Montana steak joint, with black Naugahyde booths and steaks too big to finish in one sitting. Thursday nights, you can get the large T-bone for $15. You also get the salad bar, spaghetti, and potato. One of the most popular dishes is the gourmet seafood plate, which might include a small lobster tail, crab legs, and scallops, depending on what's in season.

511 E. Park, Anaconda. ⓒ 406/563-9963. Reservations recommended. Main courses $12–$40. AE, MC, V. Daily 5pm until the last diner leaves.

Pekin Noodle Parlor *(Finds)* CHINESE   Operated by the same family since 1916, the Pekin Noodle Parlor is a time capsule from the days when its neighborhood was a bustling Chinatown, complete with opium dens and brothels around every corner. Featuring curtained booths that are former brothel stalls (the old opium den is in the basement), the Pekin does a respectable job with Chinese standards like chow mein and chop suey, and also serves a few American standards (burgers, steaks, and egg plates).

117 S. Main St. (at Main), Butte. ⓒ 406/782-2217. Reservations accepted for large parties only. Lunch $4–$15; dinner $6–$15. MC, V. Sun–Mon 5–10:30pm; Wed–Thurs 5–11pm; Fri–Sat 5pm–midnight. Closed Tues.

The Uptown Café *⋒* CONTINENTAL   The Uptown Café is a white-tablecloth restaurant in a no-tablecloth town. Despite the fact that the environment is casual and unpretentious, Barb Kornet and Guy Graham's restaurant presents five-course meals built around Montana beef and fresh seafood flown in from the Pacific Northwest. The favorite starter is Clams Maison—succulent clams prepared with white wine, chives, and butter. Other choices include soup—gazpacho if you're lucky—plus several types of salads, a pasta or vegetable dish, and the main course. We recommend the salmon or halibut, when they're available, but we wouldn't turn down a steak either. Every night until 6:30pm, the cafe also serves an early-dining special: cheese ravioli with artichokes and roasted red peppers or chicken Dijon, for example, always with a Caesar salad and French bread for only $12. It makes you wonder if this is really Butte.

47 E. Broadway, Butte. ⓒ 877/723-4735 or 406/723-4735. Reservations recommended. Lunch $5–$9; dinner $11–$28. AE, DISC, MC, V. Mon–Fri 11am–2pm; Mon–Sat from 5pm; Sun from 4pm.

BUTTE AFTER DARK

No trip to Butte is complete without a visit to the **M&M Cigar Store,** 9 N. Main St. (ⓒ **406/723-7612**). The cigar store/saloon/diner/casino Jack Kerouac said was "the end of my quest for an ideal bar" was continuously open for more than a century after it went into business in 1890, but found itself boarded up for nearly 2 lonely years after its owner filed for bankruptcy in 2003. But director Wim Wenders fixed the M&M up when he used it as a location for *Don't Come Knocking.* The renovations made the place a more attractive investment, and it reopened—with Governor Brian Schweitzer hand-delivering the liquor license—in time for St. Patrick's Day 2005. "May she never close," Schweitzer remarked on that day.

A SIDE TRIP TO DEER LODGE

Deer Lodge is home to Montana's state prison, which isn't ordinarily a recommendation for a tourist destination. And we won't recommend any places to stay, because you probably won't want to spend the night. But there is a collection of museums here that makes Deer Lodge worth a morning's stop—especially if you're a car buff or a fan of ranching life.

As you enter Deer Lodge from the west on County Road 275, you'll pass the **Grant-Kohrs Ranch National Historic Site** ✯ (© **406/846-2070;** www.nps.gov/grko), another of the National Park Service's marvelous facilities. The site preserves the rich history and traditions of ranch life in the West. The ranch itself was founded in the late 1850s when Johnny Grant, a Canadian trader, moved here, eventually building up a herd of several hundred cattle. After a few years, he sold it to legendary cattleman Conrad Kohrs, and the ranch became the headquarters for a vast cattle empire scattered across the open range of Montana, Idaho, and Wyoming. Today, the site includes 90 structures, 26,000 artifacts, and a 1,500-acre cultural landscape maintained as a small-scale working ranch. Rangers lead tours of the 1862 Kohrs manor on an hourly basis. Admission is free, but donations are appreciated. It's open to the public daily 8am to 5:30pm in summer (9am–4:30pm winter) except Thanksgiving, Christmas, and New Year's Day.

Gold was discovered near Deer Lodge in 1862. This was an early precursor of the gold rush that reached full bloom with the discoveries at Bannack and Virginia City. One of the consequences of this gold rush is downtown—the castlelike **Old Montana Prison,** at 1106 Main St. (© **406/846-3111;** www.pcmaf.org). Vigilantes initially dealt with the thievery and lawlessness that prevailed during the gold rush, but the need for a real jail was eventually solved by the construction of this prison, which took in its first prisoner in 1871. It was used until 1979, when another facility was built about 5 miles from here. You can take a self-guided tour of the prison. Cell blocks, maximum-security areas, turreted guard towers, and the imposing arches of the "Sally Port" gate are the attractions here, as well as a tribute to officers killed in the line of duty at the **Montana Law Enforcement Museum.**

The Old Prison and the Law Enforcement Museum are only two of a collection of museums in Deer Lodge, which are all covered under one admission fee ($9 adults, $5 kids 10–15, and free for kids 9 and under, with lower rates in the winter). The prison complex also houses the **Montana Auto Museum,** the **Powell County Museum, The Frontier Montana Museum,** and **Yesterday's Playthings.** The complex is open to the public daily year-round: from Memorial Day to Labor Day, from 8am to 8pm, and 10am to 4pm the rest of the year, but not all of the museums stay open during the off season. Some of the museums have different hours different times of the year; call for current information.

New for 2006 is **Cottonwood City,** a re-creation of an Old West town, blacksmith, cabins, a church, a schoolhouse, and a mortuary (you can get your photo taken in a casket). There's a working blacksmith's shop as well. The **Montana Auto Museum** houses more than 120 exquisitely restored automobiles—mostly classic Fords and Chevys, but also vintage fire trucks, motor homes, and motorcycles. The **Frontier Montana Museum** has a collection of the tools that were used to win the West. There is a nice exhibit on Colt "peacemakers" and their effect on the keeping of the peace. There are also saddles, spurs, and Desert John's Saloon, with one of the largest bottle and whiskey-memorabilia collections in the country.

The vast weapons collection at the **Powell County Museum,** 1193 Main St., includes long guns and handguns from 1776 to 1956. **Yesterday's Playthings,** 1017 Main St., is a doll and toy museum. The collections of Harriet Free and Pat Campbell are displayed here, with dolls, toys, and antiques of all descriptions: mohair Teddy bears, carriages and cradles dating back to 1835, clown dolls, and various reproductions.

For additional information on these and other activities in Deer Lodge, contact the **Powell County Chamber of Commerce,** 1171 Main St., Deer Lodge, MT 59722 (© **406/846-2094;** www.powellcountymontana.com), or **Gold West Country,** 1155 Main St., Deer Lodge, MT 59722 (© **406/846-1943;** http://goldwest.visitmt.com).

4 Dillon & the Big Hole

Dillon: 65 miles S of Butte; 141 miles N of Idaho Falls, Idaho

In early Western parlance, a "hole" was a valley surrounded by steep mountains. And Big Hole is, well, a big "hole," in this old sense of a valley. It is a vast expanse of hay meadows, sagebrush flats, and ranch land ringed by towering mountains in the distance. These hay meadows have also given the Big Hole its nickname of the "valley of 10,000 haystacks," which may be a rare case of Rocky Mountain understatement.

While there are plenty of haystacks, there aren't many people. This region is the least densely populated area in western Montana. Beaverhead County, which is as large as Connecticut and Rhode Island combined, has only about 9,000 residents, and most of those live in Dillon, the county's largest town.

Dillon is primarily an agricultural center, still dependent on local farmers and ranchers rather than tourism or industry. The population jumps from 5,000 to 15,000 to 20,000 people each year around Labor Day during the event known as **"Montana's Biggest Weekend."** Among the draws are a county fair, which is wrapped around a PRCA Rodeo that draws some of the country's best cowboys, as well as national musical acts. If you plan on attending, book a room at least 3 months in advance.

The scenic loop that takes you around this valley is one of the state's more popular driving tours, and is described in section 1 of this chapter.

ESSENTIALS

GETTING THERE   The **Dillon Airport** is located at 2400 Airport Rd. and has paved runways for light planes. See Butte and Anaconda "Essentials," earlier in this chapter, for information on the closest airport to the Big Hole Valley for commercial flights, car rentals, and train and bus service. Dillon is located on I-15, about 67 miles south of Butte and 78 miles from Anaconda.

This area is also a popular destination for snowmobilers, and visitors are encouraged to call the **avalanche advisory line** (© **406/587-6981**) before setting out on a snowmobiling excursion. For **current road conditions,** call © **800/226-7623;** for current **weather information,** call © **406/449-5204.**

VISITOR INFORMATION   The **Dillon Visitor Information Center** (operated by the Beaverhead Chamber of Commerce) is located in the Camp Fortunate Interpretive Center at 10 W. Reeder St. (P.O. Box 425), Dillon, MT 59725 (© **406/683-5511;** www.beaverheadchamber.org). You can also contact **Gold West Country,** 1155 Main St., Deer Lodge, MT 59722 (© **406/846-1943;** http://goldwest.visitmt.com), for information on the entire Big Hole Valley.

GETTING OUTSIDE

Beaverhead County has several natural hot springs, including **Jackson Hot Springs Lodge** (see "Where to Stay," later in this section) and **Elkhorn Hot Springs,** which is located about 10 miles off Route 278 on a newly paved road. Go west of Dillon on 278 about 30 miles, then turn north toward Polaris at the sign. Follow the road through Polaris to Elkhorn Hot Springs, about 5 miles farther. These waters provide a therapeutic complement to various winter activities, most notably snowmobiling, downhill skiing, and cross-country skiing.

OUTFITTERS & ORGANIZED TRIPS

Great Divide Wildlands Institute (© 406/683-4669; www.greatdividetours.com) offers a variety of scenic and historical tours, with a special emphasis on the route of Lewis and Clark and the Nez Perce through the area. Starting at $250 for two people, the packages include day trips to where Lewis first met the Shoshone and other customized historic and scenic tours in the Big Hole.

Montana High Country, 35 miles west of Dillon at 7500 Scenic By-way, Polaris, MT 59746 (© **406/834-3469;** www.mhct.com), is operated by sixth-generation Montanan Russ Kipp. The company offers year-round guiding services, including fly-fishing, horseback riding, big-game hunting, and snowmobiling. Whether you're a sportsman looking to bag that elusive elk or a family longing for some quality time together, Kipp has plenty of experience in arranging a unique outdoor adventure. His most popular trips center on southwest Montana's classic trout streams, picturesque limestone canyons, and stunning mountain ranges. Prices range from $750 for a 3-day/4-night snowmobiling package to $3,500 for a 7-day deer- and elk-hunting trip. Kipp also operates a new-for-2003 Orvis-endorsed guest lodge with double rates starting at $75 per night.

FISHING

The Big Hole, Beaverhead, and Poindexter rivers are all within easy reach of Dillon, and Jefferson is only half an hour away by car. The fishing season begins early in the year when other streams may still be clearing, and extends into October. Big Hole fishermen can find several trout species, including eastern brook, brown, and golden. The **Clark Canyon Reservoir** provides good fishing for rainbow trout. Arctic grayling, ling, and whitefish also populate the waters of the Big Hole Valley. **The Beaverhead-Deerlodge National Forest,** 420 Barrett St., Dillon, MT 59725 (© **406/683-3900**), can provide you with information on the lakes and streams in the forest.

For licenses, equipment, and advice on hot fishing spots, check with the locals in Dillon at **Frontier Anglers,** 680 N. Montana St. (© **406/683-5276**). You can arrange a trip on any of the local rivers with **Tom Smith's Backcountry Angler,** 426 S. Atlantic St., Dillon, MT 59725 (© **866/266-4974** or 406/683-3462; www.backcountry angler.com). Smith has been guiding in Montana since 1983, and he also has a pair of kitchenettes and a private log home on the Beaverhead River available for rent (call for details). In Twin Bridges (just up Mont. 41), your best bet for fishing equipment and outfitting services is the **Four Rivers Fishing Co.,** 205 S. Main St. (© **888/474-8377;** www.4riversmontana.com). Aficionados of the fishing world should stop at the **R.L. Winston Rod Co.,** also in Twin Bridges, at 500 S. Main St. (© **406/684-5674;** www.winstonrods.com), for a look at some of the finest fly rods in the world. Free tours of the company facility are given each weekday at 11am; a showroom/museum is open weekdays from 8am to 4:30pm.

HIKING

Hike along the **Continental Divide National Scenic Trail** in the **Anaconda-Pintler Wilderness** for interesting geologic discoveries, fabulous scenery, and views of wildlife: Elk, moose, mule deer, antelope, and even black bears are all indigenous to the region. Covering parts of the Bitterroot and Beaverhead-Deerlodge national forests, this 158,500-acre wilderness spans 40 miles along the Continental Divide over four counties. Highways with access to the area are U.S. 93 on the west, Mont. 38 and Mont. 1 from the north, and Mont. 43 from the east and south. The **Wise River Ranger District,** Box 100, Wise River, MT 59762 (© **406/832-3178**), can direct you to the area's most traveled trails. You can also obtain a recreation directory, which describes many of the trails in the forest. The guide is available for free from **Beaverhead-Deerlodge National Forest,** 420 Barrett St., Dillon, MT 59725 (© **406/683-3900**).

HORSEBACK RIDING
Diamond Hitch Outfitters, 3405 Ten Mile Rd., Dillon, MT 59725 (© **800/368-5494** or 406/683-5494; www.diamondhitchoutfitters.com), offers 1½-hour rides, half-day trips, and full-day trips in the Pioneer Mountains. As an alternative, evening horseback rides include a campfire cookout. More adventurous overnight and extended backcountry rides are also available. Rates range from $30 per 1½-hour ride to $1,050 for a 5-day trip.

SKIING
In addition to **Maverick Mountain,** discussed below, Dillon is fairly close to **Lost Trail Powder Mountain** (see "A Detour into the Bitterroot Valley," in chapter 6).

Maverick Mountain   Located 35 miles west of Dillon in the Beaverhead National Forest, Maverick Mountain is a small, inexpensive area that attracts mostly local skiers. It remains crowd free and has yet to become a destination ski resort. It has 24 runs with 2,020 vertical feet of skiing. Most of the runs are rated for the intermediate skier. There are some wide-open bowls, meadows, winding runs, and steep chutes. The area gets enough snow—200 inches yearly—to offer some good powder days. Rentals and lessons are available for downhill skis and snowboards. There's a child-care facility, but call ahead to reserve a spot. There are no lodging facilities at the ski area, although there are some nice accommodations nearby. Cafeteria-style meals are available at the base lodge, or you can grab a hot toddy at the Thunder Bar.

Maverick Mountain Rd. (P.O. Box 475), Polaris, MT 59746. © 406/834-3454. www.skimaverick.com. Full-day lift tickets $24 adults, $16 children 6–12, free for children 5 and under. Mid-Dec to mid-Apr Thurs–Sun and holidays 9:30am–4pm. Take Mont. 278 west off U.S. 15 to the Polaris Rd. for 13 miles.

SNOWMOBILING
The Wise River trail system features 150 miles of groomed trails in the Big Hole Valley area, including **Anderson Meadows**—which leads to backcountry lakes and a rental cabin—and **Lacy Creek,** with 10 miles of groomed and ungroomed trails to five high-mountain lakes. The Beaverhead-Deerlodge National Forest's **Wise River Ranger District,** Box 100, Wise River, MT 59762 (© **406/832-3178**), is a good source of information.

NATURE PRESERVES & WILDERNESS AREAS
One of the Bureau of Land Management's Backcountry Byways, the **Big Sheep Creek Canyon** offers the opportunity to observe the majestic bighorn sheep in their spectacular natural habitat. The 50-mile byway begins in Dell, Montana, on I-15, 24 miles north of the Montana-Idaho border, and passes beneath the high rock cliffs of Big Sheep Canyon to the head of Medicine Lodge Creek. From here, it's just a short drive down to the Medicine Lodge Valley to Mont. 324, just west of Clark Canyon Dam.

Clark Canyon Recreation Area, a man-made lake 20 miles south of Dillon on I-15, is a popular spot for water-skiing or trout fishing. Lewis and Clark's Camp Fortunate is located on the northwestern shore of the reservoir, where camping and boat-launching facilities are also available.

Two Dillon-area landmarks are designated state parks because of the historical significance attached to them as a result of the Lewis and Clark expedition. **Clark's Lookout** (© 406/834-3413) provided the explorers with a vantage point from which to view their route and is reached by taking the Dillon exit from I-15, and then following the signs. **Beaverhead Rock,** 14 miles south of Twin Bridges on Mont. 41 (© 406/834-3413), was a tribal landmark recognized by expedition scout Sacajawea. Both parks are day use only.

SEEING THE SIGHTS

Based in Dillon or elsewhere in the valley, you can branch out to see **Big Hole National Battlefield;** see section 5 of this chapter for details.

The **Pioneer Mountain Scenic Byway** is a 4-mile drive that begins on Mont. 278 west of Dillon or along Mont. 43, south of the Wise River. Only the northern 28 miles of the road are paved. Driving between the east and west Pioneer Mountain Ranges, you'll experience alpine meadows, jagged peaks, and ghost towns with numerous opportunities to camp, fish, or watch wildlife. Near Coolidge (as you drive south) you'll see the old railroad bed of the Montana Southern Railway. This was the last narrow-gauge railroad built in the U.S., to serve the Elkhorn mine.

Beaverhead County Museum   The Beaverhead County Museum is located in the center of town. It's housed in the old Union Pacific Railroad Depot and an 1870s settler's cabin moved to the spot. Inside there is a little bit of everything from the pioneer era—clothes, tools, cooking utensils, furnishings, typewriters. Like a lot of small-town museums in the West, though, this one seems more interested in preserving the names of the families who donated items than in telling a coherent historical story.

15 S. Montana St., Dillon. © 406/683-5027. $2 adults, $1 seniors and children 12–17, and free for children under 12; $5 maximum per family. Apr–Sept Mon–Fri 8:30am–5pm, Sat noon–4pm; Oct–Mar Mon–Fri 8:30am–5pm.

University of Montana-Western Art Gallery/Museum   The most exciting exhibit at this gallery and museum is the Seidensticker Wildlife Collection of big-game trophies, featuring animals from the far-flung locales of Africa and Asia as well as North American game. The museum also houses a small regional permanent collection and seasonally rotating exhibits, including student artwork.

Main Hall, 710 S. Atlantic St., Dillon. © 406/683-7232. Free admission. Open during fall and spring semesters, Mon 11am–4pm and Tues–Fri 11am–4:30pm.

WHERE TO STAY

In addition to the hotels listed below, two other chain options in Dillon are at I-15 exit 63. The **Comfort Inn,** 450 N. Interchange (© 800/442-4667 or 406/683-6831), has double rates in the $60-to-$70 range; and the **Super 8 Motel,** 550 N. Montana St. (© 800/800-8000 or 406/683-4288), has double rates of $50 to $75.

Best Western Paradise Inn   The Paradise Inn is a comfortable two-story facility set back from one of Dillon's busier streets. The standard rooms are cozy and appointed with an eye for efficiency, if a bit dated, but the penthouse suites are well worth the price, with huge bathtubs and large living areas. For families, there is one two-bedroom unit.

650 N. Montana St., Dillon, MT 59725. © 800/528-1234 or 406/683-4214. Fax 406/683-4216. 65 units. $62–$70 double; $67–$92 suite. AE, DISC, MC, V. **Amenities:** Restaurant; indoor pool; indoor Jacuzzi. *In room:* A/C, TV, dataport, coffeemaker, hair dryer, iron.

Jackson Hot Springs Lodge 🐾🐾   A frequent comment from new arrivals at this lodge, when they enter the lobby and look up at the collection of animal heads on the wall, is "This is what you really expect a lodge to look like." The establishment effortlessly combines the trappings of a classic mountain lodge with an informal, cowboy-style atmosphere. The accommodations are in a series of attractive cabins, which are large, with pine-framed beds. (There's also an RV park and campground on-site.) The grounds are landscaped with attractive gardens. On the other hand, you would not be too surprised to see a cowboy ride his horse up to the bar and order a drink—for the horse. The large hot-springs pool—75×30 feet—is free to guests and available to others for a $5 fee ($3.50, 12 and under). Don't go on Wednesdays, though, because that's when it's emptied and cleaned, and it takes all day to fill up again. There is a

Red Rock Lakes National Wildlife Refuge: A Haven for the Trumpeter Swan

Though well off the beaten path in the Centennial Valley, 28 miles east of Monida (about an hour south of Dillon), the **Red Rock Lakes National Wildlife Refuge** is often called the most beautiful wildlife refuge in the United States. The refuge was established in 1935 to protect the rare trumpeter swan, and it is here that the endangered species has been brought back from near extinction after a century of being hunted for their meat and feathers (quill pens were a hot item in the 1800s). It was feared that these beautiful creatures, which have wingspans of 7 to 8 feet, had been completely wiped out, until biologists discovered several dozen here in 1933. (They're also found along the Pacific Coast and in Alaska.)

This is the largest population in the Lower 48 states—300 to 500 of the rare birds winter in the area, with about 100 calling the refuge home. They mate for life and often return to the exact same nest each year to tend their eggs and cygnets. The best place to view the trumpeters is in the open areas near Upper Red Rock Lake, from late April to the end of September.

In addition to the swan population, the 40,000-acre refuge is home to moose, deer, elk, antelope, foxes, great blue herons, sandhill cranes, ducks, and geese; more than 50,000 ducks and geese may be seen during times of migration.

The multi-use refuge is a popular spot for hiking, mountain biking, and canoeing; check with the refuge (📞 **406/276-3536;** http://redrocks.fws.gov) for regulations concerning these activities within refuge boundaries. To reach the refuge, take I-15 to the town of Monida, then drive east on a gravel-and-dirt road 28 miles to the refuge entrance. If you are coming from West Yellowstone, travel west on U.S. 20 for about 12 miles to Mont. 87. Travel northwest on Mont. 87 for 5 miles and turn south at the Sawtell historical marker. Follow the paved road around the west shore of Henry's Lake for approximately 5 miles and then turn right at Red Rock Pass Road (an improved dirt road), following it west for about 25 miles to the refuge entrance.

small restaurant on the premises, with a menu that changes seasonally. Dinner goes for $11 to $28, depending on the meal of the day.

Main St. (P.O. Box 808), Jackson, MT 59736. © 406/834-3151. Fax 406/834-3157. www.jacksonhotsprings.com. 12 cabins. $70–$125 cabin. AE, MC, V. Pets accepted with additional fee. **Amenities:** Restaurant; lounge; outdoor hot-springs pool; massage. *In room:* No phone.

A FISHING LODGE

Craig Fellin Outfitters and Big Hole Lodge ★★ *Finds*   This is one of the finest fly-fishing lodges in the West. You can catch every species of trout—rainbow, brown, cutthroat, grayling, and brook. The Big Hole River is the only river in the Lower 48 that still has native grayling in it, and the fine guides at Fellin's will help you find them. The food is excellent and the accommodations are comfortable though not luxurious, and well-suited for the angler. Deer often loiter in front of the lodge in the evening. Fellin's is best for the experienced angler, but the guides are very patient and give beginners casting lessons at the lodge before hitting the streams. Craig is also an avid golfer, and he's installed a 300-foot par-3 golf hole on the property. You can practice your putting and casting, and then combine a half-day of fishing with a round of golf at the Old Works course in nearby Anaconda (see section 3, earlier in this chapter).

Box 156, Wise River Rd., Wise River, MT 59762. © 406/832-3252. Fax 406/832-3254. www.flyfishinglodge.com. 4 units. $2,895 per person per week; shorter packages available. Rates include all meals, drinks, fishing guide, and boat. No credit cards. **Amenities:** Lounge; fishing pool; par-3 golf hole; activities desk. *In room:* No phone.

CAMPING

The **Dillon KOA,** 1225 C.R. 324, Dillon, MT 59725 (© 406/683-2749), is only 20 miles from town and offers an RV park with fishing in the Clark Canyon Reservoir. Campers here will find 31 sites for RVs and two tent campsites. In addition to the usual bathhouse, there is a seasonal swimming pool, small grocery store, fishing supplies, propane, an RV dump station, and boat-access ramps. Rates are $22 to $31 for RV sites (which includes cable TV) and $19 to $24 for tent sites. There are also several camping cabins (which share the campground's bathhouse) at $31 to $39 double.

WHERE TO DINE

Sweetwater Coffee has freshly brewed coffee, some pastries, and light lunch fare. It's located downtown at 26 E. Bannack (© **406/683-4141**). Another recommended option is **Stageline Pizza,** at 531 E. Poindexter St. in the University of Montana-Western student union building (© **406/683-9004**). Order takeout and head down to the riverbank to enjoy a beautiful Montana sunset.

Big Hole Crossing Restaurant ★ *Finds* AMERICAN   This is a neat little restaurant in the dinky mountain town of Wisdom, with a blue-tiled counter seating area, knotty pine furnishings, a roaring fireplace, and wildlife art on the walls. The food is good yet inexpensive, although it runs toward typical beef, chicken, and seafood. It's popular with the Forest Service and BLM types for breakfast and lunch, which is usually a good sign, because they tend to work up quite an appetite wrestling mountain lions, corralling grizzly bears, and arguing with ranchers about riparian habitat improvements. The pies, cinnamon rolls, and bagels are all baked in-house and are especially good. While nobody's quite sure what it is, the sawdust pie is excellent.

105 Park St., Wisdom. © 406/689-3800. Breakfast $3–$9; lunch $3.50–$8; dinner $8–$24. MC, V. May–Nov daily 7am–9pm; Dec–Apr Mon, Thurs, Sun 8am–7pm, Tues–Wed 8am–3pm, Fri–Sat 8am–8pm.

Blacktail Station ✿ STEAKS/SEAFOOD   Located in the basement below a local watering hole called Mac's Last Cast, Blacktail Station used to be the Mine Shaft, and some of the decorations from its past life still remain—like the trophy heads. But generally it's a more upscale, more yuppie-ish place than you'd expect in agricultural Dillon; prints by Montana artist Larry Zabel now adorn the walls as well as the hard-rock mining detritus. The food is very traditional and very good. The steak almost melts in your mouth and the twice-baked potato is very popular. For dessert, surprisingly, the chefs crank out a killer Key lime pie.

26 S. Montana St., Dillon. © **406/683-6611**. Main courses $12–$45. DISC, MC, V. Daily 5–10pm.

Las Carmelitas MEXICAN   Located across the street from the old depot, Las Carmelitas focuses on traditional Mexican cuisine. Lunches are nachos, salads, enchiladas, burritos, and tacos; evening meals include chiles rellenos, mole, green chile, and other south-of-the-border standbys. The atmosphere is very basic, with square tables and metal chairs. Cold beer is available, but margaritas are not, because the establishment's liquor license allows for beer and wine only.

220 S. Montana St., Dillon. © **406/683-9368**. Lunch $6–$10; dinner $7–$12. MC, V. Mon–Fri 11am–2pm; Mon–Sat 4:30–9pm.

Papa T's *(Kids)* PIZZA   Papa T's is Dillon's version of Chuck E. Cheese's, only better. It's a converted saloon where the kids can run around without getting on anyone's nerves. There are video games lining one wall, and a little kiddies' carousel for the tykes. There's even a Ms. Pac-Man game for '80s nostalgia buffs. The food is basic American: burgers (consisting of local organic beef), chicken, Philly cheese steaks, and pizza. The formula has worked for more than 20 years. The family-owned restaurant is named for founder and patriarch Tom Lohman, whose kids all call him "Papa."

10 N. Montana St., Dillon. © **406/683-6432**. Reservations accepted for large parties only. Main courses $4.50–$17. MC, V. Daily 11am–10pm.

Sparky's Garage AMERICAN/BARBECUE   As its name suggests, Sparky's sports a garage theme, with petroliana of all kinds hanging above the red-and-green checkerboard floors. The aroma of gasoline, however, is nowhere to be smelled; instead, the scent of barbecue wafts from the kitchen. The sauce is sweet and slathered all over everything from pork ribs to chicken to pulled pork, with respectable results. There are also burgers, steaks, and baskets of fried shrimp and catfish. Beyond dinner, Sparky's is a reliable choice three meals a day near the University of Montana-Western campus, and has beer and wine only.

420 E. Pointdexter St., Dillon. © **406/683-2828**. Reservations not accepted. Breakfast $3–$7; lunch and dinner $5–$18. MC, V. Mon–Thurs 6:30am–9pm; Fri–Sat 6:30–9:30pm; Sun 6:30am–8:30pm

TWIN BRIDGES

Just up Mont. 41 a piece from Dillon, a faded billboard just outside of town proclaims Twin Bridges to be the platinum capital of the Western world, an odd designation for a town that seems to be much more famous regionally for great fishing. "Floating Flotillas & Fish Fantasies" is the name given to the tiny town's annual summer festival, held in late July or early August, with highlights that include the extremely popular floating parade on the Beaverhead, dances, and a barbecue. Locals are even given the chance to show their skills at fly-casting, and there's a tug-of-war over the river. For additional information about the Twin Bridges area and scheduled activities, visit the **Greater Ruby Valley Chamber of Commerce's website** at **www.rubyvalley chamber.com**.

WHERE TO STAY

Also see The Old Hotel, under "Where to Dine," below.

Healing Waters Fly-Fishing Lodge ★★ *Finds*   Since the grand opening in 1996, this lodge has earned a reputation as one of Montana's top fly-fishing resorts. Nestled in a cottonwood grove on 52 acres of land, the lodge and its dining, living, and fly-tying rooms—not to mention its surprisingly elegant guest rooms, each with colorful quilts, Western decor, and its own deck—are a magnet for anglers working the nearby trout waters under the tutelage an excellent staff of guides. The package here includes rooms and meals, fly-fishing and guide service, and views from the front deck of the Ruby, Tobacco Root, and Greenhorn mountains. Henry Winkler ("The Fonz") is a fan.

270 Tuke Lane, Twin Bridges, MT 59754. © **406/684-5960**. www.hwlodge.com. 9 units. $600 per person per day, double occupancy. Rate includes meals and guide services. DISC, MC, V. **Amenities:** Dining room; exercise room; fly-tying room; business center; massage. *In room:* TV, coffeemaker, hair dryer, no phone.

WHERE TO DINE

The Old Hotel ★ CONTINENTAL   This remarkable restaurant is right on the highway in an out-of-the-way spot, serving gourmet meals out of a beautifully restored brick building decorated with a Scottish motif. While the menu changes weekly, you'll always find a creative assortment of sauces accompanying the main courses; past selections have included fresh sea bass drizzled with cucumber-yogurt sauce and rack of lamb with raspberry-chipotle sauce. An excellent wine cellar features French, Italian, Australian, and California labels. The second level has been converted to a two-suite B&B: Accommodations are tailored to the needs of the angler with rates of $125 a night ($85 in winter), and omelets, oatmeal, and salmon and eggs are among the breakfasts served.

101 E. Fifth Ave. Twin Bridges, MT 59754. © **406/684-5959**. www.theoldhotel.com. Reservations recommended. Breakfast and brunch $5–$10; dinner $19–$25. DISC, MC, V. May–Oct Tues–Sat 7–10am and 5–9pm, Sun 7am–2pm; Nov–Apr Thurs–Sat 5–9pm.

5 Big Hole National Battlefield ★★

76 miles W of Dillon; 106 miles S of Missoula

The flight of the Nez Perce across Montana in 1877 is among the most heroic and epic stories of the Indian Wars period. About 800 nontreaty Nez Perce left the Wallowa area of Idaho in June 1877. In an attempt to join Sitting Bull in the relative safety and freedom of Canada, the Nez Perce eluded the pursuing forces of the United States until early October, when they surrendered—not so much from military defeat but from exhaustion and starvation. On October 5, 1877, only 431 remained.

The **Big Hole National Battlefield** commemorates the flight of the Nez Perce over 1,200 miles of some of the roughest land in the Lower 48 states, through Yellowstone National Park, across Montana's high plains, all the while outwitting and outfighting the U.S. cavalry. There were several battles along the way, but by far the largest skirmish took place here. Between 60 and 90 members of the band were killed. Only 12 of the dead were warriors—the rest were women, children, and the elderly. The U.S. military suffered 29 dead and 40 soldiers were wounded.

The Nez Perce had traditionally lived in eastern Washington, Idaho, and Oregon. They had always maintained good relations with the white explorers, assisting Lewis and Clark in 1805 by caring for the expedition's members when they arrived in their country sick, tired, and low on provisions. They gave them food, two dugout canoes, and guides. The Nez Perce were also the subjects of the first major Protestant mission effort among the Indians, when the stern and domineering Eliza Spaulding—an associate of the later-martyred Marcus Whitman—urged them to give up their traditional ways in return for eternal salvation.

The Nez Perce's problems multiplied in 1860, when gold was discovered. Most were sent to reservations, but Joseph—known as "Young Joseph"—led a nontreaty band to live on his traditional homeland in the Wallowa Valley. Pressure from settlers eventually led to an order forcing Joseph's band onto a reservation.

In the summer of 1877, several Nez Perce braves ignored advice from the tribal elders and attacked and killed four white settlers in Oregon to exact revenge for the earlier murder of the father of one of the braves. This attack raised the ire of settlers, and the cavalry was called in to hunt down the Nez Perce. On June 1, 1877, Joseph's band joined four other Nez Perce groups and crossed the swollen Snake River, fleeing to Canada.

Battles erupted in Idaho before the Nez Perce entered Montana, fleeing from U.S. Army troops under the leadership of Gen. Oliver O. Howard. When the Nez Perce reached the Big Hole Valley, they decided to make camp, thinking all the while that they left their troubles behind them in Idaho.

However, in addition to Howard's troops behind them, a second group of soldiers, under the command of Col. John Gibbon, was advancing up the Bitterroot Valley toward the unsuspecting tribe. On the morning of August 9, 1877, Gibbon's soldiers, along with a contingent of local volunteers, attacked the sleeping tribe in what is today known as the Battle of the Big Hole. Less than 48 hours after they'd set up camp, the remaining Nez Perce once again found themselves fleeing for their lives and their freedom. They headed toward Canada, but the U.S. Army troops caught up to them at Bear Paw, only 40 miles from the Canadian border. The capture of Joseph's tattered band was the last major military effort of the Indian Wars period.

The Battle of the Big Hole is somewhat unusual among Indian fights in that a number of descriptions of the battle exist, many from the Indian point of view. André Garcia, a scout and adventurer, married a Nez Perce woman, In-who-lise, who was wounded in the battle. In his marvelous book *Tough Trip Through Paradise,* he says that he visited the battlefield 2 years later and human bones and skulls were still scattered everywhere.

Begun as a military reserve in 1883, the area became a national monument in 1910 and was designated a national battlefield in 1963. Today, the National Park Service maintains an interpretive center, where rangers help visitors understand the significance of the battle that occurred at Big Hole. Guided tours, a museum, exhibits, a bookstore, movies, and three self-guided walking trails are available.

Trails begin at the lower parking lot and lead to several points of interest. **The Nez Perce Camp,** where soldiers surprised the sleeping tribe, is considered sacred ground. The **Siege Area** marks the place where soldiers were besieged for nearly 24 hours as the Nez Perce fought to save their families from certain death. A fairly steep walk will lead you to the **Howitzer Capture Site,** where soldiers suffered a heavy blow as Nez Perce warriors captured and dismantled the military weapon. This spot affords a spectacular view of the battlefield and surrounding area.

The Big Hole Battlefield represents only a small fraction of the Nez Perce's tragic flight across the West. The 1,200-mile Nez Perce (Nee Me Poo) National Historic

Trail follows the entire route of the Nez Perce War, from Wallowa Lake in northwestern Oregon to Bear Paw Battlefield in north-central Montana (see chapter 8). Crossing four states, the trail features several Nez Perce war sites with interpretive markers telling the story of the tribe's fight for freedom. The trail is administered by the U.S. Forest Service, and the Beaverhead-Deerlodge National Forest (see "Visitor Information," below) can provide you with an excellent map of the four-state area.

GETTING THERE   From Missoula, you can reach the Big Hole National Battlefield by going south on U.S. 93 through the Bitterroot, 80 miles to Lost Trail Pass. Then turn east on Mont. 43 and drive 16 miles to the site. From Butte, go south on I-15 20 miles to Mont. 43, west for 51 miles to Wisdom, then continue west on Mont. 43 for about 10 miles to the site. From Dillon, take Mont. 278 west to Wisdom, then go west on Mont. 43 for 10 miles.

VISITOR INFORMATION   Located 10 miles west of Wisdom on Mont. 43, the **Big Hole National Battlefield Visitor Center,** P.O. Box 237, Wisdom, MT 59761 (© **406/689-3155;** www.nps.gov/biho), is open daily (except on Thanksgiving, Christmas, and New Year's Day) with summer hours from 8:30am to 6pm and winter hours from 9am to 5pm. Admission costs $5 per car, $3 per bike, motorcycle, or pedestrian. Picnic tables are located at the lower parking lot, though there are no camping or overnight facilities on the premises. Fishing is allowed within the battlefield's boundaries and adjacent national forest, but there are restrictions on the private land adjoining the battle site.

You can obtain a pamphlet with an auto tour of the flight of the Nez Perce through the Big Hole, Horse Prairie, and Lemhi valleys from the **National Park Service, Big Hole National Battlefield** (see above) or the **Beaverhead-Deerlodge National Forest,** 420 Barrett St., Dillon, MT 59725 (© **406/683-3900**).

The nearest facilities—restaurants, gas stations, grocery stores, and lodgings—are located in Wisdom, 10 miles to the east.

6 The Old Mining Towns: Virginia City, Nevada City & Bannack ⟨★⟨★

Virginia City: 72 miles SE of Butte; 67 miles S of Bozeman; 84 miles NW of West Yellowstone

Virginia City and nearby Nevada City have both a boisterous and colorful past and present. They are old towns, but Virginia City never turned into a ghost town; in fact, it's one of the oldest continuously occupied towns in the West.

In 1863, a group of miners led by Bill Fairweather took $180 in their first day of gold panning from a creek, which they later named Alder Gulch after the trees growing on the bank. A gold rush soon followed and a mining town grew. The nation was in the midst of the Civil War, and the Southern sympathizers in the crowd wanted to name the new city Varina after Jefferson Davis's wife. But G. G. Bissell, a northerner and a miners' judge, said, "I'll see you damned first." He wrote "Virginia" on the founding document instead, a sort of compromise, but since Virginia housed the capital of the Confederacy, no one complained.

The restoration of Virginia City began in 1946 when Charles and Sue Bovey began the painstaking task of preserving and restoring many of the structures you see in town today. Most of the buildings were erected during Virginia City's heyday as the state's second territorial capital. In the mid-1950s, Bovey also began to rebuild Nevada City, then a true ghost town, by bringing in buildings he'd acquired from around the West.

In 1991, following the deaths of Sue and Charles, son Fred Bovey determined that he was unable to continue to operate the properties and attractions. He decided to sell the whole kit and caboodle, including millions of dollars of antiques (Sotheby's estimate: $60 million). The state of Montana and Montana Historical Society attempted to have the area designated a national park, but to no avail. Even the National Trust for Historic Preservation got into the act, declaring Virginia City an endangered historic site.

Finally, partly because of a public outcry and due to the efforts of Governor Marc Racicot, the 1997 Montana legislature took dramatic fiscal measures and agreed to fund the $6.5-million purchase (such a bargain), and added $3 million for operational expenses. Today, the cities operate under the supervision of the Montana Historical Society and its foundation.

The dusty main drag of Bannack also pays tribute to the mining era. The town grew up quickly after the state's first big gold strike occurred here in 1862, but the vein was a shallow one, and Bannack quickly turned into a ghost town. Despite its short life, Bannack has a colorful history. One writer said, "It is probable that there never was a mining town of the same size that contained more desperadoes and lawless characters than did Bannack during the winter of 1862 to '63."

GETTING THERE   Virginia City and Nevada City are 13 miles west of Ennis on Mont. 287. From Bozeman, take Mont. 84 west to Norris, then go south on U.S. 287 to Ennis, then west on Mont. 287 to the sites. From Butte, take I-90 east to the Whitehall exit (Mont. 55), then go south 27 miles to Twin Bridges. From Twin Bridges, take Mont. 287 east 30 miles to the sites. They are only about a mile apart, with Nevada City being the farther west.

Bannack is reached by driving about 15 miles west of Dillon on Mont. 278, then south on a gravel road at the sign for Bannack State Park.

VISITOR INFORMATION   There are remains of many other Montana ghost towns in this part of the state; it's just that information about them is often hard to find and the towns themselves even harder. Your best bet: Contact the **Virginia City Chamber of Commerce,** P.O. Box 218, Virginia City, MT 59755 (© **800/829-2969** or 406/843-5555; www.virginiacitychamber.com), and **Gold West Country,** 1155 Main St., Deer Lodge, MT 59722 (© **406/846-1943;** http://goldwest.visitmt.com). These two agencies can provide you with free information about the historic ghost towns of Montana. While you're at it, request copies of two brochures that will enhance your visit to the area: *Walking Tour,* a historical, block-by-block guide to Virginia City; and *A Walking Tour of Nevada City, Montana.*

Most attractions in Virginia City (and all of them in Nevada City) are run by the **Montana Heritage Commission,** P.O. Box 338, Virginia City, MT 59755 (© **406/843-5247;** www.montanaheritagecommission.com and www.virginiacitymt.com), and they're open only during the peak summer season, from Memorial Day to Labor Day.

VIRGINIA CITY

As Virginia City boomed after Bill Fairweather discovered gold, it became the site of a dramatic ordeal of Western lawlessness and revenge that has fueled a thousand cowboy movie plots. Much of Virginia City's history was driven by the vigilante movement, and the town launched the career of Wilbur Fisk Sanders, who eventually went to Washington as Montana's first U.S. senator.

By 1864, when the Montana Territory was created by President Abraham Lincoln, nearly 30,000 people were living along the gulch's 8 miles. Virginia City was named territorial capital in 1865—taking that title from Bannack, virtually a ghost town by then—and held the position until 1875. For many years after its founding, the only currency acceptable to Virginia City merchants was gold dust.

As the town boomed, the incidence of robberies and murders increased. Many of the robberies depended on inside information by people usually called "road agents." The miners' sheriff, Henry Plummer, who had "persuaded" the sheriffs in Bannack, Nevada City, and Virginia to turn over their duties to him, turned out to be the leader of the road agents. As sheriff, he knew the timing of the gold movements.

No legal relief was possible, because the nearest officials to administer an oath were 400 miles away. In 1863, when a popular miner, Dutchman Nicholas Thiebalt, was murdered for $200, the other miners were outraged. The killer, George Ives, was captured and tried by a miners' court, then hanged. The site of his hanging is preserved in Nevada City. The local residents formed "vigilance committees" to capture and bring the road agents to justice. They hanged at least 21 more of the road agents—including Plummer—and some order was restored to the area.

Virginia City is the larger of the two towns; Nevada City is entirely a ghost town, a collection of original and transplanted buildings from the period. A pair of beautifully restored trains makes seven round-trips daily between the two ($6–$10 round-trip, free for children under 7).

SEEING THE SIGHTS

Virginia City has a number of operating commercial enterprises interspersed with the historical stuff. Along the main thoroughfare you'll find the village centerpieces: the **Fairweather Inn,** the **Wells Fargo Overland Company building,** and the **Virginia City Historical Museum.** One of the oldest structures, the **Montana Post Building,** once housed the state's first newspaper; the paper's original press is still used locally for menus, playbills, and placards.

You should start your visit to Virginia City at the **Visitor Center and Museum Store,** at the end of Main Street. The center has photos and a brief explanation of the history of the town, and a friendly staff of volunteers. The government shut down gold mining for good in 1942, and a few years later the Boveys began buying up the property.

The **Virginia City Players** have been an entertainment staple in town since 1949, operating out of the Smith and Boyd Livery Stable (1900). The players are Montana's oldest professional acting company. For information on showtimes, prices, and days for the Virginia City Players, call ℂ **800/829-2969** or 406/843-5377 or visit **www. virginiacityplayers.com**.

A little farther up the hill is the **Hangman's Building.** On January 4, 1864, the building was still being constructed, and a stout beam was exposed in the unfinished structure. The vigilantes took advantage of this situation to hang four road agents. The history-oriented **J. Spencer Watkins Memorial Museum** (ℂ **406/843-5500**), also on the main street, has some photos of the vigilantes on exhibit and a nice collection of period clothing. Museum visits cost $2 per person or $5 per family.

Up above the town, looking down over the main street, is **Boot Hill,** the last resting place of several road agents, who required hasty burial after they died with their boots on.

If you *really* want to see the Old West come to life, check out a **Brewery Follies** production. Famous statewide for its funny cabaret-style revues and entertaining period melodramas, the company performs nightly during the summer. The Brewery Follies have a loyal following. For information on showtimes and prices, call © **406/ 843-5218** or visit **www.breweryfollies.com**.

WHERE TO STAY

Bennett House Country Inn   The Bennett House is an eclectically furnished B&B run by some very friendly folks. All of the rooms in the house have shared bathrooms. The nicest room is the bridal suite (aka the Rose Room), with a large bay window on the second floor. There's also one cabin, with a fully equipped kitchen and its own private bathroom.

115 E. Idaho (P.O. Box 96), Virginia City, MT 59755. © **877/843-5220** or 406/843-5220. www.bennetthouseinn.com. 6 units, 1 cabin. $75–$85 double; $95 cabin. Rates include full breakfast. MC, V. *In room:* No phone.

Fairweather Inn   This small hotel, located right in the middle of downtown Virginia City, has a great upstairs porch that's a fun place to sit and people-watch. Though most of the rooms are tastefully decorated in an Old West theme, a few of them are distinguished by odd combinations of bright paint and mismatched quilts. Only six of the hotel's 15 rooms have private bathrooms; the rest are rooming house–style.

305 W. Wallace St. (P.O. Box 205), Virginia City, MT 59755. © **800/829-2969**, ext. 4, or 406/843-5377. www.alder gulchaccommodations.com. 15 units. $60–$75 double. MC, V. *In room:* No phone.

Stonehouse Inn   Built in 1884 by a local blacksmith/rancher/miner, this Gothic Revival–style B&B is a cozy place to hang your hat while in town for a night. Clad in locally quarried stone, the gray exterior is softened by a few brightly painted accents and a sweeping porch with a rocking chair. Your options range from a masculine room, embellished with antique snowshoes and a NO SPITTING sign, to a romantic upstairs room with stained glass, a private balcony, and lace-laden decor. All of the rooms have brass beds, predominately full-size. While the bathrooms are shared, they are exceptionally spacious and feature antique commodes, showers, and tubs.

306 E. Idaho St., Virginia City, MT 59755. © **406/843-5504**. www.stonehouseinnbb.com. 5 units, none with private bathroom. $75 double. Rates include full breakfast. MC, V. *In room:* No phone.

CAMPING

The **Virginia City Campground and RV Park,** P.O. Box 235, Virginia City, MT 59755 (© **888/833-5493** or 406/843-5493; www.virginiacitycampground.com), has 17 RV sites and 27 tent sites, and is open from mid-May to the end of September. The campground has a dump station, propane sales, horseshoe pits, and a recreation field, and is in a great location just east of downtown. Tent sites are $22; RV sites, $22 to $28; cabins are $55.

WHERE TO DINE

In season, there are two restaurants in Virginia City: **Banditos,** 320 Wallace Ave. (© **406/843-5556**), a bar/restaurant specializing in Southwestern dinners, and the **Virginia City Café,** 210 Wallace Ave. (© **406/843-5311**), serving sandwiches for lunch and Irish fare for dinner.

NEVADA CITY

The distance between Nevada City and Virginia City is only a mile or so, but back in the days before the vigilance committees formed, it was a dangerous mile. Miners dared not go between the two cities after dark. A robber waylaid one miner known as Dutch Fred. When the highwayman found that Fred had only $5 with him—and paper money, not gold dust, at that—the bandit cursed and told him, "If ever you come this way again with only $5, I'll shoot you." The robber shot Dutch Fred anyhow, wounding him in the arm.

Nevada City is the site of the resurgence of law and order in these Montana mining camps. Two thousand people reportedly came to town to watch the trial of George Ives for the murder of Nicholas Thiebalt. Emotions were running high on both sides, and it was in the face of these feelings that Wilbur Fisk Sanders began his place in Montana history by courageously prosecuting Ives before the crowd. The spot where Ives was hanged is marked in town.

Today Nevada City is a tourist attraction—a collection of historic wooden buildings, including an open-air museum depicting the gold-mining and settlement period of the area's turbulent history. Nevada City also exists as the result of Charles Bovey's diligence and dedication to the preservation of history. In the mid-1950s, Bovey began to re-create an authentic Western town with buildings he'd accumulated around the West. The buildings are authentic, though their setting may not be. It looks like a perfect cowboy movie set, though, and has in fact been used for a couple of oaters, including *Missouri Breaks, Little Big Man,* and *Return to Lonesome Dove.*

Admission to the Nevada City site costs $8 (free for those under 7); the site is open daily from 9am to 6pm from Memorial Day to Labor Day. For information, call *©* **800/829-2969** or 406/843-5247.

SEEING THE SIGHTS

With your walking-tour booklet in hand, begin your excursion behind the **Nevada City Hotel,** where you can view the state's only double-decker outhouse, and stroll along the streets to see what a Western mining town might have looked like. Boardwalks pass barbershops, homes, a schoolhouse, and even an Asian section. Some of the buildings are closed, but many include period furnishings and wares.

When you hear a cacophony of horns and whistles, follow the noise to the **Nevada City Music Hall,** located next door to the hotel. There you can see the "famous and obnoxious horn machine from the Bale of Hay Saloon!" A sign on the machine begs visitors not to miss hearing "the machine that has driven 28 change-makers, 72 bartenders, and near a million tourists to the brink of insanity!" The music hall is a fascinating place to spend an hour listening to the many music machines and reading about their history. It's one of the largest collections of its kind on display in the United States today. The building was originally the Canyon Lodge Recreation Hall in Yellowstone.

Across the street is the railroad museum, where you can board the steam-powered **Locomotive No. 12** for the short train ride to Virginia City (the railroad depot there is at the west end of town). The museum has an observation car once used by Calvin Coolidge and the last "Catholic chapel car" in the world. The train runs every hour, and costs $6 to $10 for a round-trip, free for children under 7.

WHERE TO STAY & EAT

You can believe the claim of the **Star Bakery Restaurant and Emporium,** 1585 Mont. 287 (*©* **406/843-5525**), that it has the best biscuits and gravy in town, because it's also the *only* restaurant in town. Best known for its breakfasts, the cozy country restaurant serves three meals a day. The restaurant dates from 1865 and has an old-fashioned soda fountain and a gift shop. The specialty of the house, believe it or not, is fried pickles. The restaurant is closed Labor Day to Memorial Day.

Just an Experience Bed-and-Breakfast If you want something more modern than the Nevada City Hotel and Cabins (see below), this B&B is your only other choice in Nevada City proper (dare we say, "downtown Nevada City?"). Two of the rooms in the house share a bathroom, and one has a private bathroom. The rooms are large, with iron-post beds, but the cabins are larger, with enough room for six people, and include loft bedrooms for the kids, color TVs with VCR/DVD player combos, and full kitchens. The original log house here was built in 1864, but it has been remodeled and incorporated into a modern cedar-sided home. Pets are permitted outdoors only.

1570 Mont. 287, Virginia City, MT 59755. © **866/664-0424** or 406/843-5402. www.justanexperience.com. 3 units, 2 cabins. $75–$100 double. AE, DISC, MC, V. **Amenities:** Jacuzzi. *In room:* Kitchen (cabins only), no phone.

Nevada City Hotel and Cabins Entering this hotel is like taking a step back in time. Constructed in the 1860s, it was originally a stage stop near Twin Bridges, and still has the cool, musty smell of a mining-camp hotel. Most of the rooms are small and spare, but the upstairs Victorian suites are huge, furnished in rough but exquisite Victorian style, complete with polished burl wood furniture and private bathrooms. If you rent a cabin, be sure to lock your door—many tourists mistake the cabins for museum exhibits and may come exploring.

Mont. 287 (P.O. Box 205), Virginia City, MT 59755. © **800/648-7588** or 406/843-5377. Fax 406/843-5402. www. aldergulchaccommodations.com. 11 units, 17 cabins. $70 double; $77 cabin. AE, DISC, MC, V. Closed Oct to mid-May. *In room:* No phone.

BANNACK

Bannack was the site of the state's first big gold strike in 1862. With more than 60 of the town's original buildings preserved, the tumbledown town is a stark reminder of the heyday of the frontier: vigilantes stalking road agents stalking prospectors, in a favored place where the rivers yielded gold dust.

Born out of the discovery of placer gold in 1862, Bannack quickly grew to a town of 3,000 people, largely composed of those hoping to strike it rich. Blacksmiths, bakeries, stables, restaurants, hotels, dance halls, and grocery stores rapidly sprang up to complement an expanding mining industry.

Bannack became the first territorial capital and the site of the first territorial legislative session in 1864. But the placer veins in Grasshopper Creek were thin. Only a few years later, it was a ghost town, and the boosters of the capital movement had turned their attention to Virginia City and the richer mines at Alder Creek.

Notorious Henry Plummer killed his first local man in Bannack in Goodrich's saloon. The victim was Jack Cleveland, who had threatened another man about a debt, which the other man had already paid. Cleveland bragged that he wasn't afraid of him. Plummer, apparently a bystander, got to his feet, cursed Cleveland, roared, "I'm tired of this," and commenced to shooting. Cleveland got the worst of it, dying 3 hours later.

Plummer was an enigmatic outlaw. He was considered a "gentleman" by the standards of the era. He married a schoolteacher, though she left him after only 10 weeks of wedded bliss. Only a few weeks before he was hanged (see the section on Virginia City, above), Plummer held an elaborate dinner for territorial officials, including the governor and some of the vigilantes, for which he had ordered a $60 turkey from Salt

Lake City. His guests apparently saw nothing unusual about enjoying the hospitality of a man they had already decided to hang.

VISITOR INFORMATION   Designated a state park in 1954, Bannack is open year-round. Summer hours are from 8am to 9pm; winter hours 8am to 5pm. There is a seasonal visitor center, as well as camping and picnic grounds, a group-use area, and hiking trails. Other lodging facilities are available in nearby Dillon (see section 4 of this chapter). Day-use fees are $5 per vehicle ($1 for bikes), and $12 for a campsite ($10 in the off season). There are also rental cabins for $39 ($25 off season).

To get to Bannack from Dillon, drive 3 miles south on I-15, to Mont. 278. Head west 17 miles on Mont. 278, then south 4 miles when you see the sign. For additional information, call © **406/834-3413.**

A SPECIAL EVENT   Bannack Days, staged annually during the third weekend in July, is a 2-day event commemorating the history and heritage of Montana's early pioneers, with activities centering around frontier crafts, music, pioneer food, and dramas. A black-powder muzzleloader shoot, Sunday church services, and horse-and-buggy rides bring the "toughest town in the West" to life and are fun for the entire family.

8

The Hi-Line & North-Central Missouri River Country

This part of Montana is classic cattle and wheat country, the true home of the American cowboy. This vast section of Montana was once a wilderness of tall grass, rolling in the wind like the sea, home to millions of pronghorn and buffalo.

Lewis and Clark reported vast herds of the latter on the plains, but that wasn't all they saw here. When the adventurers entered Montana in 1805 just past the confluence of the Yellowstone and Missouri rivers, they saw their first grizzly bear, and Lewis made the first extensive description of the animal for science.

As you travel through this region, you'll likely be closely following the trail

of Lewis and Clark to the portage of the Great Falls. In the city of Great Falls, take time to visit the Lewis and Clark National Historic Trail Interpretive Center and experience vicariously one of the great American adventures. This portion of the state is also the landscape that Charles M. Russell memorialized in his famous Western paintings and bronzes.

But the region isn't all history and vanished mythology. There's plenty of outdoor activity, including fishing and boating on Fort Peck Lake, bird-watching at the C.M. Russell National Wildlife Refuge, rafting on the wild and scenic Missouri River, and both downhill and cross-country skiing.

1 Scenic Drives

DRIVING TOUR 1: KINGS HILL SCENIC BYWAY

The Kings Hill Scenic Byway is a 71-mile stretch of U.S. 89 through the Little Belt Mountains and the Lewis and Clark National Forest. You pick it up about 22 miles southeast of Great Falls, where U.S. 87 and U.S. 89 divide. Take U.S. 89 south toward the towns of Monarch and Neihart. From the south, take U.S. 89 north from just east of Livingston on I-90. For a leisurely tour, you can watch the wildlife and the scenery, then visit the ghost towns at Castle Town and Hughesville, and the historic mining site at Glory Hole. For a more active trip, go to **Sluice Boxes State Park** just north of Monarch to hike along the abandoned rail line there, or fish in Belt Creek. In winter, there is cross-country skiing at the Silver Crest Trail System (just north of Showdown Ski Area; see below), and snowmobiling at Kings Hill. Memorial Falls has a nature trail that is accessible to visitors with disabilities. Camping sites and national forest access points are at numerous spots along the highway.

DRIVING TOUR 2: THE CHARLES M. RUSSELL TRAIL

The Judith Basin inspired the work of one of the West's seminal artists, Charles M. Russell. This drive on U.S. 87/Mont. 200 between Great Falls and Lewistown provides an intimate glimpse at the unsettled West through Russell's eyes. The drive is

lovely in a pastoral way, but it helps to have a copy of the interpretive guide of the trail from Travel Montana's **Russell Country** (© **800/527-5348** or 406/761-5036; www. russell.visitmt.com) if you want to get the full experience. The guide uses Russell's art to illuminate the history of the basin.

These highways were designated the Russell Trail by the Montana legislature. The scruffy cowhands and toughened Indians that Russell painted have been replaced by carefully tended fields of grain, but with the help of Russell's art and a little imagination, you can put yourself back in the saddle in 1880s Montana.

From Great Falls, you go southeast through the towns of Raynesford, Geyser, and Moccasin, taking in the history of the Blackfeet, the infamous last wolves of the basin in Stanford, and the role of the railroads in Hobson. Spring and fall are the best times to match Russell's color palette with that of the scenery.

There are roadside turnouts along the highway for many of the 25 interpretive sites, including the settings for two of Russell's best-known paintings, *Buffalo in Winter* and *Paying the Fiddler*. Yogo Creek Road and Memorial Way are single-lane gravel roads included in the guide, but they are not recommended for RVs.

2 Great Falls

89 miles N of Helena; 219 miles NW of Billings

Great Falls, named for a series of waterfalls on the Missouri River, is a city of about 55,000, making it Montana's third largest (after Billings and Missoula). An important cog in the U.S. military strategy, it is the home of Malmstrom Air Force Base, which has been threatened with closure (which would devastate the city) but has also been tabbed the launching point for the X-33 VentureStar, the space shuttle of the future.

But the country around Great Falls looks much as Charlie Russell found it and painted it at the end of the 19th century. Russell made his home Great Falls, and did much of his painting in his studio there.

Nearly a century before Russell's day, Lewis and Clark came through with the Corps of Discovery in 1805, making an 18-mile portage around the falls. It is a sign of Great Falls' progress that it is now known as "The Electric City," because the falls that Lewis and Clark marveled at have been tamed by a series of dams to provide electric power.

ESSENTIALS

GETTING THERE   Great Falls serves as the hub for north-central Montana east of the Rockies. The **Great Falls International Airport** (© **406/727-3404**) has daily service from **Delta** (© **800/221-1212**), **Northwest** (© **800/225-2525**), **Horizon** (© **800/547-9308**), **United** (© **800/864-8331**), and **Big Sky** (© **800/237-7788**). Shelby, 88 miles northwest, provides the closest **Amtrak** service (© **800/872-7245**).

Great Falls is located on I-15, which runs north from Butte, where the highway intersects with I-90, passing through Helena and then Great Falls. From Missoula, you can take Mont. 200 east, or you can take I-90 a little southeast, pick up U.S. 12, and go east to Helena, then north to Great Falls. Mont. 200 is more scenic. From Billings, you can take Mont. 87 north to Lewistown and then west to Great Falls. Or you can go west on I-90 to Livingston, then take Mont. 89, which includes the Kings Hill Scenic Byway (see the driving tour above), northwest to Great Falls. From Bozeman, take U.S. 287 at Three Forks, then I-15 to Great Falls.

VISITOR INFORMATION   Request tour information from **Russell Country,** P.O. Box 3166, Great Falls, MT 59403 (© **800/527-5348** or 406/761-5036;

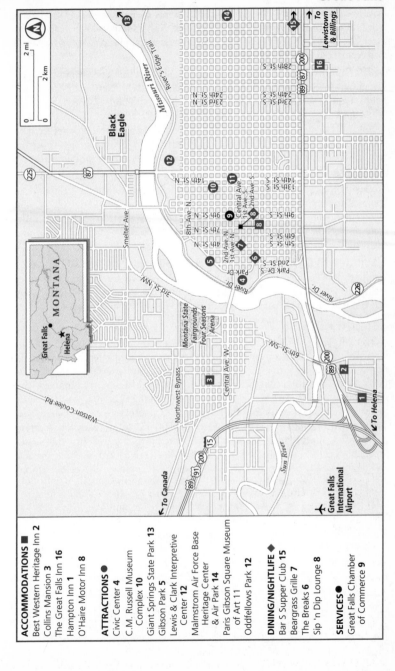

Great Falls

ACCOMMODATIONS ■
Best Western Heritage Inn **2**
Collins Mansion **3**
The Great Falls Inn **16**
Hampton Inn **1**
O'Haire Motor Inn **8**

ATTRACTIONS ●
Civic Center **4**
C.M. Russell Museum
  Complex **10**
Giant Springs State Park **13**
Gibson Park **5**
Lewis & Clark Interpretive
  Center **12**
Malmstrom Air Force Base
  Heritage Center
  & Air Park **14**
Paris Gibson Square Museum
  of Art **11**
Oddfellows Park **12**

DINING/NIGHTLIFE ◆
Bar S Supper Club **15**
Beargrass Grille **7**
The Breaks **6**
Sip 'n Dip Lounge **8**

SERVICES ●
Great Falls Chamber
  of Commerce **9**

www.russell.visitmt.com). The **Great Falls Chamber of Commerce** is at 100 1st Ave. N. (© **800/735-8535** or 406/761-4434). There is also a visitor center at the Broadwater Overlook at 15 Upper River Rd., right under the tall flagpole. For a Great Falls road report, call © **406/453-1605.**

GETTING AROUND   The best way to explore Great Falls and environs is by car. Rental franchises in town include **Avis** (© **800/331-1212**), **National** (© **800/227-7368**), **Rent-A-Wreck** (© **800/944-7501**), **Thrifty** (© **800/847-4389**), and **Hertz** (© **800/654-3131**).

You can also use public transportation. Great Falls Transit System operates seven bus lines from early morning to early evening Monday through Saturday (no service Sun and holidays). Call © **406/727-0382** or visit **www.gftransit.com** for information.

ORGANIZED TOURS   To see the town, take the 2-hour **Great Falls Historic Trolley** tour, $20 for adults, $5 children 2 to 12, with one stop at the Rainbow Falls. You pick up the tour at the High Plains Heritage Center, 472 2nd St. S. Call © **888/707-1100** or 406/771-1100 for information or browse **www.greatfallshistorictrolley. com** online. The company also does a cultural tour, a parks tour, and out-of-town day trips.

A SPECIAL EVENT   Great Falls hosts the **Lewis and Clark Festival** each year in late June; in 2006, however, it will be held in late July to commemorate the bicentennial of Lewis's journey home. Events include history workshops, tours, food booths, and children's activities. For information and tickets call © **406/452-5661.**

GETTING OUTSIDE
FISHING & BOATING

Great Falls is the unofficial dividing line for cold- and warm-water fish. You can fish for trout from Giant Springs, or take one of the many tours available on the Missouri. For half- to 7-day fishing and white-water trips on the Missouri, try **Montana River Outfitters,** 923 10th Ave. N., Great Falls (© **800/800-8218** or 406/761-1677; www. montanariveroutfitters.com). You can also paddle the Upper Missouri in 34-foot *voyageur*-style canoes with **River Odysseys West** (© **800/451-6034;** www.rowadventures. com), which offers tours in the style of the fur trappers (but with first-class tenting accommodations). Price for a 5-day trip on the Missouri is $1,295 to $1,395 per adult and $1,095 to $1,195 per child (16 or younger). The company also guides day trips and riverside hiking tours.

GOLF

The city offers two public golf courses: **Anaconda Hills** on Smelter Hill northeast of town (© **406/761-8459**) and the **Eagle Falls Golf Club** at 29th Street and River Drive North (© **406/761-1078**). Greens fees are $25 for 18 holes and $15 for 9 at both courses.

HIKING & BIKING

The 25-mile **River's Edge Trail** (www.thetrail.org) along the Missouri River starts downtown at the Oddfellows Park and runs out past Rainbow Dam and Crooked Falls, out to the Cochrane Dam. The trail is ideal for hiking, biking, running, walking, and roller skating. The **Great Falls Chamber of Commerce** (© **406/761-4434**) can provide you with information and trail maps.

WINTER SPORTS

Showdown Ski Area   Although relatively undiscovered, this is a full-service ski area, with 34 trails, two chairlifts, two surface lifts, and a 1,400-foot vertical drop. The area is perfect for beginning and intermediate skiers (30% beginner, 40% intermediate, 30% expert), with long, uninterrupted runs and lots of dry, light powder. There are ski rentals and a restaurant and bar. Family-oriented perks include a day-care center and a children's program. Adjacent to Showdown is the **Silver Crest Trail System** for cross-country skiing. **Montana Snowmobile Adventures** (© **406/236-5358**), located just off King's Hill Pass at Showdown Ski Area on the Lewis and Clark National Forest, rents snowmobiles and clothing for snowmobiling.

65 miles southeast of Great Falls on U.S. 89, near Neihart. © 800/433-0022 or 406/727-5553. For snow conditions, call 406/771-1300. www.showdownmontana.com. Full-day lift tickets $30 adults, $20 seniors 70 and over, $17 children 6–12, and free for children under 6. Early Dec to mid-Dec Fri–Sun 9:30am–4pm; mid-Dec to early Jan daily 9:30am–4pm; early Jan to early Apr Wed–Sun 9:30am–4pm. Closed Christmas, Martin Luther King Jr. Day, and Presidents' Day.

SEEING THE SIGHTS

Gibson Park, located 1 block north of the Civic Center along Park Drive, is quite nice, with a large pond, playgrounds, flower gardens, and picnic areas. This is a good place to pick up the trail system along the Missouri River. A grizzly bear chased Meriwether Lewis into the Missouri River near here in 1805. Every Wednesday evening, June through August, there is a free concert at the band shell. No word on whether the grizzly will be in attendance.

Benton Lake National Wildlife Refuge   Established in 1929 by President Herbert Hoover, the refuge is physically unimpressive, a small lake in a broad, open, treeless plain. But the 12,383 acres are important nesting grounds for waterfowl, especially mallards, pintail, teal, and canvasback. Bird-watching for waterfowl and prairie species is best early in the morning or in the evening. There's a 9-mile autotour route that takes about an hour, marked with signs to provide information about what you're seeing, but Mother Nature is constantly changing the refuge attractions.

922 Bootlegger Trail, Great Falls, MT 59404. © 406/727-7400. http://bentonlake.fws.gov. Free admission. Open daily during daylight hours. Go 1 mile north of Great Falls on Mont. 87, take a left on Bootlegger Trail, then proceed about 9 miles north to well-marked entrance.

C.M. Russell Museum Complex 🏆🏆   You can divide the world into two kinds of people—those who like cowboy art, and those who don't. It is a measure of Charlie Russell's greatness that, although he was a cowboy artist, almost everybody likes his work. This facility, which includes tours of Russell's studio and home, is one of the high points of any trip to Montana, and it's worth going out of your way to see.

Russell and the dime novelists practically invented the West. But the power of his work is that the personality of everyone and everything portrayed—American Indians, cowboys, even the landscape—shines through. Much modern "Western art" concentrates on the scenery and fierce animals without making much of a statement. Conversely, Russell had something to say about a celebrated but passing way of life, and he said it powerfully.

The museum houses the largest collection of Russell's work on the planet, hung in chronological order—starting with a trio of paintings he did when he was 13. From there, visitors get to see an amazing evolution in his vivid, self-taught style, from early watercolors, to statues made of wax and plaster and later bronze, to Christmas cards and sketches, all the way to his final, most renowned oil period before his death in 1926. The studio contains some of Russell's personal belongings, including many of the Indian artifacts he collected to help maintain his art's authenticity. A number of other excellent Western artists are shown to good advantage in the museum; besides the permanent display of works by Russell protégé Olaf Seltzer (and a collection of Browning firearms), exhibits change several times a year. The **Mint Café** serves lunch Tuesday through Saturday. You can spend an hour or all day here.

400 13th St. N. ⓒ **406/727-8787.** www.cmrussell.org. $8 adults, $6 seniors, $3 students (age 6 or older), free for kids 5 and under. May–Sept daily 9am–6pm; Oct–Apr Tues–Sun 10am–5pm. Tours May–Sept Mon–Fri 10am and 2pm; Sat–Sun 2pm. Closed major holidays.

Giant Springs State Park ☆ Lewis and Clark came upon and described the Giant Springs, purportedly the largest freshwater spring in the world. The spring now also feeds a fish-breeding facility nearby. It burbles out of the 250-million-year-old Madison Formation, a large water-bearing formation that provides a lot of groundwater throughout the northern West. The springs send out over 100,000 gallons a minute into the 201-foot-long Roe River, credited in the *Guinness Book of World Records* as the shortest in the world. The entire park covers 218 acres and has about 2 miles of trails.

The Great Falls that gave Lewis and Clark so much trouble have been dammed, but you can see a few remnants of their former glory from overlooks. In the spring, especially, you can see the power of the river flowing through the spillways at Rainbow Dam, spewing mist hundreds of feet into the air, creating the rainbows in the sunshine that so entranced the explorers. Lewis called Rainbow Falls "one of the most beautiful objects of nature." The Montana Department of Fish, Wildlife, and Parks also operates a fish hatchery and visitor center nearby (open 8am–4:30pm), where visitors can purchase hunting and fishing licenses. Call for information on ranger-led hikes and bike rides.

4600 Giant Springs Rd. ⓒ **406/454-5840.** http://fwp.state.mt.us. $5 per vehicle. Open daily during daylight hours. Take River Dr. east along the Missouri River to Giant Springs Rd. Turn left and drive about a quarter of a mile, just past the Lewis and Clark Interpretive Center.

Lewis and Clark National Historic Trail Interpretive Center ☆☆ Located on a bluff overlooking the Missouri River, this facility is hands down the best Lewis and Clark exhibit between St. Louis and the Pacific Ocean. The facility is cleverly arranged to follow the adventurers' path to each major point along the way. You start at Monticello with Thomas Jefferson's instructions to the Corps of Discovery. Then you go from one high point to the next along the journey. You visit a Mandan earth lodge, see the grizzlies, and feel the voyagers sweat as they pull their 3,000-pound boat along the 18-mile portage of the Great Falls. Of this portage Clark wrote: "To state the fatigues of this party would take up more of this journal than other notes which I find scarcely time to set down." An excellent facility, it will take several hours to see properly. The docents are wonderfully informed and entertaining. Interpretive programs are held year-round, outdoors at a "River Camp" setting during the summer months, with evening programs most Fridays at 8pm and frontiersmen demonstrating age-old skills on Saturdays.

4201 Giant Springs Rd. ⓒ **406/727-8733.** www.fs.fed.us/r1/lewisclark/lcic.htm. $5 adults, free for children under 16. Memorial Day to Sept 30 daily 9am–6pm; Oct 1 to Memorial Day Tues–Sat 9am–5pm, Sun noon–5pm. Closed major holidays.

Malmstrom Air Force Base Heritage Center and Air Park   The air park has a number of aircraft from various eras, primarily from the 1950s and 1960s, but the real attractions here are the implements of nuclear weaponry: a Minuteman III ICBM and its transporter erector. Inside, amid scads of military equipment and uniforms and a reconstruction of a World War II–era barracks, is the old command center that once controlled the base's nuclear missiles. Interpretation of the exhibits is minimal, unfortunately.

Malmstrom Air Force Base, east end of 2nd Ave. N. past 57th St. © **406/731-2705**. Free admission; civilian passes are available at the base's visitor center. Air park: Open daily during daylight hours. Museum: Mon–Fri 10am–4pm. Closed holidays.

Paris Gibson Square Museum of Art   Located in a national historic landmark building that served as Great Falls's first high school, Paris Gibson Square is now the cultural and art center of the city. The changing art shows display the works of artists from around the Northwest, as well as pieces from the permanent collection. The selection includes both contemporary and historical exhibits in a comfortable, beautifully restored space. In 2006, look for "Night Wings," with magnified digital prints of moths with accompanying sound and video.

1400 1st Ave. N. © **406/727-8255**. www.the-square.org. $5 adults and children 7 years and older, free for children under 7. Mon–Fri 10am–5pm (Tues also 7–9pm); Sat noon–5pm.

SHOPPING

There are at least 19 antiques stores in Great Falls, and the chamber of commerce can give you a map of their locations. The terrific **Dragonfly Dry Goods,** 504 Central Ave. (© **406/454-2163**), specializes in home decor, clothing, gifts, and things Western. **Hoglund's,** 306 1st Ave. S. (© **406/452-6911**), has an awe-inspiring selection of cowboy boots and hats. You can find Montana-made souvenirs or gifts at **Best of Montana,** 2912 10th St. S. (© **406/761-1233**).

WHERE TO STAY

Aside from the properties listed below, we recommend the **O'Haire Motor Inn,** downtown at 17 7th St. S. (© **800/332-9819** or 406/454-2141; www.ohairemotor inn.com), with double rates of $50 to $70; the **Hampton Inn,** 2301 14th St. SW (© **406/453-2675**), with rates of $89 to $99 double and $149 suite; and the **Best Western Heritage Inn,** 1700 Fox Farm Rd. (© **800/548-8256** or 406/761-1900), with rates $89 to $99 double and $99 to $129 suite.

Collins Mansion   Built in 1891 and listed on the National Register of Historic Places, this grand Queen Anne–style mansion was carefully converted into a stylish bed-and-breakfast in 1998. At 8,000 square feet, this gleaming white structure stands out (it sits in an otherwise typical neighborhood overlooking the west side of Great Falls) with a wraparound veranda and ornate details. All of the rooms contain period antiques and a private bathroom. The pinnacle is the Master Suite, decorated in black and gold, featuring a half-canopied queen-size bed with an antique iron frame and a city view from the bay window. The more feminine Cherub room is done in burgundy and mauve with an angelic headboard above its iron-framed queen-size bed.

1003 2nd Ave. NW, Great Falls, MT 59404. © **877/452-6798** or 406/452-6798. www.collinsmansion.com. 5 units. $80–$100 double. Rates include full breakfast. AE, MC, V. In room: A/C.

The Great Falls Inn   This is a reliable independent hotel a few miles outside downtown, located near the University of Great Falls and a medical center. The rooms are quiet and very well kept, with contemporary furnishings. All have queen-size beds, reclining lounge chairs, refrigerators, and microwaves. The inn has 12 new business-class rooms with dataports and two telephone lines. While there is a complimentary continental breakfast, there is no restaurant (or pool, for that matter), but it is more than adequate as a place for a night's sleep.

1400 28th St. S., Great Falls, MT 59405. ⓒ 800/454-6010 or 406/453-6000. Fax 406/453-6078. 61 units. $63 double. Rates include continental breakfast. AE, DC, DISC, MC, V. **Amenities:** Exercise room; Wi-Fi network; coin-op washers and dryers. *In room:* A/C, cable TV, dataport, fridge, coffeemaker, hair dryer, iron.

WHERE TO DINE

Bar S Supper Club *(Finds* STEAKS/SEAFOOD Authentic cowboy steakhouses have become endangered with the expansion of national chains in recent years, but you'll find the real deal at the Bar S, about 5 miles east of Great Falls city limits. The place has a rustic charm, with brands on the walls, lots of red vinyl and wood, and the requisite beer signs. The menu focuses almost exclusively on Montana choice beef, ranging from a 10-ounce tenderloin to a 30-ounce rib-eye, and there is also a fair amount of seafood and a smattering of poultry. Some locals come every Saturday night, and nobody leaves hungry.

8535 U.S. 89. ⓒ 406/761-9550. Reservations accepted. Main courses $7–$21. AE, DISC, MC, V. Wed–Thurs 5–9pm; Fri–Sat 5–10pm; Sun 4–9pm.

Beargrass Grille *◈◈* STEAKS/SEAFOOD After managing the landmark Depot in Missoula, Great Falls native B. J. Loucks came home and opened a slick eatery of his own, the Beargrass Grille, in 2005. The classy dining room, with white tablecloths under peach walls and prints of Paris streetscapes, contrasts with the retro-plush feeling of the adjacent lounge and more casual tapas bar. All of them feature excellent food and service, with hand-cut steaks and fresh seafood flown in from Hawaii. The dinner menu includes Thai vegetable rice and several pasta dishes as well; lunch is sandwiches, burgers, and the ever-popular pig wings served with honey-bourbon barbecue sauce—not to mention seared ahi.

518 Central Ave. ⓒ 406/453-1277. Reservations recommended. Lunch $6.25–$13; dinner $15–$25. AE, DC, DISC, MC, V. Mon–Fri 11am–2:30pm; Sat noon–2:30pm; Tues–Sat 5–10pm. Bar open later. Closed Sun.

The Breaks *◈* CONTINENTAL/FUSION The Breaks opened in 2004 in a renovated brick building that was a Model T factory in the 1920s before settling in as a Sears warehouse. Today, the space would be unrecognizable to its former occupants: a strikingly contemporary space with blue neon, colorful artwork, and heaps of industrial chic. Patrons can sit in the dim bar area or in an airier dining room with booths and tables. The food is also surprisingly creative for staid Great Falls, with good homemade soups and such entrees as garlic-rubbed jumbo scallop kabobs and buffalo short ribs marinated in gin and rubbed with garlic. Lunches are sandwiches, salads, and other light fare (including crepes stuffed with veggies, salmon, or barbecue beef). There's a nightclub with live music in the basement below.

202 2nd Ave. S. ⓒ 406/453-5980. Lunch $6.75–$9.50; dinner $9.50–$26. AE, DISC, MC, V. Mon–Sat 11am–2pm; Mon–Thurs 5–9:30pm; Fri–Sat 5–10pm. Closed Sun.

GREAT FALLS AFTER DARK

The bar scene in Great Falls is fairly sedate and typical for a city its size, with one outrageous exception: the **Sip 'n Dip Lounge** at the O'Haire Motor Inn, 17 7th St. S. (ⓒ **406/454-2141**), an authentic Tiki bar, clad in bamboo and loaded with South Seas paraphernalia of all kinds. The sip in the moniker refers to the cocktails served by the bar. The dip, however, is quite unusual: Windows behind the bar make for a view of a pool where actresses in mermaid garb swim on Friday and Saturday nights. Then you've got "Piano Pat" Sponheim tickling the ivories, as she has since 1963, delivering unusual covers of Neil Diamond, Sinatra, and Elvis tunes. This is one of the kitschiest, wackiest, and flat-out coolest nightspots in not just Montana, but the entire West.

A SIDE TRIP TO FORT BENTON

Thirty-six miles north of Great Falls on Mont. 87, you can drop down to the historic town of Fort Benton. The town faces the Missouri River, which formed its destiny. There is a pleasant waterfront park with an interesting series of murals detailing the town's history.

The Lewis and Clark expedition made a critical decision a short distance downstream from Fort Benton, where the Marias River enters the Missouri. The expedition was divided on which was the main branch of the Missouri. The vote was 30-to-2 for the Marias being the main branch. The two who went for the other branch were Lewis and Clark. Had they chosen the Marias branch, there is a good chance that the expedition would have failed, because they would not have been able to get over the Rockies before winter. A statue of the explorers at this decisive point dominates one end of Front Street in Fort Benton. A small visitor center at the Bureau of Land Management (BLM) office on Front Street offers some information about this event.

Next to the Lewis and Clark statue is the **Keelboat Mandan,** a full-scale replica 62 feet long and 13 feet wide built for the movie *The Big Sky.* In the heyday of keelboating, broad-shouldered men could push a boat upstream at a pace of about 2 miles a day. There is also a monument on the riverfront to Shep, a collie sort of dog whose master died and was sent East by train for burial. After that, Shep met every train in Fort Benton from 1936 until 1942, waiting for his master's return, until—hard of hearing and arthritic—the old dog met his end one wintry morning on the tracks.

The first steamboat reached Fort Benton in 1850, and 600 of them stopped here from 1859 to 1870. Furs, goods, and gold were all shipped through the town. **The Museum of the Northern Great Plains,** 1205 20th St. (© **406/622-5316**), tells the story of settlement. There is a vast collection of farming equipment here, testifying to the fortitude and ingenuity of the settlers on the Great Plains. **The Museum of the Upper Missouri,** at Old Fort Park and Front Street (© **406/622-5316**), has an excellent historical collection, including the rifle that the Nez Perce Chief Joseph surrendered at the Bear Paw battle, and the history and personality of Fort Benton as expressed by the artist Charlie Russell, the preacher Brother Van, and the infamous "Madame Mustache," the woman who reputedly introduced Calamity Jane to prostitution. Both museums are open Monday to Saturday from 10am to 5pm and Sunday from 1 to 5pm, from late May to late September.

The BLM manages 149 miles of the Missouri here as a federally designated Wild and Scenic River, and canoeing and keelboating are both good ways to take in the landscape. Contact the **Fort Benton Chamber of Commerce** (© **406/622-3864;** www.fortbenton.com) for a list of river outfitters.

For lodging, try the **Grand Union Hotel** ⭐⭐, 1 Grand Union Square (P.O. Box 1119), Fort Benton, MT 59442 (© **888/838-1882** or 406/622-1882; www.grand unionhotel.com), right on the river. Built in 1882 at a cost of $50,000, it was completely restored to its original splendor in 1999. Said to be Montana's oldest hotel, the Grand Union has 26 small but luxurious guest rooms (with modern conveniences: phones with dataports and TVs), a top-notch restaurant, and a brewpub. The three suites are larger. During the high season, rates start at $105 for a double and go up to $175 for the suites, a price that includes a deluxe European breakfast.

3 The Rocky Mountain Eastern Front (★

53 miles W of Great Falls

The eastern front of the Rockies is an isolated, sparsely populated section of Montana, but it is no less beautiful than the peaks and valleys to the west. A great paleontological mystery was solved here. Scientists had discovered many dinosaur fossils in the far-eastern part of the state, but no nests or eggs. When fossilized dinosaur eggs turned up along the Rocky Mountain Eastern Front—the shoreline of a shallow sea 65 million years ago—paleontologists learned that the beasts had migrated to this area to lay their eggs.

There are two towns with distinctive personalities on the front: Choteau and Augusta. Choteau bills itself the gateway to the Rockies. Named for the president of the American Fur Co., who brought the first steamboat up the Missouri, it is one of the oldest towns in Montana.

Tiny Augusta is a cheerful, friendly community. Unlike a lot of small Western towns, it is not hustling to turn itself into something else. It's only about 2 blocks long, with weathered wood exteriors on the buildings. Folks are out and about, the guy at the gas station gives you full service at the self-service pump, and everybody's on a first-name basis with just about everybody else. The pace picks up a bit the last weekend in June when the rodeo hits town.

ESSENTIALS

GETTING THERE   The closest airport is in Great Falls, about 52 miles from Choteau (see the "Great Falls" section, earlier in this chapter, for airport information). From the airport, take I-15 north to the U.S. 89 exit (about 12 miles), then go west on U.S. 89 for 40 miles to Choteau.

To reach the area by car from the northwest, drive on U.S. 2 along the southern border of Glacier National Park. At Browning, go south on Mont. 89 to Choteau. From Choteau, go southwest on U.S. 287. Two miles past the junction of Mont. 21 and U.S. 287, Augusta lies 40 miles due west of Great Falls.

VISITOR INFORMATION   For an information packet, contact the regional tourism office for **Travel Montana's Russell Country,** P.O. Box 3166, Great Falls, MT 59403 (© **800/527-5348** or 406/761-5036; www.russell.visitmt.com). In Choteau, write to the **Choteau Chamber of Commerce** at P.O. Box 897, Choteau, MT 59422 (© **800/823-3866** or 406/466-5316; www.choteaumontana.com). For hunting and fishing info, contact the **Montana Department of Fish, Wildlife, and Parks,** 4600 Giant Springs Rd., Great Falls, MT 59406 (© **406/454-5840**).

GETTING AROUND   The only way to travel this country is to drive. The closest car-rental agencies are in Great Falls.

(Tips Rental-Car Tip

A reliable four-wheel-drive vehicle is strongly recommended for touring the back roads of the Rocky Mountain Eastern Front. Many are gravel roads that turn into a slippery mush locally known as "gumbo." Car-rental companies in Great Falls and other nearby cities keep such vehicles in stock, but requests should be made weeks in advance.

OUTFITTERS & ORGANIZED TRIPS

Also see **Pine Butte Guest Ranch** and **JJJ Wilderness Ranch** (see "Where to Stay," later in this section) for learning vacations covering the region's ecology and natural history and backpacking and horse-packing trips, respectively.

High Country Adventures ★★ A Montana native, Bill Cunningham has been guiding backpacking expeditions into the Bob Marshall Wilderness since 1973, and that makes his High Country Adventures the oldest backpacking guide company in the country. It's also the Bob's only licensed backpacking outfitter, where there are dozens of licensed horse-packing guides. Cunningham goes on every trip, as does his wife, Polly. The company organizes three or four trips per summer that cover about 10 miles of trail in an average day, ranging from a week to 12 days. Breaking up the hiking are good meals, good company, and a layover day for a little fishing or mountain climbing.

P.O. Box 1404, Choteau, MT 59422. © **406/466-5699**. www.high-country-adventures.bigstep.com. Reservations required. Trips start at $850 per person per week. Rates include shuttle from airport, food, and community gear.

Timescale Adventures (Kids) Timescale Adventures runs some popular dinosaur field programs, designed for all ages and levels of interest. The 3-hour seminar is a walk along the Rocky Mountain Eastern Front covering identification of dinosaur bones and eggs, and what to do when you find one. The 2-day seminar includes a dig and instruction in fossil-preservation techniques. All of the programs originate from the **Two Medicine Dinosaur Center** in the town of Bynum, 14 miles north of Choteau on U.S. 89. The center, open daily from 9am to 6pm from Memorial Day to Labor Day (and 9am to 5pm Monday through Thursday the rest of the year), houses displays on the various dinosaurs the organization has excavated. Admission is $4 for adults and $3 for seniors and children under 12.

P.O. Box 786, Bynum, MT 59419. © **800/238-6873** or 406/469-2211. www.timescale.org. 3-hr. day tour $45 adults, $35 children under 13; 1-day program $110 per person per day; longer programs $90–$100 per person per day. Advance registration is required; space is limited.

A SCENIC DRIVE

The beautiful **Sun Canyon Drive** on Sun Canyon Road starts out along the plains west of Augusta, and then weaves up the canyon past a 1913 Bureau of Reclamation dam. During the time of Lewis and Clark, the Blackfeet called the river that carved the canyon the Medicine River, but it is now known as the Sun River. The canyon, a gray-granite jumble with snowcapped peaks in the distance, is a weekend getaway spot for residents all along the front. There are opportunities for fishing, boating, hiking, and four-wheeling in the area. The road up here is an easily navigable gravel track for the most part, but it can be very rugged in portions, especially if they've been trying to fix it. After you get to the national forest, however, the road is paved. Go figure.

SHOPPING

Latigo and Lace on Main Street in Augusta (© **406/562-3665**) is an eclectic shop overflowing with the work of Montana artists and craftspeople, plus books, cups of cappuccino, and an array of "made in Montana" collectibles. Latigo and Lace can also put your brand on a coffee mug, if you have a hankering.

WHERE TO STAY

The Bunkhouse Inn (Value) This is the cowboy way. Housed in a building that dates from 1912 and is constantly under renovation, the Bunkhouse is sort of a bed-and-breakfast without the breakfast. Proprietor Terry Taillon sends his guests to Mel's

Diner across the street. Taillon says that Mel doesn't rent rooms, so he won't serve food. That's the sort of town this is. The rooms are small and basic; there are no phones or televisions, but instead of staring at the idiot box, you can sit out on the second-floor porch watching the slow-paced bustle on Main Street. On Memorial Day weekend, you'll have a front-row seat to Montana's smallest parade as the gray-haired American Legionnaires march to the strains of Sousa marches played on a boom box carried by two of the ladies' auxiliary.

122 Main St. (P.O. Box 294), Augusta, MT 59410. ℂ 800/553-4016 or 406/562-3387. 10 units. $40–$45 double. MC, V. *In room:* No phone.

JJJ Wilderness Ranch ⭒   The Triple J is a guest ranch located in the extraordinary Sun Canyon near Gibson Reservoir. Run by the Barker family for two generations, the ranch offers everything the outdoorsy type could want—horseback riding, hiking, fishing, pack trips into the Bob Marshall Wilderness Area (at an extra charge), and pure and simple relaxation. Nestled in a forest of aspen and spruce, the rustic cabins accommodate a total of 20 guests, so you're never crowded. Though there are few amenities, it's not due to an oversight: Those who come here don't want phones and televisions.

Box 310, Augusta, MT 59410. ℂ 406/562-3653. Fax 406/562-3836. www.triplejranch.com. 7 cabins. $1,425 per adult per week, $1,005 per child 6–12 per week, double occupancy with a 1-week minimum stay. Rates include all meals and ranch activities (except pack trips), and transportation from and to the Great Falls Airport. MC, V. **Amenities:** Outdoor Jacuzzi; children's programs; activities desk; laundry service. *In room:* No phone.

Pine Butte Guest Ranch ⭒ *Finds*   Located deep in the Sawtooth Range along the Rocky Mountain Eastern Front, Pine Butte Guest Ranch is the property of The Nature Conservancy, a national land-preservation organization. Since a few endangered grizzly bears have made the 15,500-acre Pine Butte Swamp Preserve their home, the Conservancy saw fit to buy it to protect the delicate ecosystem. The preserve is the only place left in the Lower 48 states where grizzlies use both the mountain and prairie ranges as they did before settlement drove them to the remnant habitat in the mountains.

Pine Butte Guest Ranch focuses on education, running numerous workshops on appreciating and understanding the natural world. You can also do the usual dude-ranch activities—riding, hiking, swimming, and the like. Pine Butte was first home-steaded in the 1930s, but it has always been a guest ranch, not a cattle ranch, which accounts in part for the largely undisturbed habitat. Average winter winds of 80 mph have helped keep development to a minimum.

Each of the ranch's log cabins has a river-rock fireplace and is comfortably equipped with handmade furniture. However, the little time you'll be indoors will likely be spent in the lodge, with a handsome pine interior, Western decor, and a few photos of Kenneth and Alice Gleason, who owned and ran the place before the Conservancy bought it.

HC 58, Box 34C, Choteau, MT 59422. ℂ 406/466-2158. Fax 406/466-5462. www.nature.org/montana. 10 cabins. Summer $1,200–$1,500 per person per week; natural-history workshops $1,500. Rates include room, board, riding, ranch facilities, and transportation to and from Great Falls International Airport. AE, MC, V. **Amenities:** Outdoor heated pool; activities desk; washers and dryers. *In room:* No phone.

Viewforth Bed & Breakfast ⭒   The best place to stay in Augusta is, strictly speak-ing, not in Augusta, but 7 miles north. After a sojourn in Oregon, longtime Montanans Terese and Keith Blanding returned to their home state and opened Viewforth, an ele-gant Craftsman-style bungalow with a welcoming front porch. Each of Viewforth's two rooms has a mellow quality, with queen-size beds and private bathrooms, plus excellent views of Sawtooth Mountain and Castle Reef. The highlight of a stay here will likely be the time spent enjoying the silence, watching sheep graze in the pasture below as an ominous storm peers over the horizon. Breakfast here is a treat, featuring fresh-baked goods, fruit, and a hot entree such as eggs Blanding (the owners' version of eggs Benedict).

4600 U.S. 287, Fairfield, MT 59436. (℃ 406/467-3884. www.viewforth.com. 2 units. $85 double 1st night, $80 thereafter. Rates include full breakfast. No credit cards. *In room:* No phone.

WHERE TO DINE

For breakfast or lunch in Choteau, we also like the **Outpost Deli,** 819 N. Main St. (℃ **406/466-5330**), with good sandwiches and even better shakes.

Buckhorn Bar STEAKS/AMERICAN   The Dellwo family has run this bar in the same location for more than 40 years, serving a selection of steaks, chicken, and burgers. If you've got a serious appetite, your best bet is a charbroiled 16-ounce rib steak with a salad and potato for $16. The portions are remarkably large and moderately priced, the atmosphere classic woody Western, complete with dozens of antler racks overhead, cowboy-hatted patrons, and pool tables.

Main St., Augusta. (℃ **406/562-3344**. All dishes $3.25–$16. No credit cards. Daily 8am–2am. (After 11pm, only pizzas are available.)

Mel's Diner AMERICAN   Everyone in town will send you to breakfast at Mel's, a tiny place with four booths and two tables. You'll get good food at good prices: bacon and eggs, hotcakes, and biscuits and gravy for breakfast; fish and chips and burgers for lunch and dinner. You can also take your pick of ice-cream treats, shakes, and malts. The hours depend on how business is doing.

Main St., Augusta. (℃ **406/562-3408**. All dishes $1–$8. No credit cards. Daily 6am–6pm (or later).

4 Lewistown

105 miles E of Great Falls; 128 miles N of Billings

The hub of a vast agricultural region, Lewistown is not right on the way to any particular tourist destination, so if you find yourself here, you probably meant to come. The town is blessed with great downtown architecture, stately homes, and modest citizens. And there is some notable recreation here—especially hunting and fishing. Located in the center of the Judith Basin, Lewistown is surrounded by three mountain ranges—the Big and Little Snowies, the Moccasin, and the Judith. While Charlie Russell lived in Great Falls later, the Judith Basin is where he worked as a cowboy, and where he fell in love with Montana.

ESSENTIALS

GETTING THERE   Big Sky Airlines (℃ 800/237-7788) provides daily commuter airline service to **Lewistown Municipal Airport** (℃ **406/538-3264**) on a route that flies from Billings to Havre. The **Rimrock Stages bus depot,** 513 1st Ave. N. (℃ **406/538-9227**) provides service from Billings and Great Falls.

Lewistown is connected to other Montana cities by two-lane U.S. highways that radiate from the town. From Billings, go north 92 miles, then west 31 miles on U.S. 87. From Great Falls, Lewistown is 105 miles east on U.S. 87.

VISITOR INFORMATION   The **Lewistown Chamber of Commerce** has its offices adjacent to the Museum of the Central Montana Historical Association at

Symmes Park at 408 NE Main (℃ **406/538-5436;** www.lewistownchamber.com). Maps from the Bureau of Land Management, the U.S. Forest Service, and the C.M. Russell Wildlife Refuge, and local maps are all available. Information about Lewistown is also available from **Travel Montana's Russell Country** (℃ **800/527-5348**).

GETTING AROUND   Rental cars are available from **Budget** (℃ **406/538-7701**).

SPECIAL EVENTS   The **Chokecherry Festival,** held on the Saturday following Labor Day, honors that smarter-than-the-average-berry, the chokecherry, one of the few indigenous fruits of the prairie. Generally overlooked by poets and songwriters— no one has ever been the chokecherry of someone's eye, nor has life ever been a bowl of chokecherries—Lewistown attempts to place the chokecherry on its proper pedestal with parades, bake sales, pie cook-offs, and even a pit-spitting contest.

Lewistown's other big annual event is the **Montana Cowboy Poetry Gathering** ✮. Each year in mid-August, cowboys, ranchers, large animal vets, and other swaybacked and bowlegged Montana literati gather to swap lies and poems. Those who may have considered the term "cowboy poetry" an oxymoron are usually pleasantly surprised to find a relentless rhyming vitality to the poetry, along with a lot of humor, and an honest and healthy appreciation of fellow poets. For details on these events, call the **Lewistown Chamber of Commerce** at ℃ **406/538-5436.**

GETTING OUTSIDE

For information on activities in the national forest lands in this area, contact the **Lewis and Clark National Forest** (℃ **406/791-7700**).

CROSS-COUNTRY SKIING

If you're here in the winter, there is good cross-country skiing in any of the three mountain ranges that ring the valley. There are a number of trails accessible by car in the Judith Mountains north of town, on old logging and mining roads. Head north on U.S. 191 to the Maiden Canyon sign, then take a left and follow the road for 5 miles to the trails.

FISHING

High in the Big Snowy Mountains is **Crystal Lake,** about 35 miles southwest of Lewistown. This is a popular and somewhat remote recreational area that offers good fishing, hiking, and camping. You have to travel about 25 miles on gravel road to get there. Take U.S. 87 west of town for 8 miles, then turn south at the sign for Crystal Lake. After about 16 miles it runs into Forest Service Road 275, which you should follow for another 9 miles to the lake. Motorized boats are prohibited, but overnight RV and tent camping is available. For good trout fishing closer to town, try **Big Spring Creek,** which begins south of Lewistown and flows north through town to join the Judith River. You can easily access Brewery Flats on Big Spring Creek about 2 miles outside of town on Mont. 238. Flatwillow Creek in the Forest Grove area of the Little Snowies provides some rainbow and cutthroat fishing. For **flat-water fishing,** try Upper and Lower Carter's Pond, man-made ponds 6½ miles north of Lewistown on U.S. 191. There are picnic facilities and overnight camping as well. The **James Kipp Recreation Area,** 78 miles north of town on the Missouri River in the Charles M. Russell National Wildlife Refuge, also has fishing, camping, hiking, and a boat ramp. Take U.S. 191 northeast until it intersects with Mont. 19, then go north about 35 miles. Camping is $6 a night. Contact the **Bureau of Land Management** (℃ **406/538-7461**) for more information.

GOLF

The 18-hole **Judith Shadows Golf Course** (© **406/538-6062**) is an alternative-spikes-only facility located at the end of Marcella Avenue in the northeast corner of Lewistown. Greens fees are $13 for 9 holes, $22 for 18.

HIKING

At **Crystal Lake** (see "Fishing," above), there are numerous trails into the Lewis and Clark National Forest, including the Crystal Lake Loop National Recreation Trail. There is also good hiking along the Wild and Scenic Missouri River from the James Kipp Recreation Area. The **Judith Resource Area of the Bureau of Land Management,** Lewistown District Office, Box 1160, Airport Road, Lewistown, MT 59457 (© **406/538-7461**), can give you information on additional hiking trails in the nearby mountains.

SEEING THE SIGHTS

A little too cutely named, the **Charlie Russell Chew-Choo Dinner Train** (call © **800/8609646** or 406/538-8721; www.charlierussellchewchoo.com) runs from Lewistown to Denton and back every Saturday from Memorial Day through the end of September, with special holiday trains. On the 56-mile round-trip ride, the train crosses three large trestles and navigates a 2,000-foot tunnel during its 3½-hour run through the Judith Basin. The schedule varies, so call ahead. A regular summer trip with dinner is $90 per adult, $50 for children under 13.

Big Spring, located 7 miles south of Lewistown on County Road 466, is the third-largest freshwater spring in the world. The spring is the water source for the town, and is considered one of the purest in the nation. It is bottled by the Big Spring Water Company and sold at stores in the west-central part of the U.S. The spring also feeds the Montana State Fish Hatchery nearby.

Lewistown became a regional commercial center after a ranching and mining boom in the early part of the 20th century. The industry barons built large homes in a range of styles, primarily Gothic and Victorian. The first to build was J. T. Wunderlin, a gold miner and organizer of the Empire Bank & Trust. Others soon followed, creating a neighborhood of elegant homes. They lived in the **Silk Stocking District,** which is just northeast of downtown on Boulevard. (Not the section of Boulevard near Symmes Park; if you're there, you're lost.) The Lewistown Chamber of Commerce (© **406/538-5436**) can provide information on self-guided tours. The homes, however, are private residences and not open to the public. At 220 W. Boulevard, there is a plaque outside The Symmes-Wicks House (see below) describing the area. At the top of the hill overlooking the Silk Stocking District, check out the **Fergus County Courthouse** (7th Ave. and Main St.), a gold-domed mission-style courthouse built in 1906.

WHERE TO STAY

Pheasant Tales Bed-and-Bistro ⚡   While the nearby Symmes-Wicks House (see below) offers an early-20th-century experience, Pheasant Tales is a thoroughly modern, beautifully constructed and furnished guesthouse with some unique touches. Proprietors Chris and Rick Taylor are both avid pheasant hunters and anglers. After Chris began preparing gourmet meals with the birds brought down by friends, hunters told the couple that if they opened a bed-and-breakfast, they would stay there on hunting trips. Since Chris prefers fixing dinners, she instead opened a bed-and-bistro (Pheasant Tales's guests still get breakfast) specializing in eclectically prepared game birds, with impressive results. The inn is done in reddish pine, and the large rooms are comfortably furnished and have kitchenettes. With advance reservations, Chris can often prepare a gourmet dinner in the evening (starting at $25 per person). Chris will also consider requests for dinner from visitors not staying at the Pheasant Tales if they call ahead. The Taylors also breed English setters, so there is almost always a brace of puppies providing entertainment. There's an extensive deck, land to walk on, and good fishing nearby as well.

1511 Timberline Rd., Lewistown, MT 59457. ℂ **406/538-7880.** Fax 406/538-6244. www.tein.net/pheasant. 6 units. $85 double; $160 suite. Rates include full breakfast. AE, MC, V. Located 4 miles south of Lewistown. **Amenities:** Guest laundry. *In room:* Kitchenette, no phone.

The Symmes-Wicks House Bed & Breakfast ✿   Charles and Carole Wicks have beautifully restored this 1909 shingle-style, Arts and Crafts home, which sits right in the heart of the Silk Stocking District. Though you can easily see the stately exteriors of all of the surrounding homes, a stay here provides the unique opportunity to view the inside of one, replete with Tiffany glass and period antiques. Upstairs, the guest rooms are tastefully decorated, one with masculine tones, a sleigh bed, and a bathroom that's a wooden work of art. The room facing northeast has a more feminine touch. The bathroom isn't so much a room as it is a tasteful area partitioned off from the main room, with a green-marble shower as its centerpiece. In the early 20th century, there was an influx of Croatian stonecutters to Lewistown. Some of their work can be seen on this house, as well as on other buildings in the area.

220 W. Boulevard, Lewistown, MT 59457. ℂ **406/538-9068.** Fax 406/538-5331. 3 units. $70 double. Rates include full breakfast. AE, DISC, MC, V. *In room:* A/C, hair dryer, iron.

Yogo Inn   Once a train depot, the Yogo is now a very good independent hotel, with clean, quiet rooms and a hint of rustic elegance. There is a well-kept, interior courtyard that catches the sun and features a stage taken by musicians throughout the summer. The Yogo is popular with business travelers, and everything is functional but not fancy. It's the locus of the annual Montana Cowboy Poetry Gathering every August, and it books up pretty quickly for the event.

211 E. Main St., Lewistown, MT 59457. ℂ **800/860-9646** or 406/538-8271. www.yogoinn.com. 121 units. $65–$75 double. AE, DISC, MC, V. Pets accepted. **Amenities:** 2 restaurants; lounge/casino; indoor pool; indoor Jacuzzi; Wi-Fi network; coin-op washers and dryers. *In room:* A/C, TV, dataport.

5 The Hi-Line: U.S. 2

Havre: 115 miles NE of Great Falls; Fort Belknap: 46 miles E of Havre; Glasgow: 279 miles N of Billings

If you're not from Montana and find yourself on the Hi-Line, you're probably on the way somewhere else. There isn't a great deal of anything up here, except for wheat, birds, lots of ground squirrels, and the occasional pronghorn.

There are a number of National Wildlife Refuges along this drive: the gigantic **Charles M. Russell NWR,** and the smaller **Black Coulee, Bowdoin,** and **Medicine Lake**—the latter on the far-eastern border of the state. Like most of the refuges nationwide, they are managed primarily for the benefit of birds, especially migratory waterfowl. So this is a good place to bring your field guide: Even if you don't leave your car, you'll be able to identify many species, possibly including the Franklin's gull with its telltale black wingtips, the melodious western meadowlark, or the marsh hawk (or harrier, not a true hawk). The latter flies low to the ground, flapping its wings more often than the gliding hawks, and is gray when mature, brown when young, with a white bar across its rump.

The roadsides here are dotted with white crosses—memorials to people who have died in auto accidents. Maintained by friends and family, many are decorated with flowers, flags, and ribbons. There are a lot of them. Don't be fooled by the long, straight stretches of road. Drive carefully.

Call the **Havre Area Chamber of Commerce,** 130 5th Ave., Havre, MT 59501 (© **406/265-4383;** www.havremt.com) for further information about the area.

FROM HAVRE TO FORT BELKNAP

Havre probably isn't anyone's idea of a vacation spot, but it has its moments. There are some interesting historic sites, including the nearby **Bear Paw Battlefield** (see "Bear Paw Battlefield: The Nez Perce Surrender," below) the site of the last major battle of the Indian Wars. For both cultural and natural history, the best place to start is the **H. Earl Clack Museum,** located in Havre's Holiday Village Mall, 1753 W. U.S. 2 (© **406/265-4000**). The museum is open from 10am to 5pm Wednesday through Sunday (1–5pm in winter). Admission is free.

Start your driving tour of the region just south of Havre on U.S. 87, coming up from Great Falls. Drive north to Havre until you reach the junction with U.S. 2. Take U.S. 2 east until it converges with Montana's version of Route 66, a state highway running south through the Fort Belknap Indian Reservation. Take 66 through the reservation to the intersection of U.S. 191. Turn left (northeast) and drive until the road joins U.S. 2 again, about 57 miles.

SEEING THE SIGHTS

Fort Assinniboine   This well-preserved fort was established in 1879, after it was already obsolete. It was intended to protect settlers from Indian attacks, but all the tribes had already been defeated. After the defeat of Chief Joseph in the nearby Bear Paw Battle, the Fort Assinniboine troops didn't have much to worry about. After the fort closed, much of the land around it was turned into the Rocky Boys Reservation. Only guided tours are permitted because the fort is now run by Montana State University as an agricultural research station.

3 miles south of Havre on U.S. 87. © **406/265-4000** or 406/265-4383. $5 adults, $2.50 students, free for children under 6. Guided tours only, originating from the H. Earl Clack Museum in Havre daily at 5pm. Open Memorial Day to Labor Day.

Havre Beneath the Streets ⚓   This tour of Havre's boisterous history as a railroad and cowboy town provides an interesting look at the past. When a devastating fire in 1904 destroyed Havre's business district, the labyrinth of tunnels and basements under the town served as a subterranean "shopping mall." Many local businesses of the last century were located here. Their products included legal representation, food, and laundry service—not to mention honky-tonk, gambling, opium, and prostitution. There is also an aboveground railroad museum, focusing on the area's rail history.

120 3rd Ave., Havre. © **406/265-8888.** $10 adults, $9 seniors, $7 children 6–12, free for children under 6. Reservations recommended. Summer daily 9am–5pm, tours 9:30am–3:30pm; winter Mon–Sat 10am–4pm, tours 10:30am–2:30pm.

Rocky Boys Indian Reservation and the Rocky Boy Powwow   Southwest of Havre lies the home of 2,000 Chippewa and Cree Indians on this rather small plot of land at the Western Front of the Bear Paw Mountains. For years the U.S. government

Bear Paw Battlefield: The Nez Perce Surrender

One of the most remarkable events of the Indian Wars culminated at the Bear Paw Battlefield ((C) 406/357-3130), a unit of the Nez Perce National Historic Park (www.nps.gov/nepe), located 26 miles south of Chinook on County Road 240.

In 1877, in what is now northeast Oregon, the Army tried to force a band of Nez Perce Indians under the leadership of Chief Joseph onto a reservation far from their native lands. The Nez Perce decided to escape, trying to reach Canada where they hoped to join Sitting Bull's Lakota, who had already found homes there.

Joseph led 800 of his tribal members on a 1,700-mile flight through Yellowstone National Park and eventually north to this site, a mere 45 miles south of the Canadian border and freedom.

The U.S. Army under Gen. Oliver O. Howard pursued the tribe as it fled. A Civil War hero known as "the praying general," Howard, a deeply religious Christian, developed considerable hostility toward some of the Nez Perce leaders because he considered them heathens. Through a series of brilliant maneuvers, Joseph and his band of warriors, women, children, horses, and cattle escaped or defeated the army at every turn. Even Howard was forced to admit in his memoirs about the chase, "The leadership of Chief Joseph was indeed remarkable. No general could have chosen a safer position or one that would be more likely to puzzle and obstruct a pursuing foe."

They fought several battles along the way, but Col. Nelson A. Miles finally caught Joseph and his band in a snowstorm at Bear Paw, a rolling, grassy landscape achingly close to the freedom promised by the Canadian border. After a 6-day fight, Joseph surrendered on October 5, 1877. The chief's rifle is now in the Museum of the Upper Missouri in Fort Benton.

tried to keep the Cree from settling in the United States, and the tribe was homeless. In 1911, when Fort Assinniboine was abandoned, the Chippewa and Cree had part of the land set aside as a reservation. Then, as now, employment was difficult to come by. The first weekend of every August, the Rocky Boy Powwow is held near Box Elder.

From Havre, drive south on U.S. 87 and turn east at Box Elder onto Duck Creek Rd. Drive 14 miles to the Tribal Headquarters. (C) 406/395-4282.

Wahkpa Chu'gn Bison Kill   From a steep cliff above the Milk River called Wahkpa Chu'gn, the Assinniboine drove bison to their deaths to provide food for the tribe. Indians used the jump from 2,000 years ago until the 15th century. The hour-long guided tours are very informative, in part because this is one of the largest and most studied buffalo jumps in existence. Visitors are also given the opportunity to try their skill with an "atl-atl," or throwing stick.

Behind the Holiday Village Shopping Mall on U.S. 2 W. (C) 406/265-6417 or 406/265-4000. www.buffalojump.org. Tour info available at H. Earl Clack Museum. $6 adults, $5 seniors, $4 students, free for children under 6. June to Labor Day weekend, tours daily 10am–5pm, evening tour Mon–Sat at 7pm; winter tours available by reservation, weather permitting.

Chief Joseph is believed to have delivered this famous speech, translated by an interpreter:

"Tell General Howard I know his heart. What he told me before I have in my heart. I am tired of fighting. Our chiefs are killed. Looking Glass is dead. Toohoolhootze is dead. The old men are all killed. It is the young men who say yes or no. He who led the young men is dead. It is cold and we have no blankets. The little children are freezing to death. My people, some of them, have run away to the hills, and have no blankets, no food; no one knows where they are—perhaps freezing to death. I want time to look for my children and see how many of them I can find. Maybe I shall find them among the dead. Hear me, my chiefs. I am tired; my heart is sick and sad. From where the sun stands now, I will fight no more forever."

That night, White Bird and 200 of his followers slipped away to Canada. Of the 431 remaining, 21 died by the end of spring. The survivors moved to a reservation in Oklahoma, where another 47 of Joseph's people died and many more became ill. Finally, in 1885, 118 Nez Perce who agreed to convert to Christianity were allowed to relocate to the Lapwai Agency near Lewistown, Idaho. The rest, including Joseph, were settled on the Colville Reservation in Nespelem in northeast Washington State.

Joseph never gave up hope of a return to his homeland in the Wallowa Valley. He met with Pres. William McKinley in 1897, and tried unsuccessfully to purchase the land in 1900. He died at Colville in 1904 at age 64. Even in death, he wasn't returned to the Wallowa Valley, but was buried at Nespelem.

For more insight into the flight of Chief Joseph and the Nez Perce, stop at the **Blaine County Museum**, 501 Indiana St. in Chinook (© **406/357-2590**), and take a look at the interpretive displays and the 20-minute film *Forty Miles from Freedom*.

WHERE TO STAY

The **El Toro Inn**, 521 1st St. (© **800/422-5414**), is a reliable roadside motel charging about $50 for a double room. Rooms are well kept but basic, although they do have refrigerators and microwaves. On Route 2 in the eastern part of town there is a pleasant campground called the **Havre RV Park**, 1415 1st St. (© **800/278-8861**). There are showers, a saloon, a casino, laundry, and a store. Cost is about $33 for an RV, $18 for a tent.

Best Western Great Northern Inn ⓖ   This is a relatively new entry in the Havre lodging scene and a relatively upscale one. The rooms have a tad more square footage than your typical Best Western, and they have more extensive facilities than anyplace else in Havre. There is no restaurant, but you can charge your meal to your room at the restaurants across the street. There are a bridal suite with an in-room hot tub and a corporate suite. The 24-hour business center has fax, copying, and computer capabilities.

1345 1st St., Havre, MT 59501. © **888/530-4100** or 406/265-4200. Fax 406/265-3656. www.bestwestern.com/greatnortherninn. 75 units. $80–$100 double; $129–$159 suite. Rates include continental breakfast. AE, DC, DISC,

MC, V. **Amenities:** Lounge/casino; indoor pool; exercise room; indoor Jacuzzi; sauna; courtesy car; business center; Wi-Fi network. *In room:* A/C, cable TV, dataport, coffeemaker, hair dryer, iron.

WHERE TO DINE

PJ's AMERICAN   You're out on the Hi-Line, driving through Havre, so you might as well eat in a typical Montana place. PJ's is across the street from the railway station; there's a poker game in the corner with the clicketyclack of chips, and the boop-boop-boop of the electronic games of chance. The food isn't bad at all, from a menu of sandwiches for lunch and steaks and seafood for dinner, and you can play keno while you wait.

15 3rd Ave. ℭ **406/265-3211.** Breakfast and lunch $4–$6; dinner $7–$20. MC, V. Sun–Thurs 6am–9pm; Fri–Sat 6am–10pm.

Wolfie's Diner (Kids) AMERICAN   Hidden upstairs in Havre's downtown Atrium Mall, Wolfie's is our lunch pick in Havre. The basic dining room sports a 1950s theme, complete with pictures of Elvis, Marilyn, and James Dean hanging alongside a hula hoop and a leather jacket. The kitchen makes good sandwiches—we liked the Denver, with scrambled eggs, green peppers, ham, and onion on Texas toast—as well as steaks and shrimp baskets for dinner. Better yet are the hand-dipped shakes, sundaes, freezes, and whips, not to mention fresh cream puffs.

220 3rd Ave., in the Atrium Mall. ℭ **406/265-2111.** Main courses $4.50–$9. MC, V. Mon–Sat 11am–8pm.

FORT BELKNAP RESERVATION

Established in 1888, the Fort Belknap Reservation is home to the Gros Ventre and Assinniboine tribes. It was named for William W. Belknap, who was secretary of war under Pres. Ulysses S. Grant. The Gros Ventre call themselves the A'a'nin, or White Clay People. They had lived in North Dakota's Red River Valley from A.D. 1100 to 1400, gradually being pushed west by competition from other tribes. After coming to the Missouri River country in about 1730, they split into two tribes, and the southern branch became known as the Arapaho.

The Assinniboine split from the Yanktonai Sioux in the early 1600s, supposedly over a squabble. Two of the first ladies of the tribe fought about a local delicacy, a buffalo heart. They call themselves the Nakota, The Generous Ones. There is also a branch of the tribe at the Fort Peck Reservation to the east.

There is a small **museum** and visitor center at the intersection of Mont. 66 and U.S. 2 (ℭ **406/353-8372** or 406/353-8473; www.fortbelknapnations-nsn.gov). From here you can arrange a tour of the tribe's herd of more than 800 buffalo and learn a little bit about the tribe's culture ($15–$20, reservations recommended).

Nearby Snake Butte was often used as a site of vision quests, where individuals sought supernatural powers or medicine. These powers came with a price. It was said few who had them lived long lives. The Army Corps of Engineers quarried Snake Butte for stone to build the dam at Fort Peck in the 1930s.

If you head south from here to Hays, then turn to the east, you'll come to **St. Paul's Mission,** a solid stone structure established by Jesuit missionaries in 1886. Next to it is a tiny chapel built in 1931 that is dedicated to Our Lady of the Little Rockies. A local devotee has carved a statue practically identical to the supposedly miraculous one at Einsiedeld in Switzerland. To get here, take Mont. 66 south from U.S. 2 at Fort Belknap for about 40 miles to the sign for Hays. Turn left (east). Once you get to Hays, follow the road south after it turns to gravel. The mission is on the left (east) side of the street about a quarter-mile after the road turns south.

Up the road is Mission Canyon, a steep, narrow, cool gash in the otherwise open landscape. Just after entering the canyon, you'll see a natural stone arch. The very brave can climb nearly to the top, and there are several ledges where you can pose for the photographer.

FROM GLASGOW TO THE FORT PECK INDIAN RESERVATION & THE C.M. RUSSELL WILDLIFE REFUGE

People moving through the northeast extremes of Montana can find themselves a little disoriented by the sheer vastness of the horizons that stretch unbroken all the way to the Dakotas. Although this is mostly wheat country, it's not totally flat. In fact, it is sharply rolling and canyon-scored country, but it's open to the eye in all directions.

In 1879, Robert Louis Stevenson rode an immigrant train through here and later wrote: "What livelihood can repay a human creature for a life spent in this huge sameness? He is cut off from books, from news, from company, from all that can relieve existence but the prosecution of his affairs. A sky full of stars is the most varied spectacle he can hope. He may walk 5 miles and see nothing; ten, and it is as though he had not moved; twenty, and he is still in the midst of the same great level, and has approached no nearer to the object within view, the flat horizon which keeps pace with his advance."

There is a story, usually attributed to an area just over the border in western North Dakota, but in the same sort of landscape, of a lone Indian who watched patiently as a recently arrived farmer plowed into the virgin earth, turning the soil with its deep and tangled roots to begin the civilization of the already vanishing native prairie. After some time, the Indian came over to the farmer, pointed to the plowed earth, and said, "Wrong side up."

The story is probably another in the long chain of myths on which the West is built in the American imagination. But there are two contrasting sentiments made tangible here that illustrate the conflicting impulses of America: progress and preservation.

The first and easiest to spot is the Fort Peck Dam and Lake. Construction of the dam began in 1933, at the height of the Great Depression, as a way to put men to work and to provide inexpensive water to the growing agricultural area.

The dam is the largest hydraulically earth-filled dam in the world, nearly 5 miles across, backing up a lake that is 134 miles long with 1,600 miles of shoreline—more shoreline, it is said, than the entire coast of California. The dam is one of the many Corps of Engineers projects that have turned the cantankerous Missouri River that Lewis and Clark navigated into a tame and regulated lake from the Mississippi River to the Rockies.

Seven thousand men and women went to work on the dam in 1933, and at the peak of employment nearly 11,000 were employed here. Locally, the attitude toward the dam was ambivalent, as the residents were losing their homes to the slowly rising water. On the other hand, they could appreciate the need for jobs, for irrigation water, for electric power, even for a large recreational lake. The story of the dam is told at the **Fort Peck Powerhouse Museum** (© **406/526-3431** or 406/526-3411). The powerhouse looms over the landscape like a chunky Art Deco skyscraper that somehow got lost on its way to Des Moines. The museum (it's free and open 9am–5:30pm daily from Memorial Day to Labor Day weekend; closed winter) offers tours of the power plant on the hour (except for the last tour of the day, which leaves at 4:45pm). It's located on Mont. 24 at Fort Peck Dam. Nearby, the **Fort Peck Interpretive Center and Museum** on Yellowstone Rd. (© **406/526-3493;** www.pecksrex.com) houses a fine collection of dinosaur fossils and displays on the area's history in an impressive new facility that opened in 2005. The big attraction is a terrifying, fleshed-out replica of the most complete Tyrannosaurus rex skeleton ever found, unearthed nearby in 1997. It's open year-round Monday to Friday, from 9:30am to 5pm at peak season and varied hours in the off season.

SPECIAL EVENTS   **Fort Peck Lake,** backed up by the dam, is the best spot in Montana for walleye fishing. An annual competition, the **Governor's Cup,** takes place there each spring. Contact the Corps of Engineers at © **406/526-3411** or the Glasgow Area Chamber of Commerce (© **406/228-2222;** www.glasgowmt.net) for the schedule and details.

OUTFITTERS & SEEING THE SIGHTS

The tiny town of Fort Peck is Montana's only planned community, the result of its heyday as the housing base for the workers at the dam in the 1930s. It started out as a trading post in 1867, then grew with the dam, then faded when construction was finished. It is testimony to the remoteness of this region that in 1934, months after the U.S. Army Corps of Engineers had begun construction of this $100-million project (big money during the Depression), a New York supplier asked the New York army headquarters how to address some equipment it was sending out to Montana. The army solemnly replied that there was no such place as Fort Peck—it had been abandoned in the 1880s.

The **Fort Peck Theatre** is a large former cinema built in the 1930s for the workers. The surprisingly beautiful theater seats 900 people for summer stock. Its season runs approximately from the last week of June to the last week of August. Call © **406/ 526-9943** or browse **www.fortpecktheatre.org** for information and tickets.

Surrounding the many miles of shoreline at Fort Peck Lake is the **Charles M. Russell Wildlife Refuge,** named for the famous Western wildlife cowboy artist Charlie Russell. Born in 1864 in St. Louis, Russell was a working Montana cowboy at the age of 16 and drew much of his artistic inspiration from those years. He greatly admired the region's American Indians, and deplored the plowing of the grasslands. Russell knew that destroying the native grass would destroy the habitat for the animals, the bison would be lost, the Indian conquered. Russell didn't like seeing the West civilized, and he had little use for "settlers."

Turnoffs and campsites are located all along the perimeter of the refuge, as are boat ramps for anglers. Flat Creek, Rock Creek, and Nelson Creek boat ramps are easy to reach, located just off Mont. 24, which skirts the eastern side of the lake. There are 15 campgrounds scattered along the lake margin. The camping varies from rugged to semi-civilized. Only two campgrounds—the West End Campground and Downstream Campground—have flush toilets and showers; both are located near the dam. Contact the Corps of Engineers (© **406/526-3411**) for information.

The **Fort Peck Indian Reservation** is home to the Assinniboine and the Sioux. The Sioux, who had been on the reservation by themselves, were joined by the Assinniboine nation after smallpox killed more than half of the tribe farther west along the Missouri River and again threatened the tribe after it resettled near Fort Belknap. The escape from the deadly disease brought them to Fort Peck. Now the reservation is home to many non-Indians, with American Indians possessing less than half of the actual reservation.

This has been an extremely important area for the study of dinosaurs. The world's first Tyrannosaurus rex remains were discovered in 1902 just south of where the lake is in Garfield County. The **Garfield County Museum** (© **406/557-2026**) in Jordan has replicas of the T. rex skull there, along with a duckbill dinosaur and triceratops. It is open Memorial Day to Labor Day, from 1 to 5pm. Jordan is located at the intersection of Mont. 59 and Mont. 200 in the plains south of Fort Peck Lake. From Miles City, drive north on Mont. 59 for 83 miles. From Glendive, take Mont. 200 west 111 miles. From Fort Peck Dam, take Mont. 24 south 59 miles to Mont. 200, then take Mont. 200 west 36 miles.

WHERE TO STAY

The Cottonwood Inn & Suites   This motel and convention center is far and away the nicest place in Glasgow: modern and clean, if a little small in the lobby. The rooms are conventional motel rooms, with queen- or king-size beds and, for the most part, refrigerators. The restaurant, the **Prairie Rose,** is the most popular one in town. It specializes in homemade soups, bread, and pies, all made from scratch. The motel has complimentary high-speed Internet access and valet and room service, unusual out here in Hi-Line Country. There's also an adjacent RV park under the same ownership.

U.S. 2 E. (P.O. Box 1240), Glasgow, MT 59230. © **800/321-8213** or 406/228-8213. Fax 406/228-8248. www.cottonwood inn.net. 106 units. $65–$75 double. AE, DISC, MC, V. Pets accepted. **Amenities:** Restaurant; indoor pool; Jacuzzi; sauna; room service; coin-op washers and dryers; dry cleaning. *In room:* A/C, cable TV, dataport, coffeemaker, hair dryer, iron.

Fort Peck Hotel   A stone's throw from U.S. 2, this registered historic site is an intimate, old-fashioned hotel. Built in 1934 during the heyday of the WPA, it harks back to the slower way of life in Montana. There are no televisions or telephones in the rooms, a situation that tends to usher people out into the bar in the lobby for (gasp!) conversation. There is a good restaurant that serves three meals a day and has summertime dinner buffets that cater to the Fort Peck Theatre's crowds. The rooms are small but serviceable, with high ceilings and spare furnishings reminiscent of the 1930s and 1940s.

Missouri Ave. (P.O. Box 168), Fort Peck, MT 59223. © **800/560-4931** or 406/526-3266. Fax 406/526-3472. 33 units. $43 double with shared bathroom; $58 double with private bathroom; $93 for 2 adjoining rooms. AE, DISC, MC, V. Closed Dec–Mar. **Amenities:** Restaurant; lounge. *In room:* No phone.

9

Bozeman, South-Central Montana & the Missouri Headwaters

Relatively pristine, south-central Montana is a world-class playground for the outdoor recreation enthusiast. Its biggest draws are the mountains that are a haven for hikers and campers, and the fly-fishing waters of the four major rivers that run through its valleys—the Madison, Jefferson, Gallatin, and Yellowstone.

During the winter, downhill skiing takes over at Big Sky, which claims to have the largest vertical drop of any hill in the United States (4,180 ft.), and the new Moonlight Basin resort. The region is also excellent for cross-country skiing—Lone Mountain Ranch and Bohart Ranch are two of the best Nordic skiing facilities in the state.

Bozeman, home of Montana State University, provides the hip, intellectual charm and culture of a college town—good bookstores and restaurants, charming shops, even a brewpub—as well as cultural events that appeal to both the cosmopolitan and cowboy cultures. The Livingston Rodeo, one of the best in the region, complements Bozeman's Sweet Pea Festival, a celebration of music and the performing arts.

A few years ago the area around Bozeman bounded by the Bridger, Gallatin, Madison, and Tobacco ranges seemed like an undiscovered bargain for real estate opportunists. Those times have changed; the communities of Bozeman, Livingston, and Belgrade experienced a boom as newcomers moved in, attracted to the easygoing Montana lifestyle and the wide range of outdoor activities. It's also been discovered by a number of Hollywood types, such as Peter Fonda and Glenn Close, who have purchased real estate in the area. Media mogul Ted Turner is another famous part-time resident.

1 A Scenic Drive

The Bozeman–Livingston–Three Forks area is one large intersection. **Interstate 90** runs east to west through this region, and from it, three valley highways extend south or north. The westernmost of these highways, **U.S. 287,** passes through Three Forks, and runs 120 miles south along the Madison Valley to the town of Ennis (a fishing mecca) and West Yellowstone, the western gateway to Yellowstone National Park. From Bozeman, **U.S. 191** parallels U.S. 287 down the Gallatin Valley, past the resort community of Big Sky, to West Yellowstone.

The third highway, **U.S. 89,** runs 57 miles south from Livingston through the Paradise Valley to Gardiner and the north entrance of Yellowstone. Though the area is populated primarily by ranchers and there are few developed attractions, it's a beautiful drive, especially through Yankee Jim Canyon.

South-Central Montana

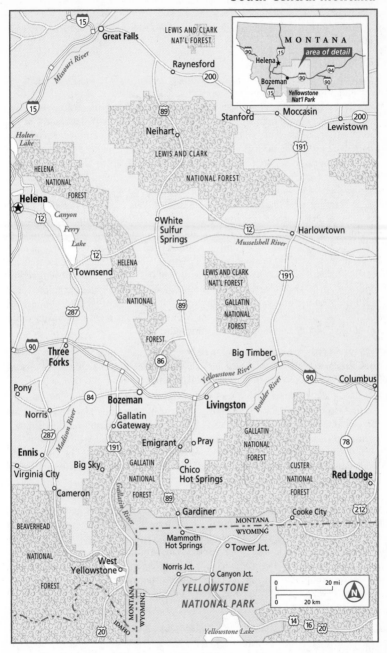

Red Lodge can be reached a few different ways, but the most scenic is by taking I-90 to exit 408 at Columbus and heading south on Mont. 78 through Absarokee and Roscoe for 48 miles.

THE BEARTOOTH SCENIC BYWAY

This loop drive takes you to altitudes of almost 11,000 feet, taking in the sights that led Charles Kuralt to call this the most scenic road in America.

Begin in Livingston. Drive south on U.S. 89, following the Yellowstone River through Paradise Valley, 53 miles to Gardiner, and then into Yellowstone National Park. Once inside the park, you can stop off at Mammoth Hot Springs, a geothermal wonderland just inside the park's northern boundary. Then, take the road from Mammoth Hot Springs east to Tower Junction, continuing east to the park's northeast entrance at Silver Gate to pick up U.S. 212 (this is the Beartooth Byway). From here, the road begins to wind upward along the Montana and Wyoming border for nearly 40 ear-popping miles until it reaches the Beartooth Pass (elevation 10,947 ft.). From that spectacular altitude, you'll see miles and miles of mountains across both Wyoming and Montana. The road then drops for 24 miles as the byway continues on to Red Lodge. From Red Lodge, drive north on Mont. 78 down into the high plains before heading back to the mountains of Bozeman, west on I-90. The entire trip takes between 6 and 8 hours, depending on the time of day you choose to drive it and the condition of the roads. *Note:* The Beartooth Byway is especially subject to the whims of Mother Nature; mudslides closed the road for almost all of its 2005 summer season. For current information, contact the **Montana Department of Transportation** (© **406/657-0209** or 406/444-9424; www.mdt.mt.gov).

2 Bozeman ★★

82 miles E of Butte; 142 miles W of Billings; 91 miles N of West Yellowstone

A college town and tourism hot spot with a friendly, semi-bohemian vibe, Bozeman was first settled in the 1860s as a farming hub. Today, its cowboy edge has been mostly chipped away, revealing a sophisticated Western chic in the form of a vibrant downtown strip filled with independent shops and restaurants. The area bustles all year long—whatever the season, the locals are always out and about. The city has also become the unofficial capital of Montana environmental politics, with several nationally important nonprofits based here.

Bozeman has experienced its greatest growth since 1990, and it shows little sign of slacking off. In fact, longtime residents worry that the town may be getting a little too hip. But it's easy to see the city's appeal. The university, Montana State, is a good one, and the downhill skiing at nearby Bridger Bowl is excellent and free of lift lines. The fact that Bozeman is less than 100 miles from Yellowstone certainly doesn't hurt, either.

But Bozeman hasn't always been a hotbed of activity. In the 1930s, for instance, local ordinances prohibited dancing anywhere in town after midnight, and in beer halls at any time. It was illegal to drink beer standing up, so all the bars had plenty of stools.

ESSENTIALS

GETTING THERE Bozeman's **Gallatin Field** (© **406/388-8321**) serves a wide region in this part of the state. Daily service is available from **Delta** (© **800/221-1212**), **Northwest** (© **800/225-2525**), **Horizon Air** (© **800/547-9308**), and **United Express** (© **800/241-6522**).

Bozeman

ACCOMMODATIONS ■
Best Western GranTree Inn **4**
Bozeman Backpacker's Hostel **9**
Bozeman's Western Heritage Inn **22**
Cooper Park Cottage **23**
Fairfield Inn **1**
Hampton Inn **2**
Hilton Garden Inn **3**
Holiday Inn **6**
Lehrkind Mansion **20**

DINING ◆
Casa Sanchez **7**
Community Food Co-op **17**
The Emerson Grill **11**
The Garage **19**
John Bozeman's Bistro **12**
Mackenzie River Pizza Co. **16**
Main Street Overeasy **14**
The Mint **5**
Montana Ale Works **21**
Naked Noodle **13**
Plonk Wine **15**
Soby's **18**

ATTRACTIONS ●
American Computer Museum **5**
Emerson Center **11**
Gallatin County Pioneer Museum **10**
Museum of the Rockies **8**
Taylor Planetarium **8**

Bus service is available through **Greyhound,** with a terminal at 1205 E. Main St. (© **406/587-3110**). **Rimrock Stages** (© **800/255-7655**) operates intrastate service.

By car, Interstate 90 handles most of the traffic. It is 140 miles along I-90 from Billings to the east and 202 miles from Missoula to the west. For **local road reports,** call © **406/586-1313**.

VISITOR INFORMATION The **Bozeman Area Chamber of Commerce** is located at 2000 Commerce Dr. (© **800/228-4224** or 406/586-5421; www.bozeman chamber.com). There's also information from Memorial Day to Labor Day at 1001 N. 7th Ave., and year-round at the **Downtown Bozeman Visitor Center** (© **406/ 586-4008;** www.historicbozeman.com) at 224 E. Main. The chamber publishes an extensive visitors guide, as well as maps detailing the area's farms and historic hot

spots. Travel Montana calls this region **Yellowstone Country.** For info from them, call
© **406/556-8680.**

GETTING AROUND   There are a number of car-rental agencies in Bozeman,
including **Avis** (© 406/388-6414), **Budget** (© 406/388-4091), **Enterprise** (© 406/
586-8010), **Hertz** (© 406/388-6939), and **National** (© 406/388-6694). For taxi
service, call **All Valley Cab** (© 406/388-9999).

SPECIAL EVENTS   Held the first full weekend each August, the **Sweet Pea Festival,** at Lindley Park and throughout Bozeman (© **406/586-4003;** www.sweetpea
festival.org), is a music, arts, and sports festival, with a parade, bands from rock to reggae, dance, art, and even a little Shakespeare. Unspooling over 6 days in early October, **Hatch** (© **406/586-2635;** www.hatchfest.com) is an audiovisual arts festival that
includes film screenings, workshops, filmmaker Q&As, and live music after dark.

GETTING OUTSIDE

Many of the outdoor activities discussed in this section take place in the **Gallatin
National Forest.** For additional information, including current road and trail conditions, contact the Bozeman Ranger District, 3710 Fallon St., Suite C, Bozeman, MT
59718 (© **406/522-2520** or 406/587-6701; www.fs.fed.us/r1/gallatin).

ORGANIZED ADVENTURES

Yellowstone Safari Company ⋆ (© **866/586-1155** or 406/586-1155; www.yellowstone
safari.com) specializes in wildlife-biologist-guided trips in Montana, at Yellowstone
and Grand Teton national parks, and along the Lewis and Clark Trail. Founded by
biologist Ken Sinay—once called "Vesuvian in his enthusiasm"—the company offers
guide services for both individuals and groups. Using specially adapted vehicles and
boats, their activities include single- and multiday safari-style expeditions to observe
wildlife and explore the natural and cultural history of the area. Full-day trips include
guides, transportation, binoculars, spotting scopes, food, and beverages. Rates depend
on group size and the kind of tour, with full-day rates varying from about $500 for
one person to about $130 per person for seven people. A half-day safari is $90 per person. Advance reservations are required, the earlier the better.

Founded in 1982 and the first of its kind, **AdventureWomen,** 15033 Kelly Canyon
Rd., Bozeman (© **800/804-8686** or 406/587-3883; www.adventurewomen.com),
offers customized trips to just about anywhere in the world for active and adventurous
women, age 30 and older. In Montana, the company guides hiking trips as well as skiing and guest-ranch trips. Rates for the weeklong outings start at $2,195 per woman.

In the guiding business since 1985, **Off the Beaten Path,** 7 E. Beall St., Bozeman
(© **800/445-2995** or 406/587-4147; www.offthebeatenpath.com), is another top-
notch local guiding outfit. The company offers about a dozen trips throughout
Wyoming and Montana each year, with an emphasis on Yellowstone and Grand
Teton, with expeditions that run the gamut from family outings to wolf watching.
The trips range from 4 to 10 days in length, and prices typically run between $350
and $500 per day.

BIKING

There are plenty of biking opportunities here, mostly off-pavement. Some of the best
mountain biking is in the Gallatin National Forest—check with the Bozeman Ranger
District office (see "Getting Outside," above) for tips on where to go.

CROSS-COUNTRY SKIING

If you want to explore on your own, many drainages provide excellent skiing around Bozeman. Some local favorites are the 10-mile, moderately difficult **Bozeman Creek to Mystic Lake Trail** that gains 1,300 feet of elevation over its course (go south of S. 3rd St. for 4 miles to Nash Rd., then east on Nash Rd. for a mile to Bozeman Creek Rd., then 1 mile south to the parking area), and the **Hyalite Reservoir Ski Loop,** a 4-mile, relatively flat track around the Hyalite Reservoir, also rated moderately difficult (see the "Hiking" section, below). The road may not be plowed or maintained in winter. Two ski mountaineering routes for the adventurous are the 14-mile **Hyalite Ski Loop** and the 5½-mile **New World Gulch to Mystic Lake Trail.** Check with the Bozeman Ranger District office (see "Getting Outside," above) for directions.

   Bohart Ranch, 16621 Bridger Canyon Rd., Bozeman, MT 59715 (© **406/586-9070;** www.bohartranchxcski.com), next to the Bridger Bowl downhill area, offers 16 miles of groomed and tracked trails for all levels of skiers. There are a biathlon range, a ski school, and ski rentals. Located in Bridger Canyon 17 miles northeast of Bozeman on U.S. 86, it's open in winter daily from 9am to 4pm, and summer daily from dawn to dusk. Cost is $13 for adults, $7 for children 7 to 12.

DOWNHILL SKIING

The nonprofit **Bridger Bowl** is just 16 miles north of town, on Mont. 86 (15795 Bridger Canyon Rd., Bozeman, MT 59715; © **800/223-9609** or 406/587-2111; www.bridgerbowl.com). Although not as steep as Teton Village in Jackson Hole, Bridger Bowl is plenty steep for most of us, and a great hill for good skiers. There is a lot of advanced and extreme terrain (40%), tempered by 60% beginner and intermediate terrain. Lift tickets cost $39 adults, $33 seniors, $13 children 6 to 12, free for those under 6 or over 72; half-day rates are available. The fixed-grip quad, two triple, and four double chairs can haul people up the hill at the rate of 7,300 an hour. With 20 feet of snowfall annually, Bridger sees a lot of powder days. Usually open from the second Friday in December to early April, daily from 9am to 4pm. There is limited lodging on the mountain; an $8 shuttle runs from Bozeman. And there are seldom any lift lines.

FISHING

The River's Edge, 2012 N. 7th Ave. (© **406/586-5373;** www.theriversedge.com), is a highly professional fly-fishing specialty shop "in the heart of Montana's blue-ribbon trout streams." They offer guided fishing trips year-round—including float fishing and walking or wading trips, plus equipment rental and shuttle service. A full-line Orvis shop, **Montana Troutfitters,** 1716 W. Main St. (© **800/646-7847** or 406/587-4707; www.troutfitters.com), offers guided float, walk and wade, and tube trips to rivers, lakes, and streams; plus 2- and 4-day fly-fishing schools. The Troutfitters are especially good at teaching youngsters the basics of the sport. **The Bozeman Angler,** 23 E. Main St. (© **800/886-9111** or 406/587-9111; www.bozemanangler.com), provides guided trips in the Madison, Gallatin, Yellowstone, Jefferson, and Missouri rivers plus numerous creeks, reservoirs, and lakes. Anglers can choose float trips in hard-sided drift boats, walk and wade, or backcountry fishing trips. From all three, full-day guided trips typically run $325 to $400 for two people, a price that includes lunch.

GOLF

Bridger Creek Golf Course at 2710 McIlhattan Rd. (© **406/586-2333;** www.bridger creek.com) is a scenic and challenging 18-hole layout, 6,400 yards from the back tees. It costs $29 for 18 holes on the weekend, $27 during the week.

HIKING

There's a beautiful and popular hiking area near Bozeman, known as the **Hyalite drainage,** in the Gallatin National Forest (see "Getting Outside," above, for contact information). The area includes Hyalite Canyon and reservoir, Palisades Falls Trail, and many trail heads for access to the national forest. A lot of the trails here are steep and difficult, though. An excellent introductory hike to get the lay of the land is the .5-mile **Palisades Falls National Recreational Trail.** From Bozeman, take 19th Avenue south for 7½ miles to the Hyalite Canyon Road, and follow the road to the reservoir. Continue east around the reservoir for 2 miles to the East Fork Road, and proceed to the Palisades Falls parking area. The trail gains 540 feet in a little more than .5 mile, which makes it very steep and gives it a rating of "most difficult" for a recreational trail.

Hyalite Reservoir itself contains cutthroat and grayling, and there are two campsites here. **The Grotto Falls Trail** is a "difficult" 1.25-mile graveled trail to Grotto Falls located 13 miles up the West Fork Road in Hyalite Canyon. For a longer hike, go the 7.25 miles up the **Hyalite Peak Trail** to the peak. There is a 3,300-foot elevation gain on this hike.

If you're interested in combining a little bird-watching with your hiking, you can get a *Birding Hotspots of the Gallatin Valley* brochure for $1 from at **Wild Birds Unlimited,** 2622 W. Main St. (© **406/586-8861**). Try the Kirk Hill nature preserve in the foothills transition zone, where you might spot a colorful western tanager or a great gray owl. Take South 19th Street south for 5 miles until the road curves west. The entrance to the preserve is on the left.

WHITE-WATER RAFTING

Montana Whitewater (© **800/799-4465** or 406/763-4465; www.montanawhitewater. com) can get you sprayed in the face by the waters of both the Yellowstone and Gallatin rivers. You paddle the raft as you fly through the nearly continuous rapids of the Gardiner section of the upper Yellowstone or through the dauntingly named rapids of Snake Bite and Mother Eater on the Gallatin. In addition to the white-water trips, the company offers more sedate scenic trips and "saddle and paddle" outings in which the morning is spent riding and the afternoon rafting. Half-day trips on the Gallatin cost $43 adults, $33 ages 12 and under; on the Yellowstone it's $33 and $23 respectively. Full-day Gallatin trips cost $75 adults and $60 ages 12 and under; and on the Yellowstone $65 and $48, respectively. Saddle and paddle jaunts range from $72 to $110.

WHERE TO FIND EQUIPMENT & SUPPLIES

It's easy to find whatever outdoor recreation equipment you need for your particular adventure. Among rental outlets we recommend are **Panda Rentals,** 621 Bridger Dr. (© **406/587-6280**), which rents bikes, rafts, canoes, skis, and snowboards; **Chalet Sports,** 108 W. Main St. (© **406/587-4595**), a full-line sporting goods store that sells skis as well as rents bikes, in-line skates, skis, and snowboards; and **Northern Lights Trading Co.,** 1716 W. Babcock St. (© **406/586-2225**), a high-end store selling gear for everything from kayaking to telemark skiing, and renting canoes, rafts, and kayaks. These stores are also great sources for advice.

SEEING THE SIGHTS

American Computer Museum ⚓ This unique museum traces the history of computing technologies from the abacus to the Apple. In an hour or so, you can catch up on more than 4,000 years of computing history and gain a newfound respect for the speed of innovation during the past few decades. Though you won't find any *T. rexes* here, you can view computing's dinosaurs: slide rules and room-size computers with a mere fraction of the power of today's super-powered miniatures.

2304 N. 7th Ave., Suite B (in the Bridger Park Mall). ℂ 406/582-1288. www.compustory.com. $4 adults, $2 children 6–12, free for children under 6. June–Aug daily 10am–4pm (Thurs until 8pm); Sept–May Tues–Wed and Fri–Sat noon–4pm, Thurs 4–8pm. Closed major holidays.

Emerson Center for the Arts and Culture Once a home for schoolchildren, this historic building (ca. 1918) was converted in 1993 into an arts and cultural center. The nonprofit organization hosts a variety of professional and contemporary art exhibits, offers a fine-arts education program, and provides retail and studio space for more than 80 artists in converted schoolrooms. There is additional gallery space a few blocks away at the **Beall Park Arts Center,** 409 N. Bozeman Ave., (ℂ **406/586-3970**). The Emerson also hosts free community events such as Lunch on the Lawn in summer, with live music and food vendors every Wednesday afternoon; special holiday activities in December; and other events and activities year-round. There's also a restaurant, **The Emerson Grill** (see "Where to Dine," below), and a theater and ballroom for a variety of programs.

111 S. Grand Ave. ℂ **406/587-9797**. www.theemerson.org. Free admission. Building daily 8am–10pm; galleries Tues–Sat 10am–5pm.

Gallatin County Pioneer Museum *Kids* Located in the old county jail, which was in use until 1982, this museum features county history, focusing in part on law enforcement (as you might expect), the area's military history, and local daily life of the past. There's a display and memorabilia from actor Gary Cooper, known as Frank in the days he grew up in Bozeman and Helena, and the lowdown on town founder John Bozeman. The museum also contains a cell from its days as the jail. There's also a collection of 11,000 historical photos and a research library devoted to Lewis and Clark. Expect to spend about an hour here if you want to dig deep.

317 W. Main St. ℂ **406/522-8122**. www.pioneermuseum.org. $3 adults, free for children under 13. June–Sept Mon–Sat 10am–5pm, Sun 1–5pm; Oct–May Tues–Fri 11am–4pm.

Museum of the Rockies *★★* This first-class museum explains the history, geology, wildlife, and people of the Rocky Mountains all the way back to the Big Bang. The centerpiece of the museum is the fabulous dinosaur exhibit, which is in the midst of a makeover that's shaping up to make it one of the premier paleontology attractions in the world. The first two phases—the **Hall of Horns and Teeth** and the **Mesozoic Media Center**—opened in 2005 and 2006, respectively. The former is centered on a life-size Torosaurus model, next to the actual 9-foot skull (the biggest land-animal noggin ever unearthed) that served as a blueprint; other displays offer an in-depth look into dinosaur biology, ecology, and theoretical behavior. The Mesozoic Media Center features interactive displays and live video feeds from archaeological sites all over the world. Phase three, the **Hall of Giants,** populated with animatronic dinosaurs, is slated for ribbon-cutting in 2007. Through the construction, visitors can also watch fossil preparers as they clean recently discovered bones.

But that's not all: In the **Martin Discovery Room,** young children can learn through play. The **Taylor Planetarium** is a state-of-the-art, 40-foot domed multimedia theater whose computer graphics simulator provides the illusion of flying through space in three dimensions. Outside, the **Living History Farm** is an early-20th-century homestead with costumed interpreters. There's also a restaurant and gift shop on-site.

600 W. Kagy Blvd. (on the Montana State University campus). © 406/994-2251. www.museumoftherockies.org. Museum $8 adults, $4 children 5–18, free for children under 5. Planetarium $3 ages 5 and up. Mid-June to early Sept daily 8am–8pm; mid-Sept to mid-June Mon–Sat 9am–5pm, Sun 12:30–5pm. Living History Farm mid-June to early Sept daily 9:30am–5pm. Closed Thanksgiving, Christmas, and New Year's Day.

SHOPPING

Main Street offers an Old West feel and New West selection, starting at about 7th Avenue and running out to I-90. The chief part of the shopping district is easily accessible on foot. Among our favorite stops here are **Vargo's Jazz City and Books,** 6 W. Main (© 406/587-5383), which sells an eclectic mass of new, used, and out-of-print books, CDs, and LPs (or the elusive, vanishing vinyl); **The Montana Gift Corral,** 237 E. Main (© 406/585-8625), which offers a wide selection of made-in-Montana gifts, in case you need a moose clock to take home; **Thomas Nygard Gallery,** 135 E. Main (© 406/586-3636), which sells pre-1950 artwork from the Northern Plains; **The Country Bookshelf,** 28 W. Main (© 406/587-0166), a terrific bookstore; and **Barkenhowell's,** 777 E. Main (© 406/586-6160), a chic dog boutique. The **Gallatin Valley Mall,** 2825 W. Main (© 406/586-4565), has department and specialty stores, art galleries, and a food court.

WHERE TO STAY

Bozeman has a full complement of chain motels, most just off I-90. In addition to the places listed below, you can stay at the **Best Western GranTree Inn,** 1325 N. 7th Ave., Bozeman, MT 59715 (© 800/624-5865 or 406/587-5261); the **Fairfield Inn,** 828 Wheat Dr., Bozeman, MT 59715 (© 406/587-2222); and the **Hampton Inn,** 75 Baxter Lane, Bozeman, MT 59715 (© 406/522-8000). The above are all at I-90 exit 306, and have rates for two in the $80-to-$120 range. New in 2005, the **Hilton Garden Inn,** 2023 Commerce Way (© 877/782-9444 or 406/582-9900), is south of I-90, exit 305, with double rates of $129 to $149. Within walking distance of downtown, we like **Bozeman's Western Heritage Inn,** 1200 E. Main St. (© 800/877-1094 or 406/586-8534), with double rates of $65 to $100. Another option is the cozy 1920s **Cooper Park Cottage,** 401 S. 5th Ave. (© 406/586-2012), which rents for $100 to $125 double.

Bozeman Backpackers Hostel _(Value_   Located in a funky Victorian that Hollywood legend Gary Cooper once called home, these bunkhouse accommodations are in a quiet residential neighborhood near downtown. The bunkrooms are coed, allowing couples to stay together, and there are also two private rooms available. The downstairs public area has a homey feel; full kitchen and bathroom facilities are available to guests.

405 W. Olive St., Bozeman, MT 59715. © 406/586-4659. www.bozemanbackpackershostel.com. 12 bunks, 2 private rooms. $16 per person; $35 private room. No credit cards. **Amenities:** Coin-operated washers and dryers. _In room:_ No phone.

Holiday Inn   The largest hotel in town, the Holiday Inn opened in 1969 when there was virtually nothing else in the immediate vicinity. It's now surrounded by other chain motels and hotels, but it remains the best. The big, open lobby has a sort of a lodge feel, with a big-screen TV that's usually surrounded by a crowd watching a ballgame, and two complimentary high-speed Internet terminals. The rooms are well kept and nicely furnished, and a few of them have terrific mountain views.

5 Baxter Lane, Bozeman, MT 59715. © 800/366-5101 or 406/587-4561. Fax 406/587-4413. www.hibozeman.com. 179 units. $89–$129 double; $129–$159 suite. AE, DC, DISC, MC, V. From I-90, take exit 306. **Amenities:** Restaurant;

lounge/casino; indoor pool; exercise room; indoor Jacuzzi; game room; courtesy car; Wi-Fi network; coin-op washers and dryers; dry cleaning. *In room:* A/C, cable TV w/pay movies, dataport, coffeemaker, hair dryer, iron.

Lehrkind Mansion ✦✦✦   Julius Lehrkind was never much of a conformist. The Swiss-born brewer wanted to live next door to his workplace, so he shunned the tonier neighborhoods on Bozeman's south side and in 1897 built a stately Queen Anne mansion right next door to his brick brewery. Former national park rangers Jon Gerster, Jr., and Chris Nixon turned "the house that beer built" into a bed-and-breakfast 99 years after the Lehrkind family moved in, with the original woodwork, plumbing, and floor plan intact. The ornate abode still sticks out in the quasi-industrial (but up-and-coming) Historic Brewery District. Surrounded by breweries that are slated to become lofts and other vestiges of the neighborhood's beery past, the Lehrkind Mansion looks like something out of a fairy tale inside and out. Gerster and Nixon have done a remarkable job capturing the house in 1890s amber: Everything, from the rare 1897 Regina music box in the parlor to the many original fixtures in the bathrooms to the amazingly preserved original carpet in the Muir Room, is from Lehrkind's day—with the exception of the hot tub out back. In 2004, the mansion got a new neighbor: a Victorian farmhouse, abandoned outside of town until Gerster and Nixon got the idea of gussying it up and making it a five-bedroom counterpart to the four-bedroom mansion. Next on the list is a tunnel between the two, just like the one Julius Lehrkind used to commute to his brewery a century ago.

719 N. Wallace Ave., Bozeman, MT 59715. ✆ **800/992-6932** or 406/585-6932. www.bozemanbedandbreakfast. com. 9 units. $119–$149 double; $169 suite. AE, DISC, MC, V. **Amenities:** Outdoor Jacuzzi. *In room:* No phone.

CAMPING

The **Bozeman KOA** (✆ **406/587-3030**) is the area's largest campground, with sites for 100 RVs and 50 tents. It is adjacent to a natural hot-springs pool (which charges a separate fee), laundry, store, and a variety of other amenities. It is located 7 miles south of Belgrade on U.S. 191, with sites from $18 to $40 and rough cabins for $45 to $60 double. There are also numerous places to camp in the **Gallatin National Forest;** contact the Bozeman Ranger District, 3710 Fallon St., Suite C, Bozeman, MT 59718 (✆ **406/522-2520;** www.fs.fed.us/r1/gallatin) for details.

WHERE TO DINE

Beyond the restaurants that follow, we're firm believers in the restorative powers of the breakfast burritos at **Soby's,** in the Bozeman Hotel at 321 E. Main St. (✆ **406/587-8857**), a favorite student haunt for breakfast and lunch. For a burger and a beer on an outdoor deck, you can't beat the **Garage,** 451 E. Main St. (✆ **406/585-8558**). In the winter, the place compensates for the cold weather with the **Soup Shack,** serving seven hot soups and an array of toppings, from a space that houses the ice-cream-oriented **Scoop Shack** in summer. The **Community Food Co-op,** 909 W. Main St. (✆ **406/587-4039**), is a locally beloved market, with a great deli, salad bar, and seating area upstairs.

Casa Sanchez MEXICAN   This 100-year-old house near the MSU campus is home to the best Mexican food in Bozeman—and it's all homemade. If you consider yourself a nacho connoisseur, Ron's Nachos has what you're looking for: a plateful of chips, chicken, salsa, and jalapeños, topped with mounds of guacamole and sour cream. Burritos, enchiladas, chimichangas, and tacos are the basic food groups on the Casa Sanchez menu. There's a large deck open in summer, but no margaritas—nor beer or wine.

719 S. 9th Ave. (at College St.). ☏ **406/586-4516.** Most dishes $8–$12. DISC, MC, V. Mon–Thurs 11am–9pm; Fri 10am–10pm; Sat 5–10pm.

The Emerson Grill ✹ ITALIAN Intimate and artsy, this dinky eatery in the Emerson Center for Arts and Culture has emerged as a local favorite, and it's an equally good bet for a quick lunch or a romantic dinner. The kitchen uses locally produced organic ingredients more often than not, creating terrific Italian fare: The menu includes flatbread pizettes, spaghetti and meatballs, and risotto as well as pepper-crusted lamb chops and calamari steaks. Lunch consists of tasty soups, grinders and focaccia sandwiches, and a few pasta dishes. Only beer and wine are available, but the selection is excellent.

207 W. Olive St., in the Emerson Center for Arts and Culture. ☏ **406/586-5247.** Reservations recommended. Lunch $6–$9; dinner $8–$26. MC, V. Mon–Sat 11am–2:30pm; Mon–Thurs 5:30–9pm; Fri–Sun 5–10pm. Closed Sun in winter.

John Bozeman's Bistro ✹✹ CONTEMPORARY AMERICAN One of the most popular and upscale restaurants in town, this restaurant offers an eclectic and innovative menu that changes on a regular basis. The offerings are all over the map, and have included buffalo, Jamaican jerk chicken, beef tenderloin, fresh fish, and many interesting vegetarian entrees. If it's available, try the red curry stir-fry, with sautéed garden vegetables, chicken, or tofu, simmered in a red curry coconut milk broth on a bed of steamed noodles. The atmosphere is inviting, a cut above casual.

125 W. Main St. ☏ **406/587-4100.** Lunch items $9–$12; dinner entrees $18–$32. AE, DC, DISC, MC, V. Tues–Sat 11:30am–2:30pm and 5–9:30pm.

Mackenzie River Pizza Co. *Kids* PIZZA These folks do pizza a decidedly new way, one which matches the decor—funky, in a slightly overdone Western style with a log structure in the middle of the dining room. The tomato-based pizzas are delicious, and there are plenty of old standbys with traditional toppings. Innovations include the pesto-based pizzas from the "Back Forty" side of the menu. Names match the ingredients: The Athenian features feta, the Thai, a peanut-ginger sauce, and the Buffalo Wing, spicy chicken and blue cheese.

232 E. Main St. ☏ **406/587-0055.** Reservations not accepted. Sandwiches $5–$6; entrees $9–$14; pizzas $10 and up. AE, MC, V. Mon–Thurs 11am–10pm; Fri–Sat 11am–11pm; Sun noon–9pm. Closes 1 hr. earlier in winter.

Main Street Overeasy BREAKFAST/SANDWICHES Chef Erik Carr opened this restaurant in 1998, and it has been a local favorite ever since, winning "Bozeman's Best Breakfast" from the weekly *Tributary* every year since 2000. The place packs 'em in for breakfast with such dishes as homemade corned beef hash, biscuits and gravy, chicken-fried steak, and cinnamon bread pudding with warm vanilla sauce. Lunches consist of large gourmet sandwiches and salads.

9 E. Main St. ☏ **406/587-3205.** Breakfast $5–$9; lunch $6–$8. AE, MC, V. Tues–Sun 7am–2:30pm. Closed Mon.

The Mint ✹✹ AMERICAN Few places meld upscale and cowboy as well as the historic Mint in downtown Belgrade, about 8 miles west of Bozeman. A local landmark since 1904, the interior is lined with black-and-white photos of cowboys, and an enormous longhorn head guards the entrance, but the blonde wood and sleek details make it a tad more formal than your typical Montana roadhouse. The specialties will rouse the carnivore in most anybody: buffalo tenderloin, a 15-ounce New York strip, and half an herb-marinated chicken. There are also daily specials, including a pasta dish and a meatless plate, and a great bar menu running the gastronomic gamut from burgers to escargot. The wine list is one of the best within a 100-mile radius.

27 E. Main St., Belgrade. ℂ 406/388-1100. Reservations recommended. Dinner $7–$31. AE, DISC, MC, V. Daily 4–10pm. Bar open later.

Montana Ale Works ℱ AMERICAN   A casual, social place to see and be seen, Montana Ale Works is a relatively new standby, a great place to unwind over hearty portions and cold libations or catch a ballgame. We like the Montana Meatloaf, a spicy slab of buffalo, beef, and pork, but other favorites include fish tacos, barbecued ribs, and plenty of steaks. After a long period of dormancy, the former railroad warehouse became a restaurant in 2000. The place hangs on to a bit of its past in the form of industrial chic decor, with brick walls and an exposed ceiling framing a vast room with plenty of nooks and crannies to find a seat. There are also pool tables, but no cigarette smoke. In the center of it all is a full bar with plenty of seating and—of course—plenty of ale: Of the 40 beers on tap, about half are brewed in Montana.

611 E. Main St. ℂ 406/587-7700. www.montanaaleworks.com. Reservations accepted. Main courses $7.50–$29. AE, DISC, MC, V. Mon–Thurs 4–10pm; Fri–Sun 4–11pm. Bar open later.

Naked Noodle ⓥⓐⓛⓤⓔ ECLECTIC/NOODLES   If you like to sample from several cuisines, or everybody in your group wants something different, this is the perfect choice. At this casual eatery in a brick- and funky art-clad space just off Main Street, you can get noodles of all kinds: Udon noodles in Thai green chile curry, Italian fettuccine Alfredo, even good old American mac and cheese. Also on the menu are a number of filling salads with the same international variety.

27 S. Willson Ave. ℂ 406/522-0800. Most items $4.75–$9.25. AE, MC, V. Mon–Sat 11am–9pm; Sun noon–9pm.

Plonk Wine ℱℱ CONTEMPORARY/ECLECTIC   A dimly lit hot spot that feels more San Francisco than Bozeman, Plonk (Euro-slang for ordinary table wine) took over the space that housed the Stockman's Bar from 1921 to 1971 (and a Hallmark shop until 2003) and molded it into an eatery that oozes with a hip, urban atmosphere. The menus (there are seven in all) change on a regular basis, but you can count on Bozeman's best selection of wine, cheese, and decadent desserts. The dinner menu always features a ravioli (its stuffing changes); you might also find bison tenderloin, Thai green curry with black tiger shrimp, or seared duck breast. Across from the well-stocked shelves of vino, there is a full bar, above which hangs a restored brand-laden mural that dates from Plonk's Stockman's Bar era.

29 E. Main St. ℂ 406/587-2170. Reservations not accepted. Lunch $8–$10; dinner $13–$20. AE, DISC, MC, V. Daily 11:30am–10:30pm. Bar open later.

BOZEMAN AFTER DARK

Bozeman is a college town, so there are lots of places to get a casual drink accompanied by loud music. Popular watering holes include **Boodle's,** 215 E. Main St. (ℂ **406/587-2901**), which has live jazz on the weekends; the lively **Crystal Bar,** 123 E. Main St. (ℂ **406/587-2888**); and the **Zebra,** 321 E. Main St. in the old Bozeman Hotel (ℂ **406/585-8851**), ground zero for the local live music scene. If it's the college bars you are after, the somewhat grungy **"Barmuda Triangle"** consists of the **Haufbrauhaus,** the **Molly Brown,** and the **Scoop,** conveniently positioned within stumbling distance of one another near the intersection of 8th Avenue and Main Street.

   Montana Shakespeare in the Parks (ℂ **406/994-3901;** www.montana.edu/shakespeare), is a professional touring company that was formed in 1973. Based in Bozeman, the troupe of 10 to 12 actors produces over 60 performances during the summer at communities throughout Montana, Wyoming, and Idaho—often in a different town each day. Some summer weekends find them at their Bozeman stage—located on the MSU campus on 11th Avenue near the corner of Grant Street—for "Shakespeare Under the Stars." Parking is available just north of the MSU field house. Call for the schedule. Performances are always free.

3 The Madison River Valley: Three Forks & Ennis ⓐⓐ

Ennis: 54 miles SW of Bozeman; 71 miles N of West Yellowstone

The Madison Valley is an almost mythical place surrounded by spectacular mountain scenery where anglers from all over gather to fish. The main attraction is the Madison River, which flows through the valley at the base of the Madison Range, a stretch of peaks that runs toward Yellowstone Park.

Besides the phenomenal fishing, the Madison Valley has tourist-worthy historical sites. **The Missouri Headwaters State Park** is at the confluence of the Jefferson, Madison, and Gallatin rivers, where Lewis and Clark paused to take shelter; **Lewis and Clark Caverns State Park,** with its spectacular underground peaks, is just up the road; and **Madison Buffalo Jump State Park** is nearby.

ESSENTIALS

GETTING THERE   The Bozeman airport, **Gallatin Field** (discussed earlier in this chapter), is the closest airport to the valley.

Greyhound stops at the Sinclair station in Three Forks at 2 Main St.

Three Forks is located on I-90, 30 miles from Bozeman, 170 miles from Billings, and 173 miles from Missoula. Three Forks is 66 miles from the capital in Helena. Ennis is 45 miles south of Three Forks on U.S. 287.

VISITOR INFORMATION   Contact the **Three Forks Chamber of Commerce,** P.O. Box 1103, Three Forks, MT 59752 (ⓒ 406/285-4753; www.threeforksmontana. com); or the **Ennis Chamber of Commerce,** P.O. Box 291, Ennis, MT 59729 (ⓒ 406/682-4388; www.ennischamber.com). **Yellowstone Country** (ⓒ 800/736-5276) is the Travel Montana tourism office for the region.

GETTING AROUND   If you're flying into Bozeman, pick up a car at the airport (see "Getting Around," in section 2, for more information). For local **road reports,** call ⓒ 406/586-1313.

GETTING OUTSIDE

There is plenty of fishing water along the road from Three Forks to Quake and Hebgen lakes along U.S. 287. The first fishing access is **Cobblestone,** just a few miles south of Three Forks on the right side of U.S. 287. If you plan to base yourself in Ennis, the **Valley Garden, Ennis Bridge, Burnt Tree,** and **Varney Bridge** fishing accesses are within minutes of town along U.S. 287. Between Ennis and Quake Lake, the accesses begin popping up frequently. **McAtee Bridge, Wolf Creek, West Fork,** and **Reynolds Pass** are all accessible from the roadside. Hebgen Lake, just south of the dam, and Quake Lake are also great fishing spots.

On Ennis's Main Street, it seems that every second door houses a fly-fishing outfitter. The **Madison River Fishing Company,** 109 Main St. (ⓒ 800/227-7127 or 406/682-4293; www.mrfc.com), has a good stock of fishing supplies and a guide service. Guided trips, for one or two people, cost $245 for a half-day and $365 for a full day; full-day trips include lunch. They also offer a free brochure that contains a map of fishing spots and various facilities along the way. Other guide services, with similar rates, include **Clark's Guide Service** (© **406/682-7474**); **Howard Outfitters** (© **406/682-4834**); and **The Tackle Shop Outfitters,** 127 Main St. (© **800/808-2832** or 406/682-4263; www.thetackleshop.com).

SEEING THE SIGHTS

Lewis & Clark Caverns ✦ These lovely limestone caverns are named for the famous explorers, but there is no evidence that their party ever saw or visited them. Discovered in the late 19th century, these caverns are a succession of vaulted chambers and passageways, thickly decorated with stalactites and stalagmites, as well as other underground formations such as massive, gleaming organ pipes; silky, delicate soda straws; intricate filigrees; and weirdly hung draperies. Plan at least 2 hours for the 2-mile guided tour through the caverns; and aboveground there are hiking trails, several picnic areas, and a large campground (see "Camping," below). A Christmas candlelight tour is held on 2 weekends in December. Reservations should be made in early December for one of the 200 or so spots available. There are three cabins on the premises with electric heat; $39 in summer and $25 in winter.

Located 19 miles west of Three Forks (midway between Butte and Bozeman) on Mont. 2. © **406/287-3541**. www. fwp.state.mt.us. Entrance fee $5 per car. Cave tours $10 adults, $5 children 6–11. Park and campground open daily year-round. Guided cave tours May 1 to mid-June daily 9am–4:30pm; mid-June to Labor Day daily 9am–6:30pm; after Labor Day to Sept 30 daily 9am–4:30pm. Tours leave as required by demand; call for group reservation.

Madison Buffalo Jump State Park This is one of a few buffalo jumps, or *pishkun,* that have been excavated. Prior to the advent of the horse, the Northern Shoshone and the Bannock drove the bison off this steep cliff to their death on the rocks below. Long rows of rocks funneled the animals to the cliff. There is a well-worn trail up to the base of the cliff, making for a short but steep hike.

23 miles west of Bozeman, off I-90 exit 283. © **406/994-4042**. www.fwp.state.mt.us. Entrance fee $5 per car. Open daily 24 hr. From the Logan exit off I-90, 7 miles south on Buffalo Jump Rd.

Missouri Headwaters State Park ✦✦ You can easily spend an hour just exploring the interpretive signage at this historic state park. Begin by following the Missouri River out from Three Forks. The headwaters themselves are no great shakes—just another river—but the sunsets from the bank of the river are breathtaking. From the headwaters, drive back toward Three Forks where, on the opposite side of the road, you'll see a parking area with interpretive markers. Allow plenty of time to read about Lewis and Clark and Sacajawea, the young Shoshone guide, as well as early American Indians, trappers, traders, and settlers. Camping and RV sites are available as well as access to hiking, boating, and fishing.

4 miles northeast of Three Forks (east on C.R. 205, then north on C.R. 286; follow signs). © **406/994-4042**. www. fwp.state.mt.us. $5 per car. Open daily 24 hr.

National Fish Hatchery The Ennis National Fish Hatchery, constructed in 1931, is probably the only place in America where you can observe two genetic mutants of ordinary rainbow trout: albino and blue. (These fish are not released into the wild trout population.) Some of the trout in the hatchery ponds weigh more than 20 pounds and are more than 5 years old. The hatchery cultivates seven different strains of rainbow trout. You can learn about the operation in the small exhibit area and tour the facility. When some of those huge adults are past their use as brood stock, they too are released into lakes and streams to test fishermen.

180 Fish Hatchery Rd., Ennis. 🕐 406/682-4847. http://ennis.fws.gov. Free admission. Daily 7:30am–5pm. The hatchery is 12 miles southwest of Ennis. Take U.S. 287 south from town to R.R. 249 and go west to Call Rd. Turn left (south), and after driving a half-mile, turn left (east) on Fish Hatchery Rd.

Quake Lake   Just before midnight on August 17, 1959, a massive earthquake measuring 7.5 on the Richter scale jolted Yellowstone and the Madison River canyon, sending large chunks of mountain into the river. A campsite just below the mountain was covered with rubble and 19 people were buried alive. The rubble that collapsed into the river created a dam and the aptly named Quake Lake. The ghostly fingers of trees that died when they were swamped still poke skyward from the lake. The visitor center on the north side of the highway offers exhibits, a video every half-hour, and an observation area from which you can see the massive slides. The area around Yellowstone and Quake Lake is still very seismically active, and southwest Montana is second only to California in terms of earthquake frequency. The visitor center has a great deal of information about the area's seismic activity and hypotheses of how it got this way.

Off U.S. 287, 27 miles northwest of West Yellowstone and 43 miles south of Ennis. 🕐 406/682-7620 or 406/823-6961. Visitor Center: $3 per car. Memorial Day to mid-Sept daily 8:30am–6pm.

WHERE TO STAY
IN THREE FORKS
Bud Lilly's Anglers Retreat   Having Bud Lilly mastermind your fishing itinerary is reason enough to stay here, but it's by no means the only reason. Formerly a railroad hotel belonging to Bud's mother, the Anglers Retreat has been refurbished and is now a cozy lodge. The three upstairs bedrooms share a bathroom with a claw-foot bathtub and shower, and each of the suites has a full bathroom with shower as well as a fully equipped kitchen. There's also a shady veranda and upper balcony overlooking a well-kept backyard; a collection of fly-fishing memorabilia, art, and antiques; and a comfortable TV room with an extensive library of fishing and Montana videos. The private cottage has its own kitchen and living area, and sleeps four. But the big draw here is the fishing. Every reservation at the Anglers Retreat includes a personalized, detailed itinerary of where to fish locally, based on your preferences and length of stay.

16 W. Birch St., P.O. Box 983, Three Forks, MT 59752. 🕐 406/285-6690. Fax 406/284-9945. 4 units, 1 cottage; 3 with shared bathroom. $65 double; $135–$176 suite; $135 cottage. MC, V. **Amenities:** Laundry facilities; videos. *In room:* A/C, kitchenette (in suites and cottage).

IN ENNIS & VICINITY
In addition to the properties discussed below, the **Rainbow Valley Motel,** 1 mile south of Ennis on U.S. 287 (Box 26), Ennis, MT 59729 (🕐 **800/452-8254** or 406/682-4264; www.rainbowvalley.com), offers large, well-maintained cabin-style rooms at rates for two of $75 to $120. There are also a couple of large cabin homes for $175 to $225 a night.

El Western Cabins & Lodges 🕊   It's a little hard to categorize this place, which has some inexpensive log duplex-style cabins as well as large, expensive two- and three-bedroom lodges. The original portion was built in 1948 and is done with knotty-pine interiors and built-in wooden cabinets. The newest lodge is the Eagle's Loft, a three-bedroom, three-bathroom, two-story cabin with vaulted ceiling and rock fireplace, plus a whirlpool tub and washer and dryer. Every unit enjoys spectacular views of the Madison Range, including Fan Mountain and the Spanish Peaks. You can't go wrong here, and the overnight cabins are as affordable as anything in the valley. There's no restaurant or lounge associated with the property, but a new conference center building with a large, inviting deck and picture windows serves both business and family groups.

4787 U.S. 287 N., P.O. Box 487, Ennis, MT 59729. ✆ 800/831-2773 or 406/682-4217. Fax 406/682-5207. www.elwestern. com. 29 units. $72–$92 double; $110–$125 kitchen cabin; $175–$250 deluxe kitchen cabin; $250–$425 lodge. AE, DISC, MC, V. From the town of Ennis, drive south 1 mile on U.S. 287. *In room:* Cable TV, dataport, kitchen, hair dryer, iron.

Potosi Hot Springs Resort 🎯🎯 *Moments*   Tucked deep in the Tobacco Root Mountains, Potosi is geared toward romance, relaxation, and outdoor recreation. It's a tricky balance, but proprietors Nick and Christine Kern pull it off more than admirably. Accommodating guests in comfy cabins with kitchens and plush furnishings, the resort provides a sea of recreational activities, as Nick guides fishing on the area's creeks and a local old-timer takes guests on horseback trips. For her part, Christine, a self-taught cook, prepares delectable dinners, anything from tiger prawns to elk medallions to an unbelievable lemon mousse. Then there are the hot springs from which the place draws its name, which fill an idyllic outdoor pool, a creek-side tub, and a private, gazebo-enclosed tub on the banks of Willow Creek. Also on-site is the Mountain Flower Spa, a creek-side yurt used as a setting for massages and herbal wraps. It's absolutely serene here in the wintertime, when a still blanket of snow covers everything except the road, which is plowed just up to the resort's driveway. Snowshoeing and cross-country skiing are the favored activities. "There's nobody up here but us," says Nick.

1 S. Willow Creek Rd., P.O. Box 269, Pony, MT 59747. ✆ 888/685-1695 or 406/685-3330. Fax 406/685-3390. www. potosiresort.com. 4 cabins. Summer $395 double ($545 with 3 meals); winter $200 ($350 with 3 meals). AE, MC, V. From Pony, drive 6½ miles southwest on S. Willow Creek Rd. Pets accepted, $10 per day. **Amenities:** Outdoor hot-springs pool; 2 hot-springs tubs (1 indoor/1 outdoor); spa; sauna; bike rentals; activities desk; laundry service. *In room:* Kitchen, hair dryer, no phone.

Wade Lake Resort   This secluded resort, which consists of five cabins, is located in a picture-perfect forested canyon on Wade Lake. The cabins are fairly primitive, with only a refrigerator, running water, heat, a gas stove, and a gas barbecue grill. A shared (but modern) bathhouse is out back. There aren't any electric outlets to plug in your computer (which we consider a major plus). Bring food to cook because the nearest restaurant is 11 miles back up the road. The area is very beautiful, though—Wade has been designated a Montana Wildlife Viewing Site. The area is rich in wildlife, with eagles and osprey nesting on the lake, and moose, elk, bear, and other locals dropping in occasionally. It also helps you remember what real quiet and real darkness are like.

P.O. Box 107, Cameron, MT 59720. ✆ 406/682-7560. www.wadelake.com. 5 cabins. $65–$110 double. No credit cards. Drive 40 miles south of Ennis to the Wade Lake turnoff, marked by a sign. Turn west on the bumpy, gravel Wade Lake Rd. and follow the signs about 6 miles to Wade Lake. **Amenities:** Cross-country skiing trails. *In room:* No phone.

CAMPING

Lewis & Clark Caverns (see "Seeing the Sights," above; ✆ **406/287-3541**) has 40 campsites ($13–$15), showers, a dump station, and fishing access on a river, plus hiking trails and interpretive programs. **Missouri Headwaters State Park** (see "Seeing the Sights," above; ✆ **406/994-4042**) has a year-round campground ($12) with 20 sites scattered along the river, plus numerous hiking trails and plenty of fishing access. Maximum trailer length is 25 feet; there's a boat ramp and dump station. Those wanting RV hookups and the usual commercial campground amenities should head to **Three Forks KOA,** on U.S. 287, 1 mile south of I-90 exit 274 (✆ **800/562-9752** for reservations, or 406/285-3611), which has a clean bathhouse, swimming pool, rec room, and playground. It's open mid-April through October, with sites for both tents and RVs at rates of $20 to $32, and basic cabins for $30 to $40.

WHERE TO DINE
NEAR THREE FORKS
Wheat Montana Bakery and Deli, 1-90 and U.S. 287 (© **406/285-3614**), is a popular breakfast and lunch spot where Montana-grown wheat is turned into bread, and the smell of bread baking alone makes it worth the stop.

Willow Creek Café and Saloon ✦ (Finds) AMERICAN   This place is a find, if you can find it—it's located 7 miles southwest of Three Forks on the Old Yellowstone Trail. It's worth the search, though, because Willow Creek is the best restaurant in the area (don't let the bullet holes in the ceiling scare you off). It began as the Babcock Saloon around 1916, and continues as a remarkable reflection of what's best in Montana: hearty meals and friendly people. The ever-popular baby back pork ribs draw repeat customers from around the country, but the local cowboys know that the beef is tops here, so the hand-pounded chicken-fried sirloin steak is their recommendation. The pasta dishes are very good and the homemade soups really taste homemade. The Sunday breakfasts are hearty and all-American.

21 Main St., Willow Creek. © **406/285-3698.** Dinner reservations recommended in summer. Lunch $4–$8; dinner $8–$20. AE, DC, DISC, MC, V. Tues–Sat 11am–9pm; Sun 8am–9pm.

IN ENNIS
Scotty's Longbranch Supper Club and Saloon ✦ AMERICAN   Scotty's has a sign that reads: NO BURGERS. NO FRIES. So don't ask. And there is classical music on the CD player. But the atmosphere otherwise is pure Western steakhouse, as is most of the food. Our choice is the steak béarnaise, when available, though veal Parmesan, crab cakes, and shrimp scampi are also on the menu. Scotty's serves twice-baked and regular baked potatoes, but like the sign says—no fries. The restaurant is located in the rear of the Longbranch Saloon.

125 E. Main St. © **406/682-5300.** Main courses $13–$27. MC, V. Mon–Sat 5:30–10pm; hours vary somewhat in winter.

4 The Gallatin Valley ✦✦

Big Sky: 53 miles S of Bozeman; 48 miles N of West Yellowstone

According to legend, the Sioux and Nez Perce once engaged in a bloody battle in the lower Gallatin Valley. On the third day of the fighting, the sun was blotted out and a booming voice told the warriors to forget old wrongs and stop fighting, because they were in the Valley of Peace and Flowers.

These days, the sun mostly shines around here, and the only booming voices heard are those calling you for your tee time or your dinner reservation. The transition of Big Sky from peace and flowers to year-round resort was not entirely without dissension, however. When legendary NBC newsman Chet Huntley—a Montana native—proposed the Big Sky ski resort, there was an outcry from the budding environmental movement. But Huntley's dream was realized in 1973, and the resort has blossomed into a world-class facility, with a second ski area—Moonlight Basin—opening in 2003.

The valley is a narrow, shining slice of Montana edged by the Absaroka and Gallatin ranges to the east and the Madison Range on the west. The Big Sky Resort covers two of the western peaks—Lone Mountain, elevation 11,186 feet, and Andesite

Mountain, 8,800 feet. Moonlight Basin's runs are also on Lone Mountain, and connect with those of Big Sky.

There are several distinct "villages" in Big Sky. The **canyon area** along U.S. 191 has a haphazard collection of motels, taverns, restaurants, gas stations, and whatnot. The **Meadow Village,** 2 miles west of the highway, includes a community of condos, a few overnight lodging places, and the golf course. The main base area for the ski resort is at the **Mountain Village,** 8 miles west of the highway, with condos, restaurants, and hotels. The Moonlight Basin development is just above Mountain Village.

The valley's summers bring excellent fly-fishing, horseback riding, and white-water rafting. This beautiful scenery may seem familiar—the Gallatin River was the setting for the film *A River Runs Through It.*

ESSENTIALS

GETTING THERE Big Sky is about 53 miles south of Bozeman's **Gallatin Field** on U.S. 191. From the airport, you can ride to the ski area with **Karst Stage** (② **800/ 517-8243** or 406/388-6404; www.karststage.com), a company that has a transportation fleet of sturdy four-wheel-drive vehicles. The ride is $35 to $40 round-trip per person in winter; summer transportation can be arranged by calling ahead. Or you can take a taxi provided by **Mountain Taxi** (② **406/995-4895**) for about $100 one-way.

GETTING AROUND A car gives you the greatest flexibility in getting around this area. For service between condominiums, hotels, restaurants, and activities within the ski area, take the **SnowExpress,** Big Sky's free local shuttle-bus system, which operates daily during the ski season.

GETTING OUTSIDE

BIKING

Big Sky Resort rents mountain bikes and offers bike rental/lift ticket combos. Call ② **406/995-5840** for details.

CROSS-COUNTRY SKIING

Big Sky Resort (see below) offers some groomed trails for cross-country skiing. But for the real deal, go to **Lone Mountain Ranch** ☀☀ (P.O. Box 160069, Big Sky, MT 59716; ② **800/514-4644** or 406/995-4644; www.lmranch.com), which has 50 miles of cross-country trails over terrain that will challenge every level of skier. Near the ranch headquarters, in the meadows, lies some flat terrain that beginners might appreciate. There's also a steeper portion to practice your telemark technique, and 12 miles of snowshoe trails. Intermediate trails with more hills make up about 60% of the area, and expert trails provide plenty of challenging downhill runs. Ski and snowshoe rentals are also available. Full-day trail passes cost $17. The entrance to Lone Mountain Ranch is off Lone Mountain Trail (the main road to the Big Sky Resort), about 4 miles west of its intersection with U.S. 191 and 2 miles east of the Meadow Village.

DOWNHILL SKIING

In 2005, Big Sky and Moonlight Basin connected their trail systems, making for a combined 5,300 acres of terrain—the largest ski area in the country. Skiers and snowboarders can buy the **Lone Peak Ticket** for a day of unlimited access to both resorts' runs for $78 adults and $59 seniors over 70 and juniors 11 to 21.

Big Sky Resort ☀ Tennis, golf, and rock climbing are all very nice, but the real reason to come to Big Sky is to ski. It's a huge hill, with more than 3,600 acres of terrain and 85 miles of trails. You can ski for nearly a vertical mile from the top of the tram at 11,150 feet elevation to the bottom of the Lone Moose lift, at 6,800 feet. There is terrain here for everybody, with 58% for advanced and expert skiers, 25% for intermediate, and 17% beginner. Big Sky gets 400 inches of snowfall, offering plenty of powder days. There's an ambitious children's program, offering lessons for kids as young as 3, and day care for kids who don't want to ski. Full ski-rental packages are available.

P.O. Box 160001, Big Sky, MT 59716. ⓒ **800/548-4486** or 406/995-5750; 406/995-5900 for snow conditions; 406/995-5743 for ski school. www.bigskyresort.com. Lift ticket $65 adults, $33 seniors (67 and over), $45 juniors 14–21, $25 for children 11–13, and free for children under 11. Late Nov to mid-Apr daily 9am–4pm.

Moonlight Basin 🄰   The first new destination ski resort in the U.S. in more than 20 years, Moonlight Basin opened in 2003 to rave reviews from hard-core skiers, but its long, steep runs may be a bit challenging for neophytes. (This makes the Lone Peak Ticket, above, a safe bet if you're on the fence about your abilities.) Six lifts serve 1,900 acres of terrain crisscrossed by about 80 trails—with a precipitous 4,150-foot drop. Most of the terrain is for the advanced skier, but there are some easier runs. Like Big Sky, the resort gets over 400 inches of snow a year. It also features a spa, kids' programs, and other outdoor activities. But the folks behind this infant of a resort look like they're just getting started. Coming in 2007: a Jack Nicklaus–designed golf course.

P.O. Box 160040, Big Sky, MT 59716. ⓒ **877/822-0430** or 406/993-6000; 406/993-6666 for snow conditions. www.moonlightbasin.com. Lift ticket $40 adults, $35 seniors (70 and over) and college students with ID, $30 juniors 11–17, and free for children under 11. Late Nov to mid-Apr daily 9am–4pm.

FISHING

According to an Indian legend, folks who drink the water of the Gallatin River will return to the valley before they die, but of course you should no longer drink untreated water out of even high mountain streams, because of the possibility of giardia, an intestinal microbe that you don't want traveling back home with you. We're not sure if eating the fish that live in the water counts toward the legend, but it's worth a try. Several guides offer trips for prices ranging from about $250 for a half-day for two to $350 full day. For details contact **Lone Mountain Ranch** (ⓒ **406/995-4644**), **Gallatin River-guides** (ⓒ **406/995-2290**), or **East Slope Anglers** (ⓒ **406/995-4369**).

GOLF

Big Sky Golf Course, Meadow Village (ⓒ **406/995-5780**), is a striking Arnold Palmer design that is fairly short, fairly open, and harder than it looks on the card. A few of the holes wander next to the West Fork of the Gallatin River, which runs through the property. Cost, which includes the cart fee, is $45 to $58 for 18 holes, $30 to $40 for 9. Tee times can be reserved up to a week in advance. In 2007, an 18-hole course designed by Jack Nicklaus is slated to open at Moonlight Basin.

HIKING

As you might expect in an area surrounded by three mountain ranges and two national forests, there is an abundance of hiking opportunities not far from Big Sky. An easy, 4-mile hike to **Porcupine Creek** is accessible nearby. Go south 2¾ miles on U.S. 191 from the intersection with the mountain village road. Turn left at the sign that announces Porcupine Creek, and go about a half-mile to the trail head. The first mile of the hike wanders along Porcupine Creek, then offers a choice of either a north or south fork. The left (north) fork goes up into the foothills, offering a view of the creek below.

If you want more of a workout, try the **Lava Lake** trail, which begins about 13 miles north of the intersection of the mountain village road and U.S. 191 on the highway. Take the Lava Lake turn. The trail climbs steeply and without much relief for 3 miles to an alpine lake in the shelter of three mountains.

And **Yellowstone National Park** is only about 40 miles south of Big Sky, and you can hike there for a lifetime.

WHERE TO STAY

Big Sky Resort, P.O. Box 160001, Big Sky, MT 59716 (ℂ **800/548-4486** or 406/995-5000; www.bigskyresort.com) handles a wide variety of lodgings—from economy to full-fledged luxury scattered among some 15 properties. The three-story **Huntley Lodge,** with 205 units, was the beginning of late NBC newsman Chet Huntley's original vision for Big Sky. It offers rooms that can sleep up to four, and several loft rooms that can accommodate six. The 97-unit **Shoshone Condominium Hotel** combines the living quarters of a condo with the amenities and services of a hotel, with sleeping for four to six. Weight-training centers, saunas, an outdoor pool, gift shops, and ski storage are included at both places. **The Summit at Big Sky,** with 213 luxury condominiums, offers European sophistication in a Western style. All three properties are slope-side and offer ski-in/ski-out convenience. Winter rates start around $200 a night double and top out at about $1,000.

Moonlight Basin (P.O. Box 160040, Big Sky, MT 59716; ℂ **877/822-0430** or 406/993-6000; www.moonlightbasin.com) offers properties ranging from condos to private residences to luxurious penthouses. **The Moonlight Lodge and Spa** (ℂ **800/845-4428**) is a magnificent mountain lodge offering luxurious penthouse suites and secluded, mid-mountain cabins; plus a sophisticated yet down-home restaurant, a relaxed-atmosphere bar, and a deli. There's also a full-service spa with treatment rooms, complete fitness center, steam rooms, heated pool, and a cascading waterfall hot tub; a concierge ready and able to organize everything from fly-fishing trips, to backcountry skiing, to dog-sled adventures; and even an ice-skating rink just outside in winter. Winter rates start at around $200 a night double during the ski season and top out well over $1,000.

In the Big Sky area, rates vary with the season and within the ski season. The highest rates are during Christmas vacation, the lowest in the spring and fall "shoulder" seasons.

Best Western Buck's T-4 Lodge   Buck's offers a woody, Western ambience on the highway a little away from the ski resort lodgings. The lodge offers large, comfortable rooms in bewildering variety. Begun in 1946 as a hunting camp, Buck's T-4 got to the valley before electricity did. It has grown somewhat randomly since then. The current lodge is thoroughly modern, including two hot tubs large enough for the kids to swim in, a game room, and all of the other amenities you want in ski- and Yellowstone-area accommodations. The best thing about the place, though, is the incredible restaurant, reviewed below. Regular motel rooms, suites, and suites with kitchenettes are available. Ask about ski packages and vacations when making reservations.

P.O. Box 160279, U.S. 191 (about a half-mile south of its intersection with Lone Mountain Trail), Big Sky, MT 59716. ℂ 800/822-4484 or 406/995-4111. Fax 406/995-2191. www.buckst4.com. 72 units. $159 double; $219 suite. Rates include hot buffet breakfast. AE, DC, DISC, MC, V. Pets accepted with additional fee ($10). **Amenities:** Restaurant; lounge; 2 outdoor hot tubs; game room; Wi-Fi network. *In room:* Cable TV, dataport, kitchenette (suites only), fridge, coffeemaker, hair dryer, iron.

Gallatin Gateway Inn ✦   Located about 28 miles north of Big Sky on U.S. 191, the Gallatin Gateway Inn is a model of historical elegance from the days of luxury railroad travel. The hotel opened in the summer of 1927, as visitors were beginning to come to Yellowstone in large numbers. The Spanish-style building recalls pre–World War II elegance, and you almost expect to see Winston Churchill relaxing on the porch with a cigar. With lavish appointments that include Polynesian mahogany woodwork, decoratively carved beams, and high arched windows, the Gallatin Gateway has maintained its proud history of lavish style and refinement. The spacious guest rooms provide a tastefully understated balance to the regal lobby. They maintain the refined historical feel, but have been updated with light colors, providing a more open and airy feeling than you usually find in hotels of this vintage. Serving dinner only, the **Porter House** restaurant's seasonally changing menu includes regional specialties showcasing ingredients from local growers, and prepares hearty dishes with an eye toward imaginative combinations and generous portions. The wine list is carefully selected to complement the food.

76405 Gallatin Rd. (U.S. 191), P.O. Box 376, Gallatin Gateway, MT 59730. ☎ **800/676-3522** or 406/763-4672. Fax 406/763-4777. www.gallatingatewayinn.com. 34 units. $71–$185 double. Rates include continental breakfast. AE, DISC, MC, V. **Amenities:** Restaurant; lounge; outdoor pool and whirlpool; angler's casting pond. *In room:* A/C, TV.

Lone Mountain Ranch ✦✦✦ *(Kids)*   Back before there was even a community of Big Sky there was Lone Mountain Ranch. Started in 1926 as a working cattle ranch, Lone Mountain Ranch rapidly blossomed into a year-round destination as a guest ranch and cross-country ski area.

In the summer, the ranch blends traditional guest-ranch activities—riding, hiking, fishing, and eating—with naturalist programs that will improve your understanding of the Yellowstone ecosystem. They'll not only guide you into the Spanish Peaks, but also into an understanding of wildflowers, bird habits and habitat, and geology. They offer guided fly-fishing trips, and the ranch was designated the Orvis-endorsed lodge of the year for 2002. Lone Mountain prides itself on a family atmosphere and has separate activities for children, including animal tracking and overnight campouts. In the winter the ranch is a cross-country ski destination, with 50 miles of trails.

The accommodations here are varied, from small cabins to the large new Ridgetop Lodge, which can host an entire family reunion. Some of the cabins are quite old, from the original ranch, while the new lodge was built in the 1990s. All are spacious with private bathrooms and attractive pine interiors. They are spread out, assuring quiet and privacy for the guests.

Lone Mountain's restaurant is good, and in the winter, there is a sleigh ride and dinner at the ranch's North Fork cabin. There is a buffet breakfast and lunch each day. Call ☎ **406/995-2782** after 3pm for dinner reservations.

P.O. Box 160069, Big Sky, MT 59716. ☎ **800/514-4644** or 406/995-4644. Fax 406/995-4670. www.lmranch.com. 23 cabins, 1 house, 6 rooms in Ridgetop Lodge. Winter: cabin or lodge room $2,040–$2,840 1st person, $1,275 2nd person, $825 each additional person; Douglas Fir House $3,975 1st person, $1,275 2nd person, $825 each additional person. Rates include 7 nights' lodging, 3 meals daily, an 8-day trail pass with unlimited access to the ranch's trail system, evening entertainment, a sleigh-ride dinner, a trail buffet lunch, and airport transfers. Summer rates are slightly higher. DISC, MC, V. From Bozeman, head south on U.S. 191 about 40 miles. **Amenities:** Restaurant; lounge; outdoor Jacuzzi; children's program; massage; cross-country ski and snowshoe trails and lessons; rafting, fishing, hiking, and climbing trips arranged; laundry service. *In room:* Coffeemaker, hair dryer, no phone.

320 Guest Ranch ✦ *(Kids)*   Bordered by the Gallatin River, the 320 Guest Ranch dates from 1898 and is one of the few cowboy-oriented accommodations in Montana that takes guests by the night (and not the week) year-round. With a full slate of activities—horseback riding, fishing in the river or a trout pond on-site, hayrides, and plenty more in the winter—the ranch is self-contained, but also offers a good base for skiing Big Sky's slopes or Yellowstone's wildlands. Accommodations come in the form of seven lodge rooms and 52 cabins and log homes on the extensive grounds (320 acres, thus the name) that range from small and fairly basic to two-bedroom log cabins on the river to even larger guest homes. The furnishings are unremarkable but fitting, and the campfire out front roars every night for marshmallows and cowboy poetry.

205 Buffalo Horn Creek (about 15 miles south of the turnoff to Big Sky Resort on U.S. 191), Gallatin Gateway, MT 59730. ✆ 800/243-0320 or 406/995-4283. Fax 406/993-4694. www.320ranch.com. 59 units, including 52 cabins and log homes. $125–$321 double; lower rates in winter. AE, DISC, MC, V. **Amenities:** Restaurant; lounge; activities desk; wireless high-speed Internet access. *In room:* Cable TV, kitchens, coffeemaker.

WHERE TO DINE

There are almost two dozen eateries at Big Sky, so you know you won't go hungry. But the closer you are to the slopes, the more expensive the food is. Restaurants range from simple snack bars to the upscale **Huntley Lodge Dining Room** (✆ **406/995-5783**), which has a good breakfast buffet in the morning and fine dining in the evening. Big Sky also has more than a dozen nightspots.

In the **Meadow Village** area, there are about a dozen restaurants, including the **Huckleberry Cafe** (✆ **406/995-3130**), which has the best breakfast in Big Sky (lunches and dinners aren't bad, either); and we also like the **Blue Moon Bakery** (✆ **406/995-2305**), which is also open for all three meals and has good sandwiches and fresh-baked pastries, along with salads, soups, and pizza, and free delivery after 5pm.

Buck's T-4 Restaurant ✮✮✮ CONTEMPORARY AMERICAN   Buck's offers an adventurous menu of "Montana cuisine," with about a half-dozen wild game dishes, including pan-seared elk chops (a bone-in elk rib chop, pan-roasted and served medium rare), and the New Zealand red deer (a chargrilled filet served with a sauce of port wine, thyme, and shallots). Our choice here, though, is any of the charbroiled steaks, served with roasted-garlic mashed potatoes. Check the Buck's T-4 website for the complete current menu. For our money, Buck's is in the running for the best-restaurant-in-Montana sweepstakes. Chef Scott Peterson has earned a reputation in the valley for culinary creativity, and various publications have named the restaurant one of the best in the Rockies.

U.S. 191 (about a half-mile south of its intersection with Lone Mountain Trail), Big Sky. ✆ 406/993-5222. www.buckst4dining.com. Reservations recommended. Entrees $16–$40. AE, DC, DISC, MC, V. Daily 6–9:30pm. Closed mid-Apr to mid-June and early Oct to late Nov.

---

5 Livingston & the Paradise Valley ✮✮

Livingston: 26 miles E of Bozeman; 110 miles W of Billings; 58 miles N of Mammoth Hot Springs in Yellowstone National Park

Livingston is caught between very cowboy and very hip. As the largest community in the Paradise Valley, it has been discovered by the Hollywood set who want to get away from it all, but unfortunately still bring some of it with them. Peter Fonda has a ranch here. You might see Dennis Quaid or Tom McGuane. Robert Redford is also a fan of the area.

The Paradise Valley is the product of the Yellowstone River, the largest undammed river in the Lower 48. Along with the two valleys paralleling it to the west—the Gallatin and Madison—this portion of Montana is a fly-fishing paradise. There are lots of fishing guides and tackle shops, and millions of acres to wander in and wonder at.

ESSENTIALS

GETTING THERE   The nearest airport is Bozeman's **Gallatin Field,** 26 miles west along I-90. It's also possible to fly into Billings's **Logan Airport,** 116 miles east along I-90.

The Gardiner entrance to Yellowstone National Park is 53 miles south on U.S. 89. For local road reports, call © **406/586-1313.** Greyhound and Rimrock Stages provide bus service. The bus depot is at 105 W. Park St. (© **406/222-2231**).

VISITOR INFORMATION   The Livingston Area Chamber of Commerce is located at 303 E. Park St. (© **406/222-0850;** www.livingston-chamber.com). For information on **Yellowstone Country,** Travel Montana's region including Livingston and the Paradise Valley, call © **800/736-5276** or 406/556-8680 (www.yellowstone. visitmt.com).

GETTING AROUND   Car-rental agents in the area include **Avis** (© 406/388-6414), **Hertz** (© 406/388-6939), and **National** (© 406/388-6694) at Gallatin Field in Bozeman. (Livingston has no car-rental outlet.) Or call a cab at **VIP Taxi** (© 406/222-0200).

GETTING OUTSIDE

Much of the outdoor recreation in this area takes place in the **Gallatin National Forest.** Check with the Livingston Ranger District, 5242 U.S. 89 S., Livingston, MT 59047 (© **406/222-1892;** www.fs.fed.us/r1/gallatin). Another good source of information on hiking, mountain biking, cross-country skiing, and snowshoeing, as well as equipment rentals and sales, is **Timber Trails Outdoors Co.,** 309 W. Park St. (© **406/222-9550**).

CROSS-COUNTRY SKIING & SNOWSHOEING

The most popular spots are in the national forest. For specific locations and current conditions, check with the Livingston Ranger District or Timber Trails Outdoors Co. (see above).

FISHING

Montana has the best trout fishing in the country, and the area around here is the best trout fishing in Montana. Livingston is the gateway to classic Montana fly-fishing in the blue-ribbon Madison River, the Paradise Valley, and the Yellowstone River. **Dan Bailey's Fly Shop,** 209 W. Park St. (© **800/356-4052;** www.dan-bailey.com), in business since 1938, offers all manner of fishing tackle for sale or rent. Bailey's can give you some tips on where to fish on your own, or provide a guide for about $375 a day, depending on where you want to go and how many are in the group. **Hatch Finders Fly Shop,** 113 W. Park St., no. 3 (© **406/222-0989;** www.hatchfinders.com), can tie your custom flies and also provide outfitters almost anywhere in the state. A full-day guided trip in the Yellowstone River area is about $375 for two anglers (plus Montana fishing licenses), $425 in Yellowstone proper.

About ¼ mile south of town on U.S. 89, **George Anderson's Yellowstone Angler** (© **406/222-7130;** www.yellowstoneangler.com) is another fully equipped equipment store and guide service. Anderson also offers a fly-fishing school. About 20 miles south of Livingston in the town of Pray is **Knoll's Yellowstone Tackle and Fly Shop,** 104 Chicory Rd. (© **406/333-4848;** www.knolls.us). Calling itself an "honest and angler-friendly" shop, here you can learn how to cast and how feathers mysteriously become fishing flies, or purchase a handcrafted rod or reel. Take U.S. 89 south to Emigrant then east and northeast on County Road 540 to Pray.

Early-season fishing before runoff starts—in late April and early May—offers excellent dry fly-fishing. In late May and June, the water on most of the rivers is running high and muddy, but the Firehole River in Yellowstone National Park has a heavy early hatch, and the fishing is good. All fishing in the park is catch and release. The rivers drop in July and August, and there are hatches daily for good fishing.

HIKING & BIKING

This area is nearly surrounded by the **Gallatin National Forest,** which has several thousand miles of hiking and biking trails, including more than 800 miles of hiking trails in two designated wilderness areas—the Lee Metcalf and Absaroka-Beartooth. Popular trails that are relatively easily accessible include **Pine Creek Falls** south of town off the East River Road. The falls themselves are a short walk from the campground at the end of the access road, and Pine Creek Lake is about 4 miles farther along. **Livingston Peak** (or Mount Baldy Trail) is east of town off Swingley Road, and the **Big Timber Canyon Trail** is north of the town of Big Timber. The Livingston Ranger District of the U.S. Forest Service and Timber Trails Outdoors Co. (see "Getting Outside" above) can provide information about trails and access routes to them. Timber Trails also rents mountain bikes, starting at about $25 per day.

HORSEBACK RIDING

Chico Hot Springs (© 406/333-4933), about 22 miles south of Livingston off U.S. 89 to the east, also offers horseback riding. **Wilderness Pack Trips,** 209 K St. (© 406/222-5128), offers 7- to 10-day horse-packing trips into Yellowstone National Park. Call for their current schedules and rates.

RAFTING

Both scenic and white-water rafting and kayaking are available on the Yellowstone River throughout the Paradise Valley. **Rubber Ducky River Rentals,** 4 Mount Baldy Dr. (© 406/222-3746; www.riverservices.com), provides guided trips June through September, or will rent boats and equipment and provide river shuttles. Chico Hot Springs (© 406/333-4933) also offers raft trips. Call for current schedules and rates.

SEEING THE SIGHTS

The main attractions in downtown Livingston are its three museums (www.livingstonmuseums.org), all of which contain gift shops.

International Fly Fishing Center You'll find some 10,000 flies on display here, plus exhibits on the history of fly-fishing, displays showing the evolution of the fishing rod, fishing-related art, and two aquarium rooms—one containing warm-water species, the other with cold-water fish. The center also offers fly-casting lessons (call for times).

215 E. Lewis St. © 406/222-9369. $3 adults, $1 children 7–14, free for children under 7. June–Sept Mon–Sat 10am–6pm, Sun noon–5pm; Oct–May daily 10am–4pm.

Livingston Depot Center ☆ This is a beautifully restored 1902 Northern Pacific railway depot, built in handsome Italianate style, that is one of the most stunning railroad stations we've ever seen (it was designed by the same architects that designed Grand Central Station in New York City). The depot houses a museum with exhibits that concentrate on the history of the railroad and how it contributed to the development of the area. There are videos and interactive displays in this thoroughly modern look at the olden days, and the museum also hosts changing exhibits on some aspect of local history, such as explorers Lewis and Clark (the depot is a designated stop on the Lewis and Clark Trail).

200 W. Park St. (℃ 406/222-2300. $3 adults, $2 seniors and students, free for children under 6. June–Aug Mon–Sat 9am–5pm; Sun 1–5pm. Closed Sept–May.

Yellowstone Gateway Museum of Park County   Located in a historic school, this museum offers artifacts from Livingston's early days—including an 1889 train caboose and a Yellowstone National Park stagecoach—and exhibits stepping back to the prehistoric people who lived in this area some 10,000 years ago.

118 W. Chinook St. (℃ 406/222-4184. $4 adults, $3.50 seniors, $3 children 6–12, free for kids under 6. June–Aug daily 10am–5pm; Sept Tues–Sat 11am–4pm; open by appointment rest of year.

SHOPPING

Livingston is a center of Western art and artists, and there are about a dozen galleries in town. For Western wildlife and fly-fishing art, try the **Visions West Gallery** at 108 S. Main St. (℃ **406/222-0337**), with woodcarvings, bronzes, and original oils. You'll find the work of Russell Chatham, a Livingston artist known for his oils and lithographs of Western landscapes, at the **Chatham Fine Art Gallery,** 120 N. Main St. (℃ **406/222-1566**). The **Danforth Gallery,** 106 N. Main St. (℃ **406/222-6510**), is a nonprofit gallery of contemporary Western art that changes its exhibits every month in the summer.

WHERE TO STAY

Right across from Livingston's downtown depot, the **Murray Hotel,** 201 W. Park St. (℃ **406/222-1350;** www.murrayhotel.com), opened in 1904 and has since put up everyone from director Sam Peckinpah to the queen of Denmark. Off the lobby, there's a good restaurant and a classic Western bar. Double rates are $72; suites are $96 to $189. A block east is the **Guest House,** 105 W. Park St. (℃ **888/222-1460** or 406/222-1460), a less expensive but serviceable motel option with double rates of $49 to $59.

Chico Hot Springs Resort 🐾🐾   Rambling over 150 magnificent acres in the Paradise Valley, just 30 miles north of Yellowstone National Park, Chico offers a taste of gentility, cowboy style. The hot springs were discovered in 1876. The lodge opened in June 1900 and has been going strong ever since. There's a bewildering variety of lodgings from small rooms that share a bathroom to their deluxe rooms, plus rustic log cabins, a standalone caboose-turned-lodging, and a five-bedroom, two-bathroom private house. The three-story original Main Lodge is furnished mostly with antiques, and houses the casually elegant restaurant. Two open-air mineral hot-springs pools are just outside and are open daily from 6am to midnight year-round. Most rooms have high-speed Internet access. In the film *Rancho Deluxe*—screenplay by local resident Tom McGuane—Sam Waterston and Jeff Bridges soak in Chico's hot pool in their cowboy hats.

1 Chico Rd., Pray, MT 59065. (℃ **800/468-9232** or 406/333-4933. www.chicohotsprings.com. 110 units. Lodge $89–$115 double; $49–$64 double with shared bathroom; $159–$199 suite; $75–$85 cabin; $169–$325 private house. AE, DISC, MC, V. Pets accepted, $10 1-time fee. **Amenities:** 2 restaurants; saloon; 2 hot-springs pools; horseback riding; rafting; hiking; fishing; evening entertainment on weekends; cross-country skiing; dog-sledding. *In room:* Coffeemaker, iron, no phone.

CAMPING

There are plenty of camping opportunities in the Gallatin National Forest, including **Pine Creek** and **Miller Creek** campgrounds to the south of town toward Yellowstone

National Park. For information, contact the Livingston Ranger District, 5242 U.S. 89 S., Livingston (© **406/222-1892;** www.fs.fed.us/r1/gallatin).

Nine miles south of Livingston is the **Livingston KOA,** 163 Pine Creek Rd. (© **800/562-2805** or 406/222-0992). Open from May to mid-October, the facility boasts an indoor heated pool, a snack bar, LP gas sales, and a bathhouse. The campground is situated along the Yellowstone River, with shady sites that cost $18 to $21 for tents and $22 to $34 for RVs. **Yellowstone's Edge,** 3502 U.S. 89 S., Livingston (© **800/865-7322** or 406/333-4036; www.mtrv.com), is located on a bluff overlooking the Yellowstone River. Open from May to mid-October, it has both pull-through sites and back-in sites along the river for RVs, plus grassy tent sites and a lodge with a store, game room, laundry room, and bathhouse. There's also a dump station and LP gas available. Tent sites cost $20 and RV sites cost $34.

WHERE TO DINE

Chatham's Livingston Bar and Grille ⭐⭐ CONTINENTAL   If you're going to eat only one meal in Livingston, this is the place to go. All the locals will direct you here. The walls are decorated with the original paintings of the owner, local artist Russell Chatham, who opened the place in 1996. Some favorites here include surprisingly fresh oysters and king salmon, as well as terrific USDA choice steaks, lamb, and duck.

130 N. Main St., Livingston, MT. © **406/222-7909.** Reservations recommended. Main courses $14–$25. AE, DISC, MC, V. Daily 5:30–9:30pm.

The Dining Room at Chico Hot Springs ⭐⭐ CONTINENTAL   As big of a draw as this beloved getaway's hot springs, Chico's resident fine-dining restaurant serves some of the best food in the Rockies. The carnivorous traveler will enjoy the selection of top-drawer beef—the Gorgonzola filet mignon and the prime rib stand out—the pan-seared salmon (served with a Thai vinaigrette) is a seafood aficionado's dream, and wine lovers won't be disappointed one bit by the award-winning list. Many of the incredibly fresh veggies originate in the resort's garden and greenhouse, and the menu always includes a vegetarian selection. Give yourself plenty of time; you'll want to linger over the food.

Old Chico Rd., Pray, MT. © **800/468-9232** or 406/333-4933. www.chicohotsprings.com. Reservations recommended. Main courses $20–$30. AE, DISC, MC, V. Summer daily 5:30–10pm; winter Sun–Thurs 5:30–9pm, Fri–Sat 5:30–10pm.

Grand Hotel ⭐ LAMB/SEAFOOD   This beautiful restaurant is located in downtown Big Timber, about 30 miles east of Livingston, in an 1890 hotel that has been beautifully restored. The ingenious menu lists starters like buffalo rellenos and calamari tempura, before giving way to main dishes like herb-roasted racks of Montana lamb, "butter-knife" filets, and cashew-and-coconut-crusted chicken breasts. The restaurant has won the *Wine Spectator* award of excellence numerous times for its all-American wine list.

139 McLeod St., Big Timber. © **406/932-4459.** www.thegrand-hotel.com. Lunch $5–$11; dinner $16–$26. DISC, MC, V. Sun–Fri 11am–2pm; daily 5–9pm.

6 Red Lodge & the Absaroka-Beartooth Wilderness

60 miles SW of Billings; 62 miles NW of Cody, Wyoming

Nestled in a steep valley at the edge of the Absaroka-Beartooth Wilderness and surrounded by the spectacular Beartooth Mountains, the community of Red Lodge is not quite a tourist town, not quite a destination ski resort, but still not the sleepy little town it once was, either. It has elements of all three, giving it a homey and still busy feel. While it is slowly losing its small-town identity in favor of a resort persona, this hasn't happened completely.

Founded as a coal-mining community in the late 1880s, it did fairly well until the mines closed in the 1930s. Today it's the beautiful scenery and outdoor activities around Red Lodge that attract us. It doesn't hurt that the town sits at the northern end of the Beartooth National Scenic Byway, which the late Charles Kuralt called the most beautiful road in America.

ESSENTIALS

GETTING THERE   To reach Red Lodge, you'll have to fly into Billings's **Logan International Airport** (✆ **406/238-3420**). From Billings, take I-94 west to Laurel, about 16 miles, then go south on U.S. 212–310. The route diverges after about 12 miles at the small town of Rockvale. Follow U.S. 212 southwest 44 miles to Red Lodge. Rental cars are plentiful at Billings' airport (see section 1 in chapter 10). For **road conditions** concerning the Red Lodge area and closures of the Beartooth National Scenic Byway, call ✆ **406/657-0209.**

VISITOR INFORMATION   Contact the **Red Lodge Area Chamber of Commerce,** 601 N. Broadway (P.O. Box 998), Red Lodge, MT 59068 (✆ **888/281-0625** or 406/446-1718; www.redlodge.com).

GETTING OUTSIDE

Many of the outdoor activities in these parts take place in the Custer National Forest. For information, contact the **Beartooth Ranger District Office** of the Custer National Forest, at the south end of town along U.S. 212 (HC49, Box 3420, Red Lodge, MT 59068; ✆ **406/446-2103;** www.fs.fed.us/r1/custer). The office is open from 8am to 5pm daily in summer, and 8am to 4:30pm Monday through Friday in winter.

GOLF

The **Red Lodge Mountain Golf Course** (✆ **406/446-3344**) is notorious for swallowing golf balls. Water comes into play on 13 of the 18 holes. The signature hole is the 238-yard, par-3 no. 6, where you hit to an island green from an elevated tee about 80 feet above the hole. Greens fees are $25 to $35 for 18 holes.

HIKING

There are some popular and challenging day hikes not far from Red Lodge. Drive south on Route 212 about 10 miles to County Road 2346, then 2 miles down that road to the **Lake Fork of Rock Creek.** From here you can do a full loop of 19 miles to the West Fork of Rock Creek trail head (or do it as an overnight backpacking trip), or just walk up a few miles to some great fishing in the streams and lakes along the way and return.

Other popular hikes leave from the trail head at the **West Fork of Rock Creek.** Head west on Red Lodge Mountain Resort's access road, known locally as Ski Run Road. When the road forks, stay left and continue for several miles past a number of campgrounds. The road turns to gravel and ends at the West Fork trail head. The hike from here to Timberline Lakes is a moderate 9 miles round-trip. If you're not feeling that energetic, you can hike for about a mile to a picturesque waterfall. The fishing in Lake Mary near the trail is very good.

And They're Off . . . to the Pig Races

Bored with the rodeo? Horse racing seems ho-hum? Just head down to the **Bear Creek Saloon & Steakhouse** (© **406/446-3481;** www.redlodge.com/bearcreek); behind the bar is Bearcreek Downs, site of the famed local pig races.

Pig races? After the famous fires in Yellowstone in 1988 created a slow tourist season, the Bear Creek Saloon & Steakhouse owners decided that a **pig race** might generate some visitor interest. There was some question over whether the races were legal, but the Montana legislature stepped in and said pig races were okay by them, provided the proceeds went to charity. So Bearcreek Downs porkers are sending Carbon County students to college—more than $60,000 has gone for scholarships so far. Pig races are held Thursday through Sunday at 5pm, from Memorial Day to Labor Day.

Even if you don't come for the piggy track meet, the Bear Creek Saloon & Steakhouse is a great place to eat. It looks and smells like an authentic Western tavern, and the grub is mostly beef. Prices range from $7 to $25, and food is served Thursday through Sunday from 5 to 10pm. The saloon is 7 miles east of Red Lodge on County Road 308.

The **Absaroka-Beartooth Wilderness area** is a 950,000-acre wilderness that extends from the boundary of Yellowstone through two national forests. It's some of the most spectacular country in the Lower 48 states. Because of its proximity to the park, it is heavily used. There are lots of great hikes, incredible vistas, and pristine lakes with excellent trout fishing. **Granite Peak,** at 12,799 feet, is the tallest mountain in Montana, but it's only one of the 28 mountains topping 12,000 feet in the Absaroka-Beartooth.

For information about the above trails, contact the **Beartooth Ranger District Office** (see "Getting Outside," above).

SKIING

Red Lodge Mountain Resort (Box 750, Red Lodge, MT 59068; © **800/444-8977** or 406/446-2610; www.redlodgemountain.com) is a relatively small, family-oriented ski area. But it's growing: The skiable terrain includes 1,600 acres of mountain, with a vertical drop of 2,400 feet. About 40% of the mountain is rated for intermediate skiers, 25% for beginners, and 35% for advanced. Of the eight lifts, two are high-speed quads. An average of 250 inches of snow falls each year, plus Red Lodge has one of the largest snowmaking operations in the Rockies. Lift tickets cost $42 for adults, $38 for juniors 13 to 18, and $15 for children 6 to 12 (free for kids under 6 and seniors 70 and over); half-day tickets are also available. The season usually runs from late November to the mid-April, with hours of 9am to 4pm.

SEEING THE SIGHTS

When it's open, the **Beartooth National Scenic Byway,** a 64-mile stretch of U.S. 212 from Red Lodge to Cooke City, is an incredible road that takes you to almost 11,000 feet elevation. Make sure a camera is handy when Pilot Peak comes into view, just outside Cooke City.

Beartooth Nature Center   The Beartooth Nature Center is the only nature center in Montana that provides a home exclusively for animals that have been injured, orphaned, or too accustomed to humans to be returned to the wild. Residents, more than 75 at a recent count, include mountain lions, wolves, coyotes, black bears, bison, and other animals native to Montana.

615 2nd Ave. E., Red Lodge. © 406/446-1133. www.beartoothnaturecenter.org. $6 adults, $5 seniors 55 and older, $2.50 children 5–15, free for children under 5. May–Oct daily 10am–5pm; Nov–Apr daily 10am–2pm.

Carbon County Peaks to Plains Museum   Highlights of this well-run and interesting museum include a simulated coal mine that recalls Red Lodge's underground past, and the Greenough Collection of cowboy and rodeo gear. There's also a Crow Indian tepee, a mountain man camp, and pioneer displays. This is the place to find out more about "Liver Eatin'" Johnston, who got his name because . . . no, it's too repulsive. You'll have to find out for yourself.

224 N. Broadway at 8th Ave., Red Lodge. © 406/446-3667. $3 adults, $2 children, free for children 5 and under. Memorial Day to Labor Day Tues–Fri 10am–5pm, Sat–Sun and holidays 1–5pm; rest of year Tues–Fri 10am–5pm, Sat 1–5pm.

WHERE TO STAY

In addition to the properties discussed below, we recommend the **Comfort Inn of Red Lodge,** 612 N. Broadway, Red Lodge, MT 59068 (© **888/733-4661** or 406/446-4469), which charges $100 double.

Chateau Rouge   The Chateau Rouge offers excellent accommodations at a very reasonable price, especially for families. Though run like a motel, the Chateau Rouge is actually a collection of privately owned condominiums. Most are two-story, two-bedroom affairs with a living room and kitchen on the first floor and the sleeping rooms upstairs. The two-story condos have large, fully appointed kitchens, while the studios have small but complete kitchens. All are attractively decorated and maintained. The only drawback—a minor one in our opinion—is that they are not air-conditioned, which can be uncomfortable on those rare summer days when the mountain temperatures reach the 90s (30s Celsius).

1505 S. Broadway, Red Lodge, MT 59068. © 800/926-1601 or 406/446-1601. Fax 406/446-1602. www.chateau rouge.com. 24 units. $75 studio; $104 2-bedroom condo, $6–$10 for each extra person; lower rates in spring and fall. AE, DC, DISC, MC, V. **Amenities:** Indoor pool. *In room:* TV.

The Pollard ★★   Built in 1893 by the Rocky Fork Coal Company at an initial cost of $20,000, The Pollard has recently undergone a magnificent restoration, integrating modern conveniences with historical character and elegance. It has been a stopover for a number of Old West celebrities, including Buffalo Bill Cody, Calamity Jane, and Jeremiah "Liver Eatin'" Johnston. The Pollard has a three-story gallery with a wood-burning fireplace. All the rooms are very large, done with manly oak furniture and ladylike flower-print comforters. Six have balconies overlooking the lobby; many have Jacuzzi tubs. The entire operation is first class.

For fine dining in Red Lodge, **The Pollard Hotel Dining Room** is a solid choice. The food is excellent—we suggest the steaks, grilled over a wood fire. Reservations are recommended. Hours are daily from 7:30am to 2pm and 5:30 to 9pm.

2 N. Broadway, Red Lodge, MT 59068. © 800/765-5273 or 406/446-0001. Fax 406/446-0002. www.thepollard.net. 39 units. $85–$95 double; $175–$265 suite. Rates include full breakfast. AE, DISC, MC, V. **Amenities:** 2 restaurants; lounge; 2 racquetball courts; large health club; Jacuzzi; sauna; limited room service; massage. *In room:* A/C, cable TV/VCR, hair dryer, iron.

Rock Creek Resort 𝓰𝓰   This property was built in 1963 as a dormitory for members of an international ski-racing camp founded by owner Pepi Gramshammer. Rock Creek retains much of the ski atmosphere that produced it, although the ski hill is a good 6 miles away, plus it's got all sorts of warm-weather recreation (a stocked trout pond, horseshoe pits, and a soccer field). The cedar-sided Beartooth Lodge, the main building, boasts a huge fireplace made of river rock and windows that offer mountain views. A wide variety of accommodations are available, from mountain lodge–style units, with lots of wood, to luxurious condominiums and three-bedroom town houses, decorated in a Western theme. Many units have wood-burning stoves or fireplaces, patios or balconies, or a private hot tub. It would be hard to find a room here without a wonderful view.

HC 49, Box 3500, Red Lodge, MT 59068. (© 800/667-1119 or 406/446-1111. Fax 406/237-9851. www.rockcreek resort.com. 88 units. $95–$295 double. AE, DC, DISC, MC, V. From Red Lodge, drive 5 south miles on U.S. 212. **Amenities:** 2 restaurants; 2 lounges; indoor pool; 4 tennis courts; weight room; Jacuzzi; sauna; bike rental; coin-op washers and dryers. *In room:* Cable TV, kitchenette (in some units), coffeemaker, hair dryer.

CAMPING

There are 16 Forest Service campgrounds available in the Red Lodge area, with sites for over 700 campers. Seven of the larger campgrounds accept reservations through the **National Recreation Reservation Service** (© **877/444-6777;** www.reserveusa. com), and the rest are first-come, first-served. For information, contact the **Beartooth Ranger District Office** of the Custer National Forest, at the south end of town along U.S. 212 (© **406/446-2103**).

Those seeking commercial campgrounds, with all the usual RV hookups and other amenities, can head to the **Red Lodge KOA,** 7464 U.S. 212 (© **406/446-2364**). It has grassy and shady sites, a heated outdoor pool, and a convenience store, and charges about $22 to $26 for tents, $24 to $34 for RVs, and $50 to $60 for basic cabins. It's open from mid-May to mid-September.

WHERE TO DINE

In addition to the restaurants discussed below, see the sidebar "And They're Off . . . to the Pig Races," above, for information on the **Bear Creek Saloon & Steakhouse,** and the "Where to Stay" section for information on the excellent restaurant at **The Pollard.**

Bogart's MEXICAN/PIZZA   Bogart's menu consists of great sandwiches, Mexican entrees, and pizza. As you might have guessed, the place is named after Humphrey himself. Other than the humble homage of naming sandwiches after some of his movies, don't expect more of a tribute. The chimichangas are toasted to a golden turn, and the chiles rellenos are excellent.

11 S. Broadway. (© 406/446-1784. Reservations not accepted. Most dishes $6–$15. MC, V. Daily 11am–9pm.

Bridge Creek Backcountry Kitchen and Wine Bar ECLECTIC   Bridge Creek is a local favorite, with a widely varied, moderately priced menu. Lunches include wraps, salads, sandwiches on fresh-baked breads, and homemade soups. At dinner you'll find fish, chicken, steaks, chops, and pasta. The wine bar is a small, bright room with an extensive wine list that for several years has received the *Wine Spectator* award of excellence. The atmosphere is casual; sort of California cafe with a Western flavor. Open at 8am daily, a coffee bar here serves a wide selection of espresso, cappuccino, latte, mocha, and iced drinks plus freshly baked pastries.

116 S. Broadway Ave. (© 406/446-9900. www.eatfooddrinkwine.com. Lunch $4–$9; dinner $10–$20. MC, V. Mon–Thurs 11am–9pm; Fri–Sat 11am–9:30pm.

Old Piney Dell ★★ *Finds* INTERNATIONAL/WESTERN   Located in a former homesteader's cabin on the banks of Rock Creek, this is where locals come for a special evening. If you like Wiener schnitzel, this place is for you—the veal is lightly breaded and delicately pan-fried to perfection. The Gorgonzola-crusted tenderloin practically melts in your mouth, and the grilled New York strip in herbed butter satisfies the heartier appetite. Chicken, lamb, pork, and fish are also on the menu, with prime rib on Fridays and Saturdays. Ask about the daily mixed grill and pasta specials, created from the best find of the day.

In Rock Creek Resort. *©* **406/446-1111.** www.rockcreekresort.com. Reservations recommended. Dinner $14–$23. AE, DC, DISC, MC, V. Mon–Thurs 5:30–9pm; Fri–Sat 5:30–10pm. Closed Mon–Tues Sept–May. From Red Lodge, drive 5 miles south on U.S. 212.

10

Billings & Eastern Montana

The plains of eastern Montana offer a more subtle beauty than the rugged mountains to the west. A land of rolling hills, dusty bluffs, and an occasional rock-walled canyon, this is classic cattle and wheat country, with grass thick and green in spring, brown and dry by fall, and blanketed by snow in winter. Temperatures can be extreme; hot in the summer under a blazing sun, and bitter cold in the winter, dipping below zero for long stretches.

Eastern Montana's history is rich: Lewis and Clark trekked along the Missouri River, and one of the most famous battles of the American West, the Battle of the Little Bighorn, was fought here.

In the old days, travel in eastern Montana was defined by the railroads. Virtually every town with 300 people and a tavern could be reached by either the main line or a spur. But the romantic days of rail travel have been replaced by the automobile, and interstates rival the rails. I-94 sweeps across the state west to east, I-15 cuts through the Rockies from Idaho to the Canadian border, and I-90 dips south from near Billings to the Crow Reservation in Sheridan, Wyoming.

1 Billings

104 miles W of Cody, Wyoming; 123 miles N of Sheridan, Wyoming; 142 miles E of Bozeman; 339 miles E of Missoula

The most populous city in Montana with around 100,000 residents, Billings might well be the most urban place in Montana or Wyoming. You'll find real shopping malls here, along with the occasional 5 o'clock traffic jam and the tallest free-standing brick building in the world (the 23-story Sheraton). Since its 1880s development by Frederick Billings as a railroad town, the city has evolved into the economic and industrial hub for the entire region.

Once a booming oil town, as well as a crossroads for the railroads, Billings has now positioned itself as the progressive medical center for all of eastern Montana, the Dakotas, and Wyoming. The economy is still based on cattle and grain, but downtown Billings boasts new banks and contemporary business centers, with many historic buildings enjoying restorations since the turn of the 21st century. Billings also has its share of scenic splendor: From the rimrocks surrounding the city you can see the Pryor Mountains, the Bighorns, and the majestic Beartooths to the west.

ESSENTIALS

GETTING THERE   Billings's **Logan International Airport** (© **406/238-3420;** www.flybillings.com) is the state's busiest, located about 2 miles north of downtown. Service is provided by **Big Sky Airlines** (© **800/237-7788** or 406/245-2300), **Delta** (© **800/221-1212**), **Horizon** (© **800/547-9308**), **Northwest** (© **800/225-2525**), **Frontier** (© **800/432-1359**), and **United** (© **800/241-6522**).

If you're traveling by car, I-90 connects Billings to Bozeman, Butte, and Missoula in the west before crossing into Idaho; I-90 east heads southeast into Wyoming. I-94 branches off I-90 10 miles east of town and runs northeast through Miles City and Glendive before reaching North Dakota. U.S. 87 heads north out of Billings to Roundup, and U.S. 310 goes south to Lovell, Wyoming.

VISITOR INFORMATION   The **Billings Area Chamber of Commerce & Visitor Center,** 815 S. 27th St. (P.O. Box 31177), Billings, MT 59107 (© **800/735-2635** or 406/252-4016; www.billingscvb.visitmt.com), has brochures, maps, and area information. Travel Montana's **Custer Country** (© **800/346-1876** or 406/628-1432; www.custer.visitmt.com) is another information source.

GETTING AROUND   Billings's downtown street system might be a bit confusing at first, but can be mastered if you remember that Montana Avenue is the dividing line between north and south. Numbered avenues run parallel to Montana, starting with 1st Avenue North and 1st Avenue South, which are located 1 block away on each side of it, and increasing from there. The numbered streets run perpendicular to Montana, their names changing from North to South as they cross it, and increase numerically from east to west. The heart of downtown lies north of Montana and is relatively compact. Its boundaries are North 27th and North 29th streets and 1st and 6th avenues North.

To access downtown from I-90, which skims the southern edge of the city, take exit 450 and go north on 27th Avenue; the Business Loop follows Montana Avenue between exits 446 and 452. Coming from the north, from Roundup, U.S. 87 turns into a four-lane road before heading west into the Heights, the northeastern part of the city. Follow this road into downtown, or turn right on Airport Road to reach Logan International Airport.

The best way to see Billings is to drive. Car-rental companies at the airport include **Enterprise** (© **800/736-8222** or 406/294-2930), **Budget** (© **800/527-0700** or 406/259-4168), **Hertz** (© **800/654-3131** or 406/248-9151), and **National** (© **800/227-7368** or 406/252-7626).

The city bus service is **MET Transit** (© **406/657-8218**). Taxi service is available from **City Cab** (© **406/252-8700**), **Yellow Cab** (© **406/245-3033**), and **Red Lodge Shuttle** (© **888/446-2191** or 406/446-2257).

Black Otter Trail Scenic Drive

The Black Otter Trail Scenic Drive, following about 3 miles along the edge of the sheer rimrock overlooking Billings, affords a spectacular view of the city and the three mountain ranges in the distance. To get there, take Montana Avenue east to U.S. 87 and turn left (north). After you pass the MetraPark arena complex on your right, turn left onto Airport Road, and shortly thereafter, left again onto Black Otter Trail. Boot Hill Cemetery is at this end of the road, and contains 40 of the unlucky residents of the town of Coulson, most of whom "died with their boots on." It's also the final resting place of the famous scout Yellowstone Kelly, who asked to be buried here above the land he scouted.

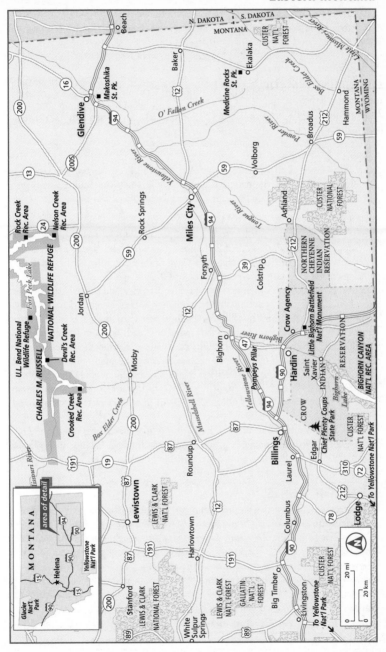

GETTING OUTSIDE

Fun Adventures Tours (© **888/618-4386**; www.montanafunadventures.com) offers hayrides and historical tours.

FISHING

Though the Yellowstone River runs through the city, it is wide, busy, and often muddy. The best nearby fishing is in the **Bighorn Canyon National Recreation Area** (see section 3, later in this chapter), 83 miles southeast of town. Fishing guides come and go pretty often in the Billings area, so to find a local one, the best bet is to ask at **The Base Camp,** 1730 Grand Ave. (© **406/248-4555**).

GOLF

Lake Hills Golf Club (© **406/252-9244**) and the **Peter Yegen, Jr., Golf Club** (© **406/656-8099**) are the two 18-hole public golf courses in Billings, with greens fees of $23 to $26, not including cart.

NEARBY PARKS & NATURE PRESERVES

In town, there is a good **multiuse trail system** popular with joggers, walkers, and bikers. Contact **Billings Parks & Public Lands** (© **406/657-8371**) for information.

An unusual side trip is to **Pictograph Cave State Park,** where you can see cave paintings made by prehistoric people over 4,500 years ago. There are over 100 pictographs, in red and black pigments made from ashes, clay, and animal fat. The meaning of the designs is continually debated—were they ceremonial, or perhaps celebrations of a successful hunt or battle (there are many images of shield-bearing warriors)? A short, but fairly steep, interpretive trail leads up to the caves, which are more like large stone alcoves than caves in the usual sense. They lie in a classic, sheer, broad sandstone canyon inhabited by rabbits and an occasional rattlesnake—so stay on the trail. From Billings, take I-90 east to exit 452 and follow the signs for 6 miles. The park is open from 8am to 8pm from May 1 to September 30, with an entrance fee of $5 per vehicle. Call © **406/247-2940** or visit www.pictographcave.org for information.

Locals go to nearby **Lake Elmo State Park,** 10 miles north of Billings on U.S. 87 (© **406/247-2940**), for picnicking, swimming, windsurfing, fishing, and volleyball. Boat rentals and windsurfing lessons are available in the summer; gas-powered boats are prohibited. Entrance fee is $5 per vehicle.

SEEING THE SIGHTS

To view some modern artists' contributions to decorating the West, drive the **Avenue of the Sculptures** along 27th Street (from I-90 exit 450 to the airport) for an outdoor art show. The first work, *The Cattle Drive Monument,* is right outside the chamber of commerce's visitor center. *The Trough,* a contemporary piece that looks like a fragment of collapsed concrete, is in front of the Norwest Bank Building at 175 N. 27th. *The Sheriff Webb Memorial Marker* is on the courthouse lawn, and finally, in front of the airport is the *Range Rider of the Yellowstone,* posed for by silent-screen cowboy actor William Hart.

Peter Yegen, Jr., Yellowstone County Museum   The small museum, located next to the airport, has a large collection housed in a 104-year-old cabin, which has had such eminent visitors as Teddy Roosevelt and Buffalo Bill Cody. Rotating exhibits describe the history and diverse cultures of Montana and the Yellowstone River Basin, from prehistory through the 1950s. Changing exhibits of contemporary local and

Billings

ACCOMMODATIONS ■
Dude Rancher Lodge **8**
Holiday Inn Grand Montana **3**
The Josephine B&B **7**
Historic Northern Hotel **14**
Sheraton Billings **9**
Sleep Inn **19**

DINING ◆
Casey's Golden Pheasant **12**
George Henry's Restaurant **6**
Juliano's **5**
McCormick Cafe **16**
Montana Brewing Company **11**
Q **17**
Walkers Grill **15**

ATTRACTIONS ●
Moss Mansion **4**
Peter Yegen, Jr. Yellowstone
    County Museum **2**
Pictograph Cave State Park **20**
Western Heritage Center **13**
Yellowstone Art Museum **10**
ZooMontana **1**

SERVICES ●
Billings Area Chamber of
    Commerce & Visitor Center **18**

Kids   Especially for Kids: Animals, Animals

The only wildlife and botanical park within 500 miles of Billings, ambitious **ZooMontana** 🐾 covers 70 acres and is continually changing and growing. The zoo concentrates on northern plains wildlife, some of which you may see on your trip through the state. There are nature trails meandering among the natural habitats of red pandas, eastern gray wolves, Manchurian sika deer, bald eagles, great horned owls, and the North American river otter; there's a petting zoo in a farm and ranch setting.

The zoo is also home to two of the 300 Siberian tigers remaining in the world, as well as to the retirees from a captive breeding program for black-footed ferrets (North America's rarest mammal). A new state-of-the-art grizzly bear habitat is opening in 2006.

Take exit 443 north off I-90, head northwest on King Avenue to Shiloh Road, then south (📞 **406/652-8100**; www.zoomontana.org). Admission is $6 adults, $3 children 3 to 15, $4 seniors over 65. Open daily May through mid-October 10am to 5pm; mid-October through April daily 10am to 4pm.

---

national artists are in the Landmarks Gallery. Also on the grounds: a vintage steam engine and a stuffed two-headed calf. The view of Billings and the surrounding countryside from the museum's deck is terrific.

1950 Terminal Circle, adjacent to Logan International Airport. 📞 **406/256-6811**. www.pyycm.org. Free admission. Mon–Fri 10:30am–5pm; Sat 10:30am–3pm. Closed Sun and national holidays.

The Moss Mansion 🐾   This massive red-sandstone mansion, built in 1901 for Billings banker Preston B. Moss, was designed by prominent New York architect Henry Janeway Hardenbaugh. It has many European influences, including a Moorish entry, a Shakespearean library, and a French Louis XVI parlor. Oak and mahogany millwork gives an elegant feel to the upstairs bedrooms. The mansion, listed on the National Register of Historic Places, has been used in various TV miniseries and Hollywood films, and was featured on A&E's *America's Castles* in 1997. Visitors view a short video about Moss and early Billings before taking the 1-hour guided tour of the home. The Moss Mansion also hosts various events during the spring and summer months, and is elaborately decorated for Christmas.

914 Division St. 📞 **406/256-5100**. www.mossmansion.com. $7 adults, $5 seniors and students with ID, $3 children 6–12, free for children under 6. Summer guided tour every hour on the hour, Mon–Sat 9am–4pm, Sun 1–3pm; winter daily 1–3pm. Closed Thanksgiving, Christmas, and New Year's Day.

Western Heritage Center   A lot of Western museums are just vast collections of dusty reminders of bygone eras. But this facility has done an excellent job of interpreting and editing its extensive collection, making the panoramic history of Western settlement accessible to casual visitors. In addition to the usual exhibits of the area's settlement by white people, the Heritage Center includes sensitive displays on the Crow tribe and on Japanese and other minority settlers. Interactive presentations include videos and recorded memories of three Yellowstone County homesteaders.

2822 Montana Ave. 📞 **406/256-6809**. www.ywhc.org. Free admission. Tues–Sat 10am–5pm; also Sun in summer 1–5pm.

Yellowstone Art Museum &&   Montana art aficionados are justifiably proud of the Yellowstone Art Museum, a leader in the contemporary Western art movement. The museum showcases the best the new West has to offer, from Deborah Butterfield's ranch sculptures to Russell Chatham's gauzy landscapes to Rudy Autio's colorful, erotic ceramics. Additionally, the museum's permanent collection—over 3,000 pieces—includes the largest public gathering of the drawings, paintings, books, and memorabilia of cowboy illustrator Will James, plus paintings and drawings by other historic regional artists such as J. H. Sharp and Charles M. Russell. Changing exhibitions have recently included modernism on the High Plains and "A Western Icon: The Art and Stories of Will James." Expect to spend up to 2 hours.

401 N. 27th St. ✆ 406/256-6804. www.artmuseum.org. $7 adults, $5 seniors and college students, $3 children 6–18, free for children under 6. Tues–Sat 10am–5pm (until 8pm Thurs); Sun noon–5pm.

SHOPPING

In the downtown area, the shopping district covers about 4 blocks on North 29th Street, Broadway, and 1st and 2nd avenues North. The area is heavy in the antiques line, but it also has a few boutiques and independent bookshops. The **Depot Antique Mall,** 2223 Montana Ave. (✆ 406/245-5595), is the first stop for antiquers. You can find just about anything in this cavernous downtown space hosting nearly 100 dealers. For contemporary art, try the **Toucan Gallery,** 2505 Montana Ave. (✆ 406/252-0122), in the city's historic district, offering prints, oils, handmade furniture, and ceramics. The fashion conscious can find clothing from around the world at the **Cactus Rose,** 202 N. 29th St. (✆ 406/252-9126). The classic Western department store, where lots of real cowboys get their gear, is **Lou Taubert Ranch Outfitters** (✆ 406/245-2248), at 123 Broadway. For outdoor clothing and equipment, check out **The Base Camp** (✆ 406/248-4555) at 1730 Grand Ave.

WHERE TO STAY

In addition to the properties discussed below, you might consider the **Holiday Inn Grand Montana,** 5500 Midland Rd. (I-90 exit 446), ✆ 877/554-7263 or 406/248-7701, with double rates of $79 to $129; or the **Sleep Inn,** 4904 Southgate Dr. (I-90 exit 447), ✆ 800/424-6423 or 406/254-0013, with double rates of $55 to $75.

Dude Rancher Lodge *Value*   The Dude Rancher has been offering real Western hospitality since it opened in 1949. The rooms, which surround an inner courtyard, are comfortable and quiet, with ranch oak furniture and king- and queen-size beds. Its downtown location puts you within walking distance of numerous restaurants, shopping, banks, the library, and the Alberta Bair Theatre.

415 N. 29th St., Billings, MT 59101. ✆ 800/221-3302 or 406/259-5561. www.duderancherlodge.com. 57 units. $48–$80 double. AE, DISC, MC, V. **Amenities:** Restaurant; room service; dry cleaning. *In room:* A/C, cable TV, fridge, coffeemaker.

Historic Northern Hotel &   The Northern has long been Billings's landmark hotel, going back to the days of the railroaders. It was the finest place to stay from its construction in 1902 until it was destroyed by fire in 1940—although it was rebuilt almost immediately. Early dignitaries who stayed here include painter C. M. Russell, Theodore Roosevelt, and Prince Olaf of Sweden. A late-1990s renovation retained and polished its elegance and style. It has a contemporary Western flair, but isn't pushy about it. For business travelers who have to use their computers, it is excellent, with comfortable desks, accessible power outlets, and dataports on the phones in the suites.

Broadway and 1st Ave. N., Billings, MT 59101. ⓒ 406/245-5121. Fax 406/259-9862. 160 units. $89 double; $109–$139 suite. AE, DC, DISC, MC, V. **Amenities:** Restaurant; lounge/casino; exercise room. *In room:* A/C, cable TV, dataport, coffeemaker, hair dryer, iron.

The Josephine Bed & Breakfast ⌀   A first-rate B&B, The Josephine is housed in a 1912 Victorian built by a wealthy rancher to give his children access to schools in Billings. Named for a steamboat that once plied the waters of the Yellowstone between here and St. Louis, the inn is located within walking distance of downtown, offering a quiet retreat amid Billings's urban bustle. Owners Bobbi and Harvey Bybee have installed high-speed Internet access, and there's a modern whirlpool tub in one room, but most rooms feature the classic, high-sided, claw-foot tubs familiar to Western movie buffs. The Captain's Room offers a masculine feel, from the pipes on the night table (but don't light one up; the entire inn is nonsmoking) to the four-poster bed. The other rooms have more feminine touches. There are a library, parlor, and dining room for breakfast, and a wraparound porch outside. Breakfasts are memorable: Harvey makes a terrific caramel-pecan French toast and his sourdough pancakes aren't bad at all, either.

514 N. 29th St., Billings, MT 59101. ⓒ **800/552-5898** or 406/248-5898. www.thejosephine.com. 5 units. $75–$160 double. AE, DISC, MC, V. **Amenities:** Wi-Fi network. *In room:* A/C, cable TV, dataport.

Sheraton Billings Hotel ⌀   Declared the world's tallest free-standing brick building by the Brick Institute of America, this 23-story tower is like a beacon in the heart of downtown—you can see it from just about everywhere. The rooms are nice, with comfortable beds, plush chairs, and the best views around, and the list of amenities is comprehensive. (It is also surprisingly pet-friendly, providing beds, leashes, and food on request.) The hotel clearly caters to the business traveler—there's a 24-hour business center, the desks are huge, rooms have high-speed Ethernet ports, and the entire hotel is encompassed by a wireless network—but it fits the bill for anyone who wants quick access to downtown.

27 N. 27th St., Billings, MT 59101. ⓒ **800/588-7666** or 406/252-7400. 282 units. $112 double; $132–$202 suite. AE, DC, DISC, MC, V. Pets under 60 lb. accepted with $50 deposit ($25 nonrefundable). **Amenities:** Restaurant; lounge; heated indoor pool; exercise room; indoor Jacuzzi; 2 saunas; game room; concierge; 24-hr. business center; Wi-Fi network; salon; room service; dry cleaning; executive level. *In room:* A/C, cable TV w/pay movies, dataport, coffeemaker, hair dryer, iron.

WHERE TO DINE

For breakfast and lunch, we like the **McCormick Café,** 2419 Montana Ave. (ⓒ **406/ 255-9555**), and its offerings of eggs, crepes, sandwiches, pizza, and numerous vegetarian dishes.

Juliano's ⌀⌀ PACIFIC RIM/CONTEMPORARY AMERICAN   One of the best restaurants in Montana, Juliano's serves excellent, original food in a casually elegant atmosphere. It's a little hard to categorize the food here. Chef Carl Kurokawa is a native of Hilo, Hawaii, and his menu describes the cuisine as "Fun American with European and Asian influences." Privately, Kurokawa says to call it "Carl food." The menu changes monthly, but you can depend on it having the fresh Hawaiian fish that Kurokawa insists on flying in. For dinner you might get locally raised lamb or Rocky Mountain elk, or maybe chicken-fried, almond-crusted calamari. At lunch there are salads—if you're feeling adventurous, try the crispy chicken and grapefruit salad— plus sandwiches and pasta dishes. The building was originally the stable of the sandstone "castle" next door, built in 1902. A pressed-tin ceiling with Bacchus hoisting a

glass covers one of the dining rooms, and there is an outdoor patio for nice days. There is an extensive wine list, and special wine dinners are presented (call for dates).

2912 7th Ave. N. ✆ **406/248-6400.** Reservations recommended. Lunch items $7–$9; dinner entrees $14–$25. AE, DC, DISC, MC, V. Mon–Fri 11:30am–2pm; Wed–Sat 5:30–9pm.

George Henry's ⚜ AMERICAN   Housed in an 1882 home, the ambience of George Henry's recalls a 1920s tearoom with a lot of stained glass and old-world charm. The food is mainly innovative and well-prepared variations on American standards, with a fairly extensive menu. The Steak Oscar—an 8-ounce filet mignon topped with crab, asparagus, and béarnaise sauce—is a popular dinner choice, but we especially recommend the broiled Grecian-style lamb chops. You also might like the orange roughy (broiled with a Parmesan crust) or the pan-fried walleye pike, topped with slivered almonds and a lemon-dill sauce. Desserts, such as the strawberry shortcake torte, are all homemade, and the wine list is 35 labels deep. The lunch menu includes lots of salads, plus sandwiches, burgers, and our choice—the quiche of the day.

404 N. 30th. ✆ **406/245-4570.** Reservations accepted. Main courses lunch $7–$9, dinner $9–$24. AE, DISC, MC, V. Mon–Fri 11am–2pm and 5:30–9pm; Sat 5:30–9pm.

Montana Brewing Company 🅺🅸🅳🆂 MICROBREWERY   A bustling bar and grill, Billings's downtown microbrewery has been won a number of medals at the Great American Beer Fest, and it's easy to taste why. Their beers, brewed in vats behind the dining room, include Custer's Last Stout, Cutthroat Rye, and several seasonal beers; nine are always available on draft. The food is pretty good, too, including pizzas (we like the Wild Boar, with jalapeños and sausage), chicken potpie, enchiladas, and a gamut of burgers and sandwiches. Despite the noisy bar area and adjacent casino, this is a pretty good place for families, and there's a kids' menu to boot.

113 N. Broadway. ✆ **406/252-9200.** Main courses $5–$10. Reservations accepted for large parties only. AE, DISC, MC, V. Daily 11am–11pm. Bar open later.

Q ⚜⚜ MEDITERRANEAN/CONTEMPORARY   An anchor in the ongoing revitalization of Historic Montana Avenue, Q is the brainchild of Suzy Schaer, for whom it is named. (Suzy Q, get it?) In sharp contrast to its peers in Billings, this eatery is very sleek and very hip, and feels more California than Montana. The room combines historic details—an original pressed tin ceiling, for one—with contemporary design—suede wall panels, custom veneers, and striking yellow lamps. The menu meshes Mediterranean and Asian influences with a contemporary American slant: Entrees include pastas, steaks, salmon, and a few vegetarian dishes. The restaurant is attached to the **Carlin Martini Bar and Nightclub,** equally hip and serving up a mean kamikaze martini.

2503 Montana Ave. ✆ **406/245-2503.** www.qcuisine.com. Reservations recommended. Main courses $13–$24. AE, DC, DISC, MC, V. Mon–Sat 4:30–10pm.

Walkers Grill ⚜⚜ AMERICAN BISTRO   Longtime Billings stalwart Walkers moved into posh new digs in 2004, taking over the first floor of a new brick loft building in the heart of downtown. Featuring the work of 26 different artists, the space itself is a masterwork of contemporary Western design, marked by barbed-wire chandeliers, wheat-field-inspired carpeting, a host stand made from a hitching post, and a bar made from a cattle guard. The food is also excellent: Chef Mike Harmon brings a bit of the exotic (tortilla-crusted catfish and Thai pasta) to the table with plenty of creative interpretations of local standards (cola-marinated buffalo flank steak and roasted leg of lamb with huckleberry-mint coulis). A tapas menu of gourmet pizzas, Asian appetizers, and small versions of main courses is also served. The wine list is extensive, including many French wines—often difficult or impossible to find on the plains.

2700 1st Ave. N. (☎ 406/245-9291. www.walkersgrill.com. Reservations recommended. Main courses $11–$25; tapas $5–$9. AE, DISC, MC, V. Daily 5–10pm; tapas bar 4–11pm.

BILLINGS AFTER DARK

Playing host to productions and live music of all kinds, the **Alberta Bair Theater,** Broadway and Third Ave. (☎ **406/256-6052;** www.albertabairtheater.org), is the prime performing arts venue in Billings. **Casey's Golden Pheasant,** 222 N. Broadway (☎ **406/256-5200**), has been around since 1935. It features a blend of blues, jazz, reggae, and rock music, and a menu of standard pub grub. On Monday nights, there is an open mic, and the locals come in to jam, as do some of the famous touring musicians. The stage has been visited by B. B. King, Chuck Mangione, Vince Gill, and Wynton Marsalis. The 3,000-square-foot ceiling Mural of Musicians pays tribute to legendary musicians—Buddy Holly, Billie Holiday, Bob Marley, and many more. **Hooligan's,** 111 N. Broadway (☎ **406/294-3495**), is a good sports bar with an Irish theme.

A SIDE TRIP TO POMPEYS PILLAR

A 150-foot-high sandstone butte 29 miles east of Billings holds the only concrete evidence left along the way of the famous journey of Lewis and Clark through the Louisiana Purchase. On July 25, 1806, Capt. William Clark carved his name and the date on the side of the rock. He noted in his famous journals for that day, "The nativs have ingraved on the face of this rock figures of animals &c near which I marked my name and the day of the month and year." Clark then walked to the top and described the panoramic view of the river and plains that can be captured from the top. Clark had to scramble up through the yucca and sagebrush, but visitors now are aided by stairways and enthusiastic and informative volunteer guides who will point out the historic sites and wildlife—from ant lions to eagles' nests.

Clark's name is now locked under a protective glass cabinet, but many others have added their names. The pillar was originally called Pompy's Tower by Clark, using the nickname he'd given the youngest member of their expedition, little Baptiste Charbonneau, the son of Sacajawea and Touissaint Charbonneau, the expedition guides. The boy traveled in Clark's dugout, and the captain called him "my boy Pomp."

The park, operated by the Bureau of Land Management, is open from Memorial Day to Labor Day, from 8am to 8pm; then into late September from 9am to 5pm; after that you have to park a half-mile away and walk in. The fee is $3 per carload during the season; free at other times. For more information call the visitor center (☎ **406/ 875-2233**) or visit www.pompeyspillar.org. To get there, go 29 miles east of Billings to I-94 exit 23.

2 The Crow Reservation

54 miles E of Billings

The beautiful Crow Reservation—the Crow People call themselves the Apsaalooke, "Children of the Large-Beaked Bird"—encompasses 3,565 square miles in southeastern Montana. It consists of seven main communities, of which Crow Agency, on I-90, is the hub of tribal management and government.

One of the main Indian Nation events of the summer-long powwow trail is **Crow Fair,** held here the third week in August. Powwows are social gatherings featuring traditional food, dress, and dances. Visitors are welcome at powwows, but flash photography is not allowed during contests, and you should always ask dancers for permission before taking their photographs. For more information contact the **Tribal Headquarters,** P.O. Box 159, Crow Agency, MT 59022 (© **406/638-2700**), or surf to www.crowfair.com.

The most famous and historic site here is the **Little Bighorn Battlefield National Monument** (see section 4, below), a somewhat ironic inclusion on this reservation. The Crow scouted for Custer, and the Little Bighorn is the site of the cavalry's most infamous defeat at the hands of the Indians.

A good place to learn about the Crow culture is at **Chief Plenty Coups State Park** (© **406/252-1289**). The tribe's last traditional chief, Chief Plenty Coups deeded his home and lands as a memorial to the Crow Nation, and the museum houses many of the Crow leader's personal items plus interpretive displays about the Crow people. From Billings, drive about 25 miles south on Mont. highways 416 and 418 to Pryor, then go a mile west, following signs. There are picnic facilities but no overnight camping. It's open May through September daily from 8am to 8pm; visitor center 8am to 5pm. Entrance fee is $2 per adult, $1 for children 6 to 12, and free for kids under 6.

3 Bighorn Canyon National Recreation Area

Fort Smith: 83 miles SE of Billings

Over eons, the Bighorn River carved a steep, sheer canyon out of the rolling plains of present-day southeastern Montana and into northwestern Wyoming. The construction of the Yellowtail Dam—named for Crow chairman Robert Yellowtail—near Fort Smith on the Crow Reservation, not only provides power and irrigation, but also marvelous recreational opportunities on and around 71-mile-long Bighorn Lake. Established on October 15, 1966, the Bighorn Canyon National Recreation Area encompasses over 120,000 acres and straddles the Montana-Wyoming border.

The lake and recreation area are remote and not easy to get to, requiring long drives on winding roads through small towns. The Wyoming and Montana portions of the recreation area are not connected by a road, although a boater can cruise easily up and down the reservoir. But it's worth the effort to get here: Steep walls soar above the deep waters, and there's superb water fun, some hiking, and tremendous photo opportunities.

ESSENTIALS

ACCESS POINTS   There are two portions of the recreation area and two different access points. On the **Montana** side, from Billings, exit I-90 at Hardin and follow Route 313 south to Fort Smith and Yellowtail Dam.

The **Wyoming** section is accessed about 3 miles east of Lovell. From I-90 north of Sheridan, head west on U.S. 14 and turn north on Wyo. 37. The route is well marked.

FEES   The daily entrance fee is $5 per vehicle.

VISITOR INFORMATION   Contact **Bighorn Canyon National Recreation Area,** P.O. Box 7458, Fort Smith, MT 59035 (© **406/666-2412;** www.nps.gov/bica).

Bighorn Canyon has visitor centers with exhibits and a descriptive film in each of its sections. Near Lovell, Wyoming, the **Bighorn Canyon Visitors Center,** 20 Hwy. 14A E., Lovell, WY 82431 (© **307/548-2251**), is open daily from 8am to 6pm in the summer and from 8:30am to 4:30pm in the winter. The **Yellowtail Dam Visitor Center** (© 406/666-3218) in Montana is open from 9am to 5pm daily from Memorial Day to Labor Day.

For additional information, contact the **Lovell Area Chamber of Commerce,** 287 E. Main St., Lovell, WY 82431 (© 307/548-7552; www.lovellchamber.com).

REGULATIONS & WARNINGS   The park has a number of black bears, which are not generally as dangerous to people as grizzlies, but can cause problems when they learn that humans carry food. Therefore, *never* feed the bears, not only for your safety but for theirs as well.

GETTING OUTSIDE
Bighorn Canyon is primarily a flat-water recreation area with excellent boating and fishing, plus swimming, water-skiing, and scuba diving. There are limited hiking trails and scenic drives.

Anglers, take note: **Fishing regulations** are tricky in these parts since the Crow Reservation encompasses nearly all of the Montana portion of the canyon. A state fishing license from whichever state you'll be fishing in is needed, and unless you are certain which it will be, it's best to get both. The visitor center has information on limits, regulations, and fishing conditions.

ON THE MONTANA SIDE
A park ranger can help you find the **Om-Ne-A Trail,** which stretches for 3 steep miles along the canyon rim. The **Beaver Pond Trail** is a short trip from the visitor center along Lime Kiln Creek.

ON THE WYOMING SIDE
The south side of the park offers some of the more sensational canyon views and is a prime viewing spot of some of the last wild horses to run free in North America. The **Horseshoe Bend** area, on Wyo. 37, has a full-service marina (© 307/548-7230), open from Memorial Day to Labor Day (sometimes a bit longer).

Leaving Horseshoe Bend, you'll pass burgundy-colored hills and enter the **Pryor Mountain National Wild Horse Range,** which has been home to wild mustangs— the virtual emblem of the West, along with the buffalo—for more than a century. Sometimes, you can catch a glimpse of a few from the road. Just across the Montana border is the **Devil Canyon Overlook,** offering a view of the river as it winds through a steep canyon of gray limestone and orange shale.

At the end of the highway is **Barry's Landing,** with a boat ramp and fishing access, and the focus for most of the recreational opportunities in the southern part of the park.

The self-guided **Canyon Creek Nature Trail** (.5 mile), which starts at Loop C of the campground at Horseshoe Bend; and the trail from **Barry's Landing** to the campground at Medicine Creek (2 miles), are the only hikes on this side of the park.

WHERE TO STAY
There are five park-service campgrounds in the recreation area; sites are free and first-come, first-served. Accommodations on the south side of the park are available in **Lovell,** 3 miles west of the intersection of Wyo. 37 and U.S. 14A (Alt. 14).

Forrester's Bighorn River Resort (© 800/665-3799 or 406/666-9199; www. forrester-travel.com) is an outfitting company owned and run by former wildlife biologist Nick Forrester and his wife, Francine, a Manhattan-trained chef. There are seven rustic but very comfortable private cabins and a lodge with a massive river-rock fireplace in the living room, cigar loft, pro shop, and dining room where Francine serves meals to soothe weary fishermen. Located about a half-mile north of Fort Smith, the cabins sit on a bluff overlooking the Bighorn River. The Forresters offer packages that include all meals and lodging starting at $450 per person per day.

4 Little Bighorn Battlefield National Monument

56 miles E of Billings

Perhaps there is no phrase in the English language that serves as a better metaphor for an untimely demise than "Custer's Last Stand." It was on this battlefield, on the dry sloping prairies of southeastern Montana, that George Armstrong Custer met his end. Though the details of the actual battle that took place on June 25, 1876, are sketchy at best, much remains for the visitor to explore and ponder in this mysterious place. The **Little Bighorn Battlefield National Monument** chronicles the history of this world-famous engagement, offering a coherent look at how the battle developed, where the members of Custer's contingent died, and how it might have looked to the swarming warriors.

ESSENTIALS

GETTING THERE   The monument is located 56 miles east of Billings. Take I-94 east to I-90 south; just past Crow Agency take exit 510 for U.S. 212. The battlefield is located a few hundred yards east.

ADMISSION & HOURS   The park and visitor center are open daily 8am to 9pm from Memorial Day to Labor Day, 8am to 6pm in spring and fall, and 8am to 4:30pm in winter. The visitor center is closed on Christmas, New Year's Day, and Thanksgiving. Admission costs $10 per vehicle; $5 for those on foot.

VISITOR INFORMATION   At the **Visitor Center** (© **406/638-2224**) just inside the park entrance, you'll see actual uniforms worn by Custer, read about his life, and view an eerie reenactment of the battles on a small-scale replica of the battlefield. For advance information, contact the Superintendent, Little Bighorn Battlefield National Monument, P.O. Box 39, Crow Agency, MT 59022-0039 (© **406/638-3204;** www.nps.gov/libi).

TOURING THE MONUMENT   It's possible to view the site in less than a half-hour, but you'll shortchange yourself with that approach. Instead, plan to spend enough time to explore the visitor center, listen to interpretive historical talks presented by rangers there, and then tour the site. You'll leave with a greater appreciation for the monument and an understanding of the history that led up to the battle.

After stopping at the **visitor center,** drive 4½ miles to the **Reno-Benteen Monument Entrenchment Trail,** at the end of the monument road, and double back. Interpretive signs at the top of this bluff show the route followed by the companies under Custer, Benteen, and Reno as they approached the area from the south, and the positions from which they defended themselves from their Indian attackers.

As you proceed north along the ridge, you'll pass **Custer's Lookout,** the spot from which the general first viewed the Indian village. This was the spot at which Custer sent for reinforcements, though he continued marching north.

Capt. Thomas Weir led his troops to **Weir Point** in hopes of assisting Custer but was immediately discovered by the Indian warriors and forced to retreat to the spot held by Reno.

The **Medicine Trail Ford,** on the ridge, overlooks a spot well below the bluffs in the Medicine Trail Coulee on the Little Bighorn River, where hundreds of warriors who had been sent from the Reno battle pushed across the river in pursuit of Custer and his army.

Farther north, the Cheyenne warrior Lame White Man led an attack up **Calhoun Ridge** against a company of the Seventh Cavalry that had charged downhill into the coulee. When Indian resistance overwhelmed the army, troops retreated back up the hill, where they were killed.

As you proceed to the north, you will find detailed descriptions of the events that occurred on the northernmost edges of the ridge, as well as white markers that indicate the places where army troops fell in battle. The bodies of Custer, his brothers Tom and Boston, and nephew Autie Reed, were found on Custer Hill.

Indian casualties during the rout are estimated at 60 to 100 warriors. Following the battle, which some say began early in the morning and ended within 2 hours, the Indians broke camp in haste and scattered to the north and south. Within a few short years they were all confined to reservations.

The survivors of the Reno-Benteen armies buried the bodies of Custer and his slain army where they fell. In 1881, the graves that could be located were reopened, and the bones re-interred at the base of a memorial shaft found overlooking the battlefield. Custer's remains were eventually reburied at the U.S. Military Academy at West Point in 1877.

The adjacent **National Cemetery,** established in 1879, incorporates a self-guided tour to some of the more significant figures buried there. In 2003, there was a dedication for a new Indian memorial, a sculpture garden dubbed "Peace Through Unity." There are also three **walking trails** within the monument for visitors wishing to explore the battle in greater depth.

A SPECIAL EVENT   The **Hardin Area Chamber of Commerce** (I-90 exits 497 and 503) sponsors **Little Bighorn Days,** around June 25 each year, but not at the monument. The events include a reenactment, parade, symposiums, and of course food. For information, call ✆ **406/665-1672.**

5 Miles City ⊛

145 miles E of Billings; 70 miles SW of Glendive

Miles City gets its name from Col. Nelson A. Miles—the commander of the Fifth Cavalry who was ordered to return bands of Indians to reservations in the summer of 1876. As the world moves on around it, Miles City has retained its Western flair for more than a century. In the early days, as portrayed in Larry McMurtry's novel *Lonesome Dove,* Miles City was a cowboy town on the verge of becoming a leading cattle market; the market came with the arrival of the Northern Pacific Railroad in 1881.

Today, Miles City maintains its cowboy traditions with its annual Bucking Horse Sale—which attracts rodeo stock contractors from all over the country—and the Range Riders Museum, a thorough collection of photographs and firearms from the old days. It's where remote ranchers come when they need barbed wire or tractor axles, and still boasts a traditional Main Street with a saloon and lunch counter. Residents take an active pride in the town's lack of parking meters—a vestige of its civility and small population.

ESSENTIALS
GETTING THERE   It's an easy 145-mile drive on I-94 from Billings. Miles City's **Frank Wiley Field** (© **406/232-1021**) is serviced by **Big Sky Airlines** (© **800/237-7788**), with connecting flights to Billings and Glendive.

VISITOR INFORMATION   The **Miles City Area Chamber of Commerce,** at 51 Pleasant St., Miles City, MT 59301 (© **406/234-2890;** www.mcchamber.com), provides maps and guides to the town. Or get an area vacation guide from **Custer Country** (© **800/346-1876** or 406/628-1432; www.custer.visitmt.com).

GETTING OUTSIDE
There's an attractive municipal swimming facility at the west end of Main Street.

FISHING & BOATING
Miles City isn't classic Montana fishing country, but there is plenty of access to the Yellowstone and Tongue rivers for walleye, sauger, catfish, crappie, and, occasionally, the unusual paddlefish (see "Paddlefishing," in section 6, below). Fishing throughout the area is best in late spring and early fall. **Twelve-mile Dam,** 11 miles south of Miles City on Mont. 59, then 1 mile south on Tongue River Road, has camping facilities and a boat launch, and a handicapped-accessible fishing platform.

Luring in floaters with Yellowstone River access, **Pirogue Island State Park** (© **406/234-0900**) is just north of Miles City. Go 1 mile north on Mont. 59, then 2 miles east on Kinsey Highway, then 2 miles south on a county road. Stop by **Red Rock Sporting Goods,** 700 S. Haynes Ave. (© **406/232-2716**), for gear and information.

GOLF
Miles City has the **Town and Country Club golf course** (© **406/234-1500**) running along the banks of the Tongue River southeast of town. It's relatively short—3,280 yards. Greens fees (including cart) are $25 to $30 for 18 holes.

SEEING THE SIGHTS
Custer County Art and Heritage Center 🌟🌟 *Kids*   The old city water plant (built between 1910 and 1924) has been reincarnated as an art-and-history museum,

---

The World-Famous Miles City Bucking Horse Sale

Ever since 1914, rodeo contractors—the men who supply the animals for the West's rodeos—have been meeting in Miles City and lining up their stock. This gathering, which began as an informal event, has now become the "World-Famous Miles City Bucking Horse Sale," held every May on the third weekend of the month. More than 200 horses are sold at auction, from untried stock to spoiled saddle horses. There are parimutuel horse races, a parade, trade show, and rodeos, as well as wild-horse racing. The downtown area is virtually closed down at night, bands play on the streets, and beer is swilled and spilled while the city's open-container ordinances are suspended inside the "people corral." Tickets cost $10 to $15. For the current schedule, call the Miles City Area Chamber of Commerce (© **406/234-2890**) or visit www.buckinghorsesale.com.

with one-time water tanks now filled with art. There are changing exhibits of traditional and contemporary art from the museum's permanent collection, plus national and regional touring exhibits. Listed on the National Register of Historic Places, the museum building is actually an attraction itself. In 1979, it was awarded the governor's trophy for best adaptation of a historic structure. The art center hosts the Western Art Roundup, an annual Western art show on the third weekend in May, and an auction each year in late September.

Waterplant Rd. off W. Main St. (just west of town). © **406/234-0635.** www.ccac.milescity.org. Free admission. May–Sept Tues–Sun 9am–5pm; rest of year Tues–Sun 1–5pm.

Range Rider Museum   The amazing thing about this collection is its size—the Western memorabilia collection fills 11 buildings and includes a frontier town, an art gallery that includes the work of Charles Russell, and a gun collection of more than 400 firearms, including an elephant gun. Items on display also include American Indian artifacts and French sabers. There are 500 photos of local celebrities in the Wilson Photo Gallery, and a replica of Old Milestown—as the town was originally called—of 1877. Of particular interest are the excellent photos of Cheyenne tribal members taken in the 1890s.

U.S. 12 (on Main St., just west of town at I-94 exit 135). © **406/232-6146** or 406/232-4483. $5 adults, $4 seniors, $1 high school and college students, 50¢ elementary and middle school students, free for children under 6. Apr–Oct daily 8am–5:30pm. Closed Nov–Mar.

WHERE TO STAY & DINE

There are several properties at I-94 exit 138 in Miles City. The **Holiday Inn Express,** 1720 S. Haynes Ave. (© **888/700-0402** or 406/234-1000), is a well-maintained facility with 52 units. There's a pool and whirlpool; rooms have dataports, irons and boards, hair dryers, and coffeemakers. Rates are $79 to $85 double, and include an expanded continental breakfast. The **Best Western War Bonnet Inn,** 1015 S. Haynes Ave. (© **800/528-1234** or 406/234-4560), has 54 units, including three suites with microwave and refrigerator; plus there's an indoor pool, hot tub, and sauna. Rates are $69 to $89 double. The **Miles City KOA Campground,** 1 Palmer St., Miles City, MT 56301 (© **406/232-3991**), is shaded by more than 70 cottonwoods and has full RV hookups, tent sites, a pool, and a store. Campsite rates range from $15 to $28; basic cabins are $30.

For a small Montana town, Miles City offers several pretty good restaurants. The **Stagecoach Station,** 3020 Stower St. (© **406/234-2288**), offers steak, seafood, great barbecue, and pasta (dinner items mostly in the $6–$15 range) with Old West hospitality and atmosphere to match—from the boot upholstery to "old Gabby" greeting you at the door. It's open daily from 6:30am to 10pm (until 11pm Fri–Sat). Getting a bit more modern is the **Airport Inn** (north of town on Mont. 59 overlooking the Yellowstone River; © **406/232-9977**), where you're greeted by a vintage airplane—a 1934 Aerocoupe—and have models dangling overhead while you eat. Try the "finger steaks" or munch on some pizza. A variety of sandwiches, burgers, and homemade soups are also served. Prices range from $3 to $9; it's open daily from 11am to 10pm. For fine dining, visit **Club 519,** 519 Main St., on the second floor of the Professional Building (© **406/232-5133**), a softly lit, quiet, comfortable restaurant serving very good steaks and seafood, with dinner prices in the $15-to-$30 range. It's open daily from 5 to 10pm.

MILES CITY AFTER DARK

The cowboys in their dress hats come out after dark in Miles City, mostly in the bars. The historic **Montana Bar** ✦, 612 Main St. (© **406/234-5809**), has a Montana map for a sign, with Miles City marked by a check. Built in 1893, this is where stockmen gathered. It was enlarged and received a new facade in 1914, but has changed little since, and is known as one of the most authentic Western bars in the state. It has a multicolored tile floor, antique back bar, pressed-tin ceiling, and a bullet hole in one leaded-glass panel. Patrons used to have to stand up to the bar and "drink like a man," but bar stools have been added for the modern tippler.

6 Glendive

222 miles E of Billings; 196 miles W of Bismarck, North Dakota

A cattle town in the 1880s, Glendive has gradually become a farming community, producing mostly sugar beets and wheat. The city's most curious attraction is paddle-fishing—dropping a line in the Yellowstone River in hopes of hooking a prehistoric monster (the state record is 142 lb.).

GETTING THERE It's a 222-mile drive on I-94 from Billings, or you can fly **Big Sky Airlines** (© **800/237-7788**) to **Dawson Community Airport** (© **406/687-3372**).

VISITOR INFORMATION The **Glendive Area Chamber of Commerce and Agriculture,** 313 S. Merrill Ave., Glendive, MT 59330 (© **406/377-5601;** www. glendivechamber.com), provides brochures and maps.

PADDLEFISHING

Thousands of anglers come every year to try to snag one of these prehistoric spoonbill sturgeons from the bottom of the Yellowstone River. The season is from May 15 to whenever the annual quota is met or June 30, whichever comes first, and the best fishing spot is at the intake diversion dam on the Yellowstone, 17 miles northeast of town on Mont. 16. Thought to be extinct until an angler snagged one here in 1962, these monsters (adults generally weigh 60–120 lb.) are "snagged"—caught on treble hooks dragged along the bottom of the river—and the limit is one fish per fisherman. Interestingly, local nonprofits accept paddlefish roe as a donation, and they sell the caviar to raise funds. You'll need both a Montana fishing license and a special tag, which several places in town sell; a concessionaire rents poles and lures. There's 30 campsites ($12) at the intake. Call **Makoshika State Park** (© **406/377-6256**) for additional information; there's a paddlefish display in the park's visitor center.

MAKOSHIKA STATE PARK

Montana's largest state park, at 11,531 acres, **Makoshika State Park** ✦✦ (© **406/377-6256**) is a few blocks from town via the railroad underpass. The name is Lakota, meaning "bad earth" or "bad land." Erosion has done wonders with the park's upper and most malleable layer, forming magnificent spires in some places and coulees that cut deep into the multicolored valleys in others. Stunted ponderosa pine trees are scattered over much of the park. The amazing thing about this state park is not necessarily the uncanny resemblance to Badlands National Park in South Dakota, but the abundance of dinosaur bones that have been removed from under the loess. Among the exhibits in the visitor center is the actual skull—not a replica or cast—from a young triceratops uncovered in the park. (If these displays pique your interest, pay a visit to the new **Makoshika Dinosaur Museum** in downtown Glendive for more on the region's prehistory; 111 W. Bell St.; ✆ **406/377-1637;** www.makoshika.com.)

A partially paved road—steep and narrow even by Montana mountain standards— winds about 2 miles to an overlook that provides a wonderful view of the badlands. Don't take your RV—the road is too narrow and there is nowhere to turn around. There are 5 miles of hiking trails, along with a number of off-trail backpacking routes. The visitor center (daily 10am–6pm, Memorial Day to Labor Day; Mon–Sat 9am–5pm and Sun 1–5pm the rest of the year) has a fine display of the history, pre-history, and geology of the park. There is also a "folf," or Frisbee golf, course and several hiking trails. The day-use fee is $5 per vehicle; campsites are $12.

WHERE TO STAY

Lodging here includes the historic **Best Western Jordan Inn,** 223 N. Merrill Ave. (✆ **888/453-6348** or 406/377-5555), with rates of $64 to $88 double; and **Days Inn,** 2000 N. Merrill Ave. (✆ **800/329-7466** or 406/365-6011), which charges $52 to $68 double, with lower rates in winter.

Charley Montana Bed & Breakfast 🐾🐾   An impeccable restoration of a majestic neoclassical mansion, Charley Montana is a top-flight B&B in what was once the palatial, 26-room abode of rancher Charles Krug. Ninety years after breaking ground in 1906, the Krug family sold the house and many of its original furnishings; innkeepers Jim and Katherine Lee are only the second owners. Jim has done wonders restoring the house to its original condition, paying particularly close attention to the woodwork inside and out. The five guest rooms include the Charles Room, the old master bedroom with the leather-bound encyclopedia from the Krug family library, as well as the Annie Suite, named for Krug's wife, with an impressive wardrobe and separate sitting area with heirloom armchairs. Transplants from the Twin Cities, the Lees are warm and gracious hosts with keen senses of humor and local history. Their 8,000-square-foot inn is located on the outskirts of downtown Glendive, cater-cornered to an old silo and a stone's throw from the old Bell Street Bridge across the Yellowstone River, now reserved for pedestrians and bicyclists.

103 N. Douglas St. (P.O. Box 1192), Glendive, MT 59930. ✆ **888/395-3207** or 406/365-2207. www.charley-montana. com. 5 units. $75–$85 double; $105 suite. Rates include full breakfast. AE, DISC, MC, V. **Amenities:** Game room; Wi-Fi network. *In room:* A/C, cable TV, hair dryer, iron.

A SIDE TRIP TO FORT UNION

Strictly speaking, the **Fort Union Trading Post National Historic Site** is in North Dakota. The Montana–North Dakota border bisects the parking lot, and the fort itself is a few paces east. But Fort Union was so important to Montana's development that it should be part of any trip through the eastern part of the state.

For 30 years after 1828, Fort Union was the edge of the frontier—the most important trading post in John Jacob Astor's beaver pelt and buffalo robe empire in the Northern Plains. This National Park Service site has been spectacularly reconstructed from pictures and descriptions. The main gate of the glistening, whitewashed wooden stockade overlooks the wide Missouri, and two tall stone bastions stand sentinel over the river at the fort's corners.

Lewis and Clark camped near here on their trip to the Pacific, on April 25 and 26, 1805. Lewis commented in his journals on the "wide and fertile vallies" and how ideal the site would be for a fort. The Bourgeois House has been converted into a modern visitor center, and contains excellent exhibits detailing the life and times of the fur traders. Artist George Catlin visited in 1832, as did Karl Bodmer in 1833, and John James Audubon in 1843. In 1867, the U.S. Army acquired the fort, and its lumber was used to expand nearby Fort Buford and fuel steamboats.

GETTING THERE & VISITOR INFORMATION   From I-94 exit 213 at Glendive, take Mont. 16 northeast to the North Dakota border, then North Dakota 58 north to the fort (it's about 75 miles). Contact **Fort Union Trading Post National Historic Site,** 15550 N. Dak. 1804, Williston, ND 58801 (*©* **701/572-9083;** www. nps.gov/fous). Admission is free and the park is open from 8am to 8pm during the summer and 9am to 5:30pm in winter.

11

Yellowstone National Park

For all the epic wonder of the geysers and the antlered elk and the towering waterfalls, visitors to our nation's first national park often bring home memories more subtle and personal: the fine grades of pastel colors in a small hot spring, or the flight of an osprey above the river, or a spider web sagging with steam droplets in the early morning light. Yellowstone isn't just about beauty. At every turn it raises questions about the mysteries of nature, awakening a curiosity you might have thought died during that long-ago biology exam.

After the initial reaction of wordless awe to a bubbling mud pot or a meadow of brightly colored wildflowers, it's human nature to want to know how it all works. And only in Yellowstone can you observe firsthand how wolves wander amid an elk herd seeking prey; or smell the sulfurous vapors venting from the volcanic caldera beneath the plateau; or touch the fireweed and pine seedlings sprouting within the forests burned by the 1988 fires.

It was a prescient move in 1872 when the U.S. Congress set aside 2.2 million acres of the West as a geothermal and wildlife preserve and "pleasuring ground

for the benefit and enjoyment of the people." Since then, Yellowstone has been the model for the creation of parks around the world. For Americans, it's become a kind of national touchstone to our wilderness past, visited by more than three million pilgrims a year.

Despite all we get out of Yellowstone, not nearly as much has been put back. There is a backlog of work to be done, from road repair to sewer improvements, and there are also issues of ecological health. Imported Mackinaw trout are crowding out the native cutthroat in Yellowstone Lake, and increasing traffic congestion interferes with the wildlife.

But there are success stories, too, such as the reintroduction of wolves to the Yellowstone ecosystem, and the devoted work of park scientists and managers. People who know the park well remain optimistic that our mistakes will not dislodge nature's plan. For 600,000 years, since the last time the Yellowstone caldera blew its top, the forces of nature have been reshaping Yellowstone and populating it with flora and fauna. These things take time. Likewise, as much time as you and your family can invest here will be richly rewarded.

1 The Gateway Towns: West Yellowstone, Gardiner & Cooke City

West Yellowstone: 91 miles SW of Bozeman; 30 miles W of Old Faithful; 320 miles NE of Salt Lake City. Gardiner: 79 miles SE of Bozeman; 163 miles SW of Billings. Cooke City: 127 miles SW of Billings.

WEST YELLOWSTONE

By making itself the headquarters for snowmobilers who want to travel the park's roads in winter, **West Yellowstone**—just outside the park's west gate—has created a year-round tourist economy and attracted an ever-growing number of big hotel chains. The quiet fly-fishing town that once was is no more: The shops are chock-full of curios, and the streets are clogged with tour buses, and, in the winter, rumbling snow machines.

One could argue that West Yellowstone made its Faustian bargain with tourism long ago, when the Oregon Short Line's *Yellowstone Special* train first arrived in 1909. Originally called Riverside, then Yellowstone, the town was grudgingly renamed West Yellowstone in 1920 when Gardiner residents complained that tourists would mistakenly believe the town was the park. This place is about shopping, not nature, and its biggest attraction is a zoolike look at wildlife in the Grizzly & Wolf Discovery Center.

ESSENTIALS

GETTING THERE The **West Yellowstone Airport,** U.S. 191, 1 mile north of West Yellowstone (© **406/646-7631**), provides commercial air service seasonally, June through September only, on Delta's commuter service by **SkyWest** (© **800/ 453-9417**). If you're driving the 91 miles from Bozeman to West Yellowstone, take U.S. 191 south (a pretty journey along the Gallatin River) to its junction with U.S. 287 and head straight into town. From Idaho Falls, take Interstate 15 north to U.S. 20, which takes you directly into West Yellowstone, a 53-mile drive.

VISITOR INFORMATION Visitor information is available by contacting the **West Yellowstone Chamber of Commerce,** 30 Yellowstone Ave. (P.O. Box 458), West Yellowstone, MT 59758 (© **406/646-7701;** www.westyellowstonechamber.com).

GETTING AROUND In West Yellowstone, **Avis** (© **800/230-4898** or 406/646-7635) operates mid-May through early October. **Budget** (© **800/527-0700** or 406/646-7882) is available year-round. **Yellowstone Taxi** (© **406/646-1111**) provides local service.

GETTING OUTSIDE

Most people arrive here on their way to the park, but there is no fence along the park's boundary, so some of the best wild country is actually to the west. Particularly if you like fishing, the rivers—the Gallatin and the Madison, particularly—are among the best in the country. The following tackle shops offer the full gamut of guided fishing trips and instruction: **Arrick's Fly Shop,** 37 Canyon St. (© **406/646-7290**); **Bud Lilly's Trout Shop,** 39 Madison Ave. (© **800/854-9559** or 406/646-7801); **Jacklin's,** 105 Yellowstone Ave. (© **406/646-7336**); and **Madison River Outfitters,** 117 Canyon St. (© **406/646-9644**).

Come winter, **cross-country skiers** hit the trails (see section 7, "Winter Sports & Activities"). Ski rentals are available in West Yellowstone at **FreeHeel and Wheel,** 40 Yellowstone Ave. (© **406/646-7744**), or **Bud Lilly's,** 39 Madison Ave. (© **406/646-7801**).

Despite a push for a ban and a new quota system in the park, **snowmobiling** is a huge draw in West Yellowstone, where sleds are more common than cars on snowpacked winter streets. In addition to driving the machines on the snowpacked roads of Yellowstone—where speed limits are strictly enforced—you can take the trails in surrounding national forests with fewer restrictions. There are tricks to riding on backcountry snow, so if you're inexperienced, rent a guide as well as a machine. All the major hotels and motels in West Yellowstone arrange snowmobile rentals that include gear, and there are numerous independent operations offering rentals and guides, including **Yellowstone Arctic/Yamaha,** 208 Electric St. (© **406/646-9636**), and **Backcountry Adventure Snowmobile Rental,** 224 Electric St. (© **800/924-7669**).

Yellowstone National Park

Moments   Frommer's Favorite Yellowstone Experiences

Witness the World's Most Famous Geologic Alarm Clock. Old Faithful is known for its reliability, but it's slowing down a little with age. Still, about once every 92 minutes, give or take, you can watch her blow, making her the most predictable geyser on the planet. While you're there, get a good look at the beautiful and historic Old Faithful Inn. See section 4, "Seeing the Highlights."

Escape to the Backcountry. If the packed benches at Old Faithful give you the impression that Yellowstone is overrun, venture into the backcountry for a dose of true wilderness. It will restore your spirits and perhaps your belief in national parks. Get advice from a ranger on how to travel safely in bear country, and then have it mostly to yourself—most of the three million annual park visitors rarely leave the roadways. See section 8, "Hiking."

Get Hooked on Yellowstone Trout. There is some fine fly-fishing water in and near the park. Try the Madison, the Gibbon, and the Firehole rivers, or troll the lakes for cutthroat, brown, rainbow, and brook trout. When a big trout slaps the twilight surface of the Yellowstone River, Izaak Walton smiles in fly-fishing heaven. See section 6, "Summer Sports & Activities."

Have a Howling Good Time at Lamar. Since wolves were reintroduced in Yellowstone in 1994, they have surprised biologists by making frequent morning and late-afternoon appearances along Slough Creek and in other parts of Lamar Valley. This especially untamed area in the northeast corner of Yellowstone is loaded with wildlife: bison, elk, coyotes, and grizzly bears. See section 8, "Hiking."

Make Like Teddy and Be a Rough Rider. At Roosevelt Lodge, visitors relive the Old West by taking organized rides on horseback, stagecoach, or wagon. A more adventurous alternative is the Old West cookout; you will arrive by either horseback or wagon for hearty meat-and-potatoes grub. See section 11, "Where to Dine in the Park."

Learn Something at the Yellowstone Institute. You can take classes on everything from bears to butterflies at the Yellowstone Association Institute, which inhabits the old Lamar Buffalo Ranch in the park's northeast corner. It's a friendly, communal way to get a more intimate knowledge of the ecosystem. See section 3, "A Park Primer."

Sleep on a Historic Pillow in the Park. Old Faithful Inn, dating from 1904, is a log cathedral within view of the geyser. Relax with a drink on the second-floor terrace, or climb the timber lattice that holds up the great roof. Original rooms may not all have private bathrooms, but it's still the nicest place to stay in the park. Ask for suite no. 3014 or room no. 229 to watch the geyser erupt from your room. See section 10, "Where to Stay in the Park."

Expect to pay $150 to $225 per day per snowmobile, and unless you have a helmet and winter gear to protect you from subzero wind chill, plan on spending another $25 for clothing. Also popular are **Snowcoach tours,** offered in vans equipped with tanklike treads to travel on snow. Check with **Yellowstone Alpen Guides Co.,** 535 Yellowstone Ave. (✆ **800/858-3502**), or with snowmobile outfitters, who often offer Snowcoach rides as well.

SEEING THE SIGHTS

Grizzly and Wolf Discovery Center   Those who haven't the patience to search out and observe the free-ranging wildlife of Yellowstone might want to try this not-for-profit educational center. The interpretive center gives a detailed explanation of these animals' history in this country, along with the difficult and controversial efforts to revive them in the wild. This is a closer look than you'll likely get with animals in the wild, but did you really come to Yellowstone to look at grizzlies imported from Alaska in an enclosure?

201 S. Canyon St. in Grizzly Park. ✆ 800/257-2570 or 406/646-7001. www.grizzlydiscoveryctr.org. $9.75 adults, $9 seniors, $5 children 5–12, free for children under 5. Daily 8am–dusk; shorter hours in winter.

Yellowstone Historic Center 🍴 Located in the historic 1909 Union Pacific depot, this is the only museum that focuses on Yellowstone's cultural history, providing an interesting snapshot into the ways of the park's first tourists, with scads of memorabilia, postcards, and concessionaire ephemera. There are also displays on the Yellowstone ecosystem, covering epochal events such as the 1959 earthquake that created Quake Lake and the 1988 fires, along with a mounted grizzly bear known in his animate days as "Old Snaggletooth."

Canyon St. and Yellowstone Ave. ✆ 406/646-1100. www.yellowstonehistoriccenter.org. $15 family, $6 adults, $5 seniors, $4 children and students, free for children under 4. Mid-May to mid-Oct daily 9am–9pm.

Yellowstone IMAX Theater   This theater is next door to the Grizzly and Wolf Discovery Center and, together, they form the centerpieces of a real estate development on the edge of the park, which includes several new hotels. Regardless, the IMAX concept works pretty well here—there are things an airborne camera can show you on a six-story-tall screen that you'll never see on your own two feet. A film called *Yellowstone* plays fairly often, with swooping views of the canyon and falls and other sights.

101 S. Canyon St. ✆ 406/646-4100. www.yellowstoneimax.com. $8 adults, $6 children 3–12, free for children under 3. Summer daily 8:30am–9pm, shorter hours rest of year; call for exact showtimes.

WHERE TO STAY

Make your reservations early if you want to visit in July or August, or if you're going to spend Christmas to New Year's here. If you're smart, you'll come in the fall, when there are plenty of empty rooms and better rates, and spend your days fishing the Henry's Fork or one of the other great streams in the vicinity. Rates for rooms often reflect the seasonal traffic, and prices fluctuate. Unless noted, all these establishments are open year-round.

    West Yellowstone Central Reservations handles booking for many of the hotels (✆ **888/646-7077**). Among the newer ones, you'll find chains like the **Marriott Fairfield Inn** (✆ **800/565-6803**), at 105 S. Electric St., with summertime doubles for $109 to $149; and the **Days Inn** (✆ **800/548-9551**), at 301 Madison Ave., around $110 a night for a double. There are three **Best Western** affiliates, ranging from $80 to $140 a night during the summer. Call ✆ **800/528-1234** for information and reservations. With two different levels of rooms, the **Stage Coach Inn,** at 209 Madison Ave. (✆ **800/842-2882** or 406/646-7381), is another good choice, with doubles for $69 to $139 and two different levels of rooms.

A good inexpensive option (with more character than the chains to boot), the 1912 **Madison Hotel,** 139 Yellowstone Ave. (*©* **800/838-7745** or 406/646-7745) has historic rooms for $37 to $56 for a double and newer motel doubles for $50 to $80.

Bar N Ranch *ﾐﾐ*   One of the oldest brands in Montana, the Bar N is an excellent new lodging option in West Yellowstone, operating a spiffed-up lodge and cabin complex since 2004. Located on 200 acres of unsullied ranchland with 2 miles of the Madison River and a fishing pond, the lodge is an image of the New West, with a great river-rock fireplace and a knotty pine banister leading up to the rooms upstairs. The lodge rooms mix equal parts Ralph Lauren and Old West, exuding a simple, elegant style with antler lamps, hardwood floors, stark white walls, and jetted tubs. The cabins are one- and two-bedroom units arranged in a half-circle around the lodge, with decor that echoes that of the lodge; all of them have fireplaces and several have in-room hot tubs. A staff guide is available to take guests fishing, rafting, or horseback riding, whatever your preference. The lodge has Wi-Fi Internet access.

890 Buttermilk Creek Rd. (P.O. Box 250), West Yellowstone, MT 59758. *©* **406/646-0300.** Fax 406/646-0301. www. bar-n-ranch.com. 7 units, 7 cabins. Lodge rooms $97–$103 double; cabins $118–$132 double; lower rates Oct–June. AE, DC, DISC, MC, V. **Amenities:** Restaurant; small outdoor pool; Jacuzzi; activities desk. *In room:* TV/DVD player, fridge, coffeemaker, no phone.

The Hibernation Station *ﾐ*   These luxury cabins, each named after a local river or stream, are furnished Western-style with hand-hewn log beds draped in down comforters, wall tapestries, fireplaces, and enormous bathrooms with jetted tubs. They can fit from two to eight people, and some have kitchenettes and jetted tubs. Just about every year a few more cabins go up, and the owners' plan also includes a big central lodge. The outdoor sculptures on some of the roofs are eye-catching if not gallery-quality, and you can rent a snowmobile and gear with your cabin.

212 Gray Wolf Ave., West Yellowstone, MT 59758. *©* **800/580-3557** or 406/646-4200. Fax 406/646-7060. www. hibernationstation.com. 44 cabins. $109–$279 cabin. AE, DISC, MC, V. **Amenities:** Jacuzzi. *In room:* TV, kitchenette.

Holiday Inn SunSpree Resort *ﾐ*   This big resort is the town's best hotel. The rooms are sizeable and comfortable, well maintained, and freshly updated. If you've been hiking or snowmobiling all day, the Jacuzzis in the King Spa suites are indispensable. At the activities desk, you can arrange fishing and rafting trips, bike and ATV rentals, and chuck-wagon cookouts. The Iron Horse Saloon serves regional microbrews, and the Oregon Short Line Restaurant serves Western cuisine including game and seafood dishes. At the center of the restaurant sits the restored railroad club car that brought Victorian gents to Yellowstone a century ago.

315 Yellowstone Ave., West Yellowstone, MT 59758. *©* **800/HOLIDAY** or 406/646-7365. www.doyellowstone.com. 123 units. $79–$144 double; $90–$200 suite. AE, DISC, MC, V. **Amenities:** Restaurant; lounge; large indoor pool; exercise room; Jacuzzi; sauna; bike rental; children's program; activities desk; self-serve laundry. *In room:* A/C, TV, dataport, microwave, fridge, coffeemaker, hair dryer, iron.

Three Bear Lodge *ﾐ*   The cozy, pine-furnished rooms of this family-style inn are located less than 3 blocks from the park entrance. The motel-style rooms are of above-average quality, reliable and clean, and there are some in-room hot tubs and a few large family rooms for those traveling with kids. Like just about every other lodging in West Yellowstone, the Three Bear offers snowmobile and Snowcoach tours in the winter, as well as van tours in the summer.

217 Yellowstone Ave. (P.O. Box 1590), West Yellowstone, MT 59758. ℂ 800/646-7353 or 406/646-7353. Fax 406/646-4567. www.threebearlodge.com. 74 units. $73–$108 double. AE, DISC, MC, V. **Amenities:** Restaurant; lounge; outdoor heated pool (seasonal); exercise room; 4 indoor Jacuzzis; sauna. *In room:* TV, coffeemaker, hair dryer, iron.

WHERE TO DINE

Just as the chain motels have arrived, so have garden-variety fast-food joints; West Yellowstone is a good place to stop for a quick bite on your way into the park. Apart from the choices listed below, **Uncle Laurie's Riverside Café**, 237 U.S. Hwy. 20 (ℂ **406/646-7040**), is a small but excellent alternative to steak-and-eggs breakfast joints. The menu migrates from breakfast calzones and huckleberry cinnamon rolls in the morning to a lunch menu of cold sandwiches, wraps, and "stinky burgers," so named for their garlic content. For the best variety of coffee drinks and baked goods, visit the espresso bar at the excellent **Book Peddler** in Canyon Square (ℂ **406/646-9358**). **Beartooth BBQ**, 111 Canyon St. (ℂ **406/646-0227**), is a fun place with a nice selection of local microbrews and top-notch slow-smoked ribs.

Bullwinkle's Saloon, Gambling and Eatery AMERICAN   Boisterous and noisy crowds, families and fishermen, and gamblers and goof-offs fill this restaurant frequently, and they don't leave hungry. Both luncheon and dinner menus are packed with traditional entrees: burgers and salads for lunch, and ribs, steaks, pastas, and seafood at dinner. Try the inexpensive and plentiful Bullwinkle's salad (shrimp included) or the house specialty, the hazelnut-crusted scallops, and check the updated fishing conditions charted on the wall. You can try small-stakes gambling on video poker machines, featured in most Montana bars.

19 Madison Ave. ℂ 406/646-7974. Lunch $5–$8; dinner $8–$24. AE, DISC, MC, V. Summer daily 11am–11pm; winter daily 11am–10pm; bar open later (until 2am).

The Canyon Street Grill *(Value)* AMERICAN   It's hard not to like an establishment whose slogan is, "We are not a fast food restaurant. We are a cafe reminiscent of a bygone era when the quality of the food meant more than how fast it could be served." With checkerboard floors and shiny red booths, this delightful 1950s-style spot serves hearty food for breakfast, lunch, and dinner. Hamburgers and chicken sandwiches are popular, accompanied by milkshakes made with hard ice cream or a crisp glass of huckleberry cream soda.

22 Canyon St. ℂ 406/646-7548. Main courses $6–$12. MC, V. May to Nov Mon–Sat 7am–10pm; Dec–Mar Mon–Sat 11am–4pm. Closed Apr.

Eino's Tavern *(Finds)* AMERICAN   Locals snowmobile out from West Yellowstone to Eino's (there's a trail that follows U.S. Hwy. 191) to become their own chefs at the grill here. It's a novel concept, and it keeps patrons coming back to this casual restaurant with a fine view of Hebgen Lake time and time again. If you want to blend in with the locals, go up to the counter and place your order for a steak, teriyaki chicken, hamburger, or hot dog, and keep a straight face when you're handed an uncooked piece of meat. Go to the grill, slap it on, and stand around, drink in hand, shooting the breeze with other patrons until your food is exactly the way you like it. Steaks and chicken come with your choice of a salad (or twice-baked potatoes in winter), and hamburgers come with chips.

8955 Gallatin Rd. (9 miles north of West Yellowstone on U.S. Hwy. 191). ℂ 406/646-9344. Reservations not accepted. Main courses $5.50–$20. No credit cards. Winter daily 9am–9pm; rest of year daily noon–9pm. Closed Thanksgiving to mid-Dec.

The Outpost Restaurant *(Kids* AMERICAN   Tucked away in a downtown mall, this rustic restaurant laden with Western bric-a-brac serves old-fashioned home-style fare, such as its hearty beef stew, with fork-size chunks of carrots and potatoes. There's also salmon, steaks, trout, liver, and an excellent salad bar. For breakfast, if you're really hungry, you can't beat the Campfire Omelette, smothered in homemade chili, cheese, and onions. The menu isn't all that adventurous, and there's none of the vices you'll find in the local taverns (no video poker, beer, wine, liquor, or smoking), but it offers solid fare in a quiet, family-friendly atmosphere. The homemade desserts include chocolate cream pie and a wild huckleberry sundae.

115 Yellowstone Ave. (in the Montana Outpost Mall). ℂ **406/646-7303**. Breakfast $4.50–$10; lunch $5–$11; dinner $7–$20. AE, DISC, MC, V. Daily 7am–10:30pm. Closed Oct 15–Apr 15.

GARDINER

Of all the towns that stand sentry on the roads into Yellowstone, Gardiner is the prototype gateway community. This is partly due to the historic stone Roosevelt Arch that marks the entrance through which the earliest visitors passed into the park. This is the only park entrance that's open to auto traffic year-round, in order to keep a connection open to Cooke City, which in winter can be reached only through the north entrance.

Gardiner sits at the junction of the Gardner and Yellowstone rivers (the town's eight-letter name has been attributed to a 19th-c. spelling error), still looking like the gritty little mining town it once was. Nobody puts on airs in the coffee shops and bars, and nobody raises an eyebrow when a bison or deer wanders through town. If you need additional information, contact the **Gardiner Chamber of Commerce,** 222 Park St., P.O. Box 81, Gardiner, MT 59030 (ℂ **406/848-7971;** fax 406/848-2446; www.gardinerchamber.com).

GETTING THERE   From Bozeman (the nearest jet service airport), take I-90 26 miles east to Livingston, then take U.S. 89 south 53 miles to Gardiner.

GETTING OUTSIDE

Gardiner is the spot to go for white-water rafting on the Yellowstone River. Several outfitters take guests on half- and full-day trips on routes skirting the park's northern boundary; the best of the bunch is the **Yellowstone Raft Company,** U.S. Hwy. 89 (ℂ **800/858-7781** or 406/848-7777), with half-day trips for $33 and full days for $72; children get on the boat for $23 half-day or $52 full day. While not a **snowmobiling** hub on the magnitude of West Yellowstone, a few motels here rent snowmobiles or offer Snowcoach tours. **Hiking** and **fishing** opportunities are bountiful in every direction from town.

WHERE TO STAY

Dinky, personable, and a bit eccentric, Gardiner has long had ultrafriendly lodging—thin-walled motels where, if you show up late, they've gone to bed and left a key in the door. These days it also has some newer, chain-affiliated properties, built to accommodate the ever-increasing traffic to the park. As with all the gateway towns, make your reservations early if you're coming during the peak season. The steep off-season decline in traffic results in discounts that can be considerably less expensive than the high-season rates quoted below, so be sure to ask.

Inexpensive motels fill up quickly during the summer months: The **Yellowstone Park Travelodge** (109 Hellroaring Rd.; ℂ **406/848-7520**) and **Super 8** (702 U.S.

Hwy. 89; ℂ **800/800-8000** or 406/848-7401) are open year-round with rates during the high season between $90 and $105 for a double. The **Best Western by Mammoth Hot Springs,** on U.S. Hwy. 89 (ℂ **800/828-9080** or 406/848-7311) is another option, with doubles for $119 to $129 in the summer.

Absaroka Lodge 🎯🎯 Every room in this lodge has its own furnished balcony with a jaw-dropping view of the Yellowstone River and the mountain scenery beyond it. The lodge's riverbank location—with a nice slope of lawn overlooking the river gorge—is just a few blocks from the village center, and the rooms are well appointed with queen-size beds. Suites with kitchenettes cost a little more; there is also a pair of cabins without balconies. Like most other properties in town, the lodge has staff ready and able to assist in arrangements with outfitters for fly-fishing, rafting, and, in the fall, hunting.

U.S. Hwy. 89 at the Yellowstone River Bridge (P.O. Box 10), Gardiner, MT 59030. ℂ 800/755-7414 or 406/848-7414. Fax 406/848-7560. www.yellowstonemotel.com. 41 units. $40–$100 double. AE, DC, DISC, MC, V. *In room:* A/C, cable TV, kitchenette.

Comfort Inn This log cabin–style hotel looks like it belongs here, unlike a lot of chain operations. The centerpiece is a 3,000-square-foot rustic lobby decorated with wild-game trophies, and a large second-floor balcony that offers views of Yellowstone scenery and passing wildlife. Family rooms that sleep six and luxurious suites with hot tubs are also available.

107 Hellroaring Dr., Gardiner, MT 59030. ℂ 800/424-6423 or 406/848-7536. Fax 406/848-7062. www.yellowstone comfortinn.com. 77 units. Summer $45–$150 double; winter $50–$80 double. AE, DISC, MC, V. **Amenities:** Restaurant; 3 indoor Jacuzzis; self-serve laundry. *In room:* A/C, TV, coffeemaker, hair dryer, iron, Jacuzzi.

Yellowstone Suites Bed and Breakfast 🎯 *Finds* This quiet B&B on the south bank of the Yellowstone River is a good alternative to the motels that line U.S. Hwy. 89. Originally built in 1904, legend has it that the second story's quarried stone exterior is actually a leftover from the Roosevelt Arch. The rooms are frilly and cozy, with a teddy-bear motif in the Roosevelt Room and a Victorian theme in the Jackson Room; the Yellowstone Suite has a television and a kitchenette. The real perks here are the impeccably gardened backyard and the breakfasts, which might feature stuffed French toast or eggs Benedict.

506 Fourth St., P.O. Box 277, Gardiner, MT 59030. ℂ 800/948-7937 or 406/848-7937. www.yellowstonesuites.com. 4 units. Summer $85–$129 double; winter $47–$79 double. Rates include complimentary full breakfast. AE, DISC, MC, V. **Amenities:** Outdoor Jacuzzi. *In room:* Kitchenette, no phone.

WHERE TO DINE

An indication that Gardiner has kept in touch with its mining-town roots is the relative dearth of fancy restaurants—you'll find mostly steakhouse fare, hearty breakfasts, and travelers' food. A few upscale eateries have shown up in recent years, but the dish-clattering local color of the park-side coffee shops is hard to beat. My favorite Gardiner lunch spot is the **Sawtooth Deli,** 270 W. Park St. (ℂ **406/848-7600**), serving up overstuffed, New York–style subs and eclectic specials.

Helen's Corral Drive-In BURGERS Okay, so it's not much to look at, and the menu's most adventurous item is a basket of fried shrimp. But proprietor Helen Gould built the place's reputation since 1960 on hamburgers and buffalo burgers that are nothing short of colossal. With a half-pound of meat, several slices of American cheese, bacon, and all the usual veggies, these burgers have been known to measure a full 7 inches from bun to bun. The monstrous things garnered the nickname, "Helen's Hateful Hamburgers," after a dissatisfied customer wrote a letter to the local paper dubbing them just that. Gould ran with it, using the intended insult as a sarcastic slogan in promotions and on T-shirts. "She put us on the map, that lady did," says Gould.

U.S. Hwy. 89 at Yellowstone St. © 406/848-7627. Reservations not accepted. Menu items $2.25–$10. No credit cards. Memorial Day to Labor Day daily 11am–11pm; shorter hours in winter.

Park Street Grill and Cafe ★★ ITALIAN/STEAKS Adding a dash of zest to the staid meat-and-potatoes dining scene, Phillip Curry's eatery is our pick for a nice dinner in Gardiner. Served in a room with an exposed pine interior, the menu here is a refreshing mix of gourmet Italian entrees, fresh seafood, and good old American chicken, pork, and beef dishes. The Crazy Mountain Alfredo is a good choice from the pasta menu: The delectable sauce is made a bit less sane with sweet and hot peppers, julienne chicken breast, and Italian sausage. Hearty appetites won't mind the buffalo tenderloin or the slow-roasted prime rib, and there's a decent selection of lighter fare as well. For dessert, the huckleberry crème brûlée is out of this world.

204 Park St. © 406/848-7989. Reservations recommended. Main courses $14–$27. MC, V. Mon–Sat 5:30–10pm. Closed late Oct to late Apr.

COOKE CITY

If little ol' Gardiner seems just a little too connected to the civilized world, you ought to spend a winter in tiny Cooke City or even tinier Silver Gate, just outside Yellowstone National Park's northeast entrance. In the winter, when the cloud-scraping Beartooth Pass closes to the north, supplies for these towns have to come through the park. Better to visit in the summer and take the breathtaking drive north over the pass (U.S. 212 toward Red Lodge), or south along the scenic Chief Joseph Highway (Wyo. 296). For 100 years, the lifeblood of this town was mining gold, platinum, and other precious metals, but now there is only park tourism, which seems a little anemic by comparison. Less than 100 residents live year-round in the town today, and Silver Gate, right next to the park entrance, has barely double that population. Contact the **Colter Pass/Cooke City/Silver Gate Chamber of Commerce** at Box 1071, Cooke City, MT 59020-1071 (© **406/838-2495;** www.cookecitychamber.com), for information and a map of hiking and snowmobiling trails in the area.

GETTING THERE From Billings, Montana, drive west on I-90 to Laurel, then south on U.S. 212 to Red Lodge, a total distance of 60 miles; then continue another 67 miles south over spectacular Beartooth Pass, dipping into Wyoming and back up into Montana at Cooke City.

WHERE TO STAY & EAT A room for the night will be less expensive than in other gateway towns, anywhere from $60 to $90 a night. The **Soda Butte Lodge,** 209 Main St. (© **800/527-6462** or 406/838-2251; www.cookecity.com), is the biggest motel in Cooke City, and it includes the **Prospector Restaurant** and a small casino; or, you can go to the cheaper, bare-bones **Alpine Motel,** 105 Main St. (© **406/838-2262;** www.ccalpinemotel.com). For a bite to eat and a great selection of beers, try the funky **Beartooth Cafe** (© **406/838-2475**), also on Main Street. In Silver Gate, the **Grizzly Lodge,** U.S. Hwy. 212 (© **406/838-2219;** www.yellowstonelodges.com) offers respectable albeit dated motel rooms on Soda Butte Creek for $50 to $75 from June through October. The **Log Cabin Café** (© **406/838-2367**) is a rustic-meets-refined eatery specializing in trout dinners.

2 Just the Facts

BEFORE YOU GO

To obtain maps and information about the park prior to arrival, contact **Yellowstone National Park,** P.O. Box 168, Yellowstone National Park, WY 82190 (© 307/344-7381; www.nps.gov/yell). Information regarding lodging, some campgrounds, tours, boating, and horseback riding in Yellowstone is available from **Xanterra Parks & Resorts,** P.O. Box 165, Yellowstone National Park, WY 82190 (© 307/344-7311; www.travelyellowstone.com). For information regarding educational programs at the **Yellowstone Association Institute,** contact **Yellowstone Association,** P.O. Box 117, Yellowstone National Park, WY 82190 (© 307/344-2293; www.yellowstoneassociation. org). The association operates bookstores in park visitor centers, museums, and information stations, and the old Lamar Buffalo Ranch in the park's northeast corner as the Institute's primary campus. They also have a catalog of publications you can order by mail.

GETTING THERE

If interstate highways and international airports are the measure of accessibility, then Yellowstone is as remote as Alaska's Denali National Park or the Serengeti Plains of Africa. But three million people make it here every year, on tour buses, in family vans, on bicycles, and astride snowmobiles, even from the other side of the world.

The closest airport to Yellowstone is in **West Yellowstone,** Montana, which sits just outside the park's west entrance. For information on flying into West Yellowstone, see "Essentials" in section 1 of this chapter.

Visitors can reach the park from the south by flying into **Jackson,** Wyoming (only 14 miles from the southern entrance to Grand Teton), then driving 56 miles through Grand Teton to the southern entrance of Yellowstone. **American** (© 800/433-7300); **Continental** (© 800/523-3273); **Delta** (© 800/221-1212); **Northwest** (© 800/225-2525); and **United** (© 800/241-6522) all have flights to and from **Jackson Airport** (© 307/733-7682).

To the north, **Bozeman,** Montana, is 87 miles from the West Yellowstone entrance on U.S. 191. Or you can drive east from Bozeman to Livingston, a 20-mile journey on Interstate 90, and then south 53 miles on U.S. 89 to the northern entrance at Gardiner. Bozeman's airport, **Gallatin Field** (© 406/388-8321), provides daily service via **Delta** (© 800/221-1212), **Northwest** (© 800/225-2525), and **United** (© 800/241-6522), as well as **Horizon** (© 800/547-9308). If you're driving to West Yellowstone from Bozeman, take U.S. 191 south to its junction with U.S. 287 and continue south into town.

Also to the north, **Billings,** Montana, is 129 miles from the Cooke City entrance. Billings is home to Montana's busiest airport, **Logan International** (© 406/247-8609), 2 miles north of downtown. Daily intrastate service is provided by **Big Sky Airlines** (© 800/237-7788 or 406/245-2300); and regional daily service is provided by **America West** (© 800/235-9292); **Delta** (© 800/221-1212), **Horizon** (© 800/547-9308), **Northwest** (© 800/225-2525), and **United** (© 800/241-6522). From Billings, it's a 65-mile drive south on U.S. 212 to Red Lodge, then 30 miles on the Beartooth Highway to the northeast entrance to the park. Keep in mind that the Beartooth Highway (U.S. 212), which takes you on a high, twisting journey over a spectacular pass, is open only from Memorial Day weekend until late October.

From **Cody, Wyoming,** it's a gorgeous 53-mile drive west along U.S. 14/16/20 to the east entrance of the park. **Cody's Yellowstone Regional Airport** (© 307/587-5096) serves the Bighorn Basin as well as the east and northeast entrances of Yellowstone National Park with year-round commercial flights via **Delta** (© 800/221-1212) and **United** (© 800/241-6522).

Most of the major auto-rental agencies have operations in the gateway cities. **Thrifty** (© 800/847-4389) and **Hertz** (© 800/654-3131) have operations in Billings, Bozeman, Cody, and Jackson. **National** (© 800/227-7368) and **Alamo Auto Rental** (© 800/462-5266) have locations in Bozeman, Billings, and Jackson. **Avis** (© 800/230-4898) has locations in Billings, Bozeman, West Yellowstone, and Jackson. **Budget** (© 800/527-0700) serves Billings, Cody, West Yellowstone, and Jackson.

ACCESS/ENTRY POINTS

Yellowstone has five entrances. The **north entrance,** near Mammoth Hot Springs, is located just south of Gardiner, Montana, and U.S. 89. In the winter, this is the only access to Yellowstone by car.

The **west entrance,** just outside the town of West Yellowstone on U.S. 20, is the closest entry to Old Faithful. Inside the park, turn south to see Old Faithful or north to the Norris Geyser Basin. This entrance is open to wheeled vehicles April through November and during the winter to snowmobiles and Snowcoaches.

The **south entrance,** on U.S. 89/191/287, brings visitors into the park from neighboring Grand Teton National Park and the Jackson area. As you drive north from Jackson, you'll get a panoramic view of the Grand Tetons. Once in the park, the road winds along the Lewis River to the south end of Yellowstone Lake, at West Thumb and Grant Village. It is open to cars May through November and to snowmobiles and Snowcoaches December through March.

The **east entrance,** on U.S. 14/16/20, is 52 miles west of Cody, Wyoming, and is open to cars May through September and to snowmobiles and Snowcoaches December through March. The drive up the Wapiti Valley and over Sylvan Pass is especially beautiful.

The **northeast entrance,** at Cooke City, Montana, is closest to the Tower-Roosevelt area, 29 miles to the west. This entrance is open to cars year-round, but beginning on October 15, when the Beartooth Highway closes, until around Memorial Day, the only route to Cooke City is from Gardiner through Mammoth Hot Springs. When it's open—or not blockaded by landslides, as it was during the summer of 2005—the drive from Red Lodge to Cooke City is a grand climb into the clouds.

Regardless of which entrance you choose, when you enter the park you'll be given a good map and up-to-date information on facilities, services, programs, fishing, camping, and more.

Note: Check **road conditions** before entering the park by calling for a road report (© 307/344-7381). There always seems to be major road construction in one part of the park or another, so be forewarned.

Tips Flying for Less

Flying into the closest airports to Yellowstone can be an expensive proposition. You can often save significant airfare dollars by flying to **Salt Lake City,** or the more distant **Denver.** Salt Lake City is 390 driving miles from Jackson, a route that takes you through rolling Idaho countryside and alongside the dramatic western slope of the Rockies, then high above it all over Teton Pass.

VISITOR CENTERS & INFORMATION

There are five major visitor and information centers in the park, and each has something different to offer. Unless otherwise indicated, summer hours are from 8am to 7pm daily.

The **Albright Visitor Center** (✆ **307/344-2263**), at Mammoth Hot Springs, is the largest and is open year-round. It provides visitor information and publications about the park, has exhibits depicting park history from prehistory through the creation of the National Park Service, and houses a wildlife display on the second floor.

The **Old Faithful Visitor Center** (✆ **307/545-2750**) is another large facility. A film on Yellowstone's thermal features is shown throughout the day in an indoor auditorium. Rangers dispense various park publications and post projected geyser eruption times here. The Park Service plans to open a state-of-the-art $15-million visitor-education center in place of the current architecturally maligned building; at press time, the hope was to cut the ribbon on a new facility by 2008.

The **Canyon Visitor Center** (✆ **307/242-2550**), in Canyon Village, is the place to go for books and an informative display about the park's geology, with a focus on the underlying volcanism. It's staffed with friendly rangers used to dealing with crowds.

The **Fishing Bridge Visitor Center** (✆ **307/242-2450**), near Fishing Bridge on the north shore of Yellowstone Lake, has an excellent display that focuses on the park's bird life. You can get information and publications here as well.

The **Grant Village Visitor Center** (✆ **307/242-2650**) has information, publications, a video program, and a fascinating exhibit that examines the role of fire in Yellowstone.

Helpful staff and park literature can also be found at several small information stations: the **Madison Information Station** (✆ **307/344-2821**); the **Museum of the National Park Ranger** (no phone; open daily in summer 9am–5pm) and the **Norris Geyser Basin Museum and Information Station** (✆ **307/344-2812;** open daily in summer 10am–5pm), both at Norris; the **West Thumb Information Station** (no phone; open daily in summer 9am–5pm); and the **Public Lands Desk** at the West Yellowstone Visitors Information Center, 100 Yellowstone Ave. (✆ **406/646-7701;** open daily 8am–8pm in summer, limited hours the rest of the year).

FEES & PERMITS

Entrance for up to 7 days costs $25 per vehicle and covers both Yellowstone and Grand Teton national parks. A snowmobile or motorcycle pays $20 for 7 days, and someone who comes in on bicycle, skis, or foot pays $12. You can buy an **annual permit** for $40, but the various national park passes are the best deal (see section 7, "Specialized Travel Resources," in chapter 2).

BACKCOUNTRY PERMITS   Backcountry permits are free, but you have to have one for any overnight trip, on foot, on horseback, or by boat. Camping is allowed only in designated campsites, many of which are equipped with food-storage poles to keep wildlife away. These sites are primitive and well situated, and you won't feel at all like you're in a campground. If designated campsites in a particular area have already been reserved, you're out of luck. So while you can make a reservation as few as 48 hours before beginning a trip, you would be wise during peak season to make a reservation well in advance (you can contact the park for reservations for the upcoming year beginning Apr 1), although it costs $20. The **Yellowstone Backcountry Office** (P.O. Box 168, Yellowstone National Park, WY 82190) will send you the useful *Backcountry Trip Planner* brochure with a detailed map showing where the campsites are. Call the office for more information at ✆ **307/344-2160.**

Pick up your permit in the park within 48 hours of your departure, at one of the following visitor ranger stations any day of the week during the summer: Bechler, Canyon, Mammoth, Old Faithful, Tower, West Entrance, Grant Village, Lake, South Entrance, and Bridge Bay. Boating permits for motorized craft can be obtained at only the last four ranger stations.

BOATING PERMITS   Any vessels used on park waters must have a permit. For motorized craft, the cost is $20 for annual permits and $10 for a 7-day pass. Fees for nonmotorized boats are $10 for annual permits and $5 for 7-day permits. Rivers and streams are closed to boats of any kind, except for the stretch of the Lewis River between Lewis and Shoshone lakes, which is restricted to hand-propelled craft. Coast Guard–approved personal flotation devices are required for each person boating.

FISHING PERMITS   Permits are required for anglers 16 and over; the permit costs $15 for 3 days, $20 for 7 days, and $35 for the season. Youths 12 to 15 years of age also must have a permit, but it's free. Children under 12 may fish without a permit. Permits are available at any ranger station, visitor center, Yellowstone Park General Store, and most fishing shops in the gateways. The season usually begins on the Saturday of Memorial Day weekend and continues through the first Sunday in November. Exceptions to this rule are Yellowstone Lake, its tributaries, and sections of the Yellowstone River. In the search for ecological equilibrium, the regulations have two key wrinkles: Any nonnative lake trout caught within the park must not be released alive and cutthroat trout are catch-and-release only.

REGULATIONS

You can get more detailed information about these rules from a park ranger, at a park visitor center, or at the park's website (www.nps.gov/yell).

BICYCLES   Bicycles are not allowed on the park's trails or boardwalks, but the park is a popular destination for pavement cyclists. Because of the narrowness of park roads and the presence of large recreational vehicles with poor visibility, it's recommended that you wear helmets and bright clothing. There are some designated off-pavement bicycling areas—contact the park for more information.

CAMPING   In any given year, a person may camp for no more than 30 days in the park, and only 14 days during the summer season. Food, garbage, and utensils must be stored in a vehicle or container made of solid material and suspended at least 10 feet above the ground when not in use.

CLIMBING   Because of the loose, crumbly rock in Yellowstone, climbing is discouraged throughout the park and prohibited in the Grand Canyon of the Yellowstone.

DEFACING PARK FEATURES   It's illegal to pick wildflowers or collect natural or archaeological objects. Only dead-and-down wood can be collected for backcountry campfires.

FIREARMS   Loaded guns are not allowed in the park. However, unloaded firearms may be transported in a vehicle when cased, broken down, or rendered inoperable, and on certain trails for access to areas outside the park, with a special permit. Ammunition must be carried in a separate compartment of the vehicle.

LITTERING   Littering in the national parks is strictly prohibited—remember, if you pack it in, you have to pack it out. Throwing coins or other objects into thermal features is illegal.

MOTORCYCLES   Motorcycles, motor scooters, and motorbikes are allowed only on park roads. No off-road or trail riding is allowed. Operator licenses and license plates are required.

PETS   Pets must be leashed and are prohibited in the backcountry, on trails, on board-walks, and in thermal areas. If you tie up a pet and leave it, you're breaking the law.

SMOKING   No smoking in thermal areas, visitor centers, ranger stations, or any other posted public areas.

SNOWMOBILING   Through 2006 and 2007, Yellowstone is allowing up to 720 snowmobiles per day, and all trips were required to be guided; a long-term plan, which may include an outright snowmobile ban, is slated for completion in 2007. Snowmo-bilers must have a valid driver's license, stay on the designated unplowed roadways, and obey posted speed limits.

SWIMMING   Swimming or wading is prohibited in thermal features or in streams whose waters flow from thermal features in Yellowstone. (An exception is Boiling River near Mammoth, where visitors can take a warm soak between daybreak and dusk except during spring runoff.) Swimming in Yellowstone Lake is discouraged because of the low water temperature and unpredictable weather. Bathing suits are required.

WILDLIFE   It is unlawful to approach within 300 feet of a bear or within 75 feet of other wildlife. Feeding any wildlife is illegal. Wildlife calls such as elk bugles or other artificial attractants are forbidden.

WHEN TO GO

During the quiet "shoulder" seasons of spring and fall, there are more bison and elk around than autos and RVs. Before the second week in June, you'll be rewarded by the explosion of wildflowers as they begin to bloom, filling the meadows and hillsides with vast arrays of colors and shapes. After that, roads become progressively busier. Traveling before peak season has economic advantages, as well, since rates at gateway-city motels are lower, as are the costs of meals. After Labor Day weekend, crowds begin to thin again and the roads become less traveled. In addition to wildlife and improved fishing condi-tions in some areas, the fall foliage transforms the area to a calendar-quality image.

In the winter, Yellowstone has a storybook beauty, as snow and ice soften the edges of the landscape and shroud the lumbering bison. Geyser basins appear even more dramatic, the frigid air temperature in stark contrast to the steaming, gurgling waters. Nearby trees are transformed into eerie "snow ghosts" by frozen thermal vapors. Wildlife cluster at the thermal areas to take advantage of the softer ground and more accessible vegetation. Lake Yellowstone's surface freezes to an average thickness of 3 feet, creating a vast ice sheet that sings and moans as the huge plates of ice shift.

The other winter sound is made by the herds of snowmobiles that roam the roads and are at the center of a contentious issue of late. (For more information on the snowmobile issue, see the box, "Snowmobiling: To Ban or Not to Ban," on p. 292.) Through winter 2006–07, Yellowstone is admitting 720 snowmobiles per day, all of which must be accompanied by a licensed guide.

You can also enter the park in tracked vehicles that deliver visitors to the beautifully rebuilt Old Faithful Snow Lodge and tour the park. From the lodge or Mammoth—which also stays open to cars during the winter—you can ski, snowmobile (assuming regulations still permit it), or visit the thermal areas. The only road within the park open for automobile traffic is the Mammoth Hot Springs–Cooke City Road.

SEASONS

Natives of the region describe weather in the Yellowstone ecosystem as predictably unpredictable. Because of the region's high elevations and changing weather systems, the park is characterized by long, cold winters and short, though usually warm, summers.

The first sticking snows typically fall by November 1, and cold and snow may linger into April and May (and even June), though temperatures generally warm up by then. The average daytime readings during spring are 40°F (4°C) to 50°F (10°C), gradually increasing to 60°F (16°C) to 70°F (21°C) by early June. Yellowstone is never balmy, but temperatures during the middle of the summer are typically 70°F (21°C) to 80°F (27°C) in the lower elevations, and are especially comfortable because of the lack of humidity. Even during the summer months, nights will be cool, with temperatures dropping into the low 40s (4–7°C). No matter how warm you expect it to be, it's a good idea to bring a warm jacket, rain gear, and water-resistant walking shoes. And, because this is high altitude, bring plenty of sunscreen and a wide-brimmed hat to protect yourself in the thin atmosphere. As summer thunderstorms are common, a tarp and an umbrella are also recommended.

During winter months temperatures hover in the single digits, and subzero overnight temperatures are common. You should bring fleece underwear, heavy shirts (not cotton!), vests and coats, warm gloves, and warm, wicking socks. The lowest temperature recorded at Yellowstone was –66°F (–54°C), in 1933.

AVOIDING THE CROWDS

One of the things you'll discover when you venture down a trail is that the majority of Yellowstone's three million annual visitors aren't going to follow you. (Less than 10% of visitors wander beyond the trail heads.) Some are afraid of grizzly bears; some are in a hurry; some just don't want the exertion. Regardless, Yellowstone rewards those who expend a bit of shoe leather: A mere half-mile from the traffic jams, you'll find few people and much better opportunities to smell the wildflowers.

If you really want a Yellowstone experience that's all your own, head for the backcountry. This is some of the deepest, most exquisite wilderness in the country, and you definitely won't be fighting a mob. While visitation at Yellowstone increases yearly, backcountry permits do not—they've been level since 1980. Our favorite areas are the Thorofare region, in the park's southeast corner at the headwaters of the Yellowstone River, and the shores of Shoshone Lake, the largest backcountry body of water in the Lower 48, but there's so much wilderness here that it's hard not to find views of your own.

EDUCATIONAL PROGRAMS

Yellowstone offers free **ranger-led educational programs** ★★ that will significantly enhance a visitor's understanding of the area's history, geology, and wildlife. Most programs run from early June through late September. Detailed information on location and times is listed in the park newsletter, which is distributed at the entrance gates. On a more informal basis, you'll run into ranger-naturalists roaming the geyser basins and along the rim of the Grand Canyon in Yellowstone, and in areas where wildlife gather in both parks, leading informative walks and answering the questions of inquisitive visitors.

Evening campfire programs are presented nightly in the summer at Mammoth, Norris, Madison, Old Faithful, Bridge Bay, Grant, and Canyon. Many of these activities are accessible to those with disabilities. It's a good idea to bring a flashlight, warm clothing, and rain gear. Rangers also conduct walking, talking, and hiking programs throughout the park, including half-day "Adventure Hikes" that cost $15.

As one would expect, there are more tours and evening programs in the **Old Faith-ful** area than anywhere else in the park. The topics of the guided walks, which can run as long as 1½ hours, usually focus on the geysers, their fragile plumbing, and their role in the Yellowstone ecosystem. A slide-show program is held in the auditorium in the evening.

Beginning in June, daily hikes in the **Canyon** area head out to the Hayden Valley and the rim of the Grand Canyon; a ranger talk on the art inspired by the falls is held several times a day at the lower platform of Artist Point. An explanation of the origins of the hot pools and mud pots is conducted daily beginning in June at the **Grant** area as part of a walk of the Lakeshore area of the West Thumb Geyser Basin. The **Lake/Fishing Bridge** agenda includes walking tours of the Mud Volcano area, and along the shores of Yellowstone Lake and Indian Pond. There is an afternoon talk at the Fishing Bridge Visitor Center about managing wildlife like grizzlies and wolves, and a discussion of fisheries management is held on the west end of the Fishing Bridge. For a full schedule, consult the park newsletter distributed at the entrance gates.

Mammoth Hot Springs is host to several interesting ranger-led programs, namely a pair of "Daily Special" talks on the park's natural wonders and a historical tour of the original site of Fort Yellowstone, established more than 125 years ago. There is also a guided tour of the hot-springs terraces. The hottest, most dynamic, and oldest geyser basin in the park is at **Norris,** where a popular 1½-hour tour begins at the Norris museum three times daily.

There are also special exhibitions at the various visitor centers around the park. *Yellowstone Revealed,* a film on the teeming microbial life in the park's hot pools, plays regularly at the Old Faithful Visitor Center, and an excellent exhibit on the park's volcanism is at the Canyon Visitor Center.

The ranger/naturalist programs are one of several activities that make up the **Junior Ranger** program. For $3, kids can pick up an activity paper at one of the visitor centers, then follow its guidelines for hiking and learning about the park. When they complete the program, their enrollment as Junior Rangers is announced to the public with great fanfare.

Photographers can get some lessons and free advice through **Kodak's photo walks and demonstrations,** which are held at various locations around the park during the summer. Check the *Yellowstone Today* newspaper for locations and times. Astronomers from the **Museum of the Rockies** in Bozeman, Montana, bring their telescopes and stories to a series of stargazing sessions throughout the park—contact the museum at © **406/994-2251** for a schedule.

The **Yellowstone Association Institute** *ৰৰৰ* (© **307/344-2294**) offers a slew of guided classes, including daylong hikes to multiday backcountry adventures, often with a historical or scientific bent. Many multiday courses are based at the old Lamar Buffalo Ranch in the park's northeast corner; students overnight in basic cabins and share a kitchen and bathhouse. The Institute has also teamed with Xanterra Parks & Resorts to offer visitors days spent exploring trails with guides and nights at the comfortable lodgings throughout the park. These **Lodging and Learning** packages are excellent options for those who want to delve into the park without too much of the traditional "roughing it." Rates (starting at about $550 per person) include box lunches, breakfast, and in-park transportation. Contact **Xanterra Parks and Resorts** (© **307/344-5566;** www.travelyellowstone.com).

In September, the Institute takes over **Roosevelt Lodge** with the **Roosevelt Rendezvous,** a series of 4-day educational experiences with a daily menu of different field trips led by park experts. There are also evening programs. Rates start at $530 per person, including a cabin and three meals a day.

SERVICES & SUPPLIES

Independent of Xanterra, Yellowstone Park General Stores is the concessionaire behind the bulk of the park's retail operations. The company operates **stores** throughout the park, including Old Faithful, Mammoth Hot Springs, Lake, Fishing Bridge, and Grant Village, that feature gift shops, grocery supplies, and soda fountains. Depending upon the location, you may find a limited supply of fresh veggies and canned goods (as at the Canyon store), plus fishing supplies, souvenirs, and, of course, ice cream. **Service stations** are located at major visitor areas: Old Faithful, Canyon, Mammoth Hot Springs, and Grant Village. Exact locations of all services and stores are listed in the park newspaper you receive at the entrance gates.

If you have medical problems while visiting the park, Yellowstone Park Medical Services provides help at the **Lake Hospital** (© 307/242-7241), an acute-care facility; the **Old Faithful Clinic** (© 307/545-7325); and the **Mammoth Clinic** (© 307/344-7965), the only year-round facility of the three.

ORGANIZED TOURS & ACTIVITIES

A number of tour companies offer bus tours of the park originating in gateway communities: **Powder River Coach USA** (© 800/442-3682), out of Cody, offers daylong trips; **Yellowstone Alpen Guides** (© 800/858-3502) takes travelers around the park from West Yellowstone. If you are looking for specialized guided trips—such as photo safaris or snowmobile tours—contact the chamber of commerce in the gateway community where you want to begin (see section 1, earlier in this chapter, for contact information).

Within the park, the hotel concessionaire, **Xanterra Parks & Resorts** (© 307/344-7311;** www.travelyellowstone.com), has a variety of general and specialized tours. Five different motorcoach tours are available from all of Yellowstone's villages. For $44, you can explore the **Circle of Fire** (Old Faithful, Yellowstone Lake, the Hayden Valley); you can cruise to the southern neighbor of Grand Teton for $48 on **Teton Vista Rendezvous;** or, for $50, you can do the **Yellowstone in a Day** tour. These are full-day tours, with stops at all the sights and informative talks by the guides. Specialty trips include photo safaris, wildlife trips up the Lamar Valley, and Yellowstone Lake sunset tours in historic buses from the 1930s.

At Bridge Bay Marina, 1-hour **Scenicruiser tours** depart throughout the day from June to the end of September for a trip around the northern end of giant Yellowstone Lake. You view the Lake Hotel from the water and visit Stevenson Island while a guide fills you in on the history, geology, and biology. Fares are $11 for adults and $6.75 for children 2 to 11. Guided fishing trips on 22-and 34-foot cabin cruisers are also available from Yellowstone Park Lodges at Bridge Bay ($66 and $85 per hour, respectively), and you can rent smaller outboards and rowboats.

Buses are replaced in the winter by **Snowcoach tours.** These are closer in size to a van than a bus, mounted on tank treads with skis in front for steering. The Snowcoach can pick you up at the south or west entrances, or at Mammoth, and take you all over the park. You can spend a night at Old Faithful and then take a Snowcoach up to Mammoth the next night, or do round-trip tours from the gates or wherever you're staying in the park. One-way and wildlife-watching trips range from $27 to $60, while round-trips cost $100 to $120. **Yellowstone Alpen Guides** (✆ **800/858-3502**) offers Snowcoach trips from West Yellowstone for $99.

One- and 2-hour **guided horseback trail rides** are available at Roosevelt Lodge and Canyon Village. Children must be 8 years old and at least 48 inches tall; adults cannot exceed 250 pounds. Tour prices are $30 for a 1-hour ride and $50 for a 2-hour ride, and there is no discount for children. Check any activity desk for times and dates. Reservations are recommended and can be made at **Xanterra Parks & Resorts** activity centers in the hotels, although not before you leave home.

FOR TRAVELERS WITH DISABILITIES

Wheelchair-accessible accommodations are located in the Cascade and Dunraven lodges and Western cabins at Canyon Village; in Grant Village; in the Old Faithful Inn and Snow Lodge and Cabins; and in the Lake Yellowstone Hotel. For a free *Visitors Guide to Accessible Features in Yellowstone National Park,* call ✆ **307/344-2017,** write to the Park Accessibility Coordinator, P.O. Box 168, Yellowstone National Park, WY 82190, or pick up the guide at the gates or visitor centers. There are **accessible campsites** at Fishing Bridge, Bridge Bay, Madison, Canyon, and Grant campgrounds, which may be reserved by calling ✆ **307/344-7311.**

Accessible restrooms with sinks and flush toilets are located at all developed areas except West Thumb and Norris. Accessible vault toilets are found at West Thumb and Norris, as well as in most scenic areas and picnic areas.

Many of Yellowstone's roadside attractions, including the Grand Canyon of the Yellowstone's south rim, West Thumb Geyser Basin, much of the Norris and Upper Geyser basins, and parts of the Mud Volcano and Fountain Paint Pot areas, are negotiable by wheelchair.

Visitor centers at Old Faithful, Grant Village, and Canyon are wheelchair accessible, as are the Norris Museum and the Fishing Bridge Visitor Center. Mammoth's visitor center is accessible via a back entry.

Handicapped parking is available at Old Faithful, Fishing Bridge, Canyon, Norris, and Grant Village, though you'll have to look for it; at some locations it is near a Yellowstone Park General Store.

3 A Park Primer

A BRIEF HISTORY

A trip to Yellowstone has changed considerably since the days of George Cowan: When he visited the park in 1877, he set a new standard for "roughing it." Cowan was kidnapped from his horse-packing camp and shot by the Nez Perce Indians, then subsisted on roots and coffee grounds as he dragged his paralyzed body for days through the wilderness.

Let's just say the United States government had a bit to learn about how to run the world's first national park. It still does, but it's getting better all the time. For more than 125 years, the National Park Service has been directing traffic at this complex intersection of wilderness and tourism, juggling the protection of powerful natural wonders while allowing for civilized comforts. And if anyone complains that the roads are potholed or the coffee is cold . . . well, George Cowan would not be sympathetic.

Yellowstone was never known as a hospitable place. Nomadic Indian bands crossed the plateau but never settled there, except for a small group of Shoshone known as

Wildlife & Where to Spot It

Biologists consider Yellowstone one of the most important wildlife habitats in the world. You'll find all sorts of creatures here, from the dramatic bald eagle and grizzly bear to the less-publicized reptiles and insects of the thermal areas. What particularly distinguishes this collection of wildlife is that the giant herds of elk, the thousands of bison, and all their brethren are free-roaming. Grizzly bears and wolves in the wild are currently extremely rare in the Lower 48.

Some claim the **bison** (buffalo) that once blanketed the Great Plains were only driven to the Yellowstone Plateau when they were hunted off the plains. Regardless, this herd is right at home here, wandering along the main thoroughfares without much regard for their human spectators. They are easy to view in the summer months, often seen munching grass, wallowing in dust pits, and even wrestling sumo-style for mates in the **Lamar, Hayden,** and **Pelican valleys;** the **Bechler River area;** and in the geyser areas **near the Firehole River.** *A caution:* Keep your distance from these behemoths. They have poor eyesight and cranky dispositions, and, like moose, they can move with sudden speed (up to 35 mph) to batter anyone who invades their personal space.

Biologists have trouble agreeing on how many **bears** there are in Yellowstone, but most will acknowledge that their numbers are on the rise. Their food supplies seem to have stabilized a bit with the wolf reintroduction (more carcasses) and procutthroat fishing regulations. In the Greater Yellowstone Ecosystem there are probably about 1,000 black bears and 600 grizzlies, but estimates vary.

Decades ago, bears foraged in open-pit garbage dumps near the lodges, or tourists hand-fed bears who begged along the park roads. When the dumps were closed in the 1970s and bear feeding was prohibited, the population of bears plummeted. Diminishing habitat around the park also had an impact. However, bears are creative omnivores, and they've found new food sources in the wild. Come spring, they tend to gravitate toward elk and bison (either the very young or very old) and wolf kills, but their diet has been assessed as being about three-quarters vegetarian.

Black bears are most commonly sighted in the spring, sometimes with cubs, in the Canyon, Tower, Madison, and Old Faithful areas, where they feed on green grass and herbs, berries, ants, and carrion. The more aggressive grizzly's unpredictable behavior makes them the likely suspect in the rare instances of bear attacks on humans, but blacks have demonstrated that they also are capable in this regard. Rangers closely monitor their movements during late spring in areas near trout-spawning streams and carrion sites to minimize the possibility of an encounter.

Odds of seeing a grizzly are best during May and June, in the Lamar and Hayden valleys, before they retreat into the backwoods for the summer. Backcountry travelers often see bears in the remote Thorofare Country on the park's southeast border, where bears (and avid anglers) journey to the Yellowstone River headwaters for the spawning cutthroat trout in the spring.

It is estimated that 60,000 **elk** (wapiti) populate the ecosystem. You should have no problem telling elk from deer or antelope by their size (typically 900 lb.), the males' large antler racks, and their chestnut-brown heads and necks, with a distinctive tan patch on their rumps. One herd can usually be located around **Mammoth Hot Springs;** others are often seen in the meadows between Old Faithful and Madison Junction.

During winter months, the northern Yellowstone herd heads to a winter grazing area near Gardiner as the southern herd descends to the National Elk Refuge near Jackson. Listen in the fall for the distinctive bugling of the males, a throaty gargle that slips into a piercing, high whistle.

Moose are more solitary than elk; they're grumpy loners, and not very patient with the tourists that flock around whenever they appear. Those appearances are usually in alder thickets and marshes around streams, particularly around Canyon and near Shoshone Lake in the backcountry. They are recognizable by their dark coats, massive antlers, and the fleshy dewlap that hangs beneath their necks like a bell. A moose is capable of traveling at 30 mph; cows will charge any perceived threat to a calf, and bulls become particularly ornery in the fall. Give them a wide berth.

The **pronghorn,** usually labeled antelope (though unrelated), is often sighted grazing near the northern entrance to Yellowstone. These fleet and flighty animals have excellent vision, and they'll take off at 45 mph when photographers try to get near. However, they're not as common a sight as they were in 1990, as the park's population of pronghorn has plummeted in recent years. The pronghorn is identified by its short, black horns, tan-and-white body, and black accent stripes.

For a long time, the **coyote** has been the predator most often spotted by park visitors, but the arrival of wolves has taken its toll on the smaller canine. Coyotes may be seen alone or in small packs—they're particularly visible in winter—with brown to gray coats that grow silvery after the snow falls. They prey on small animals like squirrels and rabbits, or larger ungulates like elk and deer that have grown old or ill. They'll also scavenge the leftovers of other predators. Biologists estimate there are around 500 coyotes in the park. You'll see them out in the open meadows of the **Hayden Valley,** and you might get lucky and see the interaction between wolves and coyotes in places like **Slough Creek.**

Gray wolves from Canada were reintroduced to the park in 1995, and it appears they're here to stay, feasting on the smorgasbord of elk in the northern end of the park. There are more than 300 wolves in the ecosystem today. The **Lamar Valley** is where they were first released, and patient observers at dawn and dusk can sometimes see the Druid Peak Pack along the river or the Rose Creek Pack on the slopes above Slough Creek. Look for ranger Rick McIntyre—he's there most of the summer—or one of the many dedicated wolf trackers on hand in springtime, and ask for advice, or check at the east gate or Mammoth Visitor Center for the best sighting opportunities.

"Sheepeaters." The first non-Indian to lay eyes on Yellowstone's geothermal wonders was probably John Colter, an explorer who broke away from the Lewis and Clark expedition in 1806 and spent 3 years wandering a surreal landscape of mud pots and geysers. When he described his discovery on his return to St. Louis, no one believed him, and he settled down to life as a farmer. Later, miners and fur trappers followed in his footsteps, occasionally making curious reports of a sulfurous world still sometimes called "Colter's Hell."

The first significant exploration of what would become the park took place in 1869, when a band of Montanans led by David Folsom completed a 36-day expedition. Folsom and his group traveled up the Missouri River, then into the heart of the park, where they discovered the falls of the Yellowstone, mud pots, Yellowstone Lake, and the Fountain Geyser. But it was an 1871 expedition led by U.S. Geological Survey Director Ferdinand Hayden that brought back astonishing photographs of Yellowstone's wonders by William Henry Jackson.

Crude health spas and thin-walled "hotels" went up near the hot springs. A debate soon followed over the potential for commercial development and exploitation of the region. Many people take credit for the idea of creating the national park—members of the Folsom party later told a story about thinking it up around a campfire in the Upper Geyser Basin. In any case, the idea caught on as Yellowstone explorers hit the lecture circuit back East. In March 1872, President Ulysses S. Grant signed legislation declaring Yellowstone a national park.

No one had any experience in managing a wilderness park, and many mistakes were made: Superintendents granted favorable leases to friends with commercial interests in the tourism industry; poachers ran amok, decimating the wildlife population; a laundry business near Mammoth cleaned linens in the hot pool.

By 1886, things were so bad that the army took control of the park; its firm-fisted management practices resulted in new order and protected the park from those intent upon exploiting it, although the military participated in the eradication of the plateau's wolf population. By 1916, efforts to make the park more visitor-friendly began to bear fruit: Construction of the first roads had been completed and guest housing was available in the area. Stewardship of the park was then transferred to the newly created National Park Service.

THE PARK TODAY

The job of the National Park Service will never be easy in Yellowstone, where rangers must preserve a natural environment for a wide range of species—including one very demanding creature, the human being. Tourists come from around the world to visit Yellowstone, some with high expectations of creature comforts in the wilderness.

It's challenge enough to provide an unimpaired view of the wildlife, scenery, and thermal features of the park to three million visitors a year. It's even harder to mitigate the environmental impact of those visitors on the forests, meadows, thermal areas, and wildlife habitat. The powers that be debate a number of issues today: the reintroduction of wolves, their protection, and their impact on livestock around the park; the invasion of Yellowstone Lake by man-introduced species such as Mackinaw trout; the crush of automobile and snowmobile traffic; the privatization of park operations; and the diminishing store of undeveloped land around the park, which traditionally provides a cushion for Yellowstone's wildlife populations.

The National Park Service is determined that the laws of nature should remain unaffected by human intrusion; that's why firefighters let the 1988 fires burn until fears arose about the loss of park buildings and human lives. A similar situation may develop with the wildlife population, which is protected within the park but not outside of it, and therefore has stretched certain food supplies to their limits. Herds of elk, deer, and bison have ballooned in size, raising questions about the ecosystem's ability to support them; some say the reintroduction of wolves and the rebounding bear population may solve the problem naturally.

When Canadian gray wolves were transplanted to the park's northeast corner in 1995, the reintroduction proved astonishingly successful: The wolves reproduced rapidly and immediately began enlarging their range, breaking into new packs and roaming beyond the park boundaries. When a few developed a taste for calves and lambs, ranchers were incensed, lawsuits began to fly, and a federal judge in Wyoming ruled in 1998 that all reintroduced wolves should be removed. This decision was overturned in 2000, and the wolves—which now number about 175 in the park—are finally entrenched in Yellowstone for the long haul.

Then there are the snowmobilers. They come from the flatlands, singing praises for the fine trail system in and around the park. For more information on the snowmobile issue, see the box "Snowmobiling: To Ban or Not to Ban," on p. 292.

There are summer traffic problems, too, particularly involving house-size motor homes and trailers navigating the narrow, twisting park roads. They create traffic jams and force bicyclists off the road. Along with cars, they interrupt the passage of wildlife like bison and elk. Traffic studies suggest the problem will worsen, and the government has shown little inclination to spend the money necessary to fix Yellowstone's beaten-up roads.

"Privatization" has been a watchword since the Reagan era, and increasingly the parks are allowing concessionaires to take over management duties, such as campground management, in order to put private dollars to work where federal funds once did the job. Critics fear that this leads to profit-driven decisions: Certainly the expansion of winter activities makes more economic than environmental sense. On the other hand, the beautiful new Old Faithful Snow Lodge is a vast improvement over the lodge it replaced, thanks to Xanterra Parks & Resorts. Park management has taken matters into its own hands by steadily increasing entrance and user fees. A good portion of these fees will be used for building maintenance, salaries, roads, and other park infrastructure needs.

PLANT LIFE OF THE PARK

The large mammals may be the stars of Yellowstone National Park, but flower-lovers will find plenty to enjoy here among the park's 1,200 native plants. Flowers and shrubs broadcast bright shades of blues, purples, yellows, and oranges throughout the park, providing a colorful accent to the forests and meadows.

The plateau's volcanoes, fires, and glaciers have created a series of tumultuous changes that have had an enormous impact on plant life. At one site in the Lamar Valley, the inspection of petrified tree stumps exhumed by erosion resulted in the identification of 27 distinct layers of forests, one atop the other.

The plants have evolved with the ever-changing Yellowstone environment. Forests once populated with hardwood, like maple, magnolia, and sycamore, are now filled with conifers, the most common of which are pine, spruce, and fir. A smattering of cottonwood and aspen thrive in the cool park temperatures.

Vegetation zones tend to reflect altitude: Lower-elevation valleys tend to be dry and grassy, with sagebrush and few trees; forests of fir dominate between about 6,000 and

7,500 feet, followed by lodgepole pine stands and then spruce and more fir up to the timberline, with open meadows where wildflowers explode in the spring. At high elevations, shrubs and carpetlike vegetation take over, and you have to lean over to examine the tiny blossoms.

Attempts by park officials to manage the ecosystem have had an impact, too. Climax forests—a plant succession leading to conifers that create a shady canopy and block the growth of seedlings—had a prolonged reign in Yellowstone because of fire suppression, which contributed to the ferocity of fires in the dry summer of 1988. However, once the fires were allowed to burn, it became clear that fire was crucial in the life cycle of lodgepole pine. Since its cones release seeds only after a burn, many of the areas that were "ravaged" in 1988 are now carpeted by an astounding one million saplings per acre.

4 Seeing the Highlights

This is a wonderland you can return to again and again, sampling a different pleasure each time. All the sites mentioned here are easily accessible along the loop tours detailed in section 5, "Driving the Park." The farther you get from the pavement, and the farther from July and August you schedule your visit, the more private your experience will be.

We've organized this list geographically, following the roadways that form a figure-8 at the heart of the park. We'll begin in the north, then move south, first along the east side, then west. Get out the oversize map you receive at the gate or by mail and follow along.

MAMMOTH HOT SPRINGS

At the park's north entrance, 5 miles south of Gardiner, Mammoth Hot Springs is home to spectacular limestone terraces, historic park buildings, and the Mammoth Hot Springs Hotel. It's one of the older park settlements, with stone buildings dating from the late 19th century, when the army was stationed here at Fort Yellowstone.

There are no geysers at **Mammoth Hot Springs Terraces** ఆ*ఆ*, but this cascading staircase of hillside hot pools, among the oldest in the park, offers a boardwalk tour of gorgeous pastels in shades of white, yellow, orange, and green, the unintentionally artistic work of microscopic bacteria in the sediments. The mineral-rich springs constantly bubble to the surface, depositing travertine as the water cools in contact with the air. It's a vivid illustration of the park's unusual geological situation: a rare geologic hot spot of seismic activity in the middle of the continent, where molten rock nearly makes it to the earth's surface.

Whether or not you spend the night at the **Mammoth Hot Springs Hotel**—not the most distinguished lodging in the park, but it has historic character—you should drop by the **Albright Visitor Center.** This building once housed Fort Yellowstone's bachelor officers, but you won't find a pool table here today; rather, you'll find displays on park history, wildlife and photography exhibits, smiling rangers dispensing advice, and numerous park publications and maps. Films on the park's origin and the art it inspired are shown throughout the day. A special treat for international visitors is the opportunity to get their visas stamped with the official Yellowstone National Park document stamp. For more information, call ℂ **307/344-2263.**

TOWER-ROOSEVELT AREA

East of Mammoth Hot Springs you enter a delicious mix of high plains, deep forest, and twisting rivers. Toward the northeast corner lies one of the most beautifully serene

⟨Moments⟩ **Hot Springs Hot Spot**
_____

Once upon a time, travelers in Yellowstone bathed, cooked, and laundered their clothes in the hot springs, but such activities are illegal nowadays. There is one spot on the east side of the road to the north entrance, however, where the public is allowed to take a dip. Called **Boiling River** 𝖆𝖆, the hot springs here run into the Gardner River and create a series of temperature-graded (around 100°F/38°C) pools. This was once a late-night skinny-dipping secret, but you can't do that anymore: There's a parking lot, gate, and posted hours (daybreak–dusk, closed during the high springtime runoff). Regardless, this is just about the best possible way to cap off a day of touring and hiking: sitting in Mother Nature's hot tub, surrounded by beautiful scenery.

valleys in the Rockies, the **Lamar Valley** 𝖆𝖆𝖆. This glacier-carved swath of grassy bottom and forested flanks sits apart from the vehicular chaos at the center of the park, a good thing because the traffic here is not automobiles, but the bison, bears, wolves, and elk whose presence has earned the valley the nickname, "The Serengeti of the United States." If you continue east and leave Yellowstone via the park's northeast entrance, you'll be heading up to the spectacular views of the **Beartooth Highway.**

The area around the Tower-Roosevelt Junction was once a favorite spot of U.S. President Theodore Roosevelt. At **Roosevelt Lodge,** visitors can enjoy the kind of simple accommodations that fit the tastes of the Bull Moose himself: those with the rustic flavor of the Old West. This is the most relaxed of the park's villages, and a great place to take a break from the more crowded attractions. Get into the cowboy spirit by taking a **guided trail ride,** a **stagecoach ride,** or a **wagon ride.** You can skip the dining room and ride out for an **Old West cookout,** served from a chuck wagon to patrons who arrive by either horseback or wagon. The nearby 132-foot **Tower Falls** 𝖆 is named for the looming volcanic pinnacles at its brink and provides an excellent photo opportunity. While in the area, take time to view the petrified forests on **Specimen Ridge,** where a wide variety of fossilized plants and trees date back millions of years. All things considered, Roosevelt is a great place to escape the hordes.

Farther south, **Pelican and Hayden valleys** are the two most prominent remnants of large, ancient lakebeds in the park. They are now vast, subalpine meadows, thriving with plant life that provides feed for sizable bison and elk populations. You might see a bear here, too.

THE GRAND CANYON OF YELLOWSTONE

Hayden Valley flanks the featured attraction of the park's center: the **Grand Canyon of the Yellowstone River** 𝖆𝖆𝖆, a colorful, 1,000-foot-deep, 24-mile-long gorge that some can't resist comparing to its larger counterpart in Arizona. Okay, then: This canyon is greener, the water clearer, the air cooler, and it has two dramatic waterfalls, the big one taller than Niagara. As it drops through this gorge, the Yellowstone River in some places moves at 64,000 cubic feet of water per second.

Volcanic explosions and glaciers surging and receding shaped the canyon. The geological story is told in the canyon itself, where hard lava flows formed the lip of the falls next to softer quartz-rich rock that gave way, allowing the river to cut deeply through the layers of red, orange, tan, and brown hue. Plumes of steam pinpoint vents along the canyon's rock spires, where viewing opportunities are extensive and varied. There are many hikes along and down into the canyon, which is 24 miles long and up to 1,200 feet deep, and you'll be surprised at how few people you encounter away from the parking areas. Many do trek down to a view of the Lower Falls on **Uncle Tom's Trail** 🎢 from the South Rim, and a short path from a parking area for Upper Falls View also offers breathtaking views. Two other favorite trails are **Inspiration Point** and **Artist Point;** both are wheelchair accessible.

Canyon Village has a sprawling 1950s look, which puts off some visitors, but the architecture is starting to come back in vogue. It's usually crowded, but you can find many useful services there, and some of the newer lodging is an improvement.

NORRIS GEYSER BASIN

If you travel south from Mammoth on the west side of the park, you pass some interesting rock formations, **Obsidian Cliff** and **Roaring Mountain,** before coming to **Norris Geyser Basin** 🎢🎢. Norris is not nearly as famous as the Mammoth terraces or the crowd of geysers around Old Faithful, but there's a lot going on here, from the steaming pools of the **Porcelain Basin** to the eruptions of **Echinus Geyser.** If you're the patient type, you can sit by the blowhole of **Steamboat Geyser** and hope that this, the largest of park geysers with a maximum height of 400 feet, will erupt. But be prepared to wait: It erupted six times between 2000 and late 2005, and only blew twice during the preceding 12 years. This is one of the hottest, most active thermal areas on the plateau, at the intersection of three faults in the earth's crust; when they shift, new geysers pop up and old ones disappear. The **Norris Geyser Basin Museum** explains geothermal features, and the nearby **Museum of the National Park Ranger** tracks the history of the park's stewards.

OLD FAITHFUL

About a quarter of the world's geysers are crowded into hills, valleys, and riverbanks around **Old Faithful** 🎢🎢, where the hot pools and spouts are divided into three areas: the **Lower, Midway,** and **Upper geyser basins.** Here you'll find burbling mud pots, radiant pools like **Chromatic Spring,** and geysers with a variety of tricks, from the angled shots of **Daisy Geyser** to the witches' cauldron of **Crested Pool.**

Finds **Petrified Wood**

With so many hot pots, mountain peaks, geysers, and bison to gawk at, it's not surprising that many visitors to Yellowstone miss some of the finest examples of petrified forest found anywhere. The trees were preserved, scientists believe, when their organic matter was replaced by volcanic material during one of the many eruptions on the plateau. Some of the tree trunks still stand, particularly in the Specimen Ridge area in the northeast area of the park, and they are a monument to the region's warmer, swampier past: sycamore, magnolias, and dogwoods are all preserved in stone. Check at the Tower Ranger Station for maps showing you where to find petrified wood. This is not a renewable resource: Don't touch or take.

But the grand old dame of geysers, the star of the show, is **Old Faithful.** Over the past 100 years, its eruptions have been remarkably consistent, blowing 15 to 23 times daily with a column averaging about 134 feet and a duration of about 40 seconds. Recent seismic activity has elongated the intervals (to about 92 min.) between eruptions a tad, but it's still the most predictable geyser in the world. Estimates posted at the visitor centers are give-or-take 10 minutes; if the last eruption was a long one, you might have to wait 2 hours for the next burst. (No big deal—there's plenty else to see here.)

Since the geyser is one of the key park attractions, the **Old Faithful Visitor Center** (© **307/545-2750**) is larger than most of its counterparts. An excellent film describing the geysers and their microscopic inhabitants is shown throughout the day in an air-conditioned auditorium—quite a relief on hot July afternoons. The Park Service hopes to close the existing visitor center by 2008 and cut the ribbon on a new state-of-the-art building, which will feature interactive exhibits and an environmentally integrated architectural style.

A National Historic Landmark, the shingled, steep-roofed **Old Faithful Inn** was built of local stone and hand-hewn timber, including a pair of interior balconies above the lobby floor. See section 10, "Where to Stay in the Park," later in this chapter, for a full description and review.

YELLOWSTONE LAKE

West of Old Faithful, over Craig Pass, or south of Canyon, through the wildlife-rich **Hayden Valley,** is gigantic **Yellowstone Lake** ⚮⚮, another natural wonder unique to Yellowstone. At 20 miles long, 14 miles wide, and more than 300 feet deep in places, it's the largest lake in the world above 7,000 feet in elevation. If you took a dip in the frigid water (not recommended), you could hardly guess that the caldera underneath the lake is filling with hot liquid magma, actually tilting the lake northward at a measurable pace. The caldera is the sunken remainder of a huge volcanic blast 600,000 years ago, and another about 700,000 years before that. Experts believe it's due to blow again sometime in the next 100,000 years—any day now, at least in geologic time. Volcanic underpinnings aside, grizzlies work the tributary streams in the spring when fish spawn (some campgrounds are closed), and lots of other wildlife congregate here, including moose and osprey.

The lake has long been a favorite fishing spot, but recent regulations have made cutthroat trout a catch-and-release species parkwide. This is part of a desperate attempt by park biologists to help the cutthroat come back against the planted Mackinaw or lake trout, which dine on small cutthroat and therefore are not to be released alive. You'll see some big sailboats braving the quirky winds of the lake, and experienced paddlers may want to **kayak** or **canoe** into the south and southeast arms of the lake, which are closed to motorboats. These deep bays are true wilderness, and great areas to fish and view wildlife. When you pick up a boating permit, you'll also get a stern warning from rangers to watch out for the changeable weather if you get out on the lake's open water. They're right to urge caution; even the best paddlers risk their lives in a sudden afternoon storm.

Lake Village, on the north shore of the lake, offers a large range of amenities, including fine restaurants at either the rustic cabins at **Lake Lodge** or the majestic 100-year-old **Lake Yellowstone Hotel.** This hotel has Greek columns and a spacious solarium overlooking the lake, the best place for a cocktail or a romantic dinner within park boundaries. It's very different from the Old Faithful Inn, but a rival for its beauty and history. Just south of Lake Village is **Bridge Bay Marina,** the park's water-activity center. Here you can obtain guided fishing trips, small-boat rentals, and dock rentals; there's also a store and tackle shop.

WEST THUMB & GRANT VILLAGE

On the south end of the lake, at **West Thumb,** the boiling thermal features extend out into the lake. You can see steaming cones and churning water created by the action of the underwater hot springs. **Fishing Cone** is rumored to be the place where fishermen once used the "hook and cook" method, immediately tossing their catch into a hot pot for instant meal preparation. Don't try it—it's illegal to drop anything into a thermal feature, and the geyser water has traces of mercury and arsenic. You can walk among the lakeshore pools at the **Central Basin** and look at the colorful, thick fudge of the **Thumb Paint Pots.**

Grant Village, named for President Ulysses S. Grant, was completed in 1984 and is the newest of Yellowstone's villages. It has some of the most modern facilities in the park, but it's also the least inspired. On the plus side, this area is a great vantage point for watching sunrises and afternoon squalls move across the lake, and you may see **river otters** and **cutthroat trout** in the old marina's waters. (Come wintertime, the otters like to use holes melted by the underwater thermal features as base camps for ice-fishing escapades.) The **Grant Visitor Center** plays a video that explores the role of fire in the Yellowstone ecosystem.

5 Driving the Park

Yellowstone has approximately 370 miles of paved roads, and in recent years the park has struggled to catch up with a backlog of maintenance—filling potholes, widening shoulders, and redoing some roads completely. The wear and tear of heavy RVs and trailers undoes the work as quickly as it's done, and since road construction is limited to the warm months of summer, drivers often encounter delays along the park's roads. If you travel in July or August, you'll share these frustrations with a lot of other drivers. But you can see a surprising number of interesting sights along the figure-eight roadways at the heart of the park. You can take in both north and south loops—together known as the **Grand Loop**—in 1 day if a quick blink at each stop is enough for you. Better, though, to take your time, or explore different areas on different trips.

THE UPPER LOOP

At 70 miles, the Upper Loop, which begins at the north entrance, is the shorter of the two loop drives. If you start by going east from **Mammoth Hot Springs** and the park headquarters, orient yourself at the **Albright Visitor Center,** then take in the **Black-tail Plateau** or rustic **Roosevelt Lodge** (a good place for lunch). If you'd prefer, take a side trip up the pretty **Lamar Valley** ✹✹✹ for wildlife viewing at least as far as Slough Creek—checking out the views of **Tower Falls** and **Mount Washburn** (the highest point in the park)—and up **Dunraven Pass** to look out over the Mirror Plateau. Then head west from Canyon Junction to Norris Junction and north to the **Norris Geyser Basin** ✹✹, with pastel pools and a few burbles and spouts, and its fine museum. You'll continue north past **Roaring Mountain** (a travertine cascade by the road; get out only if you have some extra time) and **Obsidian Cliff** (same advice), and then have dinner in the dining room at the historic **Mammoth Hot Springs Hotel** or the **Park Street Grill** in **Gardiner,** 5 miles north.

Tips **Winter Road Conditions**

Be cautious if you're planning a winter road trip to Yellowstone. Icy roads and blinding snowstorms take their toll every year. The park itself is largely closed to automobiles in the winter—only the northern entrance is open to wheeled vehicles. The road through Lamar Valley to the northeast gate is kept open to get essential supplies to Cooke City, but from there you can go no farther north into Montana, because the Beartooth Highway is impassable in winter. The rest of the park's primary roads are open during the snowy months to Snowcoaches and snowmobiles . . . and bison, which find the packed roads convenient and think nothing of lolling along with a line of frustrated snowmobilers waiting for a chance to pass. For up-to-the-minute information on weather and road conditions, call ☏ **307/344-7381.**

If you're doing only the Upper Loop on this trip, you should include the **Grand Canyon of the Yellowstone** ✿✿✿ on your tour—it's a short ways south of Canyon Village, where the loop runs west to Norris.

THE LOWER LOOP

The longer **Lower Loop** covers some of the more famous park landmarks in its 96-mile circuit. Beginning at the south entrance, you would join the loop at the **West Thumb** of Yellowstone Lake, an otherworldly shoreline of hot springs and mud pots. If you go east, the loop skirts the west shore of **Yellowstone Lake** to the handsome **Lake Hotel** at the north end, where the Yellowstone River outlet is spanned by **Fishing Bridge.** The route then encompasses the **Grand Canyon of the Yellowstone, Madison Junction** and the **Firehole Canyon Drive,** the **Lower Geyser Basin** and the **Fountain Paintpots,** the **Midway Geyser Basin,** and the **Upper Geyser Basin** and stalwart **Old Faithful,** where you can top off the day with a meal at historic **Old Faithful Inn** or the relatively new **Old Faithful Snow Lodge.** Then head east over **Craig Pass** to the lake again.

Put the two loops together and you've done the Grand Loop of approximately 166 miles. At its conclusion, you will have seen most of the major attractions in the park.

OUT OF THE LOOPS: ENTRANCES & OTHER DETOURS

Rapturous descriptions of the **Lamar Valley** ✿✿✿ elsewhere in this guide should encourage you to take a run out of the park's northeast entrance. The valley is wide and beautiful and alive, with elk and bison grazing by the river, and coyotes, wolves, and grizzly bears making guest appearances. Beyond the park gate you'll find Cooke City, a friendly little town, and then a switchback climb north on the Beartooth Highway, with its spectacular views.

Roads to the other entrances also have allure. If you head east along the north shore of Yellowstone Lake, you'll begin climbing into **Sylvan Pass,** the 8,530-foot exit route that will take you through the east gate into the beautiful Wapiti Valley and eventually to the town of Cody (see chapter 13, "Cody & North-Central Wyoming"). The north and east shores of the lake have beaches where you can sun, swim, or begin a paddling journey to the remote southern corners of the lake. The **south entrance** road skirts **Lewis Lake** and follows **Lewis River,** where you'll often see the graceful parabolas of fly-fishing lines at work. You'll also see some of the stark handiwork of the 1988 fires. Similarly, areas along the **west entrance road** are still marked by the burned husks of trees; there are also peaceful views of the **Madison River** along this road.

There are also some trips off the main roads that are worth taking. Try the short **Firehole Canyon Drive** (just south of Madison Junction, head west on the one-way loop) for a look at Firehole Falls and a dip in the idyllic spring-warmed swimming hole a bit farther down the road. For a chance at sighting wolves, drive into **Slough Creek** in the Lamar Valley in the early morning or late afternoon. Drive across the Yellowstone River just south of Canyon Village and hike from majestic overlook to majestic overlook along the **South Rim.** Drive to the **Mount Washburn** picnic area off Dunraven Pass (elevation 8,859 ft.), and if you're feeling energetic, hike 3 miles to the top of the 10,243-foot peak.

6 Summer Sports & Activities

BICYCLING

Considering the vast expanse of real estate the parks covers, the challenging terrain, and the miles of paved roads and trails, a cyclist could conclude that the park is a prime area for biking, on or off the roads.

It looks good on paper, but the reality borders on harrowing. The narrow and twisty roads have no bike lanes, so bikers continually fight for elbow room with wide-bodied RVs and trailers. Off-road opportunities are limited because bikes are allowed on only a small number of trails.

Nevertheless, plenty of bicyclists take the challenge. The following trails are available to bikers, but know that you will share the roads with hikers. The **Mount Washburn Trail,** leaving from the Old Chittenden Road, is a strenuous trail that climbs 1,400 feet. The **Lonestar Geyser Trail,** accessed at Kepler Cascade near Old Faithful, is an easy 1-hour ride on a user-friendly road. Near Mammoth Hot Springs, **Bunsen Peak Road** and **Osprey Falls Trails** present a combination ride/hike: The first 6 miles travel around Bunsen Peak; getting to the top requires a fairly short (but fairly steep) hike. A round-trip hike down to Osprey Falls adds another 3 miles—and a steep climb back up—to the journey.

Bike rentals are available in West Yellowstone at **Yellowstone Bicycles** (© 406/ 646-7815) and **FreeHeel and Wheel** (© 406/646-7744), and in Jackson at **Hoback Sports** (© 307/733-5335).

BOATING

The best place to enjoy boating in Yellowstone is on **Yellowstone Lake,** which has easy access and panoramic views. The lake is one of the few areas where powerboats are allowed; you can rent rowboats and outboard motorboats at **Bridge Bay Marina** (© 307/242-3876). Motorboats, canoes, and kayaks can be used on Lewis Lake (about 15 miles north of the south entrance).

FISHING

There are two primary types of anglers in Yellowstone. First are the fly casters, purists more interested in the artistry and seduction of fly-fishing than in keeping what they catch. There are stretches of the Yellowstone and Madison rivers where the anglers are packed tippet to tippet and the trout must be punch drunk from catch-and-release.

Then there are the powerboat fishermen who troll the deep waters of **Yellowstone Lake.** Seven varieties of game fish live in the parks: five trout species (cutthroat, rainbow, brown, brook, and lake), grayling, and mountain whitefish. Of the trout, only the cutthroat are native, and they are being pressured in the big lake by the larger lake trout. As a result, you can't keep any pink-meat cutthroat caught in Yellowstone Lake, and you must keep any lake trout. These policies have diminished the number of fishing boats on Yellowstone Lake in recent years, but they're necessary.

The Yellowstone fishing season typically opens on the Saturday of Memorial Day weekend and ends on the first Sunday in November, except for Yellowstone Lake, which has a slightly shorter season, and the lake's tributaries, which are closed until July 15 to avoid conflicts between humans and grizzly bears, both of which are attracted to spawning trout.

The **required Yellowstone fishing permit** is available at any ranger station, visitor center, or Yellowstone Park General Store in the park. Anyone older than 16 needs a fishing permit, which costs $15 for 3 days or $20 for 7 days, and $35 for the season. Fishers aged 12 to 15 also need a permit, but it's free. Casters under 12 can fish without a permit when supervised by an adult.

In June, one of the best fishing spots is on the **Yellowstone River** downstream from Yellowstone Lake, where the cutthroat trout spawn; anglers head to **Madison River** near the west entrance in July and then again in late fall for rainbow and some brown trout; in late summer, the **Lamar River** and **Soda Butte Creek** in the park's beautiful northeast corner are popular spots to hook cutthroats in September. You'll find more isolation at **Trout Lake,** a small backcountry lake about 10 miles west of the northeast entrance.

You can fish the **Yellowstone River** below the Grand Canyon by hiking down into **Seven Mile Hole,** a great place to cast (thanks to the dearth of vegetation to snag on) for cutthroat trout from July to September, with the best luck around Sulphur Creek.

Other good fishing stretches include the **Gibbon and Firehole rivers,** which merge to form the Madison River on the park's west side, and the 3-mile **Lewis River Channel** between the Shoshone and Lewis lakes during the fall spawning run of brown trout.

There is an access for anglers with disabilities at the **Madison River,** 3½ miles west of Madison Junction at the Haynes Overlook. Here you'll find a fishing platform overhanging the river's edge for 70 feet.

HORSEBACK RIDING & LLAMA TREKKING

People who want to pack their gear on a horse, llama, or mule must get permits to enter the Yellowstone backcountry, or hire an outfitter with a permit (see below). If you're looking for just a short ride, Xanterra Parks & Resorts offers 1- and 2-hour guided trail rides daily aboard well-broken, tame animals. Stables are located at Canyon Village, Roosevelt Lodge, and Mammoth Hot Springs. Roosevelt Lodge also offers **evening rides** from June into September.

If you're looking for a longer, overnight horse-packing experience, contact the park and request a list of approved concessionaires that lead backcountry expeditions. Most offer customized, guided trips, with meals, horses, and camping and riding gear provided. Costs will run from $200 to $400 per day per person, depending on the length of the trip and number of people. In Gardiner, at the north entrance to the park, **Adventures Beyond Yellowstone** (© 406/848-7287; www.abyellowstone.com) offers horseback trips in the park for groups of four or more; coming from the south side of the park, try **Press Stephens, Outfitter** (© 307/455-2250), in Dubois.

While not a horseback excursion per se, you might also try **Yellowstone Llamas** (© **406/586-6872;** www.yellowstone-llamas.com). Beasts of burden carry the heavy gear, leaving you free to wander the trails. They typically cover 5 to 8 miles per day, and serve gourmet meals with stream-chilled bottles of wine. Cost is $195 to $225 a day per adult, $145 to $175 for children 12 and under.

7 Winter Sports & Activities

Yellowstone's average snowfall of 4 feet every year provides the perfect backdrop for a multitude of winter activities. The north entrance remains open, so you can drive in from Gardiner for a day, and drive back out. You can travel throughout the park by snowmobile or Snowcoach, and spend the night either at Mammoth or at the handsomely rebuilt Old Faithful Snow Lodge. For additional information on all of the following winter activities and accommodations, as well as Snowcoach transportation and equipment rentals, contact **Xanterra Parks & Resorts** (© **307/344-7311**). There are also many activities, outfitters, and rental shops in the park's gateway towns.

CROSS-COUNTRY SKIING

The best cross-country trails in Yellowstone are the **Lonestar Geyser Trail,** a fairly level 5-mile round-trip through a remote setting, starting at the Old Faithful Snow Lodge, and the **Fern Cascades Trail,** which begins in the Old Faithful housing area on the south side of the road and winds for 3 miles through a rolling wooded landscape. Energetic skiers can tackle the 12-mile **Mallard Lake Trail,** though it may take them all day—it departs north of the Old Faithful Lodge area along the north side of the Upper Geyser Basin, then loops north and east to Mallard Lake and back to Old Faithful.

Equipment rentals, ski instruction, ski shuttles to various locations, and guided ski tours are all available at the **Old Faithful Snow Lodge** and the **Mammoth Hot Springs Hotel,** the park's two winter lodging options. Discounts are available for multiday rentals of skis or snowshoes. Ski instruction costs around $25 per person for a

---

Snowmobiling: To Ban or Not to Ban?

Before President Clinton left office in 2001, he "ended" the ongoing controversy by establishing a ban on snowmobiles in Yellowstone, effective beginning the winter of 2003–04. However, gateway communities and snowmobile manufacturers responded with lawsuits, and the Bush administration also voiced its opposition to a total ban, delighting the outfitters in West Yellowstone and Cody. In mid-2004, just 3 months later, a judge overturned a ruling enforcing the ban.

All of this means that through the winter of 2006–07, snowmobiles will continue to ramble through Yellowstone and Grand Teton; all trips will continue to be guided by licensed outfitters with a daily quota of 720 machines; and the technology will continue to meet best-available standards. If a new plan is not approved by 2007, snowmobiles will be phased out. If you're planning a trip, you can get up-to-date information by calling © **307/344-2580** or visiting www.nps.gov/yell.

2-hour group lesson; a full-day guided excursion costs $65 to $115 per person (lunch may or may not be included).

The **Yellowstone Association Institute** ✿✿✿ (✆ **307/344-2294**) offers winter courses throughout the park. Past offerings have included 3-day classes devoted to wintertime photography, cross-country skiing, and the ecology of wolf reintroduction. The institute's faculty and staff are a knowledgeable and friendly bunch, and a class is one of the best ways to acquaint yourself with the park in any season.

ICE SKATING

The **Mammoth Hot Springs ice rink** is located behind the old Mammoth Hot Springs Recreation Center. On a winter's night you can rent a pair of skates ($1 an hour; $4 per day) and glide across the ice of this outdoor rink, while seasonal melodies are broadcast over the PA system. It's cold out there, but there's a warming fire at the rink's edge.

SNOWMOBILING

Roads that are jammed with cars during the summer fill up with snowmobiles (assuming that they haven't been banned) and bison during the winter. In deference to the shaggier road warriors, moderate speed limits are strictly enforced, but this is still an excellent way to sightsee at your own pace. A driver's license is required for rental ($170 for a single rider, $180 per day for two at **Mammoth Hot Springs Hotel** or **Old Faithful Snow Lodge**), as is a guide ($215 per group for a custom day trip, rentals not included, or $210 per person for a regularly scheduled trip, rental included). A helmet is included with the snowmobile, and you can rent a clothing package for protection against the bitter cold. **Warming huts** are located at Mammoth, Indian Creek, Canyon, Madison, West Thumb, and Fishing Bridge. They offer snacks, a hot cup of coffee or chocolate, and an excellent opportunity to recover from a chill. *Caution:* Keep an eye on snow conditions. While it's true that snowmobile trails are groomed for travel, when snow cover is scanty, a normally smooth trip can become something akin to riding on a jackhammer.

Snowmobile rentals are also available in the **gateway communities** of Gardiner and West Yellowstone, Montana, and at **Flagg Ranch Snowmobiles,** at the south entrance to Yellowstone (✆ **800/443-2311**). Most rental shops accept reservations weeks in advance, so reserving at least 2 weeks ahead of time is a good idea. Plan on making reservations for the week between Christmas and New Year's at least 6 months in advance.

8 Hiking

Getting your car snarled in one "wildlife jam" after another in pursuit of a glimpse of one of the park's four-legged denizens is one way to enjoy the outdoors. Another is taking a hike, even a short one, because you'll see a whole new side of the park. There are gentle hikes where you never lose sight of the road; moderate hikes where you might spend an afternoon penetrating the forest to visit a spot of secluded beauty; and overnight trips where you can hike and camp for days without seeing anyone but the people who embarked on the journey with you.

Part of the reason so few people hike and camp in the Yellowstone wilderness is fear of bears. Bear attacks are extremely rare, and usually involve a sow protecting her cubs, but you should carry pepper spray, just in case; when you camp, secure your food and cooking gear in a tree well away from tents. Park rangers can advise you on current bear activity and safe practices. This is true wilderness, but if you equip yourself properly and learn proper techniques, you'll be safer than you are on a city street. If you go into the backcountry, you need a permit (see "Where to Go & How to Reserve a Spot," below), which also ensures that someone knows where you are.

For those who would rather sleep in a bed, there are still excellent day hikes that allow you to escape the crowd and view wildlife in its own habitat, take in the scenery, or climb a peak. Rangers at visitor centers can advise you on a hike to match your interests and abilities, and provide maps of the extensive trail system in the park. Besides a good map, always bring a good supply of water (and, if you can, a purifier or iodine pills) and rain gear.

Here is a small selection of good hikes, long and short. In addition to these individual hikes, the **Continental Divide Trail (CDT)** links many of them together as part of a continuous trail from Mexico to Canada, roughly following the spine of the continent. The Yellowstone Backcountry Office maintains a guide to CDT trails. The Howard Eaton Trail system once went all through the park, but was supplanted by the Grand Loop Road. Sections of the old trail are still maintained and will be found in trail guides, though some of them closely parallel park roads. For a more extensive list of trails and details than what follows here, pick up longtime ranger Mark C. Marschall's excellent *Yellowstone Trails* (Yellowstone Association, $9.95), or the maps provided by the park.

HIKES AROUND MAMMOTH

The **Beaver Ponds Loop Trail** starts in Mammoth at Clematis Gulch (between Liberty Cap and an old stone Park Service residence) and makes a 5-mile loop to a series of beaver ponds, where your best chances of seeing the big-tailed beasts are early morning or afternoon. There are some good views coming and going, including Mount Everts. More ambitious hikers can link up with the **Sepulcher Mountain Trail,** which features hot springs, gardens of oddly shaped limestone boulders, and scenic views from the ridges of the Mammoth area. Be in shape for this one and bring a good map of the crisscrossing trail system, because you'll cover at least 12 miles, depending on your route.

Nearby is the **Bunsen Peak Trail** ⭐⭐, a short but steep trip to the summit of this volcanic remnant, with a 1,300-foot gain in elevation. Make the hike early and you can watch the morning sun strike Electric Peak, which glows with a golden hue. The 2-mile trail passes through mosaic burns from the 1988 fires, and when you get to the top you'll have a view from 3,000 feet above the Yellowstone Valley. After topping the peak, you can take an alternative route down Bunsen's east side and come back along the Old Bunsen Peak Road Trail for a 6-mile round trip. If you're looking for more, hike the **Osprey Falls Trail** ⭐ and add 3 miles down a series of switchbacks for a great view of a 150-foot waterfall to the trek.

HIKES IN THE TOWER-CANYON AREA

The **Tower Falls** overlook is easy to get to; it's only 300 feet from the Tower Falls parking area. Walk .5 mile more along some steep switchbacks and you'll be at the less crowded base of the falls for a stunning view. You can also hike 3.5 miles to the falls from Roosevelt Lodge, a good car-free choice if you happen to be staying there. Begin on the **Lost Lake Trail** and take a left when the trail forks .5 mile from the lodge.

Just south of Canyon Village, the **Chittenden Bridge** crosses from the Loop Road to the South Rim Road near the top of the Grand Canyon of the Yellowstone. You can park and hike either the **South Rim** or **North Rim trail,** with spurs that drop steeply

Finds   An Old Faithful Secret

For a spectacular view of Old Faithful from above, take the **Observation Point Look Trail** ☆, a 2-mile jaunt (beginning at the Old Faithful Visitor Center) that will take you by numerous thermal features on the other side of the Firehole River. Follow the Geyser Hill Trail across the river and then climb the switchbacks to the observation point to watch Old Faithful burst in relative solitude.

(but briefly) down to viewing platforms at the Upper and Lower falls. If you want a more complete and less crowded view of this deep gorge, take the **7-mile Hole Trail** (which is actually 5.5 miles long) along the north canyon rim. You'll see the Silver Cord Cascade from the rim, and then drop down to the river after a couple of miles in an area where the canyon widens enough for trees. There are some active hot springs along this hike. This is quite a drop (1,400 ft.), and hikers should be prepared for a fairly demanding climb out.

Across the road from Uncle Tom's Trail parking area (the first parking area to the left after crossing the bridge to the South Rim) is the trail head for the **Clear Lake/ Ribbon Lake Loop Trail** ☆. The hike to Clear Lake is 1.5 miles, a gradual climb across a high plateau, and Ribbon Lake lies less than 2 miles beyond. Bears are often active in this area early in the year, so check with rangers for current conditions before heading out. Views of the plateau improve with each footstep, until you find yourself surrounded by a panoramic view of the mountains surrounding the canyon area. During early and late spring it's a bit more difficult because snow runoff and rain can make trails wet and muddy, but that shouldn't be an impediment to anyone interested in the spectacular views. Clear Lake itself is intimately small, and gives you the opportunity to see subsurface activity of the thermal areas below the lake. On a circumnavigation of the lake along a trail, you will see—and smell—venting activity making its way to the surface; in some spots the lake looks like a boiling pot. This trail also connects to the **Howard Eaton Trail,** an arduous, 14-mile trail to Fishing Bridge and Yellowstone Lake.

The **Mount Washburn Trail** ☆☆☆ falls into the "if you can only do one hike, do this one" category. It's a short hike to panoramic views, with wildflowers decorating the way and nonchalant bighorn sheep often browsing nearby. Trail heads are located at the summit at Dunraven Pass (elevation 8,859 ft.), and on Old Chittenden Road, where there's more parking available. Either hike is 6 miles round-trip, with an increase in elevation of 1,400 feet; however, the climbs are fairly gradual and interspersed with long, level stretches. From the summit, the park will lie before you like a map on a table: You'll see the Absaroka Mountains to the east, Yellowstone Lake to the south, and the Gallatin Mountains to the west and north. In addition to sheep, you may see marmots and red fox; bears have also made use of the area in recent years. You'll be climbing a summit that's 10,243 feet, so pace yourself, and bring warm clothing to fend off the storms that often buffet the top. The hike to the summit is an easy 90-minute walk at a steady pace, which can stretch to 2 hours if you take time for breaks. There's a day-use shelter in the base of the ranger lookout, with viewing telescopes and restrooms.

HIKES NEAR OLD FAITHFUL

The popular trail to **Lonestar Geyser** covers a little more than 2 miles of mostly level terrain to the geyser, which rewards visitors with eruptions up to 50 feet tall every 3 hours. The trail follows the Firehole River, with a forest canopy to keep it cool in the summer, widening now and then into broad riverbank meadows. The geyser erupts from a brown cone about 12 feet high, and is surrounded by a meadow pocked by steam vents and thermal features. The path begins from a parking lot on the Old Faithful–West Thumb road just south of the Kepler Cascades. It's partially paved to the geyser and open to bicyclists. If you want to try a less busy (and less scenic) route, take the **Howard Eaton Trail** just east of the Old Faithful overpass, 3 miles to the geyser. From the geyser, you can continue on—bicycles can't—over Grants Pass to join the Bechler River Trail to Shoshone Lake.

From the Biscuit Basin parking lot, you can take a fine 3-mile round-trip hike to **Mystic Falls,** which fall 100 feet to the Firehole River. Continue up switchbacks to the top of the falls and beyond, and you'll link up with the **Little Firehole Meadows Trail** to return to Biscuit Basin, with more views on the way. You can make this trip in less than 2 hours, with only a 460-foot elevation gain.

Fairy Falls plummets a more impressive 200 feet, and can be reached by hiking 2.5 miles on the Fairy Falls Trail, which begins from the Old Faithful–Madison road just south of the Midway Geyser Basin parking area. Hikers who don't mind a slightly longer haul (about 8 miles round-trip) will be rewarded with better wildlife-viewing opportunities by starting from the **Imperial Meadows** trail head a mile south of the Firehole River bridge on Fountain Flat Drive. The hike winds through an area populated by elk along Fairy Creek, then past the Imperial Geyser, where it joins the Fairy Creek Trail and travels east to the base of the falls. The total gain in elevation is only 100 feet. If you turn west instead, you'll find an unmarked trail north to the Imperial Geyser.

HIKES NEAR YELLOWSTONE LAKE

At the north end of the lake, the **Pelican Valley Trail** takes a loop north of the lake around an area loaded with elk, bison, sandhill cranes, trout, eagles, grizzlies, and the new kids on the block, wolves. You can take hikes of different length, up to a 16-mile loop, but a lot of folks, having had their fill of wildflowers and beasts, go no farther than Pelican Creek Bridge, a 7-mile round-trip. If you continue on, you'll pass through forest and "bear meadows." This is a daytime-only hiking area (9am–7pm), and it's closed in the early summer until July 4 because of bear activity.

The **Elephant Back Loop Trail** ✿ is an opportunity to get a bird's-eye view of the island-dotted expanse of Yellowstone Lake, the Absaroka Mountains, and the Pelican Valley—and maybe a moose. It's a great photo opportunity and a fairly easy 4-mile loop, beginning a mile south of Fishing Bridge Junction off the road to Lake Village.

You can walk along the north shore of Yellowstone Lake on the **Storm Point Trail** ✿ (be aware that it's occasionally closed due to grizzly bear activity). This easy, level 2-miler terminates at a point jutting into the lake where you'll find lovely panoramic views. It begins in the Indian Pond area, 3½ miles east of Fishing Bridge directly across from the Pelican Valley trail head.

HIKES TO REMOTE AREAS & OVERNIGHT BACKCOUNTRY TRIPS

The **Bechler Meadows Trail** enters the southwest corner of the park, an area rich in waterfalls, cascades, and thermal features rarely seen by human eyes. The access is by Idaho 47 from Ashton, Idaho, which will take you to the Bechler Ranger Station in the southwest corner of the park. About 5 miles into the hike, the trail makes several fords of the river as it enters Bechler Canyon, passing Collonade Falls and Iris Falls. There are places on this trail where you can view the Grand Tetons in the distance, and some thermal features bubble and churn on the Bechler River's banks. This is a camping trip—you can cover nearly 30 miles if you hike all the way into the Old Faithful area—best made late in the summer to avoid high water during creek crossings. You'll need a backcountry permit for overnight stays (see "Camping," below).

The **Slough Creek Trail,** which begins in the Lamar Valley of the park's northeast corner, takes hikers through some of the best wildlife habitat in the park. You can see elk, bison, trumpeter swans, the occasional grizzly bear, and the wolves that have quite

(Tips) Wilderness U.: Guided Backpacking with the Yellowstone Association Institute

The Yellowstone Association Institute (YAI) uses the park's backcountry as a 2.4-million-acre classroom for many of its 400 annual classes. In fact, a number of courses are guided backpacking trips into the Yellowstone wilderness.

I recently went on a YAI expedition with about 10 other customers, following the same route the Nez Perce Indians took through Yellowstone in summer 1877 while evading the U.S. Army. The 4-day adventure—which was preceded by a day in an indoor classroom in Gardiner—traversed 40 miles under the leadership of an experienced backcountry guide and park historian Lee Whittlesey, whose wry humor nicely complemented his historical insight.

We learned about the obstacles the Nez Perce faced en route to their ultimate surrender in Montana. Under the leadership of Chief Joseph, 600 to 800 people, including a good number of children and elderly persons, evaded capture from June into October, cutting through a slice of the fledgling national park known as Yellowstone in the process.

We learned about the rugged terrain the Nez Perce crossed and differing accounts of their exact path through the park. And we learned about wolf tracks. And about the "leave no trace" etiquette upheld by backcountry enthusiasts.

Most of all, we learned that the flight of the Nez Perce has been the key event in the tribe's history since 1877. The 5-month ordeal haunts many of its members to this day.

The "Flight of the Nez Perce" backcountry course has become a staple in the YAI catalog, along with guided backpacking classes about wolves, grizzly bears, waterfalls, photography, and the microbes that inhabit the park's thermal features. It's a great way to educate yourself on the topic, not to mention the ins and outs of backpacking, and you'll meet a bunch of like-minded Yellowstone lovers in the process. Trips typically last 4 days to a week and cost $400 to $700 per person. You need to bring most of your own gear. Call © 307/344-2294 or visit www.yellowstoneassociation.org for a course catalog and other information.

happily taken up residence among abundant prey. The presence of wolves has made this area more popular, and the trail is also used by horse-packers. The trail starts from the road to Slough Creek campground, following the creek's valley north, then crossing a ridge to a second valley. You can hike a few miles, or take your camping gear and head for the park boundary, 11 miles to the north.

The **Thorofare Trail** follows the eastern shore of Yellowstone Lake and then skirts the Yellowstone River up into some of the most remote and beautiful backcountry in the Rockies. It's a long, steep trail, but you'll be rewarded with views of the Upper Yellowstone Valley, Two Oceans Plateau, and abundant wildlife. Eventually you'll reach a gorgeous alpine valley just outside the park's boundary, with a ranger station known as Hawk's Rest. Fishermen love this area, as do grizzly bears, especially during the cutthroat trout–spawning season. This is the most remote roadless area in the Lower 48, a good 30 miles from the trail head at the lake, and even the most capable hikers should consider riding with an outfitter. You can cut 9 miles off the trip by getting a boat shuttle (about $280 round-trip with a maximum capacity of six people) to the mouth of the lake's southeast arm (call the marina at © **307/242-3893**), or you can come in through the Bridger-Teton National Forest to the south (check with the forest's Blackrock Ranger Station in Moran, Wyoming; © **307/543-2386**).

9 Camping

WHERE TO GO & HOW TO RESERVE A SPOT

The National Park Service has shifted management of five major campgrounds to Xanterra Parks & Resorts, the park concessionaire, which means, predictably, higher fees, but also allows you to make reservations ahead of arrival. The other seven campgrounds still managed by the park are available only on a first-come, first-served basis. These lower-cost campgrounds ($12–$14 per night) are located at Indian Creek, Lewis Lake, Mammoth, Norris, Pebble Creek, Slough Creek, and Tower Fall. We like Lewis Lake and Indian Creek, which tend to be available when others are full. Check with rangers about campsite availability when you enter the park; some campgrounds fill up as early as 8am.

Xanterra Parks & Resorts operates the large campgrounds at Bridge Bay, Canyon, Grant Village, Madison, and Fishing Bridge, where the fees are $17 per night. The **Fishing Bridge RV Park** is the only campground equipped with water, sewer, and electrical hookups for RVs and trailers, though it accepts hard-sided vehicles only (no tents or tent trailers), and the fees are $33 per night. The **Madison campground** is the first to open in early May, while **Grant Village** is closed until mid-June to avoid bear conflicts during trout-spawning season. These campgrounds are usually busier, and some, like Bridge Bay, are rather barren of trees unless you get a site on the fringes. Most campgrounds close in September, but Madison is open until mid-October, and Mammoth is year-round. If you plan to travel in July or August, make your reservations 6 months ahead of time by calling © **307/344-7311;** by writing **Xanterra Parks & Resorts,** P.O. Box 165, Yellowstone National Park, WY 82190; or by visiting **www.travelyellowstone.com**.

Camping is allowed only in designated areas and visitors are limited to 14 days between June 15 and Labor Day, and to 30 days the rest of the year, except at Fishing Bridge, where there is no limit. Checkout time for all campgrounds is 10am. Quiet hours are strictly enforced between the hours of 8pm and 8am.

There are plenty of opportunities for backcountry camping as well. Some areas in the Yellowstone backcountry include delicate habitat—the southeast arm of Yellowstone Lake is an example—and visitors must camp in designated areas for a limited time only. Check with the **Yellowstone Backcountry office** (© 307/344-2160) for rules, reservations, and advice.

WHAT TO EXPECT

Remember, these are campgrounds, not motels, so the amenities are spare. But some have showers and bathrooms and potable water. Check the chart below to determine the level of comfort at each campground. Showers and laundry facilities are available at Canyon, Fishing Bridge, and Grant Village campgrounds. In addition, campers may use the shower and laundry facilities at Lake Lodge and Old Faithful Lodge.

In the northeast area of the park, the **Tower Fall campground** is near a convenience store, restaurant, and gas station at Tower Lodge, 19 miles north of Canyon Village and 18 miles east of Mammoth. **Slough Creek campground** ⚡ is located in a remote section of the Lamar Valley near the northeast entrance; the good news is there are fewer people, good fishing, and the possibility of wolf sightings; the bad news is that restroom facilities are pit toilets. **Canyon campground** is the busiest in the park. Sites are in a heavily wooded area; the store, restaurants, visitor center, and laundry at Canyon Center are nearby. Because it's in an area of spring bear activity, attempts have been made over the years to close the RV park at **Fishing Bridge.** It's still open, but only hard-sided camping vehicles are allowed here. **Bridge Bay** is located near the shores of Yellowstone Lake, so you get tremendous views, especially at sunrise and sunset. Unfortunately, though surrounded by the forest, much of the area has been clear-cut, so there's not a whole lot of privacy. It's close to boat-launching facilities and the boat-rental operation. **Madison** ⚡ and **Norris campgrounds** are attractive, wooded locations in the heart of the park, close to wildlife activity, hiking trails, and rivers. These camp areas seem less like outdoor motels than the big campgrounds on the park's east side.

Amenities for Each Campground in Yellowstone National Park (Where Flush Toilets Are Not Available, Vault Toilets Are Provided)

Campground	# Sites	Fee	Showers/ Laundry	Flush Toilets	Disposal Stations	Generators Permitted
Bridge Bay*	432	$17	No	Yes	Yes	Yes
Canyon*	272	$17	Yes	Yes	Yes	Yes
Fishing Bridge*	344	$33	Yes	Yes	Yes	Yes
Grant Village*	425	$17	Yes	Yes	Yes	Yes
Indian Creek	75	$12	No	No	No	No
Lewis Lake	85	$12	No	No	No	No
Madison*	277	$17	No	No	Yes	Yes
Mammoth	85	$14	No	No	Yes	No
Norris	116	$14	No	No	Yes	No
Pebble Creek	32	$12	No	No	No	No
Slough Creek	29	$12	No	No	No	No
Tower Fall	32	$12	No	No	No	No

*Reserve through Xanterra Parks & Resorts, © **307/344-7311;** TDD 307/344-5395; **www.travelyellowstone.com.**

10 Where to Stay in the Park

For accommodations listings just outside the park, see section 1, "The Gateway Towns: West Yellowstone, Gardiner & Cooke City," at the beginning of this chapter.

The first thing you should know: no televisions. Private bathrooms have arrived and phones are in place, but televisions are in only two rooms in the entire park (the suites at Mammoth).

Railroad companies built most of the park's hotels and lodges around the start of the 20th century, and they would offer their primped Victorian guests a package tour that delivered them by train and stagecoach to luxurious resorts with rocking chairs on the verandas and gourmet food. A good deal of that old-style ambience has been thankfully retained at Yellowstone. Many of the newer facilities erected by the park concessionaire (in particular, the Old Faithful Snow Lodge and the new lodges at Canyon) are suitably matched to older buildings, at least on the exterior. However, the push for more features may come in the near future, and, during recent upgrades at the Lake Hotel, the wiring was installed for televisions—just in case. Many of the hotels provide beautiful examples of architecture and craftsmanship, but they're not perfect: The plaster walls transmit some sound and the bathrooms tend to be smallish. However, even the most budget-conscious traveler will find a room in the park that fits the pocketbook. Look over the descriptions below carefully, though, because some of the cheaper lodgings are primitive indeed.

Canyon Lodge and Cabins   This complex is one of the newer facilities in the park (Cascade and Dunraven lodges here both were completed in the 1990s), but it can't escape the considerable human activity in sprawling Canyon Village. However, the lodges are located a mere half-mile from the Grand Canyon of the Yellowstone and Inspiration Point, one of the most photographed spots in the park. Cascade Lodge offers simple rooms appointed with tasteful log furnishings in the three-story building; the newer Dunraven is similar, although it is more modern (with an elevator); both are located adjacent to a woodland setting. There are also clusters of cabins scattered throughout the village: clean, motel-style configurations. The cabins are single-story duplex and four-plex structures with private bathrooms that are among the largest in the park. They're a bit weathered but generally acceptable; given the sheer number of units involved, this isn't the place to "get away from it all."

In Canyon Village (P.O. Box 165), Yellowstone National Park, WY 82190. © **307/344-7311**. Fax 307/344-7456. www.travelyellowstone.com. 605 units. $142 double; $45–$132 cabin. AE, DC, DISC, MC, V. Closed Oct to late May. **Amenities:** Restaurant; lounge; activities desk; self-serve laundry. *In room:* No phone.

Tips Making Reservations

Yellowstone accommodations are normally open from May to mid-October. The winter season begins in mid-December and runs through March, with accommodations and meals available at either Mammoth Hot Springs or Old Faithful Snow Lodge and Cabins. Vacancy increases before June 20 and after September 25. Rooms are typically fully booked during the peak season in July and August, so reservations should be made up to a few months in advance. For information or reservations at any of the locations within the park, contact **Xanterra Parks & Resorts** at P.O. Box 165, Yellowstone National Park, WY 82190 (© **307/344-7311**; www.travelyellowstone.com).

Grant Village   The southernmost of the major overnight accommodations in the park, Grant Village was completed in 1984 and is one of the more contemporary choices in Yellowstone. It's not as architecturally distinctive as the Old Faithful options, consisting of six condo-style units (with motel-style rooms), but it's also less touristy and more isolated. Rooms are tastefully furnished, most outfitted with light wood furniture, track lighting, electric heat, and laminated counters. Nicer and more expensive rooms affording lake views have mullioned windows, one queen-size or one or two double beds, and full bathrooms.

On the West Thumb of Yellowstone Lake (P.O. Box 165), Yellowstone National Park, WY 82190. ⓒ 307/344-7311. Fax 307/344-7456. www.travelyellowstone.com. 300 units. $116–$120 double. AE, DC, DISC, MC, V. Closed late Sept to late May. **Amenities:** Restaurant; lounge; activities desk.

Lake Lodge Cabins *Value*   These cabins surrounding Lake Lodge stand near the lake, a relatively quiet, traffic-free area just around the corner from the Lake Yellowstone Hotel. The old Western lodge's most attractive feature is a large porch with wicker rockers that invite visitors to sit and gaze out across the water. The accommodations are in well-preserved, clean, free-standing cabins near a trout stream that threads through a wooded area. (There are nature walks around the lodge, but this is a trout spawning area, so access is usually restricted early in the summer when grizzlies emerge from hibernation.)

These cabins come in two grades: **Western** cabins provide electric heat, paneled walls, two double beds (and, in some cases, an extra twin), and combination bathrooms, while **Pioneer** cabins are smaller and sparsely furnished, with one or two double beds each and small shower-only bathrooms. A number of the cabins here have been recently renovated, making them among the freshest in the park and a good deal for the money. You'll need to head outdoors to enjoy the lake views, as the only things you can see from your cabin are other cabins. Because the dining room here is a tad short on atmosphere, you might want to make the short trek to the Lake Yellowstone Hotel for a more sumptuous meal in a more appetizing setting.

On Lake Yellowstone (P.O. Box 165), Yellowstone National Park, WY 82190. ⓒ 307/344-7311. Fax 307/344-7456. www.travelyellowstone.com. 186 cabins. $61 Pioneer cabin; $121 Western cabin. AE, DC, DISC, MC, V. Closed mid-Sept to early June. **Amenities:** Restaurant; lounge; activities desk; self-serve laundry. *In room:* No phone.

Lake Yellowstone Hotel and Cabins *🏞🏞*   The ionic columns, dormer windows, and deep porticos on this classic yellow building faithfully recall the year it was built: 1891. It's an entirely different world from the rustic Western style of other park lodgings. The facility was restored in the early 1990s, and its better rooms are the most comfortable and roomy in the park, with soul-stirring views of the massive lake.

The three- and four-story wings house the hotel rooms, and there's also a motel-style annex and an assortment of cabins. The upper-end rooms here are especially lavish for Yellowstone, with stenciled walls and traditional spreads on one queen-size or two double beds. Smaller rooms in the annex are fitted with two double beds and bring to mind a typical motel chain. The free-standing yellow-clad cabins here are a lower-priced alternative, decorated with knotty-pine paneling, and furnished with double beds and a writing table. A number of them were nicely renovated in 2004, making them among the best cabins in the park.

On the north side of the lake (P.O. Box 165), Yellowstone National Park, WY 82190. ⓒ 307/344-7311. Fax 307/344-7456. www.travelyellowstone.com. 300 units. $124–$200 double; $101 cabin; $443 suite. AE, DC, DISC, MC, V. Closed early Oct to mid-May. **Amenities:** 2 restaurants; lounge; activities desk; self-serve laundry. *In room:* No phone (cabins).

⟨Tips⟩ Rooms with a View

When staying at the **Old Faithful Inn,** if you want to watch the geyser erupt from your room, ask for suite no. 3014 or room no. 229. The suite is the "best in the house," with a spacious bathroom, bedroom, and sitting room, and goes for $390 a night. Room no. 229 is a high corner room with views of Old Faithful and the geyser basin, and because it's one of the older rooms, it costs only $81 a night. The problem with no. 229 is that you have to plan far ahead: People vie for this room, and you probably won't get it if you don't reserve it a year before your visit.

Mammoth Hot Springs Hotel and Cabins ⟨★⟩   Below the steaming terraces of Mammoth Hot Springs, this is one of two Yellowstone hotels open during both summer and winter seasons. (The other is the Old Faithful Snow Lodge.) Established in 1911, the hotel itself is less distinguished than the Lake Yellowstone Hotel or the Old Faithful Inn, but it manages to blend a wide range of rooms into a satisfying whole. Make sure you drift into the **Map Room** (named for the massive inlaid map of the United States on one of the broad paneled walls), a great place to while away an evening reading or listening to a pianist.

The only truly high-end accommodations are the suites. Standard rooms and cabins are arranged around three grassy areas, offering minimal amenities with a fair amount of charm. Some rooms have tubs only, some rooms have showers only, and some share a bathroom down the hall. The cottage-style cabins are clustered in rings adjacent to the hotel, and vary in quality; some are a bit rough, others have sun decks and hot tubs.

At Mammoth Hot Springs (P.O. Box 165), Yellowstone National Park, WY 82190. ⟨✆⟩ **307/344-7311.** Fax 307/344-7456. www.travelyellowstone.com. 212 units. $75–$107 double; $65–$100 cabin; $164 cabin with hot tub; $301 suite. AE, DC, DISC, MC, V. **Amenities:** 2 restaurants; lounge; activities desk. *In room:* No phone (cabins).

Old Faithful Inn ⟨★★★⟩   There are three hotels within viewing distance of the geyser, including a very nice new one, but this is undoubtedly the crown jewel of Yellowstone's man-made wonders. Seven stories tall with dormers peaking from a shingled, steep-sloping roof, it's an architectural wonder that was designed by Robert Reamer to blend into the natural environment—and it's been the place to stay in Yellowstone for a century, first welcoming guests in 1904.

The cavernous, log-laden lobby is striking, with an ambience that is half elegant palace and half rugged wilderness lodge. You can climb the stairs to its internal balconies, but seismic activity eventually closed the crow's nest, where a chamber orchestra initially performed for the well-dressed guests below. Only 30 miles from the west entrance and 40 miles from the south entrance, this is the first place visitors think of when they want a bed for the night, so make reservations far ahead during the busy summer months.

Guest rooms are in the main building and in wings that flank the main lodge. Original rooms are basic, appointed with conservative fabrics and park-theme art, but they might not have private bathrooms; the wing rooms offer better facilities and more privacy.

Note: Due to an ongoing renovation, the Inn had a short season in 2005, and plans called for it to be closed for part of the 2006 summer as well. Call for current information.

At Old Faithful (P.O. Box 165), Yellowstone National Park, WY 82190. ☎ **307/344-7311.** Fax 307/344-7456. www. travelyellowstone.com. 327 units. $81 double without bathroom; $106–$197 double with bathroom; $290–$390 suite. AE, DC, DISC, MC, V. Closed mid-Oct to mid-May. **Amenities:** 2 restaurants; lounge; activities desk. *In room:* No phone.

Old Faithful Lodge Cabins *Value*

These are the leftovers from the days when crude cabins littered the landscape around the world's most famous geyser. The ones closest to the geyser were hauled away years ago, but you still get a sense of what tourism was like in the park's early days, especially if you rent one of the **budget cabins,** which are just slightly less flimsy than tents and have basic beds and sinks, no more. Showers and restrooms are a short walk away. **Frontier cabins** are the better units, adding a private bathtub to other amenities. If amenities are irrelevant, these rustic, thin-walled cabins are an economical way to put a roof over your head in the park. The lodge is perhaps the busiest spot in the geyser area, featuring several snack shops and a huge cafeteria dishing up varied fast food.

At Old Faithful (P.O. Box 165), Yellowstone National Park, WY 82190. ☎ **307/344-7311.** Fax 307/344-7456. www. travelyellowstone.com. 96 cabins, some without private bathroom. $57–$85 double. AE, DC, DISC, MC, V. Closed mid-Sept to mid-May. **Amenities:** 2 restaurants; activities desk. *In room:* No phone.

Old Faithful Snow Lodge and Cabins *★★*

The rickety dormitory-style Snow Lodge is no more: It was torn down in 1998 to make way for this new, award-winning structure that could aptly be called the New Faithful Snow Lodge. Its contemporary big-beam construction and high ceiling in the lobby echo the Old Faithful Inn, and a copper-lined balcony curves above the common area, where guests can relax in wicker furniture. The designers paid attention to every last detail: The public areas have a contemporary (but appropriate) style, some of the lodge's wood was recycled from the actual mill that provided the lumber for the Old Faithful Inn in 1904, and wrought-iron bears are a prevalent touch. The modern rooms are spacious and comfortable, second only to the upper-end accommodations at the Lake Hotel. There's also a small collection of surrounding cabins with motel-style furnishings (many of which were built after the 1988 fires).

At Old Faithful (P.O. Box 165), Yellowstone National Park, WY 82190. ☎ **307/344-7311.** Fax 307/344-7456. www. travelyellowstone.com. 134 units. $161 double; $83–$128 cabin. AE, DC, DISC, MC, V. Closed mid-Oct to mid-Dec and mid-Mar to early May. **Amenities:** Restaurant; lounge; activities desk. *In room:* No phone (cabins).

Roosevelt Lodge Cabins *★* *Kids*

This is considered the park's family hideaway, a low-key operation with dinky, primitive cabins, stables, and a lodge restaurant that feels like a big ranch house. The bare-bones cabins are called Roughriders, and they're furnished with two simple beds, clean linens, a writing table, and a wood stove. A step up, the Frontier cabins have their own bathrooms and showers. The lodge is a rugged but charming stone edifice, its large, inviting porch outfitted with rockers so guests can sit back and watch the world go by. Stagecoach rides, horseback trips, and Western trail cookouts give this place a cowboy flavor, and it's a less hectic scene than the other park villages.

At Tower Junction (P.O. Box 165), Yellowstone National Park, WY 82190. ☎ **307/344-7311.** Fax 307/344-7456. 80 cabins, 14 with private bathroom. $57–$100 cabin. AE, DC, DISC, MC, V. Closed early Sept to June. **Amenities:** Restaurant; lounge; activities desk. *In room:* No phone.

11 Where to Dine in the Park

While they're not world-class establishments, Yellowstone's restaurants are well suited to their location and the appetites of their patrons: The portions definitely won't leave anyone going hungry. Most of the menus include a selection of unadventurous, all-American meat-and-potatoes grub alongside several more creative entrees. Consistency can be a problem, because the volume is high and the kitchen staffs are seasonal.

If you're not up for restaurant dining, but you don't want to cook over your camp stove the whole time, there is counter-style fast-food service at the **Yellowstone Park General Stores** as well as snack shops and cafeterias at Canyon, Mammoth, Grant Village, Lake Lodge, and Old Faithful. Try the new **Geyser Grill** at the Old Faithful Snow Lodge, or the old lunch-counter scene at the **Fishing Bridge Yellowstone Park General Store.** The **Glacier Pit Snack Bar** is a nostalgic breakfast counter at the Yellowstone Park General Store in the Canyon Lodge area, open from mid-May to late September.

Canyon Lodge Dining Room *(Kids* STEAKS/SEAFOOD   This is a spacious dining area, a tad sterile perhaps, and when it fills up, it's noisy. The salad bar is long and loaded, but otherwise the dinner fare is largely geared toward the carnivore, with a wide selection of steaks alongside some seafood and pasta selections. The breakfast buffet is a good way to start your day, with all the standard American fixings. The crowds can be large at Canyon Village, but there is a relaxed and unhurried feel to this place that you don't find at some of the park's other busy points. Families in particular might appreciate the ability to take their time with their meals.

At Canyon Lodge. (*C* 307/344-7901. Reservations required. Breakfast $4.50–$8.50; lunch $5.75–$9; dinner $9.25–$19. AE, DC, DISC, MC, V. June to mid-Sept daily 7–10:30am, 11:30am–2:30pm, and 5–10pm.

Grant Village *(* AMERICAN   Breakfast and lunch at the Grant Village restaurant are much like those at the other restaurants in the park, although the chef often surprises diners with interesting dinner items that stray from the norm. Lunch might include pan-fried trout covered with toasted pecans and lemon butter, huge burgers, and a top-notch chicken and tortilla-strip salad. The dinner menu ranges from huckleberry chicken to polenta lasagna to prime rib, but the specialty is trout, prepared in three creative ways: stuffed with crabmeat with jalapeño sauce, pan-fried with pecans, or sautéed with bacon and green onion. Quality and ambience here are comparable to those of the better dining rooms at the major park hotels.

At Grant Village. (*C* 307/344-7901. Dinner reservations required. Breakfast $4–$9; lunch $5–$8; dinner $9–$20. AE, DISC, MC, V. June–Sept daily 6:30–10am, 11:30am–2:30pm, and 5:30–10pm.

Lake Yellowstone Hotel *(*(* CONTINENTAL   This represents the finest dining Yellowstone has to offer, with a view of the lake stretching south from a vast dining room that doesn't feel crowded even when it's full. One of the best ways to start your day is with a generous breakfast buffet, but the huevos rancheros and pan-fried trout and eggs are also quite good. The dinner menu is even more inviting. Appetizers include crab cakes and lobster ravioli, while entrees include Idaho trout, bison prime rib, and, of course, several beef dishes.

The deli just off the hotel lobby by the dining room entrance serves lighter fare, including sandwiches, from an area slightly larger than a broom closet. Just down the road, the Yellowstone Park General Store offers three meals in a section of the store that is shared with tourist items; the best bets here are breakfast or a burger. Inexpensive meals are also served cafeteria-style at the Lake Lodge.

On the north side of the lake. ✆ 307/344-7901. Dinner reservations required. Breakfast $4.50–$11; lunch $5.75–$10; dinner $16–$33. AE, DC, DISC, MC, V. Mid-May to early Oct daily 6:30–10:30am, 11:30am–2:30pm, and 5–10pm.

Mammoth Hot Springs Dining Room ⛄ STEAKS/SEAFOOD
At Mammoth, there's a good balance between casual and formal because the dining room is reminiscent of an above-average neighborhood restaurant: comfortable and pleasant without too much of the hotel's Victorian past. The view of the Old Fort Yellowstone buildings and surrounding slopes is also quite enjoyable. The breakfast buffet is essentially identical to what you'll find here at other locations, featuring eggs, French toast, and the like. The lunch menu focuses on an array of sandwiches, including smoked turkey on Parmesan-crusted sourdough, a grilled vegetarian wrap, and grilled German bratwurst. The dinner menu is more substantial, with prime rib, salmon, and other upper-end standbys, and the house-smoked entrees are quite good.

At Mammoth Hot Springs. ✆ 307/344-7901. Dinner reservations required. Breakfast $4–$8.50; lunch $6–$9; dinner $9–$20. AE, DC, DISC, MC, V. Summer daily 6:30–10:30am, 11am–2:30pm, and 5–10pm.

Obsidian Dining Room ⛄ STEAKS/SEAFOOD
In the snazzy new Snow Lodge, a spacious restaurant provides a comparatively contemporary alternative to the dining room at the Old Faithful Inn. It's a little quieter, a little less expensive, and a little less formal. It still has some flash on the menu—braised lamb shank and polenta lasagna, for instance—and there is a breakfast gem in the Southwestern eggs. And this is the only place in the park that serves a leisurely breakfast until noon (albeit no lunch). All things considered, it's a huge improvement over the cramped restaurant of the old Snow Lodge.

At the Old Faithful Snow Lodge. ✆ 307/344-7901. Breakfast $4.50–$11; dinner $9–$20. AE, DC, DISC, MC, V. May to mid-Oct and mid-Dec to mid-Mar daily 6:30am–noon and 5–10pm.

Old Faithful Inn ⛄ STEAKS/SEAFOOD
The food notwithstanding, the true highlight is the gnarled log architecture of this distinguished historic inn. Breakfast is buffet or a la carte, and there's a lot to choose from. There's another buffet at lunchtime (headlined by barbecue beef and chicken), as well as a generous assortment of salads and sandwiches. The dinner menu is extensive, with four cuts of prime rib, several fish dishes, meatloaf, and pastas. The fare has gotten more distinguished in recent years, with such creative options as roasted pork loin with jalapeño cream sauce and shrimp scampi making regular appearances on the menu. However, the quality is woefully inconsistent, ranging from tremendous to mediocre on my visits in recent years.

At the Old Faithful Inn. ✆ 307/545-4999. Dinner reservations required. Breakfast $6–$9; lunch $5–$10; dinner $10–$25. AE, DC, DISC, MC, V. Mid-May to mid-Oct daily 6:30–10:30am, 11:30am–2:30pm, and 5–10pm.

Roosevelt Lodge STEAKS/SEAFOOD
This is supposed to be the cowboy alternative to the fancier cuisine served at the bigger Yellowstone hotels, but the unadventurous menu will win over only the most naive city slickers. For breakfast, it's eggs and flapjacks; lunch is burgers and sandwiches. Come suppertime, the Roosevelt beans are the standout because the short menu is dominated by middle-of-the-road American specialties, such as ribs and steaks. A better idea: Join Roosevelt's Old West Dinner Cookout, and ride by horse or wagon thorough the Pleasant Valley to a chuck-wagon dinner that includes cornbread, steak, watermelon, those famous beans, and apple crisp. It's a daily summer event (reservations required) that costs $60 to $70 for an adult, depending on the route of your horseback ride, or $50 if you go by wagon. Children pay $10 less.

At Tower Junction. ✆ 307/344-7901. Breakfast $3.25–$7; lunch $5.25–$9; dinner $9–$20. AE, DC, DISC, MC, V. July to early Sept daily 7–10:30am, 11:30am–4pm, and 5–9pm.

12

Jackson Hole & Grand Teton National Park

Grand Teton compares to Yellowstone somewhat the way a Generation X snowboarder compares to an old ski patrol graybeard: It's younger, flashier, and closer to the bars. The Tetons are a young mountain range in geologic time, and Grand Teton is a young national park, on the rolls in its present form since 1950; Yellowstone, by comparison, dates back to 1872. And whereas the geysers of Yellowstone are a pretty long drive from anywhere, you can come off a climb at Grand Teton and be in a posh Jackson eatery 20 minutes after you hit the valley floor.

That's not a knock on Grand Teton National Park. Jackson, after all, is a spiffy resort town with a little cowboy still in it. And within the park's borders are beautiful lakes and rivers, wildlife galore, and lots of recreational opportunities. In the summer, you can climb, hike, boat, balloon, backpack, raft, bird-watch, and fish. In winter, the park and nearby resorts become a magnet for skiers of every style and skill level. Jackson Hole Mountain Resort is upgrading furiously to keep its status as a premier national skier's destination, and its neighbor on the west side of the mountain, Grand Targhee, has some of the best powder in the Rockies.

1 Jackson Hole ✶✶

57 miles S of Yellowstone National Park; 432 miles NW of Cheyenne; 275 miles NE of Salt Lake City; 177 miles SW of Cody

Of the few communities in the Rockies that have successfully toed the line between promoting themselves as resort towns and retaining some semblance of indigenous character, Jackson is a standout. The million-dollar homes are sprouting all over the valley, but there is still open space, a memory of the cowboy past, and some resistance to letting in too much commercial glitz.

The remaining open spaces allow visitors to imagine what it was like early in the 19th century, when fur trappers first camped here. They were followed by ranchers, who soon became *dude* ranchers. Today, the community holds an interesting mixture of ski bums, blue bloods, nouveau riche, avid outdoor types, and even a few old-time cowboys. The cosmopolitans of this motley crew came not just with a hunger for scenery, but also with a taste for music, art, and good restaurants, too, and the selection here is unrivaled in Wyoming. The big ski hill lures a younger crowd, with the final ingredient for resort status—celebrities—supplied by transplants like Harrison Ford.

Jackson

ACCOMMODATIONS ■

Alpenhof Lodge **2**
Amangani **12**
Anvil Motel and Hostel **24**
Bentwood Inn **4**
Days Inn **6**
Four Seasons Resort
  Jackson Hole **2**
Hostelx **2**
Jackson Hole Lodge **13**
Motel 6 **8**
Red Lion Inn **9**
Rusty Parrot Lodge
  and Spa **18**
Snake River Lodge and Spa **2**
Spring Creek Ranch **11**
Super 8 **7**
Trapper 8 **26**
Virginian Lodge **10**
Wort Hotel **21**

DINING ◆

Bar T-5 **35**
Betty Rock Coffee House
  & Cafe **14**
Billy's Giant
  Hamburgers **23**
The Blue Lion **19**
Bubba's Bar-B-Que **15**
Burke's Chop House **22**
The Cadillac Grille **23**
Jedediah's House
  of Sourdough **30**
Koshu Wine Bar **16**
Mangy Moose **2**
Million Dollar Cowboy Bar **23**
Nani's Genuine Pasta House **27**
Nora's Fish Creek Inn **5**
Old Yellowstone Garage **28**
Rendezvous Bistro **6**
Shades Cafe **33**
Snake River Brewery **17**
Snake River Grill **31**
Stiegler's **1**
Sweetwater Restaurant **32**

ATTRACTIONS ●

Grand Targhee Ski Area **5**
Jackson Hole Museum **20**
Jackson Hole Mountain Resort **3**
National Elk Refuge **34**
National Museum of
  Wildlife Art **25**
Town Square **29**

307

Jackson or Jackson Hole—What's the Difference?

You'll likely see every kind of merchandise imaginable fashioned with an image of the Tetons and the words "Jackson Hole, Wyoming" scrawled over it. You may notice that on the map, the town just south of Grand Teton National Park is called Jackson. But your plane ticket says Jackson Hole. But wait a minute—the postmark just says Jackson. What gives?

The mystery of the town's name is actually pretty simple. Three mountain men ran a fur-trapping company in these parts in the 1800s: one named David Jackson, another named Jedediah Smith, and a third named William Sublette. Mountain men in those days referred to a valley as a hole. As the story goes, Sublette called the valley Jackson's Hole, because Jackson spent a great deal of time in it. That name was shortened, and when the town materialized, it was also named for David Jackson. So the city itself is Jackson, Wyoming, and it lies in the great valley that runs the length of the Tetons on the east side, Jackson Hole.

ESSENTIALS

GETTING THERE   The **Jackson Airport** (© 307/733-7682) is located north of town at the southern end of Grand Teton National Park. **American Airlines** (© 800/433-7300) flies in from Chicago, and regular service is provided from Denver and Salt Lake City by **Delta** (© 800/221-1212) and **United** (© 800/241-6522). **Northwest** (© 800/225-2525) also connects from Billings, Montana, and **Big Sky Airlines** (© 800/237-7788 or 406/245-2300) flies in from Boise, Idaho.

If you're getting here on your own wheels, come north from I-80 at Rock Springs on U.S. 189/191, or come east from I-15 at Idaho Falls on U.S. 26 and either come through Snake River Canyon on that highway or veer north over Teton Pass on Wyo. 32. If you are coming south from Yellowstone National Park, you can stay on U.S. 89, which runs north and south through both parks and into town. For up-to-date weather information and local road conditions, contact the Jackson Hole Chamber of Commerce (see below).

VISITOR INFORMATION   The **Jackson Hole Chamber of Commerce** is a source of information concerning just about everything in and around Jackson. Along with the U.S. Forest Service and National Park Service, representatives of the chamber can be found at the informative **Visitors Center,** 532 N. Cache, about 3 blocks north of Town Square with a view of the National Elk Refuge. For information on lodging, events, and activities, contact the chamber at P.O. Box 550, Jackson, WY 83001 (© 307/733-3316; www.jacksonholechamber.com). For lodging information and reservations, call **Jackson Hole Central Reservations** (© 800/838-6606; www.jacksonholewy.com).

GETTING AROUND   Once you're on the ground, major car-rental operations serving the airport include **Alamo** (© 800/462-5266 or 307/733-0671), **Avis** (© 800/230-4898 or 307/733-3422), **Thrifty** (© 800/847-4389 or 307/734-9306 or 307/733-2206), and **Hertz** (© 800/654-3131 or 307/733-2272). Also providing rentals in the area are **Dollar** (© 877/222-7736 or 307/733-9224) and **Eagle Rent-a-Car,** downtown at 375 N. Cache (© 307/739-9999), where you can rent everything from minivans to RVs to snowmobiles. Eagle also provides free pickup and delivery.

Taxi service is available from **Buckboard Cab** (© 307/733-1112). **Alltrans** (© 800/443-6133 or 307/733-3135) offers shuttle service from the airport and national park tours. Many of the hotels and car-rental agencies in the Jackson area offer free shuttle service to and from the airport.

The **Southern Teton Area Rapid Transit (START)** offers bus transport from Teton Village to Jackson daily for $3 (half price for seniors, students, and those ages 9–13; children 8 and under ride free). Service includes about 70 trips a day between downtown and Teton Village in the winter, 10 in the summer, and shuts down around 12:30am year-round. For specific schedule information, contact START at © 307/733-4521 or browse **www.startbus.com**.

SPECIAL EVENTS   Held annually in late May, **Old West Days** is a 4-day event dedicated to Jackson's frontier past, with a shootout, cowboy poetry readings, a parade, and a rodeo. The other big annual event is the **Jackson Hole Fall Arts Festival,** a 10-day extravaganza in September with special events every day. Contact the Jackson Hole Chamber of Commerce (see above) for further information on either.

GETTING OUTSIDE
SPORTING GOODS & EQUIPMENT RENTALS

Jackson adventurers may like to flirt with danger, but generally they like to do so fully equipped and handsomely attired. Serious climbers with serious wallets will appreciate the gear at **Teton Mountaineering** ✦ at 170 N. Cache St. (© 800/850-3595 or 307/733-3595), a block from the square, where you can get carabiners, killer Nordic skis, and high-grade fleece jackets. Fishermen are lured to **High Country Flies** ✦ at 185 N. Center St. (© 877/732-7210 or 307/733-7210; www.highcountryflies.com), and the **Jack Dennis Outdoor Shop** on the square at 50 E. Broadway (© 800/570-3270 or 307/733-3270; www.jackdennis.com). **Adventure Sports,** at Dornan's in the town of Moose (© 307/733-3307), has a small selection of mountain-bike, kayak, and canoe rentals, and advice on where to go with the gear. When snowboards are put away for the summer, the **Boardroom** switches to BMX bikes and skateboards, at 225 W. Broadway (© 307/733-8327). **Hoback Sports,** 520 W. Broadway Ave. (© 307/733-5335), has a large selection of skis, boards, and summer mountain bikes for rent and sale. Equally hip, with a smaller but high-quality selection of bikes and skis, is **Edge Sports,** 490 W. Broadway (© 307/734-3916). **Skinny Skis,** at 65 W. Deloney Ave. off Town Square (© 307/733-6094), is a year-round specialty sports shop and has an excellent selection of equipment and clothing. For a supply of inexpensive, serviceable factory seconds at severely discounted prices, head north to the little town of Moose near the entrance to Grand Teton National Park and shop **Moosely Seconds** ✦ (© 307/739-1801).

BIKING

You can rent a bike and pick up maps at several of the shops listed above, or take a guided trip in Yellowstone, Grand Teton, or the national forest with **Teton Mountain Bike Tours** (© 800/733-0788; www.tetonmtbike.com) or Hoback Sports' **Fat Tire Tours,** 40 S. Millward St. (© 307/733-5335), which places bikes in the Snow King chairlift for an easy ride up the mountain.

CLIMBING

The sight of the 13,770-foot Grand Teton towering above the valley has been setting hearts pumping for generations. A century ago no one had reached the top; now, thousands have, often carefully roped and cared for by professional guides. Experienced guides and established routes assure a modicum of safety, but climbing accidents and deaths still occur. There are two reliable, long-standing guide services: **Exum Mountain Guides,** P.O. Box 56, Moose, WY 83012 (© **307/733-2297;** www. exumguides.com), and **Jackson Hole Mountain Guides,** 165 N. Glenwood St., Jackson, WY 83001 (© **800/239-7642;** www.jhmg.com). Expect to pay $500 to $600 for a guided 2-day climb of Grand Teton or $120 for a class. Those who need to practice their moves on a rainy day should try the **Teton Rock Gym,** at 1116 Maple Way in Jackson (© **307/733-0707**).

CROSS-COUNTRY SKIING

With five Nordic centers and a couple of national parks at their feet, plus the 3.5-million-acre Bridger-Teton National Forest, cross-country skiers have plenty of choices. If you're new to cross-country skiing, you might choose to start on the groomed, level trails at one of the Nordic centers. If, however, you have experience in the steep, deep powder of untracked wilderness, visit or call the National Park Service in **Grand Teton National Park** (© **307/739-3600**) or the **Bridger-Teton National Forest** in downtown Jackson at 340 N. Cache (© **307/739-5500**) and check in before you go.

The local ski shops are an excellent source of unofficial advice about the area's backcountry. Keep in mind that many of the trails used by cross-country skiers are also used by snowmobiles. The **Jackson Hole Nordic Center,** 7658 Teewinot, Teton Village (© **307/733-2629**), located on the flats just east of Teton Village, is a small part of the giant facility that includes some of the best downhill skiing around (see "Downhill Skiing," below). The price of a downhill pass includes the price of skiing on the cross-country trails.

Teton Pines Cross Country Skiing Center (© **307/733-1005**) offers 8 miles of groomed trails. **Spring Creek Ranch Touring Center,** 1800 N. Spirit Dance Rd., Jackson (© **800/443-6139**), located below the ridge resort (see "Where to Stay," later in this chapter) maintains about 10 miles of groomed trails, and you don't have to be a guest to enjoy them.

At **Grand Targhee** (© **307/353-2304**), you can rent or buy anything you need in the way of cross-country ski equipment and take off on the resort's 8 miles of groomed trails. (See listing below for a description of the resort's downhill-skiing facilities.)

For those seeking instruction, lessons are available at the Nordic centers, or you can check the schedule of **Teton Parks and Recreation** (© **307/733-5056**), which takes visitors on cross-country ski outings (about $10) every Tuesday from mid-December to mid-March.

For cross-country information in **Grand Teton National Park,** call © **307/739-3600,** or 307/739-3611 for recorded weather information. Also, see section 2, "Grand Teton National Park."

DOG SLEDDING

If your idea of mushing is not oatmeal but a pack of yipping dogs, you might want to try your hand at dog sledding. **Jackson Hole Iditarod Sled Dog Tours,** P.O. Box 1940, Jackson, WY 83001 (© **800/554-7388** or 307/733-7388; www.jhsleddog.com), associated with Iditarod racer Frank Teasley, offers both half- and full-day trips in five-person sleds (the fifth companion is your guide) and you can take a turn in the driver's stand. The half-day ride costs around $150 per person, gives the dogs an 11-mile workout, and includes a lunch of hot soup and cocoa before you head back to the kennels. For around $300 a head, you can take the full-day excursion out to Granite Hot Springs, a 22-mile trip total. You get the hot lunch, plus your choice of freshly barbecued trout or steak for dinner. Another outfitter, **Washakie Outfitting** (C **800/249-0662;** www.dogsledwashakie.com), leads trips in the national forests around Togwotee Pass. These trips fill up quickly, so call several days in advance to reserve a spot.

DOWNHILL SKIING

Low temperatures, black-diamond runs, remote location, and an intimidating vertical drop haven't scared skiers away from Jackson Hole—this is what *attracts* them. The two largest ski resorts in the area have been expanding, putting in faster chairs, and eliminating long waits in lift lines. The quality of snow on the mountain can vary, but skiers who seek challenges will not be disappointed. All resorts are open daily.

Jackson Hole Mountain Resort 🎿🎿   This resort is booming, with scads of new hotels and timeshares going up at the mountain's foot in recent years, more than doubling the guest capacity in just a few short years. There is special grandeur to this ski resort, from its spectacular mountaintop views to its daring black-diamond runs to its 400 annual inches of powder. Take the tram to the top of **Rendezvous Mountain** and plunge down Tensleep Bowl if you want to get a taste of skiing on the edge. You'll find an inexhaustible supply of steep runs that require skiing expertise. There are lesser runs to the north, including gentler journeys down the sides of **Apres Vous Mountain** that will better suit an intermediate skier. At the bottom, two small chairs serve beginning skiers. (**Note:** At press time, ownership was planning to close the resort's tram after summer 2006, though there will still be lift access to Rendezvous Bowl.)

Crowded days have been few in recent years—lucky for skiers, if not the owners. With 2,500 acres of skiable terrain, there's plenty of room. Ten lifts, a gondola, and an aerial tram are available from early December to the beginning of April. (The resort turns into a mountain-biking playground come summer.) For an orientation, join the Mountain Hosts, who gather groups at the top of the Rendezvous lift to escort newcomers on a 2-hour tour.

The competition among ski resorts compels growth—not just on the slopes, but also in the resort villages below. A variety of restaurants, lodging, a medical clinic, shops, and entertainment—from sleigh-ride dinners to a skating rink—make it unnecessary to leave the complex during a ski vacation.

If you've never skied in powder up to your kneecaps, make an early-morning trip to the **Hobacks Zone,** just under Cheyenne Bowl. The ski patrol closes it off as soon as the snow gets tracked out.

3395 W. Village Dr. (P.O. Box 290), Teton Village, WY 83025. C **888/DEEP-SNO** or 307/733-2292; 307/733-2291 for snow conditions; 800/443-6931 for central reservations. www.jacksonhole.com. Full-day lift tickets $70 adults, $56 young adults (15–21), $35 seniors over 64 and children under 15. AE, DISC, MC, V. Early Dec to early Apr daily 9am–4pm. From Jackson, take Wyo. 22 west to Wyo. 390 and go north to Teton Village, about 5 miles.

Grand Targhee Resort 🎿   The Grand Targhee resort has struggled at times, changing ownership, wheeling and dealing with federal land managers, and sparring with local conservationists over expansion plans and real-estate development. None of that affects the snow, however, which is terrific. Or the deep, forgiving powder from

November through spring (more than 500 in. annually), and a more peaceful, less-crowded village that provides a worthy alternative to Teton Village. Many skiers break up a Jackson ski trip by driving over Teton Pass for a day or two on these slopes.

This may also be a better place for less-aggressive skiers. There is a beginner's powder area and hundreds of acres of wide-open powder slopes for intermediates and other cruisers. You can take a high-speed quad to the adjacent Peaked Mountain and ski in thigh-deep, untracked snow. A problem you might encounter is, oddly enough, fog. Now and then the mountain gets socked in with gray moisture, forcing skiers to ski below the thick blanket. The **Lost Groomer Chute,** a run that takes full advantage of the weather moving west to east, will provide the most insatiable powder hound with enough dust.

Here are a few of the other treats at Targhee: You can ride a sleigh on a starlit evening to a roundtable dinner in a snow-buried yurt; your kids can enroll in the Powder Scouts program, which gives kids ages 6 to 12 a full day of instruction, food, and skiing for $90; and a spa offers everything from massage to a mineral mud wrap, along with hot tubs, sauna, exercise room, and heated outdoor pool.

Ski Hill Rd., Box SKI, Alta, WY 83422. ✆ **800/TARGHEE** or 307/353-2300. www.grandtarghee.com. Full-day lift tickets $55 adults, $35 seniors (62 and older), $34 children 6–14, free for children under 6. AE, DISC, MC, V. Mid-Nov to Apr daily 9am–4pm. From Jackson, take Wyo. 22 over Teton Pass into Idaho, then Idaho 33 north to Driggs, then follow the signs west (back into Wyo.) to Targhee Resort, about 38 miles.

Snow King Resort   If you enter Jackson from the north on a winter night, the lit slopes of Snow King are an appealing sight. Snow King offers a variety of recreation, from tubing hill to ice rink to snowboard park. Plus, it's conveniently located near the heart of town. It's the oldest ski hill in Wyoming, operating since 1939, and the hotel has attractive, moderately priced rooms. The only problem is the skiing itself: A limited number of fairly steep runs don't offer much variety. The beginner's slope is small and amounts to only 15% of the terrain, and there's not enough intermediate snow to satisfy all levels of ability. The two other area resorts are much bigger, with more and longer runs and a greater variety of challenges. "Town Hill," as it's known, has 400 acres of skiable terrain, a triple chair, two double chairs, and two surface tows.

400 E. Snow King, Jackson, WY 83001. ✆ **800/522-5464** or 307/733-5200; 307/734-2020 for snow conditions. www.snowking.com. Lift tickets $35 adults, $25 seniors 60 and older and children under 14. AE, DISC, MC, V. Late Nov to late Mar daily 10am–4pm. Take Cache St. south to Snow King Ave. Turn left and follow the signs to the resort.

FISHING

Yellowstone and Grand Teton national parks are home to some fabled fishing spots (see the park sections for details), but some of the best angling in the region is found outside the park boundaries.

The **Snake River** emerges from Jackson Lake Dam as a broad, strong river, with decent fishing from its banks in certain spots—like right below the dam—and better fishing if you float the river. Fly-fishermen should ask for advice at local stores on recent insect hatches and good stretches of river, or hire a guide to keep them company. **High Country Flies** 🎣, 185 N. Center St. (✆ **307/733-7210;** www.highcountry flies.com), has a vast selection of high-quality fishing gear, flies, and fly-tying supplies, along with lessons, guided trips, and free advice if you just want to gab about where to cast. The **Jack Dennis Outdoor Shop** on Town Square, at 50 E. Broadway (✆ **307/733-3270;** www.jackdennis.com), is a much bigger store with room to display some big boats, and it also offers lessons and guides. **Westbank Anglers,** 3670

N. Moose-Wilson Rd. (© **307/733-6483;** www.westbank.com), is another full-service fly shop. The going rate for guided fishing is about $375 for a full day for two people.

GOLF

More than one American president has played a round of golf in Jackson, which despite its short putting season has some world-class links. The **Jackson Hole Golf and Tennis Club** (© **800/628-9988** or 307/733-3111), north of Jackson off U.S. 89, has an 18-hole course that's been rated one of the nation's top resort courses. Greens fees run $125 for 18 holes before 1pm (and going down as it gets later, all the way to $45 after 6pm), with cart and range balls included. The **Teton Pines Resort and Country Club,** 3450 N. Clubhouse Dr. (© **800/238-2223** or 307/733-1005), designed by Arnold Palmer and Ed Seay, is a challenging course and prime real estate; greens fees are $170 to $190 for 18 holes. Both are open to the public.

HIKING

One benefit of having so many mountain ranges converging around Jackson is that you have *choices*—especially when it comes to hiking. The most popular place to go for a stroll in the vicinity of Jackson is **Grand Teton National Park,** which shows off some glorious aspen colors in the fall. Less traveled are the forests that abut the park, particularly **Bridger-Teton National Forest** just east of Jackson. Bridger-Teton and its east-side counterpart, **Shoshone National Forest,** encompass a huge piece of mountain real estate, including glaciers, 13,000-foot peaks, and some of the best alpine fishing lakes in the world. Among the mountain ranges included in these forests are the **Absarokas,** the **Gros Ventre,** the **Wyoming,** and the **Wind River Range,** or "Winds," as they're called by locals, which stretch about 120 miles from just southeast of Jackson near Pinedale to the South Pass area and the Red Desert. The **Greater Yellowstone Visitor Center** at 532 N. Cache in downtown Jackson provides all of the hiking and access information you'll need for the national forest as well as for the Gros Ventre and Teton wilderness areas. Call the Forest Service (© **307/739-5500**) for additional information.

HORSEBACK RIDING

Some hotels, including those in Grand Teton National Park, have stables and operate trail rides for their guests. For details, contact **Jackson Hole Trail Rides** (© **307/733-6992**), **Spring Creek Ranch Riding Stables** (© **800/443-6139**), or the **Mill Iron Ranch** (© **307/733-6390**). Rides cost around $50 for 2 hours.

KAYAKING, CANOEING & SAILING

With the Snake and Hoback rivers and the lakes of Grand Teton National Park, it's no surprise to see all kinds of watercraft towed or tied to the roofs of SUVs in Jackson. Canoeists and kayakers enjoy the upper Snake River, from Jackson Lake Dam down to Moose, and expert kayakers are attracted to the ride through Snake River Canyon and Hoback white water. Beginners should be wary of the upper Snake—snags and spring currents have claimed lives, so a guide is advisable. Canoeists paddle Jenny Lake and, with a small portage or two, String and Leigh lakes. The big lake, **Jackson,** attracts sailboats and sea kayaks, but beware of the sudden afternoon eruptions of gusty wind and thunderstorms.

Several operators in Jackson run schools and guide services for beginners, intermediates, and advanced paddlers. The two major outfits are the **Snake River Kayak and Canoe School,** 225 N. Cache St. (© **800/KAYAK-01;** www.snakeriverkayak.com);

and **Rendezvous River Sports,** 945 W. Broadway (© **307/733-2471;** www.jhkayak school.com).

RAFTING

There are two parts to the Snake River—the smooth water north of Jackson, and the white water of the canyon, to the south and west. A rafting trip down the upper Snake, usually from Jackson Lake Dam or Pacific Creek to Moose, is not about wild water but about wildlife: Moose, bald eagles, osprey, and other creatures come to the water just like we do. Several operators provide scenic float trips, charging $40 to $50 for a half-day, $70 to $90 for a full day. Ask at **Barker-Ewing** (© **800/365-1800**); **Grand Teton Lodge Company** (© **307/543-2811**); and **Signal Mountain Lodge** (© **307/543-2831**).

SNOWMOBILING

Though West Yellowstone is the most popular base for snowmobiling in the Yellowstone area, Jackson has a growing contingent of snowmobile aficionados and outfitters. You don't really need a guide to tour Togwotee Pass and the Granite Hot Springs area if you stick to groomed trails. Snowmobilers also head for the rugged Gros Ventre Mountains and the Greys River area, 45 miles west of Jackson. The operators who rent snowmobiles (including the necessary clothing and helmets) also have guides to take you on 1-day and multiday tours of Jackson Hole and the surrounding area. **High Country Snowmobile Tours, Wyoming Adventures,** and **Rocky Mountain Snowmobile Tours** share a website and reservation service (© **800/647-2561;** www.snowmobiletours.net), offering guided trips in Jackson Hole, Yellowstone, and the surrounding wildlands. **Jackson Hole Snowmobile Tours,** 515 N. Cache St. (© **800/633-1733;** www.jacksonholesnowmobile.com), offers 1-day trips in Yellowstone and multiday trips along the Continental Divide. A typical guided, full-day outing costs from $200 to $300, with pickup and drop-off service, equipment, fuel, a continental breakfast, and lunch at Old Faithful included. Also in Jackson, snowmobiles can be rented at **Leisure Sports,** 1075 S. U.S. Hwy. 89 (© **307/733-3040**).

WHITE-WATER RAFTING

The Snake River Canyon's fame has not diminished its Class IV allure to expert paddlers—but they avoid the midday crowds and take their white-water jollies more toward twilight. If you want to join them jolting over Lunch Counter Rapids, but you'd rather be in a raft steered by somebody who knows what they're doing (you'll be asked to paddle, and you may feel like your life depends on it), contact **Barker-Ewing** (© 800/365-1800), **Charlie Sands Wildwater** (© 800/358-8184), **Dave Hansen Whitewater** (© 800/732-6295), **Jackson Hole Whitewater** (© 800/648-2602), **Lewis and Clark Expeditions** (© 800/824-5375), or **Mad River Boat Trips**

Tips Boating Regulations

If you're going to set out in your own boat, you should know that before launching in the park, you'll need a boat permit. Ask at the visitor center at Moose, or call the **National Park Service** at © **307/739-3600** for information. Once you get outside the park, you're in the jurisdiction of the **Bridger-Teton National Forest,** with offices in Jackson at 340 N. Cache (© **307/739-5500**).

(© 800/458-7238). Generally, a full-day trip runs $70 to $90, lunch included, and a half-day trip costs $40 to $50.

OFFBEAT BUT MEMORABLE WAYS TO SEE THE TETONS
AERIAL TOURING

For a much quicker climb to the tops of the mountains, call **Jackson Hole Aviation** (© 307/733-4767; www.jhaviation.com), at the Jackson Hole Airport, or **Teton Aviation,** Driggs Airport, Driggs, ID 83422 (© 800/472-3100 or 208/354-8131). You'll get a new perspective on the immensity of the Grand Teton (though you won't get too close—the park has some air-space restrictions). Jackson Hole Aviation offers airplane trips ($120 an hour), and Teton has 1-hour flights in planes and gliders ($185–$225) that take you to 11,800 feet on the west side of the Grand.

BALLOONING

It used to be that only anglers were up at the crack of dawn in Jackson, but now you can add balloonists. The folks at the **Wyoming Balloon Company,** P.O. Box 2578, Jackson, WY 83001 (© 307/739-0900; www.wyomingballoon.com), like to fire up early, in the still air that cloaks the Teton Valley around 6am. Their "float trips" stay aloft for a little more than an hour, cruising over a 3,000-acre ranch with a full frontal view of the Tetons. The journey concludes with a champagne toast at the landing site. Flights in a balloon cost $225 per adult and $175 per child 6 to 12 (not recommended for kids 5 and under).

EXPLORING THE AREA

Jackson Hole Aerial Tram Rides   Here you can see the Tetons from an elevation above 10,000 feet, but don't expect a private tour. During busy summer days the tram carries 45 passengers, packed in like the skiers that take the lift in the winter. The top of Rendezvous Mountain offers an incredible view, but it can get pretty chilly, even in the middle of summer, so bring a light coat. *Note:* At press time, ownership was planning to close the resort's tram after summer 2006.

At Jackson Hole Mountain Resort, 7658 Teewinot, Teton Village. © 307/739-2753. www.jacksonhole.com. Tickets $19 adults, $15 seniors 65 and over, $8 children 6–12, free for children 5 and under. Late May to mid-June and Sept daily 9am–5pm; mid-June to Aug daily 9am–6pm. Tram runs approximately every half-hour.

Jackson Hole Museum   Dedicated volunteers maintain this repository of early photographs, artifacts, and other items of historical significance, and they'll guide you through the collections. You can browse the exhibits or go down the street to the Historical Society at Glenwood and Mercil to do some research. At the museum, you'll find collections of trade beads, antique pole furniture, pistols, and Indian artifacts, spread out in 3,000 square feet of floor space.

105 N. Glenwood St. (at the corner of Deloney St.). © 307/733-2414. www.jacksonholehistory.org. Admission $6 families, $3 adults, $2 seniors, $1 students and children. Mon–Sat 9:30am–6pm; Sun 10am–5pm. Closed Oct–May.

National Museum of Wildlife Art ♠   If you don't spot this museum on your way into Jackson from the north, consider that a triumph of design: Its jagged, red-sandstone facade is meant to blend into the steep hillside facing the elk refuge. Within this 50,000-square-foot castle is some of the best wildlife art in the country, as well as exhibits on the elk refuge wildlife and a 200-seat auditorium where there are regular slide shows and lectures on a wide range of subjects. There are 14 exhibit galleries that display traveling shows and collections dating from the 19th century to the present,

---

Kids **Especially for Kids**

Snow King may not have the best skiing in the valley, but it caters to kids and families. In the summer, kids can frolic on the **Snow King's Alpine Miniature Golf Course and Alpine Slide** (② 307/733-5200). A round of 18 holes is $7 for those aged 7 and up and $3 for 6 and under.

The **Alpine Slide** is the golf course's untamed neighbor. It's a wild ride down the 2,500-foot ophidian highway running from the top of the blue-and-yellow chairlift to the bottom of Snow King Mountain; it's like a water slide without the water. A trip down the slide runs $10 per person.

In the winter, there are ski schools for kids with day-care options at all the ski resorts. Once again, Snow King has something extra: an ice-skating rink, which opens in October and features skating and hockey until spring. For prices and hours, call ② 307/733-5200.

---

including John James Audubon and local great Carl Rungius. The museum houses a repository of internationally acclaimed wildlife films, and in the winter it's the takeoff point for sled tours of the elk refuge (you can also view the wildlife through spotting scopes on the balcony). There's a good little cafe, too.

2820 Rungius Rd. (3 miles north of town on U.S. Hwy. 89, across from the National Elk Refuge). ② 307/733-5771. www.wildlifeart.org. Admission $8 adults, $7 students and seniors, free for children under 18 when accompanied by an adult. Daily 9am–5pm, except Sun only 1–5pm during spring and fall.

WILDLIFE-WATCHING

National Elk Refuge ☆   It's not exactly nature's way, but the U.S. Fish and Wildlife Service makes sure that the elk in this area eat well during the winter by feeding them alfalfa pellets. It keeps them out of the haystacks of area ranchers and creates a beautiful tableau on the peaceful flats along the Gros Ventre River: thousands of elk, some with huge antler racks, dotting the snow for miles. Drivers along U.S. Hwy. 89 might also see trumpeter swans, coyotes, moose, bighorn sheep, and, lately, wolves. As autumn begins to chill the air in September, you'll hear the shrill whistles of the bull elk in the mountains; as snow begins to stick on the ground, they make their way down to the refuge. Although the cultivated meadows and pellets help the elk survive the winter, some biologists say this approach results in overpopulation and the spread of diseases such as brucellosis.

Regardless, this is a great opportunity to see these magnificent wapiti up close. Each winter from mid-December until March, the Fish and Wildlife Service offers **horse-drawn sleigh rides** that weave among the refuge elk. Rides early in the winter will find young, energetic bulls playing and banging heads, while late-winter visits (when the Fish and Wildlife Service begins feeding the animals) wander through a more placid scene. Rides embark from the Greater Yellowstone Visitor Center (532 N. Cache St.) between 10am and 4pm on a first-come, first-served basis. Tickets for the 45-minute rides cost $15 for adults and $11 for children 6 to 12, and can be purchased at the visitor center. Ask about a combination pass for the sleigh ride and the Wildlife Art Museum.

Located 3 miles north of Jackson on U.S. Hwy. 26/89. ② 307/733-9212. http://nationalelkrefuge.fws.gov. Free admission. Visitor center: summer daily 8am–7pm; winter daily 8am–5pm.

SHOPPING

In recent years stores like **Gap** (on Town Square; *©* 307/733-7927) and **Eddie Bauer** (55 S. Cache St.; *©* 307/733-7336) have opened factory-outlet stores in Jackson, and among the ever-changing array of shops (rents are high; so is turnover) you can find everything from American Indian crafts to cowboy boots to Oriental rugs. But these are what you'll find in most resort towns. The areas where Jackson excels are its art galleries and outdoor-wear shops.

Standouts in the outdoor-clothing category include **Teton Mountaineering** (170 N. Cache St.; *©* 307/733-3595), also a great spot for climbing, camping, and winter gear; and **Moosely Seconds** (in Moose; *©* 307/739-1801), where you'll find surprisingly deep discounts on quality outdoor wear.

Collectors, tired of bighorn sheep on the crags and weather-beaten cowboys on their horses, often dismiss Western art. But while Jackson has plenty of that genre in stock, some of its two dozen galleries are more adventurous and sophisticated. The beauty of Tom Mangelsen's wildlife photography has been somewhat diluted by its display in airports and malls, but Jackson is where he started, and at the **Images of Nature Gallery,** 170 N. Cache St. (*©* 307/733-9752), you'll find some of his work signed and numbered. The **Center Street Gallery,** 30 Center St. (*©* 307/733-1115), has the lock on abstract Western art in Jackson. A mile north of town, at 1975 U.S. 89 (toward the park), is the **Wilcox Gallery** (*©* 307/733-6450), which showcases more than 20 painters and sculptors from across the nation.

WHERE TO STAY

The thin-walled, dimly lit motels of the past are just memories now—Jackson lodgings these days come with palatial trappings and, in some cases, prices that start at $500 a night. Prices are generally discounted in off season (spring/fall), but not during ski season.

Clustered together near the junction west of downtown where Wyo. 22 leaves U.S. Hwy. 26/89 and heads north to Teton Village is a colony of chain franchises: **Motel 6** (600 S. U.S. Hwy. 89; *©* 307/733-1620) and **Super 8** (750 S. U.S. Hwy. 89; *©* 800/800-8000 or 307/733-6833). Also in the vicinity are the more upscale and expensive **Days Inn** (350 S. U.S. Hwy. 89; *©* 800/329-7466 or 307/733-0033), with private hot tubs and fireplaces in suites; and the **Red Lion Inn** (930 W. Broadway; *©* 800/844-0035 or 307/734-0035). High-season prices for the motels range from $80 to $175. Rooms at the Red Lion during high season run from $199 to $329 a night.

On the inexpensive end of the scale, the **Anvil Motel,** 215 N. Cache St. (*©* 800/234-4507 or 307/733-3668; www.anvilmotel.com) offers hostel beds in the dormstyle "Bunkhouse" for $25 a night. This is one of the cleanest and best-kept hostels in the West, with ski lockers, a communal kitchen, and a hot tub. The motel is a good deal, too, with high-season doubles for $82 to $125.

IN JACKSON

Jackson Hole Lodge   Although it sits near one of the busiest intersections in Jackson and it's packed into a small space, this lodge is quiet and well designed, so its location in the heart of town becomes a plus. The pool is not just for splashing—you can lap its 40-foot length, sit in one of the whirlpools, take a sauna, or sit out on your own sun deck. The rooms are more comfortable and complete than what you'll find at a chain property, blending Western ambience with scads of in-room options. Best of all are the condo lodgings, with two upstairs bedrooms, a full kitchen, and a living room with foldout couch. This gives families a little space, and it's also affordable.

420 W. Broadway, Jackson, WY 83001. © 800/604-9404 or 307/733-2992. Fax 307/739-2144. www.jacksonhole lodge.com. 59 units. $79–$139 double; $129–$309 condo. AE, DC, DISC, MC, V. **Amenities:** Indoor pool; 2 Jacuzzis; sauna; game room. *In room:* A/C, cable TV, kitchen, coffeemaker.

Rusty Parrot Lodge and Spa 🏵🏵

The name sounds like an out-of-tune jungle bird, but since 1990 the Rusty Parrot has shown excellent pitch, cultivating a country lodge and spa right in the heart of busy Jackson. Located across from Miller Park, the Parrot is decorated in the nouveau Western style of peeled log, with an interior appointed with elegant furnishings and river-rock fireplaces. One very attractive lure is The Body Sage Spa, where you can get yourself treated to all sorts of scrubs, wraps, massages, and facials. The breakfast that comes with your room includes omelets, fresh pastries, fruits, cereals, and freshly ground coffee; food also appears later in the day, but the lodge likes to make that a surprise (sorry). Rooms are gigantic, and several have private balconies.

175 N. Jackson St. (P.O. Box 1657), Jackson, WY 83001. © 800/458-2004 or 307/733-2000. www.rustyparrot.com. 31 units. $275–$385 double; $550–$650 suite. Rates include full breakfast. AE, DC, DISC, MC, V. **Amenities:** Restaurant; lounge; outdoor Jacuzzi; spa; Wi-Fi network. *In room:* TV.

Trapper Inn

The employees here are some of the most helpful you'll find in Jackson, and they'll tip you off on the best deals in the valley. Just 2 short blocks from the Town Square, the Trapper is hard to miss if you're walking north on Cache from the Town Square. On the west side of Cache, you'll notice the Trapper on the bronze sign. You can walk anywhere downtown within minutes. The rooms are spacious, featuring cozy quilts and stately lodgepole-pine furnishings. There is a family room and a Jacuzzi king suite as well. At press time, the owners were working on a third building slated to open in late 2006.

235 N. Cache St., Jackson, WY 83001. © 888/771-2648 or 307/733-2648 for reservations. www.trapperinn.com. 54 units. $107–$179 double. AE, DC, MC, V. **Amenities:** Jacuzzi; self-serve laundry. *In room:* A/C, TV, fridge, coffeemaker.

Virginian Lodge 🏵

It's not brand-new. It's not a resort, it doesn't have a golf course, and the highway is right outside the door. Since its overhaul in 1995, however, the Virginian is one of the better motels in Jackson: The prices remain reasonable, the interior courtyard (with a large grassy play area and central pool) is a world away from the Broadway-facing exterior, and it's a busy, cheerful place to stay. You can get a room with a private Jacuzzi or a kitchenette, and many have "dry" bars and sofa sleepers.

750 W. Broadway, Jackson, WY 83001. © 800/262-4999 or 307/733-2792. Fax 307/733-4063. www.virginian lodge.com. 170 units. $95–$109 double; $125–$185 suite. AE, DC, DISC, MC, V. **Amenities:** Restaurant; lounge; outdoor pool; Jacuzzi; game room; Wi-Fi network; self-serve laundry. *In room:* A/C, TV, kitchenette.

Wort Hotel 🏵🏵

Located on Broadway just off the Town Square, the Wort stands like an old tree. Opened in the early 1940s by the sons of Charles Wort, an early-20th-century homesteader, the Tudor-style two-story building was largely rebuilt after a 1980 fire. Nowadays, it has an old-fashioned style to it, both in the relaxed **Silver Dollar Bar** (distinctively graced with 2,032 silver dollars) and the quiet, formal dining room. In the manner of an old cattle-baron hotel, the lobby is graced by a warm, romantic fireplace; another fireplace and a huge, hand-carved mural accents a mezzanine sitting area, providing a second hideaway. The rooms aren't Tudor at all—the Wort labels them "New West." Brass number plates and doorknobs welcome you into comfortable, air-conditioned guest rooms with modern decor, thick carpeting, and armoires. The Silver Dollar Suite features a wet bar inlaid with the same silver dollars found in the bar below.

50 N. Glenwood St., Jackson, WY 83001. © 307/733-2190. www.worthotel.com. 60 units. $165–$275 double; $325–$550 suite. AE, DISC, MC, V. Valet parking $10 daily. **Amenities:** Restaurant; lounge; exercise room; Jacuzzi; Wi-Fi network. *In room:* A/C, cable, TV, coffeemaker, iron.

NEAR JACKSON

Amangani 🐾🐾🐾 Cut into the side of East Gros Ventre Butte, Amangani's rough rock exterior blends incredibly well so that the lights from its windows and pool appear at night to glow from within the mountain. The style is understated and rustic, but every detail is done with expensive style. Walking through the high-ceilinged corridors or lounging by the outdoor pool, you know not to strike up a casual conversation with your neighbor—this place is all about class and privacy, not to mention superlative views. Hotelier Adrian Zecha has resorts like this around the world, from Bali to Bora Bora, and while the designs are tailored to the landscape, the approach is the same: personal service, luxury, and all the little touches. To name a few of the latter, there are CD players in every bedroom, cashmere throws on the day beds, and stunning slate and redwood interiors.

1535 NE Butte Rd., Jackson, WY 83002 (on top of East Gros Ventre Butte). © 877/734-7333 or 307/734-7333. www.amanresorts.com. 40 units. $750–$1,300 double. AE, DC, DISC, MC, V. **Amenities:** Restaurant; lounge; year-round outdoor pool; exercise room; spa; Jacuzzi. *In room:* A/C, TV/VCR, dataports, minibar, hair dryer, iron, safe.

Bentwood Inn 🐾🐾 *Finds* This B&B is an architectural marvel. Built from 200-year-old timber cleared from Yellowstone to make room for a rest area, the inn is a 6,000-square-foot log mansion with 43 corners. The parlor, centered about a three-story river-rock fireplace, is an ideal place to while away a thunderstorm, but the real beauty here is outside, situated just east of the Snake River on 3 acres of cottonwood and pine forest with a breezy deck and back lawn. The rooms themselves, all with remote-controlled gas fireplaces, private balconies, and Jacuzzi tubs, are extensions of the innovative design, with touches equally urban and rural, from ornate tile work to longhorn skulls above the bed. Innkeepers Bill and Nell Fay (the former designed the inn himself) pay a great deal of attention to detail and it shows. The breakfasts are simultaneously hearty and gourmet, and the fridge is always stocked with a wide range of soft drinks and libations. One room is pet-friendly.

4 miles west of Jackson on Teton Village Rd., P.O. Box 561, Jackson Hole, WY 83001. © 307/739-1411. Fax 307/739-2453. www.bentwoodinn.com. 5 units. $195–$295 double; $245–$325 suite. Rates include complimentary full breakfast and evening cocktails. AE, DISC, MC, V. **Amenities:** Game room. *In room:* Cable TV/VCR, hair dryer, iron.

Spring Creek Ranch 🐾🐾 Perched atop East Gros Ventre Butte, 1,000 feet above the Snake River and minutes from both the airport and downtown Jackson, this resort commands a panoramic view of the Grand Tetons and 1,500 acres of land populated by deer, moose, and the horses at its riding facility in the valley below. It seems a little less exclusive now that Amangani has opened next door. But Spring Creek still has much going for it: The rooms, divided among nine buildings with cabinlike exteriors, all have wood-burning fireplaces, Native American floor and wall coverings, and balconies with views of the Tetons. Most rooms have a king- or two queen-size beds, and the studio units boast kitchenettes. In addition to its own rooms, the resort arranges accommodations in the privately owned condominiums and vacation homes that dot the butte—large, lavishly furnished, and featuring completely equipped kitchens. The resort also has an "Adventure Spa," offering a combination of guide service and post-outing treatments, and in-house naturalists who lead guests into the parks.

1800 Spirit Dance Rd. (on top of the East Gros Ventre Butte), Jackson, WY 83001. © **800/443-6139** or 307/733-8833. www.springcreekranch.com. 125 units. $310 double; $375–$1,200 condo; $2,000–$2,200 home. AE, MC, V. **Amenities:** Restaurant; outdoor pool; tennis court; spa; Jacuzzi; concierge; activities desk; complimentary shuttle; room service. *In room:* A/C, TV/VCR, kitchenette, fridge, coffeemaker.

IN TETON VILLAGE

Teton Village is gradually becoming the self-contained resort town now typical of better ski resorts—it has everything you need, from food to powder to a massage, a short limp from the chairlifts. The village is located on the west side of the Snake River, surrounded by ranchlands that have been protected from development. While lodging in the town of Jackson tends to be a little cheaper in the winter than the summer, the ratio is reversed at Teton Village—rooms by the ski hill get more expensive after the snow falls. For a wide range of basic condos and deluxe vacation homes, contact **Jackson Hole Resort Lodging,** 3200 W. Village Dr., P.O. Box 510, Teton Village, WY 83025 (© **800/443-8613** or 307/733-3990; www.jhresortlodging.com).

Very Expensive

The Alpenhof 🌟🌟 No other spot in the village has quite the Swiss-chalet flavor of this long-standing hostelry, which has a prize location only 50 yards from the ski resort tram. Four stories tall, with a pitched roof and flower boxes on the balconies, it offers a little old-world atmosphere, as well as excellent comforts and service. The management continues to upgrade, most recently redoing the dining room and deluxe accommodations with brightly colored alpine fabrics, newly constructed handcrafted Bavarian furnishings, and tiled bathrooms with big, soft towels. Among the accommodations, you can choose from two junior suites with wet bars and five rooms with fireplaces, and many rooms have balconies or decks. Economy rooms offer two doubles or one queen-size bed, while deluxe units are larger. The resident **Alpenrose** restaurant specializes in fondue.

3255 W. Village Dr., Teton Village, WY 83025. © **800/732-3244** or 307/733-3242. Fax 307/739-1516. www.alpenhof lodge.com. 42 units. $159–$429 double; $439–$529 suite. AE, DC, DISC, MC, V. Closed Nov. **Amenities:** 2 restaurants; lounge; outdoor pool; Jacuzzi; sauna. *In room:* TV, dataport, hair dryer, iron.

Four Seasons Resort Jackson Hole 🌟🌟🌟 The newest—and most deluxe—lodging option in Teton Village, the ultra-stylish Four Seasons opened in December 2004 and immediately set a new standard for ski-in, ski-out luxury. From a year-round slopeside pool (landscaped to resemble a mountain creek), to the cowboy-hatted doorman, to the rooms, stately, luxurious, and definitively Western, this is one of the top slopeside properties in the country. The range of rooms starts at the high-end and goes up from there, but even the standard kings are large and plush, and every unit has a balcony or a fireplace. One especially notable perk: the hotel's "Base Camp," a full-service outdoor activity concierge who can arrange customizable outings involving mountain biking, hiking, fishing, and ballooning, and outfit you in style. In the winter, the service transforms into a first-rate ski concierge, and s'mores and hot chocolate are served alongside heated towels outside at the pool. The eating and drinking facilities are also a cut above, and range from casually hip to extraordinarily extravagant.

7680 Granite Loop, P.O. Box 544, Teton Village, WY 83025. © **307/732-5000.** Fax 307/732-5001. www.fourseasons. com. 140 units. $400–$750 double; $700–$4,000 suite; lower rates spring and fall. AE, DC, DISC, MC, V. Valet parking $18 daily. **Amenities:** 2 restaurants; 3 lounges; year-round outdoor pool; exercise room; 3 Jacuzzis; sauna;

extensive equipment rental; spa; game room; concierge; activities desk; business center; shopping arcade; salon; 24-hr. room service; dry cleaning. *In room:* A/C, cable TV/DVD player w/pay movies, dataport, kitchen, fridge, coffeemaker, hair dryer, iron, safe.

Snake River Lodge and Spa ℱ Major renovations were completed in 2003, and this perpetually changing establishment looks to have gained some stability under the ownership of RockResorts. Wooden walls, stone floors and fireplaces, and a stuffed bison accent the main reception area. The main lodge provides accommodations where classy overshadows rustic, with exposed wooden-beam ceilings, down comforters, and luxurious furnishings. There are three levels of suites, from oversize versions of the standard rooms to three-bedroom versions with top-of-the-line kitchens, good sound systems, and Jacuzzi tubs. The 17,000-square-foot **Avanyu Spa** is a new addition, featuring everything from hydrotherapy to free weights. Winter visitors can ski directly to a locker room with whirlpool and sauna, and drop their skis off for an overnight tune-up.

7710 Granite Loop Rd. (Box 348), Teton Village, WY 83025. © **866/975-ROCK** or 307/732-6000. Fax 307/732-6009. www.rockresorts.com. 130 units. $289–$459 double; $400–$1,250 suite; lower rates in spring and fall. AE, MC, V. **Amenities:** Restaurant; lounge; indoor/outdoor pool; health club and spa; Jacuzzi; children's programs; concierge; room service; dry cleaning. *In room:* TV, kitchenette, coffeemaker, hair dryer, safe.

Moderate

Hostel X ℱ *Value* If you came to Wyoming to ski, not to lie in the lap of luxury, get yourself a room at Hostel X and hit the slopes. Owned and operated by the Wilson family since 1967 and called "the soul of Jackson Hole," it's a great bargain for those who don't need the trimmings, and it's not a dormitory, either—comfortable but simple private rooms (about the caliber of a roadside motel) hold up to four people; they have either one king-size bed or four twins. There's also a good place to prep your skis, a library, a kids' playroom stocked with toys, and a common room with chessboards, a Ping-Pong table, a fireplace, Internet access, and TV. You can walk to the Mangy Moose and other fun spots, and nobody will be able to tell you apart from the skiers staying at the Four Seasons.

3315 W. Village Drive, Teton Village, WY 83025. © **307/733-3415.** Fax 307/739-1142. www.hostelx.com. 55 units. $58 double. MC, V. Closed early Apr to late May and Oct to early Dec. **Amenities:** Game room; self-serve laundry. *In room:* No phone.

NEARBY GUEST RANCHES

Though there have been ranches in the valley for more than a century, many of Jackson Hole's residents have always made part of their living hosting visitors from Europe and the eastern U.S. who came to hunt, see the sights, and enjoy the outdoors. Somewhere around 1900, the term "dude ranching" came into discourse, and Jackson joined Sheridan and Cody as popular Wyoming destinations for folks who wanted a cowboy experience. You can come out to work hard on horseback, move cattle, eat wranglers' grub, and pay dearly for it; but many of the dude ranches offer a more relaxed vacation, with riding, river floating, fine food, and plenty of boots-up porch time.

Flying A Ranch ℱ Nestled at 8,300 feet between the Gros Ventre and Wind River ranges of Wyoming, the Flying A stuns its visitors with panoramic views. Quaking aspen, stream-fed ponds, and curious antelope are hardly disturbed by this exclusive operation, which hosts only 14 guests at a time. Built in the 1930s, the ranch cabins have been carefully restored, with evocative touches that include wood-burning stoves, handmade pine furniture, and regional artwork. Typical of a dude ranch, everything is included: unlimited horseback riding, fly-fishing (with lessons, if you wish), mountain biking, guided hikes, gourmet meals, and unlimited hot-tub time. The cabins are rustic on the outside but have complete bathrooms and fireplaces, porches, and views. The quiet intimacy of this small operation is underlined by an adults-only policy. It's a 50-mile drive from the ranch to Jackson for shopping and sightseeing excursions.

771 Flying A Ranch Rd., Pinedale, WY 82941 (50 miles southeast of Jackson on U.S. 191). Ⓒ **888/833-3348** in winter, or 307/367-2385. www.flyinga.com. 7 cabins. $1,300–$1,950 per person per week. Rates include all meals and ranch activities. No credit cards. **Amenities:** Restaurant; Jacuzzi; activities desk. *In room:* Kitchenette, hair dryer, iron, no phone.

Heart 6 Ranch (Kids)

Slightly more than an hour's drive north of Jackson, just east of the Moran Junction, is the Heart 6, a fistful of fun for families. The Heart 6 isn't the fanciest of the guest ranches in and around Jackson Hole, but it's certainly not short on entertainment. Fishing, horseback riding, hiking, or just enjoying the fantastic views lead the long list of outdoor activities. A naturalist from the Park Service is also on hand to educate guests on the local wildflowers. The ranch offers an airport-shuttle system, Saturday trips to the rodeo in Jackson, and extensive children's programs for tykes 3 and over; babysitting service is also available with prior notice. On rainy days, kids and adults alike can enjoy the recreation center, with bumper pool, foosball, and Ping-Pong.

16985 Buffalo Valley Rd. (35 miles north of Jackson and 5 miles east of Grand Teton National Park on U.S. 26/287), Moran, WY 83013. Ⓒ **888/543-2477** or 307/543-2477. www.heartsix.com. 15 cabins. $1,550–$1,750 per person per 6-night stay June–Aug; $75–$200 double Sept–May. Summer rates include all meals. DISC, MC, V. **Amenities:** Restaurant; outdoor heated pool; Jacuzzi; game room; activities desk. *In room:* No phone.

Lost Creek Ranch (★★)

The Lost Creek is so popular that one guest has stipulated in his will that his family will inherit annual trips after his demise. Reservations are at a premium with a short season and a maximum capacity of about 50 guests. If you manage to wrangle a reservation, however, this ultraplush ranch offers a wide range of outdoor activities, crowned by sumptuous gourmet meals. All the usual dude-ranch activities are included, and then some: hiking, riding, evening entertainment, and touring the parks are all part of the package.

After all that activity, you can pamper yourself in the spa (not included in the room rates, aside from fitness classes): get a massage, a sea-salt body scrub, or a facial, or else take a yoga class or work out. If you want to get away from the kids, there's a lounge with billiards and cards and a skeet-shooting range.

Duplex cabins, representing the height of rustic elegance, can be rented or subdivided; each section is outfitted with queen-size and twin beds and a private bathroom. There's also a two-bedroom cabin with a fireplace that sleeps six.

P.O. Box 95, Old Ranch Rd. (off U.S. 89, 20 miles north of Jackson), Moose, WY 83012. Ⓒ **307/733-3435.** Fax 307/ 733-1954. www.lostcreek.com. 10 cabins. $5,840–$13,710 per cabin per week. Rates include all meals, float trips, and rodeo. Call for discounted off-season rates. AE, DC, DISC, MC, V. Closed mid-Sept to May. **Amenities:** Outdoor heated pool; tennis courts; health club and spa; outdoor Jacuzzi; sauna; children's program; activities desk; laundry service. *In room:* Fridge, coffeemaker, hair dryer, microwave, no phone.

Red Rock Ranch (Kids)

This working cattle ranch makes room for families who want a fun experience amid the peaceful wilderness of the Gros Ventre Mountains east of Grand Teton National Park. With excellent catch-and-release fly-fishing on a private stretch of Crystal Creek, horseback riding in the mountains, and activities that include overnighters for the kids, cookouts with live music, and weekly country dances, this guest ranch northeast of Jackson is a great spot to bring the whole bunch. All nine cabins (one or two bedrooms) are comfortable log structures built in the 1950s, each busily decorated with Western trappings and a charming woodstove.

The kids will have a blast here. The **Children's Riding Program** (for those 6 and older) is a great learning experience and takes kids all over the ranch by horseback, but the overnight camp-out is the real Western treat. After a horseback ride, the kids (with the help of a couple of wranglers) set up camp and cook supper over an open fire. The night is spent playing games, telling stories, and looking up at a million stars.

P.O. Box 38, Kelly, WY 83011 (30 miles northeast of Jackson on U.S. 26/287). © 307/733-6288. www.theredrock ranch.com. 9 cabins. $1,650 per adult per week; $350–$1,250 per child per week. Rates include all meals and horseback riding. Minimum 6-day stay (Sun–Sat). No credit cards. Closed Sept–May. **Amenities:** Restaurant; lounge; outdoor heated pool; Jacuzzi; sauna; game room; activities desk. *In room:* Fridge, coffeemaker, no phone.

CAMPING

There aren't a lot of campsites for trailers close to this resort town anymore, because property values attract more upscale investments. In town, the **Wagon Wheel Campground** (© 307/733-4588) is about 5 blocks north of Town Square at the Wagon Wheel Motel and has RV sites for $47 to $50 and tent sites for $25. There's also the **Snake River Park KOA Campground,** on U.S. 89, 10 miles south of town (© 307/ 733-7078), and the **Teton Village KOA** (© 307/733-5254), 12 miles northwest of Jackson in Teton Village, both with sites for about $33 for tents, $45 for RVs. If you're looking to set up a tent when the parks are full, **Curtis Canyon Campground** (© 307/739-5500) is a great campground up behind the elk refuge in Bridger-Teton National Forest, and it will cost only $12 a night.

See also section 2, "Grand Teton National Park," for details on camping in Grand Teton National Park.

WHERE TO DINE

Jackson has more dining options than all of the other towns in this book combined, running the gamut of cuisine and price. You'll find the predictable steak/seafood/pasta menus—usually injected with a few de rigueur wild-game dishes, too—but you'll also find more unusual choices. In addition to the choices reviewed below, you can get a quick bite at **Shades Cafe,** 82 S. King St. (© 307/733-2015), which serves good coffee, sandwiches, and other breakfast and lunch entrees. At the other end of the spectrum is **Bubba's Bar-B-Que,** 515 W. Broadway (© 307/733-2288), a late-night hangout dishing out ribs and other meats. If you need a good shot of espresso with your morning paper, stop at the **Betty Rock Coffee House and Cafe,** 325 W. Pearl Ave. (© 307/733-0747), where you can sit outside on the deck. For an old-fashioned chuck-wagon dinner, mosey out with the **Bar-T-5 Covered Wagon Cookout and Wild West Show** (© 800/772-5386 or 307/733-5386).

EXPENSIVE

The Blue Lion ✦✦ ECLECTIC   In the fast-moving, high-rent world of Jackson dining, The Blue Lion stays in the forefront by staying the same. Owned and operated by Ned Brown since 1978, the restaurant is located in a two-story blue clapboard building—it looks like a comfy family home—across from a park. Inside, in intimate rooms accented with soft lighting, diners enjoy slow-paced and elegant meals. The menu features rack of lamb and wild-game specialties, such as grilled elk loin in a peppercorn sauce. Fresh fish is flown in daily for dishes such as the nori-crusted ahi.

160 N. Millward St. ℭ **307/733-3912.** Reservations recommended. Main courses $15–$33. AE, DC, DISC, MC, V. Summer daily 6–10pm; winter daily 6–9pm.

Burke's Chop House ℱ STEAKS/GAME/SEAFOOD   Formerly the chef at the steakhouse under the Million Dollar Cowboy Bar, Michael Burke struck out on his own and opened this ambitious eatery in downtown Jackson in February 2004. The sleek dining room, punctuated by plenty of dark wood, a few antique car parts and scenic photographs, and a sweeping bar, provides an understated setting for the unpretentious but excellent fare. The menu includes smoked baby back pork ribs with homemade bourbon barbecue sauce, cornmeal-crusted trout, and a nice selection of steaks and chops. The buffalo tenderloin and filets are particularly satisfying.

72 S. Glenwood St. ℭ **307/733-8575.** Reservations recommended. Main courses $16–$36. AE, DC, DISC, MC, V. Daily 6–10pm.

The Cadillac Grille ℱ CALIFORNIA ECLECTIC   The nostalgic neon and hip American cuisine give this restaurant a trendy air that attracts see-and-be-seen visitors as well as locals. The chefs work hard on presentation, but they also know how to cook, despite the wide-ranging variety of dishes, from fire-roasted elk tenderloins to pancetta-crusted Alaskan halibut. A *Wine Spectator* favorite, the wine list is equally long and varied. The Grille's upscale dining room is one of three options at this address; you can also eat at the posh bar, or the '50s-themed confines of **Billy's Giant Hamburgers,** where a great burger runs about $6. For the best of both worlds, order a burger at the bar.

55 N. Cache St. ℭ **307/733-3279.** Reservations recommended. Lunch $5–$18; dinner $16–$29. AE, MC, V. Daily 11:30am–3pm and 5:30–9:30pm.

Old Yellowstone Garage ℱ ITALIAN   Since relocating west from Dubois in 2000, the Old Yellowstone Garage has continued its 10-year tradition of serving up delectable Italian in a casual Western atmosphere. The self-dubbed "slow food" served here includes starters such as *cozze mie* (mussels in a garlic–white wine sauce), calamari, and antipasti plates. The dinner menu includes risotto (prepared differently every day), San Remo (deep-fried zucchini stuffed with mascarpone), and slow-cooked lamb shank, a wintertime favorite. Wood-oven pizzas round out the menu (and *are* the menu on Sun), the specialty being the *pizze bianca,* with homemade cheeses and fresh herbs. All of this is served up in a room with hardwood floors, big windows, tables, and booths, marked simply on the outside with the letters OYG.

175 Center St. ℭ **307/734-6161.** Reservations recommended. Main courses $15–$36. AE, DISC, MC, V. Tues–Sun 6–10pm.

Snake River Grill ℱℱℱ CONTEMPORARY AMERICAN   This is a popular drop-in spot for locals, including some of the glitterati who sojourn in the area—Harrison Ford and Calista Flockhart, to name two. The front-room dining area overlooks the busy Town Square, but there's a more private, romantic room in the back. It's an award-winning restaurant for both its wine list and its menu, which features regular fresh-fish dishes (ahi tuna is a favorite), crispy pork shank, and some game-meat entrees such as venison chops and Idaho trout. The pizzas—cooked in a wood-burning oven—are topped with exotic ingredients such as duck sausage or eggplant with portobello mushrooms.

Town Square, Jackson. ℭ **307/733-0557.** Reservations recommended. Main courses $20–$40. AE, MC, V. Summer daily 5:30–10pm; shorter hours rest of year. Closed Nov and Apr.

Stiegler's *Finds* AUSTRIAN/CONTINENTAL   Austrian cuisine isn't exactly lurking beyond every street corner, waiting to be summoned with a Julie Andrews yodel, but the discerning Austrian will certainly appreciate Stiegler's. Since 1983, Stiegler's has been confusing, astonishing, and delighting customers with such favorites as venison St. Hubertus, bratwurst, and schnitzel, as well as less recognizable (and not as heavy as Austrian food's reputation might suggest) delicacies. Each plate is served with at least three veggies for a terrific presentation and variety of tastes. The desserts are more familiar: apple strudel and sweet vanilla cream-cheese crepe. Peter Stiegler, the Austrian chef, invites you to "find a little *Gemütlichkeit*"—the feeling you get when you're surrounded by good friends, good food, and, of course, good beer. The inviting copper bar has its own menu ($10–$19, with great burgers) and there are intimate tables and booths inside and a poolside patio outside.

Teton Village Rd. at the Aspens. ℭ **307/733-1071.** Reservations recommended. Main courses $18–$30. AE, MC, V. Tues–Sun 5:30–9:30pm. Closed Mon.

MODERATE

Koshu Wine Bar ✹✹ *Finds* ECLECTIC   Housed in the back half of the Jackson Hole Wine Company, this small, sleek dining room serves ingenious, addictive, Asian-inspired creations. The Far East is just a starting point, with dishes that meld dozens of influences into dishes such as ahi tartare and pork ribs; the menu changes on a near-daily basis. Thanks to its location in a wine store, patrons can choose from 800 varieties of wine at retail price (plus a nominal corking fee).

200 W. Broadway in the back of the Jackson Hole Wine Company. ℭ **307/733-5283.** Reservations recommended. Main courses $15–$30. AE, MC, V. Daily 6–10:30pm. Bar open later.

Mangy Moose *Kids* AMERICAN   Coming off the slopes at the end of a hard day of skiing or snowboarding, you can slide right to the porch of this Teton Village institution. Good luck getting a seat inside, but if you like a lot of noise and laughter, a beer or a glass of wine, and tasty food you'll be patient—it beats getting into your car and driving into town. The decor matches the pandemonium: It looks like an upscale junk shop, with bicycles, old signs, and, naturally, a moose head or two hanging from the walls and rafters. The food is customary Wyoming fare (steak, seafood, and pasta)—we're big fans of the buffalo meatloaf and the fresh Idaho trout. There is often live music on weekends in the saloon, and an affiliated cafe, the RMO Cafe, serves coffee, breakfast, and lunch in a separate room from 7am to 5pm.

1 W. Village Dr., Teton Village. ℭ **307/733-4913.** Reservations recommended for larger parties. Main courses $11–$26. AE, MC, V. Daily 5:30–10pm.

Nani's Genuine Pasta House ✹✹ *Finds* ITALIAN   The setting is simple, but the food is extraordinary at Nani's, where you are handed two menus: a "Carta Classico" featuring pasta favorites such as *amitriciana* (tomato, onion, guanciale, and freshly ground black pepper) and fresh mussels in wine broth, and a list of specialties from a different featured region of Italy. Depending on when you visit, it might be Sicily, where Head Chef Camille Parker's family has its roots, or Emilia-Romagna, where prosciutto, Parmesan, and balsamic vinegar are culinary staples. Parker ventures to Italy annually for research, and you can literally taste her passion. Your only problem with her restaurant might be finding it—it's tucked away behind a little relic of a motel, and rarely does it fill to the rafters.

242 N. Glenwood St. ℭ **307/733-3888.** Reservations recommended. Main courses $13–$33. MC, V. Daily 5–10pm.

Nora's Fish Creek Inn ☆ *(Finds)* AMERICAN   If you like to eat among locals, and if you like to eat a lot, Nora's is the place to hang out in Wilson, 6 miles northwest of Jackson—just look for the 15-foot trout on the roof. Rough but pleasant to look at, it's an institution, and if you come here often, you'll start to recognize the regulars, who grumble over their coffee and gossip about doings in the valley. Breakfast is especially good, when there are pancakes and huevos rancheros that barely fit on the huge plates. Prices are inexpensive compared to those at any of the other restaurants in town. Dinner is fish, fish, and more fish, namely fresh Idaho trout.

5600 W. Wyo. 22, Wilson. ☎ **307/733-8288.** Reservations accepted for dinner. Breakfast $5–$8; lunch $4–$9; dinner $12–$21. AE, DISC, MC, V. Mon–Fri 6:30am–2pm; Sat–Sun 7am–1:30pm; June–Sept daily 5–9pm; mid-Dec to Mar dinner daily 5:30–9pm; no dinner Oct to mid-Dec and Mar–May; breakfast and lunch hours are the same year-round.

Rendezvous Bistro ☆☆ AMERICAN/SEAFOOD   Taking over a building that once housed a Denny's franchise, the Rendezvous opened in 2001 and garnered a fast local following. It's easy to see why: The place is contemporary yet casual, the food is affordable but very good, and the service is excellent. Climb into one of the intimate booths and order a dozen oysters on the half shell and slurp away, but save some room for a main course, ranging from steak frites to tuna tartare to a whole Maine lobster. It might sound formal, but it's really not—the beauty is that the food is the best upscale value in town, while the atmosphere is very laid-back.

380 S. Broadway. ☎ **307/739-1100.** Reservations recommended. Main courses $9–$20. AE, MC, V. Sun–Thurs 5:30–10pm; Fri–Sat 5:30–11pm. Closed mid-Apr to mid-May and Sun in winter.

Sweetwater Restaurant ☆ AMERICAN   Although this little log restaurant serves American fare, it does so in a decidedly offbeat way. The eclectic menu includes, for example, a Greek salad, a Baja chicken salad, and a cowboy-grilled roast beef sandwich. During the summer, there's outside dining. The dinner menu is just as quirky and livened by nightly specials; try the unique chile-lime crab cakes before diving into a giant grilled salmon filet glazed with tequila, lemon, and honey or buffalo pot roast with jack cheese grits. Vegetarians will want to sample the spinach and feta casserole. The lunch slate is full of creative salads and sandwiches.

85 King St. ☎ **307/733-3553.** Reservations recommended. Lunch $8–$11; dinner $16–$25. AE, DISC, MC, V. Daily 11:30am–3pm and 5:30–10pm; shorter hours in winter.

INEXPENSIVE

Jedediah's House of Sourdough *(Kids)* AMERICAN   You feel like you've walked into the kitchen of some sodbuster's log cabin home when you enter Jedediah's—the structure was built in 1910 and now resides on the National Register of Historic Places. Bring a big appetite for breakfast, and a little patience—you might have to wait for a table, then you might have to wait for food while you stare at the interesting old photos on the wall. But it's worth it, especially for the rich flavor of the sourjacks (sourdough pancakes) served with blueberries. Lunches include soups, salads, and burgers and sandwiches—on sourdough, of course. The sourdough starter here is also historic: It dates from the 1870s.

135 E. Broadway. ☎ **307/733-5671.** Reservations not accepted. Breakfast $3–$9; lunch $5–$8. AE, DC, DISC, MC, V. Daily 7am–2pm.

Snake River Brewery ☆ *(Value)* MICROBREWERY   One of the West's best microbreweries, the industrial-meets-contemporary-looking establishment offers a menu of pasta, applewood-fired pizzas and paninis, and salads. The real standouts are the beers, especially Custer's Last Ale and Snake River Pale Ale. This place is a local's favorite and a great lunch spot, with daily $6 specials like turkey-and-brie wraps and chipotle barbecue sandwiches.

265 S. Millward St. ✆ **307/739-BEER**. Reservations not accepted. Most dishes $6–$12. AE, DISC, MC, V. Daily 11:30am–11pm. Bar open later.

JACKSON AFTER DARK

Talented musicians from well-known orchestras participate in the **Grand Teton Music Festival** ✸ (✆ **307/733-3050;** www.gtmf.org) held in summer in the amphitheater next to the tram lift. Tickets are usually available on short notice, especially for the weeknight chamber music performances, which are often terrific.

Wyoming's only year-round professional theater company performs at the **Pink Garter Mainstage Theatre,** 50 W. Broadway Ave. (✆ **307/733-3670;** www.offsquare. org), and produces classic and contemporary comedies and dramas. Tickets (typically $10–$30) for all shows should be reserved.

Those less impressed with dramaturgy should head down to the **Silver Dollar Bar,** at 50 N. Glenwood St. in the Wort Hotel (✆ **307/733-2190**), for a drink with one of the real or wannabe cowpokes at the bar. And, yes, those 2,032 silver dollars are authentic. At the very famous **Million Dollar Cowboy Bar** on the Town Square, at 25 N. Cache St. (✆ **307/733-2207**), you can dance the two-step to live bands. If you want some high-octane dancing fun, head west to Wilson and the **Stagecoach Bar** (✆ **307/733-4407**) on Wyo. 22 on a Sunday night. It's the only night there's live music in this scruffy bar and hamburger joint, and the place is jammed wall to wall.

2 Grand Teton National Park ✸✸✸

12 miles N of Jackson

Since people often think of Grand Teton in conjunction with either Yellowstone National Park or Jackson Hole, they imagine it's been around since the days of exploration, trappers, and ranch homesteads. But it's a fairly new park, about 50 years old, just as the dramatic Tetons are a fairly young mountain range—a mere 10 million years old, give or take a millennium.

It's also a small park, at least by Yellowstone standards, comprising the eastern slope of this brief mountain range and a portion of the Snake River plain below. It lacks the unique geothermal features of its northern neighbor, but few mountains stand in such dramatic relief as the towering Cathedral Group, Les Trois Tetons (or "the three breasts," as some lonesome French trappers named them): **Mount Owen, Teewinot,** and **Grand Teton.** The Grand, as the locals call it, rises highest, to 13,770 feet, and it has lured climbers since the Depression era, when young Paul Petzoldt and a friend scrambled their way to the top in tennis shoes, to the astonishment of locals. Now commercial guides take hundreds of people to the summit every year, while adventurers find new and more difficult climbs in the range, or new ways of challenging themselves, like snowboarding or paragliding off the summits.

But Grand Teton is not merely an amusement park for risk-takers. There are beautiful lakes where you can sail or fish, and hikes that take you to waterfalls and panoramic views of the valley and mountains. There are historic sites like Menors Ferry, built a century ago to get folks across the Snake River, and some beautiful old lodges where you can experience holidays the way our grandparents did. Alpine wildflowers explode during the late spring, and hikers will often see elk, moose, trumpeter

Jackson Hole & Grand Teton National Park

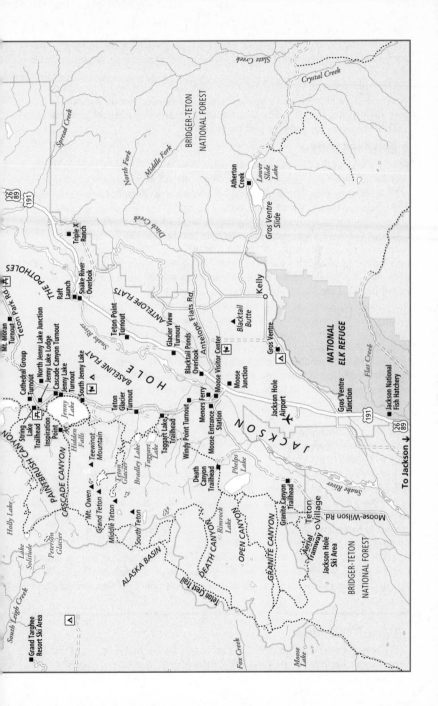

swans, bald eagles, and the occasional bear. There are peaceful nights under the stars when you might hear a chorus of coyotes yapping, or, more recently, the husky howls of wolves.

More than Yellowstone, Grand Teton is a modern park, beset by complex issues that sometimes pit wilderness values against modern conveniences like the commercial airport that operates here, or other uses, like the irrigation water behind Jackson Lake Dam or the cattle that graze the park's meadows.

A BRIEF HISTORY

Your first look at the Tetons, rising like spears from the Snake River plain, will take your breath away. Geologists say these mountains are still growing along a crack in the earth's crust that thrusts the range upward from the west as the valley sinks to the east. The lakebed sediments of the valley floor are actually "younger" than the pre-Cambrian rock of the peaks. Recent earthquakes in the area indicate the fault is still active. Like much of the Rocky Mountains, this range has been sculpted by glaciers, which gouged out the deep U-shaped valleys between the peaks. When the ice sheet that covered Jackson Hole melted for the last time, 15,000 years ago, it left a depression and a big mound of debris—called a terminal moraine—that formed a natural dam at the end of Jackson Lake.

The receding layers of ice created beautiful glacial lakes like Phelps, Taggart, Bradley, Jenny, String, and Leigh; polished the sides of Cascade Canyon; and honed the peaks to their present jagged state. The glaciers live on, the most prominent being the five that have survived on Mount Moran.

The first human inhabitants of the region appeared about 12,000 years ago. Among the tribes that hunted here were the Blackfeet, Crow, Gros Ventre, and Shoshone. Summers were spent here hunting and raising crops; winters meant migration to warmer climes. The trappers and explorers who followed the tribes into the valley were equally distressed by the harsh winters and short growing season, which made Jackson Hole marginal ranchland at best. These early homesteaders quickly realized that their best hope was to market the beauty of the area, which they began doing in earnest as early as a century ago.

The danger of haphazard development soon became apparent. There was a dance hall at Jenny Lake, hot-dog stands and piles of debris along the roads, and vacation homes going up on prime wildlife habitat. In the 1920s, Yellowstone park officials and conservationists met to discuss how the Grand Teton area might be protected, and eventually they enlisted philanthropist John D. Rockefeller, Jr., to acquire lands for a future park. In 1929 a park was established to protect the mountains, while Rockefeller continued buying up ranches at the base of the Tetons, using a dummy corporation to hide his involvement. Wyoming's congressional delegation fought hard against park designation in the valley as Jackson Hole public opinion swayed like a

---

⌐Tips **Travel Tip**

If you're considering a visit to the area's parks before mid-June, you should begin your exploration in Grand Teton before working north to Yellowstone. Elevations are slightly lower and snow melts earlier, so trails are more navigable and temperatures a bit more moderate.

pendulum, so President Franklin D. Roosevelt created the Jackson Hole National Monument in the 1940s. In 1950 the park was expanded to its present form.

JUST THE FACTS
ACCESS/ENTRY POINTS

Like the range of mountains it protects, Grand Teton National Park is a strip of real estate centered on a north-south axis. Teton Park Road, the primary thoroughfare, skirts along the lakes that pool at the mountains' base. From the **north,** you can enter the park from Yellowstone National Park, which is connected to Grand Teton by a wilderness corridor called the **John D. Rockefeller Jr. Memorial Parkway** through which the U.S. 89/191/287 runs for 8 miles, where you may see wildlife through the trees, some of which are bare and blackened from the 1988 fires. When you come this way, you will already have paid your entrance to both parks, so there is no entrance station, but you can stop at **Flagg Ranch,** approximately 5 miles north of the park boundary, and get park information. December through March, Yellowstone's south entrance is open only to snowmobiles and Snowcoaches.

You can also approach the park from the **east,** via U.S. 26/287. This route comes from Dubois, 55 miles east on the other side of the Absaroka and Wind River mountains, and crosses **Togwotee Pass,** where you'll get your first—and one of the best— views of the Tetons towering above the valley. Travelers who come this way can continue south on U.S. 26/89/191 to Jackson without paying an entrance fee, though they are within the park boundaries.

Finally, you can enter Grand Teton from Jackson in the **south,** driving about 13 miles north on U.S. 26/89/191 to the Moose turnoff and the park's south entrance. Here you'll find the park headquarters, a visitor center, and a small community that includes dining, rental cabins, and shops.

For details on how to fly into the region, see "Getting There" in section 1, "Jackson Hole."

VISITOR INFORMATION

There are three visitor centers in Grand Teton National Park. The **Moose Visitor Center** (© 307/739-3399) is a half-mile west of Moose Junction at the southern end of the park; it's open from 8am to 7pm daily from June to Labor Day, and 8am to 5pm the rest of the year. (Groundbreaking for a dazzling new facility at Moose, dubbed the **Grand Teton Discovery and Visitor Center,** took place in June 2005. The $22-million project is scheduled to open to the public in 2007.) The **Colter Bay Visitor Center** (© 307/739-3594), the northernmost of the park's visitor centers, is open 8am to 8pm from early June to Labor Day, and from 8am to 5pm after Labor Day to early October. There is also **Jenny Lake Visitor Center** (© 307/739-3343), open from 8am to 7pm daily from early June to Labor Day and from 8am to 5pm after Labor Day to early October. Maps and ranger assistance are available at all three, and there are bookstores and exhibits at Moose and Colter Bay.

To receive park maps and information prior to your arrival, contact **Grand Teton National Park,** P.O. Drawer 170, Moose, WY 83012 (© 307/739-3600). Other key park numbers include emergency park dispatch (© 307/739-3300), and recorded information on climbing (© 307/739-3604) and campgrounds (© 307/739-3603). The park's website is **www.nps.gov/grte**.

Other sources of useful information include **Travel Montana,** P.O. Box 200533, 301 S. Park Ave., Helena, MT 59601 (© 800/847-4868; www.visitmt.com);

Wyoming Division of Tourism, I-25 at College Drive, Cheyenne, WY 82002 (© **800/225-5996;** www.wyomingtourism.org); **Yellowstone Country,** 1822 W. Lincoln St., Bozeman, MT 59715 (© **800/736-5276); Jackson Chamber of Commerce,** P.O. Box 550, Jackson, WY 83001 (© **307/733-3316;** www.jacksonhole chamber.com); and **Park County Travel Council,** P.O. Box 2454, Cody, WY 82414 (© **307/587-2297;** www.pctc.org).

FEES & BACKCOUNTRY PERMITS

There are no park gates on U.S. 26/89/191, so you get a free ride through the park on that route. But if you want to get off the highway and explore, you'll pay $20 per automobile for a 7-day pass for entry into both Grand Teton and Yellowstone national parks. If you expect to visit the parks more than once within a year, you can buy a $40 annual permit, but we consider the various national park passes, which are also honored here, to be a better deal (see section 7, "Specialized Travel Resources," in chapter 2). For information on camping fees at Grand Teton National Park, see "Camping," later in this chapter.

Backcountry permits are required from the Park Service for overnight use of backcountry campsites. The permits are free, but they can be reserved only from January 1 to May 15 (and the reservation itself costs $15); thereafter, all backcountry permits are issued on a first-come, first-served basis up to 24 hours before your first night out. Permits are issued at the Moose and Colter Bay visitor centers and the Jenny Lake ranger station. Reservations may be made by writing the **Permits Office,** Grand Teton National Park, P.O. Drawer 170, Moose, WY 83012. Phone reservations are not accepted, but information is available by calling © **307/739-3602.**

Boating permits are required if you bring your own boat (for motorized craft, $20 for an annual permit and $10 for a 7-day permit; for human-powered vessels, $10 for an annual permit, and $5 for a 7-day permit). You can get permits at Moose or Colter Bay; the cost is included in the price of a boat rental. Motorized boats are permitted on Jenny, Jackson, and Phelps lakes; sailboats, Windsurfers, and jet skis are allowed on Jackson. Boats paddled by humans are permitted on most park lakes and the Snake River.

State of Wyoming **fishing licenses** are required for fishers over 14 years of age. An adult nonresident license costs $10 per day, $75 for the season. Youth fees (ages 14–18) are $3 per day, $15 for the season. (A Wyoming resident pays $15 for a season permit, and a $10 Conservation Stamp is also required for all licenses except the 1-day variety.) You can buy them at sporting-goods stores or park visitor centers. The entirety of the Snake River is open for fishing from April 1 to October 31; Jackson Lake is closed all of October. Because the Snake River flows into, and exits, Jackson Lake, different regulations apply to various sections of the river, and several are closed; the prudent angler will become knowledgeable of these laws to avoid a hefty fine.

REGULATIONS

The rules here are similar to those in most national parks. It is illegal to damage or collect natural, archaeological, or historical objects, and even picking wildflowers is prohibited. Pets must be leashed and are not allowed more than 50 feet from roadways; on trails, boats, or boardwalks; or in the backcountry. They are allowed in campgrounds, but must be restrained at all times.

Loaded guns are not permitted in the park. However, unloaded firearms may be transported in a vehicle when cased, broken down, or rendered inoperable. Ammunition must be carried in a separate compartment of the vehicle.

SEASONS

Spring is an excellent time to visit the park—but remember that spring starts later in Wyoming than in most other parts of the country. In **May** and **June,** mild days and cool nights intersperse with occasional rain and snow. The snow level usually remains above valley elevation until mid-June. Wildflowers are in bloom, and, on a clear day, the snow-covered Tetons stand out boldly against a crisp blue sky. Better yet, trails are virtually devoid of hikers, though at higher elevations snow might still block the paths; check in at one of the ranger stations for trail conditions.

Summer is the most intense season at Grand Teton, with flowers blooming, fish and wildlife feeding, and all sorts of activity crammed into a few months of warm weather, from July to early September.

In **September,** sunny days and cooler nights alternate with rain and occasional snowstorms, and by the middle of the month, fall colors begin to make their way across the landscape.

The first big snow usually arrives by the beginning of **November** (though it's not unheard of in July!). In winter months, temperatures stick in the single digits, with subzero overnight temperatures common.

AVOIDING THE CROWDS

Summer is the busy time here, but crowds thin in the park after Labor Day, and you can enjoy sunny days and brilliant aspen yellows well into October. When there are crowds, you can avoid them by staying away from the centers of activity, which are Colter Bay, Jenny Lake, and Moose. Check out the overlooks, photograph the sites, and take in a few educational exhibits, then abandon the paved areas for unpaved trails.

TIPS FOR TRAVELERS WITH DISABILITIES

Visitor centers at Moose, Colter Bay, Jenny Lake, and Flagg Ranch provide interpretive programs, displays, and visitor information in several formats, including visual, audible, and tactile. Large-print scripts, Braille brochures, and narrative audiotapes are available at Moose and Colter Bay.

Accessible parking spaces are located close to all visitor center entrances; curb cuts are provided, as are accessible restroom facilities.

Campsites at Colter Bay, Jenny Lake, and Gros Ventre campgrounds are on relatively level terrain; Lizard Creek and Signal Mountain are hilly and less accessible. Picnic areas at String Lake and Cottonwood Creek are both accessible, though the toilet at Cottonwood is not.

Accessible dining facilities are located at Flagg Ranch, Leeks Marina, Jackson Lake Lodge, and Jenny Lake Lodge.

More information is available by contacting **Grand Teton National Park,** P.O. Drawer 170, Moose, WY 83012 (✆ **307/739-3600;** www.nps.gov/grte).

VIEWING THE PEAKS

Grand Teton National Park is famous for its mountains, and rightly so. The Cathedral Group is composed of **Grand Teton** (elevation 13,770 ft.), **Teewinot** (elevation 12,325 ft.), and **Mount Owen** (elevation 12,928 ft.). Nearby, almost as impressive, are **South Teton** (elevation 12,514 ft.) and **Middle Teton** (elevation 12,804 ft.).

If you come from the north and Yellowstone National Park, you will have paid a park-entry fee and be entitled to explore along **Teton Park Road,** west of the Snake. You'll be looking at mountains as you drive the east shore of Jackson Lake, and you'll

---

(Tips   Seeing the Park for Free

Those who are only passing by and never plan to get far from their cars can see the full spectacle of these mountains without paying a park entry fee. If you come from the east, you will pass no tollbooths on your way south on U.S. 26/89/191, but there are frequent pullouts on the west side of the road that give you a panoramic overview of the Snake River and the Tetons. For that matter, you get a more distant, but equally grand, view of the mountains coming over **Togwotee Pass** on U.S. 26/287.

---

find plenty of opportunities to pull over and snap your shutter. Four miles south of Colter Bay, you can take an unpaved, 1-mile road heading east from the highway to the **Grand View Overlook.** A large, flat area at the end of the road offers a commanding view of the Grand Tetons, and an excellent picnic spot. This road is great for autos, hikers, and bicycles, but not for large RVs.

You'll also get excellent views of the Cathedral Group on the trails and roads that ring **Jenny Lake** (see "Seeing the Highlights," below).

Signal Mountain, southeast of Jackson Lake, may not rank up there with the other Tetons, but you can drive right up it to an excellent lookout spot. Navigating the twisting, narrow road pays off at the summit, where you can gaze out over the valley, Cascade Canyon, Jackson Lake, and the Tetons.

Slightly north of Jenny Lake is the underrated, yet astoundingly humbling, **Mount Moran** (elevation 12,605 ft.), the fourth-largest peak in the range; its curiously flattened, sheared-off summit is the result of erosion back in geologically volatile times.

SEEING THE HIGHLIGHTS
JACKSON LAKE & THE NORTH END OF THE PARK

A great many people enter Grand Teton National Park from the north end, emerging from Yellowstone's south entrance with a 7-day park pass that gets them into Grand Teton as well. Yellowstone is connected to Grand Teton by a wilderness corridor called the **John D. Rockefeller Jr. Memorial Parkway** where the highway runs for 8 miles. Along it, you'll see an interesting area of meadows sometimes dotted with elk; the Snake River as it runs into Jackson Lake; and forests that in some places still show the impact of the 1988 fires. Some people complain about the sight of blackened tree trunks, but others are heartened to see the mosaic shapes of natural burn and the soft green of new trees sprouting.

Along the parkway, not far from Yellowstone, you'll pass your first lodging option, **Flagg Ranch** (see "Where to Stay in the Park," later in this chapter), with gas, restaurants, and other services. In the winter, this is a busy staging area for the Snowcoach and snowmobile crowds, but the new snowmobile quotas led the place to close its rental cabins come fall starting in 2003.

JACKSON LAKE   The north end of the park is dominated by giant **Jackson Lake,** a huge expanse of water that fills a deep gorge left 10,000 years ago by retreating glaciers. Though it empties east into the Snake River, curving around in the languid **Oxbow Bend**—a favorite wildlife-viewing float for canoeists—the water from Jackson Lake eventually turns south, then west through Snake River Canyon and into Idaho. In 1911, potato farmers downstream were instrumental in getting Congress to fund Jackson Lake Dam, which raised the lake about 40 feet and waterlogged the forest around the shoreline. Stream flow is now regulated at the dam for both farmers and rafters in the canyon, and, for better or worse, we have an irrigation dam in a national park. The dead trees have long since been cleared out and the dam was rebuilt with an eye for aesthetics in 1989. In general, the lake looks quite natural, except when water level plummets in the fall.

LEEKS MARINA   As the road follows the east shore of the lake from the north, the first development travelers encounter is **Leeks Marina,** where boats can launch, gas up, and moor from mid-May to mid-September. A casual restaurant serves light fare and pizza during the summer. But drivers also have the option of stopping at numerous picnic pullouts along the lake.

COLTER BAY   Just south of Leeks is **Colter Bay,** a busy outpost of park services where you can get groceries, postcards and stamps, T-shirts, and advice. If this is your first stop in the park, get maps and information at the **Colter Bay Visitor Center.** Here you can view park and wildlife videotapes and attend a park-orientation slide program throughout the day. Ranger-led activities include museum tours, park-orientation talks, natural history hikes, and evening amphitheater programs. Colter Bay has lots of overnight options, from its cabins to its old-fashioned tent camps to its trailer park and campground. There are also a general store and do-it-yourself laundry, two restaurants, a boat launch and boat rentals, and tours. You can take pleasant short hikes in this area, including a walk around the bay or out to **Hermitage Point** (see "Hiking," below).

The **Indian Arts Museum** ✪ (✆ **307/739-3594**) at the Colter Bay Visitor Center is worth a visit, though it is not strictly about the Native American cultures of this area. The artifacts are mostly from Plains Indian tribes, but there are also some Navajo items from the Southwest. The collection was assembled by David T. Vernon, and includes pipes, shields, dolls, and war clubs sometimes called "skull crackers." Visiting Indian artists work in the museum all summer long and sell their wares on-site. Admission is free.

JACKSON LAKE JUNCTION   From Colter Bay, the road veers east and then south again past **Jackson Lake Lodge** (see "Where to Stay in the Park," later in this chapter), a slick, 1950s-style resort with a magnificent view of the Tetons and brushy flats in the foreground where moose often roam. Numerous trails originate here (see "Hiking," below), heading both to **Jackson Lake** and east to **Emma Matilda Lake.** The road then becomes **Jackson Lake Junction,** where you can either continue west along the lakeshore or go east to the park's **Moran Entrance Station.** Here the park's odd entrance configuration comes into play: If you go out through the Moran entrance you are still in the park, and may turn south on U.S. 26/89/191 and drive along the Snake River to Jackson, making most of your journey within the park's borders, though you might not know it.

SIGNAL MOUNTAIN   But if you're here to enjoy the park, you'd probably turn west on **Teton Park Road** at Jackson Lake Junction, and arrive after only 5 miles at **Signal Mountain.** Like its counterpart at Colter Bay, this developed recreation area, on Jackson Lake's southeast shore, offers camping sites, accommodations in cabins and multiplex units, two restaurants, and a lounge with one of the few live televisions in the park. This is also the place to fill up on gasoline and provisions from the small convenience store. Boat rentals and scenic cruises of the lake also originate here.

If you turn east instead of west off Teton Park Road at Signal Mountain, you can drive up a narrow, twisting road to the top of the mountain, 700 feet above the valley, where you'll have a fine view of the ring of mountains—Absarokas, Gros Ventres, Tetons, and Yellowstone Plateau—that create Jackson "Hole." Note also the potholes created in the valley's hilly moraines left by retreating glaciers. Below the summit, about 3 miles from the base of the hill, is **Jackson Point Overlook,** a paved path 300 feet long leading to the spot where the Hayden Expedition's photographer, William Henry Jackson, shot his famous wet-plate photographs of Jackson Lake and the Tetons more than a century ago—proof to the world that such spectacular places really existed in the Rockies.

JENNY LAKE & THE SOUTH END OF THE PARK

JENNY LAKE Continuing south along Teton Park Road, you move into the park's southern half, where the tallest peaks rise abruptly above a string of smaller lakes strung together in the foothills—**Leigh Lake, String Lake,** and **Jenny Lake,** which is the favorite of many park visitors. At North Jenny Lake Junction you can take a turnoff west to **Jenny Lake Lodge** (see "Where to Stay in the Park," later in this chapter)—the road then continues as a one-way scenic loop along the lakeshore before rejoining Teton Park Road about 4 miles later.

Beautiful **Jenny Lake** gets a lot of traffic throughout the summer, both from hikers who circumnavigate the lake on a 6-mile trail and from more sedentary folks who pay for a boat ride across the lake to Hidden Falls and the short, steep climb to **Inspiration Point** (see "Hiking," below). The parking lot at **South Jenny Lake** is often jammed, and there can be a long wait for the boat ride, so you might want to get there early in the day. There are also a tents-only campground, a visitor center, and a general store stocked with a modest supply of prepackaged foods, and even less fresh produce and vegetables. You can take a fairly level and easy hike around the south end of the lake to Hidden Falls or grab a ride with the **Jenny Lake Boating Company** (② **307/734-9227**); round-trips cost $7.50 for adults and $5 for children 7 to 12 (free for kids 6 and under).

SOUTH OF JENNY LAKE South of the lake, Teton Park Road crosses open sagebrush plains with never-ending views of the mountains. You'll pass the **Climbers' Ranch** (see "Climbing," later in this chapter)—an inexpensive dorm-lodging alternative for

---

Tips **Insider Tips**

Some of the best spots aren't highlighted on the map. On the west side of the road from Signal Mountain to the Jenny Lake cutoff, a little over a mile north of the Spring Lake–Jenny Lake scenic drive cutoff, is an unmarked, unpaved road that leads to **Spalding Bay.** You'll travel through bumpy moose habitat before curling down a steep hill to a back bay of the lake, where you'll find a small campsite, a boat launch with parking for trucks and boat trailers, and a primitive restroom. Use of the campsite requires a park permit, but we think this site provides an excellent opportunity to find seclusion with excellent views of the lake and mountains. The road is easily negotiable by an automobile or sport-utility vehicle; we would not recommend an RV or towed trailer.

climbers—and some trail heads for enjoyable hikes to **Taggart Lake** and elsewhere. Look closely in the sagebrush for the shy pronghorn, more commonly (and incorrectly) labeled antelope. This handsome animal, with tan cheeks and black accent stripes, can spring up to 60 mph. Badgers also roam the brush here; you might encounter one of the shy but ornery creatures in the morning or at twilight.

The **Teton Glacier Turnout** presents a view of a glacier that grew for several hundred years until, within the past century, it reversed direction, pressured by hotter summer temperatures, and began retreating.

MOOSE VISITOR CENTER   The road arrives at the park's south entrance again, actually well within the park's boundaries—and the **Moose Visitor Center,** which is also park headquarters. If you are approaching the park from the south rather than the north, this is where you can find maps, advice, and some interpretive displays; a new facility is on tap for 2008 across the street from the existing one.

Just behind the visitor center is **Menors Ferry.** Bill Menor had a country store and operated a ferry across the Snake River at Moose back in the late 1800s. The ferry and store have been reconstructed, and you can buy items similar to the ones Menor used to sell here. Nearby is a historic cabin where a group of locals met in 1923 and planted the seed for the protection of the natural and scenic quality of the area, an idea that eventually led to the creation of the national park.

Also in this area is the **Chapel of the Transfiguration.** In 1925, this chapel was built in Moose so that settlers wouldn't have to make a long buckboard ride into Jackson. It's still in use for Episcopal services spring through fall and is a popular spot for weddings, with a view of the Tetons through a window behind the altar.

DORNAN'S   This is a small village area just south of the visitor center on an inholding of private land owned by one of the area's earliest homesteading families. There are a few shops and a semigourmet grocery store, a post office, a bar where there is sometimes live music, and, surprisingly, a first-rate wine shop.

OTHER PARK HIGHLIGHTS

The highway route through the park on the east side of the Snake has several turnouts for shutterbugs (better have a wide-angle lens!). Among the stops you can make are the **Glacier View Turnout** (where you can view an area that was filled with a 4,000-ft.-thick glacier 150,000 years ago) and the **Blacktail Ponds Overlook** (a beaver-dam subdivision). Gazing out across **Snake River Overlook** at the plateaus that roll from riverbed to valley floor lends vivid insight into the power of the glaciers and ice floes that sculpted this landscape. If you want to go a ways off-road and down to the river, you can try the dirt **Schwabacher Road** or the newly repaved **Deadman's Bar Road.**

Only 5 miles north of Jackson on U.S. 26/89/191, you can turn east on the **Gros Ventre River Road** and follow the river east into its steep canyon; a few miles past the little town of Kelly, you'll leave the park and enter the **Bridger-Teton National Forest.** In 1925, a huge slab of mountain broke off the north end of the Gros Ventre Range on the east side of Jackson Hole, a reminder that nature still has an unpredictable and violent side. The slide left a gaping open gash in the side of Sheep Mountain, sloughing off nearly 150 million cubic feet of rock and forming a natural dam across the Gros Ventre River half a mile wide. Two years later, the dam broke, and a cascade of water rushed down the canyon and through the little town of Kelly, taking several lives. The town of **Kelly** is a quaintly unconventional community with a large number of yurts.

Up in the canyon formed by the Gros Ventre River there are a roadside display with photographs of the slide area and a short nature walk from the road down to the residue of the slide and **Lower Slide Lake,** with signs identifying the trees and plants that survived or grew in the slide's aftermath.

RANGER-LED ACTIVITIES

It's got to be the best bargain in the world: National parks offer all sorts of free presentations and guided hikes throughout the summer days, and the rangers are generally personable and knowledgeable. At Grand Teton, these range from a ranger-led 3-mile hike from the Colter Bay Visitor Center to Swan Lake, to a relaxed evening chatting with a ranger on the back deck of the Jackson Lake Lodge, with the Tetons as a dramatic backdrop and spotting scope for watching moose and birds. Numerous events are held during the summer at Colter Bay, South Jenny Lake, and the Moose Visitor Center. Check the daily schedules in the park's newspaper, *The Teewinot,* which you can pick up at any visitor center.

From Moose, rangers lead visitors out to the "lek"—the mating ground of the strutting grouse, whose males' displays are dramatic to say the least—during the springtime mating season. In winter, **guided snowshoe hikes** begin at the Moose Visitor Center.

At the Taggart Lake trail head, there are **wildflower walks** led by rangers who can tell you the difference between lupine and larkspur, daily in June and July, and guided morning hikes to Hidden Falls from Jenny Lake (you take the boat across the lake), among other activities.

Youngsters 8 to 12 can join **Young Naturalist programs** at Colter Bay or Jenny Lake and learn about the natural world for 2 hours while hiking with a ranger. Signups are at the visitor centers (the fee is a mere $1), and the kids will need basic hiking gear.

There are also evening **campfire gatherings** at the Gros Ventre, Jenny Lake, Signal Mountain, Lizard Creek, and Colter Bay campground amphitheaters on a variety of park-related topics.

OTHER ORGANIZED TOURS & ACTIVITIES

The **Teton Science School** ✸ (© 307/733-4765; www.tetonscience.org) is a 30-year-old institution with a cabin campus in the park that offers summer programs for students and adults that discuss the ecology, geology, and wildlife of the park, with workshops in photography and tracking, too. The school's **Wildlife Expeditions** (© 307/773-2623; www.wildlifeexpeditions.org) offers trips in open-roofed vans, on rafts and sleighs, and by foot. These tours bring visitors closer to the wildlife than they're likely to get on their own, and guests sometimes participate in radio tracking and other research projects. The **Grand Teton Natural History Association** is a not-for-profit organization that provides myriad information about the park, including information for travelers through its bookstores at visitor centers in and around the park. These materials are available by writing the association at P.O. Drawer 170, Moose, WY 83012 (© 307/739-3606; www.grandtetonpark.org).

HIKING
DAY HIKES

Many people cross Jenny Lake, either by boat or on foot around the south end, to hike up into **Cascade Canyon** ✸✸, a steep but popular journey that takes you first to **Hidden Falls** (less than 1 mile of hiking if you take the boat; 5 miles if you walk around) or another .5 mile to **Inspiration Point.** Skip the boat shuttle to avoid the crowds;

Tips **Picture-Perfect**

A meadow near the summit of Signal Mountain presents an excellent opportunity to look to the west for photos of both Mount Moran and the Tetons. The best time to take those photos is before 11am, when the sun will be mostly at your back, or in the early evening, when the sun will backlight the crests to the west.

---

the easy hike around the south end of the lake is refreshing, uncrowded, and a good prelude to heading up the canyon. Most people go no farther than Inspiration Point, but if you're physically up to it you really should go on. It's a steep climb to the entrance of the canyon, followed by a gentle ascent though a glacially sculpted canyon. At a fork in the trail around 4 miles from Inspiration Point you can follow either the north fork of Cascade Creek to Lake Solitude (3 miles) or the south fork to Hurricane Pass (5 miles). Try the north fork for a more relaxed day hike. Wildflowers carpet the area, ducks nest along Cascade Creek, and moose and bear may be spotted. The round-trip up into the canyon is about 4.5 miles.

A less-taxing alternative to the Cascade Canyon trip discussed above is a detour to **Moose Ponds,** which begins on the Inspiration Point trail. The ponds, located 2 miles from the trail head, are alive with birds. The area near the base of Teewinot Mountain is populated with elk, mule deer, black bears, and moose. The trail is flat (at lake level), short, and easy to negotiate in 1 to 1½ hours. The best times to venture forth are in early morning and evening.

Just down the road from South Jenny Lake is the trail head to **Taggart Lake,** a particularly interesting hike that winds through a recovering burn area to a glacial lake. The hike from the parking lot to the lake (a decent fishing spot) is only 1.6 miles along the eastern route, and rarely crowded. After reaching the lake, you can return by the same trail or continue the loop on the **Taggart Lake Trail,** which leads around one end of the pond and loops back to the trail head through a more heavily forested area. This route adds .8 mile to the trip, and the elevation gain is 467 feet. At its highest point, the trail overlooks all of Taggart Lake and the stream that flows from it.

Upon reaching Taggart Lake, a second alternative is to continue north 1.4 miles to **Bradley Lake,** the smaller of the two, and then return to the Taggart Lake trail head. Like others in Grand Teton, this hike is best made during the early morning or early evening hours when it is cooler and there is less traffic.

Yet another hike in this busy area begins at the **Leigh Lake trail head,** next to String Lake at the String Lake Picnic Area. This trail head is between Leigh Lake and Jenny Lake (String Lake is a smaller body of water between the two). The Leigh Lake trail is well marked and relatively flat, and goes through a forested area that is always within sight of the lake. Picnickers willing to hike roughly .4 mile from the String Lake Picnic Area to the edge of the lake will find themselves eating in a less-congested area that provides spectacular views of the Tetons. The trail continues along the shore of Leigh Lake, but is rather uninteresting; a better option, if time allows, is to return to the picnic area, cross the String Lake inlet, and explore the western edge of Jenny Lake.

Just footsteps from the entrance to the Signal Mountain Lodge is a sign marking the trail head for the 3-mile **Signal Mountain Summit Trail** ✸, which is not generally described in commercial trail books. Though it's well marked, it's not well traveled, since most visitors drive their automobiles in this area. The trail begins steeply, and subsequently opens onto a broad plateau covered with lodgepole pines, grassy areas, and wildflowers. Cross the paved road and you'll arrive at a large, lily-covered pond at the opening of a meadow, home to frogs and waterfowl. The trail then winds along the south and east perimeter of the pond before turning east and heading toward the summit, a climb that will take up to 2 hours. Shortly after passing the pond, you'll come to a fork in the road that converts the trip into a loop trail. Take the northern route and you'll travel the rim of the mountain, meandering to the summit through a forest of sagebrush and pine trees. On the return, the southern trail skirts large alpine ponds where you'll find waterfowl, moose—and, perhaps, black bears.

The day hikes at the north end of the park are less crowded. The easy but lengthy trip to **Two Ocean Lake** begins off the Pacific Creek Road north of Moran Junction and eventually circumnavigates the lake, with much of the mostly level walk through cool conifer forest. Or, located near Colter Bay Visitor Center, the **Hermitage Point trail head** branches out into trips ranging in distance from 1 to 9 miles, mostly in lodgepole pine, with recurring views of the lake and the peaks on the other side. With careful planning, you can start the day with a hike from Colter Bay that leads past **Cygnet Pond** across **Willow Flats** to Jackson Lake Lodge (for lunch). Then, take the same path back to Colter Bay in time for the evening outdoor barbecue—all told, that's 9.3 miles round-trip.

Among the loops you can take from the Hermitage Point trail head are trails to **Swan Lake** and **Heron Pond** (which share the same point of origin), the kind of country where wildflowers, Canada geese, moose, beaver, and bears all thrive. The two most prominent flowers here are heart-leaf arnicas and Indian paintbrush. Don't be put off by the fact that the first 600 feet of the Swan Lake/Heron Pond trails are steep; after reaching the top of a rise, the terrain levels out and has only moderate elevation gains from that point on. Within minutes, this trail opens to a broad meadow covered with sagebrush and, later in the summer, blooming wildflowers. Here you'll find one of the most spectacular views of Mount Moran, and the peaks reflect on the surfaces of the water.

Finding swans at Swan Lake requires a trip to the south end, where a small island affords isolation and shelter for nests. There are also osprey, kingfishers, and white pelicans in this neck of the woods. The distance from Swan Lake through a densely forested area to the Heron Pond intersection is .3 mile; Hermitage Point is 3 miles from this junction, along a gentle path that winds through a wooded area popular with bears. Circumnavigation from the Colter area is doable in 2 hours.

A shorter hike in the Colter area, the **Lakeshore Trail** is a wide, shady thoroughfare that skirts the bay, leading to gravelly beaches that present views across Jackson Lake of the entire Teton range. The views leap out at you when you arrive at the end of the trail; water gently laps at the shore and, thankfully, you're out of the dense roadside traffic. This 2-mile loop can be completed in about 1 hour of brisk walking.

LONGER HIKES

If you decide a day hike isn't enough, you must get an overnight permit and camp in one of the various camping zones reserved through the visitor centers. Much longer trips can be strung together into the mountainous backcountry, crossing the mountains' spine to **Teton Canyon** on the Idaho side, or, at the north end of the park, exploring deep into the **Jedediah Smith Wilderness.**

Within the park, you can go far beyond the day hikes described above—extending a Cascade Canyon hike, for instance, by going north to Lake Solitude, then coming down into **Paintbrush Canyon** (where you can camp, with a permit) and out at String Lake. You can also take the tram to the top of the ski area in Teton Village and follow the **Teton Crest Trail** north into the park, eventually dropping down through **Death Canyon** (another camping area) to **Phelps Lake** (also a camping zone, the closest one to civilization). A trip like this is more than 20 miles and will take several days.

The Park Service has a helpful brochure that delineates the 20 or so backcountry camping zones and lakeshore sites. You'll need to reserve sites, and rangers can brief you on the quality of different routes, the areas where you're likely to encounter bears, and "leave no trace" camping techniques.

OTHER SPORTS & OUTDOOR ACTIVITIES

For lovers of outdoor recreation, Grand Teton National Park offers one of the most accessible play lands of rock and water in the Lower 48. In addition to hiking, mountaineers and technical climbers can attack the highest hills; paddlers glide across the smooth waters of the lakes or splash along the livelier flow of the Snake River; and boaters will find waters open to motorized vessels and sailboats.

BIKING The roads in Grand Teton were not built with bicyclists in mind, though the flats of the valley seem perfect for pedaling. The problem is safety—there are huge RVs careening about, and some roads have only narrow shoulders. Teton Park Road has been widened somewhat, but traffic is heavy here; road bikers should try **Antelope Flats Road,** beginning at a trail head 1 mile north of Moose Junction and going east. Sometimes called **Mormon Row,** this paved route crosses the flats below the Gros Ventre Mountains, past old ranch homesteads and the small town of Kelly. It connects to the unpaved **Shadow Mountain Road,** which actually goes outside the park into national forest, climbing through the trees to the summit. Total distance is 7 miles and the elevation gain is 1,370 feet, and you'll be looking at Mount Moran and the Tetons across the valley.

Mountain bikers have a few more options, but keep in mind that bikes are prohibited on backcountry trails and boardwalks. Try **Two-Ocean Lake Road** (reached from the Pacific Creek Rd. just north of Moran Junction) or the **River Road,** a 15-mile dirt path that parallels the Snake River's western bank. Ambitious mountain bikers may want to load their overnight gear and take the **Grassy Lake Road,** once used by Indians, west from Flagg Ranch 50 miles to Ashton, Idaho. Books and maps with biking routes are available from at **Adventure Sports** (© 307/733-3307) in Moose, where you can also rent bikes.

BOATING Boaters have quite a few opportunities here. Motorboats are permitted on Jenny, Jackson, and Phelps lakes. Rafts, canoes, dories, and kayaks are allowed on the Snake River within the park. No boats are allowed on Pacific Creek or the Gros Ventre River. Bigger boats find room on Jackson Lake, where powerboats pull skiers, sailboats move noiselessly in summer breezes, and fishermen ply the waters in search of wily trout. Those who venture on the big lake need to be aware that the weather can change suddenly, and late-afternoon lightning is not uncommon; sailors should be particularly wary of the swirling winds that accompany thunderstorms. **Scenic cruises** ✪ of Jackson Lake are conducted daily by the **Grand Teton Lodge Company** (© **307/543-2811**), and breakfast and dinner cruises run twice weekly, both leaving from the **Colter Bay Marina** from May through September. See "Fees & Backcountry Permits," earlier in this chapter, for information on boat permits. Boat and canoe rentals, tackle, and fishing licenses are available at **Colter** and **Signal Mountain.** Shuttles to the west side of Jenny Lake, as well as cruises, are conducted by **Jenny Lake Boating Company** (© **307/733-9227**).

CLIMBING Every year there are rescues of climbers who get trapped on Teton rock faces, and many years there are fatalities. Yet the peaks have a strong allure for climbers, even inexperienced ones, perhaps because you can reach the top of even the biggest ones in a single day. But it isn't easy. The terrain is mixed, with snow and ice year-round—knowing how to self-arrest with an ice axe is a must—and the weather can change suddenly. The key is to get good advice, know your limitations, and if you're not already skilled, take some lessons at the local climbing schools (see "Getting Outside," in section 1).

Climbers who go out for a day do not have to register or report to park officials, so they should be sure to tell friends where they're going and when they'll be back. Overnight climbers must pick up a free permit. Climbing rangers who can lead rescue efforts are on duty at the **Jenny Lake Ranger Station** at South Jenny Lake from June until the middle of September. The American Alpine Club provides inexpensive dormitory beds for climbers at the **Grand Teton Climbers' Ranch** (© **307/733-7271;** www.americanalpineclub.org). Guided climbs of Grand Teton are offered by **Jackson Hole Mountain Guides** (© **800/239-7642;** www.jhmg.com) and by **Exum Mountain Guides** in Moose (© **307/733-2297;** www.exumguides.com).

CROSS-COUNTRY SKIING You can ski flat or you can ski steep in Grand Teton. The two things to watch out for are hypothermia and avalanches. As with climbing, know your limitations and make sure you're properly equipped. Check with local rangers and guides for trails that match your ability. Your options include the relatively easy **Jenny Lake Trail,** starting at the Taggart Lake Parking Area, about 9 miles round-trip of flat and scenic trail that follows Cottonwood Creek. A more difficult ski is the **Taggart Lake–Beaver Creek Loop,** a 3-mile route that has some steep and icy pitches coming back. About 2 miles of the **Moose-Wilson Road**—the back way to Teton Village from Moose—is unplowed in the winter, and is an easy trip through the woods. You can climb the winding, unplowed road to the top of Signal Mountain have some fun skiing down. There is an easy ski trail from the Colter Bay Ranger Station area to Heron Pond—about 2.75 miles, with a great view of the Tetons and Jackson Lake. Get a ski-trail map from one of the visitor centers.

FISHING The lakes and streams of Grand Teton are popular fishing destinations, loaded with lively cutthroat trout, whitefish, and Mackinaw (lake) trout in Jackson, Jenny, and Phelps lakes. You'll most likely catch fish under 20 inches, fishing deep with trolling gear from a boat during hot summer months. The Snake River runs for about 27 miles in the park, and has cutthroat and whitefish up to about 18 inches. It's a popular drift-boat river for fly-fishing. If you'd like a guide who knows the holes, try **Jack Dennis Sports** (© **307/733-3270**), **Triangle X-Osprey Float Trips** (© **307/733-5500**), or **Westbank Anglers** (© **307/733-6483**). The going rate is $350 for a full day for two people. **Signal Mountain** (© **307/542-2831**) offers guided half-day trips on motorized craft in **Jackson Lake** for one or two people for $200. As an alternative, stake out a position on the banks below the dam at **Jackson Lake,** where you'll have plenty of company and just may snag something. You'll need a Wyoming state fishing license (see section 13, "The Active Traveler," in chapter 2). The going rate for a guided trip for two is $375 a day.

IN 1896 "BUFFALO BILL" FOUNDED CODY, WYOMING AS A HOSPITALITY TOWN...

Col. William F. "Buffalo Bill" Cody

AND IT'S BEEN ONE EVER SINCE

Even 100 years after his heyday, Buffalo Bill's Wild West spirit lives on in Cody, Wyoming, Yellowstone National Park's east gate. With an unmatched variety of attractions available, you're sure to find the perfect fit for you. Start the day touring the Buffalo Bill Historical Center's five world-class museums. Or for the outdoor enthusiast, golf, fly fish, horseback ride or float the river. Then enjoy a Best of the West trolley tour, experience the old west at Old Trail Town and watch a gunfight reenactment at the historic Irma Hotel. Top the day off at the Cody Nite Rodeo, filled with bucking broncs and bulls every night June through August. Or you might prefer our Cowboy Music Review, a Branson-style music variety show. And there's a wide selection of art galleries, fine restaurants, and lodging available.
Cody still puts "wild" in the Wild West.

Buffalo Bill's
🦬 CODY/YELLOWSTONE COUNTRY 🦬
www.yellowstonecountry.org
836 Sheridan Ave. · Cody, Wy 82414 · 800-393-2639

UNITED
EXPRESS

SKYWEST
DELTA CONNECTION

RAFTING & FLOAT TRIPS   The upper end of the Snake River in the park can be deceptive—its smooth surface runs fast during the spring, and there are deadly snags of fallen trees and other debris. Check with rangers before putting your boat in—they'll discourage you if they think your skills may not match the river—and proceed with caution. It's a wonderful river for wildlife, too, with moose, eagles, and other animals coming, like you, to the water's edge. There are many commercial float operators in the park who will allow you to relax more and look around. They run mostly from mid-May to mid-September (depending on weather and river-flow conditions). These companies offer 5- to 10-mile scenic floats, some with early-morning and evening wildlife trips. Try **Solitude River Trips** (© 800/733-2871), **Barker-Ewing Float Trips** (© 800/365-1800), **Grand Teton Lodge Company** (© 307/543-2811), and **Signal Mountain Lodge** (© 307/543-2831).

CAMPING

Since Grand Teton is so much smaller than its counterpart to the north, the mileage between campgrounds is much shorter. As a consequence, selecting a site in one of the five National Park Service campgrounds within the park becomes a matter of preference (rather than geography) and availability. Fees in all campgrounds are $15 per night, and all have modern comfort stations. Campgrounds operate on a first-come, first-served basis, but reservations are available to groups of 10 or more by contacting the **Grand Teton Lodge Co.,** P.O. Box 240, Moran, WY 83013 (© **307/543-3100**). You can get recorded information on site availability by calling (© **307/739-3603**). Reservations for **trailer sites** at Colter Bay campground may also be made by contacting the **Grand Teton Lodge Co.** Additionally, **Grand Teton Campground** is a concessionaire-operated campground located in the **Flagg Ranch** complex on the John D. Rockefeller Jr. Memorial Parkway. The area has 97 sites with utility hookups, 74 tent sites, showers, and a laundry. For reservations, contact **Flagg Ranch,** P.O. Box 187, Moran, WY 83013 (© **800/443-2311**).

All the campgrounds but Jenny Lake can accommodate tents, RVs, and trailers, but there are no utility hookups at any of them. **Jenny Lake Campground,** a tents-only area with 51 sites, is situated in a quiet, wooded area near the lake. You have to be here first thing in the morning to get a site.

The largest campground, **Gros Ventre,** is the last to fill, if it fills at all—probably because it's located on the east side of the park, a few miles from Kelly on the Gros Ventre River Road. It has 372 sites, a trailer dump station, a tents-only section, and no showers. If you arrive late in the day and you have no place to stay, go here first.

Signal Mountain Campground, with views of the lake and access to the beach, is another popular spot that fills first thing in the morning. It has 86 sites overlooking Jackson Lake and Mount Moran, as well as a pleasant picnic area and boat launch. It has no showers or laundry, but there's a store and service station nearby.

Colter Bay Campground and Trailer Village has 350 sites (some with RV hookups), a general store, showers, and a laundry. The area has access to the lake but is far enough from the hubbub of the village to offer a modicum of solitude; spaces are usually gone by noon.

Lizard Creek Campground, at the north end of Grand Teton National Park near Jackson Lake, offers an aesthetically pleasing wooded area near the lake with views of the Tetons, bird-watching, and fishing (not to mention the mosquitoes: bring your repellent). It's only 8 miles from facilities at Colter Bay and has 60 sites that usually fill by 2pm.

Amenities for Each Campground in Grand Teton National Park

Campground	# Sites	Fee	Showers	Laundry	Flush Toilets	Disposal
Colter Bay	350	$15	Yes	Yes	Yes	Yes
Gros Ventre	372	$15	No	No	Yes	Yes
Jenny Lake*	51	$15	No	No	Yes	No
Lizard Creek	60	$15	No	No	Yes	No
Signal Mountain	86	$15	No	No	Yes	Yes

* *tents only*

WHERE TO STAY IN THE PARK

If you plan to visit Grand Teton during a "fringe" season—usually the best, least-crowded time to go, in the fall or spring—you better check first to see if the inn is open. Three different companies run the lodgings in the park, and they all run on different schedules. In early May, you'll find padlocks on the doors everywhere but at Flagg Ranch, which technically isn't in Grand Teton anyway, but in the limbo of the John D. Rockefeller Jr. Memorial Parkway. Likewise in late fall: By mid-October, there are hardly any beds available in the park, and you'll be bunking in Jackson.

You can get information about or make reservations for Jackson Lake Lodge, Jenny Lake Lodge, and Colter Bay Village through the **Grand Teton Lodge Company,** Box 240, Moran, WY 83013 (✆ **800/628-9988** or 307/543-2811; www.gtlc.com); for **Signal Mountain Lodge,** contact Signal Mountain Lodge Co., Box 50, Moran, WY 83013 (✆ **307/543-2831;** www.signalmountainlodge.com); and reservations at **Flagg Ranch** are made though Flagg Ranch, Box 187, Moran, WY 83013 (✆ **800/443-2311;** www.flaggranch.com).

EXPENSIVE

Jackson Lake Lodge 🏨🏨   Much the way that Old Faithful Inn or the Lake Hotel captures historical eras of Yellowstone tourism, Jackson Lake Lodge epitomizes the architectural milieu of the period when Grand Teton became a park. That era was the 1950s, an age of right angles, flat roofs, and big windows. While not as distinctive as Yellowstone's standouts, the lodge is more functional and comfortable than its northern counterparts. The setting is sublime, overlooking Willow Flats with the lake in the distance, and, towering over it without so much as a stick in the way, the Tetons and Mount Moran. You don't even have to go outside to see this impressive view—the lobby has 60-foot-tall windows. Guest rooms are in the three-story main lodge and in cottages scattered about the property, some of which have large balconies and mountain views. Lodge rooms are spacious and cheery, and most offer double beds, electric heat, and newly tiled bathrooms. Both the lodge and cottage rooms are comparable to an upper-tier chain hotel, with an American Indian motif. For a premium, the view rooms provide guests with a private picture window facing the Tetons.

P.O. Box 240, Moran, WY 83013. ✆ **800/628-9988** or 307/543-3100. www.gtlc.com. 385 units. $141–$249 double; $425–$575 suite. MC, V. Closed mid-Oct to mid-May. **Amenities:** 2 restaurants; lounge; heated outdoor pool; airport shuttle; activities desk. *In room:* Dataport, hair dryer, iron.

Jenny Lake Lodge 🏨🏨🏨   My favorite property in any national park, this lodge justifiably prides itself on seclusion, award-winning food, and the individual attention that come with a cabin resort kept intentionally small. The property is a hybrid of mountain-lake resort and dude ranch, with various extras included in its prices, such as horseback rides, meals, walking sticks, umbrellas, and cool cruiser bicycles. The cabins, each named for a resident flower, are rustic on the outside and luxurious within—decorated with bright braided rugs, dark wood floors, beamed ceilings, cushy plaid armchairs, and tiled bathrooms. Rooms have one queen-size, one king-size, or two queen-size beds. Some were old dude ranch cabins from the 1920s, and some were built on the property in 1992; the latter have larger bathrooms and more modernity, but not as much character.

Catering to an older, affluent, and exceedingly loyal clientele, the style here is a throwback: a blend of peaceful rusticity and occasional reminders of class and formality (jackets for men are "appreciated"). Generally, though, if you aren't sweating the prices, Jenny Lake Lodge offers a wonderful chance to unwind in a fairly isolated, feet-up-on-the-rail atmosphere with scenery and service that can't be matched.

Box 250, Moran, WY 83013. (℄ **800/628-9988** or 307/543-3100. www.gtlc.com. 37 units. $475 double; $635–$680 suite. Rates include MAP (modified American plan). AE, MC, V. Closed mid-Oct to May. **Amenities:** Restaurant; lounge; activities desk. *In room:* Dataport, coffeemaker, fridge.

MODERATE

Colter Bay Village ☆ *Kids*   You might call this the people's resort of Grand Teton, with simpler lodgings, lower prices, and a lively, friendlier atmosphere that seems particularly suited to families. Situated on the eastern shore of Jackson Lake, Colter Bay Village is a full-fledged recreation center. Guest accommodations are in rough log cabins perched on a wooded hillside; they are clean and simply furnished with area rugs on tile floors and reproductions of pioneer furnishings—chests, oval mirrors, and extralong bedsteads with painted headboards.

If you want to take a trip back to the early days of American auto travel, when car camping involved unwieldy canvas tents on slabs by the roadside, you can spend an inexpensive night in "tent cabins." (Sleeping bags, pillows, and blankets are available to rent.) The shower and bathroom are communal. Overall, the village provides an excellent base of operations for visitors because it has the most facilities of any area in the park.

P.O. Box 240, Moran, WY 83013. (℄ **800/628-9988** or 307/543-3100. www.gtlc.com. 166 units. $74–$139 log cabin; $37 tent cabin. MC, V. Closed late Sept to late May. **Amenities:** 2 restaurants; activities desk; self-serve laundry. *In room:* No phone.

Dornan's Spur Ranch ☆   An outfitter's camp since the 1940s, Dornan's is now a collection of year-round cabins built in the 1990s. Located at a family-owned operation in Moose that also includes a market, a wine shop, an outdoors store, guide services, and dining, the dozen cabins here are a good option for families and larger groups. All of the units have tub/shower combinations, fitting lodgepole pine furnishings, and fully equipped kitchens. Two of the cabins are right on the Snake River, but they're often booked a year in advance during peak season.

P.O. Box 39, Moose, WY 83012. (℄ **307/733-2522.** www.dornans.com. 12 units. $155–$230 up to 6 people. AE, DISC, MC, V. **Amenities:** 2 restaurants; lounge. *In room:* Kitchen.

Flagg Ranch Resort ☆   A few years ago this resort just outside Yellowstone National Park was showing its age—the sort of place where a hunter would rent a drafty room to collapse in after a few days in the woods. Not anymore: It's all fixed up, transformed into a self-contained resort on the Snake River with log-and-luxury ambience. The newest accommodations are duplex and four-plex log cabins constructed in 1994 featuring king-size beds, spacious sitting areas with writing desks and chests of drawers, wall-to-wall carpeting, and bathrooms with tub/shower combinations and separate vanities.

The only livestock on the ranch these days are the herds of snowmobiles that gather here in the winter to warm up before entering Yellowstone; however, the cabins are now closed during winter. In the summer, there are float trips, horseback rides, and excellent fishing in Polecat Creek or the Snake River. The lodge is a locus of activity, with its double-sided fireplace, fancy dining room, gift shop, espresso bar and pub with large-screen television, convenience store, and gas station. A campground and RV facility are situated on the grounds amid a stand of pine trees.

P.O. Box 187, Moran, WY 83013. © 800/443-2311 or 307/543-2861. www.flaggranch.com. 92 cabins; 171 campsites. $150–$170 cabin double; $20 tent site; $45 RV site. AE, DISC, MC, V. Closed mid-Oct to mid-May. **Amenities:** Restaurant; lounge; activities desk; self-serve laundry.

Signal Mountain Lodge *Finds*   Signal Mountain has a different feel—and different owners—from the other lodgings in Grand Teton, adding to the sense that any place you choose to stay in this park is going to give you a fairly unique atmosphere. What they all have in common is the Teton view, and this lodge, located right on the banks of Jackson Lake, might have the best. To top it off, it's got lakefront retreats, which you can really inhabit, with stoves and refrigerators and foldout sofa beds for the kids. Other accommodations, mostly rustic log cabins, come in a variety of flavors, from motel-style rooms in four-unit buildings set amid the trees to family bungalows with decks, some enjoying beach frontage. These carpeted units are nicely maintained, featuring handmade pine furniture, electric heat, covered porches, and tiled bathrooms; some have fireplaces. Recreational options include rafting and fishing, and sailboat tours on the lake. A convenience store and gas station are on the property.

P.O. Box 50, Moran, WY 83013. © 307/543-2831. www.signalmountainlodge.com. 80 units. $99–$255 double. AE, DISC, MC, V. Closed late Oct to early May. **Amenities:** 2 restaurants; activities desk. *In room:* Kitchenette.

WHERE TO DINE

The Bear's Den *Kids* AMERICAN   Served at the main lodge at Flagg Ranch, the food at this oasis is better than what's typically found in what most refer to as a "family restaurant," and servings are generous. The dinner menu includes fish, chicken, and beef dishes, as well as home-style entrees such as ranch beef stew and chicken potpie; lunch and dinner are unadventurous but hearty. The ambience is also pleasant during both winter and summer months; wooden chairs and tables with colorful upholstery liven up this newly constructed log building.

At Flagg Ranch, John D. Rockefeller Jr. Pkwy. © 800/443-2311. Breakfast $4.50–$10; lunch $4–$9; dinner $11–$20. AE, DISC, MC, V. Summer 7–11am, 11:30am–4:30pm, and 5–9:30pm.

Jenny Lake Lodge Dining Room *✿✿✿* CONTINENTAL   The finest meals in either park are served here (or, for that matter, *any* park), where a *cordon bleu* chef creates culinary delights for guests and, occasionally, a president of the United States. Only breakfast and dinner are served here, and both are spectacular. The five-course dinner is the bell-ringer, though; guests choose from appetizers that might include elk carpaccio or roasted Japanese eggplant; salads with organic greens, pecans, and dried cherries; and entrees such as pan-roasted squab, herb-rubbed rabbit leg, or a venison strip loin. Desserts are equally creative and tantalizing. Price is no object, at least for guests, because meals are included in the room charge; nonguests should expect a hefty bill. If you're wearing shorts and hiking boots, you'll feel a bit underdressed.

At Jenny Lake Lodge. ℂ 307/733-4647. Prix-fixe breakfast $19; lunch main courses $8–$17; prix-fixe dinner $60, not including alcoholic beverages. AE, MC, V. Summer daily 7:30–9am, noon–1:30pm, and 6–8:45pm.

John Colter Cafe Court DELI/FAST FOOD   Here you find the two sit-down restaurants in the village (although there's also a snack shop in the grocery store). Three meals are served daily during the summer months. The **deli** serves sandwiches, chicken, pizzas, salads, and soup, with prices that range from $5 for a sandwich to $13 for a blue plate special for dinner. The **Chuckwagon Steak and Pasta House's** breakfast menu dishes up everything from plain eggs to a chuck-wagon omelet, with a vast, scrumptious all-you-can-eat buffet available. Lunch is a soup-and-salad bar, and hot sandwiches; dinner is a buffet with a nightly special each evening. Among the dinner entrees are trout, lasagna, pork chops, beef stew, and New York strip steaks. The ambience is very casual and straightforward because these restaurants cater mostly to families.

Across from the visitor center and marina in Colter Bay Village. ℂ 307/543-2811. Breakfast $3–$6; lunch $5–$10; dinner $8–$18. MC, V. Daily 6:30am–10pm. Closed Oct–Apr.

The Mural Room 🎄🎄 BEEF/WILD GAME   Jackson Lake's main dining room is quiet and fairly formal, catering to a more sedate crowd as well as corporate groups; it's also more expensive than other park restaurants. The floor-to-ceiling windows provide stellar views across a meadow that is moose habitat, to the lake and the Cathedral Group. Walls are adorned with hand-painted Western murals (what else?).

The food is the perfect complement to the view, and markedly superior to most of what you'll find in Yellowstone. Three meals are served daily in summer. Breakfast items include a continental breakfast, Belgian waffles, and vegetarian eggs Benedict. Dinner might be a grand five-course event that includes a shrimp cocktail, French onion soup, and Caesar salad, followed by an entree of Idaho trout, buffalo prime rib, vegetable lasagna, or rack of lamb. Aside from the dining room at Jenny Lake Lodge and Lake Hotel in Yellowstone, this is the most romantic and upscale eatery in either park. An inexpensive option, the luncheonette-style **Pioneer Grill,** is next door.

At Jackson Lake Lodge. ℂ 800/628-9988 or 307/543-2811, ext. 3463. Breakfast buffet $13; lunch $6–$13; dinner $17–$32. MC, V. Summer daily 7–9:30am, noon–1:30pm, and 5:30–9pm. Closed mid-Oct to May.

Signal Mountain Resort 🔺Value SANDWICHES/MEXICAN/CONTINENTAL There are actually two restaurants here, serving delicious food in the friendliest style in the park. The fine dining room and lounge are called **Peaks** and **Deadman's Bar,** respectively, and the **Trapper Grill** supplements the Continental fare with Mexican entrees, pizzas, and plump sandwiches. You eat up the scenery, too, with a view of Jackson Lake and Mount Moran.

Bargain hunters flock to the bar for the decadent nachos supreme: a foot-tall mountain of chips, cheese, chicken, beef, beans, and peppers that runs a mere $14. You'll easily fill four people for that price, leaving you plenty of change for the bar's signature blackberry margaritas. Because the bar has one of three televisions in the park and is equipped with cable for sports nuts, the crowd tends to be young and noisy. Full meals are served in the proper dining room, with an emphasis on sustainable cuisine. Entrees include free-range chicken with wild mushroom risotto, Mediterranean pasta, and filet mignon wrapped in applewood smoked bacon, the most expensive entree. Also under the Signal Mountain umbrella is the pizzeria at **Leeks Marina** (ℂ 307/543-2494), just a few miles north of Colter Bay.

At Signal Mountain Resort. ℂ 307/543-2831. Breakfast $6–$9; lunch $6–$10; dinner $10–$33. AE, DISC, MC, V. Summer daily 7–10am and 11:30am–10pm.

3 A Side Trip to Dubois & the Wind River Range

86 miles NE of Jackson

For years, Dubois was a kind of doppelgänger to Jackson, a blue-collar logging town with some quietly wealthy folks living on nice ranches up the nearby draws. Now the sawmill is closed, and wealthy folks who want to stay ahead of the latest real estate fashion are wandering over Togwotee Pass and buying up the beautiful Upper Wind River Valley. That means Dubois is poised for some serious development, but it hasn't quite happened yet, which dismays some residents and pleases others. Lying as it does along one of the Yellowstone access roads, Dubois is just far enough from the park entrances to be spared the West Yellowstone gateway syndrome, and if locals keep their heads, they'll protect the great trout streams, uncluttered wilderness, and small-town ambience from uncontrolled growth. So far, so good. It's a fun town, often with several bands playing in the bars on weekends. **To get there** from Jackson, go north on U.S. 26/89/191 to Moran Junction, then east over Togwotee Pass on U.S. 26/287.

The **Rustic Pine Steakhouse,** 123 E. Ramshorn (© **307/455-2772**), does a good job with beef, seafood, and pasta; or you can get a great salad and sandwich on home-baked bread (and great barbecue ribs) at **Cafe Wyoming,** 106 E. Ramshorn (© **307/455-3828**), hidden off the parking lot of Dubois Hardware with a pleasant porch overhanging Horse Creek.

In the lake-dotted Whiskey Basin, just south of town, one of the largest extant herds of bighorn sheep migrate down in the winter to get away from the deep snows, and so there is a **National Bighorn Sheep Interpretive Center,** 907 W. Ramshorn (© **888/209-2975;** www.bighorn.org) located just off the highway in the center of town. Just across the park at the **Dubois Museum,** 909 W. Ramshorn (© **307/455-2284;** www.duboismuseum.org), is a look at the past of the town, the Sheepeater Indians, and other interesting artifacts with local flavor. The museum is open from 9am to 5pm daily May through September. Contact the **Dubois Chamber of Commerce,** P.O. Box 632, Dubois, WY 85213 (© **307/455-2556;** www.duboiswyoming.org), for additional information on the community.

WHERE TO STAY

Brooks Lake Lodge ⚜   For many years, this remote and historic mountain lodge, once an overnight stop on the road to Yellowstone, languished; in 1989, it was painstakingly restored and reopened to a good deal of well-deserved hype. It sits above the shores of Brooks Lake, a prize fishing lake surrounded by soaring pinnacles. This is the entry point to some of the most remote and challenging wilderness in the Rockies, packed with elk, trout, and grizzly bears. Yet the handsome lodge, with its hand-stripped timbers and deep porch overlooking the lake, is as cozy and comforting as

---

(*Tips* **Travel Tip**

Before arriving in Dubois, practice pronouncing the name without sounding like a city slicker. There are many ways to pronounce it, but only *Doo*-boys is correct. Sure, there is the inclination to say Doo-*bwah,* but quell that urge—this isn't France.

anyone could ask. You can lounge or take advantage of the riding stock, guided up steep trails to incredible views.

Accommodations are seven guest rooms in the lodge (one room is a suite with a Jacuzzi and a fireplace) and eight cabins along the tree line. The cabins, each decorated with a distinct frontier motif, are comfortable, spacious affairs that have large decks or porches with views of the lake, and Western pine furniture.

458 Brooks Lake Rd., Dubois, WY 82513. *C* 307/455-2121. www.brookslake.com. 12 units, 3 family cabins. Summer $275–$325 per person per night; winter $200–$250 per person per night. Rates include all meals. AE, MC, V. Closed Apr–May and Oct–Nov. **Amenities:** Restaurant; activities desk; spa; exercise room. *In room:* Coffeemaker, hair dryer, iron, no phone.

13

Cody & North-Central Wyoming

Deep, broad valleys, cupped by daunting mountain ranges, provide some of the most livable pockets of the Rocky Mountain West. Not only do the mountains provide some protection from howling storms, but their snowmelt keeps streams running through the summer and their beauty supplies a spectacular backdrop for the communities nestled below.

Such a valley runs down the center of Wyoming, cradled by the Bighorn Mountains in the east and the Absarokas and Yellowstone Plateau in the West. Though the area around the town of Cody gets only about 10 inches of moisture annually, founder William "Buffalo Bill" Cody recognized a century ago that with a few dams and ditches in the right places, the mountains' snowpack could supply water year-round. His legacy continues to shape the basin's economy today: A great summer scene of cowboy fun attracts hordes of visitors, and green fields of sugar beets and grains stretch for miles from the mouth of the Wapiti Valley.

While Cody was staking claims to water rights along the Shoshone River in the early 20th century, the U.S. Bureau of Reclamation was storing that water behind the Buffalo Bill Dam, the world's tallest when it was completed in 1910. The reservoir today irrigates some 93,000 acres in central Wyoming, and the swift winds that skim the lake's surface attract the bravest of windsurfers.

In the post–"Buffalo Bill" era, the charms of north-central Wyoming have taken many a visitor by surprise on their journey to and from Wyoming's famous national parks. And quite a few travelers find reason to linger longer in the nearby valleys, exploring a wealth of American Indian and Wild West history, geology, mountain scenery, outdoor recreation, and small-town charm. Highlights include fun-loving Cody, the Bighorn Canyon National Recreation Area, the gushing hot springs of Thermopolis, and the forests and rivers of Shoshone National Forest and other public lands.

The combination of stunning scenery and historic cattle operations makes the Cody area a natural center for dude ranches, where visitors can saddle up and swing a lariat. Or you can mount a more stationary seat in the stands at one of the summer rodeos. Cody's rodeo grounds light up every night in the summer, and nearly every town in the basin has its special rodeo weekend. On the Wind River Indian Reservation, the evening outdoor entertainment is often a powwow, featuring drum groups, colorful garb, and traditional dancing, with visitors welcome, and food stands offering Indian tacos and other treats.

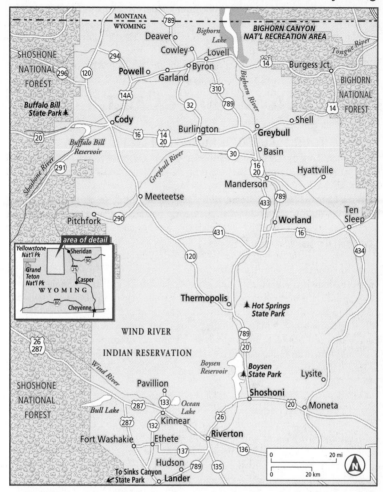

1 Scenic Drives

The two-lane roads of north-central Wyoming follow the contours of a craggy land-scape, tracking the twists and turns of the river and switchbacking over the mountain passes; the roads are narrow but generally not too crowded, except for the constant stream of traffic to Yellowstone's east entrance. **U.S. 14/16/20,** the east entrance road (also called the Yellowstone Hwy.), is the major east-west route through this region. The breathtaking views as it snakes through the Wapiti Valley and up over Sylvan Pass into Yellowstone make the traffic and seemingly interminable road repairs worthwhile. West of Cody, almost any road you take will reward you with a canyon or a climb, but many of them narrow into rough dirt byways as they delve deeper into the forest. **Wyo. 291** does that, as it follows the **South Fork of the Shoshone River** upstream toward the white-capped peaks of Yellowstone's Thorofare country. Along the way are prominent volcanic rock formations like Castle Rock, a succession of picturesque ranches, and sometimes a lucky glimpse of bighorn sheep, before the road finally dead-ends on the fringes of the Absaroka Range.

Cody is also an alternative starting point for the **Chief Joseph Scenic Highway,** which links up to the Beartooth Scenic Byway into Montana (see section 1, "A Scenic Drive," in chapter 9).

Note: Most of the sights mentioned in the following driving tours are discussed in greater detail later in this chapter.

DRIVING TOUR 1: BIGHORN MOUNTAIN LOOP

This moderately easy day trip will open your eyes to an extraordinary mountain range, on a route that encompasses the towns of **Powell** and **Lovell,** as well as the scenic **Shell Canyon** area. Begin in Cody by taking U.S. 14A northeast to Lovell and the **Bighorn Canyon National Recreation Area** (see section 3, in chapter 10, for more information on this recreation area). A side trip north along Wyo. 37 provides views of the wild horses of the Pryor Mountain National Wild Horse Range and Bighorn Lake from the Devil Canyon Overlook.

After crossing the Bighorn River, U.S. 14A rises through the foothills and up the steep flanks of the Bighorns, not far from the footpaths of prehistoric travelers who built the **Medicine Wheel,** a 74-foot stone circle with 28 spokes. Like other mysterious wheel designs in the Rockies, it may have served ancient peoples as an astronomical key or a long-distance travel marker. To get here, turn off U.S. 14A at the Medicine Wheel sign and hike 1.5 miles from the parking area to the site. American Indian spiritual leaders still conduct ceremonies here. Visitors are asked not to remove offerings or disturb American Indians using the site for prayer or fasting. For more information, contact the Medicine Wheel Ranger District of the Bighorn National Forest (© 307/548-6541).

Once you have crested the divide of the Bighorn Mountains, take U.S. 14 southwest at Burgess Junction toward Shell Canyon and the towns of Shell and Greybull. The road drops sharply through steeply cut canyons, and you can stop at the **Shell Falls Interpretive Center** and follow a paved path to a close-up view of the creek, tumbling and twisting amid tall granite slabs. As the road flattens out near the town of Shell, you're surrounded by the deep red sandstones of the **Chugwater Formation,** set off by the rich greens of cultivated fields. This area enfolds some well-packed dinosaur fossil beds. U.S. 14/16/20 takes you back to Cody, toward the embrace of the Absaroka Mountains and Yellowstone. This driving tour can be enjoyed year-round, though winter drivers should proceed cautiously on the steep grades around Burgess Junction.

DRIVING TOUR 2: BIGHORN BASIN LOOP

This all-day trip keeps to the Bighorn River Basin, navigating rolling sagebrush hills, cultivated farmlands, hot-spring terraces, and one-pump (formerly one-horse) Western towns.

Depart from Cody and travel south along Wyo. 120 to the tiny burg of **Meeteetse** on the banks of the Greybull River. From here, continue on Wyo. 120 to **Thermopolis,** self-proclaimed home of the world's largest free-flowing hot springs (New Zealand does not agree). After a relaxing soak and a brief drive east for a glimpse of the bison herd that roams **Hot Springs State Park,** travel northeast on U.S. 16/20 to **Worland,** an important agricultural center. Then, drive east along U.S. 16 to **Ten Sleep,** which lies at the base of another steep-sided canyon cutting down through the Bighorn Mountains. You may want to hike and cast a line in Ten Sleep Creek.

Here, take the Nowood Road north, which joins Wyo. 31 to Manderson and follows the base of the Bighorns. From Manderson, follow U.S. 16/20 north to Basin, take Wyo. 30 west to the junction of Wyo. 120, and continue north to Cody. Along the way, you'll enjoy views of the Bighorn River and the Greybull River Valley. Winter isn't too harsh on this loop, which could include a detour south of Meeteetse on Wyo. 290 to the **Wood River Ski Touring Park.** If it's summer, rangers at Hot Springs State Park have a map and key to Legend Rock petroglyph sites north of Thermopolis, where you can hike around the cliffs.

2 Cody ⟨★⟩

52 miles E of the east entrance of Yellowstone; 177 miles NE of Jackson; 214 miles NW of Casper

The legendary scout and entertainer William F. "Buffalo Bill" Cody really knew how to put on a show, and he also knew where to put a town. Cody, founded by its namesake in 1887, is beautifully situated near the juncture of rivers that pour from the rugged Absaroka Range. Every summer, the town of Cody stages a cow-town circus that would do the founder proud, entertaining throngs of visitors on their way to and from Yellowstone 52 miles west. And the drive to the park is sublime: Theodore Roosevelt called the Wapiti Valley "the most scenic 50 miles in the world."

Stop by Cody before the mid-May opening of Yellowstone's east entrance and it's rather lifeless. For 3 months every summer, though, the town parades its Western charm for masses of travelers. When the sun goes down, the lights come on at the rodeo grounds, and nightly the broncs do a little busting of their own. A world-class museum, a reassembled Old West town, and retail shops all attract visitors. Though lacking the resort density and sophistication of Jackson, Cody's Western charm feels more authentic.

The Mystery of Buffalo Bill's Grave

Buffalo Bill's legend looms large over Cody, but some locals believe that it's more than his spirit looking down from the surrounding peaks. Rumor has it that Buffalo Bill is buried not atop Lookout Mountain in Golden, Colorado, but on Cedar Mountain, just outside of Cody. After the legendary showman's 1917 demise, the mayor of Denver and the *Denver Post* arranged to buy his body as the centerpiece to a tourist attraction. As the story goes, a trio of Cody residents took it upon themselves to see to it that Cody be laid to rest outside the town that bears his name. They swapped Buffalo Bill's body (which sat on ice for 6 months in Denver before the funeral) with that of an anonymous old cowboy who died in Cody without any kin. While there's more than one story floating around regarding the true whereabouts of Cody's grave, longtime Cody residents (and many of Buffalo Bill's descendants) swear that a nameless cowboy is buried on Lookout Mountain in Colorado and that William F. Cody's final resting place is where he wanted it—in Cody, Wyoming.

ESSENTIALS

GETTING THERE Cody's **Yellowstone Regional Airport** (✆ 307/587-5096), serves the Bighorn Basin as well as the east and northeast entrances of Yellowstone National Park with year-round commercial flights via Delta/United feeder **SkyWest** (✆ 800/864-8331) through Salt Lake City and Denver.

If you're driving from **Cheyenne,** travel north on I-25 to Casper, then west on U.S. 20/26 to Shoshoni, where U.S. 20 turns north to Thermopolis. From there, it's another 84 miles to Cody on Wyo. 120. From **Jackson,** take U.S. 191 to the West Thumb Junction in Yellowstone, drive east along the northern boundary of Yellowstone Lake, and continue on U.S. 14/16/20 to Cody. Coming from the southwest, drive north from Rock Springs on U.S. 191 to Farson, Wyo. 28 to Lander, Wyo. 789 to Thermopolis, and Wyo. 120 to Cody.

VISITOR INFORMATION For printed information on this area of Wyoming, contact the **Park County Travel Council,** 836 Sheridan Ave., P.O. Box 2454, Cody, WY 82414 (✆ 307/587-2777; www.pctc.org), or the **Wyoming Business Council Travel and Tourism Division,** I-25 at College Drive, Cheyenne, WY 82002 (✆ 800/ 225-5996 or 307/777-7777; www.wyomingtourism.org).

GETTING AROUND If you haven't come by car, you'll probably need to rent one; there's little public transportation. **Budget** (✆ 800/527-0700 or 307/587-6066), **Thrifty** (✆ 800/367-2277 or 307/587-8855), and **Hertz** (✆ 800/654-3131 or 307/ 587-2914) maintain desks at Yellowstone Regional Airport.

SPECIAL EVENTS The Buffalo Bill Historical Center is a tremendous resource for unique events in Cody. The April festival of **Cowboy Songs and Range Ballads** features storytelling, poetry, and some fine yodeling and balladry. In mid-June, the **Plains Indian Powwow** brings alive the Robbie Powwow Garden on the south end of the Buffalo Bill Historical Center parking lot with whirling color. Traditional dance competitions are coupled with craft shows and American Indian food, and non-Indians are welcomed into round dances. Call the Buffalo Bill Historical Center (✆ 307/ 587-4771) for information.

Every July 1 to July 4, during the **Cody Stampede,** the streets are filled with parades, fireworks, street dances, barbecues, and entertainment, capped by a top-notch rodeo. Call ✆ 800/207-0744 or 307/587-5155 for tickets (see **www.cody stampederodeo.org** for more information). For 2 days in July, the cool rhythms of jazz and the brassy sound of big band and swing music take over the lawn of the Elks Club, 1202 Beck Ave., and other venues during the **Yellowstone Jazz Festival.** Featured musicians come from afar, and all varieties of jazz are heard from 11am until dark. Call ✆ 307/587-2777 for information.

In mid-August, the Buffalo Bill Historical Center (✆ 307/587-4771) stages the **Buffalo Bill Celebrity Shootout,** where celebrities and local shooters test their skills in trap, skeet, sporting clays, and five-stand shooting. In late September, Cody hosts the **Western Design Conference** (✆ 888/685-0574) at the Cody Auditorium and the Buffalo Bill Historical Center, a gathering of artisans to show off their work in Western-style furniture, decor, and clothing.

GETTING OUTSIDE

If you'd rather not drive in Yellowstone's heavy summer traffic, guided tours of the park are available locally through **Grub Steak Expeditions,** P.O. Box 1013, Cody, WY 82414 (✆ 800/527-6316 or 307/527-6316; www.grubsteaktours.com), and

Powder River Tours (© **800/442-3682,** ext. 114, or 307/527-3677). Bob Richard, Grub Steak's proprietor (and one of the most knowledgeable guides you'll find), can spin a tale with the best of them. His roots in the area run deep; he's a third-generation Cody resident and former Yellowstone ranger.

Cody has fewer organized recreation options than Jackson does, but there is no shortage of places to go outdoors. **Buffalo Bill State Park,** located along the canyon and reservoir 6 miles west of Cody, is a hot spot for outdoors buffs, with opportunities for hiking, fishing, and a variety of watersports, particularly windsurfing. The park also has facilities for camping and picnicking.

BIKING

If you want to explore the area on two wheels, cruiser rentals are available for $20 for a half-day at **Core Mountain Sports,** 1019 15th St. (© **307/527-7354**). Although there isn't a marked network of bike paths in the Cody area, you can ride on the Forest Service trails west of town off U.S. Hwy. 14/16/20 in the Shoshone National Forest. For specific trail information, the **Forest Service** (© **307/527-6921**).

CROSS-COUNTRY SKIING

If you favor a groomed course for cross-country skiing, try the **North Fork Nordic Trails** in Shoshone National Forest near the east entrance to the park off U.S. 14/16/20. You can circuit 25km (16 miles) of trails adjacent to the Sleeping Giant downhill area and the Pahaska Tepee resort.

FISHING

Yellowstone's legendary fly-fishing waters are a short drive away, but the smaller streams west of Cody are also excellent angling destinations: **the Clark's Fork of the Yellowstone, the North and South Forks of the Shoshone,** and **Sunlight Creek.** They're located northwest of Cody along Chief Joseph Highway—go north on Wyo. 120, 17 miles to Wyo. 296 (which is Chief Joseph). To the east, the warmer and slower **Bighorn River** and **Bighorn Lake** nurture catfish, walleye, and ling for boat fishermen. For advice on the trout streams near Cody, ask at **Tim Wade's North Fork Anglers,** 1107 Sheridan Ave. (© **307/527-7274;** www.northforkanglers.com), where they stock gear and clothing and also guide day trips ($300–$350 for two) and overnight excursions. If you like to troll or cast from a boat, **Buffalo Bill Reservoir,** 6 miles west of Cody on Yellowstone Highway (U.S. 14/16/20), has produced some big Mackinaw, as well as rainbow, brown, and cutthroat trout. You have a shot at landing a 10-pound rainbow at **Monster Lake** (© **800/840-5137;** www.monsterlake. com), a private 150-acre body of water on the Fraser Ranch 10 miles south of Cody. It's strictly catch-and-release for these lunker rainbows (and brooks, browns, and salmon), and there's a hefty fee per rod.

GOLF

The **Olive Glenn Golf and Country Club,** 802 Meadow Lane, is an 18-hole PGA championship course that is open to the public daily from 6am to 9pm. Greens fees are a modest $20 for 9 holes, $35 for 18. Call © **307/587-5551** for tee times.

RAFTING

There aren't lots of Class IV, serious white-water rapids on the rivers around Cody, but the upper stretches of the North Fork of the Shoshone River run pretty fast in the spring. Contact **Wyoming River Trips,** 1701 Sheridan Ave. (© **800/586-6661** or

307/587-6661; www.wyomingrivertrips.com), or **Core Mountain Sports,** 1019 15th St. (℃ **307/527-7354**). Prices run from about $25 to $50, depending on the length and difficulty of the trip.

SNOWMOBILING

The most popular Cody snowmobiling trails originate from nearby Pahaska Tepee Resort, located 51 miles from Cody on U.S. 14/16/20 (see the listing in "Where to Stay," below). The **Pahaska Tepee Trail** connects to the Yellowstone National Park trails and the lengthy Continental Divide Snowmobile Trail, and offers breathtaking views including Avalanche Peak (10,566 ft.) and Cody Peak (10,267 ft.). Don't take it if you're afraid of heights. The **Sunlight trail system** is located 36 miles north of Cody and winds through the wilds to a stunning view of the Beartooth Mountains. You start from a parking area at the junction of Wyo. 296 and U.S. 212 and follow the Beartooth Scenic Byway east for 16 miles to a warming hut. To the east, there are 70 miles of snowmobile routes in the Bighorn Mountains. Snowmobiles can be rented at **Pahaska Tepee Resort** and in Cody at **Mountain Valley Engine Service,** 422 W. Yellowstone Ave. (℃ **307/587-6218**).

WINDSURFING

The **Buffalo Bill Reservoir** (see "Seeing the Sights," below) sucks wind from three mountain gorges, making one of the top 10 windsurfing destinations in the continental United States, according to *Outside* magazine. The temperature is tolerable June through September. There is a boat ramp near the campground on the north side of the reservoir just off U.S. 14/16/20.

SEEING THE SIGHTS

Beyond the attractions listed below, herpetology buffs will surely want to check out the **Wild West Rattlesnake Museum,** 1420 Sheridan Ave. (℃ **877/836-6688**), home to over 20 different rattlesnake species and five cobras, among other reptiles, accompanied by interpretive displays and demonstrations. If your tastes in wildlife lean to the horned instead of the scaled, stop by the visitor center for the **Foundation for North American Wild Sheep,** next to the Buffalo Bill Historical Center at 720 Allen Ave. (℃ **307/527-6261;** www.fnaws.org), with exhibits on the four different wild sheep that call North America home.

Buffalo Bill Historical Center ☆☆☆ Nicknamed the "Smithsonian of the West," this vast museum is top-drawer, casting a scholarly eye on the relics of the West's young history while offering some flash and entertainment for the easily distracted. From its beginnings in a rustic log building, it's grown into a thoroughly impressive modern edifice that now houses five different museums in all.

The **Buffalo Bill Museum** is a monument to one of the earliest manifestations of America's celebrity culture, displaying the wares that turned a frontier scout and buffalo hunter into a renowned showman. Posters trumpet his world-famous Wild West shows featuring "Custer's Last Rally" and "Cossack of the Caucasus," and there are some grainy film clips of the show itself. The **Whitney Gallery of Western Art** showcases work by the adventurous artists who carried their palettes to the frontier to record firsthand the wilderness beauty, the proud Indian cultures, and the lives of trappers and cowboys in the 19th century. Bygone Western artists such as Frederic Remington, Charlie Russell, Albert Bierstadt, and Gutzon Borglum share exhibition space with contemporary practitioners. The **Plains Indian Museum** is devoted to the history of

Plains tribes, including the Blackfeet, Cheyenne, Crow, Gros Ventre, Shoshone, and Sioux. Interactive exhibits explain the migrations and customs of the tribes and display art and artifacts, including cradleboards, ceremonial dresses and robes, pipes, and beadwork. Situated in an eye-catching rotunda populated by dozens of engaging exhibits, the new **Draper Museum of Natural History** focuses on man's investigation of nature over time, with specific attention on the Greater Yellowstone Ecosystem (there's a map composed of 27,000 tiles) and many interactive displays. The **Cody Firearms Museum** displays weaponry dating from 16th-century Europe in its collection of more than 5,000 pieces.

The center also features rotating special exhibitions, and its research library is an unparalleled resource for all things Western. Expect to spend anywhere from 2 hours to 2 days here, depending on just how deep your interest lies.

720 Sheridan Ave. ℂ **307/587-4771.** www.bbhc.org. Admission $15 adults, $13 seniors, $10 students, free for children under 6; maximum $40 per family. Admission is good for 2 consecutive days. Group tour rates available by request. Open daily year-round, peaking at 7am–8pm June to mid-Sept; call for seasonal hours.

Buffalo Bill Reservoir
The **Buffalo Bill Dam** drops like a slim concrete knife 328 feet into the gorge carved by the Shoshone River west of Cody, and you can walk out atop the dam and look down the steep canyon or back across the deep blue water of the reservoir. Several workers died building it, and when it was completed in 1910, it was the tallest dam in the world. The lake behind it serves anglers, boaters, and windsurfers while providing irrigation water to farmers downstream. An octagonal visitor center perched next to the dam provides exhibits on the reservoir, wildlife, and area recreation. There is a boat launch along the north lakeshore off U.S. Highway 14/16/20 and a clean, spacious campground that lacks only adequate shade.

6 miles west of Cody on U.S. Hwy. 14/16/20 at the top of Shoshone Canyon. ℂ **307/527-6076** for visitor center. Free admission. May–Aug daily 8am–8pm; Sept daily 8am–6pm. Closed rest of year.

Cody Nite Rodeo ★★ (Kids)
If you want to see an authentic Wyoming rodeo, Cody (the self-proclaimed "Rodeo Capital of the World") offers a sure thing: a nightly tussle between bulls, broncs, and cowboys, as well as roping, cutting, and kids' events such as the "calf scramble"—about 100 young patrons chasing a bewildered young cow. Pay an extra $2, and you get a seat just above the chutes in the Buzzard's Roost. The 6,000-seat stadium sits out on an open terrace above the Shoshone River west of town—not a bad place to be on a cool Wyoming evening beneath the stars. Once a year, some of the nation's top rodeo competitors show up for the Fourth of July Cody Stampede (see "Special Events," above). Before the rodeo, there's a kiddie area with rides, games, and rodeo activities.

Stampede Park (on U.S. Hwy. 14/16/20 as you head west of town toward the Wapiti Valley). ℂ **800/207-0744** or 307/587-5155. Admission $15 adults, $8 children 7–12, free for children under 7. June–Aug nightly at 8:30pm; gates open at 7pm.

Cody Trolley Tours ★
An informative, witty look back at Cody's colorful past with a focus on the town's founding father himself, Buffalo Bill, these hour-long tours in a restored trolley take visitors on a loop that includes historic homes, public art, and Buffalo Bill Reservoir. The owner-operators, Mike and Margie Johnson, deliver a running commentary that is augmented by visual aids and recorded snippets that will keep the kids interested. While the couple's narration occasionally comes off as an economic development pitch for Cody, it also packs a dense serving of fun facts and trivia into the 60-minute drive.

1192 Sheridan Ave. (tours begin and end on the front porch of The Irma Hotel). © 307/527-7043. www.codytrolley tours.com. Admission $15 adults, $13 seniors, $6 children 6–17, free for children under 6. Ask about a combination ticket for the Buffalo Bill Historical Center. Tours offered mid-June to late Sept Mon–Sat at 11am, 3pm, and 6:30pm; Sun 11am and 3pm.

Museum of the Old West at Old Trail Town *Kids*

Walking the authentically creaky boardwalks here, you'll pass by gray storefronts and clapboard cabins gathered from ghost towns around the region and assembled on the original town site of Cody City, a short jog from the rodeo grounds. Soft-spoken archaeologist Bob Edgar hasn't wasted any paint on these relics, which include an 1883 cabin from Kaycee where Butch Cassidy and the Sundance Kid once conspired, a saloon decorated with bullet holes, and what must be the largest collection of worn-out buckboard carriages in the U.S. Also on-site: the relocated graves of a number of Western notables, including John "Liver-eatin'" Johnston, the model for Robert Redford's *Jeremiah Johnson*.

1831 Demaris Dr. © 307/587-5302. Admission $6 adults, $5 seniors, $2 children 6–12, free for children under 6. May 15–Sept 15 daily 8am–8pm; call ahead for hours at other times of year.

Tecumseh's Old West Miniature Village and Museum *Kids*

You have to pass through a trading post of Western tourist plunder and handcrafted beadwork to get to this finely detailed miniature diorama of Wyoming and Montana history. Described by proprietor Jerry Fick as his "lifetime work," the room-size landscape depicts everything from fur trappers floating the rivers to Custer's last moments at Little Big Horn. There is also a sizable collection of Indian and pioneer artifacts and taxidermy.

142 W. Yellowstone Ave. © 307/587-5362. www.tecumsehs.com. Admission $3 adults, $1 children 7–18, free for children under 7; $10 maximum per family. June–Aug daily 8am–8pm; call for hours in winter.

WHERE TO STAY

A good accommodations resource is **Cody Guest Houses,** 927 14th St. (© **800/587-6560;** www.codyguesthouses.com), which manages about 40 properties, from Victorian B&Bs to three-bedroom houses. Rates range from $99 to $450 a night. If you're on a budget, try **Bison Willy's Base Camp,** 1625 Alger St., Cody, WY 82414 (© **877/587-0629** or 307/587-0629; www.bisonwillys.com), a home converted into a hostel of sorts with dormitory-style bunks going for $20 a night and private rooms for $75. There's a communal kitchen, a "beer deck," and a dog kennel on-site.

Buffalo Bill Village Resort: Comfort Inn, Holiday Inn and Buffalo Bill Village Historic Cabins *&*

Consisting of three distinct lodging options at the same convenient location, the Buffalo Bill Village has something for everybody. The Holiday and Comfort inns are similar to their chain brethren elsewhere, while the village of historic cabins offers a rustic exterior and a more Western feel, with modern conveniences inside. The former two are priced nearly identically and have similar amenities (the rooms at the Holiday Inn won awards for its 2004 renovation, but the Comfort Inn includes continental breakfast in the rate). The one- and two-bedroom cabins at Buffalo Bill Village are simply equipped—with a bed, phone, and TV—and surrounded by plenty of room for the kids to roam around. The cabins themselves first housed the contractors who built the city around 1920, and became the centerpiece of this family-owned resort in the 1950s. (The Holiday Inn followed in the '70s, the Comfort Inn in the '90s.) Also on-site is an Old West–style boardwalk where you can shop for curios or sign up for tours and river trips, and there's an outdoor heated pool and several restaurants.

17th St. and Sheridan Ave., Cody, WY 82414. ℭ **800/527-5544.** Fax 307/587-2795. Comfort Inn: 75 units; $69–$169 double. Holiday Inn: 189 units; $69–$169 double. Buffalo Bill Village Historic Cabins: 83 units; $59–$159 double. AE, DC, DISC, MC, V. Historic Cabins closed Oct–Apr. **Amenities:** Restaurant; lounge; outdoor pool; fitness room; activities desk; courtesy car; shopping arcade; coin-op washers and dryers; dry cleaning. *In room:* A/C, cable TV, dataport and high-speed Internet access, coffeemaker, hair dryer, iron.

The Irma Hotel *Overrated*   Buffalo Bill's entrepreneurial gusto ultimately left him penniless, but it also left us this century-old hotel (named for his daughter) in the heart of town. Cody hoped to corral visitors who got off the train on their way to Yellowstone, and one of his lures was an elaborate cherrywood bar, a gift from straight-laced Queen Victoria. You can still hoist a jar on Her Royal Majesty's slab in the Silver Saddle Saloon or spend the night in a renovated room that might have once housed a president or prince.

Suites are named after local characters from the town's early days: The Irma Suite, on the corner of the building, has a queen-size bed, a writing table, a vanity in the bedroom area, a small sitting area, and an old-fashioned bathroom with a tub/shower combination. While The Irma's aura will surely please history buffs, those acclimated to ultramodern convenience will probably want to look elsewhere. But the hotel's location in the middle of town and the regular schedule of reenacted gunfights out front help compensate.

1192 Sheridan Ave., Cody, WY 82414. ℭ **800/745-4762** or 307/587-4221. www.irmahotel.com. 73 units. $69–$92 double; $96–$119 suite. AE, DC, DISC, MC, V. **Amenities:** Restaurant; lounge. *In room:* A/C, cable TV, dataport.

The Mayor's Inn 🌟🌟   This two-story A-frame, built in 1905 for Mayor Frank Houx, found itself in the path of a wrecking ball in 1997. However, before it was demolished, it was sold and moved on a truck to its current location, just a few blocks away. It's now one of Cody's best B&Bs, with rooms such as the Yellowstone, featuring a lodgepole-pine bed frame and black-and-white photos of the park's early years, and the Hart Mountain Suite, with romance and floral decor in spades. There's also a carriage house (breakfast not included) with a well-equipped kitchen and a fully licensed bar on the enclosed back porch, the perfect spot to unwind after a day of sightseeing. The breakfasts here are a hearty treat, featuring sourdough flapjacks and buffalo sausage.

1413 Rumsey Ave., Cody, WY 82414. ℭ **888/217-3001** or 307/587-0887. Fax 307/587-0890. www.mayorsinn.com. 5 units. $100–$155 double; $205 suite. Rates include complimentary full breakfast. AE, DISC, MC, V. **Amenities:** Restaurant; lounge. *In room:* A/C, TV, in-room hot tub, hair dryer, no phone.

GUEST RANCHES & RESORTS

Pahaska Tepee Resort 🌟   Buffalo Bill's hunting lodge, only 2 miles from the east entrance to Yellowstone, was dubbed with his Lakota name, Pahaska (longhair), when he opened the lodge to park visitors in 1905. Near the top of the beautiful Wapiti Valley along U.S. Hwy. 14/16/20, Pahaska is a popular stop for people visiting the Yellowstone area. The cabins are scattered on the hill behind the historic (and colorfully decorated) lodge. Accommodations have limited amenities and might best be described as "minimotels" with two to five rooms, each with a private entrance. Some bathrooms have only showers, some have tubs—it's best to ask in advance.

183 Yellowstone Hwy., Cody, WY 82414. ℭ **800/628-7791** or 307/527-7701. Fax 307/527-4019. 47 units. Mid-June to Aug $90–$135 double, $495 condo, $895 lodge; off season $93–$140 double, $495 condo, $900 lodge; lower rates spring and fall. DISC, MC, V. Closed Oct–May. **Amenities:** Restaurant; lounge. *In room:* Kitchen.

Rimrock Ranch ❀ Tucked along Canyon Creek at 6,300 feet above sea level, Rimrock Ranch has an intimate feel not found on larger dude ranches. The cabins, nestled alongside the creek, are fairly modern and definitely a cut above some of the more "rustic" cabins in the area. The weekly package includes backcountry rides, rodeo trips, fishing, cookouts, and river floats. A small outdoor pool perches next to the lodge with a view down the canyon. In summer, horse-packing trips are available; in the winter, there are snowmobile packages.

2728 North Fork Rte., Cody, WY 82414. ℭ **800/208-7468** or 307/587-3970. Fax 307/527-5014. www.rimrock ranch.com. 8 cabins. Mid-May to mid-Sept $1,475 per adult per week; $1,200 per child 6–18 per week. Rates include all meals. MC, V. Drive 25 miles west of Cody on U.S. 16/20/14 (aka Yellowstone Hwy.); ranch is on the south side of highway. **Amenities:** Outdoor heated pool; outdoor Jacuzzi; game room; courtesy car; washer and dryer. *In room:* No phone.

7D Ranch ❀❀ Beautiful Sunlight Creek runs through this venerable ranch, which has a homey, lived-in quality missing in slicker operations. The Dominick family has run the spread for three generations, and they know the nooks and crannies of the Sunlight Basin and the Beartooth Mountains, which guests explore on daylong rides, hikes, and fishing expeditions. Riding and casting lessons, naturalist-led wildflower walks, weekly square dances, and bonfires are all part of the package. And the cabins, cheerfully decorated with heaps of frontier charm, have more personality than the bulk of the 7D's peers. September is adults-only, but the rest of the season the ranch is family-friendly, with numerous children's activities.

Sunlight Basin, Box 100, Cody, WY 82414. ℭ **866/587-3997** 307/587-9885. www.7dranch.com. 11 cabins. May–Sept $1,560 per double cabin per week. Rates include all meals. MC, V. Drive north from Cody on Wyo. 120 to Wyo. 296, then west. Ranch is 50 miles from Cody via Sunlight Rd. **Amenities:** Children's program; game room. *In room:* No phone.

WHERE TO DINE

For its size, Cody may have more good restaurants than any of the gateways, especially considering that the town virtually shuts down from November to May. The town's finest restaurants aren't all meat-and-potatoes operations, either, although there's no shortage of good prime rib. Note that all the restaurants listed in this section are open year-round.

If you need something less than a formal meal, such as a plateful of fuel food or a jolt of caffeine for a busy day, Cody has a good supply of familiar fast-food joints and a few informal, inexpensive places. **Peter's Cafe Bakery,** at 1219 Sheridan Ave. (ℭ **307/527-5040**), across the street from The Irma, serves a full breakfast starting at 6:45am, with fresh-baked bagels, pastries, and espresso, plus subs and burgers for lunch and dinner. There is also the eclectic **Beta Coffeehouse,** 1132 12th St. (ℭ **307/527-7879**), for coffee drinks and fresh-baked muffins and bagels. One of the best places day or night to get a steak or beer and a burger (or Rocky Mountain oysters!) is the thoroughly Western **Proud Cut Saloon,** 1227 Sheridan Ave. (ℭ **307/527-6905**), where lots of rodeo riders keep a running tab.

Cassie's Supper Club ❀ WESTERN Cassie's is the sort of classic roadhouse you might expect and look for in the West: big platters of beef, four bars serving drinks, and ornery roadhouse decor with taxidermy, antelope skulls, and assorted cowboy ephemera. This place has the routine down, having been in business since 1922. Located along the highway west of town in what was once a "house of ill fame," Cassie's is now very respectable and very busy. Besides the requisite steaks, there's seafood (including a great walleye dinner), pasta, and chicken, plus a full menu of specialty drinks. In the Buffalo Bar, a 20-foot mural depicts horses, cowboys, and shootouts. The dance floor bustles to the twang of live country music every night in summer.

214 Yellowstone Ave. (© 307/527-5500. Reservations recommended. Main courses $7–$20 lunch, $18–$40 dinner. AE, DISC, MC, V. Daily 11am–11pm; shorter hours in winter.

Maxwell's Restaurant *Kids* ECLECTIC AMERICAN   A family restaurant in which "family" does not translate to "bland," Maxwell's has some spicy chicken and pasta dishes to go with its salads, seafood, and beef. The gourmet pizzas aren't a bad choice, nor is the pork tenderloin Marsala, sautéed in a light wine sauce with portobello mushrooms. You can even order a Philly cheese steak for lunch, uncommon in Wyoming. The low-backed booths and varnished wood tables are sometimes packed with boisterous families, raising the noise level and waitress stress, but it's a friendly crowd. The bread and dessert are homemade daily.

937 Sheridan Ave. (© 307/527-7749. Lunch $6.50–$8.50; dinner $8–$23. AE, DISC, MC, V. Daily 11am–9pm. Closed Sun in winter.

The Mayor's Inn Dining Room *Finds* AMERICAN   Besides The Irma and the Buffalo Bill Village, The Mayor's Inn is the only establishment in Cody with hotel rooms, a restaurant, and a bar. The restaurant is a great pick for a leisurely dinner: Innkeepers Dale and Bill Delph focus on just one seating an evening. The antiques-laden dining room has a nice air to it, and Bill showcases his culinary chops with rib steaks, seared buffalo medallions, and a regularly changing menu of flavorful preparations he dubs "regional fusion."

1413 Rumsey Ave. (© 307/587-0887. Reservations recommended. Dinner main courses $15–$20. AE, DISC, MC, V. Summer Thurs–Sat 6–9pm.

Tommy Jack's *Finds* CAJUN   A geographically unusual eatery just off Cody's main drag, Tommy Jack's dishes up surprisingly authentic Cajun specialties—such as gator, crawfish, étouffée, gumbo, and catfish—with more than a hint of the bayou. The place opened in 2001, and locals now love it, with tourists quickly catching on. It helps that the eponymous proprietor is a Louisiana native, and that crawfish is flown in several times a week. It also helps that the service is excellent, the glass-block-and-brick room is comfortable and inviting, and the requisite cornbread is fluffy and sweet.

1134 13th St. (© 307/587-4917. Lunch $5–$9; dinner $10–$22. AE, DISC, MC, V. Mon–Sat 11am–10pm; Sun 10am–2pm and 5–9pm.

CODY AFTER DARK

The **Cody Stage,** 1110 Beck Ave. (© **307/587-7469**), is a local theater that stages several plays each year.

For those with less cultured aims, Cody has a lively nightlife, headed by **Cassie's** (see "Where to Dine," above), with a dance floor laden with real and wannabe cowboys and cowgirls. Downtown, the historic **Silver Dollar Bar,** at 1313 Sheridan Ave. (© **307/527-7666**), has tasty burgers, live music, pool tables, and numerous TV screens. Housed in a converted brick garage, **Cooter Brown's,** in the alley behind 1134 13th St. (© **307/587-6261**), draws in hordes of hip, young Wyomans with DJs, bands, and regular drink specials.

3 A Side Trip around the Bighorn Basin

Greybull: 40 miles E of Cody; 60 miles W of Sheridan

The prehistoric past of this region is written in the rock, and nowhere in Wyoming is that more true than in **Greybull,** named for a legendary albino bison sacred to American Indians. The town lies amid red-rock formations rich in fossils and archaeological treasures. **The Greybull Museum** (325 Greybull Ave.; ✆ **307/765-2444**) houses one of the largest fossil ammonites in the world, as well as petrified wood, agates, and American Indian artifacts. This fine museum is open Monday through Saturday, 10am to 8pm from June to Labor Day, and more restricted hours in the winter, with free admission. Just north of town you'll find a spectacular 15-mile-long, 2,000-foot-high natural fortress named **Sheep Mountain,** a textbook example of a "doubly plunging anticline," geolingo for a natural arch folded into layered rock.

Greybull is a gateway town to the Bighorn Mountains on scenic U.S. 14 up Shell Canyon. Just 7 miles outside of town heading east is the **Stone Schoolhouse,** listed on the National Register of Historic Places. The one-room schoolhouse was built in 1903 of locally quarried sandstone, and in recent years was converted to a bookstore/gallery, though its hours are unpredictable. Less than a mile farther along the highway, turn south on Red Gulch Road and drive 5 miles to a signed parking area where you can view dinosaur tracks. Driving east from Greybull, U.S. 14 climbs through steep and beautiful **Shell Canyon** (see Driving Tour 1, in section 1, "Scenic Drives").

Fifty miles south of Greybull and east through little Hyattville brings you to the **Medicine Lodge State Archaeological Site** (✆ **307/469-2234**), where prehistoric peoples decorated the sandstone cliffs along Medicine Lodge Creek with carved petroglyphs and painted pictographs of hunting scenes. You can fish the small stream for brown trout. There is a shady, inexpensive, 26-site campground here, open May through October, with no RV hookups. To reach the site and campground, take Wyo. 789/U.S. 16/20 for 20 miles from Greybull to Manderson, then drive 22 miles along Wyo. 31 to Hyattville. In Hyattville, drive north and turn right onto Cold Springs Road. Follow the signs 5 miles to the site. The day-use fee is $4 per vehicle; campsites are $12.

4 Thermopolis

84 miles S of Cody; 130 miles NW of Casper; 218 miles E of Jackson

Steaming water cascades over pastel-colored terraces and down to the Bighorn River at Hot Springs State Park, one of the undiscovered treasures of Wyoming. Trumpeted as the largest hot springs in the world (it's not quite: New Zealand's Whakarewarewa rightfully claims that honor), the 134°F (57°C) water from the Big Spring supplies two indoor/outdoor pool facilities, two hotels, and a state-run soaking spa. The town of Thermopolis grew up around the hot springs after it was sold to the U.S. government by the tribes of the Wind River Indian Reservation in 1896. Developers dreamed of a health spa to rival Saratoga, but it never quite happened. What did happen is a small, peaceful town with a great place to soak or slide, a nearby canyon of exciting white water, and surrounding hills holding a trove of dinosaur bones and prehistoric petroglyphs.

ESSENTIALS

GETTING THERE The closest airports are the **Riverton Regional Airport** (55 miles south of Thermopolis, off U.S. 26 W. at 4700 Airport Rd.; ✆ **307/856-1307**)

and Cody's **Yellowstone Regional Airport** (84 miles northeast on Wyo. 120 to U.S. 14/16/20, north to 3001 Duggleby Dr.; ✆ **307/587-5096**). There is a small airport in Thermopolis used by private fliers.

United (✆ **800/554-5111**) and **Frontier** (✆ **800/432-1359**) fly into Riverton, with several daily connecting flights to Denver and north to Worland. Cody service is provided by United and Delta feeder **SkyWest** (✆ **800/864-8331**).

To reach Thermopolis from Cody, drive 84 miles southeast on Wyo. 120. From Cheyenne, drive north on I-25 to Casper (178 miles), west on U.S. 20/26 to Shoshoni (98 miles), and north on U.S. 20 to Thermopolis. From Rock Springs, take U.S. 191 to Farson, Wyo. 28 to Lander, and Wyo. 789 through Riverton and Shoshoni to Thermopolis.

VISITOR INFORMATION The **Thermopolis–Hot Springs Chamber of Commerce** (✆ **800/SUN-N-SPA** or 307/864-3192; www.thermopolis.com) sends out packets of information about local attractions.

GETTING AROUND If you've arrived by plane at one of the area airports, you'll need to rent a car to get around. **Hertz** (✆ **800/654-3131**) maintains counters at both the Riverton and Cody airports.

GETTING OUTSIDE

Hot Springs State Park (see the detailed listing below) offers a variety of outdoor activities, from splashing in mineral water to picnicking on the lawn. South and upstream on the Bighorn River is twisting **Wind River Canyon,** a tricky but bountiful fishing and floating section (you'll need permits from the Wind River Indian Reservation), topped by 19,000-acre **Boysen Reservoir,** about 20 minutes from Thermopolis on U.S. 20. The campgrounds ($12 a site, plus the requisite $4 day-use fee) on the largely treeless shore of this state park can be a bit buggy and hot in August, but the water attracts boaters to sail, fish, and water-ski. There are three small public beach areas, on the reservoir's northeastern and western shores. For more information on the park, contact **Boysen State Park,** Boysen Route, Shoshoni, WY 82649 (✆ **307/876-2796**), or call Wyoming State Parks and Historic Sites headquarters in Cheyenne at ✆ **307/777-6323.**

FISHING

Whether you like fishing lakes or streams, this area has trophy-size opportunities—Boysen grows record-setting walleye, as well as trout and perch, while the Bighorn River grows some fat brown and cutthroat trout. Check locally to be sure you've got the right fishing license: The canyon requires a tribal permit; the reservoir and other stretches of river require a state license—both available at local sporting-goods stores. If you have your own boat, or hire an outfitter, you can float and fish from the bottom of the canyon at the Wedding of the Waters (where there's a wheelchair-accessible boat ramp) to Thermopolis. During the warmest part of summer, algae can darken the river and hamper fishing, but spring and fall are anglers' dreams.

GOLF

The Legion Golf Course is a 9-hole course that overlooks the city from Airport Hill. Call ✆ **307/864-5294** to book a tee time at affordable prices—9 holes for $12 to $14. The pro shop offers cart rentals, a driving range, and lessons.

HIKING

A boardwalk allows you to explore the bulbous travertine terraces without scalding your soles in the hot-spring water that flows over them. The paths extend to a suspended footbridge across the Bighorn River and a riverside walkway below. For more earnest hikers, there is the approximately 6-mile **Volksmarch Trail,** one of several around the state that are marked with a trademark brown-and-yellow insignia. This one loops through the park and downtown Thermopolis. Just north of town off U.S. 20 you can hike **T Hill** for a bird's-eye view of Thermopolis, the Wind River Canyon, and the Owl Creek Mountains. The 2-mile round-trip up **Roundtop Mountain** is another rewarding hike, culminating in spectacular views of the Hot Springs and Thermopolis, with the trail head beginning near the Monument Hill Cemetery on Airport Road.

WHITE-WATER RAFTING 🐟🐟

The tribes of the **Wind River Indian Reservation** virtually gave away the hot springs, but not the canyon upstream, through which the Wind River tumbles and twists (for reasons no one can explain, the Wind River becomes the Bighorn River as it leaves the canyon). A Shoshone-owned company now takes rafters through rapids named after historic tribal figures like Chief Washakie and Sharp Nose. "Sphincter Rapid" is not an Indian name, but it tells you there are some Class III to IV white-water thrills ahead. You can run half the canyon or the whole thing, take a more leisurely fishing trip, or camp overnight with **Wind River Canyon Whitewater,** 210 Hwy. 20 S., Thermopolis (© **888/246-9343** or 307/864-9343 in season, 307/486-2253 during off season; www.windrivercanyonraft.com). White-water trips run $30 to $38 for a half-day or $75 for a full day.

HOT SPRINGS STATE PARK 🐟🐟

Few state parks in Wyoming are as nice as **Hot Springs** (© **307/864-2176**), with its shady trees, striking flower gardens, and a stretch of the Bighorn River running through it, as well as a roaming buffalo herd and the main event: the magnificent hot springs, with some of its water funneled into swimming pools and slides. It's located at the north side of town off U.S. 20 and admission is free. The park's only shortcoming is that you can't camp overnight, which must please nearby private campgrounds and lodgings. As a Wyoming tourist attraction, the hot springs places a distant third to Yellowstone and Grand Teton national parks, but the sparse crowds allow Thermopolis to retain its small-town style.

At the north end of the park, you can climb a few stairs to look down into the bottomless blue-green depths of the Big Spring—the placid surface belies the fact that the spring pumps out around 15 million gallons a day.

SOAKING IN THE BATHS

You can't just plop yourself down in this 134°F (57°C) water, but there are three bathing facilities in the park. To get to them, take the loop road—at the north end are the bathing areas. First, and simplest, is the **State Bath House** (© **307/864-3765**), a small spa open to the public free of charge thanks to famed Shoshone Chief Washakie. When the tribes sold the federal government the hot springs in 1896—it would later become state property—Washakie noted that the springs had always been a place of peace and neutrality among tribes, and should therefore always be free to all people. The small, clean indoor and outdoor pools aren't for frolicking or swimming laps— just soaking, wading, and perhaps conversing with some of the old-timers who come

---

Gift of the Waters Historical Indian Pageant

An annual production, the pageant reenacts the sale of the hot springs and surrounding lands by the Shoshone and Arapaho peoples to the federal government in 1896. The pageant portrays the sale as an act of peace and neighborly
brotherhood. In fact, the tribes were starving and desperate. Indians from
Wind River play some of the roles in the pageant. The pageant is performed
annually during the first weekend in August, along with a powwow. Contact
the **Thermopolis Chamber of Commerce** (© **800/SUN-N-SPA** or 307/864-3192)
for information.

---

here. Soaks are limited to 20 minutes per session. You can rent a towel, locker, and
bathing suit for under a dollar each, and it's open Monday through Saturday from
8am to 5:30pm, Sunday from noon to 5:30pm. On either side of this peaceful place
are the more raucous commercial pools.

STAR PLUNGE The big lure at the Plunge are its three big slides—the kids'
favorite "Little Dipper," the outdoor "Super Star," and the enclosed "Blue Thunder,"
the latter a 300-foot spin around a 60-foot tower that will thrill you to your claustro-
phobic, free-falling toes. Indoor and outdoor pools, hot tubs, Jacuzzis, a snack bar, and
an arcade make this the favorite of the young set. On a crowded summer afternoon,
there are lines at the slides, splashing all around, and a teenage volume level, but you
can still find stillness in the "vapor cave." For more information call © **307/864-
3771.** Admission is $9 for children over 4 and adults, $4 for children 4 and under, $7
for seniors. It's open daily from 9am to 9pm. Closed late November to mid-December.

HELLIE'S TEPEE SPA The Spa (© **307/864-9250**), sometimes called Hot
Springs Water Park, is a little more peaceful under its big dome than its neighbor to
the east, but it has its share of lively teens and a contingent of young families. The
slides are not as big here, but you can hear yelps of delight as bodies zip down the
twisting indoor open tube. There is a fast-moving open slide outdoors, too, and often
a wet basketball game in the roomy outdoor pool. Soaking pools, a steam room, a
sauna, and a game room complete the scene. Admission is $9 for ages 6 to 62, $5 for
ages 4 to 5, $7 for 63 and over, and free for children 3 and under. Open daily from
9am to 9pm.

SEEING THE SIGHTS

Hot Springs County Historical Museum and Cultural Center The original
cherrywood bar from the Hole-in-the-Wall Saloon—Butch Cassidy's hangout—is the
biggest draw at this local museum, which has some gems among the musty clutter that
you learn to expect of rural repositories of historical artifacts. Alongside a trove of
Native American weaponry and art, various modes of transportation are represented,
including a caboose and a stagecoach used to tour Yellowstone. Other exhibits trace
the local economic threads, primarily coal mining, petroleum extraction, and agriculture. On the lower level are a fully outfitted print shop, general store, and dentist's
office. The museum's cultural center features local artwork and crafts on a rotating
basis. Expect to spend an hour.

700 Broadway. © 307/864-5183. www.trib.com/~history. $4 adults, $2 seniors and children 6–12, free for children
under 6. Memorial Day to Labor Day Mon–Sat 9am–8pm, Sun 1–6pm; Rest of year Tues–Sat 9am–5pm.

Legend Rock Petroglyph Site ✦ *(Finds)*   Petroglyphs—prehistoric drawings inscribed in rock—are scattered throughout the foothills of Wyoming's mountains. Legend Rock is one of the richest petroglyph sites in the Rockies, and it is managed—rather informally—by state agents at Hot Springs State Park (✆ **307/864-3765**). Visitors can pick up a gate key at the park and then drive up Wyo. 120 to the Hamilton Dome turnoff, then continue 8 miles west, partly on a dirt road, to the site. There you can hike up and down Cottonwood Creek to find pecked representations of turtle-like creatures, birds, hunters, and musicians. To get a good view of some of the panels you need to scramble up on ledges. Weather has taken its toll on this soft sandstone, and so have souvenir hunters—hands off, please! Be sure to ask for a map to the site when you pick up the key between 9am and 5pm at the park office; the route is not well marked. You can drive down by the creek, but you're better off, particularly when it's wet and muddy, parking up by the gate and taking the short hike down.

Near Hamilton Dome, 27 miles northwest of Thermopolis. For information contact Hot Springs State Park (✆ **307/ 864-3765**) or the Thermopolis Chamber of Commerce (✆ **800/SUN-N-SPA**).

Outlaw Trail Ride   Butch Cassidy was a well-known character around Thermopolis, although not by any means the only outlaw who favored this rugged country. Visitors who want to relive a Wild West getaway can join the annual Outlaw Trail Ride in August, and journey 100 miles up through the dry, hidden canyons of Hole-in-the-Wall country. Only about 100 people can participate in the weeklong event, and it's popular, so book well in advance. You must BYO horse and sleep on the ground.

Outlaw Trail, Inc., Box 1046, Thermopolis, WY 82443. ✆ **888/362-RIDE** or 307/864-2287. www.rideoutlawtrail.com. $875 per rider. The ride occurs annually in mid-Aug.

Wyoming Dinosaur Center & Dig Sites ✦ *(Kids)*   This dinosaur museum is located right at the site where modern-day paleontologists have unearthed dinosaur bones from the Jurassic period. There are 20 full skeletons on display at the center, as well as eggs, shells, and other remnants from around the world. Except in winter, visitors can take guided tours of dig sites, and then watch workers clean and prepare bones in the laboratory at the center. Visitors can also get dirty with the center's Dig for a Day program ($125 per person); call for a schedule.

110 Carter Ranch Rd., Thermopolis, WY 82443. ✆ **800/455-3466** or 307/864-2997. www.wyodino.org. Museum: $6 adults 14–59, $3.50 children 4–13 and seniors, free for children under 4. Dig site: $10 adults 19–59, $7 children 4–18 and seniors, free for children under 4. Summer daily 8am–6pm; winter daily 10am–5pm. Closed major holidays.

WHERE TO STAY

Thermopolis has a number of motels and campgrounds with a little age on them, so if you're arriving in the busy summer season you should have a reservation, or risk landing in a room with the amenities of a closet. Recently, chain affiliates have taken a new interest in lodgings here, so the choices are growing.

Best Western–The Plaza Hotel ✦   If you'd rather not have a wildebeest staring at you on your way to breakfast (see Holiday Inn of the Waters, below), but still want to be in the park (and just an easy walk from the pools), try this alternative, a funky old brick place that once operated as a hostel but now has been nicely fixed up. The 1918 structure is on the National Register of Historic Places and the aura is more urban inn than chain motel. Several of the rooms and suites still have working fireplaces, and new owners have completely renovated the inner courtyard.

116 E. Park St. (P.O. Box 866), Thermopolis, WY 82443. ✆ **888/919-9009** or 307/864-2939. www.bestwestern.com. 36 units. $85–$130 double; reduced rates in winter. Rates include continental breakfast. AE, DC, DISC, MC, V. **Amenities:** Outdoor pool; Jacuzzi. *In room:* A/C, TV, coffeemaker, hair dryer, iron.

Holiday Inn of the Waters *(Kids)*   This is no cookie-cutter Holiday Inn—it's a hot-springs resort along the Bighorn River within Hot Springs State Park. The huge volume of superheated water that surges from the upturned sandstones is piped into the outdoor Jacuzzi next to the big pool. If lolling under the stars doesn't soften you up, take a turn in the health club and submit to the ministrations of a licensed masseuse. Unique to this Holiday Inn are its location in the park, several antiques-furnished rooms, and frequent promotions (2 nights, dinner, and champagne for two for $170–$190 from Sept–May). Certainly no other Holiday Inn has a restaurant like the Safari Room, arrayed with enough big-game trophies from around the world to make Ernest Hemingway blush and vegetarians gag.

Hot Springs State Park, Thermopolis, WY 82443. ✆ **800/HOLIDAY** or 307/864-3131. www.holidayinn.com. 80 units. $79–$130 double. AE, DC, DISC, MC, V. **Amenities:** Restaurant; lounge; outdoor pool; health club; Jacuzzi; sauna; massage; coin-op washers and dryers. *In room:* A/C, cable TV, coffeemaker, hair dryer, iron.

Roundtop Mountain Motel *(Value)*   The Roundtop is the best of the budget bunch in Thermopolis, offering lodging in either a motel room or a log cabin. A redwood deck and patio complement some of the newly renovated units, and kitchenettes are available, which puts the Roundtop ahead of its competition. Though not directly adjacent to the hot springs, the motel is located downtown and within a short drive or walk of the mineral baths.

412 N. 6th, Thermopolis, WY 82443. ✆ **800/584-9126** or 307/864-3126. Fax 307/864-3905. www.roundtopmotel.com. 12 units. Summer $65–$69 double; winter $35–$49 double. DISC, MC, V. *In room:* A/C, cable TV, kitchenette.

Super 8 Thermopolis *(Kids)*   The tile-roofed Southwest style of architecture distinguishes this new motel from other Super 8's, and from the many older, somewhat drab lodgings in Thermopolis. Inside, the decor is not particularly distinguished, but there is a big indoor pool, a pleasant lobby and eating area for the full breakfast, and a honeymoon suite with a marble Jacuzzi. And it's a good bet for kids, offering eight family rooms, each with a bunk bed, two queen-size beds, a VCR, and a Nintendo for only $10 extra.

Lane 5 S., Hwy. 20, Thermopolis, WY 82443. ✆ **800/800-8000** or 307/864-5515. Fax 307/864-5447. www.super8.com. 52 units. Summer $79–$95 double, $175 suite; winter $65–$75 double, $145 suite. Rates include full breakfast. AE, DC, DISC, MC, V. **Amenities:** Indoor heated pool; Jacuzzi; coin-op washers and dryers. *In room:* A/C, cable TV, hair dryer.

CAMPING

The **Fountain of Youth RV Park** (✆ **307/864-3265**) has tent and RV sites available almost year-round (closed Nov–Jan) and is located 1½ miles north of town by the river on U.S. 20. The campground features a large hot mineral spring pool, barbecue grills, showers, laundry room, dump station, and camp store. RV sites cost about $25 (tent sites are lower), and MasterCard and Visa are accepted. Facilities are wheelchair accessible and an EMT is on-site. When things are busy in the summer, you may find yourself overhearing the unmuffled conversation of the Harley riders parked in the next slot. Open April through October, the **Eagle RV Park** (✆ **888/865-5707** or 307/864-5262; www.eaglervpark.com) offers RV sites for $23, tent sites for $17, and log cabins for $34—and peace and quiet. It's located at 204 S. U.S. 20, just south of Thermopolis.

WHERE TO DINE

Pumpernick's *(Finds* AMERICAN The three rooms where meals are served at Pumpernick's clearly weren't designed as a restaurant, but the bric-a-brac-bedecked quarters add a friendly intimacy to good food. In the summer, you can escape the elbows by eating outside in the roomy adjacent arbor. Pumpernick's serves three-egg omelets to breakfast noshers, then crepes and plump specialty sandwiches for lunch. Dinner features generous portions of T-bone steaks and seafood, including rainbow trout and steamed shrimp. The place bakes its own breads, which it uses for hoagies, soup bowls, and dinner loaves. Try the Hertle Turtle for a melt-in-your-mouth chocolate treat.

512 Broadway. ℂ **307/864-5151.** Breakfast $2–$8; lunch $3–$7; dinner $9–$17. AE, DISC, MC, V. Summer Mon–Sat 7am–9pm; winter Mon–Sat 7am–8pm. Closed Sun year-round.

5 Wind River Valley

Lander: 160 miles SE of Jackson; 117 miles N of Rock Springs; 163 miles S of Cody

The deep curve of the Wind River Valley is shaped by the snowcapped Wind River Range to the West and the Absaroka and Owl Creek ranges on the east, forming a cottonwood-lined bottom that many consider one of the most beautiful areas in Wyoming. A sizable portion of the valley belongs to the Eastern Shoshone and Northern Arapaho tribes of the **Wind River Indian Reservation,** where there is considerable poverty, but also productive ranches and spectacular wilderness reaching up to the Continental Divide. The largest towns are Riverton and Lander, but there are smaller communities like Dubois, Shoshoni, Fort Washakie, and the historical gold-mining town of Atlantic City.

RIVERTON

Notched in a big bend of the Wind River is **Riverton,** a settlement that was carved out when the federal government opened the northern portion of the reservation to non-Indian people a century ago. Riverton has established itself as a retail commercial center for west-central Wyoming. Contact the **Riverton Area Chamber of Commerce,** 213 W. Main St., Riverton, WY 82501 (ℂ **307/856-4801;** www.riverton chamber.org), for information, including useful suggestions for day trips in the area and a list of events. That calendar includes a summer **Riverton Rendezvous and Balloon Rally,** held during the second and third week in July, when colorful balloons from all over the Rockies rise against the majestic backdrop of the Wind River Range, and the town puts on arts and crafts fairs, a demolition derby, a family dinner with live entertainment, and even a treasure hunt. Also in July, there is the nostalgic **1838 Rendezvous** staged at the junction of the Wind River and the Little Wind River, with black-powder shooting, Indian dancing, tomahawk throws, and bead-trading. A **cowboy poetry gathering** is held here in September, and there is the February **Wild West Winter Carnival** with drag races, ice sculpting, and fishing derbies on the frozen surface of Boysen Reservoir.

GETTING THERE From Thermopolis, take U.S. 20 south through scenic Wind River Canyon to Shoshoni, then U.S. 26 south to Riverton.

WHERE TO STAY If you plan to stay overnight in Riverton, your best bet is the **Holiday Inn** (ℂ **800/HOLIDAY** or 307/856-8100). Located at 900 E. Sunset, it has

121 rooms that typically rent for $75 to $100 double. Or you could head 24 miles farther west on Wyo. 789 to **Lander** (see below).

SHOSHONI

Shoshoni, which translates as "Little Snow," is located 22 miles east of Riverton on U.S. 26. Peek behind the shabby exterior of the little town and you'll find what are reputedly the state's best milkshakes at the endearing **Yellowstone Drug Store,** 127 Main St. (© 307/876-2539); some interesting sites for rockhounds amid abandoned copper mines in the Owl Creeks to the north; and, on Memorial Day weekend, the state's premier **Old Time Fiddlers' Contest.** Contact the **Shoshoni Chamber of Commerce,** Box 324, Shoshoni, WY 82649 (© 307/876-2556), for more information.

LANDER

If you head 24 miles farther west of Riverton on Wyo. 789, you hit **Lander,** tucked snugly into the foothills of the Wind River Range where the three fingers of the Popo Agie River draw together. When railroads were the nation's primary mode of travel, Lander was "where the rails end and the trails begin": the takeoff point for backcountry trips to hunt, fish, or explore the lake-dotted wilderness that climbs to the Continental Divide. The trains are gone, but this is still where you put on your hiking or riding boots. For more information, contact the **Lander Area Chamber of Commerce,** 160 N. 1st St., Lander, WY 82520 (© **800/433-0662** or 307/332-3892; www.landerchamber.org).

Just west of town on Wyo. 131 is **Sinks Canyon State Park** (© **307/332-3077**), where the Middle Fork of the Popo Agie disappears into a limestone cave and reappears farther down the canyon at a pool with an overlook where you can feed kibble to giant trout (no hooks allowed!). Day use is $4. The park has a nature trail, a visitor center with naturalist displays, a campground ($12 a night), and tumbling waterfalls for those willing to hike some switchbacks. For a different kind of experience, drive south 37 miles on U.S. 287 to the **South Pass City Historical Site** (© **307/332-3684**), which re-creates a gold-mining town from the 1860s, and where Esther Hobart Morris became the nation's first female justice of the peace. There is a $4 day-use fee.

Lander has a justly famous **Fourth of July parade and Pioneer Days Rodeo** (© **800/433-0662**), and later in July it hosts the **International Climber's Festival** (© **307/3491561;** www.climbersfestival.org). Slide shows by climbing greats, clinics, an equipment show, and climbers testing their mettle on the walls of Sinks Canyon and Wild Iris draw hundreds of serious climbers to the event. Some of the climbers are resident here, partly thanks to the **National Outdoor Leadership School** ✦, which has been teaching outdoor types responsible ways of enjoying the wilds for more than 40 years, and now has branches all over the world. For course offerings from India to the Rocky Mountains, write the school's Lander headquarters at 284 Lincoln St., Lander, WY 82520 (© **800/710-6657** or 307/332-5300; www.nols.edu).

If you want an exotic element to your trail adventure, try the **Lander Llama Company,** 2024 Mortimore Lane, Lander, WY 82520 (© **800/582-5262** or 307/332-5624; www.llamahiking.com). Their naturalist-led Red Desert trip is as enlightening as it is enjoyable, incorporating ancient American Indian history and fossil viewing with stunning Wyoming scenery. If you'd prefer to horse around, check out **Allen's Diamond Four Ranch,** P.O. Box 243, Lander, WY 82520 (© **307/332-2995;** www.diamond4ranch.com), for guided horseback tours in the Popo Agie Wilderness and Wind River Range. The ranch's overnight accommodations are bare-bones—woodstoves, propane lights, bring your own bedding—but the emphasis is on riding, fishing, and seeing the high country. There are special programs for kids.

Winter transforms this country into a snowmobiler's playground, with 250 miles of the **Continental Divide Trail** from Lander to Yellowstone. Call the **Wind River Visitors Council** (© **800/645-6233;** www.wind-river.org) or the Lander Area Chamber of Commerce (see above) for information on this and other trails.

WHERE TO STAY & EAT

As far as lodging and grub go, there are quite a few options in Lander, from pizzerias and roadside motels to supper clubs and historic B&Bs. The **Budget Host Pronghorn Inn,** 150 E. Main St. (© **307/332-3940**), is a reliable choice, with frontier-style trappings and a riverfront setting. Standard doubles run $60 to $78 in the high season. The Lander Llama Company (see above) rents **The Bunk House,** a stylishly rustic cabin (with a kitchenette) on the Popo Agie River, for $95 a night, with a five-guest limit. For dining, try the **Gannett Grill,** 126 Main St. (© **307/332-8228**), with a more-interesting-than-it-sounds menu of thick burgers, sandwiches, pizza, and salads. Next door is **Cowfish,** 128 Main St. (© **307/332-7009**), which specializes in beef and seafood, and has an organic garden and a microbrewery on-site.

WIND RIVER INDIAN RESERVATION

Note: The starting point for a tour of the Wind River Indian Reservation is Fort Washakie, located 14 miles north of Lander on U.S. 287, or 146 miles from Jackson (U.S. 26/89/191 to Moran Junction, then U.S. 287 over Togwotee Pass to Dubois and then on to the reservation).

More than 2 million acres of the **Wind River Indian Reservation** surround the town of Riverton, encompassing an area that stretches 70 miles east to west and 55 miles north to south. Wyoming's sole reservation is home to more than 2,500 Eastern Shoshone and 5,000 Northern Arapaho tribal members, governed by a council made up of representatives from both tribes.

The Shoshone were given a huge reservation to buffer westward travelers from more hostile tribes to the north like the Sioux and Blackfeet. A reservation that once included parts of Wyoming, Utah, and Colorado was reduced greatly when non-Indians discovered gold, grazing land, and water on tribal lands. Today, the Wind River Indian Reservation is a still-sizable 2.2 million acres, including oil and gas fields, several small communities, and some of the most pristine wilderness—and best fishing—in the United States.

The Northern Arapaho came to Wind River in the late 1870s for what they thought was a temporary placement before moving to their own reservation farther east. However, government promises were forgotten or ignored, and the Arapaho settled in to stay. The two tribes have unrelated languages and a history of warfare, but their relationship has gradually improved.

There is poverty and high unemployment on the reservation, but there is pride, too, quite evident at the powwows. Outsiders are welcome at these dances, which are held May through September at various sites (the Wind River Visitors Council can provide a schedule; © **800/645-6233;** www.wind-river.org) where you'll see a more open, friendly side of the Arapaho and Shoshone, as long as you are respectful. Sun dances are more spiritual affairs, and while visitors are not banned, these moving ceremonies are not for tourists, and no photographs or videos are allowed.

Services for visitors are not well developed on the reservation, but you can learn more about the Shoshone tribe at the **Shoshone Tribal Cultural Center** (© 307/ 332-9106) in Fort Washakie, and about the Arapaho tribe at the **St. Stephen's Mission** (© 307/856-7806). At St. Michael's Mission, in Ethete (5 miles east of Fort Washakie), there is a **museum** (© 307/332-2660) of Arapaho cultural artifacts.

Sacajawea, the famed Shoshone scout for the Lewis and Clark expedition, is supposedly buried on a reservation that bears her name, west of Fort Washakie. There is some debate about whether she is buried there, but it's a beautiful cemetery on a hill, and worth a visit (ask for directions in Fort Washakie). You might also stop by nearby **Roberts Mission**—John Roberts was an Episcopal minister who lived most of his life on the reservation and had a tremendous influence on the tribes, founding a school and recording useful historical and anthropological information about the tribes. Chief Washakie, the venerated Shoshone chief, is buried in a cemetery along the Little Wind River on the north side of Fort Washakie. He lived to be over 100 and was buried with full honors by the U.S. Army—the only Indian chief to be so honored.

In late June, American Indians from around the country converge at Fort Washakie for **Shoshone Treaty Days,** a celebration of American Indian tradition and culture. The **Eastern Shoshone Powwow and Indian Days** follow a week later, with one of the West's largest powwows and all–American Indian rodeos, including thrilling bareback relay horse races.

There are hundreds of lakes in the reservation's high country, and in the summer they come alive with trout—browns, cutthroats, brook, and golden. You can purchase a reservation fishing permit at local sporting-goods stores and find your way with maps to Bull and Moccasin lakes by car, or pick up USGS topographical maps and head for the high country on foot. Check with the fly-tying experts at **Rocky Mountain Dubbing Company,** 115 Poppy St. (© **307/332-2989;** www.rmdstore.com), on U.S. 287 just south of Lander, for permits, maps, equipment, and advice. If you want a guided multiday fishing trip, contact **Paradise Outfitters** (© **307/856-2950**).

14

Sheridan & Eastern Wyoming

As you enter Wyoming from the east, the plains begin to roll like ocean swells, rising and falling until they break against the Rockies. As the elevation rises, the grass grows shorter. Rains taper from dependable downpours to sporadic cloudbursts. The wind races across the surface, combing down the grass and sculpting the snow.

Bison once roamed these prairies in enormous herds, and people were few. But the modern era brought rapid change. In the 18th century, Indian bands mounted horses that had escaped from Spanish conquistadors and enjoyed a brief era of prosperity on the plains, hunting buffalo with great skill. Then the white people arrived: trappers searching for beaver pelts, and pioneers who wanted to either settle here or just pass through on their way to Utah, California, or Oregon. But it was the Texas trail drives, moving north, not west, that most shaped the history and culture of eastern Wyoming.

The landscape hasn't changed much since then. There are still widely scattered settlements; a few small, irrigated fields; and lots of grass and cattle. The billboards announce "Welcome to the Cowboy State," but these days it's more often the coal and oil and gas beneath the prairies that subsidize the human population in

these wide-open spaces. But the cowboy life is still vibrant, and friendly to visitors: You can see rodeos or join a cattle drive, or just buy a hat and pair of boots and pretend. You can explore the mostly unchanged landscapes where cattle barons and their hired guns battled homesteaders in the Johnson County War, where outlaw Butch Cassidy and the Hole-in-the-Wall gang did their "work," and Indian chiefs Crazy Horse and Red Cloud clashed with the cavalry.

Adventurers come to climb **Devils Tower,** a natural skyscraper of volcanic rock that suddenly rises over 1,000 feet from the flatlands of eastern Wyoming. Visitors also come to hike and fish in the Bighorn Mountains, a handsome range somewhat overshadowed by the peaks of the Continental Divide farther west.

You can explore this region by interstate—I-25 runs north-south, while I-90 dips down from Montana and then east to Devils Tower—or take small highways like U.S. 18 and Wyo. 59 to reach smaller towns and more remote country. But since Sheridan is often the target of travelers to the area, this chapter begins there, exploring south to Buffalo and then east to Gillette and Devils Tower. Then we backtrack to Casper for a look at Wyoming's second-largest city.

1 Sheridan

144 miles N of Casper; 130 miles S of Billings; 156 miles E of Cody

Sheridan looks right at home where the Rockies meet the plains, its deep roots evident in its well-preserved historic downtown. The Bighorn Mountains cast afternoon shadows in this direction, across the ranches in the foothills where "dude" ranching was defined and perfected. One of the largest of Wyoming's small towns, with about 16,000 residents, Sheridan, named after Civil War general Phil Sheridan, retains its small-town charm with century-old buildings along Main Street and the mansions of cattle barons.

The source of prosperity in more recent times lies in the massive coal deposits to the north and east. After decades of production, the big strip mines are in a slow decline, and tourism is on the rise, with an influx of adventurous mountain bikers, rock climbers, paragliders, snowmobilers, and cross-country skiers who are lured by the Bighorns. Ranching these days is less about beef and more about providing saddle time for vacation dudes and retreats for wealthy corporate kings. Or queens—Queen Elizabeth of England, who has distant relations here, stopped by in the 1980s, and like any sensible horsewoman would, she dropped by **King's Saddlery,** known worldwide for hand-tooled tack and ropes.

ESSENTIALS

GETTING THERE   The **Sheridan County Airport** (© 307/674-4222), just southwest of town on **Airport Road** (take exit 25 off I-90), has daily service from Denver and Billings on **Big Sky Airlines** (© 800/237-7788).

If you drive from Billings, take I-90 south 130 miles to Sheridan. From Sheridan you can continue south on I-25, sliding along the eastern side of the Bighorn Mountains, 147 miles to Casper, or drive the full 325 miles to Cheyenne. From Yellowstone and Cody, follow U.S. 14 across the basin and over the Bighorns, and drop into Ranchester, where you'll take I-25 15 miles south to Sheridan.

VISITOR INFORMATION   **Sheridan Travel and Tourism,** P.O. Box 7155, Sheridan, WY 82801 (© 888/596-6787 or 307/673-7120; www.sheridanwyoming.org), is located at the State Information Center, off I-90 at exit 23. Across the street is the **Wyoming Game and Fish Visitors Center** (© 307/672-7418), with information on wildlife habitats, fishing, hunting regulations, and the best places to spot wildlife.

GETTING AROUND   You can rent a car from **Avis** (© 800/831-2847) or **Budget** (© 800/527-0700) at Sheridan's airport. Or call **Sheridan Taxi** (© 307/674-6814).

GETTING OUTSIDE

The **Bighorn National Forest** offers some of the best outdoor recreation in the country, with hundreds of miles of marked trails for hiking, mountain biking, cross-country skiing, snowshoeing, and snowmobiling; plus campgrounds, fishing streams, and fantastic wildlife-viewing opportunities. For maps and advice, contact the forest headquarters and Tongue Ranger District office, 2013 Eastside 2nd St. (© 307/674-2600; www.fs.fed.us/r2/bighorn).

For advice on local hot spots for hiking, mountain biking, fishing, camping, and the like, plus topographical maps, check with **Big Horn Mountain Sports** ☆, 334 N. Main St. (© 307/672-6866; www.bighornmountainsports.com). This extremely well-stocked sporting-goods store sells equipment and supplies, and also rents practically anything you might need for fly-fishing, backpacking, camping, snowshoeing, downhill and cross-country skiing, and snowboarding. Affiliated with the shop is a full-service mountain-bike facility (© 307/672-2453), with sales, repairs, and rentals. Big Horn Mountain Sports also coordinates fly-fishing classes and guided trips.

Ron Spahn of **Spahn's Big Horn Mountain Bed and Breakfast** (© 307/674-8150) offers daylong tours of the area, with a focus on the off-the-beaten-path sites that are representative of the "real West," looking at Indian history and modern social problems, mining and environmental issues, outlaw hide-outs, and the wild horses of the Pryor Mountains. Ron drives customers in a four-wheel-drive vehicle and offers a field lunch and an engaging, educated perspective. His tours run $95 per person with a $325 minimum.

EQUESTRIAN EVENTS

Polo? In Wyoming? Well, they ride horses, don't they? Introduced by early English cattle barons, the tradition continues with matches every summer Sunday at the **Big Horn Equestrian Center,** south of Sheridan toward the town of Big Horn at 351 Bird Farm Rd. (© 307/674-8687; www.bighornpoloclub.com). Admission is free (unless a benefit match is scheduled).

FLY-FISHING

The Tongue River is the Bighorns' blue-ribbon stream. There are browns, rainbows, and brook trout up to 20 inches. Inquire at the **Game and Fish Division,** 700 Valley View Dr. (℗ **307/672-7418**), for local catch limits and licenses. For equipment needs, advice, and guided trips, contact the **Fly Shop of the Big Horns,** 227 N. Main St. (℗ **800/253-5866;** www.troutangler.com).

GOLF

Dubbing itself "The Golf Capital of Wyoming," Sheridan offers several excellent courses with views of the Bighorn Mountains, including one of the state's best, **The Powder Horn** 🏌🏌, 6 miles south of Sheridan in Big Horn (℗ **307/672-5323;** www.thepowderhorn.com). The course includes 27 beautiful holes that mix Scottish-style golf with plenty of wide-open fairways and target golf. Greens fees for 18 holes run $51 to $71 plus $14 per seat for a cart. There are also the 9-hole **Sheridan Country Club** (west of Sheridan at 1992 W. 5th St.; ℗ **307/674-8135**), with greens fees of $16 to $20; and the 18-hole **Kendrick Golf Club** (on Big Goose Rd.; ℗ **307/674-8148**), charging $15 to $22.

SEEING THE SIGHTS

Bradford Brinton Memorial Ranch 🏌   From a distance, surrounded by cottonwoods and dwarfed by the hills and horizon, the Brinton ranch house doesn't look much different from most other two-story, white wood-frame homes. But the house, dating from the late 1800s, is not the real reason to visit. Yes, this 20-room residence offers a fine example of how a "gentleman rancher" lived in the early 1900s—the tables are set with china and the shelves filled with gold- and leather-bound volumes—but on the walls hangs a first-class art collection. Here you'll see *Fight on the Little Bighorn* by Frederic Remington, and *When Ropes Go Wrong* by Charles M. Russell. Will James, John Audubon, and a host of other notable Western artists show up in one of the best but least-known Western art collections in the Rockies.

239 Brinton Rd., Big Horn (10 miles south of Sheridan on U.S. 87). ℗ **307/672-3173.** www.bradfordbrintonmemorial. com. $4 adults, $3 children 13–18 and seniors 62 and over, free for children under 13. Memorial Day to Labor Day daily 9:30am–5pm; Sept and Dec Sat–Sun 10am–4pm.

King's Saddlery and Museum 🏌   Don King's Main Street emporium is a cowboy's candy store, with an extensive collection of Western tack, and any size, length, and lay of ropes. Wander the shop to see the tools of the modern cowboy, and watch the King brothers hand-tool leather. Then step back in time to their museum, housing one of the largest collections of Indian artifacts and cowboy trappings—including high-back saddles, chaps, Spanish bits, silver spurs, and quirts. Don is often around to chat. Next door is the Kings' **Bozeman Trail Gallery,** 190 N. Main St., which displays Western-subject paintings and sculpture; a gift shop is on the other side of the saddlery.

184 N. Main St. ℗ **800/443-8919** or 307/672-2702. Free admission. Mon–Sat 8am–5pm.

Sheridan Inn   The majestic Sheridan Inn was hailed as the finest hotel between Chicago and San Francisco when it opened in 1893, and visitors today can step back to that time as they explore the restored first floor and get a glimpse of its grandeur on guided tours through the yet-to-be-restored second and third floors. Modeled after Scottish hunting lodges, the hotel had dormer windows for each of the 62 rooms, and three impressive river-rock fireplaces. The back bar was imported from England, and the building boasted the town's first electric lights, running water, and telephone. Buffalo

Bill Cody led the grand march for the first dance on opening night, and Cody returned annually to stand on the long veranda auditioning riders for his *Wild West Show*. The Sheridan Inn has hosted a variety of other visiting celebrities and dignitaries, including Calamity Jane, Pres. Theodore Roosevelt, Will Rogers, and Ernest Hemingway. Although it hasn't operated as a hotel since 1965, the Sheridan houses a restaurant—and the handsome and historic bar still serves drinks. Fundraising is underway for a complete restoration of the hotel that will allow overnight stays.

Broadway and 5th St. (✆ 307/674-5440. www.sheridaninn.com. $2 self-guided tour of the 1st floor and museum; $5 guided tour of all 3 floors. Lobby and museum Mon–Fri 10am–2pm; guided tours daily in summer.

Trail End State Historic Site   The Kendrick Mansion, the only example of Flemish Revival architecture in Wyoming, sits on 3¾ acres of manicured grounds. John Kendrick, orphaned in Texas, arrived in Wyoming at age 22 on a cattle drive. By 1912 he'd built a 200,000-acre cattle ranch and amassed a net worth of $1 million. The next year, he completed construction on a home so large it took a ton of coal a day to warm its 20 rooms. He later became Wyoming's governor, then U.S. senator. Visitors today can marvel at materials not common in pioneer Wyoming: silk, mahogany, Italian marble, Georgia pine beams, and a maple floor in the ballroom. Also on the grounds is a carriage house, which serves as a community theater.

400 Clarendon Ave. (✆ 307/674-4589. www.trailend.org. $4 adults over 18. June–Aug daily 9am–6pm; Mar–May and Sept to mid-Dec daily 1–4pm.

The Ucross Foundation   Retreats for writers, artists, and musicians are not all that common in the West, but Ucross has gained an international reputation by providing a quiet, beautiful setting for seclusion and creativity. This ranchland, 27 miles east of Sheridan, was once the headquarters of the Pratt and Ferris Cattle Company, established in 1879. Now over half of the 22,000-acre ranch is protected with a conservation easement with The Nature Conservancy. You don't need an artist's residency to stop in and visit **Big Red,** a magnificently restored structure that once served as the main ranch house but today is a showcase of antique furniture; and the **Big Red Gallery,** which every year mounts four exhibits. If you're in the area on the Fourth of July, this is the place to be; more than 4,000 people show up for the fireworks.

30 Big Red Lane, Clearmont. (✆ 307/737-2291. Fax 307/737-2322. www.ucrossfoundation.org. Free admission. Mon–Fri 8:30am–4pm. From Sheridan, drive 27 miles east on U.S. 14 to junction with U.S. 16.

WHERE TO STAY

The Sheridan area has a great range of lodging establishments, running the gamut from modern hotels to Victorian B&Bs to authentic dude ranches. The two best chain properties are the **Best Western Sheridan Center,** 612 N. Main St. (✆ 877/743-7432 or 307/674-7421), with double rates of $114 to $129 in the summer, $74 to $79 in the winter; and the historic **Mill Inn,** I-90, exit 25 (✆ 888/357-6455 or 307/672-6401; www.sheridanmillinn.com), a converted flour mill with double rates of $85 to $100 summer, $65 to $75 winter.

Piney Creek Inn   Why settle for a generic motel room when you can stay in the "Hideaway" cabin nestled in the trees and warmed by a fireplace and Jacuzzi? Why pay for two motel rooms when a family can easily fit in the "Pine Lodge" cabin with its gnarled-pine spiral staircase leading to the loft bedroom? The cabins have kitchenettes and gas grills, and a campfire pit and hammocks are under the pines to complete the picture. Owners Vicky and Mel Hoff try to keep their rates low and their service high.

They'll connect you with local horse stables, or point you toward trails to hike. Piney Creek was once one of Wyoming's best-kept secrets, but good news travels fast; be sure to book at least 3 months in advance.

11 Skylark Lane, P.O. Box 456, Story, WY 82842. ℂ 307/683-2911. www.pineycreekinn.com. 2 units, 2 cabins. $85–$95 double; $135–$145 suite; $125–$175 cabin. Rates include full breakfast. MC, V. 7 miles west of I-90 from exit 33 or 44. **Amenities:** Outdoor Jacuzzi. *In room:* Kitchenette, fridge, coffeemaker.

Spahn's Big Horn Mountain Bed and Breakfast 🏕🏕 Spahn's Big Horn Mountain B&B prides itself on being the oldest B&B in Wyoming, and it's certainly one of the best. Picture this: a four-story log cabin surrounded by pines; a common room with a crackling fire, shelves of books, and a piano; and outside, a deck with a 100-mile view of prairie stretching to the east. The rooms glow with varnished peeled logs, and have such country comforts as patchwork quilts and claw-foot tubs. Ron Spahn (he's run the place for 20 years with his wife, Bobbie) leads evening wildlife safaris in search of moose, elk, and deer on Monday and Thursday; he also takes customers on daylong tours of the area (see "Getting Outside," above). The secluded "Eagle's Nest" guest cabin is perfect for honeymooners. The property is smoke-free.

P.O. Box 579, Big Horn, WY 82833. ℂ 307/674-8150. www.bighorn-wyoming.com. 4 units. $100–$165 double. Rates include full breakfast. MC, V for reservation deposit only; payment by cash or check. 15 miles southwest of Sheridan via U.S. 87 and Wyo. 335. *In room:* Fridge (in some units), no phone.

GUEST RANCHES

HF Bar Ranch 🏕 *Kids* With reasonable rates and plenty of activities for children, the HF Bar Ranch really caters to families—nannies are encouraged to come along at half-price (but are allowed only limited activities). This hospitable ranch is a real hoedown of old-fashioned fun, with weekly hayrides and dances. Ice and wood are delivered daily to each of the cabin's front porches, and hearty family-style meals are served in the main lodge. Guests can take daily trail rides or arrange a pack trip to the remote and rustic "mountain camp" 15 miles into the Bighorns. The sports enthusiast of the group can fish the miles of stream banks, shoot on one of the six sporting-clay courses, or hunt pheasant and chukar on a private bird reserve.

1301 Rock Creek Rd., Saddlestring, WY 82840. ℂ 307/684-2487. www.hfbar.com. Reservations required at least 6–12 months in advance. 30 cabins. $215 per person per day; free for children under 5. June to mid-Sept, 1-week minimum stay required. Rates include all meals and ranch activities. Round-trip transfers from Sheridan airport can be arranged for an additional $12 per family. No credit cards. Take I-90 35 miles south of Sheridan to exit 47. Drive west on Shell Creek Rd. and Rock Creek Rd. for 12 miles to ranch. **Amenities:** Dining room; indoor heated pool; children's program; activities desk; massage; babysitting; laundry service. *In room:* Coffeemaker, no phone.

Paradise Guest Ranch 🏕 Aptly named, this dude ranch 45 miles south of Sheridan adds modern conveniences to the ambience and activities you expect on a ranch. The log cabins not only have decks with views of the surrounding valley, mountains, or streams, but also come equipped with their own washers and dryers. As with most resort ranches in the West, several trail rides depart daily for guests of all levels of ability. And if you're riding all day, you can get a chuck-wagon dinner. There are ample after-dark activities for the entire family, with evening entertainment in the ranch's French Creek Saloon and recreation center.

Box 790, Buffalo, WY 82834. ℂ 307/684-7876. www.paradiseranch.com. 18 cabins. $1,375–$1,675 per adult per week; $525–$1,575 per child (age 12 and under) per week. Rates include all meals and ranch activities and round-trip transportation to the Sheridan airport. No credit cards. Closed Nov to mid-May. From Buffalo, drive 13 miles west on U.S. 16, then turn right at Hunter Creek Rd. to the road leading to the ranch. **Amenities:** Dining room; lounge. *In room:* Kitchenette, fireplace, washer and dryer.

CAMPING

The **Sheridan/Bighorn Mountain KOA Campground,** 63 Decker Rd. (© **800/ 562-7621** for reservations, or 307/674-8766), ½ mile north of Sheridan at the Port of Entry exit, offers quiet and shady tent and RV sites, plus all the usual commercial campground amenities, including an outdoor swimming pool and miniature golf. The campground is open from May to mid-October, with rates from $17 to $35. For those who prefer roughing it, the **Bighorn National Forest** has several primitive camp-grounds in the area, with sites costing $10 per night. Contact the Sheridan office (© **307/674-2600**) for further information.

WHERE TO DINE

Empire Grill ⭐⭐ ECLECTIC/STEAKS   The Empire Grill upped the ante for Sheridan's meat-and-potatoes dining scene when it opened in 2002 and won a fast local following. In a slick space with checkerboard floors and an air of intimacy, the kitchen here plates up a wide variety of dishes: for starters, wonton salads, almond-crusted brie, and "Rocky Mountain Shrimp" served in Tabasco-lime-garlic butter; and entrees like chipotle glazed prawns with andouille sausage, pork loin glazed with a port-cherry sauce, and chicken breast with a tequila-cream sauce on a bed of linguine. The food and service are both excellent, and the wine list sophisticated. Lunch brings gourmet sandwiches, pastas, and such unusual pizzas as pepper bacon and Thai curry. (The pizzas are also served for dinner.)

5 E. Alger St. © **307/674-4300**. Reservations recommended. Lunch $5.50–$10; dinner $9–$25. AE, DISC, MC, V. Tues–Fri 11am–2pm and 6–9pm; Sat 11:30am–2pm and 6–9pm.

Oliver's ⭐⭐ CONTEMPORARY AMERICAN   Like the Empire Grill, Oliver's brings some big-city flair to the cowboy environs of Sheridan. Opened in 2002 by Matt Wallop, the son of former U.S. Senator Malcolm Wallop, the monthly-changing menu has some Western touches among its wide range of influences. You might get spiced buffalo ravioli, or a chile-rubbed New York strip, served with tortilla sauce, or maybe macaroni and cheese made with Gouda, white cheddar, and Parmesan. Like the menu, the space itself is contemporary, with a San Francisco–inspired design that melds elegant and industrial with a hint of the West. There is also a nice inventory of wines and such tantalizing desserts as espresso crème brûlée.

55 N. Main St. © **307/672-2838**. Main courses $12–$39. Reservations recommended. AE, DISC, MC, V. Mon–Thurs 5:30–10pm; Fri–Sat 5:30–11pm; Sun 10am–2:30pm. Bar open later.

Sanford's Grub & Pub CAJUN   The maze of rooms at Sanford's, located in a 1907 historic building, is decorated like the dorm room of a junkman's son: Televisions, beer signs, and license plates are crammed to the rafters. You might even say the same about the dinner menu, which leans toward Cajun dishes, with really good jambalaya and Cajun-flavored burgers and steaks—try the New York strip Cajun-style. But the restaurant also has a whole lot of other things, including some items, like fried okra, that you wouldn't expect to see above the Mason-Dixon line. Sanford's is a good spot for beer drinkers, with a seemingly unlimited selection of bottled beers, plus the restaurant's own Cloud's Peak Raspberry Wheat, a stout, and an amber ale.

1 E. Alger St. (at N. Main St.). © **307/674-1722**. Reservations not accepted. Burgers and sandwiches $5–$9; main courses $10–$19. AE, DC, DISC, MC, V. Daily 11am–10pm (9pm in winter).

Waldorf A'Story Deli ⭐ *Finds* AMERICAN   Located in the Piney Creek General Store—which sells bait and auto supplies as well as canned escargot and 200 varieties of hot sauce—this funky place fills to the rafters with locals and tourists alike because of its terrific food. American breakfast standards and plump sandwiches give way to gourmet pasta and steak specials at night; you might get shrimp scampi or country-fried steak one night, chicken penne and filet mignon the next. The atmosphere is fun, fast-paced, and friendly, among the eclectic clutter of antique sewing machines, tree-stump barstools, and stuffed animals and snowshoes hanging from the wood beams that crisscross the corrugated ceiling.

19 N. Piney Rd., Story. © 307/683-2400. Reservations not accepted. Breakfast $2.50–$8; lunch and dinner $5–$10. MC, V. Mid-June to mid-Sept daily 7:30am–9pm; mid-Sept to mid-June Mon–Thurs 11am-3pm; Fri 11am–7:30pm; Sat–Sun 7:30am–5pm. 7 miles west of I-90 from exit 33 or 44.

SHERIDAN AFTER DARK

The doors of the legendary **Mint Bar,** 151 N. Main St. (© **307/674-9696**), first swung open in 1907. The place operated as a speak-easy until Prohibition ended, then evolved into the prototypical Western bar; "Meet me at the Mint" became a catch-phrase in these parts. It's still decorated just as it was in the 1940s, with all sorts of taxidermy and historic photos. There's an 8-foot, 4-inch Texas rattlesnake skin (said to have sheathed an 80-pounder) above the bar and plenty of local color seated in front of it.

WYO Theater   Built in 1912, the WYO is a model for other old theaters in the West. It was a broken-down movie palace facing the wrecking ball in the early 1980s when locals stepped in and saved it, restoring the proscenium and reviving live enter-tainment in Sheridan. Classical music, local choral groups, touring dance companies, and popular performers like Michael Martin Murphey and Baxter Black fill the house.

42 N. Main St. © 307/672-9084. www.wyotheater.com. Tickets usually $7–$18.

2 Buffalo ⊛

35 miles S of Sheridan; 182 miles E of Cody

Though Sheridan remains the busy hub of this Wyoming region, it is surrounded by interesting little towns like Dayton, Story, and Ranchester, plus one big enough to deserve its own slot: Buffalo. A short drive south of Sheridan on I-90, this old ranch-ing town is near the site of the infamous Johnson County War (a battle among settlers over the use of rangeland), and not far from the Hole-in-the-Wall country favored by Butch, Sundance, and other outlaws.

Though this was a favorite area of Indian bison hunters, it was not named for a shaggy beast: The original settlers drew names from a hat, and the winner had writ-ten his New York hometown.

The historic downtown area is compact enough to explore on foot. Follow the **Clear Creek Centennial Trail** on a wheelchair-accessible path from downtown to a pleasant grassy area where it joins a 3-mile unsurfaced road to the base of the Bighorn Mountains. Maps are available from the **Buffalo Chamber of Commerce,** 55 N. Main St., Buffalo, WY 82834 (© **800/227-5122** or 307/738-2444; www.buffalo wyo.com). You'll see the old **Occidental Hotel** at 10 N. Main (see "Where to Stay," below). At the excellent **Jim Gatchell Memorial Museum,** 100 Fort St. (© **307/684-9331;** www.jimgatchell.com), you'll find American Indian artifacts like arrowheads and medicine rattles, as well as cavalry items and the bridle Tom Horn braided while awaiting execution. The museum is open daily from 9am to 6pm June through

Range Wars

The Johnson County War was a struggle between immigrant homesteaders and the cattle barons over the open range. One of the skirmishes in that struggle took place at the **TA Ranch**—ask to see the bullet holes—which now hosts guests (Box 313, Buffalo, WY 82834; © **307/684-5833;** www.taranch.com; 13 rooms, $185 per person double). The ranch is located 13 miles south of Buffalo on U.S. 87.

August, and weekdays from 9am to 4pm the rest of the year ($4 adults, $2 children ages 6–16, free for kids 5 and under).

Buffalo lies on the route of the Bozeman Trail, a 19th-century shortcut to the gold country of Montana that cut right through the hunting grounds of several resentful tribes. The U.S. Army built forts to protect travelers, and engaged in skirmishes with the resident Sioux, Cheyenne, and Arapaho. The largest fort was **Fort Phil Kearny** (exit 44 off I-90; © **307/684-7629;** www.philkearny.vcn.com), where soldiers endured repeated raids by hostile Indians. Though the original fort is gone, the site today is a national historic site with a visitor center and tours of two major battle sites nearby: the 1866 Fetterman Massacre, in which Crazy Horse and his band overwhelmed a small army contingent; and the Wagon Box Fight, which went the other way. The visitor center is open from 6am to 8pm Monday through Saturday from May to September; and noon to 4pm Wednesday through Sunday the rest of the year; with a $2 admission.

Robert LeRoy Parker (Butch Cassidy) and his partner, Harry Longabaugh (Sundance Kid), assembled their infamous group of bandits known as the Wild Bunch to rob trains and banks, and steal herds of horses and cattle. One of their favorite places to hide was the **Hole-in-the-Wall,** a red-rock canyon area above the Middle Fork of the Powder River. The Hole-in-the-Wall is located about 45 miles south of Buffalo near the town of Kaycee. Take I-25 south from Kaycee to the Triple T Road exit, continue south 14 miles to County Road 111, then go west 18 miles to County Road 105, then north 8 miles to the U.S. Bureau of Land Management directional sign for Hole-in-the-Wall. It's a 3-mile hike into the actual site. The Hole itself is no more than a notch in a butte, disappointing to folks used to Disney-like re-creations of outlaw hide-outs. But for the intrepid on horse or in four-wheel-drive vehicles, you can explore the spacious **Outlaw Cave.** There are tepee rings in the surrounding area and large pictographs and stenciled handprints under a rock overhang.

Note: Most of this area is private land. Be sure to check with the U.S. Bureau of Land Management office in Buffalo (© **307/684-1100**) before exploring on your own.

Just a few miles northwest of Buffalo along I-90 is **Lake DeSmet,** an excellent fishing and boating destination, with opportunities for picnicking and camping.

WHERE TO STAY

The Occidental Hotel ⊘⊘   The Occidental started as a tent in 1879 and evolved into a hotel that was demolished and rebuilt in 1900. It was lost in a poker game in 1919 to the Smith family, ranchers who ran it as a hotel for more than 50 years. It closed in 1980, and the dust and cobwebs took over for 20 years. But new owners John and Dawn Wexo breathed new life into the place: After 8 years and $1.2 million of restoration, the grand hotel reopened in 2002. The rooms—often fashioned out of two or three of the old rooms—are stylish and decorated with original furnishings and reproduction wallpaper. We like the masculine Teddy Roosevelt Suite, with an original sink and tub, and the dinky Hole-in-the-Wall room, with brick walls and tasteful decor. We also like the historic saloon downstairs, its woodwork pocked with bullet holes from Buffalo's Wild West days past.

10 N. Main St., Buffalo, WY 82834. ℂ 307/684-0451. www.occidentalwyoming.com. 16 units. Summer $110–$165 double, $200 suite; winter $75–$125 double, $150 suite. AE, DISC, MC, V. Pets accepted (fenced yard outside). **Amenities:** 2 restaurants (fine dining/cafe); lounge; Wi-Fi network. *In room:* A/C, cable TV.

3 Gillette

103 miles E of Sheridan; 243 miles E of Billings

Gillette is now "Energy Capital of the Nation," boasts the local convention and visitors bureau, but just a century ago it was a huge sea of open range. Where there were once herds of cattle, you can now see several massive surface coal mines, like the RAG Coal West–Eagle Butte Mine. The mine, which opened in 1978, shipped its 250-millionth ton of coal on April 15, 1998, and continues to produce more than 40 million tons a year. The huge coal mines, along with recently discovered coal-bed methane gas, have made Gillette a prosperous community, which means that this is a pleasant place to live (or visit), with a variety of modern facilities, including a first-class swimming pool and water park. There is still plenty of undeveloped plains habitat, too, particularly in the 1.8-million-acre **Thunder Basin National Grassland.** Anyone who likes geological wonders, and anyone who enjoyed *Close Encounters of the Third Kind,* will want to visit the nearby **Devils Tower National Monument.**

ESSENTIALS

GETTING THERE   **Great Lakes Airlines** (ℂ **800/554-5111**) offers daily commuter flights from Denver to the **Gillette-Campbell County Airport** (ℂ **307/686-2280**), off U.S. 14/16.

By road, Gillette is 103 miles east of Sheridan via I-90 and 61 miles from Devils Tower National Monument.

VISITOR INFORMATION   Contact the **Gillette Convention and Visitors Bureau,** 1810 S. Douglas Hwy. #A, Gillette, WY 82718 (ℂ **800/544-6136** or 307/686-0040; www.visitgillette.net).

GETTING AROUND   You can rent cars from **Avis** (ℂ **307/672-8588**), **Hertz** (ℂ **307/686-0550**), or **Enterprise** (ℂ **307/686-5655**); or get a taxi from **City Cab** (ℂ **307/685-1000**).

GETTING OUTSIDE

Golf addicts can get their fix at either the **Gillette Golf Club,** 1800 Country Club Rd. (ℂ **307/682-4774**), or the **Bell Nob Golf Course,** 1316 Overdale (ℂ **307/686-7069**). The former is a 9-hole course; Bell Nob has 18.

Bird-watchers will enjoy the waterfowl of **McManamen Park,** near the corner of Gurley Street and Warlow Drive. **Hunters** are drawn here to bag elk, mule deer, pronghorn, and upland birds. Numerous hunting guides operate in the Gillette area; contact the Gillette Convention and Visitors Bureau (see above) for assistance in finding one.

SEEING THE SIGHTS

If you are impressed by big holes and big machinery, you've come to the right place. The RAG Coal West–Eagle Butte Mine has an impressive overlook near mile marker 100 on U.S. 14/16, about 1 mile north of Gillette's airport. The mine company and the Gillette Convention and Visitors Bureau jointly sponsor **free summer tours** to the mine site, where you can see the massive equipment used to extract the coal. Tours take place June through August, Monday through Friday, at 9 and 11am. Reservations should be made by calling ☎ **800/544-6136** or 307/686-0040.

The **Campbell County Rockpile Museum** ⚘, 900 W. 2nd St. (☎ **307/682-5723**), is the place to go to learn something about the history of this area. Displays include artifacts of the area's past such as saddles, rifles, arrowheads, and the like, but we prefer the big stuff—antique vehicles, including several Ford Model Ts, and a wagon collection that includes a horse-drawn hearse and an old sheep wagon. Kids like the vintage tractors they can climb on, as well as the other hands-on displays, including one that helps children identify the area's animals. There's also a "Grandma's Attic" section, where kids can dress up in historical (and funny-looking) fashions from days gone by. Adjacent to the museum building is a historic schoolhouse, completely furnished, that dates to the early 1900s; and a furnished homesteader's cabin from the same era. Both of these buildings were relocated to the museum grounds from other parts of the county. Finally, for those who like firecrackers—we mean really, really big firecrackers—don't miss the 10-minute big-screen video on coal mining that shows what dynamite can really do! Admission to the museum is free. June through August, it's open Monday through Saturday from 9am to 7pm; the rest of the year it's open Monday through Saturday from 9am to 5pm.

The **CAM-PLEX,** a massive event pavilion, has been the host in recent years of the National High School Rodeo Finals, as well as an array of other exciting events. Call ☎ **307/686-3025** to find out what's scheduled.

WHERE TO STAY & DINE

Lodging rates in Gillette are highest in summer, and sometimes as much as a third less at other times. The largest lodging property in town is the **Best Western Tower West Lodge,** 109 N. U.S. 14/16, Gillette, WY 82716 (☎ **800/762-7375** or 307/686-2210), which charges $60 to $110 double. The **Clarion Western Plaza,** 2009 S. Douglas Hwy., Gillette, WY 82718 (☎ **307/686-3000**), charges $59 to $105 double; and **Days Inn,** 910 E. Boxelder Rd., Gillette, WY 82718 (☎ **800/329-7666** or 307/682-3999), charges $50 to $120 double.

Among restaurants we like in Gillette are **The Prime Rib Restaurant & Steakhouse,** 1205 S. Douglas Hwy. (☎ **307/682-2944**), an upscale steak and seafood place where you can get tender, slow-roasted prime rib, charbroiled filets, sautéed halibut, and shrimp scampi, among other items, as well as a wine list that's garnered acclaim from *Wine Spectator.* Lunch prices are in the $6-to-$10 range, and most dinner entrees cost $9 to $21. The restaurant is open Monday through Friday from 11am to 10pm, Saturday and Sunday from 4 to 10pm.

4 Devils Tower National Monument ⚘

62 miles NE of Gillette; 230 miles SE of Billings; 110 miles W of Rapid City, South Dakota

Once upon a time, so the Kiowa legend goes, seven sisters were playing with their brother when he suddenly turned into a bear. Fleeing, the girls scrambled onto a small rock and prayed. The rock started to grow, pushing them into the sky. While the bear clawed at the rock's sides, trying to get at the girls, the rock thrust them so high that they became the points of the Big Dipper. Rising 1,267 feet above the Belle Fourche River below, the formation became named (in various spellings) Mato Tipila, or "Bear Lodge." The site is sacred to the Lakota and other tribes native to the northern plains.

Col. Richard I. Dodge, who commanded a military escort to a U.S. Geological Survey party that visited the Black Hills in 1875, is credited with giving the formation its current name. In his book *The Black Hills*, written the year after his journey, Dodge described Devils Tower as "one of the most remarkable peaks in this or any other country." In 1906, Congress declared it the nation's first national monument. The tower was further popularized in the 1977 movie *Close Encounters of the Third Kind*.

While the 50-million-year-old tower itself is composed of hard igneous rock, much of the remaining exposed rock within the 1,347-acre monument is composed of soft sediments from the warm, shallow seas of the Mesozoic era. These colorful bands of rock encircling the igneous core include layers of sandstone, shale, mudstone, siltstone, gypsum, and limestone.

Any visitor will understand immediately the allure of this striated column of volcanic rock. It's especially evocative in the evening—as darkness shrouds the surrounding hills, Devils Tower stands above the horizon, glowing amber.

ESSENTIALS

GETTING THERE From Gillette, take I-90 east to Moorcroft (exit 154) and follow signs to Devils Tower; from Jackson, take U.S. 26/287 to Riverton, then U.S. 26 to Casper, then I-90 through Gillette to Moorcroft; from Sheridan, take I-90 to Gillette, then see above.

VISITOR INFORMATION Contact **Devils Tower National Monument,** P.O. Box 10, Devils Tower, WY 82714-0010 (© **307/467-5283;** www.nps.gov/deto). The **Devils Tower Natural History Association,** P.O. Box 37, Devils Tower, WY 87214-0037 (© **307/467-5283**), operates a bookstore at the monument's visitor center and offers a variety of publications.

VISITOR CENTER Open from early April to late November only, the visitor center is located 3 miles from the monument's entrance, with exhibits about the tower's history and geology.

FEES & REGULATIONS The entrance fee is $10 per vehicle or $5 per person on foot, motorcycle, or bike. Disturbing any wildlife or gathering items such as rocks or flowers is prohibited. Especially do not feed, chase, or disturb prairie dogs; they bite and may carry diseases. Abandoned prairie-dog holes are often homes to black widow spiders and rattlesnakes.

Impressions

A dark mist lay over the Black Hills, and the land was like iron. At the top of the ridge I caught sight of Devils Tower upthrust against the gray sky as if in the birth of time the core of the earth had broken through its crust and the motion of the world was begun. There are things in nature that engender an awful quiet in the heart of man; Devils Tower is one of them.

—N. Scott Momaday, author of House Made of Dawn

SEEING THE MONUMENT

It's easy to experience much of what Devils Tower has to offer in less than a day. Rangers recommend that you allow 2 to 4 hours to walk a trail, stop at the visitor center, and view the prairie dogs.

Surrounded by ponderosa pines and bathed in blue sky, the towering rock obelisk is visible for miles, and it's easy to imagine the reaction of the first lonely American Indian scouts and French fur trappers who stumbled upon this stunning geologic anomaly a few centuries ago. The paved 1.3-mile round-trip **Tower Trail,** rated easy, goes all the way around the formation, offering close-up views of the tower on fairly level ground. Wayside exhibits tell the Devils Tower story. It connects to the 1.5-mile **Joyner Ridge Trail,** which has some wide-open grassland that makes for a sublime view of the tower.

Home to the feisty black-tailed **prairie dog,** the grounds of Devils Tower National Monument are perfect for picnicking and viewing wildlife. You can watch the sociable prairie dogs in their colony, or "town," just inside the park's east entrance station. The critters excavate elaborate networks of underground passageways, then guard their burrows with warning "barks" when predators such as hawks, eagles, bullsnakes, coyote, red fox, and mink come too close. Walk the leisurely .5-mile round-trip **Valley View Trail** to see a prairie-dog town, or savor a picnic lunch among the wildflowers at the monument's picnic area on the banks of the sleepy Belle Fourche River.

CLIMBING THE TOWER

Climbers have been wedging their fingers in the tower's cracks for more than a century, at a rate in recent years of about 5,000 climbers annually. (About one-third actually make it to the summit.) Climbers must register with a ranger before starting and upon their return; otherwise, there are no permits or requirements for climbing the tower. Be prepared for sudden storms; carry rain gear and a flashlight. Rockfall is common, so helmets are advised. Ask a ranger for additional safety and climbing information; the visitor center has a list of the guides permitted to lead climbs up the tower. We recommend Frank Sanders' **Above All Climbing Guides and Instruction** (*©* **888/314-5267;** www.devilstowerclimbing.com), which specializes in working with novice climbers and has rates starting at $150 per day. Above All has a climbing gym on the monument boundary where its introductory packages begin and always has at least one guide for every two customers. A voluntary climbing ban is observed each June out of respect for American Indian religious ceremonies that are held on Devils Tower at that time.

WHERE TO STAY

Immediately outside of the monument's boundaries, climbing guru Frank Sanders runs the **Devils Tower Lodge,** P.O. Box 66, Devils Tower, WY 82714 (*©* **888/314-5267** or 307/467-5267; www.devilstowerlodge.com), an eclectic four-room bed-and-breakfast in the former superintendent's residence. The rooms all have own private bathrooms; the facilities are geared toward climbers and the communal mood makes guests feel as if they're staying in a home instead of an inn. Rooms are $115 to $170 a night, full breakfast included. Mastercard and Visa are accepted. In Hulett, try the **Hulett Motel,** 202 Main St., Hulett, WY 82720 (*©* **307/467-5220;** www.hulettmotel. com). Double rates are $65 to $85 year-round; Discover, Mastercard, and Visa are accepted. Rooms are clean and well maintained, and there's also a row of trim and tidy cabins on the Belle Fourche River.

CAMPING   Located a mile from the monument's headquarters, **Belle Fourche Campground** is open April through October and rarely fills up except for Sturgis Motorcycle Rally time in August. Its 30 sites accommodate RVs (up to 35 ft. long) and tents on a first-come, first-served basis. Each campsite has a cooking grill, table, and nearby drinking water. There are no showers, RV hookups, or dump stations. Sites costs $12 per night, and there are three group sites, which cost $2 per person per night, with a six-person minimum. The adjacent Valley View Trail skirts a giant prairie-dog town, and the campground's amphitheater offers excellent interpretive ranger programs.

Those looking for a commercial campground with RV hookups, hot showers, and all the usual amenities will find the **Devils Tower KOA,** P.O. Box 100, Devils Tower, WY 82714 (© **800/KOA-5785** or 307/467-5395; www.devilstowerkoa.com), just outside the monument entrance. Open May through September, it offers 56 RV sites, 100 tent sites, and 11 camping cabins (which share the bathhouse and other campground facilities). Rates for two adults are $24 to $45 in hookup sites, $21 for tents, and $52 for cabins. Amenities include a heated swimming pool, self-service laundry, game room, cafe, two interesting gift shops, horseback rides, hayrides, summer rodeos, and a nightly showing of *Close Encounters of the Third Kind,* filmed in part at Devils Tower.

5 Casper

153 miles S of Sheridan; 178 miles NW of Cheyenne; 300 miles S of Billings; 240 miles NW of Denver

Casper is a pleasant little city between the Great Plains and Rocky Mountains that owes much of its success to the oil and gas industry. Its first oil refinery was built in 1895, and though, like most boom towns Casper has had its share of ups and downs, the petroleum industry continues to help the economy keep rolling along. But what keeps many residents here, and what makes the community of interest to many visitors, is not what's under the ground but what is on the ground.

Casper has a small but fun ski area, and there is a lot of wildlife in the vicinity, including more than 75% of the world's pronghorn. Also look for mule and white-tailed deer, fox, and a variety of birds. The North Platte River, which meanders through the city, is a premier year-round trout fishery.

This is also an ideal spot to see the real history of the West. Casper stands at the crossroads of westward expansion, and you stand in the ruts of the Oregon, Mormon, California, and Pony Express trails. Fur traders stopped here in 1812 on their way back East, building a hovel from rocks and buffalo hides, perhaps the first building constructed by non-Indians in Wyoming. Later, pioneers and Mormons crossed the North Platte River here. Then came the oil miners, and Casper boomed.

Today, Casper is the second-largest city in the state, with about 50,000 residents. It was also the hometown of U.S. Vice President Dick Cheney and his wife, Lynn.

ESSENTIALS

GETTING THERE   Casper's **Natrona County International Airport,** 8500 Airport Pkwy. (© **307/472-6688**), 12 miles northwest of Casper on U.S. 20/26, has daily flights from **Delta** (© **800/221-1212**), **Northwest** (© **800/225-2525**), and **United** (© **800/241-6522**).

To reach Casper from **Sheridan,** drive 153 miles south on I-25. From **Cheyenne,** take I-25 north for 178 miles. From **Jackson,** take U.S. 191 to the Moran Junction, then drive 255 miles east on U.S. 26/287.

VISITOR INFORMATION Visit the **Casper Area Convention and Visitors Bureau,** 992 N. Poplar St., Casper, WY 82601 (© **800/852-1889** or 307/234-5362; www.casperwyoming.info).

GETTING AROUND Rent a car with **Avis** (© 307/237-2634) and **Budget** (© 307/266-1122) at the airport. Need a cab? Call **RC Cab** (© 307/235-5203).

SPECIAL EVENTS Casper draws its largest crowds during the 5-day **Central Wyoming Fair and Rodeo,** which takes place each summer in mid-July. Call © **307/235-5775** for details. On the third weekend of July each year, the **Beartrap Summer Festival** (© **307/266-5252;** www.beartrapsummerfestival.com) takes place on top of Casper Mountain, with blues and bluegrass musicians plus the Wyoming Symphony Orchestra.

GETTING OUTSIDE

To escape the heat of the summer or ski a few runs in the winter, head up **Casper Mountain,** being sure to stop at the pullouts to take in the view of the plains stretching north toward the Bighorn Mountains. The mountain rises 8,000 feet above sea level, and there are campgrounds, hiking trails (try Garden Creek Falls), ski tracks, groomed snowmobile tracks, and mountain-biking trails. Another popular destination for outdoor recreation is **Muddy Mountain.** Much of the public land here is under the jurisdiction of the **Bureau of Land Management,** 2987 Prospector Dr., Casper, WY 82604 (© **307/261-7600**). The office has maps and other information available, and is open Monday through Friday from 7:45am to 4:30pm. Another good source for information, as well as equipment sales and rentals of cross-country skis and snowshoes, is **Backcountry Mountain Works,** 4120 S. Poplar St., at Sunrise Center (© **307/234-5330**). At **Mountain Sports,** 543 S. Center St. (© **800/426-1136** or 307/266-1136), you'll find winter and summer outdoor equipment (including camping supplies), plus rentals of skis ($12 a day) in the winter and mountain bikes ($24 a day) year-round. The **Ugly Bug Fly Shop,** 240 S. Center St. (© **307/234-6905**) is a great angler's resource, with advice, gear, and guides.

There are some great hiking opportunities on Casper Mountain, including the **Braille Trail,** which enables visually impaired visitors to enjoy the beauty of Beartrap Meadow, with interpretive Braille markers describing the area's ecology. The Casper Area Convention and Visitors Bureau (see above) can provide you with maps detailing this and other hiking trails.

Edness Kimball Wilkins State Park (© **307/577-5150**) is a pleasant day-use park just 6 miles east of Casper off I-25, where you'll find huge old cottonwoods over the North Platte River. The park has hard-surfaced walking paths, a canoe- and raft-launch ramp, a swimming area, picnic tables, and a playground. There is also an accessible fishing pier, and excellent bird-watching opportunities for species including cormorants, yellow-billed cuckoos, golden and bald eagles, and numerous ducks. The park is open daily from 7am to 10pm; admission costs $4 per vehicle.

SKIING

A cheerful little ski area is a big plus in an area of sometimes howling winters, and Casper has a fine one in the **Hogadon Ski Area** ⊛ (© **307/235-8499**), situated atop Casper Mountain (drive south on Wyo. 258 from I-25 to Casper Mountain Rd.). It has a 600-foot vertical rise to a top elevation of 8,000 feet. Two double chairs and a Poma lift cover its 60 acres of groomed trails, and there are also on-site equipment rentals, a snack bar, and a ski and snowboarding school. Nearby, a county-owned

---

(Fun Fact Historical Footnote

Both the city of Casper and Fort Caspar Museum and Historic Site were named for Lt. Caspar W. Collins, who was killed in an Indian attack here in 1865. However, it's the city and not the fort that is misspelled. Most of the army post communications were misspelled and the city picked up the incorrect spelling when it incorporated in 1889.

---

cross-country ski area (© 307/237-8098) is groomed for skating and track skiing. The ski area generally opens around the first of December and closes sometime in April. Lift tickets are $30 for adults, $26 for students (ages 12–18), and $17 for children (ages 5–11). During ski season, Hogadon is open Wednesday through Sunday, plus holidays (except Christmas Day), from 9am to 4pm.

SEEING THE SIGHTS

Casper Planetarium   This planetarium offers a multimedia jaunt into space, with changing programs ranging from a basic exploration of the night sky to trips through the solar system. There are also other astronomy-related programs, such as one on the possibility of life beyond Earth; plus special kids' shows. The planetarium also offers telescope-user workshops, instruction on how to build your own rocket, and lectures. There are hands-on science displays and exhibits of meteorites and tektites, plus a gift shop.

904 N. Poplar Ave. © 307/577-0310. $2.50 per person per program. June–Aug showings daily at 4, 7, and 8pm; Sept–May Sat at 7pm. Call for additional holiday programs.

Fort Caspar Museum and Historic Site   Come to Fort Caspar for a look at what the "good old days" in these parts were really like. The first occupation of this site was in 1847 when Brigham Young and the Mormon Pioneer party constructed a ferry to cross the North Platte River. The post also served as a relay station for the Pony Express, and the transcontinental telegraph crossed the river here. The U.S. Army occupied the site in 1862, naming the post Platte Bridge Station. While attempting to reach an army supply train on July 26, 1865, members of the Sioux and Cheyenne tribes attacked Lt. Caspar W. Collins and troops from the fort. Collins and 26 other soldiers were killed during battles that day, and the fort was later renamed Fort Caspar to honor the lieutenant.

Today the site includes the reconstructed fort buildings furnished as they would have appeared in 1865—the mess hall, telegraph hall, officers' quarters, store, blacksmith shop, stables, commissary, and the like. A modern museum features exhibits on the social and natural history of central Wyoming. During the summer there are living-history programs and lectures. Allow 1 or 2 hours.

4001 Fort Caspar Rd. © 307/235-8462. $2 adults, $1 for ages 6–17, free for children under 6. June–Aug Mon–Sat 8am–7pm, Sun noon–7pm; shorter hours rest of year. The museum is open year-round, but the fort buildings are open May–Sept only.

National Historic Trails Interpretive Center ★★   This excellent facility opened in Casper in 2002, using state-of-the-art exhibits to give us modern travelers an idea of what life on the "road" was like to the emigrants who passed through here in the mid-1800s on the Oregon, Mormon, California, and Pony Express trails. A number of engaging multimedia exhibits cover the pioneer story from the packing of the wagons to the ferrying of the rivers—the latter is demonstrated by a faux wagon that visitors ride across the Platte River, simulated with motors and a movie. Be sure to take in the informative 18-minute film that tells the trails' history with real-life accounts of pioneers' journeys before the railroad rendered the trails obsolete. The final "exhibit" is the trails themselves, leaving from this spot and marked by BLM markers, for those that want to see a landscape that's changed little in the past 200 years. Allow 2 hours.

1501 N. Poplar St. © 307/261-7700. www.wy.blm.gov/nhtic. $6 adults, $5 seniors 60 and over, $4 students over 18, $3 children 6–17, $1 children 3–5, free for children under 3. Apr–Sept daily 8am–7pm; Oct–Mar Tues–Sat 9am–4:30pm.

Nicolaysen Art Museum and Discovery Center   This attractive facility presents changing exhibitions of works by national and regional artists, with an emphasis on art by Western artists or with a Rocky Mountain West theme. There are one large and six small galleries, and three exhibitions take place simultaneously, for a total of a dozen different shows each year. Works range from traditional Western to contemporary. The Discovery Center is a hands-on self-guided studio with about a dozen stations, some often related to the current exhibits, where participants of all ages can create their own art. Allow 1 or 2 hours.

400 E. Collins Dr. (Collins and Kimball). © 307/235-5247. www.thenic.org. Free admission. Tues–Sat 10am–5pm; Sun noon–4pm.

Tate Geological Museum   You like rocks? If so, this is the place to come. You can see a vast collection of Wyoming jade, a variety of minerals, and meteorites here. The Tate also has a section on dinosaur excavations from the Natrona County area, including a *T. rex* skull, and the leg and skull of a brontosaurus. There's also an interactive computerized weather station, plus "please touch" exhibits of fossils and minerals.

125 College Dr. © 307/268-2447. Free admission. Mon–Fri 9am–5pm; Sat 10am–4pm.

WHERE TO STAY

In addition to the lodging properties discussed below, reliable chains in Casper include the **Days Inn,** 301 E. "E" St., Casper, WY 82601 (© **800/329-7666** or 307/234-1159), with double rates of $72; and the attractive **Holiday Inn,** 300 W. "F" St., Casper, WY 82601 (© **800/465-4329** or 307/235-2531), with double rates of $85 to $109. The **Ivy House Inn,** 815 S. Ash St., Casper, WY 82601 (© **307/265-0974**), is a Cape Cod–style B&B with five rooms that go for $55 to $105 double.

Moments Time Travel

Historic Trails West, P.O. Box 428, Mills, WY 82644 (© **307/266-4868;** www.historictrailswest.com), organizes trips that take you back in time as you rattle in a wagon, or sway in the saddle, along the Oregon, California, Pony Express, and Mormon trails. Trips range in length from 3 hours ($35 adults, $25 children 10 and under) to all day ($85 adults, $65 children 10 and under), which includes lunch. Prices are slightly higher for those who opt to ride horses instead of sitting in the wagons. There are also overnight and multiday wagon-train trips, plus a 5-day wagon trail, at $895 adults, $695 children 10 and under. Trips are scheduled May through October.

Hotel Higgins ✦   Built by area oil tycoon John Higgins in 1916, the Hotel Higgins is a small historic hotel—listed on the National Register of Historic Places—that is plain on the outside but beautiful within, and a wonderful place to soak up the post-Victorian ambience of the early-20th-century American West. It has mahogany and oak woodwork with distinctive decorative touches that include alabaster chandeliers, beveled glass doors, and terrazzo tile floors. Standard rooms are somewhat small by today's standards (as is the case in most historic hotels), decorated with antiques, including some original pieces from the hotel. The brass, iron, or massive wooden beds have attractive quilted bedspreads, and dressers are oak or walnut.

416 W. Birch St. (P.O. Box 577), Glenrock, WY 82637. ℭ **800/458-0144** or 307/436-9212. www.hotelhiggins.com. 9 units. $70 double; $80 suite. Rates include continental breakfast. AE, DC, DISC, MC, V. From Casper, take I-25 south for 20 miles to the first Glenrock exit. **Amenities:** Restaurant; lounge. *In room:* Cable TV, no phone.

Parkway Plaza Hotel & Convention Centre   This sprawling hotel is a friendly and busy place, with all the amenities you'd expect of a major convention center and 25,000 square feet of meeting space. There are a variety of units here, ranging from luxurious suites and minisuites to spacious standard rooms and some smaller units. All have attractive modern American hotel decor—pleasant but somewhat nondescript—and some of the older, smaller rooms are set way back from the lobby, and therefore a healthy walk. Some units have kitchenettes.

123 W. "E" St. (P.O. Box 823), Casper, WY 82602. ℭ **800/270-7829** or 307/235-1777. Fax 307/235-8068. www. parkwayplaza.net. 288 units. $80 double; $95–$325 suite. AE, DC, DISC, MC, V. Pets accepted, $25 deposit. **Amenities:** 2 restaurants; lounge; indoor heated pool; weight room; spa; indoor Jacuzzi; airport shuttle; salon. *In room:* A/C, cable TV, dataport, kitchenette (some units), coffeemaker, iron.

WHERE TO DINE

In addition to the restaurants discussed below, you can get a good burger or traditional American breakfast at a reasonable price at **Johnny J's,** 1705 E. 2nd St. (ℭ **307/234-4204**), a '50s-style diner open daily from 6am to 9pm (10pm Fri–Sat).

Bosco's Italian Restaurant ✦ ITALIAN   Other than cowboy cooking—translate that as beef, beef, and more beef—the only cuisine that seems to shine throughout Wyoming is Italian. This friendly little restaurant is no exception. It serves excellent food, and stays open as long as the customers keep coming (usually about 10pm). The scampi is excellent, or you can create your own fettuccini dish from ingredients such as fresh vegetables, smoked salmon, and shrimp. The menu also includes veal and gluten-free dishes for those with wheat allergies.

847 E. "A" St. ℭ **307/265-9658.** Reservations recommended. Lunch items $5–$9; dinner entrees $8–$21. AE, DC, DISC, MC, V. Tues–Fri 11am–2pm and 5pm–close; Sat 5pm–close.

The Paisley Shawl ✦ CONTINENTAL   This is the area's best fine-dining establishment. Located inside the historic Hotel Higgins, 20 miles east of Casper, The Paisley Shawl is the dining complement to a very good guest inn/restaurant combination. Specialties include shrimp scampi, chargrilled steaks, and an apple-marinated pork tenderloin. Set inside the hotel's former ballroom—next to a fun little bar—the restaurant is expansive, with seating for 60. There aren't many restaurants in Wyoming that make you feel as if you're indulging yourself by dining there. This is one of them.

In the Hotel Higgins, Glenrock. ℭ **800/458-0144** or 307/436-9212. www.hotelhiggins.com. Reservations recommended on weekends. Lunch $5–$10; dinner $12–$25. AE, DC, DISC, MC, V. Mon–Sat 11am–2pm and 6–9pm; Sun brunch 10am–4pm. From Casper, take I-25 south for 20 miles to the first Glenrock exit.

Wonder Bar AMERICAN   A Casper stalwart where drinkers once rode their horse to the bar in the 1940s, the Wonder Bar has reinvented itself as a slick, smoke-free microbrewery in recent years. The menu includes half-pound burgers with all sorts of toppings as well as salads, sandwiches, pasta, seafood, and meatloaf. We skipped the W.B.B.F.B.—a 5-pound burger that costs $22—in favor of some tasty fish tacos. The brewery makes four beers, including a stout and a wheat.

256 S. Center St. (℃) 307/234-4110. www.thewonderbar.net. Reservations accepted. Main courses $6–$14. AE, DC, DISC, MC, V. Tues–Fri 11am–2pm and 5pm–close; Sat 5pm–close.

6 Fort Laramie National Historic Site

125 miles SE of Casper

On a hot day in 1834, mountain man William Sublette stopped his pack train laden with goods for the Green River rendezvous. Looking at the confluence of the Laramie and Platte rivers, then to the east, across the dusty plains, and then to the west, toward the mountains, he decided that this was a good place for a trading post. Over the next 15 years, the fort served as a hub of the buffalo trade, then as a way station for weary travelers who needed a break on their way to the Pacific.

In 1849—the year of the California gold rush—the U.S. Army bought the fort to "defend" the rising tide of immigrants from the "savages." The Indian Wars hadn't really started yet, not until 1854, when a lame Mormon-owned cow wandered off and was eaten by a starving Miniconjou. A young lieutenant marched into the Sioux camp and demanded that the cow-eater be turned over for swift justice; soon his troops opened fire on the village, and the wars had begun. Many battles later, the Indian tribes gathered here to negotiate the Treaty of 1868, which gave the Sioux and their allies the Powder River country and the Black Hills for "as long as the grass shall grow and the buffalo shall roam."

Soon thereafter, gold was discovered in the Black Hills, and the promise was broken. The army corralled the Indians onto reservations, the railroad replaced the wagon trails, and the beaver and the buffalo were exterminated; the fort closed down in 1890. It wasn't until 1938 that Franklin Roosevelt designated Fort Laramie a national historic site. In its time, travelers from Jim Bridger to Mark Twain had stopped at the fort; today almost 100,000 tourists ramble through many of the site's 22 original structures.

For an in-depth look at life at the fort, stop by the **visitor center** and watch the 18-minute video about the fort and its role in the settlement of the West. You'll see historical photos there, and a gift shop sells a wide selection of Western-themed books and gift items. Pick up a paper copy of the self-guided tour of the fort's historic buildings, or for $3 rent the audio tour, which not only tells the history of the fort but also brings it alive with the voices and sounds of the past.

Some of the more notable (and restored) buildings you'll see are the **cavalry barracks,** where dozens of soldiers slept, crowded into a single room; **Old Bedlam,** the post's headquarters, which later served as housing for officers, bachelors, and married couples; the **guardhouse,** a stone structure that housed the fort's prisoners; and the **bakery.**

Living-history programs are conducted every summer, from June to mid-August, when rangers dress in period costumes, give talks, and answer visitors' questions.

Before leaving the fort, consider driving to the **Old Bedlam Ruts** (ask for a map from the visitor center), 2 miles northwest of the fort. The bumpy gravel road allows you to view the rutted trail marks left by the wagon trains of early Western settlers. Look for Laramie Peak and the grave of Mary Homsley, one of the many who died along the trail.

The grounds and buildings are open daily from sunrise to sunset. From mid-May to mid-September, the visitor center is open daily from 8am to 7pm, and daily from 8am to 4:30pm the rest of the year. Admission costs $3 for adults, free for those 16 and under. To get to the fort from Casper, take I-25 east past Douglas to U.S. 26 (exit 92), and head east to Wyo. 160, which you take southwest 3 miles to Fort Laramie. For more information, contact **Fort Laramie National Historic Site,** National Park Service, 965 Gray Rocks Rd., Fort Laramie, WY 82212 (© **307/837-2221;** www.nps.gov/fola).

15

Southern Wyoming

Southern Wyoming has long been less a destination than a land passed through. All the famous trails—the Bozeman, the California, the Emigrant, the Mormon, the Overland, and the Pony Express—lead somewhere else. Even today, if you stand on a hill just outside the state capital of Cheyenne, where two major interstates intersect, you'll see a cluster of mega–gas stations crowded with RVs, autos, and semis, fueling up before speeding east or west.

In the middle of the 19th century, nearly a half-million people passed through Wyoming on the Oregon Trail. They paused at Independence Rock only long enough to rest and to carve their names in the stone (it's still there—west of Casper on Wyo. 220). This cross-state journey, which can now be done in less than a day, took a month in the 1840s. Along this route travelers left wagon tracks, cast-iron stoves, worn-out boots, crippled livestock, and their dead. It was no easy passage: On average, they dug 10 graves for every mile of trail.

By 1868, the railroad had forged across the plains, following the more southerly route of the Overland Stages. The arrival of the railroad brought shantytowns of gambling tents, saloons, and brothels, known as "Hell on Wheels." Left behind as the rails moved on, the makeshift towns collapsed, and a cycle of booms and busts began. New discoveries of coal, oil, gold, or uranium would spur a revival, followed by another bust.

Today that legacy colors the character of towns along I-80, which follows the same path used by the first transcontinental railroad. A new generation of miners dig coal and trona (a gray-white or yellowish mineral used in cleaning agents) and keep the oil and natural gas flowing. Mineral money builds sparkling new schools and government buildings, but there is still a rough-and-ready quality to the downtown districts.

But unlike the old days, the communities now have a better grip on the landscape. **Cheyenne** is the state capital, home to thousands of government workers. The remnants of the ranching families that once dominated the area come out in force every year for **Frontier Days,** a rodeo extravaganza known the world over. West over the pass in **Laramie,** the University of Wyoming is a cultural and intellectual nexus. From Laramie west, I-80 climbs around Elk Mountain and races across the high desert—an expansive (some might say bleak) view from behind the windshield, and a sometimes-harrowing drive during winter blizzards.

Cross-country travelers often miss the unexpected beauty in this land because they steadfastly stick to the interstate instead of the two-lane roads that lead to chalk buttes and rust-colored mesas. Take an off-ramp and head north among the stirring buttes of the Red Desert, read the ancient archaeological record at Fossil Butte, hike the mountain cirque of the Snowy Range, or dip in the clear waters of Flaming Gorge. On summer afternoons, the dry air turns humid, the sky blackens, and lightning dances on the red rims. When the sun breaks again, the cliffs burn copper.

1 Scenic Drives

I-80 runs the length of southern Wyoming along the same path followed by the first transcontinental railroad: straight, fast, convenient, but not often scenic. To the curious eye, though, there are interesting sights along the way.

Geology buffs will be interested in the road cuts made by the interstate—eons of geologic history are revealed. Historians will appreciate the remnants left more than a century ago: Take exit 272, 41 miles west of Laramie, and visit **Little Arlington,** where you'll find what's left of an old stage station and a log cabin, back in the trees. Here along the interstate you'll also see Wyoming's latest contribution to the nation's energy pool: a wind farm of spinning propellers lining the ridges like an infantry on stilts.

But to break the monotony of the long drive across southern Wyoming, you need to take a loop off the interstate. There's plenty of great scenery out there, including the landscapes you'll see on the following trips. Many of the sights mentioned here are discussed in further detail later in this chapter.

DRIVING TOUR 1: THE SNOWY RANGE SCENIC BYWAY: LARAMIE TO SARATOGA

The **Snowy Range Road** (Wyo. 130), designated the nation's second scenic byway, twists up and over the Medicine Bow Mountains south of I-80 and west of Laramie, through corridors of pines and between snow banks (even in midsummer), and tops Snowy Range Pass at 10,847 feet. During the winter, heavy snows block the pass, but you can reach a ski area (both Alpine and Nordic) on the Laramie side, 6 miles past Centennial.

To reach the Snowy Range Scenic Byway from Laramie, take exit 311 off I-80 and head west along Snowy Range Road. Once past the little town of Centennial, the road switchbacks uphill at a steep grade. As you top the pass, you'll see sharp granite peaks to the north, often skirted by snow, bordering a group of snowmelt-fed lakes. This is the top of the range, with elevations more than 12,000 feet above sea level. On a summer day you'll have plenty of company at the turnouts—people stopping to look, to fish, to hike a nature trail, to picnic. Half a day of vigorous hiking (if you're adjusted to the altitude) will get you atop Medicine Bow Peak, the highest summit in the range. The road then descends the east side of the range, following French Creek to the **Upper North Platte River** (known as the Miracle Mile), which is popular with anglers. When you come to a T in the road, turn right on Wyo. 130 and drive 8 miles north to **Saratoga,** a friendly little town where many boats are launched to fish the excellent waters of the Platte. Continue north from here to rejoin I-80 at Walcott.

FINISH THE LOOP: A DIFFERENT WAY BACK TO LARAMIE You can return on I-80 to Laramie, or take a more adventurous route by going north from Walcott on U.S. 30/287 toward Medicine Bow. This road follows the rail line and, as such, bypasses the mountains—in the winter, it's often a better route than the interstate. The landscape is sagebrush plains and hills, where antelope roam. Every 20 miles or so, you'll hit a crumbling town. One community with a little life still left in it is **Medicine Bow,** location of the Virginian Hotel (another model for Owen Wister's *The Virginian*) and of a watering hole with character, the Diplodocus Bar. Take a look at the bar itself—a solid slab of Wyoming jade, 40 feet long. Some of the great historic dinosaur discoveries were made in this area, at nearby Como Bluff. Continue east to finish the loop in Laramie.

DRIVING TOUR 2: THE RIVERS ROAD & HIGHWAY 70: LARAMIE TO BAGGS

This scenic drive goes from Laramie to the town of Baggs along Wyo. 230 and a recently completed stretch of Wyo. 70. **Wyo. 230** (also known as "The Rivers Road") winds its way southwest from Laramie along the Laramie River to the town of **Mountain Home,** where the road dips south into Colorado. Here it makes a loop along Colo. 127/125 for 18 miles and reenters the state of Wyoming on the other side of the Medicine Bow Mountains. The route then continues northwest along Wyo. 230 to the old logging town of Encampment. This last portion offers beautiful river scenery with aspen and lodgepole pines, and opportunities for trout fishing. From Encampment, take Wyo. 70 west to Baggs across 58 miles of Carbon County land in the Sierra Madre Mountain Range. Because of the altitude, views can stretch for miles around this virtually uninhabited belt of southern Wyoming. But the altitude also causes road closures in the winter. Wyo. 70 climbs to 9,955 feet to Battle Pass, named for a nearby conflict that took place in 1841. Here it crosses the Continental Divide before descending to the small towns of **Savery, Dixon,** and **Baggs,** a trio of hamlets with a combined population of less than 500. Early settlers came to the area in search of gold and silver. The history of Baggs also includes a different kind of business: Outlaw Butch Cassidy pulled off several robberies here, and quick-triggered livestock detective Tom Horn frequented the area during the late 1800s.

At Baggs, turn north off Wyo. 70 onto Wyo. 789, then drive north for 51 miles through high-plains ranching country. At Creston Junction, you'll rejoin I-80. From here, you can either drive west to Rock Springs and the Utah border or return east to Laramie. You won't have traveled as far as you think, but you'll have seen a lot more along this route than you would have staring at the back of an 18-wheeler along the interstate.

2 Cheyenne

93 miles N of Denver; 180 miles S of Casper

Cheyenne is located in the southeast corner of the state. Legend has it that when Gen. Grenville M. Dodge's surveying crew trudged across the prairie, picking a route for the transcontinental railroad, night came, they were tired, they stopped and said, "Good as any," and thus was born the present site of Cheyenne.

By horse or by highway, you can't miss Cheyenne, not only the largest city in Wyoming (population: 53,000) but also its capital. Visitors enjoy the many historical and political sights, from the **Capitol Building** to the **Historic Governors' Mansion.** But Cheyenne's biggest event, hands down, is that wild and woolly weeklong cowboy extravaganza, **Cheyenne Frontier Days.**

ESSENTIALS

GETTING THERE   Great Lakes Aviation (© 800/554-5111) flies daily into the **Cheyenne Regional Airport** (© 307/634-7071) on East 8th Avenue, but most people choose to fly directly in and out of **Denver International Airport** (© 800/247-2336), 101 miles south of Cheyenne in Colorado on I-25, and rent a car to drive into Wyoming from there.

By bus, you can get here with **Greyhound** (© 800/554-5111). **Powder River Transportation** (© 307/635-1327) buses leave for intrastate destinations from the bus terminal at 222 Deming St., under the I-80 overpass at U.S. 85.

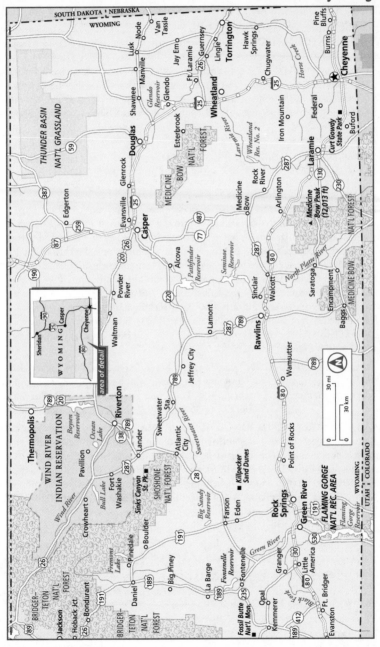

To get to Cheyenne from **Casper,** take I-25 south for 180 miles. From **Rock Springs** in the southwest part of the state, take I-80 east for 258 miles.

VISITOR INFORMATION   The **Cheyenne Area Convention and Visitors Bureau** in the lovingly restored Cheyenne Depot at 121 W. 15th St. (ℭ **800/426-5009** outside Wyoming, or 307/778-3133; www.cheyenne.org), has a variety of brochures and local maps, including the *Cheyenne Historic Downtown Walking Tour,* and the *Downtown Cheyenne Map.* Just outside of town, you can also get information at the **Wyoming Information Center,** operated by the Wyoming Division of Tourism, located just off I-25 at College Drive.

GETTING AROUND   Avis (ℭ 800/332-1212 or 307/632-9371) and **Hertz** (ℭ **800/654-3131** or 307/634-2131) have airport counters. For a taxi, call **Need-A-Ride Cab** (ℭ **307/778-0222**) or **Capital City Cab** (ℭ **307/632-8294**).

CHEYENNE FRONTIER DAYS 🐾🐾

In the world of rodeo, there are three must-see classics: The Pendleton Round-up, the Calgary Stampede, and the "Daddy of 'em All," Cheyenne Frontier Days. Since the inaugural event in 1897, it has grown into one of the largest rodeos in the world. The Frontier Days committee and thousands of volunteers organize this 10-day-long Western spectacle of parades, rodeo, dances, and concerts each summer, the last full week of July. It's safe to say that this is the most vivid demonstration of Western hospitality you'll encounter in the modern world.

Though the rodeo lasts for a full 10 days, picking and choosing activities carefully can save you a lot of time and money. Rodeo ticket prices range anywhere from $11 to $23 per person, and nightly shows featuring popular country music acts cost $18 to $42.

VISITOR INFORMATION   Contact the **Cheyenne Frontier Days Ticket Office** for brochures, ticket forms, and information on all shows and activities during upcoming Frontier Days celebrations at Cheyenne Frontier Days, P.O. Box 2477, Cheyenne, WY 82003 (ℭ **800/227-6336** or 307/778-7222; www.cfdrodeo.com).

GETTING AROUND DURING THE FESTIVAL   Parking is provided at Frontier Park for $10 per vehicle, but shuttle parking is also available and makes much more sense. The shuttle picks up visitors at several locations and delivers them to the rodeo grounds; round-trip fare is $6 per carload. The city also runs a special bus service to Frontier Park from downtown Cheyenne that stops at nearby campgrounds and hotels. Contact the **Cheyenne Area Convention and Visitors Bureau** (ℭ **307/778-3133**) for bus stop locations and scheduled pickups.

The Pancake Breakfast   Since their inception in 1952, these free breakfasts have become increasingly popular. Legend holds that a cement mixer churns up enough pancake batter to cook 100,000 flapjacks for 30,000 people. The breakfasts are held downtown at the Cheyenne Depot Plaza on the corner of Lincolnway and Capitol and served by the local Kiwanis Club, including, sometimes, an unassuming governor.

Cheyenne City Center parking lot, corner of Lincolnway and Capitol. Free admission. During Frontier Days, Mon, Wed, and Fri 7–9am.

The Parade   With the exception of Buffalo Bill's walk through the streets of Cheyenne in 1898 and a docile march led by Theodore Roosevelt in 1910, Cheyenne's Frontier Days Parade in its early days was similar to a stagecoach holdup. Guns blazed as cowboys rode through the streets with little regard to form or style. In 1925, things

ACCOMMODATIONS ■

Best Western Hitching Post Inn **9**
Holiday Inn **17**
Lincoln Court **8**
Little America Hotel & Resort **7**
Motel 6 **6**
Nagle Warren Mansion Bed & Breakfast **19**
The Plains Hotel **16**

DINING ◆

Little Bear Inn **1**
Luxury Diner **13**
Whipple House **20**

ATTRACTIONS ●

Cheyenne Botanic Gardens **5**
Cheyenne Depot Museum **14**
Cheyenne Frontier Days Old West Museum **3**
Cheyenne Gunslingers **15**
Frontier Park **4**
Historic Governor's Mansion **18**
Wyoming State Capitol **12**

SERVICES ●

Cheyenne Area Convention and Visitors Bureau **14**
Cheyenne Municipal Airport **11**
Wyoming Information Center **10**

took a turn toward civility when the "Evolution of Transportation" theme was introduced. Today, many horse-drawn vehicles make their way through the streets of Cheyenne as part of the Old-Time Carriage section of the parade. In addition to the carriages and antique cars, marching bands, local clubs, and various Plains Indians groups march. Viewing sites are as near as the closest curb, but you'll want to claim a position 45 minutes before the start.

The parade starts at Capitol Ave. and 24th St., runs down Capitol Ave. to 17th Ave., and continues up Carey Ave. to the finish at Carey Ave. and 24th St. Free admission. During Frontier Days, Sat, Tues, and Thurs, commencing at 9:30am.

The Rodeo   An anthropologist might see rodeo as a fading ritual to a passing way of life, but don't tell that to the fans who pack the stands at Frontier Days. It's actually one of the most popular spectator sports in the nation, as American as apple pie and baseball. Cheyenne's annual rodeo draws people from across the nation, and the best of the best cowboys.

Spectators from around the world pack into the stands to watch events like steer wrestling, barrel racing, team roping, and the classic event—and Wyoming's state symbol—saddle bronc riding. It's enormous fun, but part of the attraction is that these men and women put themselves in harm's way, working enormous animals with a wild streak. In a world where risk is often an illusion created by entertainers, this is the real thing. Champion bull-rider Lane Frost died in the ring at Frontier Days in 1989.

Daily ticket prices start at $11 for bleachers at the far end of the arena; $15 for seats closer to the roping gates; and $23 for the center of the action—the bucking chutes. Each night after the rodeo, top country stars take the stage. Concert tickets range from $18 to $40.

Frontier Park, exit 12 off I-80. ℂ **800/227-6336** or 307/778-7222. Tickets $11–$23. During Frontier Days, daily at 1pm.

SHOPPING

The can't-miss retailers in Cheyenne are **Sierra Trading Post,** 5025 Campstool Rd. (ℂ **307/775-8050**), for outdoor gear and close-outs of all kinds; the **Wrangler,** 1518 Capitol Ave. (ℂ **307/634-3048**), for cowboy boots and Western duds; and **Wyoming Home,** 210 W. Lincolnway (ℂ **307/638-2222**), for Western furnishings and decor.

SEEING THE SIGHTS

Stop in at the **Nelson Museum of the West** at 1714 Carey Ave. (ℂ **307/635-7670;** www.nelsonmuseum.com) to see a collection of cowboy trappings, American Indian artifacts, taxidermy trophies, and Western memorabilia. The **Cheyenne Botanic Gardens,** 710 S. Lions Park Dr. (ℂ **307/637-6458;** www.lbotanic.org), is a showcase of lush flowerbeds.

Cheyenne Depot Museum   Newly opened in 2003, this museum details Cheyenne's beginnings as a dusty railroad town and the tells the story of how rails shape this part of the West. Exhibits include fascinating historical photographs, models, and the original cargo scales used when the depot was active (late 1800s to 1980s). The Union Pacific Depot was restored to its original condition and is worth visiting even if you're not a railroad buff—but if you are, start here and then pick up the brochure *Tracking Trains in Cheyenne* from the information center in the depot lobby: It's a great resource for trainiacs, covering historic rail landmarks and the best places to gawk at the real thing.

121 W. 15th St., in the Union Pacific Depot. ℂ 307/632-3905. www.cheyennedepotmuseum.org. $4 adults, free for children under 13. Memorial Day to Labor Day Mon–Fri 8am–7pm, Sat 9am–5pm, Sun 10am–5pm; Rest of year Mon–Fri 9am–5pm, Sat 10am–5pm, Sun 11am–5pm.

Cheyenne Frontier Days Old West Museum   Frontier Days has been around long enough that folks have become interested in its history, so sponsors established this museum to warehouse memorabilia from the rodeo and other historical artifacts. The Old West Museum, located next door to the rodeo arena, is a convenient place to take a break from the action. There are carriages, temporary exhibits, photos, a video-screening room, and a treasure-trove of rodeo gear.

4610 N. Carey Ave., Frontier Park. ℂ 307/778-7290. www.oldwestmuseum.org. $5 adults, free for children under 13. Mon–Fri 9am–5pm; Sat–Sun 10am–5pm; longer hours during Frontier Days.

Cheyenne Gunslingers (Kids)   June through July, this nonprofit Cheyenne group puts on an Old West shootout downtown in "Gunslinger Square." You'll recognize it by the stage set of an Old West saloon, jail, and gallows. The volunteer actors love to ham it up. Their shows include jailbreaks, near-hangings, and shootouts—starring corrupt judges, wily villains, and white-hatted good guys. It's not necessarily the most accurate portrayal of the Old West (and it's not intended to be), but it is great entertainment for the family.

Gunslinger Sq., Lincolnway and Carey. © 307/635-1028. www.cheyennegunslingers.org. Free admission. June–July, shows at 6pm, Sat at noon; during Frontier Days, the show runs twice daily at noon and 6pm at the Soda Saloon at 203 W. 17th St.

Cheyenne Street Railway Trolley   No longer used as a mode of mass transit, the local trolley offers visitors a ride around Cheyenne's main tourist sites, including the Governors' Mansion, the Wyoming State Capitol, and the historic homes of the area's late-19th-century cattle barons.

Purchase tickets at the Cheyenne Area Convention and Visitors Bureau, 121 W. 15th St. © 800/426-5009 or 307/778-3133. Tour $8 adults, $4 children 4–12, free for kids 3 and under. Mid-May to mid-Sept 2-hr. tours Mon–Sat 10am and 1:30pm; Sun 1:30pm.

Historic Governors' Mansion   If you're interested in the political history of the state, you should continue 6 blocks from the capitol to the Historic Governors' Mansion. Built in 1904, it housed Wyoming's first families until 1976; today, many of the rooms have been restored to their 1905 appearances. Over the years, the decorative styles mixed, and you'll find everything from Chippendale to Colonial Revival to Art Nouveau. There's even a steer-horn chair in the entrance hall.

300 E. 21st St. © 307/777-7878. Free admission. Tues–Sat 9am–5pm. Closed noon–1pm in winter and Sat on 3-day weekends.

Wyoming State Capitol   In the summer, when the streets of Cheyenne are shaded by large old oaks, it's easy to come upon the capitol building a bit by surprise. It's not a large capitol, as such things go, but it's a traditional one, with a gold-leaf dome and carved stone. The main structure was built in 1888; the wings were added in 1917, but otherwise, the stately building has undergone little change over the years. Inside you can admire the beautiful woodwork, stained glass, and sparkling marble floors, and view historical photos and exhibits on the state's wildlife. Outside, you can stop by three statues: a monument to the first female justice of the peace, Esther Hobart Morris; a bronze bison; and the *Spirit of Wyoming*—the wild bucking horse emblazoned on every license plate in the state.

Capitol Ave. at 24th St. © 307/777-7220. Self-guided tours Mon–Fri 8:30am–4:30pm, except holidays.

WHERE TO STAY

Thanks to its crossroads location, there's a plethora of accommodations in Cheyenne, from basic motels to ornate B&Bs. The chain properties include **Holiday Inn,** adjacent to the junction of U.S. 85 and I-80 at 204 W. Fox Farm Rd. (© 307/638-4466), offering double rooms for $89 to $99 ($199 during Frontier Days); and **Motel 6,** 1735 Westland Rd. (© 800/466-8356 or 307/635-6806), with double rates of about $40 ($89 during Frontier Days). The 1950s-style **Lincoln Court,** 1720 W. Lincolnway (© 307/638-3302), is another reliable bet, with double rates of $50 to $60 ($130 during Frontier Days).

A reservation caution: Hotels fill up quickly during Frontier Days, and rack (published) rates are much higher.

Best Western Hitching Post Inn   Located along the motel strip on Lincolnway near the junction of I-25 and I-80, the Hitching Post is where most of the legislators stay during their annual sessions at the capitol, so it has an air of importance and deal-making. With that comes some of the best service in town. It also has spacious, well-appointed rooms. In 2005, the property converted 10 former apartments on-site into luxury suites with two bedrooms and, for the most part, full kitchens. Monday through Saturday, there is live entertainment in the lounge.

1700 W. Lincolnway, Cheyenne, WY 82001. (℃ **800/221-0125** or 307/638-3301. Fax 307/778-7194. 176 units. $89–$109 double; $150 suite; during Frontier Days $220 double, $300 and up suite. AE, DC, DISC, MC, V. **Amenities:** 2 restaurants; lounge; indoor pool; shopping arcade; business center; Wi-Fi network; coin-op washers and dryers; dry cleaning. *In room:* A/C, cable TV, dataport, kitchen, fridge, coffeemaker, hair dryer, iron.

Little America Hotel and Resort 𝒜   This is one of the largest hotels in Wyoming and a noteworthy oasis. The main building and low-rise brick lodges are surrounded by an executive golf course, duck pond, and mature evergreens. The main building harbors a tasteful lounge warmed by a fireplace and Navajo rugs; shops offer boutique clothing, jewelry, and Western souvenirs; there's a stuffed penguin, the hotel's unoffi-cial mascot, in the hall. Accommodations, in four low-rise brick lodges, all refurbished since 2000, provide 31-inch TVs, balconies, and bathrooms with tub/shower combos and marble counters. Rooms come in three categories: standards, minisuites with king-size beds, and executive suites. Meals are available in the Western Gold Dining Room (the house specialty is prime rib) and the lounge, and the coffee shop is open from 5am to 1am with very modest prices. The Olympic-size pool is open summer only, but a fitness center and jogging path can be used year-round.

2800 W. Lincolnway (I-80 at I-25), Cheyenne, WY 82009. (℃ **800/445-6945** or 307/775-8400. Fax 307/775-8425. www.cheyenne.littleamerica.com. 188 units. $86–$189 double; during Frontier Days $129–$200 double. AE, DC, DISC, MC, V. **Amenities:** 2 restaurants; lounge; outdoor heated pool; exercise room; shopping arcade. *In room:* A/C, cable TV, dataport, fridge, coffeemaker, hair dryer, iron.

Nagle Warren Mansion Bed & Breakfast 𝒜𝒜   This gem of an inn is the center-piece of an increasingly hip stretch on 17th Avenue. Originally built in 1888 by famed architect Erasmus Nagle (it was the first house in the state with indoor plumbing), the mansion was converted into an elegant bed-and-breakfast in 1997. Grand and spa-cious, the three-story structure oozes luxury, from the furnishings (almost exclusively regional antiques) to the stately spire that anchors the building's southeast corner. The rooms, named after the mansion's former residents, feature lavish, late-19th-century style, tempered by a few modern perks—CD players, televisions, and modem-ready phones. Half of the rooms are located in the main building, and half are in the adjoin-ing carriage house (the latter have fireplaces), but they all have their own unique allure.

222 E. 17th St., Cheyenne, WY 82001. (℃ **800/811-2610** or 307/637-3333. www.naglewarrenmansion.com. 12 units. $98–$165 double; during Frontier Days $275 double. Rates include full breakfast. AE, DC, MC, V. **Amenities:** Lounge; exercise room; Jacuzzi; complimentary bikes; courtesy car; Wi-Fi network; massage; dry cleaning. *In room:* A/C, cable TV w/VCR, dataport, hair dryer, iron, safe.

The Plains Hotel 𝒜   Built in 1911, the stalwart Plains Hotel went through a long period of decline before enjoying a complete overhaul that was finished in 2003, giv-ing its rooms, lobby, and restaurant a much-needed face-lift in the process. Under a stained-glass ceiling, the lobby is a multipillared space with its original tile floor and a retouched mural on the walls ringing the ceiling. Rooms run the gamut from stan-dard (with a king-size bed or one or two queen-size) to larger parlor suites (a king-size or two queen-size) to true two-room suites, one of which is done up in high cowboy style thanks to the help of *American Cowboy* magazine. The rooms on the whole are nice and fresh, with a subtle Western motif, with bathrooms that vary in terms of amenities and quality—some are a bit old, some have showers only, and others feature the vanities in the rooms. The elevators are also quite dinky: As the story goes, they built them that way so people couldn't take their horses up to their rooms.

1600 Central Ave., Cheyenne, WY 82001. (C) 866/275-2467 or 307/638-3311. Fax 307/635-2022. www.theplains hotel.com. 131 units. $89–$129 double, $139–$199 suite; during Frontier Days $169–$199 double, $225–$350 suite. AE, DC, DISC, MC, V. **Amenities:** Restaurant; lounge; exercise room; business center. *In room:* Cable TV, hair dryer, iron.

CAMPING

The biggest campground is the **Restway Travel Park,** 4212 Whitney Road, 2 miles east of Cheyenne ((C) **800/443-2751** or 307/634-3811). Catering to RV and tent campers alike, Restway boasts a heated swimming pool, miniature golf, and a store stocked with basic supplies; nightly rates run from about $15 for a basic tent site to $35 for a site with full hookups during Frontier Days. For something a bit different, head to **Terry Bison Ranch,** located 6 miles south of Cheyenne via I-25, exit 2 ((C) **307/ 634-4171;** www.terrybisonranch.com), a working buffalo ranch with tent ($18 per night) and RV sites ($24 per night), as well as a bunkhouse, guest cabins, gift shop, and restaurant. The ranch also offers cabins, lodge rooms, and a variety of tours.

WHERE TO DINE

Little Bear Inn ☞ STEAKS/SEAFOOD   A Cheyenne stalwart since 1958, the Little Bear's story actually begins in the 1870s. The original Little Bear was a way station (read: saloon and casino) for travelers, traders, and outlaws, with a colorful history right up until it closed in the 1950s when the county sheriff came down on gambling. (The proprietor figured that people wouldn't come all that way just for the food.) In less than a decade, the new one opened about 20 miles closer to town than the original, and has been a Cheyenne institution ever since, serving up quality steaks and seafood in an atmosphere of antiquated elegance—and a side of Western character. For the adventurous, the menu includes frog legs and Rocky Mountain oysters, as well as a creative array of steaks that includes buffalo, Italian preparations, and a breaded New York strip.

700 Little Bear Rd. (near I-25, exit 16). (C) 307/634-3684. Main courses $12–$19. AE, DISC, MC, V. Sun–Thurs 5–9pm; Fri–Sat 5–10pm.

Luxury Diner ⓕ*inds* AMERICAN   A favorite blue-collar breakfast counter, the Luxury Diner is a real down-home greasy spoon. We say that affectionately, of course; the food is good, the coffee always hot, and the waitresses sassy. Breakfast is served all day. The pie: apple. The special: meatloaf. It's the real thing—no Buddy Holly posters, no 45s dangling from the ceiling for that "retro" look. In fact, the small dining area ran as a trolley from 1896 to 1912, before becoming a diner in 1926. Pictures of trains cover the walls, Christmas lights blink around the trim, and the menu says, "Friendliest place in town." It's right.

1401-A W. Lincolnway. (C) 307/638-8971. Breakfast $2–$8; lunch $4–$8. AE, MC, V. Daily 6am–4pm.

The Whipple House ☞ CONTINENTAL   Located in the majestic Victorian mansion (1883) from which it draws its name, The Whipple House is Cheyenne's most romantic and intimate restaurant. Praised by locals and tourists alike, the food here is classic, savory, and rich. There's an ample selection of steaks and seafood on the menu here, and a formidable wine list to boot. Our favorites: for lunch, the Burger Robert, with Gorgonzola cheese and a tantalizing tomato relish; for dinner, the lamb chops, glazed with mint and garlic and served in a blackberry sauce.

300 E. 17th St. ⊘ **307/638-3551.** Lunch $7–$9; dinner $11–$33. AE, DC, DISC, MC, V. Mon–Fri 11am–2pm; Mon–Sat 5–9pm. Closed Sun.

CHEYENNE AFTER DARK

The **Atlas Theatre,** 211 W. Lincolnway (⊘ **307/635-0199**), is Cheyenne's prime performing arts venue. The hippest watering hole in town is **Snake River Brewery,** 121 W. 15th St., in the Union Pacific Depot (⊘ **307/634-7625**), a sports bar/microbrewery that serves good barbecue and other pub fare; it has a partnership with the brewery of the same name in Jackson. In front of the depot on summer Friday evenings, free **concerts** are staged from 4:30 to 7:30pm.

3 Laramie ⟨★

49 miles NW of Cheyenne; 360 miles SE of Yellowstone/Grand Teton; 207 miles E of Rock Springs; 124 miles N of Denver

Though the political capital is 49 miles to the east, Laramie is the cultural and intellectual capital of Wyoming. It's home to the state's only university, public or private. Unlike Jackson, which has a prefabricated feel designed to appeal to visitors, Laramie has an earnest charm that seems to have developed by accident, and it has been this way for nearly a century. Located just east of the beautiful Medicine Bow Mountains, at an altitude of more than 7,000 feet, Laramie is sometimes buffeted by chill winds. But it has university-town amenities like bookstores and coffee shops, and a few Western features to boot, including outlying ranchlands and some rowdy downtown bars.

ESSENTIALS

GETTING THERE The **Laramie Regional Airport** (⊘ **307/742-4164**), west of town along Wyo. 130, services daily flights on **Great Lakes Aviation** (⊘ **800/554-5111**) from Denver.

Or go **Greyhound** (⊘ **800/231-2222**) at **Tumbleweed Express,** a bus depot/convenience store at 4700 Bluebird Lane (⊘ **307/742-9663**). The bus stops at several Wyoming cities along I-80, including Rock Springs and Cheyenne.

Laramie is an easy 49-mile drive from Cheyenne on I-80; driving from Salt Lake, it's just more than 300 miles once you hit Evanston. The fastest route from the Yellowstone–Grand Teton area is via U.S. 287 south for 259 miles to Rawlins and I-80 east for 101 miles to Laramie.

VISITOR INFORMATION Contact the **Albany County Tourism Board,** 210 Custer St. (⊘ **800/445-5303;** www.laramie-tourism.org), or the **Laramie Area Chamber of Commerce** (⊘ **307/745-7339;** www.laramie.org).

GETTING AROUND Hertz (⊘ **800/654-3131** or 307/745-0500) and **Enterprise** (⊘ **800/736-8222** or 307/721-9876) maintain outlets in Laramie. Taxi service is available through **Taxi, LLC** (⊘ **307/761-8294**).

SPECIAL EVENTS **Jubilee Days** (⊘ **307/745-7339;** www.laramiejubileedays.com) is a Western party that runs early to mid-July with rodeos, parades, and fireworks. The **Wyoming Snow Sculpting Competition** (⊘ **307/745-7339**) is held in frosty February.

GETTING OUTSIDE

Curt Gowdy State Park, named for the television sportscaster who hailed from Wyoming, is quite pleasant, if not spectacularly beautiful. Located 23 miles southeast of Laramie, the 1,645-acre park is a great spot for a picnic ($4 day-use fee). Or stay the night in one of the five campsites for $12 per night. There are two lakes here, but no swimming is allowed (they provide part of Cheyenne's water supply). Boating is permitted, but no rentals are available at the park. Call © 307/632-7946 for further information. To get to the park, take I-80 east until you see the exit for Wyo. 210, the scenic back road to Cheyenne.

About 10 miles southeast of Laramie, on the edge of the Medicine Bow National Forest, are **Pole Mountain** and the **Vedauwoo Recreation Area** (© 307/745-2300). Vedauwoo and the Happy Jack trail head near the Summit exit of I-80 have some excellent summer and winter recreational opportunities. The name Vedauwoo (pronounced *Vee*-duh-voo) is Arapaho for "earth-born." The rock formations—soft-edged blocks shaped like stools, turtles, and mushrooms—were considered the sacred creations of animal and human spirits, and young Indian men sought visions there. Today rock climbers pursue their quests for challenging climbs here, and find tough technical pitches. Other folks see a great place to mountain bike, hike, and scan the vistas. To get there, take I-80 east toward Cheyenne, past the second biggest Abe Lincoln head in these parts (10 miles outside town) to exit 329, the Vedauwoo turnoff.

SEEING THE SIGHTS

The **Laramie Plains Museum,** 603 Ivinson Ave. (✆ 307/742-4448; www.laramie museum.org), is housed in a gorgeous three-story Queen Anne Victorian home built by Laramie settler Edward Ivinson, with furnishings from the 1890s. Admission is $5 adults and $3 children 6 to 12 (free for under 6). The **Wyoming Children's Museum and Nature Center,** 968 N. 9th St. (✆ 307/745-6332; www.wcmnc.org), has enough things to keep kids busy, including a frontier general store where children can handle things and do face painting. Admission is $3 children 4 to 12 ($1 for those under 4) and $2 adults.

University of Wyoming The only 4-year college in the state, the University of Wyoming was born in 1887 with the funding of Old Main, its first building. At that time, there were five professors, two tutors, and 42 students on the 20-acre campus, which included Prexy's Pasture, where the school's first president kept his cows. Today, the University of Wyoming has more than 2,000 faculty and staff members and an enrollment of about 13,000. The university has boomed along with oil and gas prices and the coal-bed methane market, with the legislature loosening the purse strings in recent sessions.

A campus tour is worth the effort, if for no other reason than to check out the campus architecture, which ranges from the solid sandstone castles of a century ago to the spaceship designs of today (stop at the **Visitors Services Center,** 1408 Ivinson Ave., for a map). To catch a glimpse of student life in Laramie, swing by Prexy's Pasture. Those visiting during the school year may also want to contact the **calendar line** (✆ 307/766-5000) to find out what's on the schedule.

With no pro sports teams in Wyoming, the college's athletic programs take on special importance. Fans drive from all over the state to root for the **Cowboys** as they compete against Mountain West Conference foes. For event information and tickets, contact the ticket office (✆ 307/766-4850; www.wyomingathletics.com).

The university plays an important role with its museum spaces, and most of the exhibits are free. Located in the Knight Geology Building, in the northwest corner of Prexy's Pasture, the **Geological Museum** (✆ 307/766-2646; www.uwyo.edu/geomuseum) has plenty of dinosaur fossils. It's open Monday through Friday from 8am to 5pm, Saturday and Sunday from 10am to 3pm. Also worth visiting is the **Rocky Mountain Herbarium** (✆ 307/766-2236; www.rmh.uwyo.edu), open Monday through Friday from 8am to 5pm (7:30am–4:30pm when school is out of session). The **Insect Museum** (✆ 307/766-2298; in the Ag Building, just north of Prexy's Pasture) is primarily a research facility and a bit esoteric to the average visitor; call for current hours. The **Centennial Complex** (on the east side of campus, east of 15th St.) houses the **UW Art Museum** (✆ 307/766-6622; http://uwadmnweb.uwyo.edu/ArtMuseum), with works by Audubon, Charlie Russell, Thomas Moran, and even Gauguin. It's open Monday through Saturday from 10am to

5pm, as well as Sundays 1 to 5pm in the summer. Also in this building is the **American Heritage Center** (℃ 307/766-4114; http://ahc.uwyo.edu), a top-notch research facility with extensive collections of Western-history materials and some unexpected archives, like some of Jack Benny's papers, open Monday through Friday from 8am to 5pm (7:30am–4:30pm when school is out of session).

Wyoming Territorial Prison State Historic Site Formerly a penitentiary where Butch Cassidy served time, the Territorial Prison transmogrified into an experimental livestock station before becoming the historical park it is today. Almost everything having to do with frontier life before the start of the 20th century can be found here, from a funky frontier town, to stagecoach rides, to a ranching exhibit with a home-steader's cabin and farm animals.

975 Snowy Range Rd. (just east of I-80, exit 311). ℃ 307/745-6161. www.wyoprisonpark.org. Admission $5, $2.50 for children 12–17. May–Oct daily 9am–6pm; call for winter hours.

SHOPPING

Since Laramie is a university town, it has its fair share of bookstores. There is of course a big chain, **Hastings Books, Music, and Video,** at 654 N. 3rd St. (℃ 307/745-0312), but there are also some fine and idiosyncratic locals, including the peaceful **2nd Story Books** and **Personally Recommended Books,** both at 105 E. Ivinson Ave. (℃ 307/745-4423). To see what's hot on campus, visit the **University Bookstore** 1 block north of Ivinson Avenue and 13th Street (℃ 800/370-2676).

If you're looking for the gear you need for an adventure in the Medicine Bow, try **Cross-Country Connection** at 222 S. 2nd St. (℃ 307/721-2851) for skiing and climbing equipment (you can rent skis here, too). For Western clothing and souvenirs, hit **Martindale's,** downtown at 217 E. Grand Ave. (℃ 307/721-4100).

Downtown Laramie is also home to all kinds of artists and craftspeople. **Earth, Wind, and Fire** (℃ 307/745-0226), at 216–220 S. 2nd St., is a pottery lover's dream come true. **Grand Bazaar,** at 111 E. Grand Ave. (℃ 307/742-9382), is another excellent gallery. The prime antiques store is **Antique Fever,** 211 S. 2nd St. (℃ 307/721-8398).

WHERE TO STAY

Among the chain properties in town are **Travelodge,** 165 N. 3rd St. (℃ 800/942-6671 or 307/742-6671), with rooms for $50 to $75 double; and **Comfort Inn,** 3420 E. Grand Ave. (℃ 307/721-8856), with double rates from $69 to $109. Outside of the chains, the **Sunset Inn,** 1104 S. 3rd St. (℃ 800/308-3744 or 307/742-3741), is a small motel with an outdoor pool and indoor hot tub. Doubles cost $40 to $70.

A. Drummond's Ranch Bed-and-Breakfast 𝄐 *Finds* A short drive from either Laramie or Cheyenne, the Drummonds' house sits above peaceful hills of pine and sage. Here you can ride mountain bikes or horses in summer, cross-country ski in win-ter, or even take a llama to lunch. That's right. For $70 per person, the Drummonds will pack your lunch by llama. Or guests can bring their own horses, and owner and horse-lover Taydie Drummond can set your steed up with its own bed-and-breakfast.

Inside, guests relax in the living room or sit on the porch and gaze. The inn isn't par-ticularly historic, large, or quaint, but it feels exactly like what it is: a home. It's a grand place to kick back, take walks, and pet the animals. Second-story rooms have two beds and share a bathroom. The aptly named Hummingbird Room looks out over Colorado's Rocky Mountain National Park, 75 miles away. Those in love will want to stay in the Carriage House Loft, with its private deck, hot tub, gas fireplace, and steam sauna.

399 Happy Jack Rd., Laramie/Cheyenne, WY 82007 (25 miles east of Laramie off I-80). ℭ **307/634-6042.** www.adrummond.com. 4 units. $72–$124 double; $164–$200 carriage-house room. Rates include full breakfast. MC, V. **Amenities:** Bike and horse rentals. *In room:* TV/VCR, coffeemaker, hair dryer, iron.

The Brick Bed & Breakfast ⨁ In 1905, wealthy landowner Ora Haley built this stately Victorian for his daughter and her husband, who occupied it for about 20 years. Since that time, the home—with walls three bricks thick—has served as a sorority house, an apartment building, and a real-estate office before Pennie and Gary Espeland converted it into a comfortable B&B in 2004. The home still has many original fixtures and furnishings, plus a bit of Western charm in the form of a buffalo-hide rug in the foyer and an elk trophy mounted on the staircase to the rooms on the second floor. The rooms share two bathrooms and are cozy and classy; the Emma J. Room features ranch antiques and access to the back deck, and the inn's popular hot tub. Breakfasts include crème brûlée pancakes and Pennie's "Kickass Quiche"; other little extras include fresh brownies and an evening cocktail hour.

105 S. 5th St., Laramie, WY 82070. ℭ **800/788-4626** or 307/745-4390. 4 units, all with shared bathroom. $89–$129 double. Rates include full breakfast. AE, MC, V. **Amenities:** Outdoor Jacuzzi; Wi-Fi network. *In room:* No phone.

Vee Bar Guest Ranch ⨁⨁ A jewel of a guest ranch, the Vee Bar is definitely pricey, but perfect for those looking to delve into the ranching lifestyle as they get away from it all. The property itself, 800 acres in all, features lush fields, cottonwood and willow groves, and a stretch of the crystalline Little Laramie River. Alongside the historic main lodge, the accommodations here are comfortable cabins and a trio of "Riverside Suite" duplexes that manage to balance the rustic with the convenient. Two of the free-standing cabins are more than a century old, restored and furnished with antiques of local origin; the third is modern (1990), but blends into the old-fashioned atmosphere with ease. Activities such as horseback riding, fishing, river tubing, and overnight camp-outs are included, as are all meals. For breakfast, expect flapjacks, eggs, and bacon; for dinner, steaks and seafood. Guests can unwind in the historic John Wayne Saloon.

2091 Wyo. 130, Laramie, WY 82070. ℭ **800/483-3227** or 307/745-7036. Fax 307/745-7433. www.vee-bar.com. 9 cabins. $2,900 per week for 2 people; $1,100 per week each additional person. 3-night packages also available. Rates include all meals and activities. In the fall, winter, and spring (and summertime Sat), single-night stays are available for $150 for a double room. AE, DISC, MC, V. Located 21 miles west of Laramie via Snowy Range Rd. (Wyo. 130). **Amenities:** Restaurant; lounge; exercise room; Jacuzzi; children's programs; Wi-Fi network; self-serve laundry. *In room:* No phone.

CAMPING

The **Laramie KOA,** off I-80 at 1271 W. Baker St. (ℭ **307/742-6553**), is open April through October, depending on the snows. There are 100 pull-through sites here, as well as a rec room, small store, and unobstructed mountain views. Full hookups cost $22 to $29. There is also a campground at Curt Gowdy State Park (see "Getting Outside," above).

WHERE TO DINE

Thinkers and talkers fuel up on good java at the **Coal Creek Coffee Company,** 110 E. Grand Ave. (ℭ **307/745-7737**); there is sometimes live music in the evenings. You can get pasta or pizza at **Grand Avenue Pizza,** 301 E. Grand Ave. (ℭ **307/721-2909**), which hides in an old corner space downtown.

Altitude Chophouse & Brewery ⨁ AMERICAN/MICROBREWERY This downtown eatery, effortlessly melding woodsy and swank, features tree stumps for bar stools and blue banners hanging from the rafters to dampen the sound of friendly chatter. The smoke-free atmosphere is a rich complement to the excellent fare, which includes pub standards (burgers, pizzas, and cheese sticks) as well as excellent steaks and seafood. We like the cedar plank salmon and the Cajun-spiced pork loin, but the steaks are also held in high regard. The prices are right, and the beers aren't bad at all, either.

320 S. 2nd St. © 307/721-4031. Reservations accepted. Main courses $7–$16. AE, DC, MC, V. Mon–Sat 11am–10pm. Bar open later.

Sweet Melissa *(Finds* VEGETARIAN   A meatless menu in Wyoming might sound like something of an oxymoron, but this funky cafe by the rail yard will satisfy most any patron, carnivorous or not. The three-bean chili is terrific, and makes us long for another trip to Laramie, but the menu also includes salads, eggplant subs and hummus sandwiches, lentil loaf, mushroom fajitas, and several pasta dishes. The establishment does not serve beer, wine, or liquor, but has a nice selection of teas.

213 S. 1st St. © 307/742-9607. Reservations accepted for large parties only. Main courses $5–$9. No credit cards. Mon–Sat 11am–9pm.

4 A Side Trip for the Outdoor Enthusiast: The Snowy Range & Carbon County

Snowy Range: 32 miles W of Laramie

You can very quickly leave behind the dry plains around Laramie and find yourself up among lakes, forest, and substantial peaks in the north end of the Medicine Bow Mountains, known as the **Snowy Range.** Just take Wyo. 130 west, through the foothill town of Centennial, past the **Snowy Range Ski Area** (© 800/462-7669; www.snowyrange.com), and up into the mountains, where peaks rise well over 10,000 feet. Though **Medicine Bow Peak** is 12,013 feet tall, it's a relatively easy day climb, starting at the parking lot by Lake Marie and covering about 5 miles. You can loop around the west side of the hollow in which the peak stands and return on the east side among the lakes. Trails are well marked and you'll meet people as you hike. Just keep an eye on the thunderheads, as you'll be above timberline, exposed to lightning. For **detailed trail maps,** contact the **Medicine Bow National Forest,** 2468 Jackson St. in Laramie (© 307/745-2300; www.fs.fed.us/r2/mbr).

If you drive on over the Snowies—it takes only about an hour—you'll drop down into the valley of the **North Platte River,** with its old mining and timber towns such as Encampment and Saratoga. **Saratoga** is the roost of several fishing outfits that guide on the North Platte, one of the finest trout fisheries in the state. If you spend the night, you'll probably enjoy the creaky, old-fashioned style of the historic **Hotel Wolf** at 101 E. Bridge St. (© 307/326-5525; www.wolfhotel.com), with double rates of $47 to $90, or the **Saratoga Inn,** 601 E. Pic Pike Rd. (© 800/594-0718; www.saratogainn.com), with its own hot-spring-fed pool, golf course, and double rates of $79 to $99. At the foot of the mountains in Centennial, try the **Old Corral Hotel** (© 866/653-2677 or 307/745-5918; www.oldcorral.com), with $69 to $79 for a double with Western decor, or the rustic **Brooklyn Lodge** (© 307/742-6916; www.brooklynlodge.com), a log-laden B&B with rockers and wagon-wheel tables; double rates are $150. Another area attraction of note is **Woods Landing** (© 307/745-9638; www.woodslanding.com), a historic Western dance hall built on 24 boxcar springs—when the dance floor is full, the place literally bounces. A restaurant and a complex of rustic rental cabins ($45–$95 double) are on-site.

CAMPING

Medicine Bow National Forest (© 307/745-2300; www.fs.fed.us/r2/mbr) maintains a number of semiprimitive campgrounds June through September, scattered throughout the range west of Laramie. Fees range from $7 to $10 per night.

FISHING

The Upper North Platte River cuts right through Saratoga, and those in the know consider it one of the state's top trout-fishing spots. **Stoney Creek Outfitters,** 216 E. Walnut, Saratoga (© 307/326-8750; www.fishstoneycreek.com), charges $425 for a full-day, two-person float-fishing expedition.

5 Rock Springs

258 miles W of Cheyenne; 178 miles S of Jackson

Rock Springs began as a stage station on the Overland Trail, named after a natural spring that dried up after extensive mining in the area. In 1894, Jack London wrote of Rock Springs: "It seems to be a mining town. . . . It seems to be the Wild and Woolly West with a vengeance." It's still true: Rock Springs shows the rougher side of Wyoming, powered by a coal-burning power plant, freight trains roaring through, and all-night truckers stopping for coffee, adding to a blue-collar sensibility.

For more than a century, boom followed bust followed boom, and in the late 1970s, oil, gas, and coal caused the area population to skyrocket. So did the crime rate, and corruption raised its ugly head. But things have improved dramatically since.

The city is not far from some fine outdoor attractions: **Fossil Butte National Monument** (see section 7) and **Flaming Gorge National Recreation Area** (see section 6 for more information).

ESSENTIALS

GETTING THERE   Great Lakes Aviation (© 800/554-5111) flies into **Rock Springs-Sweetwater County Airport,** 15 miles east of town on I-80 (© 307/352-6880), and the **Greyhound** bus rumbles in at 1695 Sunset Dr. (© 307/362-2931).

Rock Springs sits at the intersection of U.S. 191 and I-80. From Cheyenne, drive I-80 west for 258 miles. From Jackson, take U.S. 191 south for 178 miles.

VISITOR INFORMATION   The Rock Springs Chamber of Commerce, 1897 Dewar Dr. (© 800/463-8637 or 307/362-3771; www.rockspringswyoming.net), puts a positive spin on Rock Springs and its immediate area.

GETTING AROUND   Avis (© 800/331-1212 or 307/362-5599) and **Hertz** (© 800/654-3131 or 307/382-3262) maintain counters at the airport. For a **taxi,** contact **City Cab** (© 307/382-1100).

SEEING THE SIGHTS

While strolling around town, pop into the **Community Fine Arts Center,** at the Sweetwater County Library, 400 "C" St. (© 307/362-6212), which contains a few original paintings by Grandma Moses and Norman Rockwell. The **Rock Springs Historical Museum,** at 201 "B" St. (© 307/362-3138), is a fine piece of Romanesque architecture housing exhibits covering the city's rough-and-tumble past. The **Western Wyoming Community College Natural History Museum,** 2500 College Dr. (© 307/382-1600), has several dinosaur displays and a few fish and plant fossils. All three museums are free.

WHERE TO STAY

The two hotels listed below may not be the fanciest in the state, but they have swimming pools and well-maintained modern rooms. The **Inn at Rock Springs,** 2518 Foothill Blvd. (© **800/442-9692** or 307/362-9600), offers rooms for $50 to $80 double. You'll get a free continental breakfast every morning, as well as a heated outdoor pool and hot tub at the **EconoLodge,** at I-80 exit 104 (© **800/548-6621** or 307/382-4217), for $55 to $75 double.

WHERE TO DINE

Bitter Creek Brewing MICROBREWERY   LIFE IS TOO SHORT TO DRINK CHEAP BEER, reads the sign behind the oak bar. If you agree, then Bitter Creek is the place for you. In four fermenting vats adjacent to the bar, they concoct their own special microbrews, including the popular Mustang Pale Ale, and the cleverly named Coal Porter, a darker beer with a slight chocolate aftertaste. The ever-changing menu includes gourmet salads, pizzas, and pasta dishes.

604 Broadway. © **307/362-4782.** Lunch $5–$9; dinner $10–$18. AE, MC, V. Mon–Thurs 11:30am–10pm; Fri–Sat 11:30am–11pm; Sun 11:30am–8pm.

6 Flaming Gorge National Recreation Area ★

24 miles W of Rock Springs

By May 1869, the Union Pacific had laid its tracks across Wyoming and pinned them to the eastbound rails with a golden spike. The town of Green River, 15 miles west of Rock Springs, was only a year old. And that May, 10 frontiersmen and ex-soldiers climbed off the train, led by a veteran who'd lost his arm in the Civil War. They jumped into stout wooden boats and set off down the Green River. As they slid through red canyons with the cliffs peaking high above, almost singed yellow along the rims, they named the place "Flaming Gorge."

The expedition continued down the Green, which merged into the Colorado River, and then continued on into the Grand Canyon, weaving through boulders, portaging sandbars, and being sucked through rapids. Three men decided to hike out rather than risk the rapids. They were later found bristling with arrows. The remaining seven survived. And the leader would go on to map and record the *Great American Desert* and later to help organize and then direct the U.S. Geological Survey. The one-armed Civil War veteran, the famous river runner, was, of course, John Wesley Powell.

Today a 455-foot dam, 15 miles into Utah, backs the river onto itself for 91 miles, nearly to the town of Green River. Each summer, jet-boaters, water-skiers, and anglers skim the surface of the reservoir, while paddlers drop in below the dam for scenic and adventurous floats in the wake of Powell's boats.

ESSENTIALS

GETTING THERE   Take I-80 west from Rock Springs for 15 miles to the town of **Green River** at the junction of Wyo. 530. (See "A Driving Tour," below, for information on driving through the area.)

VISITOR INFORMATION   For information before you arrive, contact the **District Ranger** (© **435/784-3445;** www.fs.fed.us/r4/ashley). Once you're in the area, stop at the U.S. Forest Service's **visitor center** in Green River at 1450 Uinta Dr. (© **307/875-2871**) to pick up maps and brochures.

Impressions

The river enters the range by a flaring, brilliant red gorge, that may be seen from the north a score of miles away . . . We name it Flaming Gorge.
—Explorer Major John Wesley Powell, May 26, 1869

ADMISSION & REGULATIONS   Admission to the 190,000-acre Flaming Gorge National Recreation Area is $2 per vehicle per day. The Forest Service's regulations here are mostly common-sense, aimed at preserving water quality and protecting the forest and historic sites. In addition, Wyoming and Utah fishing and boating regulations apply in those states' sections of the recreation area. Leashed dogs are permitted on trails.

A DRIVING TOUR

As you drive south from Green River on Wyo. 530, the cactus and sagebrush-filled **Devils Playground** badlands and the rock formations of **Haystack Buttes** will be to your right. Wyo. 530 runs the length of the recreation area's west side and provides access to the Flaming Gorge Reservoir at the **Buckboard Crossing Area,** 20 miles south, where a full-service marina operates during the summer.

From Wyo. 530, pick up Utah 44 just across the state line in Manila, Utah. Utah 44 runs south then east for 27 miles to pick up U.S. 191. Along this route you'll catch glimpses of Utah's Uinta Mountains to the west and may see bighorn sheep in nearby **Sheep Creek Canyon,** which has been designated a special geological area by the Forest Service because of its dramatically twisted and upturned rocks. A mostly paved 11-mile loop road cuts off from Utah 44, offering a half-hour tour of this beautiful, narrow canyon, with its lavish display of rocks that have eroded into intricate patterns, a process that began with the uplifting of the Uinta Mountains millions of years ago. This loop may be closed in winter.

Eventually, you'll come to the **Red Canyon Overlook** on the southern edge of the gorge, where a rainbow of colors adorns 1,000-foot-tall cliffs. The **Red Canyon Visitor Center** (open 9:30am–5pm in summer) is nearby, as is **Flaming Gorge Dam.**

To head back to Wyoming, take U.S. 191 away from the eastern edge of the gorge. From the junction of Utah 44 and U.S. 191, it's 16 miles to the border. Once you're at the state line, it's 30 miles to the turnoff for **Firehole Canyon,** an access to the gorge that offers views of the magnificent spires known as **Chimney Rocks.** Keep going north on U.S. 191 and you'll hit I-80 again.

GETTING OUTSIDE

For more information about the Utah portion of Flaming Gorge National Recreation Area, including additional outdoor recreational activities and outfitters, lodging options, and other nearby sites of interest, see *Frommer's Utah.*

BOATING   Three marinas on **Lake Flaming Gorge** provide boat rentals, fuel, launching ramps, and boating and fishing supplies. **Cedar Springs Marina** (© 435/889-3795; www.cedarspringsmarina.com) is 2 miles west of Flaming Gorge Dam; **Lucerne Valley Marina** (© 435/784-3483; www.flaminggorge.com) is on the west side of the lake, 7 miles east of Manila; and **Buckboard Marina** (© 307/875-6927) is also on the west side of the lake, off Wyo. 530, 22 miles north of Manila.

CAMPING   The U.S. Forest Service maintains about 20 RV and tent campgrounds in the area ($6–$32), and there are also many primitive riverside sites. Contact the **Forest Service visitor center** in Green River (© 307/875-2871) for more information.

FISHING   You might want to bring along a muscular friend if you plan to fish Lake Flaming Gorge, which is famous as the place to catch record-breaking trout, such as the 51-pound 8-ounce lake (Mackinaw) trout caught in 1988, the 26-pound 2-ounce rainbow caught in 1979, or the 33-pound 10-ounce brown caught in 1977. You'll also see other cold-water species such as smallmouth bass and kokanee salmon. Fishing is popular year-round, although ice-fishermen are warned to make sure the ice is strong enough to hold them. For fishing information and excursions, call **Conquest Expeditions** (© **435/784-3370;** www.conquestexpeditions.com).

7 Killpecker Sand Dunes & Fossil Butte National Monument

Killpecker Sand Dunes: 40 miles N of Rock Springs; 140 miles SE of Jackson

KILLPECKER SAND DUNES

North of Rock Springs and east of Eden (we're not kidding . . . it's a small town) swell the **Killpecker Sand Dunes**—the largest active dunes in North America. Here hikers can scale and descend the heaving hills of white sand, where the noon heat shimmers and the midnight cold cuts. Rock climbers trek to **Boar's Tusk,** a standing volcanic plug, while ethnography buffs seek the **White Mountain Petroglyphs,** and photographers with high-powered telephoto lenses should be on the lookout for wild horses.

Bird-watchers will especially enjoy the **Seedskadee Wildlife Refuge,** where they may see geese, sandhill cranes, and great blue herons along the miles of marshes along the Green River.

GETTING THERE   To get to the dunes, drive Wyo. 191 north from Rock Springs 36 miles to Eden. Turning east, you'll bump along at least 20 miles of gravel road. Bring a compass, plenty of emergency water, and a map. It's best to contact the Bureau of Land Management (© **307/352-0256**) before blazing the trail on your own. *Note:* When it rains, the bentonite on these rough roads turns to glue, and smart drivers stop trying.

FOSSIL BUTTE NATIONAL MONUMENT

Standing at the base of Fossil Butte, gazing up 1,000 feet at the rust- and ocher-stained cliffs, with the crackling desert wind rattling sage and tumbleweeds, you'd never guess that eons ago you'd have been looking up from the bottom of a subtropical ocean. Some 50 million years ago, during the Eocene Epoch, millions of fish wriggled across what's now the sky. With the ebb and flow of millennia, they sifted into the mud and fossilized.

Today, visitors join paleontologists during the summer to dig for the ancient remains of fish, insects, turtles, birds, and even bats. You can also hike (be watchful for rattlesnakes) on two short trails—the 1.5-mile Fossil Lake Trail and the 2.5-mile Quarry Trail. This is also a prime wildlife-viewing area, where you're likely to see pronghorn, mule deer, white-tailed prairie dogs, and ground squirrels, and you might be lucky enough to spot moose, elk, and beaver as well. A variety of birds are also seen here, including Canada geese, great blue herons, Clark's nutcrackers, yellow-headed blackbirds, great horned owls, and red-tailed hawks.

The excellent **Fossil Butte Visitor Center** ⚐ (© **307/877-4455**) exhibits more than 75 fossils, including a 13-foot-long crocodile and the oldest known bat, plus it offers video programs. It's open daily from 8am to 7pm June through August, but only until 4:30pm the rest of the year, and closed during winter holidays and bad snow.

GETTING THERE From Green River, head west on I-80 to U.S. 30 (exit 66), which you follow north about 40 miles. Past Kemmerer, follow the signs to the visitor center (about 3½ miles). Admission to both the monument and visitor center is free. Advance information is available from Superintendent, Fossil Butte National Monument, P.O. Box 592, Kemmerer, WY 83101-0592 (© **307/877-4455;** www.nps.gov/fobu).

ALSO WORTH A LOOK No need to rush through Kemmerer, an old mining town with a pleasant central square and some fine old buildings, set along the Hams Fork River. Why not visit the very first **JCPenney store** (© **307/877-3164**) and the original home of its founder, James Cash Penney. The store, despite being small and historic, is a regular JCPenney, open year-round. The house is open May to September only, with free admission. The "mother" store is on the town's central square, at 722 JC Penney Dr.; the home is 1 block north.

Appendix:
Montana & Wyoming in Depth

Spectacular scenery combines with a genuine frontier history to create what we consider the real American West. The land is mostly uncluttered—even the so-called cities are little more than overgrown cow towns—and the setting is one of rugged beauty: the remote wilderness of Yellowstone's Thorofare country, the Gallatin valleys where Sacajawea led Lewis and Clark, and the sandstone arroyos of famed outlaw Butch Cassidy's Hole-in-the-Wall country.

There's a little more pavement here than there was 75 years ago, but the open horizon and hospitality—along with a pronounced independent spirit among the locals—still exist in Montana and Wyoming. Your first visit will likely be centered on the scenery, the outdoor recreation, and the region's Wild West history, but these two states have even more to offer.

1 The Natural Environment

In Montana and Wyoming, the earth seems to have turned itself inside out, its hot insides leaking into hot springs and geysers, its bony spine thrust right through the skin of the continent to form the Continental Divide, making it a geologist's dream. And to a biologist it's heaven, one of the last regions in the United States with enough open space for animals like elk and pronghorn and grizzly bears to roam free.

Plains, basin, and range alternate in this high-altitude environment that is in large part defined by its extremes of weather and climate. These changing landscapes make Montana and Wyoming two of the best vacation spots in the country for travelers who like their scenery dynamic and dramatic.

The western side of both states is mountainous, dragging moisture from the clouds moving west to east and storing it in snowpack and alpine lakes. Because the ridge of the Rockies wrings moisture from the atmosphere, you find deeper, denser forest extending far to the west, while on the east side, the lodgepole pine, spruce, and fir forests give way to the Great Plains, a vast, flat land characterized by sagebrush, native grasses, and cottonwood-lined river bottoms.

But a lot of the landscape dates back more than 100 million years to when the collision of tectonic plates buckled the earth's crust and thrust these mountains upward. Later, glaciers (of which some vestiges remain) carved the canyons. The tallest peaks in Wyoming are located within the Wind River Range, which rises from the high plains of South Pass and runs northwest to the Yellowstone Plateau. Nine of the peaks in the Winds have elevations over 13,000 feet; **Gannett Peak,** at 13,785 feet, is the highest in the state. Several other mountain ranges are found to the south of Yellowstone—including the Absarokas and the stunning Tetons—and from Yellowstone north into Montana run other dramatic ranges, including the Gallatin, Madison, Mission, Bitterroot, Cabinet, and Beartooth, where you'll find Montana's highest point, **Granite Peak,** at 12,799 feet.

The **Continental Divide** enters Montana from Canada and traces a snaking path through the two states. Both Montana and Wyoming have rivers flowing west to the Pacific and east to the Atlantic.

Here you'll also find the headwaters of major river systems—the Flathead and Clark Fork heading west into the Columbia from Montana, along with the Snake from Wyoming; the Yellowstone, North Platte, and Madison joining the Missouri bound east; and the Green from Wyoming emptying into the Colorado heading south. These rivers are the lifeblood of the region, supplying irrigation, fisheries, and power from dams. Montana also boasts the country's largest freshwater body of water west of the Mississippi River: **Flathead Lake. Yellowstone** and **Jackson lakes** are Wyoming's two largest natural bodies of water.

Montana is the greener of these two states, with more abundant alpine wilderness and bigger rivers. Wyoming, however, has been dealt a more interesting hand of natural wonders: Waterfalls, geysers, and other geothermal oddities at Yellowstone; as well as the natural landmark of clustered rock columns that rise more than 1,280 feet above the surrounding plains at **Devils Tower,** near the state's Black Hills region of the northeast. At Wyoming's Red Desert, south of Lander, the Continental Divide splits to form an enclosed basin where no water can escape, and nearby you find **Fossil Butte National Monument,** an archaeological treasure chest of fossilized fish and ancient miniature horses.

The states are characterized by long, cold winters and short summers of hot days and chilly nights. Temperature ranges are dramatic, and are largely dependent on elevation. Except along the far western edge of Montana, precipitation here is less than 30 inches a year. It's considerably less as you journey east and south. But the snowpack in the high mountains—over 300 inches accumulate in some areas—melts through the summer and keep the rivers running.

2 The Northern Rockies Today

The northern Rockies have been discovered by a new group of immigrants, many seeking a quieter, less stressful life away from the crowds, pollution, and crime of city life. But these newcomers are quite different from the settlers who discovered this region a hundred or more years ago. Those people were homesteaders, putting down roots, raising families, and building communities. The much greater wealth and mobility of today's Americans have brought a different crowd. Many come only for a particular season. A growing number make their livings long-distance, often via a computer modem. Cities with scenery and recreation are thriving—Missoula, Jackson, Bozeman—and new residents are bringing some cosmopolitan tastes. Once they're here, these newcomers often resist growth—trying to shut the gate behind them.

Whether Wyoming and Montana can build year-round economies with tourism as the engine remains to be seen. The natives know the value of patience and withholding judgment, and in many cases that's what they're doing in regard to the newcomers and the new economy—they know that if you wait 5 minutes the weather will likely change, and so may a lot of other things.

3 History 101

MONTANA

IN THE BEGINNING The first people believed to have wondered at the land we now call Montana was Folsom Man, who arrived sometime after the end of the last Ice Age about 12,000 years ago, and lived here until superseded by the Yuma culture about 6,800 years ago.

Then, about 3,000 years ago, a more modern American Indian culture began to emerge, eventually evolving into the Kootenai, Kalispell, Flathead, Shoshone, Crow, Blackfeet, Chippewa, Cree, Cheyenne, Gros Ventres, and Assiniboine that lived across the state when Europeans first encountered them.

Buffalo provided food, clothing, shelter, and ornamentation for the tribes. There have been more than 400 *pishkun,* or buffalo jump sites, uncovered in Montana, and you can see a few of them preserved on your travels through the state.

EUROPEAN EXPLORERS The first European known to enter Montana was Pierre Gauliter, Sieur de Varennes de la Verendrye.

Verendrye had heard of a river that flowed to the western sea and was looking for the Northwest Passage. He came in 1738, but retreated. His sons, Pierre and François, returned in 1743 and described the "shining mountains," generally believed to be the Bighorns of southern Montana and northern Wyoming. But threats of a looming Indian war discouraged the brothers and they returned to Montreal. No other white men are known to have come here for another 60 years.

When they finally did arrive, they were with the expedition of Lewis and Clark. The explorers reached the mouth of the Yellowstone River on April 26, 1805, and pushed upriver to the Shoshone, where they were warmly greeted, the result of having coincidentally brought Shoshone chief Cameahwait's long-lost sister Sacajawea with them as one of their guides.

SETTLEMENT The first industry in Montana, at least for non-Indians, was trapping. John Jacob Astor, Alexander Ross, and William Ashley brought in their hearty *voyageurs* to clear the country of beaver for the European hat market.

The first steamboat landed at Fort Benton—the westernmost navigable section of the Missouri River—in 1859. Until 1862, four cargo boats a year landed there, increasing to 39 a year after gold was discovered at Bannack.

The discovery of gold opened Montana's Wild West era for real, a period you

Montana Dateline

- **11,000 B.C.** Earliest evidence of humans in Montana.
- **A.D. 1620s** Arrival of the Plains Indians.
- **1803** The eastern part of Montana becomes a territory through the Louisiana Purchase.
- **1805–06** Explorers Lewis and Clark journey through the northern Rockies to and from the Pacific coast.
- **1864** Montana becomes an official territory. Gold is discovered at Last Chance Gulch in Helena.
- **1876** Defeat of George A. Custer at the Battle of the Little Bighorn.
- **1877** Chief Joseph of the Nez Perce tribe surrenders to U.S. soldiers in the Bear Paw Mountains.
- **1880** The Utah and Northern Railroad enters Montana.
- **1883** The Northern Pacific Railroad crosses Montana.
- **1889** Montana, on November 8, becomes the 41st state in the Union.
- **1893** The University of Montana in Missoula and Montana State University in Bozeman are founded.

continues

can see preserved in the Bannack/Virginia City/Nevada City area. The lure of easy money plus the fact that these towns were some 400 miles from official justice attracted outlaws, con artists, and ladies of the night from all over the West.

In 1864, just as gold was discovered in Last Chance Gulch in present-day Helena, the Montana Territory was formed and Sidney Edgerton became the first territorial governor. The capital was moved to Virginia City and a constitutional convention was called as the first step toward statehood. A constitution was drafted and sent to St. Louis for printing, but was lost somewhere along the way.

In 1884, another constitution was drafted. This one didn't work either, for one reason or another, and in 1889, the now well-practiced delegates came up with a third one. Taking no chances, they prefaced it with the Magna Carta, the Declaration of Independence, the Articles of Confederation, and the U.S. Constitution. Montana finally became a state in November 1889.

TROUBLE BETWEEN THE INDIANS & THE SETTLERS

Montana's Indian tribes were not at first invariably hostile to the whites, and signed a number of treaties signaling their peaceful intentions. But the influx of settlers and the confinement of tribes to the reservation resulted in dissatisfaction among the original inhabitants, and escalating hostilities against the whites. In 1876, the War Department launched a campaign against the Sioux and Cheyenne. At the end of June that year, this culminated in the **Battle of the Little Bighorn** and the death of all of the command under Gen. George Armstrong Custer.

The Indian victory was only a temporary setback for the whites, however, and by 1880 all the Indians had been forced onto reservations. The last action of the Indian War period occurred in Montana with the heroic flight of Chief Joseph's Nez Perce from their northern Idaho reservation toward Canada in 1877.

INDUSTRIALIZATION

When copper was first discovered in the silver mines in Butte, no one could have foretold its effects on Montana's future. When copper wiring became an integral part of several new electrical technologies, Butte copper became an important resource for America. One of the first men to profit was Marcus Daly, an Irish immigrant, who arrived in Butte in his mid-30s and purchased his first mine, which yielded incredibly large amounts of the purest copper in the world. Soon a smelter was built near the source at Warm Springs in Anaconda, the town that took its name from the company Daly founded.

William A. Clark, another coppermine baron, was a Horatio Alger type. An

- **1910** Glacier National Park is established.
- **1914** Women's suffrage amendment passes.
- **1917–19** Missoula native Jeannette Rankin, a Republican, becomes the first woman elected to U.S. Congress and votes against U.S. participation in World War I.
- **1940** Fort Peck Dam is completed. Jeannette Rankin is again elected to the U.S. House of Representatives;

she is the only member of Congress to vote against U.S. involvement in World War II.
- **1965** Construction of Yellowtail Dam is completed.
- **1973** Montana's third state constitution goes into effect; it includes the right to a clean and healthful environment and the goal of preserving the cultural integrity of the state's American Indians.
- **1983** Anaconda Copper Mining Company shuts down.

- **1986** Montana spends $56 million on environmental protection programs.
- **1995** Wolves are reintroduced into Yellowstone National Park. Daytime speed limits are abolished (but later reestablished).
- **1996** Recluse Theodore Kaczynski, dubbed the Unabomber, is arrested at his cabin near Lincoln and is later sentenced to life in prison for sending a series of

average youth from Pennsylvania, he rooted around in mines until his efforts took him to Montana. He had a keen business acumen that prompted him to purchase mining operations, electric companies, water companies, and banks. He quickly amassed a great deal of wealth; then his inflated ego drove him to the political arena. His was the major voice in the territorial constitution proceedings in 1884, and when Montana held its last territorial election, Clark was determined to get into public office as Montana's representative.

A war commenced between Daly and Clark, rooted in Clark's determination to hold political office and Daly's unwillingness to see him do it. Montana finally became a state in 1889, after 5 tough years of appeals to the U.S. Congress. The bellicose millionaires were so set on controlling the young state's political interests that they purchased or created newspapers to give themselves a printed voice. They stuffed money into the pockets of voters and agreed on nothing. In Montana's first congressional election, Clark fell three votes shy of his bid, and the legislature adjourned without selecting a second senator, leaving Montana with only half of its due representation in Washington.

The fight for capital status came along in 1894. Helena had been the capital, but the constitution held that the site must be determined by the voters. Daly wanted his newly created Anaconda to be the capital; Clark was happy with the status quo. The fact that Anaconda was ruled by the strong arm of the Anaconda Mining Company caused voters to turn to the diversified ways of Helena. For once in his life, William Clark was not only rich but also appreciated by the masses. Or so it seemed.

With his thirst for public office revitalized, Clark did his best to buy his way into the U.S. Senate, and actually pulled it off. Daly, infuriated by the way his bitter enemy achieved his seat, demanded an investigation by the Senate. The investigation uncovered a wealth of improprieties on Clark's part, so he resigned. Down, but not out, Clark took a deep breath and plunged immediately back into the thick of things. Once when Robert Burns Smith, governor of Montana and hardly an ardent admirer of Clark's, was out of town, Clark arranged for his friend A. E. Spriggs, the lieutenant governor, to appoint Clark to the Senate. This lunatic act embarrassed the state of Montana, causing Smith to nullify the appointment upon his return. Meanwhile, Daly had sold his Anaconda Copper Company to Standard Oil to form the Amalgamated Copper

mail bombs that killed three people.
- **1998** The $6-million Lewis & Clark National Historic Trail Interpretive Center opens in Great Falls.
- **2000–01** A series of forest fires—mostly wildfires but some caused by careless humans—drive thousands of people from their homes and do millions of dollars in damage.
- **2003** Wildfires burn 140,000 acres in Glacier National Park.
- **2005** The grizzly bear is delisted as an endangered species.

Company, and Clark was now up against a nameless, faceless opponent.

He chose to link his fate with another, younger copper king, Augustus Heinze, hoping to form an alliance that Amalgamated couldn't match. At this time, Heinze was more influential than the older, less active Clark, and the team of Heinze and Clark soon had complete control of the mining world in Montana. It seemed as if Clark's last wish—to garner the Senate post he had been denied for so long—would be realized with Heinze's help. And so it was—Clark served his state as a senator from 1901 to 1907.

Though the discovery of copper in Montana was important economically, today it is also considered by many as just another chapter in the history of the state's misuse of natural resources. Montana's copper-mining industry also brought its share of unmitigated disaster to future generations. Marcus Daly died in 1900 without control of his beloved Anaconda Copper Company. Augustus Heinze sold his interest in mining in 1906 and lost his fortune on Wall Street. William Clark died in 1925 at the age of 86 in New York with a net worth estimated at $150 million. Their legacy: a reputation as the ultimate robber barons and polluters.

THE 20TH CENTURY At the beginning of the 20th century, Montana experienced a boom of a different type. The Indian Wars had ended, and white settlers declared the land a safe and fertile haven for farming. The U.S. government helped things along in 1909 when it passed the Enlarged Homestead Act, giving 320 acres to anyone willing to stay on it for at least 5 months out of the year for a minimum of 3 years. Homesteaders arrived from all over the country to stake a piece of land.

Sentiment for the homesteaders was never good, and the generalization that homesteaders were stupid, dirty people became increasingly popular. Even the renowned cowboy artist Charlie Russell, who had no stake in the matter, expressed anti-farming sentiments. The truth is, Montana's agricultural backbone was created by these extraordinary people who came west to establish farms. Wheat became—and still is—the major crop in such areas as the Judith Basin in the center of the state and Choteau County north of Great Falls.

As more and more homesteaders came to settle in Montana and farming became a mainstay of the state's economy, women began to emerge from their submissive roles in the home and take part in a suffrage movement on a large scale. In the

Wyoming Dateline

- **18,000 B.C.** Earliest evidence of humans in Wyoming.
- **A.D. 1807** John Colter explores the Yellowstone area, coming as far south as Jackson Hole.
- **1812** Fur trader Robert Stuart discovers South Pass, the gentlest route across the northern Rockies.
- **1843** Pioneers begin traveling west on the Oregon Trail through Wyoming.
- **1848** U.S. Army moves into Fort Laramie to protect Oregon Trail travelers from Indians.
- **1852** The first school in the state is founded at Fort Laramie.
- **1860** The Pony Express begins its run from Missouri
- to California, through Wyoming.
- **1867** The Union Pacific Railroad enters Wyoming.
- **1868** The Treaty of Fort Bridger creates the Shoshone Reservation in northwest Wyoming.
- **1868** The Territory of Wyoming is created by Congress.

middle of it all was young Jeannette Rankin from Missoula. In 1914, voters narrowly passed the amendment for women's suffrage; 2 years later, Rankin, a Republican, became the first woman elected to the U.S. Congress. Though her stay was brief, she was there long enough to vote against United States involvement in World War I. In 1940, she was again elected to the U.S. House of Representatives, and, as an avowed pacifist, became the only member of Congress to vote against American involvement in World War II.

When the Great Depression hit Montana, farming was enduring some rather dry difficulties, and jobs were nowhere to be found. Roosevelt's New Deal was a lifesaver. Without the jobs created by the Civilian Conservation Corps and the Works Progress Administration, the state might have never recovered its economic balance. Of particular help was construction of the Fort Peck Dam in the mid-1930s, which employed more than 50,000 workers. The earth-filled dam, the largest of its kind in the world, took almost 5 years to complete.

Since the 1950s, the story of Montana has been an evolving one, with tourism and agriculture playing key roles. While farming and cattle-ranching methods have become much more sophisticated, many of the younger generation, expected to carry on the farming tradition, have opted to settle in the larger cities. Though agriculture still drives the economic engine of the state, tourism makes a huge financial contribution. The face of ranch life has changed, with many ranches now filled with guests paying to participate in ranch activities.

WYOMING

IN THE BEGINNING The earliest indications of man in what is now Wyoming date back some 20,000 years. No one knows the identity of these early inhabitants, nor can anyone say with certainty who created the Medicine Wheel in the Bighorn Mountains or the petroglyphs found in various parts of the state. The earliest identified settlers were the Crow, Sioux, Cheyenne, and Arapaho—tribes that came from the east—as well as the Shoshone and Bannock, who came from the Great Basin, more closely related to the peoples of Central America. The lifestyles of these tribes were greatly changed by the arrival of two European innovations—the horse and the gun. The first white men in Wyoming were fur trappers, and the first of them was John Colter, who left the Lewis and Clark expedition in 1806 to wander south through Yellowstone and possibly Jackson Hole.

SETTLEMENT The Oregon Trail and other major pioneer routes west cut right

- **1869** Wyoming Territorial Legislature grants women the right to vote and hold elective office.
- **1870** Esther H. Morris becomes the nation's first female justice of the peace.
- **1872** Yellowstone National Park is established as the nation's first national park.
- **1884** First oil well is drilled in Wyoming.
- **1886–87** Great blizzard decimates ranches of eastern Wyoming, sending many "cattle barons" into bankruptcy.
- **1889** The state constitution is adopted.
- **1890** Wyoming becomes the nation's 44th state.
- **1892** The Johnson County War breaks out over a dispute about cattle rustling.
- **1897** The first Cheyenne Frontier Days rodeo is staged.
- **1906** Devils Tower is established by President Roosevelt as the country's first national monument.
- **1910** Buffalo Bill Dam is completed.
- **1925** Nellie Taylor Ross becomes the nation's first female governor.

continues

through Wyoming and the territories of the Sioux, Shoshone, Arapaho, and other tribes. Without much regard for the people they were displacing, the non-Indians killed a great deal of the game the Indians depended on; Indian bands, in turn, harassed and sometimes attacked the travelers. Indian tribes were increasingly pushed west into tighter spaces, and there was warfare among tribes.

In a series of treaties, beginning with the Fort Laramie Treaty of 1851, the tribes gave up rights to some of their homelands in return for reservations and other considerations. The discovery of gold in areas like the Black Hills and South Pass, and the routes of settlers, led to numerous treaty violations and continued conflict. Tribes in the east were being evicted and shipped west. Treaties that might have protected Indian rights were modified and broken, and U.S. Army troops were sent in to keep the peace. Some tribal leaders, recognizing the inexorable advance of the whites, decided the only alternative was to fight the invaders.

TROUBLE BETWEEN THE INDIANS & THE SETTLERS   Sitting Bull and Crazy Horse of the Hunkpapa Sioux joined forces with members of the Cheyenne and Arapaho tribes along the Little Bighorn River. It was here in June 1876 that a huge gathering of Indians defeated George Custer and his men.

Inevitably this led to a backlash, a series of attacks on Indian communities, culminating in the death of Sitting Bull and the massacre of Big Foot and his Sioux followers in 1890 at Wounded Knee, South Dakota. Chief Washakie of the Shoshone was one of the few great Indian leaders still alive, though his star was diminished by his decision to ally his tribe with the whites. That alliance got his people one of the finest reservations in the West, and the only one in Wyoming—Wind River. Then the U.S. Army moved the now threadbare Arapaho, traditional enemies of the Shoshone, to Wind River "temporarily," and the two tribes began an uncomfortable coexistence that continues to this day.

INDUSTRIALIZATION & THE 20TH CENTURY   Big cattle operators moved into Wyoming in the 19th century, controlling the territory's economy and political scene through organizations like the Cheyenne Social Club. A couple of severe winters in the 1880s and the influx of new settlers building fences raised tensions. When the cattle "barons" brought in hired guns to clear out the newcomers, the Johnson County War of 1892 erupted. The wealthy cattlemen claimed the newcomers were rustlers. But that show of muscle was futile in halting the longtime decline of the big livestock owners.

- **1927** Man claiming to be Butch Cassidy visits Wyoming from Washington, suggesting that the outlaw was not killed in Bolivia as was generally believed.
- **1929** Grand Teton National Park is established, consisting of only the peaks.
- **1929** Oil thefts discovered on federal land at Teapot Dome, a scandal that rocks the Harding Administration.

- **1950** National forest and private lands are added to form Grand Teton National Park as it is today.
- **1965** Minuteman missile sites are completed near Cheyenne.
- **1973** The Arab oil embargo sends oil prices skyrocketing, instigating a huge oil-drilling boom in Wyoming.
- **1988** Five fires break out around Yellowstone National

Park, burning through the summer and blackening approximately one-third of the park.
- **1995** Wolves are reintroduced into Yellowstone.
- **1996** The National Park Service institutes a voluntary ban on climbing Devils Tower during June to respect American Indian religious ceremonies.

Though the ranch community would long dominate Wyoming politics, the true economic hammer in the state would soon be the energy industry. The state's fate has been closely tied to oil, gas, and coal, with the economy rising and falling in synch with world prices. The boom and bust of the energy industry has prompted repeated calls for a more diversified economy, and in recent years Wyoming's tourism industry has begun to have an impact. Wyoming remains a predominantly rural state where you have a job in the energy industry or, like your parents and grandparents, work the ranch.

- **1998** Gay University of Wyoming student Matthew Shepard murdered.
- **2002** The $10-million National Historic Trails Center opened in Casper.
- **2003** Geothermal activity in Yellowstone is especially intense, with Norris Geyser Basin and the bottom of Yellowstone Lake two loci of action.
- **2004** The state enjoys a nearly $1-billion surplus in its annual budget, thanks to increased drilling and mining activity.

Index

A Guide for Every Type of Traveler

FROMMER'S® COMPLETE GUIDES

For independent leisure or business travelers who value complete coverage, candid advice, and lots of choices in all price ranges.

These are the most complete, up-to-date guides you can buy. Count on Frommer's for exact prices, savvy trip planning, sight-seeing advice, dozens of detailed maps, and candid reviews of hotels and restaurants in every price range. All Complete Guides offer special icons to point you to great finds, excellent values, and more. Every hotel, restaurant, and attraction is rated from zero to three stars to help you make the best choices.

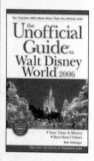

UNOFFICIAL GUIDES®

For honeymooners, families, business travelers, and anyone else who values no-nonsense, *Consumer Reports*–style advice.

Unofficial Guides are ideal for those who want to know the pros and cons of the places they are visiting and make informed decisions. The guides rank and rate every hotel, restaurant, and attraction, with evaluations based on reader surveys and critiques compiled by a team of unbiased inspectors.

FROMMER'S® IRREVERENT GUIDES

For experienced, sophisticated travelers looking for a fresh, candid perspective on a destination.

This unique series is perfect for anyone who wants a cutting-edge perspective on the hottest destinations. Covering all major cities around the globe, these guides are unabashedly honest and down-right hilarious. Decked out with a retro-savvy feel, each book features new photos, maps, and neighborhood references.

FROMMER'S® WITH KIDS GUIDES

For families traveling with children ages 2 to 14.

Here are the ultimate guides for a successful family vacation. Written by parents, they're packed with information on museums, outdoor activities, attractions, great drives and strolls, incredible parks, the liveliest places to stay and eat, and more.

Visit Frommers.com

Frommer's is a registered trademark of Arthur Frommer, used under exclusive license.

WILEY

Now you know.

THE NEW TRAVELOCITY GUARANTEE

**EVERYTHING YOU BOOK WILL BE RIGHT, OR WE'LL WORK
WITH OUR TRAVEL PARTNERS TO MAKE IT RIGHT, RIGHT AWAY.**

*To drive home the point,
we're going to use the word "right" in every single sentence.*

Let's get right to it. Right to the meat! Only Travelocity guarantees everything about your booking will be right, or we'll work with our travel partners to make it right, right away. Right on!

Here's a picture taken smack dab right in the middle of Antigua, where the guarantee also covers you.

The guarantee covers all but one of the items pictured to the right.

For example, what if the ocean view you booked actually looks out at a downright ugly parking lot? You'd be right to call – we're there for you. And no one in their right mind would be pleased to learn the rental car place has closed and left them stranded. Call Travelocity and we'll help get you back on the right track.

Now, you may be thinking, "Yeah, right, I'm so sure." That's OK; you have the right to remain skeptical. That is until we mention help is always right around the corner. Call us right off the bat, knowing that our customer service reps are there for you 24/7. Righting wrongs. Left and right.

Now if you're guessing there are some things we can't control, like the weather, well you're right. But we can help you with most things – to get all the details in righting,* visit **travelocity.com/guarantee**.

*Sorry, spelling things right is one of the few things not covered under the guarantee.

I'd give my right arm for a guarantee like this, although I'm glad I don't have to.

travelocity
You'll never roam alone.